Multidisciplinary Computational Intelligence Techniques:

Applications in Business, Engineering, and Medicine

Shawkat Ali
CQUniversity, Australia

Noureddine Abbadeni
King Saud University, Saudi Arabia

Mohamed Batouche
University of Constantine, Algeria

Managing Director:	Lindsay Johnston
Senior Editorial Director:	Heather A. Probst
Book Production Manager:	Sean Woznicki
Development Manager:	Joel Gamon
Development Editor:	Hannah Abelbeck
Acquisitions Editor:	Erika Gallagher
Typesetter:	Adrienne Freeland
Cover Design:	Nick Newcomer, Lisandro Gonzalez

Published in the United States of America by
Information Science Reference (an imprint of IGI Global)
701 E. Chocolate Avenue
Hershey PA 17033
Tel: 717-533-8845
Fax: 717-533-8661
E-mail: cust@igi-global.com
Web site: http://www.igi-global.com

Library of Congress Cataloging-in-Publication Data

Multidisciplinary computational intelligence techniques: applications in business, engineering, and medicine / Shawkat Ali, Noureddine Abbadeni, and Mohamed Batouche, editors.
p. cm.
Summary: "This book explores the complex world of computational intelligence, which utilizes computational methodologies such as fuzzy logic systems, neural networks, and evolutionary computation for the purpose of managing and using data effectively to address complicated real-world problems"-- Provided by publisher.
Includes bibliographical references and index.
ISBN 978-1-4666-1830-5 (hardcover) -- ISBN 978-1-4666-1831-2 (ebook) -- ISBN 978-1-4666-1832-9 (print & perpetual access) 1. Computational intelligence. 2. Evolutionary computation. I. Ali, Shawkat, 1969- II. Abbadeni, Noureddine, 1970- III. Batouche, Mohamed, 1964-
Q342.M856 2012
006.3--dc23

2012003207

British Cataloguing in Publication Data
A Cataloguing in Publication record for this book is available from the British Library.

Editorial Advisory Board

Table of Contents

Chapter 6
Application of Multi-Objective Evolutionary Algorithms to Antenna and Microwave Design Problems 75
Sotirios K. Goudos, Aristotle University of Thessaloniki, Greece

Chapter 7
Using Computational Intelligence for Improved Teleoperation over Wireless Network 102
Salman H. Khan, National University of Sciences & Technology (NUST), Pakistan
Arsalan H. Khan, Northwestern Polytechnical University (NPU), P.R. China
Zeashan H. Khan, Center for Emerging Sciences, Engineering and Technology (CESET), Pakistan

Chapter 8
Bangla Music Genre Classification 124
Ashfaqur Rahman, Centre for Intelligent and Networked Systems, Central Queensland University Rockhampton, Australia

Chapter 9
Automatic Recognition and Localization of Saudi License Plates 139
Lama Hamandi, American University of Beirut, Lebanon
Khaled M. Almustafa, Prince Sultan University, Kingdom of Saudi Arabia
Rached N. Zantout, Prince Sultan University, Kingdom of Saudi Arabia
Hasan R. Obeid, Zawya, Lebanon

Chapter 10
Numerical Integration Using Swarm Intelligence Techniques 171
Naceur Khelil, Laboratory of Applied Mathematics, Universite Mohamed Khider de Biskra, Algeria
Leila Djerou, LESIA Laboratory, Universite Mohamed Khider de Biskra, Algeria
Mohamed Batouche, CCIS-King Saud University, Saudi Arabia

Chapter 11
A Multilevel Thresholding Method Based on Multiobjective Optimization for Non-Supervised Image Segmentation 182
Leila Djerou, LESIA Laboratory, Universite Mohamed Khider de Biskra, Algeria
Naceur Khelil, Laboratory of Applied Mathematics, Universite Mohamed Khider de Biskra, Algeria
Nour El Houda Dehimi, L.B.M. University, Algeria
Mohamed Batouche, University Mentouri–Constantine, Algeria

Chapter 12
On the Use of Particle Swarm Optimization Techniques for Channel Assignments in Cognitive Radio Networks 202
Hisham M. Abdelsalam, Cairo University, Egypt
Haitham S. Hamza, Cairo University, Egypt
Abdoulraham M. Al-Shaar, Cairo University, Egypt
Abdelbaset S. Hamza, University of Nebraska-Lincoln, USA

Detailed Table of Contents

It is widely accepted that the presence of some of the firm's attributes or characteristics attracting premiums in terms of average returns is pervasive and not restricted to a few individual markets. However, the way to derive these premiums by sorting firms based on their characteristics that are known associated with share returns is not without controversy. This chapter takes a different approach by adopting a novel Multi Self-Organising Maps to cluster shares first and then identify fundamental factors afterwards. It finds that firm's size and book-to-market ratio attributes do have explanatory power over share average returns. There is also lack of evidence for other factors in explaining the share average returns.

This chapter presents an efficient approach to personalized pronunciation assessment of Taiwanese-accented English. The main goal of this study is to detect frequently occurring mispronunciation patterns of Taiwanese-accented English instead of scoring English pronunciations directly. The proposed assessment help quickly discover personalized mispronunciations of a student, thus English teachers can spend more time on teaching or rectifying students' pronunciations. In this approach, an unsupervised model adaptation method is performed on the universal acoustic models to recognize the speech of a specific speaker with mispronunciations and Taiwanese accent. A dynamic sentence selection algorithm, considering the mutual information of the related mispronunciations, is proposed to choose a sentence containing the most undetected mispronunciations in order to quickly extract personalized mispronunciations. The experimental results show that the proposed unsupervised adaptation approach obtains an accuracy improvement of about 2.1% on the recognition of Taiwanese-accented English speech.

Chapter 3
A Bees Life Algorithm for Cloud Computing Services Selection 31
Salim Bitam, Mohamed Khider University – Biskra, Algeria
Mohamed Batouche, University Mentouri – Constantine, Algeria
El-Ghazali Talbi, University of Lille 1, France

In recent years, the scientific community has begun to model and solve complex optimization problems using bio-inspired methods. Such problems cannot be solved exactly by traditional methods within a reasonable complexity in terms of computer capacities or computational times. However, bio-inspired methods provide near optimal solutions in realist conditions such as cost, capacity, and computational time. In this chapter, the authors propose a new population-based algorithm called the Bees Life Algorithm (BLA). It is applied to solve the cloud computing services selection with quality of service (QoS) requirements. It is considered as swarm-based algorithm, which closely imitates the life of the bee colony. It follows the two important behaviors in the nature of bees, reproduction and food foraging. Bees life algorithm can be applied to the combinatorial optimization problems as well as to the functional optimization problems. An experimental study has been conducted in order to demonstrate the performance and the efficiency of the proposal and its robustness. After comparisons with genetic algorithm (GA) as referential algorithm in this field, the obtained results showed the BLA performance and effectiveness. Finally, promising future research directions are examined to show the BLA usefulness for research in the cloud computing and computational intelligence areas.

Chapter 4
Cloud-Based Intelligent DSS Design for Emergency Professionals 47
Shah J. Miah, Victoria University, Australia

Computational Intelligence (CI) has become a well-established research field of computer science in which multi-disciplinary problems are studied to design an effective computing solution. As a known computer-based CI approach, decision support systems (DSS) has gained popularity as a computing solution to structured and unstructured problems in organizations' managerial improvement. DSS design needs to meet the domain-specific demands of emergency professionals on both an on-site and a real-time basis using the support of the most up-to-date technological provisioning platform. The advantages of cloud computing may offer promising support (e.g. Internet or web-based provisioning) for DSS services to meet the emergency professionals' decision needs. This chapter introduces requirements of a cloud-based CI approach for domain-specific decision support through the functionalities on an anywhere and anytime basis. The chapter highlights the context of intelligent DSS design in terms of support in determining the priorities of taking action, both for medical emergency professionals and natural disasters workers, as potential application areas identified in this study.

Chapter 5
Occlusion Handling in Object Detection 61
Farjana Z. Eishita, University of Saskatchewan, Canada
Ashfaqur Rahman, Central Queensland University Rockhampton, Australia
Salahuddin A. Azad, Central Queensland University Rockhampton, Australia
Akhlaqur Rahman, American International University, Bangladesh

Object tracking is a process that follows an object through consecutive frames of images to determine the object's movement relative other objects of those frames. In other words, tracking is the problem of estimating the trajectory of an object in the image plane as it moves around a scene. This chapter presents research that deals with the problem of tracking objects when they are occluded. An object can be

partially or fully occluded. Depending on the tracking domain, a tracker can deal with partial and full object occlusions using features such as colour and texture. But sometimes it fails to detect the objects after occlusion. The shape feature of an individual object can provide additional information while combined with colour and texture features. It has been observed that with the same colour and texture if two object's shape information is taken then these two objects can be detected after the occlusion has occurred. From this observation, a new and a very simple algorithm is presented in this chapter, which is able to track objects after occlusion even if the colour and textures are the same. Some experimental results are shown along with several case studies to compare the effectiveness of the shape features against colour and texture features.

Antenna and microwave design problems are, in general, multi-objective. Multi-objective Evolutionary Algorithms (MOEAs) are suitable optimization techniques for solving such problems. Particle Swarm Optimization (PSO) and Differential Evolution (DE) have received increased interest from the electromagnetics community. The fact that both algorithms can efficiently handle arbitrary optimization problems has made them popular for solving antenna and microwave design problems. This chapter presents three different state-of-the-art MOEAs based on PSO and DE, namely: the Multi-objective Particle Swarm Optimization (MOPSO), the Multi-objective Particle Swarm Optimization with fitness sharing (MOPSO-fs), and the Generalized Differential Evolution (GDE3). Their applications to different design cases from antenna and microwave problems are reported. These include microwave absorber, microwave filters and Yagi-uda antenna design. The algorithms are compared and evaluated against other evolutionary multi-objective algorithms like Nondominated Sorting Genetic Algorithm-II (NSGA-II). The results show the advantages of using each algorithm.

The role of computational intelligence techniques in applied sciences and engineering is becoming popular today. It is essential because the autonomous engineering applications require intelligent decision in real time in order to achieve the desired goal. This chapter discusses some of the approaches to demonstrate various applications of computational intelligence in dependable networked control systems and a case study of teleoperation over wireless network. The results have shown that computational intelligence algorithms can be successfully implemented on an embedded application to offer an improved online performance. The different approaches have been compared and could be chosen as per application requirements.

Bangladesh is very rich in its musical history. Music documented the lives of the people from the ancient times. This chapter provides a guideline for classifying Bangla songs into different genres using a machine learning approach. Four different genres, namely Rabindrasangit, Folk song, Adhunik song, and Pop music, were used in the experiments. A set of second order features are used for representing the trend of change of primary features computed over the timeline of the song. The features are incorporated into a number of classification algorithms and a classification framework is developed. The uniqueness of the genres is clearly revealed by high classification accuracies achieved by the different classifiers.

In this chapter, localizing Saudi license plates in images and recognizing characters automatically in those plates are described. Three algorithms to recognize English and Arabic characters in Saudi license plates are presented. The three algorithms rely on processing information from lines strategically drawn vertically and horizontally through a character. In most of the cases, all letters and numbers were able to be recognized. Furthermore, two approaches for localization, "object adjacency" and "character recognition," are described in this chapter. The algorithms were successfully applied to images containing Saudi License plates as shown through the results presented. A hybrid approach is also presented in which vertical alignment was used to aid the recognition phase in correctly recognizing characters. The hybrid method is only applicable to new Saudi license plates since they contain redundant information in both Arabic and English sections.

This chapter proposes quadrature methods (PSOQF) for approximate calculation of integrals within Particle Swarm Optimization (PSO). PSO is a technique based on the cooperation between particles. The exchange of information between these particles allows to resolve difficult problems. Riemann quadrature formula (RQF) will be discussed fifor, followed by Trapezoidal quadrature Formula (TQF). Finally, a comparison of these methods presented is given.

The aim of this work is to provide a comprehensive review of multiobjective optimization in the image segmentation problem based on image thresholding. The authors show that the inclusion of several criteria in the thresholding segmentation process helps to overcome the weaknesses of these criteria when used separately. In this context, they give a recent literature review, and present a new multi-level image thresholding technique, called Automatic Threshold, based on Multiobjective Optimization (ATMO). That combines the flexibility of multiobjective fitness functions with the power of a Binary Particle Swarm Optimization algorithm (BPSO), for searching the "optimum" number of the thresholds and simultaneously the optimal thresholds of three criteria: the between-class variances criterion, the minimum error criterion and the entropy criterion. Some examples of test images are presented to compare with this segmentation method, based on the multiobjective optimization approach with Otsu's, Kapur's, and Kittler's methods. Experimental results show that the thresholding method based on multiobjective optimization is more efficient than the classical Otsu's, Kapur's, and Kittler's methods.

Efficient utilization of open spectrum in cognitive radio networks requires appropriate allocation of idle spectrum frequency bands (not used by licensed users) among coexisting cognitive radios (secondary users) while minimizing interference among all users. This problem is referred to as the spectrum allocation or the channel assignment problem in cognitive radio networks, and is shown to be NP-hard. Accordingly, different optimization techniques based on evolutionary algorithms were needed in order to solve the channel assignment problem. This chapter investigates the use of particular swarm optimization (PSO) techniques to solve the channel assignment problem in cognitive radio networks. In particular, the authors study the definitiveness of using the native PSO algorithm and the Improved Binary PSO (IBPSO) algorithm to solve the assignment problem. In addition, the performance of these algorithms is compared to that of a fine-tuned genetic algorithm (GA) for this particular problem. Three utilization functions, namely, Mean-Reward, Max-Min-Reward, and Max-Proportional-Fair, are used to evaluate the effectiveness of three optimization algorithms. Extensive simulation results show that PSO and IBPSO algorithms outperform that fine-tuned GA. More interestingly, the native PSO algorithm outperforms both the GA and the IBPSO algorithms in terms of solution speed and quality.

This chapter presents an intelligent method of optimising the radiation beam of wireless sensor nodes in Wireless Sensor Network (WSN). Each node has the feature of a monopole antenna. The optimisation involves selection of nodes to be organised as close as possible to a uniform linear array (ULA) in order to minimise the position errors, which will improve the radiation beam reconfiguring performance. Instead of utilising random beamforming, which needs a large number of sensor nodes to interact with each other and form a narrow radiation beam, the developed optimisation algorithm is emphasized to only a selected number of sensor nodes which can construct a linear array. Thus, the method utilises radiation beam reconfiguration technique to intelligently establish a communication link in a WSN.

In order to implement clustering under the condition that the number of clusters is not known a priori, the authors propose a novel automatic clustering algorithm in this chapter, based on particle swarm optimization algorithm. ACPSO can partition images into compact and well separated clusters without any knowledge on the real number of clusters. ACPSO used a novel representation scheme for the search variables in order to determine the optimal number of clusters. The partition of each particle of the swarm evolves using evolving operators which aim to reduce dynamically the number of naturally occurring clusters in the image as well as to refine the cluster centers. Experimental results on real images demonstrate the effectiveness of the proposed approach.

Most recently, IT-enabled education has become a very important branch of educational technology. Education is becoming more dynamic, networked, and increasingly electronic. Today's is a world of Internet social networks, blogs, digital audio and video content, et cetera. A few clear advantages of Web-based education are classroom independence and availability of authoring tools for developing Web-based courseware, cheap and efficient storage and distribution of course materials, hyperlinks to suggested readings, and digital libraries. However, there are several challenges in improving Web-based education, such as providing for more adaptivity and intelligence. The main idea is to incorporate Semantic Web technologies and resources to the design of artificial intelligence in education (AIED) systems aiming to update their architectures to provide more adaptability, robustness, and richer learning environments. The construction of such systems is highly complex and faces several challenges in terms of software engineering and artificial intelligence aspects. This chapter addresses state of the art

Semantic Web methods and tools used for modeling and designing intelligent tutoring systems (ITS). Also it draws attention of Semantic Web users towards e-learning systems with a hope that the use of Semantic Web technologies in educational systems can help the accomplishment of anytime, anywhere, anybody learning, where most of the web resources are reusable learning objects supported by standard technologies and learning is facilitated by intelligent pedagogical agents, that may be adding the essential instructional ingredients implicitly.

A. A. M. Nurunnabi, SLG, University of Rajshahi, Bangladesh
A. B. M. S. Ali, CQUniversity, Australia
A. H. M. Rahmatullah Imon, Ball State University, USA
Mohammed Nasser, University of Rajshahi, Bangladesh

The use of logistic regression, its modelling and decision making from the estimated model and subsequent analysis has been drawn a great deal of attention since its inception. The current use of logistic regression methods includes epidemiology, biomedical research, criminology, ecology, engineering, pattern recognition, machine learning, wildlife biology, linguistics, business and finance, et cetera. Logistic regression diagnostics have attracted both theoreticians and practitioners in recent years. Detection and handling of outliers is considered as an important task in the data modelling domain, because the presence of outliers often misleads the modelling performances. Traditionally logistic regression models were used to fit data obtained under experimental conditions. But in recent years, it is an important issue to measure the outliers scale before putting the data as a logistic model input. It requires a higher mathematical level than most of the other material that steps backward to its study and application in spite of its inevitability. This chapter presents several diagnostic aspects and methods in logistic regression. Like linear regression, estimates of the logistic regression are sensitive to the unusual observations: outliers, high leverage, and influential observations. Numerical examples and analysis are presented to demonstrate the most recent outlier diagnostic methods using data sets from medical domain.

Rao M. Kotamarti, Southern Methodist University, USA
Mitchell A. Thornton, Southern Methodist University, USA
Margaret H. Dunham, Southern Methodist University, USA

Many classes of algorithms that suffer from large complexities when implemented on conventional computers may be reformulated resulting in greatly reduced complexity when implemented on quantum computers. The dramatic reductions in complexity for certain types of quantum algorithms coupled with the computationally challenging problems in some bioinformatics problems motivates researchers to devise efficient quantum algorithms for sequence (DNA, RNA, protein) analysis. This chapter shows that the important sequence classification problem in bioinformatics is suitable for formulation as a quantum algorithm. This chapter leverages earlier research for sequence classification based on Extensible Markov Model (EMM) and proposes a quantum computing alternative. The authors utilize sequence family profiles built using EMM methodology which is based on using pre-counted word data for each sequence. Then a new method termed *quantum seeding* is proposed for generating a key based on high frequency words. The key is applied in a quantum search based on Grover algorithm to determine a candidate set of models resulting in a significantly reduced search space. Given Z as a function of M models of size N, the quantum version of the seeding algorithm has a time complexity in the order of $O(\sqrt{Z})$ as opposed to $O(Z)$ for the standard classic version for large values of Z.

Chapter 18
Improving the Efficiency of Large-Scale Agent-Based Models Using Compression Techniques 301
Mitchell Welch, University of New England, Australia
Paul Kwan, University of New England, Australia
A.S.M. Sajeev, University of New England, Australia
Graeme Garner, Office of the Chief Veterinary Officer, Department of Agriculture, Fisheries and Forestry Australia, Australia

Agent-based modelling is becoming a widely used approach for simulating complex phenomena. By making use of emergent behaviour, agent based models can simulate systems right down to the most minute interactions that affect a system's behaviour. In order to capture the level of detail desired by users, many agent based models now contain hundreds of thousands and even millions of interacting agents. The scale of these models makes them computationally expensive to operate in terms of memory and CPU time, limiting their practicality and use. This chapter details the techniques for applying Dynamic Hierarchical Agent Compression to agent based modelling systems, with the aim of reducing the amount of memory and number of CPU cycles required to manage a set of agents within a model. The scheme outlined extracts the state data stored within a model's agents and takes advantage of redundancy in this data to reduce the memory required to represent this information. The techniques show how a hierarchical data structure can be used to achieve compression of this data and the techniques for implementing this type of structure within an existing modelling system. The chapter includes a case study that outlines the practical considerations related to the application of this scheme to Australia's National Model for Emerging Livestock Disease Threats that is currently being developed.

Chapter 19
Embedded System for Heart Disease Recognition using Fuzzy Clustering and Correlation 327
Helton Hugo de Carvalho Júnior, Instituto Federal de Educacao, Ciencia e Tecnologia, Campus Campos do Jordão, Brazil
Robson Luiz Moreno, UNIFEI, Brazil
Tales Cleber Pimenta, UNIFEI, Brazil

This chapter presents the viability analysis and the development of heart disease identification embedded system. It offers a time reduction on electrocardiogram – ECG signal processing by reducing the amount of data samples without any significant loss. The goal of the developed system is the analysis of heart signals. The ECG signals are applied into the system that performs an initial filtering, and then uses a Gustafson-Kessel fuzzy clustering algorithm for the signal classification and correlation. The classification indicates common heart diseases such as angina, myocardial infarction and coronary artery diseases. The system uses the European electrocardiogram ST-T Database – EDB as a reference for tests and evaluation. The results prove the system can perform the heart disease detection on a data set reduced from 213 to just 20 samples, thus providing a reduction to just 9.4% of the original set, while maintaining the same effectiveness. This system is validated in a Xilinx Spartan®-3A FPGA. The FPGA implemented a Xilinx Microblaze® Soft-Core Processor running at a 50 MHz clock rate.

Chapter 20
Parallel Evolutionary Computation in R 351
Cedric Gondro, The Centre for Genetic Analysis and Applications, University of New England, Australia
Paul Kwan, University of New England, Australia

Evolutionary Computation (EC) is a branch of Artificial Intelligence which encompasses heuristic optimization methods loosely based on biological evolutionary processes. These methods are efficient in finding optimal or near-optimal solutions in large, complex non-linear search spaces. While evolutionary algorithms (EAs) are comparatively slow in comparison to deterministic or sampling approaches, they are also inherently parallelizable. As technology shifts towards multicore and cloud computing, this overhead becomes less relevant, provided a parallel framework is used. In this chapter the authors discuss how to implement and run parallel evolutionary algorithms in the popular statistical programming language R. R has become the de facto language for statistical programming and it is widely used in biostatistics and bioinformatics due to the availability of thousands of packages to manipulate and analyze data. It is also extremely easy to parallelize routines within R, which makes it a perfect environment for evolutionary algorithms. EC is a large field of research, and many different algorithms have been proposed. While there is no single silver bullet that can handle all classes of problems, an algorithm that is extremely simple, efficient, and with good generalization properties is Differential Evolution (DE). Herein the authors discuss step-by-step how to implement DE in R and how to parallelize it. They then illustrate with a toy genome-wide association study (GWAS) how to identify candidate regions associated with a quantitative trait of interest.

Chapter 21
Fuzzy Image Segmentation for Mass Detection in Digital Mammography: Recent Advances and Techniques 378
Hajar Mohammedsaleh H. Alharbi, King Abdulaziz University, Kingdom of Saudi Arabia
Paul Kwan, University of New England, Australia
Ashoka Jayawardena, University of New England, Australia
A. S. M. Sajeev, University of New England, Australia

In the last decade, many computer-aided diagnosis (CAD) systems that utilize a broad range of diagnostic techniques have been proposed. Due to both the inherently complex structure of the breast tissues and the low intensity contrast found in most mammographic images, CAD systems that are based on conventional techniques have been shown to have missed malignant masses in mammographic images that would otherwise be treatable. On the other hand, systems based on fuzzy image processing techniques have been found to be able to detect masses in cases where conventional techniques would have failed. In the current chapter, recent advances in fuzzy image segmentation techniques as applied to mass detection in digital mammography are reviewed. Image segmentation is an important step in CAD systems since the quality of its outcome will significantly affect the processing downstream that can involve both detection and classification of benign versus malignant masses.

Compilation of References 403

About the Contributors 436

Index 446

Preface

The amount of digital data is becoming almost double in every year. Managed well, the data can be used to extract new sources of knowledge for our daily business. How? The straightway solution is Computational Intelligence. During the last few years, there have been growing interests in developing and applying Computational Intelligence techniques to solve in many real world complex problems. However, these techniques are facing many challenges. This book presents a number of diverse methods and applications of Computational Intelligence techniques in the fields of business, engineering and medicine.

Multidisciplinary Computational Intelligence Techniques: Applications in Business, Engineering, and Medicine provides researchers, practitioners, students, and technologists with current trends of intelligent techniques. It will help researchers to exchange and share their views on the latest developments in the field. This book will also help those who are from outside the computer science discipline (from business, medicine, and engineering for instance) to understand how and what intelligent techniques can be used in their own areas. Researchers, instructors, designers of information systems, users of these systems, and graduate students will also benefit from this book where they can find the fundamental knowledge as well as a set of potential applications.

Many Computational Intelligence books focus on theories or narrow specific application areas. The motivation for this book is to provide a mix of theory and applications to the readers in order to show the practical value of computational intelligence techniques. In this regard, this book is a special contribution in the Computational Intelligence field. The contributors feel the book to be an unique publication that systematically presents a cohesive view of all the important aspects of modern Computational Intelligence. The scholarly value of this book and its contributions to the literature in the information technology discipline are that:

- It increases the understanding of modern Computational Intelligence methodology and techniques.
- It identifies the recent key challenges which are faced by Computational Intelligence users in business, engineering, and medicine.
- It helps the new comers to the Computational Intelligence field understand the essence of computational intelligence.
- It describes the most recent applications on Computational Intelligence techniques across business, engineering, and medicine.

The book is suitable to any one who needs an informative introduction to the current development, basic methodology, and advanced techniques of Computational Intelligence. It serves as a handbook for researchers, practitioners, and technologists. The text is appropriate for senior undergraduates and postgraduates students in Computational Intelligence. It facilitates discussion and idea sharing. It helps researchers exchange their views on experimental design and the future challenges on such discovery techniques.

A B M Shawkat Ali
CQUniversity, Australia

Noureddine Abbadeni
King Saud University, Saudi Arabia

Mohamed Batouche
University of Constantine, Algeria

Acknowledgment

Editors of this book are especially grateful to authors who have directly contributed for this book. We also thank all reviewers around the globe for carefully reading and constructively reviewing each chapter of this book. Their valuable feedback resulted in significant improvements to the quality of the final outcome. We are thankful to the editorial advisory board members for their guidance. We would like to acknowledge the great support received from our publisher IGI Global. We thank our universities for their support. Finally we are grateful to our family of each of us for their consistent and persistent supports to bring this book to its final form.

A B M Shawkat Ali
CQUniversity, Australia

Noureddine Abbadeni
King Saud University, Saudi Arabia

Mohamed Batouche
University of Constantine, Algeria

Chapter 1
Which Fundamental Factors Proxy for Share Returns?
An Application of the Multi Self-Organising Maps in Share Pricing

Bob Li
Deakin University, Australia

Yee Ling Boo
Deakin University, Australia

ABSTRACT

It is widely accepted that the presence of some of the firm's attributes or characteristics attracting premiums in terms of average returns is pervasive and not restricted to a few individual markets. However, the way to derive these premiums by sorting firms based on their characteristics that are known associated with share returns is not without controversy. This chapter takes a different approach by adopting a novel Multi Self-Organising Maps to cluster shares first and then identify fundamental factors afterwards. It finds that firm's size and book-to-market ratio attributes do have explanatory power over share average returns. There is also lack of evidence for other factors in explaining the share average returns.

1. INTRODUCTION

In recent years, it has become increasingly common to sort firms based on their attributes or characteristics, such as size, book-to-market ratio (B/M) and dividends yield (yields), to form empirical asset pricing portfolios. Investigators then use them to examine whether asset pricing models can explain the dispersion in firm's share returns. For instance, after Fama and French (Fama and French (1993, 1995, 1996)) show that their three-factor model can explain more than 90% of the returns of these portfolios and that the unexplained portion of returns is economically small,

DOI: 10.4018/978-1-4666-1830-5.ch001

subsequently, a large number of asset-pricing tests have used portfolios sorted on both size and B/M. Other firm characteristics used to form portfolios include return standard deviation, profit margin, liquidity, relative past return performance, profit margin, earnings-price ratio, and firm industry (Campbell et al (2008), Chava and Jarrow (2004), Fama and French (1988) and Zmijewski (1984)).

Forming portfolios based on characteristics has some advantages. For instance, it can generate a large dispersion in returns. However, it subsequently presents a challenge to any asset pricing model and has sparked a debate about whether this practice is appropriate. Lo and MacKinlay (1990) point out that the ad-hoc nature of the sorting technique - sorting on characteristics that are known to be correlated with returns generates a data snooping bias. Berk (2000) suggests that the characteristics that researchers rely on to share sorting may be mechanically linked to share returns. In addition, Conrad et al. (2003) demonstrate that the increasing popularity for researchers to sort stocks on multiple characteristics, and consequently to form larger number of portfolios, exacerbates the data-snooping bias. Such practice results in the return dispersion weakening or even disappearing in out-of-sample tests because the relation between returns and the characteristic is not robust over time.

Apart from the data-snooping concern, Daniel and Titman (2005) suggest that firm characteristics, such as B/M, serve as a "catch-all" factor. These characteristics capture the differences in the sensitivities of stocks' returns to a number of different fundamental factors. Consequently, factors based on firms' characteristics will be bound to have an explanatory power over share returns in the empirical testings using characteristics sorted portfolios. However, these testings are unable to tell us whether other factors, perhaps more fundamental ones can be equally important variables in explaining share returns. Stein (1996) suggests that "*the return differentials associated with the book-to-market ratio and other predictive variables be thought of as compensation for fundamental risk. While there seems to be fairly widespread agreement that variables such as book-to-market do indeed have predictive content, it is much less clear that this reflects anything to do with risk.*" Therefore, one cannot rely on the prevailing sorting practice in which shares sorted according to firms' characteristics are used to identify fundamental factors in empirical asset pricing. It is primarily this criticism that motivates this study.

In this paper, we propose a novel computational approach to identify fundamental factors that capture the sensitivities of stocks' returns. Such approach is well motivated economically, and more importantly, alleviates some of the problems inherent in the prevailing asset pricing practice.

This study makes the following contributions to the finance literature. Firstly, it overcomes the ad-hoc nature of sorting shares into portfolios based on their known characteristics. Secondly, it validates the well known fundamentals, such as size and B/M, in predicting share returns.

The remainder of the paper proceeds as follows. Section 2 describes the proposed methodology to be used in the study. Subsequently, Section 3 delineates the data. Section 4 reports the modelling findings. Section 5 proposes future research direction and Section 6 concludes.

2. PROPOSED METHODOLOGY: THE MULTI SELF-ORGANISING MAPS (SOM) BASED CLUSTERING APPROACH

Clustering approach is well known and often used to allocate mutual funds and hedge funds into style categories (Brown and Goetzmann (1997), Brown and Goetzmann (2003)) and empirical evidence suggests that clustering approach outperforms many traditional classification techniques based on investment objectives. More recently, it has been used in asset-pricing studies (Brown et al. (1998), Brown et al. (2008) and Ahn et al. (2009)). The underlying concept is that stocks with similar past returns will be placed in one category (cluster), whist the common practice in asset pricing is to 'factorise' stocks by sorting them into *ex ante* classes based on firms' characteristics. Brown et al. (1998) argue that: "*securities are grouped together to minimise the sum-of-squared errors over the time period of the estimation. For example, two securities whose returns nearly match each other each observation period over a given time interval will cluster together.*" (p. 5). Thus, clustering algorithm is a natural fit with the theoretical returns generating process of stocks, with additional benefits being the potential increase in accuracy and precision for the estimate. We argue that the risk categories we discover using clustering are not *ad-hoc*. Instead, they are endogenously determined using statistical techniques, and that they are readily interpretable in terms of the characteristics of the underlying securities. In this way we shall circumvent the criticism of the characteristics sorting approach.

The proposed clustering approach is innovatively based on Self-Organising Maps (SOM). It was initiated by Kohonen (2001), and it is well reported that SOM has been successfully and widely applied in many domains, such as healthcare, marketing, engineering, etc. In addition, it has also applied in the field of finance, for pricing new shares (Han et al. (2008)) and estimating hedge ratio (Hsu and Chen (2008)). The SOM is an unsupervised artificial neural network that is regularly used for performing clustering tasks. It is a brain inspired approach that iteratively organises and maps large input data into different clusters. In other words, high dimensional data, such as share returns data, could be mapped into lower dimensional clusters and therefore dimensionality reduction could be achieved. This shows that SOM is appropriate for cluster analysis in which underlying hidden patterns of large and high dimensional data such as share returns data could be identified. In addition, SOM has several advantages over the other clustering methods. For instance, it has self-learning capabilities; preservation of the topological relationship of the data and most importantly effective visualisation for abstracted high dimensional data.

A typical SOM architecture is shown in Figure 1. The input layer consists of input vectors and the output layer, which is also the feature map, consists of output nodes. They are completely connected as every node in the input layer is connected to every node in the output layer but not to other nodes in the same layer (Larose (2005)). In the SOM, input vectors are connected to an array of neurons, in which weights connecting input vectors to certain regions of the array of neurons will be adjusted and strengthen during a competitive learning process (Smith (1999)). Such learning process is the principle mechanism in SOM, where the output nodes compete among themselves to be the winning node. In this case, the winner of the competition is the output node that has the smallest Euclidean distance to the input node and therefore becomes the centre of its neighbourhood. Subsequently, the winning node earns the most "reward" and cooperatively shares its "reward" with its neighbouring nodes. Specifically, the "reward" refers to the learning received and thus the winning node receives the most learning with its neighbours receiving less the further away they are from the winning node. That means, these nodes participate in learning and therefore demonstrates adaptation as weights are adjusted to increase the chance of winning the competition again. In brief, SOM exhibits three characteristic processes, namely competition, cooperation and adaptation (Larose, 2005).

Let us denote an input vector $x_n = x_{n1}, x_{n2}, \ldots, x_{nm}$ where m is the set of field values for n number of records and a weight vector $w_j = w_{1j}, w_{2j}, \ldots, w_{kj}$ where the current set of k weights for a particular output node j. In addition, the size of the neighbourhood around winning node g at time t is denoted by $N_g(t)$. The steps of the SOM algorithm are as follows:

Figure 1. A typical self-organising maps (SOM) architecture

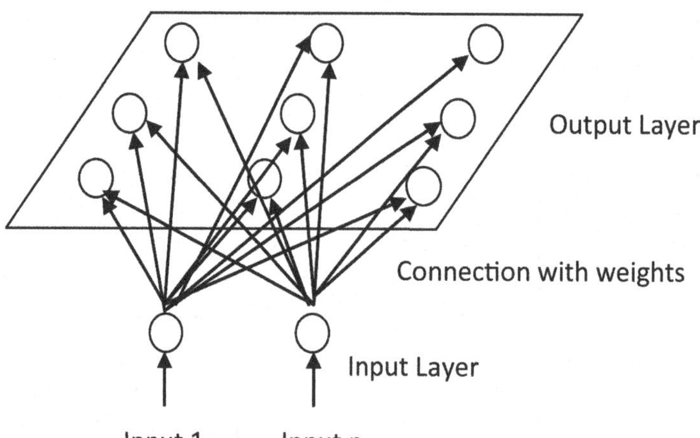

Step 1: Initialise weights to small random values between 0 and 1, neighbourhood size $N_g(0)$ appropriately and set parameter functions that control the learning rate, $\alpha(t)$ and $\sigma^2(t)$ to be between 0 and 1.

Step 2: Present input vector x_n through input layer for competition process. For each output node j, calculate the similarity distance via Euclidean distance,

$$D(w_j, x_n) = \sqrt{\sum_{i=1}^{n} (w_{ij} - x_{ni})^2}.$$

Step 3: For cooperation process, select the smallest value of $D(w_j, x_n)$ as the winning node g. Identify all the output nodes j within the neighbourhood size $Ng(t)$.

Step 4: For adaptation process, adjust the weights connecting the input layer to the winning node and its neighbouring nodes according to the learning rule: $w_{ij}(t+1) = w_{ij}(t) + \eta[x_{mi} - w_{ij}(t)]$ where the learning rate $\eta = \alpha(t)$ $\exp(-\|r_j - r_g\| / \sigma^2(t))$ for all output nodes j within the neighbourhood size N_g. $r_j - r_g$ is the physical distance (number of nodes) between output node j and winning node g.

Step 5: Continue from Step 2 for φ iterations and then decrease the learning rate η and neighbourhood size N_g. Stop when weights have stabilised and termination criteria are met.

Our proposed methodology is a SOM-based clustering approach, as depicted in Figure 2. The novelty of our clustering approach has introduced multiple SOMs that individually take into consideration of the different types of attributes in asset pricing. In particular, each attributes is separately clustered with multiple SOM, and subsequently associated via the unique identifiers of each record. Furthermore, we statistically summarise and describe the associated clusters that basically form the asset pricing portfolios. The extracted portfolios could then be interpreted, deduced and compared with standard asset pricing portfolios. Such approach has given the opportunities to explore and scrutinise each attributes and therefore the outlooks of each of the attributes are provided. Moreover, the associated clusters offer a global picture of the portfolios in which the attributes are linked together. Thus, the characteristics of different portfolios are extracted and multiple perspectives of the asset pricing portfolios could be presented. To the best of our knowledge, this approach is fairly new in describing the asset pricing portfolios in comparison to traditional clustering approaches. We advocate for a holistic view to extract asset-pricing portfolios and therefore enriching the existing clustering approaches in this particular problem.

Figure 2. The Multi-SOM based Clustering Approach

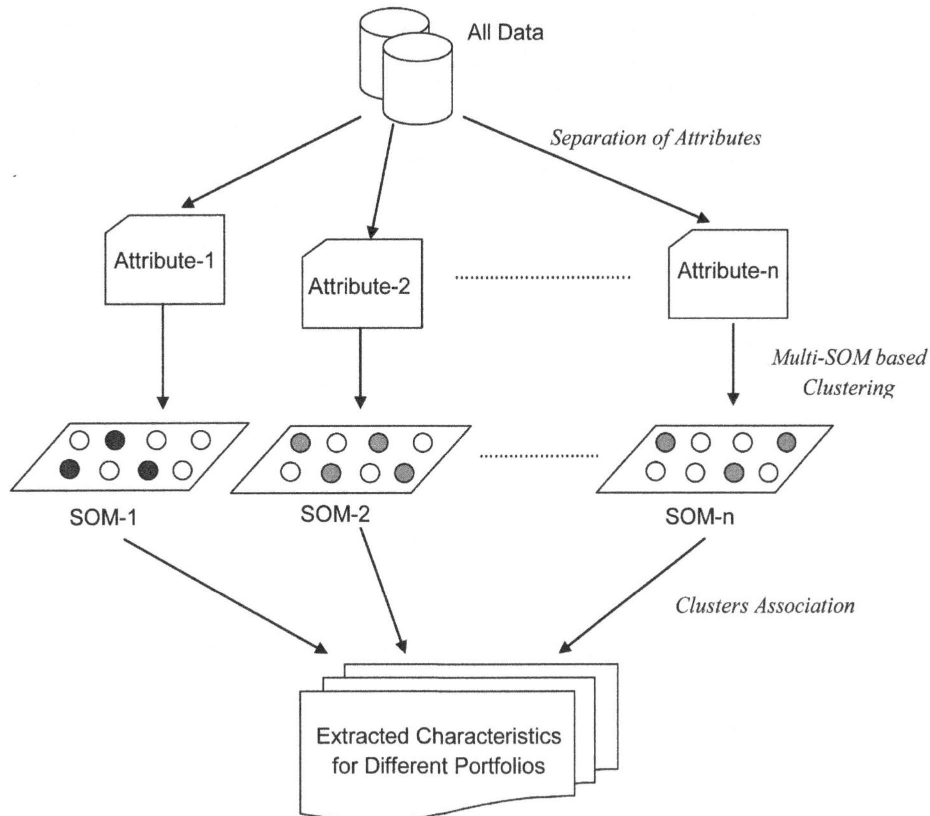

3. DATA

The dataset consists of shares traded on the New York Stock Exchange (NYSE), the American Stock Exchange (AMEX) and the National Association of Securities Dealers Automated Quotations System (NASDAQ) recorded on the Centre for Research in Security Prices (CRSP) and COMPUSTAT from January 1995 to January 2005. CRSP is the source for stock monthly prices and returns. COMPUSTAT is the source for relevant accounting data. To be selected into the dataset, a share must have:

- COMPUSTAT book common equity (B), dividends common equity (D), current accounts (CA) and current liabilities (CL), net income (NI) and sales (Sales) for year *t-1*;
- Relevant accounting data appeared on COMPUSTAT for at least two years in order to avoid the survival bias inherent in the way COMPUSTAT add firms to their database (Banz and Breen (1986));
- CRSP monthly prices for December of year *t-1*;
- To be an ordinary common equity (Share Type of 10 or 11 in the CRSP datafile), which means American Depository Receipts, Real Estate Investment Trust and units of beneficial interest are excluded.

Based on the above data, six attributes for a share are clarified to each share through the following procedures. These attributes include firm's size, B/M, yields, liquidity ratio (liquidity) and profit margin (PM). In December of year *t-1*, a firm size is obtained by multiplying its share price in December of year *t-1* by the number of shares outstanding. B/M is obtained by dividing a share's book common equity for the fiscal year ending in calendar year *t-1* by its size. Yields is a ratio of a share's common equity dividends to its share price. Liquidity is a ratio of a share's current assets to its current liabilities and profit margin is obtained by dividing net income with its sales. Following the common practice in the finance literature (Campbell *et al.* (2008), Fama and French (1988, 1993, 1996)), once obtaining all share's attributes, shares are then sorted independently by their attributes. For instance, all shares are broken into three B/M groups based on the breakpoints for the bottom 20% (Low), middle 60% (Neutral) and top 20% (High) of the ranked values of B/M. Similarly, the same shares are also broken into three size gropes based on the breakpoints for the bottom 20% (Small), middle 60% (Medium) and top 20% (Large) of the ranked values of size. Similar procedures apply to other three attributes as well.

The study period is from 1995 to 2004. Because portfolios are constructed in December year *t-1*, to avoid problems associated with firms reporting delays, the accounting data used in estimation of the share attributes is sourced in year *t-1*. This is to ensure that all accounting information has been made available to all investors at the time of the estimation. Subsequently, the beginning year of the data sample if from 1994. Table 1 provides the data sample size of the study.

Over the ten-year study period, the average size of our sample universe is 6138 shares. Understandably, the sample size reduces with an increase of the number of attributes. This is due to the availability of firm's accounting data. The average number of shares with two attributes over the ten years study period is 5572. Mainly due to the fall of the percent of firms paying dividends (Fama and French (2001), Petersen (2009)), the sample size reduces to 1173 for shares with all five attributes (the last row in the table). Also, the number of shares declines during and after the 2001 recession (from March to November 2001 according to the National Bureau of Economic Research (NBER)), resulting from the burst of the "internet bubble". The most recent recession caused by the Global Financial Crisis is not included in the study as otherwise it would compromise the generality.

4. MODELLING RESULTS

This study is an application of the Multi SOM. The modelling process is quite straightforward. In each year over the 10-year study period, shares with similar return patterns are clustered together through Multi-SOM. Table 2 presents the characteristics of the clusters. It is noticeable that the average share return in clusters differs quite distinctively, ranging from 960% in Cluster 7 to -38% in Cluster 4.

Among the seven clusters, three of them have the average share returns over 100%. This means that if an investor happens to hold a portfolio of shares in these three clusters, this investor can at least double his/her investment. It is widely accepted in the finance literature that the presence

Table 1. Sample size

Year	1995	1996	1997	1998	1999	2000	2001	2002	2003	2004
(i). Size and B/M	6054	6176	6465	6235	5823	5646	5399	4916	4566	4442
(ii). (i) plus Liquidity	4856	5020	5338	5181	4763	4564	4380	3959	3627	3551
(iii). (ii) plus PM	4777	4951	5252	5108	4708	4516	4329	3919	3584	3515
(iv). (iii) plus Yields	1433	1442	1420	1374	1253	1099	1003	908	865	935

Table 2. Cluster characteristics

	Cluster 1	Cluster 2	Cluster 3	Cluster 4	Cluster 5	Cluster 6	Cluster 7
Return	0.22	-0.04	0.54	-0.38	1.1	2.63	9.6
Std. Dev.	0.09	0.07	0.1	0.17	0.3	0.7	1.32

Note: T-test results are all significant at the 1% level.

of the premiums of holding certain types of shares is pervasive. That is investors are compensated with return premiums for bearing certain types of shares associated with higher risk characteristics, such as small in size and high in B/M (the value shares), etc. In other words, these factors have more explanatory power to the share returns. To test whether these factors indeed proxy for share returns, we can simply assess whether the shares in the higher return clusters have the same attributes as indicated in the literature. The results are presented in Table 3 and Table 4.

Among 7 clusters, the cluster with the highest return, Cluster 7, is the smallest with 9 shares in the cluster. In terms of share size, among these 9 shares, 6 of them have small size; 3 of them have medium size. Most noticeably, none of them can be categorised as a large size. The cluster with the biggest number of shares is Cluster 1, in which there are 3970 shares. Among them, 735 shares are value shares (high B/M) and 722 are growth shares. There are 3085, 1704, 2201, 682 and 80 shares located in Cluster 2 to 6 respectively.

If a fundamental factor does have explanatory power to the share returns, it is expected that certain pattern can be observed in the attribute distribution of such factor. In the finance literature, it is well established and widely accepted that the presence of the size factor, where firms with small size have higher average returns than large size shares (Banz (1981), Basu (1983), Chan and Chen (1991), Fama and French (1993), Jaffe et al (1989) and Reinganum (1981)). If such is a case, then the 3 clusters with the relative higher returns (Cluster 5-7) ought to contain a disproportionate number of shares with small size attribute. Table 4 confirms the size factor. The figures in the table are the percentage changes of the numbers of shares allocated in the cluster compared to the numbers of shares that should be allocated based on the attributes clarification described in the data section. This is based on the hypothesis that if no fundamental factor has any explanatory power to share returns, the distribution of the attributes in clusters should not deviate from the proportion of attributes clarified in the data sample. And more importantly, no clear pattern of weight change in attributes can be found.

The results in Table 4 stand in sharp contrast to this hypothesis. It illustrates a clear pattern where an overweight of small size shares is quite distinctive among the 3 higher return clusters. Particularly in the highest return cluster, Cluster 7, the number of shares with small size attribute is outweighed by 2.33 times. At the same time, there is a clear underweight pattern for large size shares among the 3 higher return clusters. This observation suggests that investors can achieve higher return on their investment by forming a portfolio consisting of shares with small size attribute.

The results in Table 4 also illustrate a pattern that an overweight of high B/M shares among the 3 higher return clusters. This finding also confirms the existence of the value factor, in which investors can earn high return by tilting their investment with high B/M. For the other 3 attributes, liquidity, PM and yields, the modelling results fail to find any pattern through clusters, which contradicts the current literature. This finding casts doubt on whether these attributes have explanatory power on share returns. The next natural question is how to reconcile this contradictory finding. One explanation might be that the presence of the size

Table 3. Number of shares and attributes in each cluster

		Cluster 1	Cluster 2	Cluster 3	Cluster 4	Cluster 5	Cluster 6	Cluster 7
size	Small	635	554	331	539	200	39	6
	Medium	2390	1886	1022	1290	405	39	3
	Large	945	645	351	372	77	2	0
B/M	Low	722	585	374	523	137	17	2
	Neutral	2513	1968	953	1202	367	24	3
	High	735	532	377	476	178	39	4
Liquidity	Low	963	589	334	314	106	8	1
	Medium	2301	1846	1036	1367	446	54	5
	High	706	650	334	520	130	18	3
PM	Low	634	522	332	582	185	30	2
	Medium	2490	1909	1022	1229	381	35	6
	High	846	654	350	390	116	15	1
Yields	Low	625	530	391	599	177	18	4
	Medium	2422	1970	1002	1221	382	36	3
	High	923	585	311	381	123	26	2

Table 4. Weight change for the share attributes in the clusters

		Cluster 1	Cluster 2	Cluster 3	Cluster 4	Cluster 5	Cluster 6	Cluster 7
size	Small	-0.20	-0.10	-0.03	0.22	0.47	1.44	2.33
	Medium	0.00	0.02	0.00	-0.02	-0.01	-0.19	-0.44
	Large	0.19	0.05	0.03	-0.15	-0.44	-0.88	-1.00
B/M	Low	-0.09	-0.05	0.10	0.19	0.00	0.06	0.11
	Neutral	0.05	0.06	-0.07	-0.09	-0.10	-0.50	-0.44
	High	-0.07	-0.14	0.11	0.08	0.30	1.44	1.22
Liquidity	Low	0.21	-0.05	-0.02	-0.29	-0.22	-0.50	-0.44
	Medium	-0.03	0.00	0.01	0.04	0.09	0.13	-0.07
	High	-0.11	0.05	-0.02	0.18	-0.05	0.13	0.67
PM	Low	-0.20	-0.15	-0.03	0.32	0.36	0.88	0.11
	Medium	0.05	0.03	0.00	-0.07	-0.07	-0.27	0.11
	High	0.07	0.06	0.03	-0.11	-0.15	-0.06	-0.44
Yields	Low	-0.21	-0.14	0.15	0.36	0.30	0.13	1.22
	Medium	0.02	0.06	-0.02	-0.08	-0.07	-0.25	-0.44
	High	0.16	-0.05	-0.09	-0.13	-0.10	0.63	0.11

and value factors subsumes somehow the explanatory power of other factors. This explanation is consistent with the explanation offered by Fama and French (1993). The other important finding from the results is that no attribute can be used to explain the reason behind that low returns. The average returns for both Cluster 2 and 4 are negative, however, there is no pattern at all to indicate which attribute contributes such bad performance.

Table 5. Weight change for the share attributes in the clusters – Equal distribution

		Cluster 1	Cluster 2	Cluster 3	Cluster 4	Cluster 5	Cluster 6	Cluster 7
size	Small	0.34	0.54	0.63	0.96	1.37	2.38	2.33
	Medium	-0.43	-0.44	-0.45	-0.47	-0.50	-0.60	-0.63
	Large	0.94	0.79	0.72	0.46	0.12	-0.56	-0.44
B/M	Low	0.56	0.67	0.70	0.79	0.53	0.38	2.33
	Neutral	-0.42	-0.42	-0.48	-0.50	-0.51	-0.75	-1.00
	High	0.70	0.59	0.73	0.71	1.00	1.88	0.67
Liquidity	Low	0.88	0.60	0.70	0.29	0.44	0.19	-0.44
	Medium	-0.47	-0.45	-0.44	-0.44	-0.39	-0.27	-0.44
	High	0.53	0.74	0.64	1.04	0.74	0.63	1.78
PM	Low	0.39	0.51	0.65	1.03	1.01	1.81	1.22
	Medium	-0.42	-0.44	-0.47	-0.49	-0.45	-0.67	-0.44
	High	0.87	0.80	0.76	0.43	0.35	0.19	0.11
Yields	Low	0.36	0.52	0.80	1.08	1.02	0.75	1.78
	Medium	-0.43	-0.40	-0.46	-0.51	-0.51	-0.63	-0.63
	High	0.94	0.69	0.56	0.44	0.52	1.13	0.11

To address the concern over whether our findings are due to the specific way that the sample data is ranked based on their attributes, 2 tests of the robustness were carried out. The first robustness test re-clarifies shares into the three sub-attribute groups (i.e. Low/Small, Neutral/Medium and High/Large) evenly. The other is to re-clarify shares based on the breakpoints for the bottom 10% (Low), middle 80% (Neutral) and top 10% (High). Table 5 reports the modelling results for the first test (the second test results are not reported here as similar findings are reported).

The results from Table 5 confirm our previous findings, only with more distinctive results. One question might be asked is that why we don't report our findings with these more distinctive results? The answer for this question is in finance literature shares are rarely sorted into groups evenly. We followed the general practice and reported the results based on that. Our other robustness test also confirms our findings. Subsequently, our findings are robust.

5. FURTHER RESEARCH

The proposed SOM-based clustering approach has opened up several potential future research works. It is necessary to consider the issues of computational complexity and scalability of the approach to deal with large number of stock data. In addition, hierarchical clustering approach could be further investigated for presenting stock data in hierarchical structure. Such hierarchy enables the creation of taxonomy of the characteristics of share returns data. The emerging studies in the field of incremental learning have provided a new perspective for analysing the time series data. The time dimension in share returns data is a prospective application for exploring the incorporation of incremental learning with the proposed SOM-based clustering approach.

6. CONCLUSION

In the finance literature, the common practice is to sort and group shares ad hoc based on share's attributes. Then portfolios formed based on these groups or a combination of them are used to assess whether asset pricing models have explanatory power over the dispersion of share returns. Sorting shares based on the attributes that are known associated with share performance poses a challenge to asset pricing and causes a concern over data-snooping bias.

In this study, we turn the table around. We adopt a novel Multi-SOM approach to cluster shares first and then identify share's attributes or fundamental factors. It is explicitly data-driven and therefore should be immune to the problems embedded with the sorting technique.

Our results show that there is a strong presence of firm size attribute in explaining high share returns. Another firm's factor, book-to-market ratio, has also explanatory power over share returns. These findings are consistent with the large body of finance literature. However, the significance of our findings is that they are from a totally different approach, which only enhances the robustness of the literature. On the other hand, the modelling results fail to find evidence in supporting the other factors - liquidity, profit margin and dividends yields, having any explanatory power over share returns. This is inconsistent with current finance literature. An explanation of this inconsistence and examinations on whether other fundamental factors, such as default risk, leverage, industrial characteristics, also possess explanatory power over share performance as documented in the literature are left for further studies.

REFERENCES

Ahn, D. H., Conrad, J., & Dittmar, R. F. (2009). Basis assets. *Review of Financial Studies*, *22*(12), 5133–5174. doi:10.1093/rfs/hhp065

Banz, R. W. (1981). The relationship between return and market value of common stocks. *Journal of Financial Economics*, *9*(1), 3–18. doi:10.1016/0304-405X(81)90018-0

Banz, R. W., & Breen, W. J. (1986). Sample-dependent results using accounting and market data: Some evidence. *The Journal of Finance*, *41*(4), 779–793. doi:10.2307/2328228

Basu, S. (1983). The relationship between earnings yield, market value and return for NYSE common stocks: Further evidence. *Journal of Financial Economics*, *12*(1), 129–156. doi:10.1016/0304-405X(83)90031-4

Berk, J. B. (2000). Sorting out sorts. *The Journal of Finance*, *55*(1), 407–427. doi:10.1111/0022-1082.00210

Brown, S. J., & Goetzmann, W. N. (1997). Mutual fund styles. *Journal of Financial Economics*, *43*(3), 373–399. doi:10.1016/S0304-405X(96)00898-7

Brown, S. J., & Goetzmann, W. N. (2003). Hedge funds with style. *Journal of Portfolio Management*, *29*(2), 101–112. doi:10.3905/jpm.2003.319877

Brown, S. J., Lajbcygier, P., & Li, B. (2008). Going negative: What to do with negative book equity stocks? *Journal of Portfolio Management*, *35*(1), 98–102. doi:10.3905/JPM.2008.35.1.95

Campbell, J. Y., Hilscher, J. D., & Szilagyi, J. (2008). In search of distress risk. *The Journal of Finance*, *63*(6), 1467–1484. doi:10.1111/j.1540-6261.2008.01416.x

Chan, K. C., & Chen, N. (1991). Structural and return characteristics of small and large firms. *The Journal of Finance*, *46*(4), 1467–1484. doi:10.2307/2328867

Chava, S., & Jarrow, R. A. (2004). Bankruptcy prediction with industry effects. *Review of Finance*, *8*(4), 537–569. doi:10.1093/rof/8.4.537

Conrad, J., Cooper, M., & Kaul, G. (2003). Value versus glamour. *The Journal of Finance*, *58*(5), 1969–1996. doi:10.1111/1540-6261.00594

Daniel, K., & Titman, D. (2005). *Testing factor-model explanations of market anomalies*. Working Paper, Kellogg School of Management, Northwestern University.

Daniel, K., & Titman, D. (2006). Market reactions to tangible and intangible information. *The Journal of Finance*, *61*(4), 1605–1643. doi:10.1111/j.1540-6261.2006.00884.x

Fama, E. F., & French, K. R. (1988). Dividend yields and expected stock returns. *Journal of Financial Economics*, *33*(1), 3–56. doi:10.1016/0304-405X(93)90023-5

Fama, E. F., & French, K. R. (1993). Common risk factors in the returns on stocks and bonds. *Journal of Financial Economics*, *33*(1), 3–56. doi:10.1016/0304-405X(93)90023-5

Fama, E. F., & French, K. R. (1995). Size and book-to-market sectors in earnings and returns. *The Journal of Finance*, *50*(1), 131–155. doi:10.2307/2329241

Fama, E. F., & French, K. R. (1996). Multifactor explanation of asset pricing anomalies. *The Journal of Finance*, *51*(1), 55–84. doi:10.2307/2329302

Fama, E. F., & French, K. R. (2001). Disappearing dividends: Changing firm characteristics or lower propensity to pay? *Journal of Applied Corporate Finance*, *14*(1), 67–79. doi:10.1111/j.1745-6622.2001.tb00321.x

Han, X., Wang, L., Shi, X., & Liang, Y. (2008). *SOM2W and RBF neural network-based hybrid models and their applications to new share pricing*. Paper presented at the meeting of the IEEE International Conference on Natural Computation, Washington, DC.

Hsu, Y., & Chen, A. (2008). *Clustering time series data by SOM for the optimal hedge ratio estimation*. Paper presented at the meeting of the IEEE International Conference on Convergence and Hybrid Information Technology, Busan, Korea.

Jaffe, J., Keim, D. B., & Westerfield, R. (1989). Earnings yields, market values, and stock returns. *The Journal of Finance*, *44*(1), 135–148. doi:10.2307/2328279

Jevtic, N. (2001). *Interactive tutorial on neural networks*. Retrieved from http://sydney.edu.au/engineering/it/~irena/ai01/nn/som.html

Kohonen, T. (2001). *Self-organizing maps*. Espoo, Finland: Springer-Verlag.

Larose, D. T. (2005). *Discovering knowledge in data: An introduction to data mining*. John Wiley & Sons, Inc.

Petersen, M. A. (2009). Estimating standard errors in finance panel data sets: Comparing approaches. *Review of Financial Studies*, *22*(1), 435–480. doi:10.1093/rfs/hhn053

Reinganum, M. R. (1981). Misspecification of capital asset pricing: Empirical anomalies based on earnings' yields and market values. *Journal of Financial Economics*, *9*(1), 19–46. doi:10.1016/0304-405X(81)90019-2

Smith, K. A. (1999). *Introduction to neural networks and data mining for business applications*. Australia: Eruditions Publishing.

Stein, J. (1996). Rational capital budgeting in an irrational world. *The Journal of Business*, *69*(4), 429–455. doi:10.1086/209699

Zmijewski, M. E. (1984). Methodological issues related to the estimation of financial distress prediction models. *Journal of Accounting Research*, *22*, 59–82. doi:10.2307/2490859

Chapter 2
Efficient Pronunciation Assessment of Taiwanese-Accented English Based on Unsupervised Model Adaptation and Dynamic Sentence Selection

Chung-Hsien Wu
National Cheng Kung University, Taiwan, R.O.C.

Hung-Yu Su
National Cheng Kung University, Taiwan, R.O.C.

Chao-Hong Liu
National Cheng Kung University, Taiwan, R.O.C.

ABSTRACT

This chapter presents an efficient approach to personalized pronunciation assessment of Taiwanese-accented English. The main goal of this study is to detect frequently occurring mispronunciation patterns of Taiwanese-accented English instead of scoring English pronunciations directly. The proposed assessment help quickly discover personalized mispronunciations of a student, thus English teachers can spend more time on teaching or rectifying students' pronunciations. In this approach, an unsupervised model adaptation method is performed on the universal acoustic models to recognize the speech of a specific speaker with mispronunciations and Taiwanese accent. A dynamic sentence selection algorithm, considering the mutual information of the related mispronunciations, is proposed to choose a sentence containing the most undetected mispronunciations in order to quickly extract personalized mispronunciations. The experimental results show that the proposed unsupervised adaptation approach obtains an accuracy improvement of about 2.1% on the recognition of Taiwanese-accented English speech.

DOI: 10.4018/978-1-4666-1830-5.ch002

INTRODUCTION

Pronunciation is a difficult part for language learners to be proficient in Second Languages (L2) due to the influence of First Languages (L1) and thus require necessary instructions from professional personnel. Computer Assisted Language Learning (CALL) systems (Menzel *et al.* 2000) (Mak *et al.* 2003) were introduced to provide automatic learning and evaluation for the needs of L2 learners (Derwing *et al.* 2000)(Coniam *et al.* 1999)(Kalikow *et al.* 1972). Computer Assisted Pronunciation Training (CAPT) is an important topic of CALL, focusing on rectifying pronunciation errors. To evaluate pronunciation proficiency of non-native speakers, pronunciation scoring is mostly used in CAPT systems to score the speech input. On the other hand, mispronunciation detection also provides additional useful information for L2 learners, e.g., local pronunciation mistakes might be more helpful for pronunciation rectification compared to a global score for a whole sentence.

In the past decade, automatic speech recognition (ASR) systems were employed to score the pronunciation in CAPT systems. SPELL(Hiller *et al.* 1993) used word pairs for pronunciation scoring at phone level to assess and improve L1 pronunciation in modules for teaching consonant production, vowel quality, rhythm and intonation, in three European languages (English, French and Italian). Hamada el al. (Hamada *et al.* 1993) used dynamic programming and vector quantization to compare non-native utterance with native recoding at word level. The capacity of text-dependent approaches was restricted because training materials cannot be updated without other new utterances from native speakers. ASR using hidden Markov models (HMMs) has also been adopted for scoring a whole sentence instead of smaller pieces. In an HMM, the state is not directly visible, but output, dependent on the state, is visible (Baum *et al.* 1967). Each state has a probability distribution over the possible output tokens. Therefore the sequence of tokens generated by an HMM gives some information about the sequence of states. HMMs have been known for their application in temporal pattern recognition such as speech, handwriting, and gesture recognition. Neumeyer *et al.* (Neumeyer *et al.* 1996) used HMM log-likelihood, segment duration and timing for pronunciation scoring of the whole sentence. Eskenazi (Eskenazi, 1996) used HMM log-likelihood to score the pronunciations of non-native speech compared to the corresponding native speech. For further analysis on pronunciation, the goodness of pronunciation (GOP) measure (Witt and Young, 2000) was proposed to score each phoneme in an utterance based on HMM likelihood and several studies brought other features or methods, such as phoneme posterior score, duration, and speech rate, for phone-level pronunciation scoring (Franco *et al.* 2000) (Mak *et al.* 2003)(Neri *et al.* 2006a) (Nakagawa *et al.* 2003).

The concept of mispronunciation network was proposed by Ronen *et al.* (Ronen *et al.* 1997). In (Neri *et al.* 2006a), HMMs for native and non-native speakers were trained and used to evaluate the pronunciations by the ratio of HMM scores of non-native to native speakers. Franco *et al.* (Franco *et al.* 2000) used the log-likelihood ratio to evaluate the recognized results based on the native and nonnative acoustic models. Tsubota *et al.* (Tsubota *et al.* 2002) adopted pronunciation error network to detect mispronunciations of Japanese students, and used Linear Discriminant Analysis (LDA) for evaluation. Neri *et al.* also introduced some work using LDA to discover the learners of Dutch having the problems on vowel pronunciation and the confusion between fricatives and plosives (Neri *et al.* 2004)(Neri *et al.* 2006b). Kim *et al.* (Kim *et al.* 2004) included the probable mispronunciations in recognition to detect the pronunciation errors and gave advice for correction. Afterward, Tepperman and Narayanan used prosodic features to detect the stresses in the pronunciation automatically (Tepperman and Narayanan, 2005). SENSEI (Chandel *et al.* 2007) proposed an assessment on articulations, stresses, and grammars for call center agents.

In CAPT systems, users were asked to complete a fixed course for pronunciation assessment. However, each individual might have different and unique mispronunciation patterns, which are termed as "personalized mispronunciations" in this chapter. If the course for pronunciation assessment can be chosen from the representative sentences with the potential mispronunciations, the assessment and evaluation will be more efficient. Therefore in this study a dynamic sentence selection algorithm is proposed for efficient pronunciation assessment. In the past years, sentence selection methods have been widely used in many NLP research topics. Several studies applied sentence selection methods to select a balanced sentence set from a large corpus. For example, the Text-to-Speech (TTS) (Wu *et al.* 2007) conversion systems used the greedy algorithm to select the sentences for speech database recording (Isogai *et al.* 2005)(Bozkurt *et al.* 2003). Schelffer *et al.* (Scheffer *et al.* 2001) presented an effective learning approach to significant sentence selection for manual annotation included in the training set. Ji and Grishman (Ji and Grishman, 2006) proposed a semi-supervised learning method involving bootstrapping and self-training algorithms.

This study proposes an efficient approach to assessing personalized pronunciations of English with Taiwanese accent. The proposed assessment method tries to detect frequently occurring mispronunciations rather than to score the overall pronunciations of a testee. An unsupervised model adaptation algorithm is adopted to adapt the acoustic models to recognize the surface form rather than the base form from Taiwanese-accented English speech. The adaptation makes use of the prior knowledge of universal mispronunciation and phone confusion matrices to determine which model should be adapted based on the recognized speech segments. To reserve more time for teachers to teach and rectify the pronunciations of the L2 speakers, efficient pronunciation assessment is achieved using the proposed dynamic sentence selection to quickly targeting their mispronunciations by choosing suitable materials for the testees. The experimental results show that the proposed unsupervised adaptation method attains an improvement on the recognition accuracy for Taiwanese-accented English speech. Eventually, dynamic sentence selection can significantly decrease the number of sentences in assessment with comparable precision rates on mispronunciation detection.

This chapter is organized as follows. In the next section, Mispronunciation Detection is described with a flow chart of the proposed pronunciation assessment method. The Dynamic Sentence Selection method used for efficient assessment is then detailed. Experiments are presented to show the performance of the proposed mispronunciation detection method and the effectiveness of sentence selection. Finally, discussions, future research directions and conclusion are given.

MISPRONUNCIATION DETECTION

Figure 1 illustrates the block diagram of the proposed method for the assessment on English pronunciations of Taiwanese speakers. The detected mispronunciations can be used to improve the English pronunciation proficiency for the Taiwanese students. In this diagram, the user is asked to pronounce a prompted sentence for evaluation. The speech utterance is recognized through an English ASR referring to a phone lattice generated from the prompted textual sentence, and the mispronunciations in this utterance are detected.

Utterance Verification

The input speech utterance is first verified to avoid speech that are irregular or inconsistent with the prompted text, such as false start, hesitation, and repair. The verification is performed using the frame-based log-likelihood. The input speech

Figure 1. Diagram of the proposed pronunciation assessment method based on mispronunciation detection for Taiwanese-accented English speech

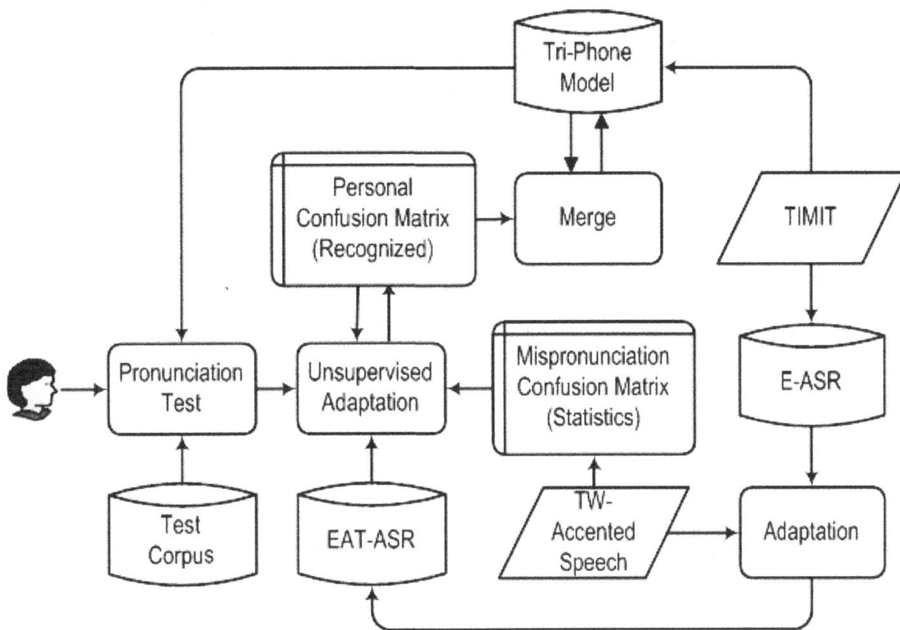

segments are forcedly aligned and verified based on the *average phone confidence score*. The *average phone confidence score* is computed for each input utterance and compared to a threshold. If the average phone confidence score exceeds the threshold, the input speech is accepted for further mispronunciation detection. Otherwise, the input speech is rejected and a new speech input is required. The *average phone confidence score* ρ is computed as:

$$\begin{aligned}\rho &= \frac{1}{N}\sum_{i=1}^{N}\rho_i \\ &= \frac{1}{N}\sum_{i=1}^{N}\frac{1}{d_i}\sum_{t=t_i}^{t_i+d_i-1}\log P(q_i \mid y_t)\end{aligned} \tag{1}$$

where N is the number of phones in the evaluation sentence. ρ_i denotes the confidence score of the ith phone calculated by averaging the frame-based log posterior probabilities. d_i is the number of frames in the ith phone. q_i represents the acoustic model of the ith phone, and t_i is the starting frame of the ith phone. y_t is the spectral feature vector of the input speech at time t. The frame-based posterior probability $P(q_i|y_t)$ is estimated as:

$$\begin{aligned}P(q_i \mid y_t) &= \frac{P(y_t \mid q_i)P(q_i)}{P(y_t)} \\ &= \frac{P(y_t \mid q_i)P(q_i)}{\sum_{j=1}^{J}P(y_t \mid q_j)P(q_j)}\end{aligned} \tag{2}$$

where J is the number of phone models. $P(q)$ is the probability of choosing the phone model q from all phone models, and is assumed to be uniform. Equation (2) can be rewritten as:

$$P(q_i \mid y_t) = \frac{P(y_t \mid q_i)}{\sum_{j=1}^{J}P(y_t \mid q_j)} \tag{3}$$

Figure 2. Procedure for the development of the test corpus

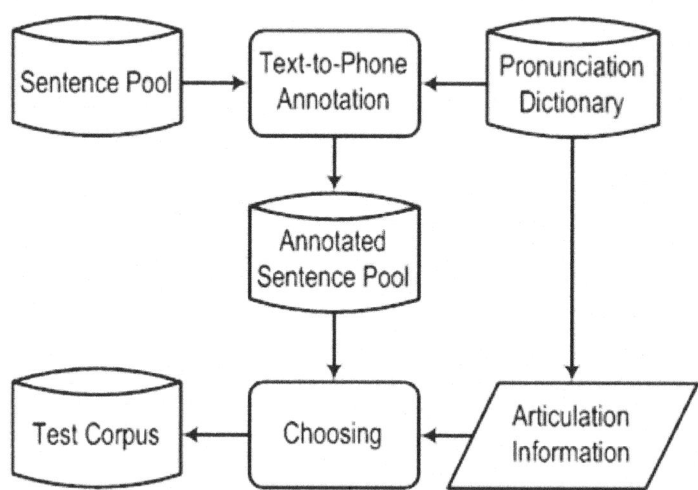

Unsupervised Adaptation for Speaker Dependency

Instead of recognizing what is supposed to be pronounced (the base form of the speech) for a prompted sentence, the actually pronounced speech (the surface form of the speech) should be recognized for mispronunciation detection. For achieving such a goal, an unsupervised adaptation mechanism (Su *et al.* 2008) is employed to adapt the models using pronounced speech to fit the Taiwanese accented speech and determine the corresponding surface form for the speech. The adapted models can boost the recognition results for more reliable pronunciation assessment and the recognized results are more reliable for adaptation iteratively. Speaker-adaptive acoustic models and personalized articulation patterns (Wu *et al.* 2011) were proposed for articulation-disordered speech recognition.

A test corpus is developed for evaluation of English pronunciations, which covers the phone concatenations as many as possible. Figure 2 illustrates the procedure of choosing the test sentences from a collected sentence pool. According to the phone models, the criteria for choosing the sentences consider that the appearance frequency of each phone should be at least 25 and the sentences can cover most cases of the inter-phone concatenations. An appearance function that considers the appearance frequency and the inter-phone concatenations is introduced, and the appearance function of a sentence W is defined as:

$$AppFC(W = k_1 ... k_n) = \sum_i C(k_i) P(k_{i-1}, k_i, k_{i+1}) \tag{4}$$

where k_i is the ith phone in sentence W with n phones, $C(k_i)$ represents the appearance frequency of phone k_i in the selected sentences, and $P(k_{i-1}\ k_i\ k_{i+1})$ denotes the appearance probability of tri-phone "$k_{i-1}\ k_i\ k_{i+1}$". In the beginning, the counts of all phones are set to 1, and the tri-phone probabilities are initialized as they are in the TIMIT database. As a sentence selected at each iteration, $C(k_i)$ and $P(k_{i-1}\ k_i\ k_{i+1})$ are updated with the numbers of appearances of phones k_i and the probabilities of tri-phones ($k_{i-1}\ k_i\ k_{i+1}$) in the sentence. Therefore, the sentences in the pool can be scored by $AppFC(W)$ and the sentence with the lowest value is selected. The test corpus is determined when each phone occurs at least 25 times. Table 1 lists the statistics of the test corpus.

Table 1. Statistics of the test corpus

	#
Sentences	83
Phones	1126
Mean Phone Frequency (±Var.)	28.15±2.4
Minimum # of Phones in a sentence	25
Maximum # of Phones in a sentence	34

In pronunciation assessment, each speaker is asked to utter a sentence from the test corpus. Each utterance is used to adapt the acoustic models for speaker-dependent modeling. An unsupervised adaptation mechanism is proposed to determine which phone models should be adapted using the utterance segment. The reliability for recognizing the phone segments f as phone x (surface form) from the input speech utterance is examined, and the adaptation is performed on the pairs with high reliabilities. The reliability is determined as:

$$P(f \mid x) > \sum_{m} P(f \mid m)P(m \mid x) \tag{5}$$

where m represents all possible mispronunciations of phone x obtained from the training database as shown in Table 2. $P(f|m)$ is the recognition likelihood of phone speech segment f recognized by the acoustic model of phone m. $P(m|x)$ is the occurrence probability of mispronunciation m with respect to phone x. For incrementally adapting the acoustic model of phone x, an iterative approach is proposed as follows.

$$P_l(f \mid x) > \sum_{m} P_{l-1}(f \mid m)P(m \mid x) \tag{6}$$

Equation (6) provides an iterative condition to determine if the acoustic model of phone x should be adapted at the lth iteration using the phone speech segment f. In the proposed adaptation method, the iterations are repeated until no more segments satisfying the above condition for model adaptation using MLLR.

Speech Recognition Using Phone Lattice

In mispronunciation detection, each speech utterance is recognized using a phone lattice generated from the prompted sentence. Figure 3 shows a predicted phone lattice generated from a given sentence "this is a book". In this figure, symbols B, E and SP denote the tags of Begin, End and Short Pause, respectively, and the other symbols denote the English phones. In the phone recognition process, given the input speech S along with the prompted sentence W, the recognized phone sequence $\hat{x}$ is obtained as follows.

$$\begin{aligned}\hat{X} &= \arg\max_{X} P(X \mid S, W) \\ &\approx \arg\max_{X} P(S, W \mid X)P(X) \\ &\approx \arg\max_{X} P(S \mid X)P(W \mid X)P(X)\end{aligned} \tag{7}$$

where $P(W|X)$ represents the probability of the prompted sentence W generated from the proposed mispronunciation detection model given a phone sequence X, and $P(S|X)$ and $P(X)$ are the likelihood outputs of the acoustic phone models and the language model for the phone sequence X, respectively. However, the language model $P(X)$ can be ignored due to the known prompts, and the optimal recognized phone sequence $\hat{X}$ from the phone lattice is calculated as:

$$\hat{X} = \arg\max_{X} P(S \mid X)P(W \mid X) \tag{8}$$

To estimate the probability $P(W|X)$, a mispronunciation detection model is proposed and trained using the "English across Taiwan" (EAT) database, which was collected by the *Association for Computational Linguistics and Chinese Language Processing* (*ACLCLP*) in Taiwan. Speech

Table 2. Extracted mispronunciations for Taiwanese speakers

Original phone	Mispronounced phone	Example	Correct Pronunciation	Mispronunciation	Frequency
[a]	[o]	Tom	[tam]	[tom]	46.15%
[a]	[ɔ]	Stock	[stak]	[stɔk]	53.85%
[æ]	[a]	Staff	[stæf]	[staf]	28.57%
[æ]	[ɛ]	Bang	[bæŋ]	[bɛŋ]	11.11%
[æ]	[ə]	Sapphire	[`sæfaɪr]	[`səfaɪr]	60.32%
[ʌ]	[a]	Luck	[lʌk]	[lak]	78.57%
[ʌ]	[ɔ]	Gut	[gʌt]	[gɔt]	21.43%
[ɔ]	[a]	Wrong	[rɔŋ]	[raŋ]	100%
[aɪ]	[ɪ]	Crisis	[`kraɪsɪs]	[`krɪsɪs]	100%
[e]	[ɛ]	Led	[led]	[lɛd]	100%
[ɛ]	[ɪ]	Error	[`erɚ]	[`ɪrɚ]	100%
[ɪ]	[i]	Lift	[lɪft]	[lift]	40.00%
[ɪ]	[e]	Republic	[rɪ`pʌblik]	[re`pʌblik]	60.00%
[i]	[ɪ]	Tea	[ti]	[tɪ]	100%
[o]	[a]	Dome	[dom]	[dam]	8.33%
[o]	[ɔ]	Holy	[holɪ]	[hɔlɪ]	91.67%
[u]	[ʊ]	Mood	[mud]	[mʊd]	100%
[ɚ]	[ə]	Father	[`faðɚ]	[`faðə]	100%
[ð]	[l]	This	[ðɪs]	[lɪs]	89.66%
[ð]	[d]	This	[ðɪs]	[dɪs]	10.34%
[θ]	[s]	Thank	[θæŋk]	[sæŋk]	100%
[ŋ]	[n]	Ring	[riŋ]	[rin]	100%
[k]	del	Sink	[sɪŋk]	[sɪŋ]	75.00%
[k]	[kə]	Sink	[sɪŋk]	[sɪŋkə]	25.00%
[d]	del	Red	[rɛd]	[rɛ]	76.79%
[d]	[də]	Red	[rɛd]	[rɛdə]	23.21%
[l]	del	Hotel	[ho`tɛl]	[ho`tɛ]	3.65%
[m]	[n]	Lame	[lem]	[len]	100%
[n]	del	Rain	[ren]	[re]	100%
[r]	[ə]	Star	[star]	[starə]	100%
[s]	del	This	[ðɪs]	[ðɪ]	77.27%
[s]	[z]	Exist	[ɪg`zist]	[ɪg`zizt]	22.73%
[t]	del	Rat	[ræt]	[ræ]	76.40%
[t]	[tə]	Rat	[ræt]	[rætə]	23.60%
[z]	del	Topaz	[`topæz]	[`topæ]	4.73%
[z]	[s]	Days	[dez]	[des]	95.27%

Figure 3. An example of the phone lattice for recognition based on the possible mispronunciations for the sentence "This is a book"

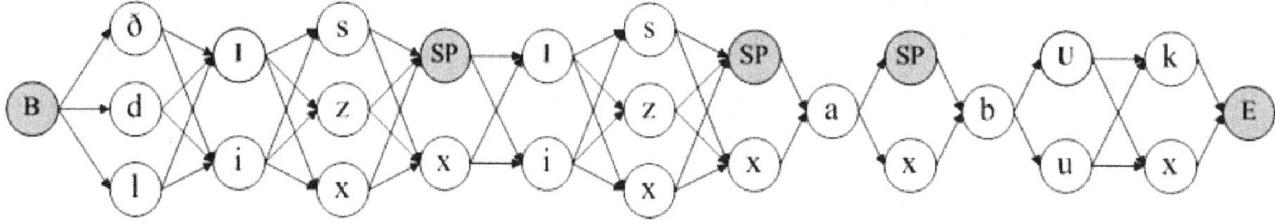

utterances in the EAT database were manually annotated by six English teachers to identify the mispronunciations with Taiwanese accent. The database was divided into 3 parts, and each part was annotated by two English teachers for cross validation. If they have different annotations, they will discuss to reach a final agreement. Table 2 lists the mispronunciations extracted from manual transcriptions. The table contains 36 types of mispronunciations composed of 24 English phones out of 40 canonical English phones and the symbol "del" marks the deletion error.

DYNAMIC SENTENCE SELECTION FOR EFFICIENT ASSESSMENT

In pronunciation assessment, for a beginner in English learning, the speaker sometimes needs to pronounce the same sentence several times. The reason for multiple pronunciations of one prompted sentence is due to the casually pronounced or disfluent pronunciations, such as false start, hesitation, and repair in the speech input. In the recording procedure, the time for a speaker to record all sentences for the test database takes about half an hour. In this section, a dynamic sentence selection is proposed for efficiency purpose.

Sentence Scoring

Sentence selection is adopted to select the sentences from the test corpus based on the detected mispronunciations from the already tested sentences. The system chooses a sentence s with J phones having the highest score computed by summing up the information of all the phones and their mispronunciation types:

$$Score(s_1^J) = -\sum_{j=1}^{J}\sum_{k=1}^{K} p_{jk} \log(p_{jk}) \tag{9}$$

where K is the number of different types of mispronunciations of the jth phone in sentence s. p_{jk} means the probability counted from the already tested sentences for the kth mispronunciation of the jth phone. Sentence scored by Equation (9) helps choose the most informative sentence from the un-tested sentences to update the probabilities of the mispronunciations of a phone. The most informative sentence in the test corpus is defined as the sentence containing the most number of phones having not been tested yet.

Mutual Information-Based Inference for Sentence Selection

From the EAT database, analytical results reveal that Taiwanese speakers who mispronounce a phone are likely to mispronounce other phones with similar/associated pronunciation types. Mispronunciations are classified into *Letter-to-sound Conversion Errors* and *Phonological Errors*. The *Letter-to-sound Conversion Errors* result from difficult orthographic phoneme conversion in English, while the *Phonological Errors* represent the mispronunciation due to the influence of Mandarin pronunciations. Since there is no difference between long and short vowels in Mandarin phones, duration is not important information to distinguish two Mandarin phones. Accordingly, if a speaker mispronounces [i] into [**I**], he/she might very likely mispronounce [u] into [**U**]. To discover these associated mispronunciation pairs, Mutual Information (MI) is adopted to calculate the mutual relations between two mispronunciations:

$$I(V;U) = \sum_{V}\sum_{U} P(V,U)\log\frac{P(V,U)}{P(V)P(U)} \tag{10}$$

where V and U are mispronunciations. $P(V)$ and $P(U)$ denote the probability of mispronunciation pairs V and U, and $P(V, U)$ represents the joint probability of V and U. $P(V)$ is estimated as:

$$P(V) = \frac{count(V)}{\sum_{s=1}^{S}\sum_{A} count(A \mid s)} \quad (11)$$

where A represents all mispronunciations from speaker s, and S is the total number of speakers. $count(V)$ is the count of mispronunciation V in the database.

$$P(V,U) = \frac{count(V,U)}{\sum_{s=1}^{S}\sum_{A}\sum_{B} count(A,B \mid s)} \quad (12)$$

where A and B are the mispronunciations for speakers. $count(V,U)$ is the number of co-occurrences of mispronunciations V and U in the EAT database. Fifty-three highly associated mispronunciation pairs were extracted from EAT corpus. Table 3 shows the top 10 of the 53 mispronunciation pairs. The mispronunciation X can be determined by the mispronunciation set $Y = \{y_1, y_2 ... y_r\}$ which are associated with X in the 56 pairs. The probability of an un-observed variation X can be obtained from the probabilities of its associated set Y in the EAT database, according to the Bayes' rule:

$$\begin{aligned} P(X) &= \frac{P(X \mid Y)}{P(Y \mid X)} P(Y) \\ &\approx \sum_{r=1}^{|Y|} W_r \frac{P(X \mid y_r)}{P(y_r \mid X)} P(y_r) \end{aligned} \quad (13)$$

$P(X|Y)$ is the probability for X while Y occurs, and $P(Y|X)$ is probability for Y while X occurs. W_r is a weighting factor estimated for X with different association rules in the variation set, and is computed as the co-occurrence frequencies for all variations with X from the EAT database:

$$W_r = \frac{P(X, y_r)}{\sum_{r=1}^{|Y|} P(X, y_r)} \quad (14)$$

The probability of an un-observed mispronunciation X is estimated from all its associated and observed mispronunciations as

$$\tilde{P}(X) \approx \sum_{r=1}^{|Y|} W_r \frac{P(X \mid y_r)}{P(y_r \mid X)} \tilde{P}(y_r) \quad (15)$$

$P(\cdot)$ indicates the probabilities estimated from the sentences tested by the speaker so far, and $\tilde{P}(\cdot)$ means the probability estimated from the EAT database as the prior knowledge. In determining the convergence of probability distributions of the mispronunciations for an un-observed phone, the probability of un-observed mispronunciation can be calculated using Equation (15) to obtain the approximated probability from the probabilities of the associated mispronunciations. The approximated probabilities are used for convergence determination in the assessment process. If the probability distributions of mispronunciations for a phone with un-observed mispronunciations converge, the mispronunciations of the phone are considered to be stabilized; otherwise the probability of the un-observed mispronunciation is set to 0.

EXPERIMENTS

In the experiments, HMM Toolkit (HTK) (Young, 2000) was used to train the acoustic models using the TIMIT corpus. The TIMIT corpus is comprised of 6,300 sentences recorded by 438 males and 192 females and defines 62 English phones including some context-dependent phones. Since the speech samples for some of the 62 English phones in the Taiwanese-accented database were insufficient to train a model, the 62 English phones were reduced to 40 phones without considering the effects of stresses. In this experiment, 4,620 sentences used in the TIMIT database were selected for training 42 acoustic models, containing 40 mono-phone models, one silence model and one short pause

Table 3. Top-10 mispronunciation pairs with high mutual information

Rank	Mispronunciation X	Mispronunciation Y	MI
1	[d]→del	[t]→del	0.027197
2	[i]→[ɪ]	[u]→[ʊ]	0.021327
3	[ð]→[l]	[t]→[tə]	0.020642
4	[ɚ]→[ə]	[o]→[ɔ]	0.018868
5	[k]→del	[t]→del	0.018647
6	[e]→[ɛ]	[i]→[ɪ]	0.018561
7	[o]→[ɔ]	[t]→[tə]	0.016998
8	[ð]→[l]	[i]→[ɪ]	0.016304
9	[ð]→[l]	[r]→del	0.016176
10	[r]→del	[t]→[tə]	0.016136

model. The acoustic features used in ASR were composed of 12 Mel-Frequency Cepstral Coefficients (MFCCs), 12 ΔMFCC, 12 ΔΔMFCCs, Energy, ΔEnergy, and ΔΔEnergy. Each acoustic model contains 3 states, each with 16 Gaussian mixtures. The second speech database used herein is the EAT database, which consists of 83,043 long and short English sentences and English words recorded by 1,164 university students in Taiwan. These students majoring in English were classified as more proficient in English pronunciation by the English teachers, while the others are classified as less proficient. The EAT database is used to adapt the universal acoustic models trained from the TIMIT database to fit the Taiwanese accent. 500 correctly pronounced utterances with balanced phone frequencies were chosen for adaptation via Maximum Likelihood Linear Regression (MLLR) algorithm (Franco *et al.* 1997).

In the experiments, 15 subjects of the university students were involved to evaluate the performances of the proposed approach for mispronunciation detection. Among these 15 subjects aged from 18 to 24 years, 7 subjects (4 females and 3 male) major in English, and the other 8 subjects (3 females and 5 males) were randomly chosen from other departments. Each of them was asked to utter 83 sentences in the test corpus as the test database, and the utterances were manually annotated with the actual pronunciations by the English teachers. The speech utterances in the test database were sequentially selected for pronunciation assessment in the following experiments. The order of the input speech in the test database for evaluation was determined by the sentence selection method.

Evaluation of ASR Performance

In the proposed mechanism, ASR plays an important role in mispronunciation detection. This section evaluates the performances of ASRs in different situations. In the following, the recognition results for different ASRs and the forced-alignment-based segmentation on speech utterance were evaluated. Table 4 shows the recognition results for ASR before and after adaptation, performed on the TIMIT database, the entire EAT database, and 600 sentences with no mispronunciations from the EAT database, different from the 500 correctly pronounced utterances with balanced phone frequencies for adaptation. The recognition rates of the adapted ASR obtained a decrease of 2.87% on the TIMIT database but an increase of 4.04~5.59% on the EAT database. On the other hand, the ability of utterance segmentation using forced-alignment also affects the detection performance. To evaluate the accuracy on utterance segmentation, the segmented result was compared to the manually annotated segments. If the difference is within 20ms, the boundary was regarded as correct. Table 5 presents the segmentation results on the two manually annotated databases. These results indicated that adaptation using accented utterances can improve the recognition performance on Taiwanese-accented English speech.

Threshold Determination for Utterance Verification

Utterance verification was used to check if the input speech utterance matches the prompted textual sentence. In this experiment, the Receiver Operating Characteristic (ROC) curve was used to select an optimal threshold for input utterance verification. The threshold was determined based on the utterances recorded by six subjects. Each sentence in the test corpus corresponds to 15 utterances from the subjects and the confidence scores for each "Matched Input" were calculated by averaging the 105 scores (Every 2 out of the 15 utterances are chosen to calculate a score, and there are 105 combinations). Each utterance can be paired with the other 82 prompted sentences to obtain 82 confidence score of the un-matched utterances. The score for each "unmatched input" was averaged over the 82 confidence scores. The histogram of the scores to the speech utterance with the matched text and un-matched texts are shown in Figure 4 with a score step of 0.5. The threshold was determined by minimizing the summation of the False Rejection Rate (Type I error) and the False Alarm Rate (Type II error). With the ROC curve shown in Figure 5, a threshold of -3 was chosen for a false rejection rate of 4.82% and a false alarm rate of 7.23% which achieves the minimum summation value.

Detection of Mispronunciations

This experiment examined the performance of the whole system on mispronunciation detection. For performance evaluation of mispronunciation detection, the annotated six test databases with utterances recorded by the subjects were used to evaluate the performance. The detected mispronunciations were compared to the human-

Table 4. Recognition results of English ASR

	EAT (600 sent. without mispronunciations)	EAT (All)	TIMIT
Original ASR	72.59%	69.32%	78.23%
Adapted with Accented Utterances	78.18%	73.36%	75.45%

Table 5. Segmentation result using forced-alignment

	EAT(without mispronunciations)	EAT (all)
Original ASR	74.20%	70.62%
Adapted with Accented Utterances	81.37%	74.25%

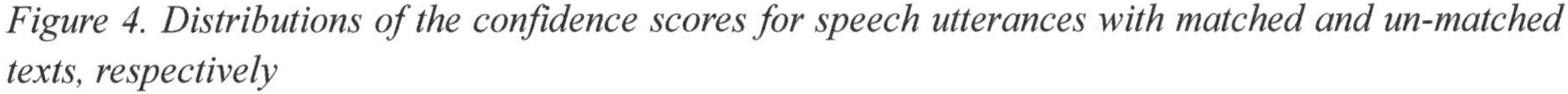

Figure 4. Distributions of the confidence scores for speech utterances with matched and un-matched texts, respectively

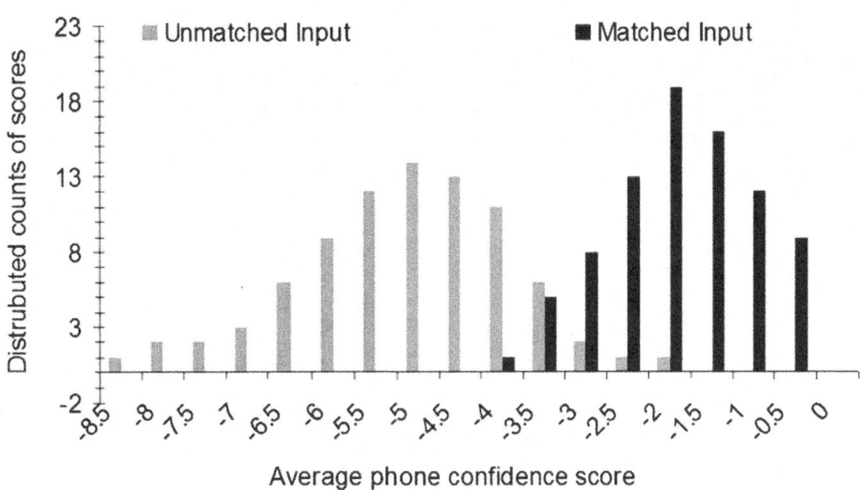

annotated results. The detection performance measured by the precision and recall rates is calculated as follows.

$$\text{Precision} = \frac{C(\text{Detected Variations} \cap \text{Annotated Variations})}{C(\text{Detected Variations})} \tag{16}$$

$$\text{Recall} = \frac{C(\text{Detected Variations} \cap \text{Annotated Variations})}{C(\text{Annotated Variations})} \tag{17}$$

The mispronunciations detected for all subjects were performed on all utterances in the test database. The phone recognition rate is determined by comparing the recognition results to the manually transcribed phone sequences. Table 6 lists the phone recognition rates, recall rates, and precision rates for the subjects. In this experiment, ASR without using the phone lattice obtained from the word lexicon achieved a recognition accuracy of about 74.9% and the recall and precision rates were 71.0% and 64. 1%. Table 7 shows the results without the proposed unsupervised adaptation which was used for speaker-adapted speech recognition. Phone recognition, recall and precision rates were respectively decreased by 2.5%, 2.2% and 1.4% comparing to the results in Table 6. According to the results, the proposed unsupervised adaptation method can obtain improvement on accented speech recognition. Table 8 lists the results using the phone lattice in recognition. The results show obvious increases of about 8.1%, 10.1% and 14.9% for recognition, recall and precision rates, respectively. The use of the phone lattice restricted the possible results and forced the recognizer to choose the predicted phone sequence. In this case, the frequent mispronunciations extracted from the EAT database was suitable for detecting possible Taiwanese-accented mispronunciations.

Sentence Selection for Detection

To evaluate the performances on sentence selection, several experiments were conducted to compare with the no-selection and the counting-based selection methods. Dynamic selection is the proposed method, no-selection uses the total sentences in the test corpus, and counting-based selection chooses the sentences containing the

Figure 5. ROC curve for the determination of the scores in speech verification

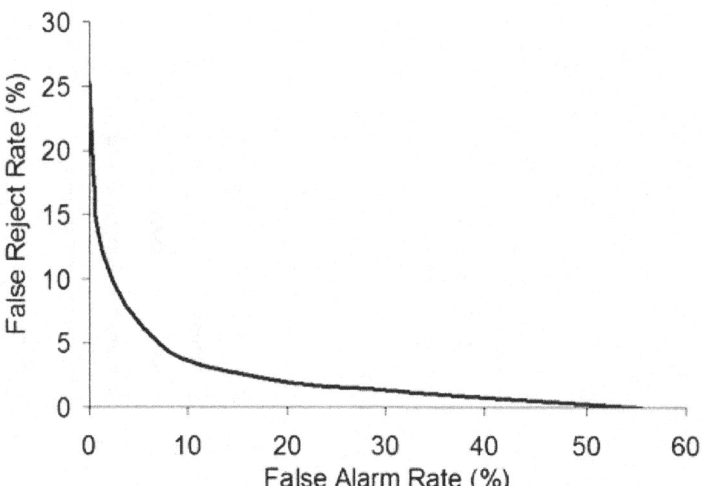

most phones that are not tested so far. The performances are evaluated based on the distribution of pronunciations. For each subject, the distribution of a speaker's pronunciations in the test database was taken as a ground truth. In evaluation, as each time a sentence is chosen and tested by the subject, the distance between the current pronunciation distribution and the ground truth is computed. The measurement for the ith iteration is calculated as:

$$M_i = |D_i - D_{i-1}| \tag{18}$$

where D_i indicates the distance from the current mispronunciation distribution to the initial matrix, which is obtained by the possible mispronunciations from the EAT databases. D is computed using the Euclidean distance:

$$D_i = \sqrt{\sum_{k=1}^{K} (pron_i^k - pron_0^k)^2} \tag{19}$$

where K is the number of all pronunciations, and $pron^k_i$ indicates the frequency of the kth pronunciation in the ith iteration. Figure 6 and Figure 7 illustrate the measures of the 15 subjects using counting-based and dynamic selection methods, respectively. The black solid lines indicate the averages measures and the "I" mark the confidence interval of 95% (±2σ).

Table 6. Detection accuracies throughout the whole test corpus

	Phone recognition rate	Detection accuracy (recall)	Detection accuracy (precision)
Sub 1	75.6%	70.4%	63.7%
Sub 2	73.2%	69.1%	67.2%
Sub 3	78.5%	72.3%	65.2%
Sub 4	74.2%	75.2%	62.5%
Sub 5	73.8%	72.9%	62.2%
Sub 6	73.7%	68.8%	64.5%
Sub 7	76.2%	67.4%	63.1%
Sub 8	73.8%	71.5%	62.9%
Sub 9	76.4%	72.0%	65.1%
Sub 10	73.1%	69.4%	66.3%
Sub 11	77.2%	72.4%	62.7%
Sub 12	73.1%	71.0%	64.5%
Sub 13	73.7%	72.5%	63.8%
Sub 14	74.9%	69.4%	63.4%
Sub 15	75.6%	70.3%	64.3%
Average	74.9%	71.0%	64.1%

Table 7. Detection accuracies throughout the whole test corpus (without unsupervised adaptation)

	Phone recognition rate	Detection accuracy (recall)	Detection accuracy (precision)
Sub 1	73.8%	69.4%	61.2%
Sub 2	70.5%	68.1%	64.4%
Sub 3	74.6%	70.2%	63.0%
Sub 4	72.8%	71.5%	63.8%
Sub 5	71.2%	69.2%	62.5%
Sub 6	69.5%	65.2%	61.3%
Sub 7	74.2%	72.4%	63.4%
Sub 8	71.0%	68.3%	62.5%
Sub 9	73.1%	70.1%	64.1%
Sub 10	70.3%	67.3%	61.6%
Sub 11	74.0%	69.0%	62.5%
Sub 12	71.7%	65.8%	61.3%
Sub 13	71.9%	66.3%	60.9%
Sub 14	72.6%	67.6%	62.9%
Sub 15	73.5%	70.7%	64.7%
Average	72.3%	68.7%	62.7%

Table 8. Detection accuracies throughout the whole test corpus (with the phone lattice)

	Phone recognition rate	Detection accuracy (recall)	Detection accuracy (precision)
Sub 1	83.0%	82.5%	78.7%
Sub 2	81.9%	80.6%	77.1%
Sub 3	85.3%	84.5%	80.3%
Sub 4	83.1%	82.1%	79.8%
Sub 5	83.8%	81.4%	79.2%
Sub 6	81.2%	79.1%	77.9%
Sub 7	83.7%	81.6%	79.3%
Sub 8	82.5%	81.3%	77.2%
Sub 9	84.7%	82.5%	81.4%
Sub 10	82.8%	79.9%	78.1%
Sub 11	82.8%	80.4%	79.7%
Sub 12	81.4%	78.8%	77.5%
Sub 13	81.4%	80.5%	78.6%
Sub 14	82.5%	80.2%	79.2%
Sub 15	84.2%	82.0%	80.7%
Average	83.0%	81.2%	79.0%

Table 9 shows the mispronunciation detection rates of the subjects using three different strategies for sentence selection and the no-selection method is regarded as the baseline system. In this table, the counting-based selection method converged in about 54.8 sentences and the recall rate achieved 76.2% on average, while the dynamic selection method converged in about 26.7 sentences and the recall rate achieved 76.6% on average. Selecting the next sentence according to the tested results is helpful on reaching the goal of testing and discovering the mispronunciations of a specific speaker. The *t-test* was performed to examine the significances among these three methods. For baseline and counting-based method, $t = 1.36 > 1.35 = P_{(0.9,14)}$; the counting-based selection can significantly reduce the number of test sentences at a confidence level of 90%. For counting-based and the proposed dynamic selection methods, $t = 1.72 > 1.345 = P_{(0.9,14)}$; the proposed method can significantly reduce the number of test sentences used in counting-based selection method at a confidence level of 90%. For the baseline and the proposed dynamic selection methods, $t=3.78>2.98=P_{(0.995,14)}$; the reduced quantity of test sentences used in proposed method is significant compared to the baseline selection method. Table 9 indicates that the number of the tested sentences can be reduced to be less than half of the number of sentences used in the baseline method and the average recall rate achieved a decrease of only 2.5% (averaged over 15 subjects).

Table 10 compared the results of counting-based and dynamic selection methods to the random selection method, which randomly selected the same number of sentences as the other two selection methods. The results of random-selection method were averaged over 5 tests. The

Figure 6. Measures of mispronunciation distributions using counting-based selection

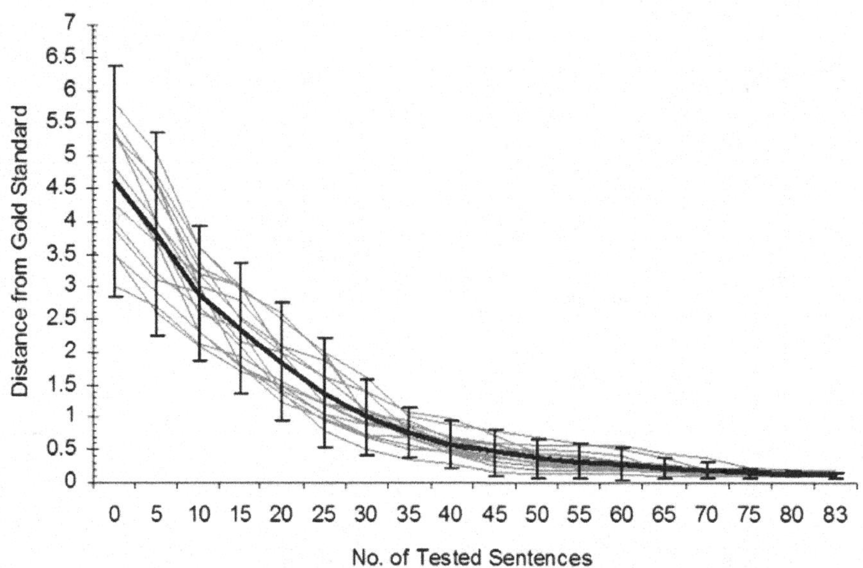

t-test is used to examine the significances on precisions compared to random selection method. For counting-based and dynamic selection methods, the precisions are significantly higher than the random selection method at a confidence level of 97.5% ($t_{(counting\text{-}based)} = 2.33 > 2.145 = P_{(0.975,14)}$ and $t_{(dynamic)} = 2.26 > 2.145 = P_{(0.975,14)}$, respectively). For the same number of sentences, the precision rates of detected mispronunciations for random selection method were 15.4% and

Figure 7. Measures of mispronunciation distributions using dynamic selection

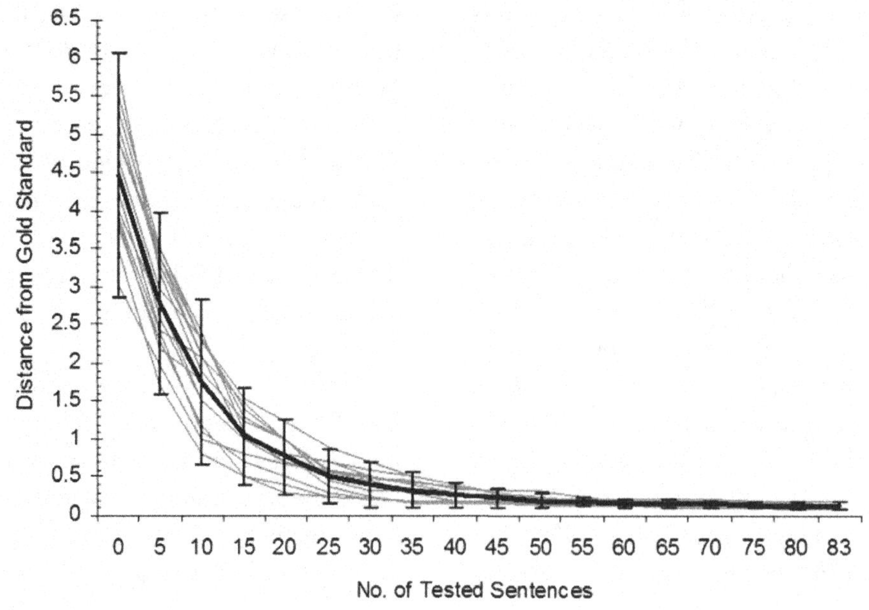

Table 9. Relation between the number of tested sentences and the precision rate of detection

	No-selection		Counting-based selection		Dynamic selection	
	# sent.	Precision	# sent.	Precision	# sent.	Precision
Sub 1	83	78.7%	64	75.2%	32	75.8%
Sub 2	83	77.1%	52	75.5%	21	74.4%
Sub 3	83	80.3%	61	76.8%	29	77.5%
Sub 4	83	79.8%	50	77.7%	26	76.3%
Sub 5	83	79.2%	46	76.9%	21	78.1%
Sub 6	83	77.9%	51	76.1%	30	75.6%
Sub 7	83	79.2%	52	75.3%	25	72.3%
Sub 8	83	77.5%	62	74.9%	29	78.1%
Sub 9	83	81.6%	54	77.0%	28	75.5%
Sub 10	83	78.1%	55	78.3%	33	77.3%
Sub 11	83	80.7%	48	76.6%	24	76.2%
Sub 12	83	77.5%	60	74.5%	27	78.0%
Sub 13	83	78.3%	55	76.2%	22	76.4%
Sub 14	83	79.4%	59	75.4%	30	77.8%
Sub 15	83	80.9%	53	77.3%	24	80.5%
Average	83	79.1%	54.8	76.2%	26.7	76.6%

Table 10. Compare different selection methods with random selection method using the same test sentences

	# sent.	Precision		# sent.	Precision	
		Counting-based	Random		Dynamic	Random
Sub 1	64	75.2%	60.5%	32	75.8%	50.6%
Sub 2	52	75.5%	61.3%	21	74.4%	42.3%
Sub 3	61	76.8%	59.2%	29	77.5%	49.4%
Sub 4	50	77.7%	58.2%	26	76.3%	44.9%
Sub 5	46	76.9%	60.2%	21	78.1%	39.2%
Sub 6	51	76.1%	60.5%	30	75.6%	40.3%
Sub 7	52	75.3%	59.8%	25	74.3%	41.7%
Sub 8	62	74.9%	57.4%	29	78.1%	42.0%
Sub 9	54	77.0%	62.1%	28	75.5%	39.8%
Sub 10	55	78.3%	62.9%	33	77.3%	45.2%
Sub 11	48	76.6%	61.6%	24	76.2%	42.4%
Sub 12	60	74.5%	60.2%	27	77.9%	43.9%
Sub 13	55	76.2%	62.8%	22	76.4%	40.7%
Sub 14	59	75.4%	61.7%	30	77.8%	51.1%
Sub 15	53	77.3%	63.6%	24	75.9%	43.3%
Average	54.8	76.2%	60.8%	26.7	76.5%	43.8%

32.7% smaller than the counting-based and dynamic selection methods.

DISCUSSION

We have shown an efficient framework for evaluating personalized English mispronunciations of Taiwanese speakers with a dynamically selected test corpus. The efficiency described in the proposed approach is evaluated by comparing the performances between different selection methods and the corresponding precision rates. Experimental results showed that using selection method in reducing the evaluation time achieved a significant improvement in obtaining the speaker-dependent mispronunciations. The number of used test sentences could be less than half from conventional evaluation procedure but can still maintain comparable accuracies. Different inventories of pronunciations between languages cause people to produce accented pronunciations while speaking L2. On the other hand, an unsupervised adaptation method is proposed to adapt the acoustic models with the speech corpus containing mispronunciations and accents. In this work, a corpus-driven prior knowledge about mispronunciations is extracted from an English speech corpus (EAT) collected in Taiwan, including 36 aggregations of mispronounced phone pairs. In addition, pronunciation property of a native language also leads to specific mispronunciation types while learning other languages.

FUTURE RESEARCH DIRECTIONS

While the predefined mispronunciations was arguable for lacking of flexibility for portraying detailed pronunciation inventory for a speaker, in future research directions, additional treatment to dealing with this problem is to collect more data from interesting domains or to consider more information related to phonology. Integrating the expertise knowledge and corpus-driven method into mispronunciation inference could also provide an adaptable CAPT which induces real pronunciations independent of a restricted domain. In addition, with the wide applications to many other research topics based on the detected mispronunciations, personalized mispronunciations can provide CAPT systems a criterion for the design of a specific training course for specific users. Detected mispronunciations can also be used to improve the accuracy of ASR. For example, modeling personalized mispronunciations provides ASR a constraint on repairing the recognition results instead of using universal mispronunciation models. In the future, mispronunciation detection from un-annotated utterances will be investigated. Discovering the association of pronunciations between different languages will also be studied for further improvement of the approach.

CONCLUSION

Distinct from most previous work on pronunciation evaluation, this study introduced an efficient approach to assessing mispronunciations from Taiwanese-accented speech instead of GOP-based scoring. The proposed unsupervised adaptation eliminates the existing problem of inconsistencies between the mispronunciation and the universal acoustic models. With accented speech adaptation, uttered speech for the prompted sentences can be recognized and the pair of unmatched phones can therefore be considered as mispronunciations. On the other hand, a dynamic sentence selection exploiting entropy and mutual information is exploited to reduce the time for evaluation, thus more attention can be put on teaching or rectifying the students' pronunciations. Experimental results show that the proposed unsupervised adaptation obtains an improvement on recognizing English utterances with Taiwanese accents. The proposed dynamic sentence selection method also effectively decreased the number of sentences necessary in the test corpus, while maintained a comparable detection rate with significance at confident levels of above 90%.

REFERENCES

Baum, L. E., & Eagon, J. A. (1967). An inequality with applications to statistical estimation for probabilistic functions of Markov processes and to a model for ecology. *Bulletin of the American Mathematical Society*, *73*(3), 360–363. doi:10.1090/S0002-9904-1967-11751-8

Bozkurt, B., Ozturk, O., & Dutoit, T. (2003). Text design for TTS speech corpus building using a modified greedy selection. In *Proceedings of Eurospeech, 2003*, 277–280.

Chandel, A., Madathingal, M., Parate, A., Pant, H., Rajput, N., Ikbal, S., ... Verma, A. (2007). Sensei: Spoken language assessment for call center agents. *ASRU 2007.*

Coniam, D. (1999). Voice recognition software accuracy with second language speakers of English. *System*, *27*, 49–64. doi:10.1016/S0346-251X(98)00049-9

Derwing, T. M., Munro, M. J., & Carbonaro, M. (2000). Does popular speech recognition software work with ESL speech? *TESOL Quarterly*, *34*(3), 592–603. doi:10.2307/3587748

English Across Taiwan (EAT). (n.d.). Retrieved from http://www.aclclp.org.tw/use_mat.php#eat

Eskenazi, M. (1996). Detection of foreign speakers' pronunciation errors for second language training - preliminary results. In *Proceedings International Conference on Spoken Language Processing*, (pp. 1465-1468). Philadelphia, USA

Franco, H., Abrash, V., Precoda, K., Bratt, H., Rao, R., & Butzberger, J. (2000). The SRI EduSpeak system: Recognition and pronunciation scoring for language learning. In *Proceedings InSTILL 2000*, (pp. 123-128). Dundee, Scotland.

Hamada, H., Miki, S., & Nakatsu, R. (1993). Automatic evaluation of English pronunciation based on speech recognition techniques. *Transactions of the IEICE of Japan. E (Norwalk, Conn.)*, *76-D*(3), 352–359.

Hiller, S., Rooney, E., Laver, J., & Jack, M. (1993). SPELL: An automated system for computer-aided pronunciation teaching. *Speech Communication*, *13*, 463–473. doi:10.1016/0167-6393(93)90045-M

Isogai, M., Mizuno, H., & Mano, K. (2005). Recording script design for corpus-based TTS system based on coverage of various phonetic elements. In *Proceedings of ICASSP 2005.*

Ji, H., & Grishman, R. (2006). Data selection in semi-supervised learning for name tagging. In *Proceedings of ACL 06 Workshop on Information Extraction Beyond Document*, Sydney, Australia.

Kalikow, D. N., & Swets, J. A. (1972). Experiments with computer-controlled displays in second-language learning. *IEEE Transactions on Audio and Electroacoustics*, *20*, 23–28. doi:10.1109/TAU.1972.1162353

Kim, J. M., Wang, C., Peabody, M., & Seneff, S. (2004). An interactive English pronunciation dictionary for Korean learners. In *Proceedings of the 8th International Conference on Spoken Language Processing*, Jeju Island, Korea.

Mak, B., Siu, M., Ng, M., Tam, Y. C., Chan, Y. C., & Chan, K. W. (2003). PLASER: Pronunciation learning via automatic speech recognition. In *Proceedings of HLT-NAACL, 2003*, 23–29.

Menzel, W., Herron, D., Bonaventura, P., & Morton, R. (2000). Automatic detection and correction of non-native English pronunciations. In *Proceedings of InSTILL 2000*, Dundee, Scotland.

Nakagawa, S., Mori, K., & Nakamura, N. (2003). A statistical method of evaluation pronunciation proficiency for English words spoken by Japanese. In *Proceedings Eurospeech 2003*, Geneva, Switzerland, (pp. 3193-3196).

Neri, A., Cucchiarini, C., & Strik, H. (2004). Segmental errors in Dutch as a second language: How to establish priorities for CAPT. In *Proceedings InSTIL/ICALL Symposium*, (pp. 13-16).

Neri, A., Cucchiarini, C., & Strik, H. (2006a). ASR corrective feedback on pronunciation: Does it really work? In *Proceedings Interspeech*, (pp. 1982–1985).

Neri, A., Cucchiarini, C., & Strik, H. (2006b). Selecting segmental errors in L2 Dutch for optimal pronunciation training. *International Review of Application in Linguistics Language Teaching*, *44*, 357–404. doi:10.1515/IRAL.2006.016

Neumeyer, L., Franco, H., Weintraub, M., & Price, P. (1996). Pronunciation scoring of foreign language student speech. In *Proceedings International Conference on Spoken Language Processing*, (pp. 1457-1460). Philadelphia, USA.

Ronen, O., Neumeyer, L., & Franco, H. (1997). Automatic detection of mispronunciation for language instruction. In *Proceedings Eurospeech '97*, Vol. 2, Rhodes, Greece, (pp. 649-652).

Scheffer, T., Decomain, C., & Wrobel, S. (2001). Active hidden Markov models for information extraction. In *Proceedings of the Fourth International Symposium on Intelligent Data Analysis*, (pp. 301-109). Lisbon.

Su, H. Y., Wu, C. H., & Tsai, P. J. (2008). *Automatic assessment of articulation disorders using confident unit-based model adaptation* (pp. 4513–4516). ICASSP.

Tepperman, J., & Narayanan, S. (2005). *Automatic syllable stress detection using prosodic features for pronunciation evaluation of language learners*. In ICASSP 2005, Philadelphia, PA, March.

TIMIT Corpus. (n.d.). Retrieved from http://www.ldc.upenn.edu/Catalog/CatalogEntry.jsp?catalogId=LDC93S1

Tsubota, Y., Kawahara, T., & Dantsuji, M. (2002). CALL system for Japanese students of English using pronunciation error prediction and formant structure estimation. In *Proceedings InSTILL 2002.*

Witt, S. M., & Young, S. J. (2000). Phone-level pronunciation scoring and assessment for interactive language learning. *Speech Communication*, *30*, 95–108. doi:10.1016/S0167-6393(99)00044-8

Wu, C. H., Hsia, C. C., Chen, J. F., & Wang, J. F. (2007). Variable-length unit selection in TTS using structural syntactic cost. *IEEE Trans. Audio, Speech, and Language Processing*, *15*(4), 1227–1235. doi:10.1109/TASL.2006.889752

Wu, C. H., Su, H. Y., & Shen, H. P. (2011). Articulation-disordered speech recognition using speaker-adaptive acoustic models and personalized articulation patterns. *ACM Transactions on Asian Language Information Processing*, *10*(2). doi:10.1145/1967293.1967294

Young, S. (2000). *The HTK book*. Microsoft Corporation.

Chapter 3
A Bees Life Algorithm for Cloud Computing Services Selection

Salim Bitam
Mohamed Khider University – Biskra, Algeria

Mohamed Batouche
University Mentouri – Constantine, Algeria

El-Ghazali Talbi
University of Lille 1, France

ABSTRACT

In recent years, the scientific community has begun to model and solve complex optimization problems using bio-inspired methods. Such problems cannot be solved exactly by traditional methods within a reasonable complexity in terms of computer capacities or computational times. However, bio-inspired methods provide near optimal solutions in realist conditions such as cost, capacity, and computational time. In this chapter, the authors propose a new population-based algorithm called the Bees Life Algorithm (BLA). It is applied to solve the cloud computing services selection with quality of service (QoS) requirements. It is considered as swarm-based algorithm, which closely imitates the life of the bee colony. It follows the two important behaviors in the nature of bees, reproduction and food foraging. Bees life algorithm can be applied to the combinatorial optimization problems as well as to the functional optimization problems. An experimental study has been conducted in order to demonstrate the performance and the efficiency of the proposal and its robustness. After comparisons with genetic algorithm (GA) as referential algorithm in this field, the obtained results showed the BLA performance and effectiveness. Finally, promising future research directions are examined to show the BLA usefulness for research in the cloud computing and computational intelligence areas.

DOI: 10.4018/978-1-4666-1830-5.ch003

1. INTRODUCTION

A new computing view called cloud computing has been emerged in these last few years. It is based on providing dynamically services using very large scalable and virtualized resources over the Internet. In order to provide those services, these resources can be divided in delivered applications, in computing hardware infrastructure and in computing platform located in different and remote datacenters. The datacenter hardware and software are known as cloud (Figure 1).

On the one hand, cloud computing allows users to run applications remotely from the cloud using a simple browser which are usually include information technology services referred as to Software-as-a-Service (SaaS) (Furht & Escalante, 2010). On the other hand, Infrastructure-as-a-Service (IaaS) refers to where the application is carried out via useful functions and services provided in the cloud. It is a set of virtualized computers with guaranteed processing power, sufficient storage and efficient performance in terms of latency and bandwidth for an Internet access in time. Between SaaS and IaaS, there are cloud platform services also known as Platform-as-a-Service (PaaS) deliver operating system, programming language and solution stack. It aims at improving the applications deployment cost and reducing its complexity.

It can be seen that the cloud resources use can be simplified by the services use which should be selected in the interest of the end-users. For example, Amazon Elastic Compute Cloud (EC2) (Amazon, 2011) is an IaaS cloud, and is the most well known cloud. Through the use of virtual machines EC2 clients create as many (virtual) machines they require and then host all their required services within the machines. EC2 clients are charged per CPU hour per virtual machine.

Figure 1. Cloud computing structure

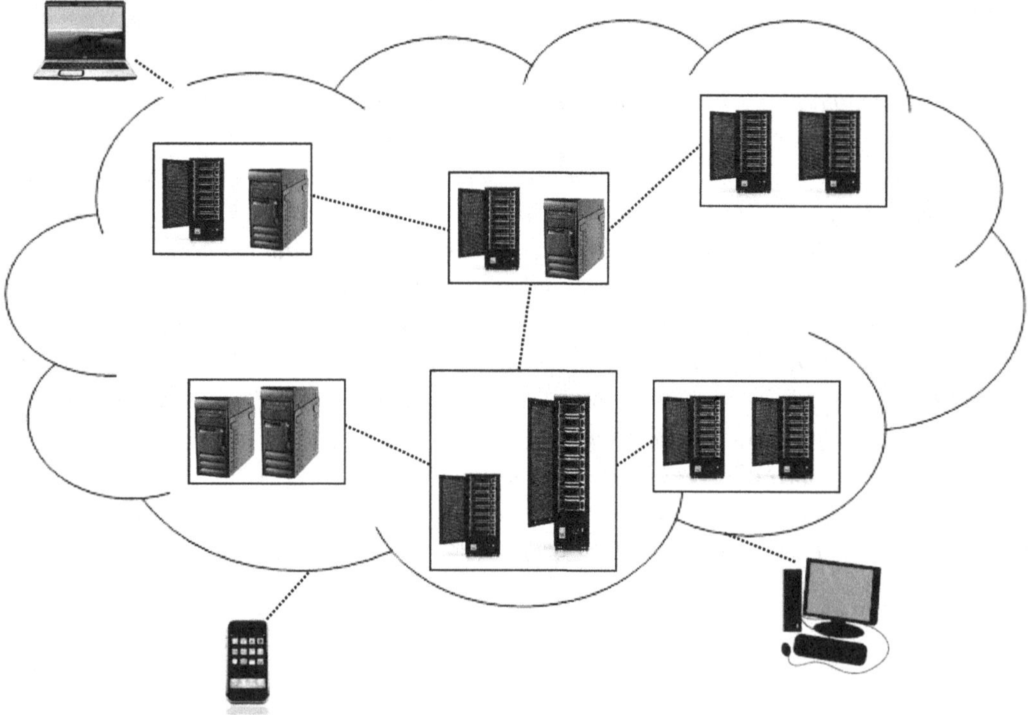

It is even possible to create a cluster within EC2 by requesting EC2 to create multiple instances of a base virtual machine and then installing the required cluster software into each machine (Goscinski & Brock, 2010).

Moreover, Google App Engine (Google, 2011) is a PaaS cloud that provides a complete Web service hosting environment to clients. Unlike EC2, App Engine clients do not need to address hardware configurations or software installations. With App Engine, clients create their own services and the services are run on Google's servers. While easier to use than EC2, App Engine is very limited in what programming languages can be used to construct services. Hence, it is required of clients to know at least one of the languages before attempting to use App Engine. Finally, there is no explicit discovery service in App Engine. The only option for clients that use App Engine is the use of discovery services that are external to App Engine, such as Universal Discovery, Description, Integration approach (UDDI) (UDDI, 2011) (Goscinski & Brock, 2010).

In order to design and develop easy tools to select cloud services, it is advised to return to basic nature of the cloud. In this way, the center of the cloud computing model is the network (Smith, 2010). It serves as the linkage between the end-users consuming cloud services and the provider's datacenters providing the cloud services. Through this network (Internet), cloud services are widely distributed to serve end-users using service-oriented applications (SOA). In other words, composite applications consist of a set of abstract cloud services known service classes are deployed. At service run time, a concrete cloud service called service instance or candidate is selected and invoked for each service class (Wang et al., 2011).

In another side, generally a cloud provider stores a huge preprocessed imagery on several datacenters scattered in many locations. These datacenters should serve tens of thousands of queries per second with low latency. Because of this scalability, the cloud could lead to very high latency and to an exponential complexity especially for end-users who are a long distance from cloud providers. Moreover, cloud services providers could supply same task but with different QoS parameters. Therefore, the same request chooses between several concrete cloud services instances combinations with the same functionality but with various QoS capacities. The user request can be associated with some end-to-end QoS requirements such as cost, response time, bandwidth etc (Wang et al., 2010).

Selection algorithm of concrete cloud services instances should ensure aggregated QoS values of the selected services which match the user requirements, and obviously, users hope to subscribe the combination of services with optimal QoS performance, while satisfying their QoS constraints. Note that, the number of combinations increased exponentially with the growing number of concrete services instances for each task which brings more challenges of the QoS-aware cloud services selection problem.

Consequently, it is mandatory to ensure a process of performance improvement of the data which is usually needed for cloud computing services delivery into the global network connectivity in terms of low latency and high input/output bandwidth. To do that, an efficient and optimal service instances selection policy should be found to assign end-user service requests to the different datacenters which form the cloud provider. It is the purpose by the proposition in this chapter, of a new bee swarm optimization algorithm called Bees Life Algorithm (BLA). It takes advantages of the global search principle represented in the bee reproduction over the crossover between the queen and several drones. It takes also, the advantages of the local search principle appears in the mutation operator in one hand, and in the other hand by a greedy food source foraging principle carried out by the bees when they search their food.

The rest of this chapter is organized as follows: the next section gives brief summaries of the state of the art approaches applied to select cloud services and the problem statement. Section 3 gives detailed description of the proposed algorithm. It starts with an explanation of the bees' life in nature as an inspiration idea. Next, cloud services selection with BLA is presented and followed by details of its steps and operators. In order to evaluate our proposal, an implementation using C++ programming language has been realized. In addition, to make the algorithm more suitable for this problem, we redefine the BLA parameters. Afterwards, a set of experiments is executed and given rise to the test results. Then, the performance comparisons with the conventional algorithm based on the QoS metrics are included and discussed in section 4. Finally, we list some future research directions and then we conclude the chapter.

2. BACKGROUND

2.1. Related Work

There are many existing approaches applied to solve cloud services selection problem in the literature. (Wang et al., 2011) had proposed an efficient QoS-aware services selection approach based on cloud model. It is used to compute the uncertainty of QoS and used mixed integer programming to identify the more suitable web services. This approach is subject of future development to help real-world service users to find appropriate services according to their QoS requirements.

(Goscinski & Brock, 2010) had proposed a new technology which makes possible the provision of service publication, discovery and selection based on dynamic attributes which express the current state and characteristics of cloud services. It is through the combination of dynamic attributes, Web service and Brokering, authors created Web service based technology that allowed quick and easy publication, discovery and selection. They provided a higher abstraction of clouds that offers publication of services, discovery and selection based on attribute values that describe dynamically state and characteristics of services that expose cloud resources, and easy to use interface for clients and service providers. They proposed a proof of concept implementation that allowed the easy publication, discovery, selection and use of an existing cluster via a simple interface using Web pages which demonstrated that the proposed technology is feasible. However, this approach was not useful for applications with QoS requirements.

In the research activity of (Alrifai & Risse, 2009), an efficient heuristic for the QoS-based service composition has been proposed. It is based on the combination of global optimization with local selection methods. This proposal reduces the efforts and improves the computational time, while achieving close to optimal results. The number of service levels is fixed and need to be defined beforehand which can be considered as drawback for dynamic services appearance.

There are many research activities based on particle swarm optimization to select services especially the web services. It can be adapted to the cloud computing services selection because of its novelty in the computing science. For example, (Wang et al., 2010) suggested an improved Particle Swarm Optimization Algorithm (iPSOA) to select a combination of composite web services with optimal QoS guarantees. On the purpose of making this proposal more suitable for QoS-aware web service selection, authors redefined the parameters, such as position, velocity and updating operations. They proposed a non-uniform mutation strategy to enhance the population diversity in the aim at overcoming the prematurity of the original PSO. Therefore, all other particles search along the direction of the global best one except for itself, whose evolution direction is blind, so it is easy to miss the optimal solutions and to result in prematurity. Moreover, they tried to improve the convergence speed in global and local level by the proposition of the adaptive weight adjustment and local best first strategies respectively.

In the former strategy, particle velocity is adjust and may be trapped by the local optimal solution in the case of particle high speed otherwise; it may affect the convergence speed for the slow velocity. Here, a weighted sum of each attributes for the QoS of a composite web service is adopted to evaluate the particle fitness. After selecting the candidate service randomly for each task, which would cost lots of time until the right one is selected; the local best first strategy is launched in order to improve the convergence speed and then the entire population has very high probability to reach high fitness value. It is enlightened by the combining global optimization with local selection approach. Experimental results showed that iPSOA offers a feasible and practically optimal approach that can be implemented in QoS-aware Web Services Selection problem. However, the proposed algorithm does not take adaptive termination of algorithms into account.

Also, PSO has been applied to the services selection by (Li et al., 2011) in order to overcome the defects such as inefficient and non-global optimization. They presented Web services selection which based on user's preference and grouping particle swarm optimization. This approach profited of PSO advantages of particle clustering which aims to improve the global search capability in Web services and avoid rapid convergence or premature. In addition, it used the fuzzy constraint to express the user's preferences to help him to select their preferences. The experimental results of this approach exhibited an improvement of the performance of services selection.

In (Zhang et al., 2007) a structure of genetic algorithm characterized by the special relation matrix coding scheme of chromosomes and the population diversity handling with simulated annealing was presented and called DiGA. It considered that the functions of a composite service can be divided into some component functions with each task. The construction of a tasks sequence gives rise to an execution path of a composite service. For each path, it is possible to construct various composite services to the specific function.

The proposed genetic algorithm (GA) used a special relation matrix coding scheme of chromosomes. It has the function to express not only the relation among tasks but also paths information. It is motivated by the ability to represent simultaneously the composite service re-planning, cyclic paths and many web service scenarios, such as probabilistic invocation, parallel invocation, sequential activation, and to improve the fitness function.

In addition, the population diversity can be measured using the concept of information entropy (Yasuhiro & Mitsuo, 1998). In order to ensure the population diversity, DiGA performed simulated annealing algorithm (SA) in (Romeo & Sangiovanni-Vincentelli, 1991) as an effective and powerful stochastic optimization technique. It helped to converge asymptotically to the optimal solution in a local area search. The genetic algorithm used the roulette wheel selection to choose two individuals "parents" ready to the crossover and mutation operators with different probabilities. Authors carried out two set of experiments of genetic algorithm to compose service in which the former used simulated annealing algorithm and the latter selected composite service only with native genetic algorithm.

The DiGA obtained results showed that the service composed by the GA with simulated annealing is better than the one composed by the GA without it. Nevertheless, it can be seen that the execution time of the GA with simulated annealing is longer than the GA without it at the cost of simulated annealing. It is obviously clear that this approach can be improved to take into account the services selection with QoS requirements.

2.2. Problem Statement

2.2.1. QoS Metric Definitions

(ISO8402, 2011) defined the quality of service (QoS) as the collective effect of service performance determining the end-user satisfaction. It consists of set of metrics allow the cloud service evaluation which are tunable by the provider such as service cost, average end-to-end delay of service delivery and average bandwidth of service transmission and others (Menasce, 2004). In this chapter, the last three QoS metrics are considered to satisfy the end-user requirements. Their definitions are given as follows:

Service cost is known as the fee that a service user has to pay to the service provider for the service invocation. It is composed of the transmission cost and the service cost and it is measured in the provider or in an international currency.

Average end-to-end delay of service delivery abbreviated delay is defined as the time which separates the end-user request and the obtained service. It depends on the request/response transmission, waiting time and request processing. It is measures in seconds.

Average bandwidth of service transmission abbreviated bandwidth is determined as the estimated throughput capacity of the network medium used to deliver successfully service packets. It is calculated by the total number of delivered packets divided by its total transmission time. It is measures in kilobits per second.

2.2.2. Formal Model of the Cloud Services Selection Problem

a. Concepts of Abstract Service and Concrete Service

The cloud contains a collection of service providers where each one scatters in the cloud a set of datacenters which may provide the different services in atomic services or in composite services format. Note that in service run time, one datacenter cannot provide a service either because it is busy or because the service is not available in this time. In this chapter, we consider the service is available in the different datacenters to limit the QoS metrics in three objectives as aforementioned.

The concept of the service requested by the end-user known as abstract composite service may aggregate atomic or other composite services and may be provided by more than one datacenter that meets a user's QoS constraints and maximizes the total utility (Yu et al., 2007). It represents the service request established by the client in its abstract format. The required abstract service class refers to:

$$SC = \{S_1, \ldots, S_i, \ldots, S_n\}$$

A concrete composite service which serves the end-user as real result can be defined as an instantiation of an abstract composite service class. It is a set of selected service candidates and refers to selected service instances:

$$SI = \{s_{11}, \ldots, s_{ij}, \ldots, s_{nt}\}$$

It can be obtained by binding each abstract service class S_i in SC to a concrete service instance s_{ij} provided by the datacenter labeled by 'j' to form SI.

b. Notations of QoS Metrics

For any concrete atomic service instance s_{ij}, we can define the QoS metrics:

Cost function: $Cost(s_{ij})$: $SI \rightarrow R^+$
Delay function: $Delay(s_{ij})$: $SI \rightarrow R^+$ and
Bandwidth function: $Bandwidth(s_{ij})$: $SI \rightarrow R^+$

They represent cost, delay and bandwidth of the selected service instance 'i' supplied by the datacenter 'j' to the end-user (client), respectively.

In addition, the selected service instance set SI is subjected to the following functions:

$$\text{Cost(SI)} = \Sigma\, s_{ij} \in \text{SI Cost}(s_{ij}) \quad (1)$$

$$\text{Delay(SI)} = \Sigma\, s_{ij} \in \text{SI Delay}(s_{ij}) \quad (2)$$

$$\text{Bandwidth(SI)} = \min\,(\text{Bandwidth}(s_{ij})),\ s_{ij} \in \text{SI} \quad (3)$$

c. Fitness Function

In order to evaluate the individual, a fitness function is defined. It is also, called objective function. Thus, each concrete composite service candidate *SI* has an associated fitness function *F(SI)*, which is defined by a weighted sum of the QoS attributes relevant to this candidate.

In this context, the fitness function of the cloud services selection is formulated as follows:

$$\text{Minimize } F(\text{SI}) = w_1 .\ \text{Cost(SI)} + w_2 .\ \text{Delay(SI)} + w_3 .\ \text{Bandwidth(SI)} \quad (4)$$

where w_1, w_2, and w_3 are the weights for each QoS attribute given by the user according to their importance.

3. BEES LIFE ALGORITHM

As population-based metaheuristic, our proposal (BLA) is presented in this section. First, the life of bees in nature is reviewed as an inspiration source of this algorithm. It will be followed by the detailed description of the BLA. Furthermore, the encoding of individual and population are presented with the stopping criterion. After that, the explanation of BLA two parts "reproduction" and "food source foraging" are mentioned. Finally, the BLA pseudo-code is then proposed.

3.1. Bee in Nature

As a social and domestic insect, the bee (Apis mellifera) is native to Europe and Africa. Living in the beehive is society which contains between 60,000 and 80,000 elements. The bees feed on nectar as a source of energy in their lives and use pollen as a source of protein in the rearing larvae (Api, 2011).

The observation of many facts and phenomena related to the life of bees shows that the organization follows the principles of intelligence and economy without any failures, and that would surely considered perfectly when applied to human societies as source of inspiration.

3.1.1. Bee Colony Components

The bee colony contains generally, a single breeding female called Queen, a few thousands of males known as the Drones, a several thousands of sterile females called Workers, and many young bee larvae called Broods give rise to others.

a. Queen

It is the fertile female individual of the beehive. The principal role of the queen is the reproduction by the egg laying (Laidlaw & Page, 1986). It mates with 7 to 20 drones out on sunny in a reproductive operation called mating flight. It stores the sperms in her spermatheca and then it laid up to 2000 eggs per day.

The fertilized eggs become female (worker) however, the unfertilized eggs become male (drones). It comes from a fertilized egg, identical to that of the worker, but lays in a special cell called "Royal cell". Throughout development, the larva will be fed exclusively on royal jelly. This regime allows the formation of a new queen which is raised exclusively in spring, to replace an old or sick queen. It is rare to observe a queen on the outside on the beehive, while it is relatively easy to find it inside but surrounded by many workers that protect and feed it.

b. Drones

They come from the development of unfertilized eggs during the breeding season in the spring to early summer. Their number is approximately two thousand and five hundred per colony with size larger than female size. Drones' role is strictly limited to the fertilization of young queens through the nuptial flight. Those which mate with the queen die shortly after. Their lifespan is about 90 days.

c. Workers

Workers are female bees but non reproductive individuals. They live from 4 to 9 months in the cold season which their number reaches 30000 workers but in summer, they exist approximately 6 weeks when their number reaches 80000. Worker is responsible of the beehive defense using its barbed stinger. Consequently, it dies after stinging.

We can enumerate the worker activities by the day criterion as follow: cell cleaning (day 1-2), nurse honeybee (day 3-11), wax production (day 12-17), guard honeybees (day 18-21), foraging honeybees (day 22-42). Worker insures the habitual activities of the bee colony such as honey sealing, pollen packing, water carries, fanning honeybees, queen attendants, drone feeding, egg moving, mortuary honeybees, honeycomb building and propolozing.

d. Broods

The young of the honeybees are named broods. They will be born after the laying of egg by the queen in special honeycomb cells: the brood frames. After that, the workers add royal jelly on the brood heads as alimentation until 3 days. Few female larvae are selected to be future queens. In this case, they are flooded by royal jelly over 6 days. The unfertilized eggs give born to the broods. The young larvae are spinning by cocoon, capping the cell by the older sisters; it is the pupa stage. Then, they reach the develop stage in which they receive nectar and pollen from foragers until leaving the beehive and spending its life as forager.

3.1.2. Bee Behaviors

Bees are characterized by several behaviors such as honeycomb building, beehive guarding and defense, honey sealing, pollen packing etc. The most two important behaviors in their life are the foraging and the reproduction. They will be presented in the two following sub-sections.

a. Reproduction

The reproduction phenomenon at the honeybee colony guarantees by the queen which mating with seven to twenty drones (Adam et al., 1972). This is the mating-flight (Rinderer & Collins, 1986). It carries out far from the nest in the air. First, the queen initializes with some queen energy and then, performs a special dance. Drones follow and mate with the queen.

They make their sperms in the queen spermatheca. It forms the genetic pool of the colony. Next, queen returns to the nest either when the energy is within some threshold, or when her spermtheca is full (retrieving at random a mixture sperms: about 5000000 spermatozoa). Three days after her last mating-flight, the queen starts to lay her eggs, which are produced in her ovaries. A good queen lays 1500 to 2000 eggs per day (Adjare, 1990). Broods are made up of fertilized eggs and unfertilized eggs. For the former, it will give birth to queens or workers; however, for the later the drones are generated.

b. Food Source Foraging

This behavior is observed when bees searching food source. Some bees called "scouts" navigate and explore the region in aim to find a food source. If yes, they come at the dance floor in the beehive to share this discovery its nest mates via the language of dance which can be round or waggle relating to the discovery distance. Some bees are recruited and then, become foragers. Their number is proportional to the food quantity information communicated by the scouts.

They calculate the amount of food sources and take its decision. Either, recruited bees continue the exploitation by the memorization of the best food found location, or they abandon. In this last case, foragers become unemployed bees; either scouts or onlooker bees according to a probabilistic dividing.

Note that the bees share a communication language of extreme precision, based on two kinds of dances: the round dance when food is very close. The second type is the waggle dance carried out when the food is distant (Seeley, 1995). The nature of the food is indicated by the odor of the bee when it is rubbed. The amount of food depends on the wriggling of the bee. The more is the wriggling, the more is the quantity (Bitam et al., 2010).

3.2. Bees Life Algorithm Description

3.2.1. Basic Explanation

Bees Life Algorithm presented in (Figure 2), starts with bee population initialization step which contains N bees (individuals) chosen randomly in the search space. The population fitness is evaluated in the second step. A bee population contains 1 queen, D drones and W workers in which the fittest bee represents the queen, the D fittest following bees represent the drones and the remaining bees are the workers. Consequently, the sum of the different bee individuals (1, D and W) equal to the population size (N). D and W are considered as a two user-defined parameters. Each cycle of a bee population life consists of two bee behaviors: reproduction and food foraging respectively.

In reproduction behavior, the queen starts mating in the space by mating-flight with the drones using crossover and mutation operators. Next, queen starts breeding N broods in step 4. Then, the evaluation of the brood fitness is performed (steps 5). If the fittest brood is fitter than the queen, it will be considered as the new queen for the next population. Moreover, D best bee individuals are chosen among the D fittest following broods and the drones of the current population to form the drones of the next population.

After that, W best bee individuals are chosen among the W fittest remaining broods and the workers of the current population in order to ensure the food foraging (steps 6 to 8). In step 9, the W workers search food source in W regions of flowers. We consider that each worker represents one region and there are other bees for each region recruited and employed to search the best food source among the different food sources in the region (step 10).

The recruited bees represent neighbor solutions in the search space used to ensure neighborhood search. BLA uses more recruited bees for the B best regions among W regions. B is user-defined parameter. For each region in step 11, only the bee with the highest fitness will be selected to form the next bee population. The evaluation of the new population fitness is executed in step 12. If the stopping criterion is not satisfied, a new bee life cycle is performed, and then we rerun the third step and so on. The BLA pseudo-code is presented as follows:

3.2.2. Individual Encoding and Stopping Criterion

Starting with the studied services selection in cloud computing, the individual represents a single solution which is a set of concrete cloud service *SI* selected at random as the preliminary step of BLA algorithm. It is established according to the end-used abstract services class *SC*. For example:

If $SC = \{S_1, \ldots, S_i, \ldots, S_n\}$ then

$$SI = \{s_{11}(c_1,d_1,bw_1), \ldots, s_{ij}(c_j,d_j,bw_j), \ldots, s_{nt}(c_t,d_t,bw_t)\},$$

when, $s_{ij}(c_j,d_j,bw_j)$ is the ith selected service instance from the datacenter *'j'* which is characterized by

Figure 2. A bees life algorithm pseudo-code

1. Initialize population (N bees) at random
2. Evaluate fitness of population (fittest bee is the queen, D fittest following bees are drones, W fittest remaining bees are workers)
3. ***While*** stopping criteria are not satisfied (Forming new population)
   /* **reproduction behavior** */
4. Generate **N** broods by **crossover** and **mutation**
5. Evaluate fitness of broods
6. If the fittest brood is fitter than the queen then replace the queen for the next generation
7. Choose D best bees among D fittest following broods and drones of current population (Forming next generation drones)
8. Choose W best bees among W fittest remaining broods and workers of current population (to ensure food foraging)
   /* **food foraging behavior** */
9. Search of food source in W regions by W workers
10. Recruit bees for each region for **local search** (more bees for the best B regions)
11. Select the fittest bee from each region
12. Evaluate fitness of population (fittest bee is the queen, D fittest following bees are drones, W fittest remaining bees are workers)
13. ***End while***

the cost c_j, the delay d_j, and the bandwidth bw_j between the customer and the provider location calculated by formulas (1), (2) and (3). The abstract composite service class structure *(SC)* is expressed using one-dimensional vector of abstract atomic service (S_i) requested by the end-used. Besides, each concrete atomic service instance (s_{ij}) is represented by vector structure included in a global vector structure determined the concrete composite service instance *(SI)* as two-dimensional structure. Here, we choose to apply a dynamic stopping criterion to ensure iteration arresting just after reaching the optimal individual. The BLA iterations are carried out and stopped only when the fitness does not change during *Ns* times after obtaining the best solution. It is the stagnation state. The number *Ns* is a user parameter. Note that a maximum iterations number (*Mt*) is also limited, even if *Ns* is not reached where ($0<Ns\leq Mt$).

3.2.3. BLA Reproduction Operators

In the reproduction part of the BLA two major operators are applied: crossover and mutation.

a. Crossover

Crossover operator helps to ensure the diversity in the solution search process. It is considered as one of the most important tool which guarantees the local optima escape. Crossover is a binary operator in which the queen is selected and one drone is randomly chosen to generate two new individuals. This process is repeated until reaching N individuals with crossover probability of P_c. In this chapter, we applied two-point crossover. Parents are splitting at these two points chosen randomly to create offspring after exchanging the extremities with correction if offspring do not belongs to the search space. In other words, in the first parent, concrete atomic services from the first point until the second point are altered with those in the other parent which are located between the same point positions as shown in (Figure 3).

b. Mutation

To take advantage of the history of previous iterations, mutation operator is proposed. It is a unitary operator in which the offspring has the chance to be mutated according to the mutation probability of P_m. Mutation helps to prevent the population from stagnating at any local optima.

We propose the mutation operator in which a selected atomic service will be chosen randomly and altered by another concrete atomic service selected at random in the datacenter (Figure 4). If the new individual do not belongs to the search space, a correction process is carried out.

3.2.4. Greedy Approach for Local Search

In the foraging part of BLA, local search (neighborhood search) approach is executed. It moves the individual in the search space to reach a neighbor individual by applying a local change. In other words, it starts from a candidate solution and then iteratively moves to a neighbor solution. At each iteration, it follows a searching process of making the optimal choice between solutions

Figure 3. 2-point crossover operator

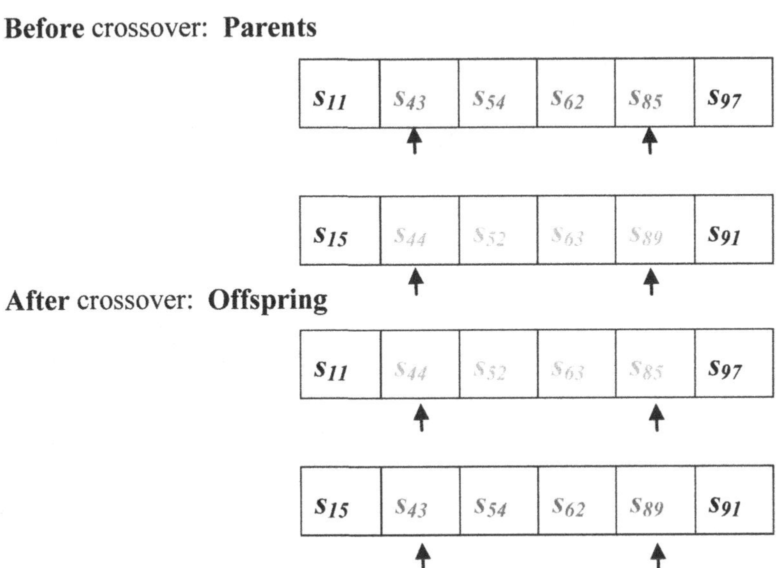

Figure 4. Mutation operator

Offspring **before** mutation:

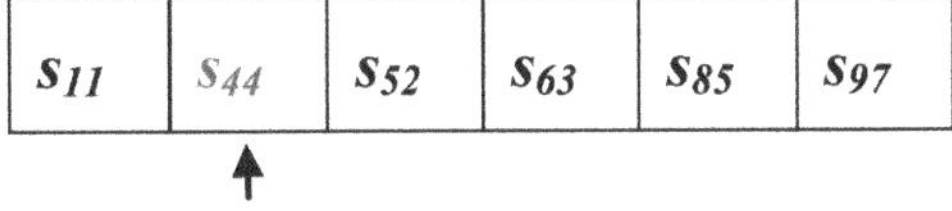

Offspring **after** mutation:

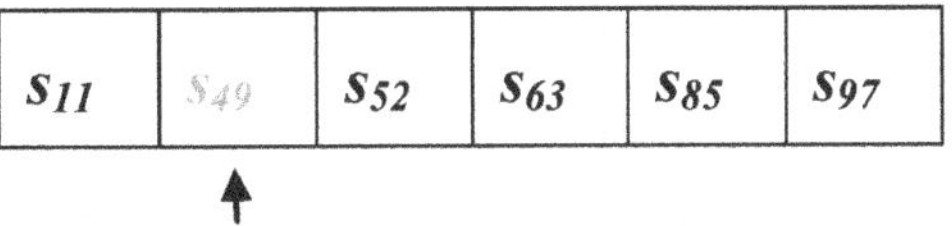

in the neighborhood with the hope of finding the global optimum.

We propose to use a greedy approach to generate neighbor individual. In this approach, one concrete service is randomly selected and replaced by another selected service in the nearest datacenter (Figure 5).

4. EXPERIMENTAL STUDY

4.1. Execution Environment

In order to evaluate the performance and the effectiveness of BLA to select the optimal cloud composite services, a series of tests have been performed on virtual cloud computing environment contains 22 datacenters as atomic service providers. End-used establishes 5 abstract composite services requests (SCs). Each one can be served in more than one datacenter in atomic services formats to give rise to 5 concrete composite services.

Tests are executed in an Intel Pentium Dual CPU T4500 with 2.30 GHz and 4.00 GB RAM under operating system Linux distribution Ubuntu 10.10. First, the proposed algorithm has been implemented using C++. This programming language choice is motivated by the integration feasibility of BLA implemented module in the cloud platform layer. For each service provider, a cost, delay and bandwidth values are defined (Figure 6).

We mention that DCj(Cj,Dj,BWj) means: DataCenter j (Cost, Delay, Bandwidth) provides atomic service "s_{ij}" in datacenter "j" to the end-user "i" as mentioned above.

4.2. BLA Parameter Settings

In this experimental study, we have chosen the following parameters as empirical values: the population size (N) varies from 10 to 50 individuals (solutions). In the reproduction behavior and as presented in section 3.1.1, the drones' number (D) changed from 7 to 20. Consequently, the workers' number (W) should alter from 2 to 29 respecting the bee population size (N = 1 + D + W) as mentioned in section 3.2.1. The crossover and mutation rates are fixed to 95% and 1% respectively.

During the food foraging behavior, promising regions (B) among those visited by workers are equal to the workers' number until reaching 15 regions. But beyond 15 workers (i.e. 15-29), B is set to 15. For each promising region, we have chosen 50 foraging bees however; only 30 are disseminated to the remainder regions. In order to evaluate each individual, we apply the fitness function Equation (4) in which the QoS weights are set to $w_1 = 1$, $w_2 = 0.5$ and $w_3 = 0.5$. They reflect the importance assigned to the cost which is followed by the delay and the bandwidth. The

Figure 5. Greedy approach for local search

Original individual:

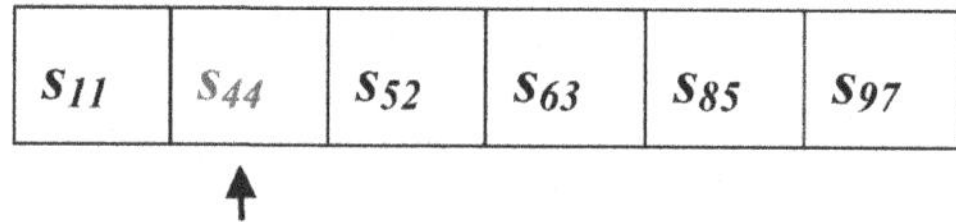

Neighbor individual:

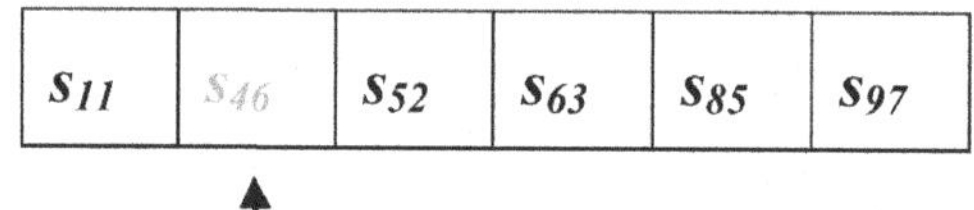

Figure 6. Cloud experimentation area

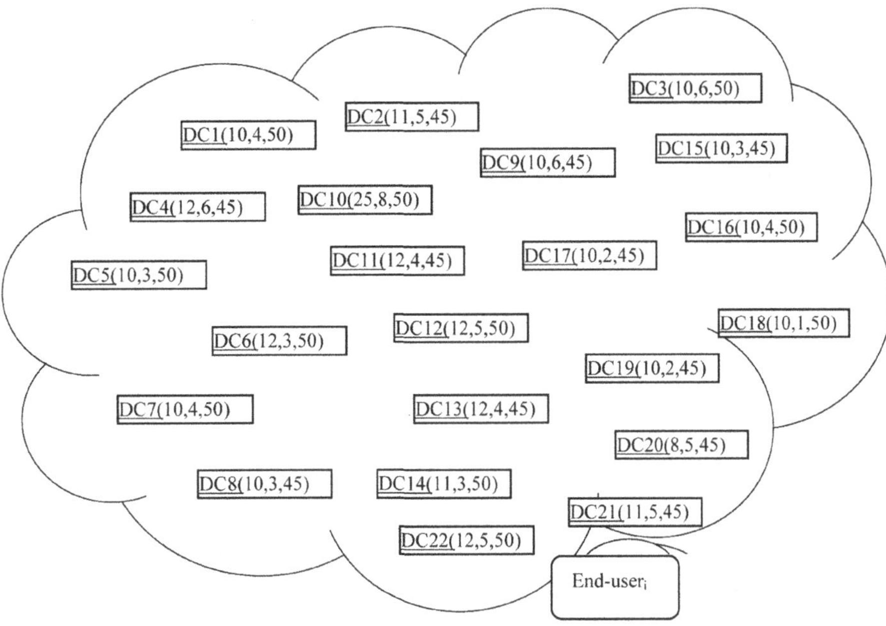

stagnation state is defined by *Ns* parameter mentioned in section 3.2.2. It is varied from 10 to 70 to evaluate BLA complexity through the iteration number and *Mt* = 200 as the maximum iterations number in the worst case.

4.3. Results and Discussions

After BLA and GA tests executions with the same parameter settings according to the cloud data presented in (Figure 6), the concrete composite services selected by these two algorithms are depicted in Table 1. Note that 'sj' in this table means the selection of concrete atomic service in datacenter 'j' for our unique end-user. Also, the best solutions found (best concrete composite service) in terms of cost, delay, and bandwidth are listed in the Table 2. Moreover, (Figure 7) shows the fitness evolution versus population size and (Figure 8) depicts fitness function against to the iterations number.

Table 1. Best selected concrete composite services given by BLA and GA

Algorithm	Selected concrete composite services
GA	SI1(s1,s9,s8,s7,s5,s6) SI2(s1,s9,s8,s7,s5,s4) SI3(s1,s9,s8,s14,s15,s19) SI4(s1,s9,s8,s14,s15,s16,s17) SI5(s1,s9,s8,s14,s15,s16,s18)
BLA	SI1(s1,s9,s8,s7,s5,s6) SI2(s1,s9,s8,s7,s5,s4) SI3(s1,s9,s8,s7,s5,s20,s19) SI4(s1,s9,s8,s7,s5,s20,s16,s18) SI5(s1,s9,s8,s7,s5,s20,s16,s19)

Table 1 and 2 show that the best fitness is the fitness obtained by BLA (146.5) compared with the fitness given by GA (168). Moreover, despite the modest value of delay reached by BLA, it presents the best cost due to its important weight factor (w_1=1) and its value compared to the other metrics. We remark also, that the BLA selected

Table 2. Best results given by BLA and GA

Algorithm	Fitness	Cost	Delay	BW.
GA	168	123	25	45
BLA	**146.5**	**110**	28	**45**

Figure 7. Fitness function evolution versus population size

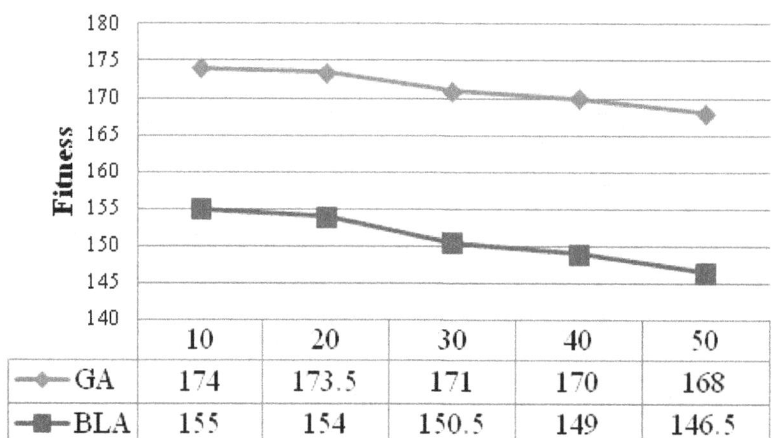

cloud service fitness is always better than those of GA even for different population size (Figure 7). In addition, BLA reaches rapidly to the optimal value and then provides less complexity than GA (Figure 8).

The obtained results exhibit that BLA is able to select cloud services with the best fitness that expresses the lowest cost and a reasonable latency and bandwidth.

It is due to the generality of the proposed algorithm that is a global optimization using the crossover operator which guarantees the diversity of the solution. Also, it ensures the local optima escape. Moreover, BLA carries out a local search represents in the mutation operator and in the neighborhood search approach which help to take advantage of the search history conducted by local search.

Figure 8. Fitness function evolution versus iterations number

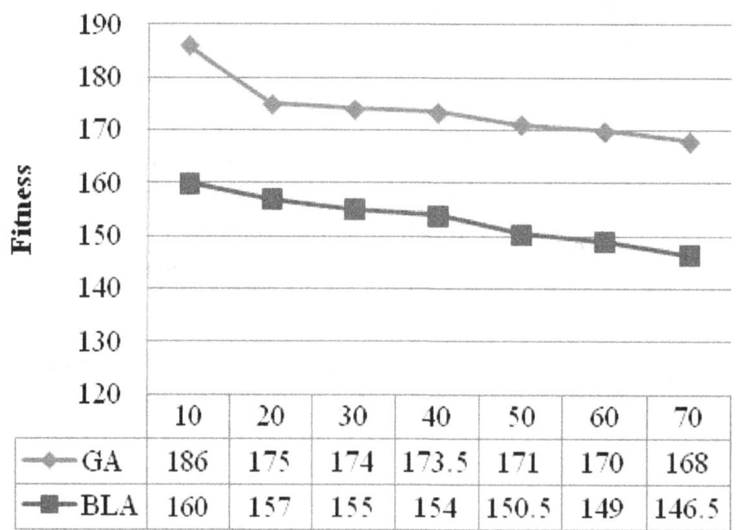

5. FUTURE RESEARCH DIRECTIONS

As computational intelligence techniques, Bees Life Algorithm can help researchers and designers in the cloud computing to select optimally services requested by the end-users. Also, it can be applied in other research areas after adaptation to overcome various optimization challenges. In continuation of this research activity, BLA can be embed into a real software framework which supports distributed computing on large data sets on cloud clusters of computers. At first, it can ensure the services selection viability in the cloud and then, the system can be considered by the standard process of such applications. Besides, we are interested in extending our study for providing a services selection system in dynamic environments which treats a new service request when the system is serving. Because of the handling of large data sets in different datacenters, the performance can be improved if a parallel BLA is designed and implemented as future promising research direction. Furthermore, we propose to implement BLA to solve other NP-hard cloud computing problems such as the job scheduling and data replication problems.

6. CONCLUSION

In this chapter, cloud computing services selection with QoS requirements has been studied and solved with Bee Life Algorithm as a new swarm optimization approach inspired by nature life of bees. Cost, delay and bandwidth have been investigated in this work as the major objectives in the cloud computing which should be improved to satisfy end-users with service time and expense reduction. In order to prove the reliability and the efficiency of this proposal, an implementation and a set of tests of BLA have been carried out. The obtained results of BLA prove the efficiency and the performance of this proposal in terms of quality of solution and complexity which are confirmed after comparisons against genetic algorithm as conventional algorithm in this context.

REFERENCES

Adams, J., Rothman, E. D., Kerr, W. E., & Paulino, Z. L. (1972). Estimation of the number of sex alleles and queen matings from diploid male frequencies in a population of apis mellifera. *Genetics*, *86*, 583–596.

Adjare, S. O. (1990). Beekeeping in Africa. *FAO Agricultural Services Bulletin, 68*(6). FAO of the United Nations.

Alrifai, M., & Risse, T. (2009). Combining global optimization with local selection for efficient QoS-aware service composition. *Proceedings of the 18th International Conference on World Wide Web*, (pp. 881-890).

Amazon. (2011). *Amazon elastic compute cloud.* Retrieved September 24, 2011, from http://aws.amazon.com/ec2/

API. (2011). *Apis mellifera.* Retrieved September 25, 2011, from http://en.wikipedia.org/wiki/Apis_mellifera/

Bitam, S., Batouche, M., & Talbi, E.-G. (2010). A survey on bee colony algorithms. *24th IEEE International Parallel and Distributed Processing Symposium, NIDISC Workshop,* Atlanta, Georgia, USA, (pp. 1-8).

Furht, B., & Escalante, A. (2010). Cloud computing fundamentals. In *Handbook of cloud computing*. Springer. doi:10.1007/978-1-4419-6524-0_1

Google. (2011). *Google app engine.* Retrieved September 24, 2011, from http://code.google.com/appengine/

Goscinski, A., & Brock, M. (2010). Toward dynamic and attribute based publication, discovery and selection for cloud computing. *Future Generation Computer Systems*, *26*, 947–970. doi:10.1016/j.future.2010.03.009

ISO. (2011). *ISO 8402:1994: Quality management and quality assurance*. Retrieved September 24, 2011, from http://www.iso.org/iso/iso_catalogue/catalogue_tc/catalogue_detail.htm?csnumber=20115/

Laidlaw, H. H., & Page, R. E. (1986). Mating designs. In Rinderer, T. E. (Ed.), *Bee genetics and breeding* (pp. 323–341). Academic Press, Inc.

Li, S., Shen, P., & Yang, S. (2011). A grouping particle swarm optimization algorithm for Web service selection based on user preference. *IEEE International Conference on Computer Science and Automation Engineering (CSAE)* Shanghai, China, (pp. 315-327).

Menasce, D. A. (2004). Composing Web services: A QoS view. *IEEE Internet Computing*, *8*(6), 88–90. doi:10.1109/MIC.2004.57

Rinderer, T. E., & Collins, A. M. (1986). Behavioral genetics. In Rinderer, T. E. (Ed.), *Bee genetics and breeding* (pp. 155–176). Academic Press, Inc.

Romeo, F., & Sangiovanni-Vincentelli, A. (1991). A theoretical framework for simulated annealing. *Algorithm*, *6*, 302–345. doi:10.1007/BF01759049

Seeley, T. D. (1995). *The wisdom of the hive*. Cambridge, MA: Harvard University Press.

Smith, D. M. (2010). *Hype cycle for cloud computing*. Gartner Rep. no.: G00201557.

UDDI. (2011). Universal discovery, description, integration. Retrieved September 24, 2011, from http://uddi.org/pubs/uddi-v3.0.2-20041019.htm/

Wang, S., Zheng, Z., Sun, Q., Zou, H., & Yang, F. (2011). Cloud model for service selection. *Proceedings of INFOCOM2011 Workshop on Cloud Computing,* Shanghai, China, (pp. 677-682).

Wang, W., Sun, Q., Zhao, X., & Yang, F. (2010). An improved particle swarm optimization algorithm for QoS-aware web service selection in service oriented communication. *International Journal of Computational Intelligence Systems*, *3*(1), 18–30. doi:10.2991/ijcis.2010.3.s1.2

Yasuhiro, T., & Mitsuo, G. E. (1998). Entropy-based genetic algorithm for solving TSP. *The Second International Conference on Knowledge-based Intelligent Electronic Systems,* (pp. 285–290).

Yu, T., Zhang, Y., & Lin, K.-J. (2007). Efficient algorithms for Web services selection with end-to-end QoS constraints. *ACM Transactions on the Web (TWEB)*, *1*(1).

Zhang, C., Su, S., & Chen, J. (2007). DiGA: Population diversity handling genetic algorithm for QoS-aware web services selection. *Computer Communications*, *30*, 1082–1090. doi:10.1016/j.comcom.2006.11.002

Chapter 4
Cloud-Based Intelligent DSS Design for Emergency Professionals

Shah J. Miah
Victoria University, Australia

ABSTRACT

Computational Intelligence (CI) has become a well-established research field of computer science in which multi-disciplinary problems are studied to design an effective computing solution. As a known computer-based CI approach, decision support systems (DSS) has gained popularity as a computing solution to structured and unstructured problems in organizations' managerial improvement. DSS design needs to meet the domain-specific demands of emergency professionals on both an on-site and a real-time basis using the support of the most up-to-date technological provisioning platform. The advantages of cloud computing may offer promising support (e.g. Internet or web-based provisioning) for DSS services to meet the emergency professionals' decision needs. This chapter introduces requirements of a cloud-based CI approach for domain-specific decision support through the functionalities on an anywhere and anytime basis. The chapter highlights the context of intelligent DSS design in terms of support in determining the priorities of taking action, both for medical emergency professionals and natural disasters workers, as potential application areas identified in this study.

INTRODUCTION

Computational Intelligence (CI) became one of the rapidly growing fields in the computer science discipline, in which different problems are studied in order to develop intelligent solutions for effective management. Decision support systems (DSS), as one kind of intelligent solution, has gained a great deal of attention by many current research studies, employing different artificial intelligence (AI) techniques based on targeted objectives. Previous studies in CI revealed two main objectives of research (Duch, 2007) the first is an attempt to understand the problem domain in terms of analyzing and extracting intelligent behavior to possible optimization; and the second

DOI: 10.4018/978-1-4666-1830-5.ch004

objective is towards modeling and designing intelligent systems. However, the intelligent systems design should focus not only on the problem analysis and relevant technology design, but also on how to meet the client's domain-specific on-site information demands within the new technological provisioning platform that would provide better user access and flexibility.

The advantage of cloud computing is that it is capable to offer a cloud-based (e.g. Internet or web-based provisioning) DSS service to meet the emergency professionals/workers' decision needs. Other known benefit is that it can bring access and service flexibility both for service users and service providers. With the benefit, it is important to understand and develop conceptual approach for designing the services. The study is relevant to such a service design, namely an intelligent DSS application design for the provision of cloud computing. The intelligent service approach would be able to provide domain-specific decision support to the decision makers through cloud-based functionalities on an 'anywhere-anytime' basis. This initiative could offer a new, shared provision where decision makers can actively perform their effective decision making, and help in liaising with relevant authorities by prioritizing action during real emergency problems while in the emergency location or on the move.

Cloud computing[1] is used as a modern architecture of shared computing service. The services offered are mainly supported through computing utility rental by service providers. After the introduction of web-based utility services by *Amazon.com*, many web service providers became increasingly interested in the cloud-computing platform for launching new services to meet clients' demands. A cloud-based provision involves minimal labor and implementation expense (Santos, Gummadi & Rodrigues, 2009). Recent studies provide examples of the proliferation of cloud computing through two main services. Firstly, Nurmi, Wolski and Grzegorczyk (2010) described an open-source software framework for cloud computing in which computing resources are considered as an "Infrastructure as a Service". Cloud providers such as *Amazon, Flexiscale,* and *GoGrid* offer "Infrastructure as a Service" for clients to access a virtual machine. These providers allow businesses to host resource services. Secondly, cloud providers such as *Google* offer a "Software as a Service" that provides use of applications over the Internet (Santos et al. 2009). In addition, Santos et al. (2009) addressed requirements of confidentiality and integrity in data access and process, and deliberately proposed a trusted cloud computing platform for facilitating a "closed box execution and storage" in a virtual environment (p.2). This implies that the cloud-based provision must provide secure functionalities with a concurrent trusted storage facility. In the same way, it is important to formalize the growing requirements of new problem-specific intelligent application design with better service benefits. This is the main focus of the chapter.

In particular for natural disaster management, Bessis, Asimakopoulou & Xhafa (2011) described a roadmap that guides employment of collective computational intelligence for disaster management. From a disaster manager's decision-making point of view, this study identified various crucial issues such as information collection, combined interactions at different decision making levels, and designing a pervasive approach for action taking or controlling (Bessis et al., 2011). Our study is motivated by factors beyond the challenges here for emergency professionals in managing natural disasters. As such, two practical instances (in particular for medical and natural disaster emergency situations) are highlighted here in this study and give rise to the research question: *how can we outline user specific requirements to design intelligent DSS exploring new technological provisions?*

For medical emergency management, previous studies identify design requirements of mobile clinical decision support systems (CDSS) for emergency triage decision support. In most cases, such CDSS are limited in the boundary of decision support: for example, the process of categorization of casualties based on their need for medical treatment (Padmanabhan et al. 2006). Michalowski, Rubin, Slowinski & Wilk (2003) developed a mobile CDSS for emergency decision support of different acute pain presentations. This client-server architecture-based CDSS model operates from wireless handheld devices and allows clinicians to interact with the existing hospital information systems for obtaining clinical data. In another case, Dong et al. (2008) described a "Novel Computer Triage Program" in which the objective was to identify a link between a DSS and a memory-based triage by nurses at the point of care. Findings from Dong's study suggested that there is significant inconsistency by nurses using memory-based triage when compared with a computer-based DSS. Padmanabhan et al. (2006) also described a mobile CDSS prototype design called "iTriage" (Intelligent Mobile Decision Support Triage prototype) for handheld devices. Though it is beyond the scope of the present study, the application of a DSS design in a shared platform, particularly for emergency medical staff working outdoors or at an accident location, can add value to service and practice improvement to medical professionals. This can help make effective decisions, for instance, on the number of beds available in the emergency departments of the closest hospitals for quick air-lifting with life support.

In the area of natural disaster emergencies, Buzolic, Mladineo & Knezic (2009) developed a DSS solution for disaster communications through decision processes in the phases of preparation, prevention, and planning of a protection system from natural and other catastrophes, as well as in phases throughout interventions during an emergency situation in the telecommunications field. The DSS model is based on the GIS technology that captures the necessary location-specific data. Similarly, Mirfenderesk (2009) described a DSS designed to assist mainly in a post-disaster situation. As a post-disaster measure it can identify a vulnerable population and assist in the evacuation of the population at risk (Mirfenderesk, 2009). Apart from these DSS approaches, there are some projects on developing disaster management solutions such as MIKE 11, designed by the Danish Hydraulic Institute (Kjelds & Muller, 2008), and SoKNOS, *Service-Oriented ArchiteCtures Supporting Networks of Public Security*, a service-oriented architecture-based solution design by the German federal government (*SoKNOS*, 2011), but these are still in the embryonic or conception stage of design. There remain issues in designing a comprehensive decision process with collective information sharing for disaster impact assessments to meet emergency requirements, especially for the safety of human and other living beings in emergencies. Field workers/ emergency disasters professionals can transfer forecasting details directly from the emergency zone and can request further resource support to address the crucial needs of emergency victims.

The discussion in this chapter intends to particularize the two aforementioned application areas, in which requirements of cloud-based DSS solutions are highlighted. The chapter will be organized in the following way. The background section provides an overview of emergency management problems and relevant computational solutions. Then the next section discusses the main concerns of such intelligent DSS design. The section after that presents a discussion of the overall chapter, the delimitations of the proposed approach in the chapter, and an outline of further research directions.

BACKGROUND

New technological provisions should be developed with the view of supporting framework for users. Cloud computing has recently emerged as a paradigm that can offer support with technological benefits for emergency professionals. The main objective is to enable individual computational technology as an application to meet a combined and collective emergency decision support needed. The benefit would be, for this instance, in enabling decision support to users/emergency professional including emergency health workers, health officials, natural disaster workers, and other relevant professionals.

EMERGENCY PROBLEM SIGNIFICANCE

A United Nations report (United Nations, 2005) claimed that natural disasters claim an average of 85,541 lives per year and affect 230 million individuals. In a relative study by Oxfam, it is suggested that this figure could grow by more than 50% by 2015 to an average of 375 million affected by climate-related disasters every year (Bessis et al., 2011). At various government and non-government levels recognition is growing on the need to work together on the prevention of and timely response to disasters occurring on an international scale (European Union, 2010). It is implied that emergency problems created as a result of climatic events and other catastrophic incidents need urgent responses by authorities. To protect the human communities and structures from the impact of disasters, teams from both government and non-government agencies need to work closely together, using the combined effort of different groups such as medical teams, civil protection, police, fire and rescue services, health and ambulance services. The relevant management requires real time responses – in order to take appropriate decisions and actions (Graves, 2004; Otten, Heijningen & Lafortune, 2004).

The need for decision making is not only for pre- and post-emergency situations, but also where "the need for information exchange during an emergency situation is present; however it can be very diverse and complex" (Carle, Vermeersch & Palma, 2004) cited in (Bessis et al., 2011, p.77). Carle et al. (2004) also report that there are frequent quotes regarding the lack and inconsistent views of information shared in emergency operations" (Bessis et al., 2011, p.77).

Studies suggest that there are many small communities that "do not have the resources, personnel and expertise to develop a set of requirements to assist them in managing their activities as they pertain to emergency response" (Bui & Lee, 1999) cited in (Bessis et al., 2011, p.77). Different emergency management approaches are not sufficient enough to address the unstructured and decentralized nature of such situations (Bessis et al., 2011).

A number of ICT-based collaborative computer-based systems have been developed to assist the requirements of many organizations to bring together their intellectual resources and the sharing of accurate information in a timely manner (Graves, 2004; Howard, Kiviniemi & Samuelson, 2002). These initiatives do not support meeting the immediate demand of the collective communities when managing any disasters in a comprehensive manner. One of the reasons for this is the need for multiple decisions to be taken in real time, as well as the necessity for correct and up to date information (Asimakopoulou, Bessis, Varaganti & Norrington, 2009; Bessis et al., 2011).

COMPUTATIONAL INTELLIGENCE METHODS

Studies investigated the use of different CI methods to address different business problems. The CI methods use different AI techniques including neural network, fuzzy logic, and evolutionary computing algorithms. Based on the analysis and nature of the problem domain, CI then applies the technique to bring possible optimization subject to user requirements. The neural network can simulate the function of the human brain that can process "many pieces of data at once and learn to recognize patterns" (Stair & Reynolds, 2005, p.426). It is suggested that some hospitals use neural networks for predicting the likelihood of contracting cancer. At the same time, different computational problem-solving methods have increasingly attracted more and more attention, for example, case-based reasoning, rules-based reasoning, hybrid reasoning, and so on. Each method offers benefits for problem areas. Case-based reasoning involves planning ahead to solve a new problem using previous experiences. Kolodner (1992) described case-based reasoning as a means of adapting old methods to meet new demands using old cases to explain new situations. Case-based reasoning attracts attention for different problem solving reasoning because it is capable of directly addressing the problems (Kolodner, 1992). A rule based reasoning use if-then conditions simply to find possible ways of solving problems. It implies that problem situation leads to identify ways of action taking.

The following Table 1 illustrates several application areas where different AI (Artificial intelligence) methods have been employed.

CLOUD COMPUTING APPLICATIONS

The term "cloud computing" has been in existence since October 2007 when Google and IBM jointly announced their collaboration (IBM website announcement, 2010 cited in Vouk (2008), and has become popular mainly due to benefits such as reduced IT overhead and flexibility in offering cheaper user access.

Fitzgerald and Dennis (2010) described cloud-based design as a "circuit-switched service architecture" that is easier to implement for organizations because "they move the burden of network design and management inside the cloud" (p.297). This implies that end users can have service through the cloud without any technological burden.

Cloud computing refers to a computing platform in which target users have the option to use their services through an Internet-based infrastructure (Fitzgerald & Dennis, 2010). Hayes (2008) described cloud computing as a software application migration from local PCs "to distant Internet servers, users and developers alike go along for the ride" (p.9). Many studies described cloud computing as a modern architecture of shared computing service. The shared computing services are mainly supported through computing utility rental by the third party organization, that is, Internet service providers. After the introduction of web-based utility services by Amazon.com, many service providers made different cloud computing platforms with novel features available for launching new services to meet their client groups' demands. Santos et al. (2009) described the two key benefits of cloud-based provision as minimal labor and implementation expense. From an end-user's perspective, Marston et al. (2011) described cloud computing as Software as a Service.

From a management perspective, the five key advantages (Marston et al., 2011) of a cloud-based system are as follows:

- A lower cost of entry for widespread deployment of IT services;
- An almost immediate access to technological resources, with no upfront capital investments;
- Lower IT barriers to innovation, as can be witnessed from the many promising start-ups;
- Easier for enterprises to extend their services – which are increasingly reliant on accurate information to meet instant client demand; and
- New classes of applications and service delivery.

Jiang, Fang & Huang (2009) introduced a cloud-based application for forest pest infection management for admin and operational professionals. The study identified different functions

Table 1. Use of AI in different application areas

AI techniques	*Application Types*	*Application domains*
Rules-based/data mining techniques (Wang, Qu, Liu & Cheng, 2004) The rules based technique based on data mining periodically mines from database elements and all the association rules of elements satisfy the relevant control rules. Practitioners can maintain and modify the standard condition in application environment database by adding recently frequent syndromes (Wang et al., 2004).	Diagnosis tool	Practice of traditional Chinese medicine
Knowledge-based techniques (Refea, Hassen & Hazman, 2003) The knowledge-based technique is established on heuristic rules resulting of experience of relevant experts. Most of the time knowledge-based technique is used for classification and reasoning such as in the purpose of fault diagnosis. It involves set of activities such as knowledge acquisition, criteria selection, selection of user interface, knowledge hierarchy building, program code writing, program validating and testing, documentation, and maintenance (Refea et al., 2003)	Management and planning tool	Irrigation and fertilization scheduling – agricultural management
Rules-based /decision tree approach (Yang, Lim & Tan, 2005) The decision tree creates diagnostic rules depending on the human experiences or classifications using leaf and decision nodes. Leaf nodes or answer nodes contain class name and decision nodes specify some possible outcome of the test nodes. For diagnosing abnormal vibration for rotating machinery, a decision table based on the cause-symptom matrix is used (Yang et al., 2005) as leaf-decision nodes for testing diagnostic outcomes.	Diagnosis tool	Diagnosing cause of abnormal vibration for rotating machinery
Rules-based; fuzzy logic (Roussel, Cavelier & van der Werf, 2000) To estimate the potential environmental effect of pesticide applications, the study uses authors' expert perception in an expert system called Ipest-B (B for Brittany). With respect to pesticide effects fuzzy logic uses three types of input variables: pesticide properties, site-specific conditions and characteristics of the pesticide application. It yields four output variables: first one reflects rate of application of pesticide, the other three reflect risk for three major environmental compartments (groundwater, surface water and air) (Roussel et al., 2000).	Advisory tool	Minimizing environmental damage from pesticides
Fuzzy logic based (Gutierrez-Estrada, De Pedro Sanz, Lopez-Luque & Pulido-Calvo, 2005) Fuzzy logic utilizes many valued form of logic such as in-between values. According to the definition (Gutierrez-Estrada et al., 2005), a fuzzy set is divided by partitions, which describe a point as a function of its membership. In the developed expert system application, fuzzy logic controller has two input fuzzy sets and one output fuzzy set (Gutierrez-Estrada et al., 2005). This explicit relationship between the partitions of the input fuzzy sets and the output fuzzy set is creased from human experience to provide conclusions.	Diagnosis tool	Assist in diagnosing eel pathologies
Neural network based (Patel, McClendon & Goodrum, 1998) The neural network can automatically extract and encode the knowledge from the data (Patel et al., 1998). According to the definition by Patel et al. (1998) a neural network can be developed using samples of data from the problem domain in the form of inputs and associated outputs.	Management tool	Managing tools for egg collection and packaging. Helps reduce human workload, reduce control cost
Object-oriented approach and rules based (Ellison, Ash & McDonald, 1998) Object-oriented approach uses factors that are identified from the problem domain. Each object is then characterized by a set of attributes relevant to factors with an associated value or set of values. For inheriting the characteristics of the objects it is then organized into a tiered dependency network (Ellison et al., 1998).	Management tool	Used by grape growers for managing diseases such as Botrytis cinerea

both for forest pest professionals and government administrators. It is therefore realized that the use of cloud-based services for the effective decision support of multiple parties is still largely overlooked, given the potential benefits. As such it is important to discuss the requirement of a conceptual approach of cloud provision to improve decision making onsite. In theory we represent a convergence need of decision making with collaborative participation through the use of cloud-based services.

DSS FOR DISASTER MANAGEMENT

As pointed earlier many decision supports needed for disaster management have been identified for computer-based solution development. DSS development for medical professionals involves limitations in the boundary of decision support. San Pedro et al. (2005) described the process of categorization of casualties based on their need for medical treatment or attention. Findings from Dong's study suggested that there is significant inconsistency by nurses using memory-based triage when compared with a computer-based DSS. Padmanabhan et al. (2006) also described a mobile CDSS prototype design called "iTriage" (Intelligent Mobile Decision Support Triage prototype) for handheld devices. The study evaluated the impact on the quality of the process and outcomes from using "iTriage" implemented on PDA (Personal digital assistant) handheld devices. Though it is beyond the scope of the present study, the application of a DSS design in a shared platform, particularly for emergency medical staff working at an accident location, can add value to service and practice improvement as medical professionals can make an effective decision on number of beds available in the emergency departments of the closest hospitals for quick air-lifting with life support.

In the disaster management domain, recent studies have proposed DSS that satisfy the requirements of decision making in aspects such as effective incident information management (Peng, Zhang, Tang & Li, 2011), disaster information exchange through virtual communities (Lu & Yang, 2011), disaster information management for public safety (Lee, Bharosa, Yang, Janssen & Rao, 2011), flood early warning systems (Lee et al. 2011) and knowledge sharing requirements for emergency management (Maio, Fenza, Gaeta, Loia & Orciuoli, 2011). All of the mentioned DSS approaches offer support decision making based on specific needs at different stages of the disaster management domain. It is revealed that research addressing requirements of developing a generic DSS framework for disaster events handling at all stages is still limited and emergent both to researchers and practitioners in this field.

MAIN FOCUS OF THE CHAPTER

Identifying two major trends of cloud computing from the study (Marston et al. 2011) we represent an effective cloud computing application in this study. The identified trends are defined as:

1. To improve solution efficiency, utilizing the power of modern computing, and
2. To improve business agility, whereby a computing solution can be used to gain competitive development.

According to the concept of efficiency, it is argued that effective use of computing resources located in geographical areas mainly offers cheaper access to different services through cloud. On the other hand, the concept of business agility implies that cloud computing must be able to play differing roles for businesses, enabling the use of CI approach on the Internet as flexible access points. The principles given in the above mentioned study supports outline a solution framework for emergency professionals in that case-based reasoning can have application to learning from past

Table 2. The underlying structure of the cloud function

Stakeholders	*Underlying structure*	*Services*
Internal management and government decision makers	Data centre	Different forecasting and decision making services
Emergency professional /field workers	Original resources of cloud (server access, monitoring and management software tools)	Majority is for cloud such as core operation with live updates and development, action taking resource allocation

problems, and rules-based reasoning can be used for different action taking decisions. In addition, drawing from Jiang et al. (2009), it is therefore useful to outline a cloud function structure. Table 2 shows the functions of the underlying structure for the proposed solution.

Hernandez and Serrano (2001) proposed a generic model for emergency management systems employing knowledge-based reasoning. The intelligent system is capable of assisting with the information needs of different human agents. The employed methodology is based on three management aspects: "what is happening?" means that the system is acquiring current situations; "what may happen?" means that the system evaluates the current situations in order to access the best possible actions and explanations for managers; and "what to do?" means that the system finds answers to take action to address problematic situations (Hernandez & Serrano, 2001). It is argued that the management aspects are significant for outlining a comprehensive solution in emergency situations.

Figure 1 illustrates proposed conceptual model below. We consider the solution aspect as an information sharing platform in between multiple agents. The main focus is on the decision making interactions between the key decision makers. There are four dimensions for structuring and identifying information flow for decision making. Top box (in the Figure 1) identifies the need for information collaboration form different established sources regarding the emergency situations, for instance, Bureau of Meteorology (BOM) for latest climate updates. The right-hand side Box defines internal authorities' involvement into different action taking, for instance, government managers who coordinate emergency situation management. This dimension involves complex decision making for allocating resources and planning action taking. Bottom box identifies local audience or victims if they have any access to main system for rapid messaging or alert signals. Finally the emergency professionals (At left-hand side) are the key agents who need to have access all of the information support for different effective action taking. This decision making service is vital for the relevant stakeholders groups as they are directly related to action taking activities. In relation to Table 2 the middle box of Figure 1 holds the intelligent DSS software on cloud. In summary, emergency professionals obtain relevant information from the cloud while the data centre can still be located at the station. The internal information management can have concurrent access to different updates in order to bring the latest instructions and action-taking decisions for emergency professionals.

We argue a rule based with case based reasoning technique that can be helpful to address such information sharing for each agent in the proposed architecture. Case-based reasoning learns from previous situation similar to the current problem and subsequently uses to solve the new problem (Kolodner, 1992). Such reasoning has application in emergency situation management and its decision making as it helps to understand and solve new problems. Then again, developing useful rules from various cases can be useful for similar

Figure 1. A conceptual model of cloud-based intelligent DSS

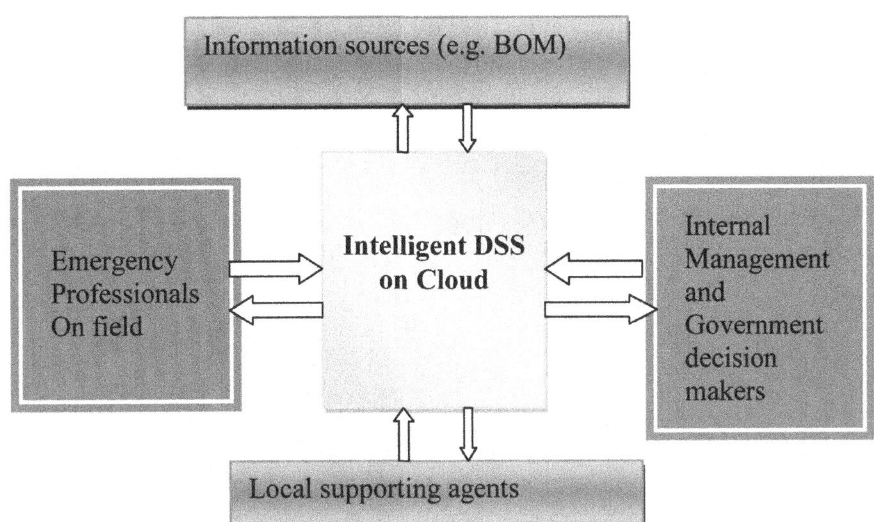

situations and its decision making so that rules could be used when they matched cases exactly, while cases could be used when rules are not applicable instantly (Kolodner, 1992). For representing potential deployment units, we illustrate medical instances that have shown in the Figure 2.

Figure 2 shows a schematic deployment diagram of the cloud computing model. The model illustrates how the computing resources as a node in the cloud can be accessed from a variety of platforms through the Internet. Medical emergency professional can get access to cloud data through the Internet browser via their mobile devices. Internet browser has HTTP connectivity to cloud server. Cloud server holds the DSS application that has different database connectivity such as SQL or JDBC to existing databases such as hospital databases.

DISCUSSION AND RECOMMENDATION

The chapter discussed the potential of a cloud-based computational intelligence technique as an application for the requirements of emergency professionals. In the context of a decision-support application, the chapter identified the requirements of emergency professional in terms of support for the determination of priorities in taking action, in real time and at field level. The proposed concept suggested the combined use of rule-based and case-based reasoning for ensuring appropriate collaboration in the decision-making design. This initiative reinforces a shift from the traditional client-server based application design to a cloud-based flexible provision, which allows mobility and interactive live use for emergency situations. At the same time, decision makers can actively perform their effective decision making, liaise with relevant authorities for sharing data (e.g. relevant climate forecasting, weather conditions) and prioritize action-taking on real problems while in the emergency location or on the move.

The chapter presented a conceptual solution approach for the target problem area in which decision making needs coordination and cooperation. We attempted to establish a theoretical foundation for designing and evaluating a solution within a real management environment. We explored different CI techniques and their usage in application

Figure 2. Potential system units of the emergency data requirements for an emergency cloud DSS

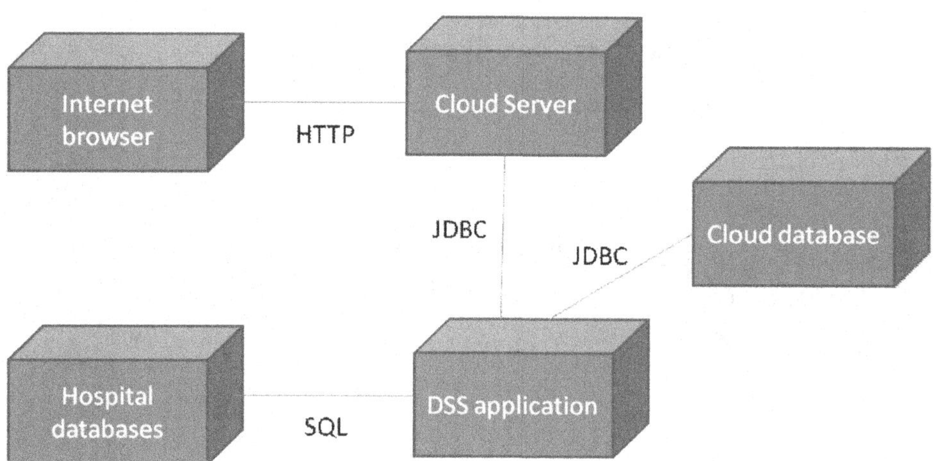

areas. It is argued that both traditional and current emergent initiatives are far from a solution that can address collaboration issues of decision makers at different levels when in the situation of a given emergency event.

FUTURE RESEARCH DIRECTIONS

The chapter introduced an emergent requirement of cloud based intelligent application design. While the findings presented in this chapter are based on a review of previous relevant research, it only represents an early stage analysis of innovative systematic solution development in the target application area. Further research will be required for designing specific knowledge repository that will be capable of working with new technological provision. The interactive user's provision in cloud based application design can also be a challenge relevant to emergency situations. In this purpose, user specific provision are required to define for each user groups for enabling better decision making or action taking through collaboration. An in-depth study will also be required for system integration considering a wide range of emergency situations and to ensure compatibility of different components within an operating environment.

Further to evaluate the CI technique in a solution framework, a test environment for such solution design will be required for ensuring appropriate information generation according to the stakeholder's requirements. This test will also help identify technical difficulties of the CI technique and various process-oriented challenges associated with user's acceptance and satisfaction.

CONCLUSION

The chapter discussed the need for a cloud-based intelligent DSS solution for emergency management. We reinforced the requirement of a comprehensive approach for the target problem area in which decision making needs coordination and cooperation. A generic model was introduced as an example. However, professionals at the problem domain may have their own opinions about a variety of different system that may be used involving different management concerns that were not covered in the chapter. Many organizations may not have appropriate resources and infrastructure associated with emergency management. Although the cloud-based solution can support flexibility and easier access to real-time data, it involves security and privacy of information and data resources including access control policy concerns.

Although intelligent techniques have grown to a sophisticated level, the combination of these services with cloud-based computing is still in the emergent stage. Many relevant tools and technologies are still being developed. The topic area introduced in the chapter of emergency professionals' decision making is still just a concept. There is a need for considerable research on initial design and testing prior to implementation of the relevant technology in practice. The author attempts to bring an application area of multidisciplinary computational intelligence techniques to enhance readers' knowledge in the field.

REFERENCES

Amazon EC2. (n.d.). Retrieved on January 12, 2012, from http://aws.amazon.com/ec2/

Asimakopoulou, E., Bessis, N., Varaganti, R., & Norrington, P. (2009). A personalized forest fire evacuation data grid push service – The FFED-GPS approach. In Asimakopoulou, E., & Bessis, N. (Eds.), *Advanced ICTs for disaster management and threat detection: Collaborative and distributed frameworks* (pp. 279–295). Hershey, PA: IGI Global.

Bessis, N., Asimakopoulou, E., & Xhafa, F. (2011). A next generation emerging technologies roadmap for enabling collective computational intelligence in disaster management. *International Journal of Space-Based and Situational Computing, 1*(1), 76–85. doi:10.1504/IJSSC.2011.039109

Bui, T., & Lee, J. (1999). An agent-based framework for building decision support systems. *Decision Support Systems. International Journal (Toronto, Ont.), 25*(3).

Buzolic, J., Mladineo, N., & Knezic, S. (2009). Decision support system for disaster communications in Dalmatia. *International Journal of Emergency Management, 1*(2), 191–201. doi:10.1504/IJEM.2002.000520

Carle, B., Vermeersch, F., & Palma, C. R. (2004). *Systems improving communication in case of a nuclear emergency*. International Community on Information Systems for Crisis Response Management (ISCRAM2004) Conference, 3–4 May 2004, Brussels, Belgium.

Dong, S. L., Bullard, M. J., Meurer, D. P., Colman, I., Blitz, S., Holroyd, B. R., & Rowe, B. H. (2008). Emergency triage: Comparing a novel computer triage program with standard triage. *Academic Emergency Medicine, 12*, 28. Retrieved from http://onlinelibrary.wiley.com/doi/10.1197/j.aem.2005.01.005/pdf

Duch, W. (2007). What is computational intelligence and where is it going? In W. Duch, & J. Mandziuk (Eds.), *Challenges for Computational Intelligence, volume 63 of Studies in Computational Intelligence,* 2007, (pp. 1–13). Berlin, Germany: Springer.

Ellison, P., Ash, G., & McDonald, C. (1998). An expert system for the management of Botrytis cinerea in Australian vineyards. *Agricultural Systems, 56*, 185–207. doi:10.1016/S0308-521X(97)00035-8

European Union. (2010). *Reinforcing the European Union's disaster response capacity*. Retrieved on 12, January, 2012, from http://ec.europa.eu/governance/impact/planned_ia/docs/28_echo_eu_disaster_response_capacity_en.pdf

Fitzgerald, J., & Dennis, A. (2010). *Fundamentals of business data communications* (10th ed.). John Wiley & Sons, Inc.

Gadomski, A. M., Bologna, S., & Costanzo, G. D. (2001). Towards intelligent decision support systems for emergency managers: The IDA approach. *International journal of Risk Assessment and Management, 2*, 224-242.

Google App Engine. (n.d.). Retrieved on January 12, 2012, from http://code.google.com/appengine/

Graves, R. J. (2004). *Key technologies for emergency response*. International Community on Information Systems for Crisis Response (ICSCRAM2004) Conference, 3–4 May 2004, Brussels, Belgium.

Gutierrez-Estrada, J. C., De Pedro Sanz, E., Lopez-Luque, R., & Pulido-Calvo, I. (2005). SEDPA, an expert system for disease diagnosis in eel rearing systems. *Aquacultural Engineering, 33*, 110–125. doi:10.1016/j.aquaeng.2004.12.003

Hernandez, J. Z., & Serrano, J. M. (2001). Knowledge-based models for emergency management systems. *Expert Systems with Applications, 20*, 173–186. doi:10.1016/S0957-4174(00)00057-9

Heyes, B. (2008). Cloud computing as software migrates from local PCs to distant Internet servers, users and developers alike go along for the ride. *Communications of the ACM, 51*(7), 9–11.

Howard, R., Kiviniemi, A., & Samuelson, O. (2002). *The latest developments in communications and e-commerce IT barometer in 3 Nordic countries*. CIB w87 Conference, 12–14 June 2002, Aarhus School of Architecture. International Council for Research and Innovation in Building and Construction.

Jiang, S., Fang, L., & Huang, X. (2009). An idea of special cloud computing in forest pests' control. *Lecture Notes in Computer Science, 5931*, 615–620. doi:10.1007/978-3-642-10665-1_61

Kjelds, J. T., & Müller, H. G. (2008). *Integrated flood plain & disaster management using the MIKE 11 decision support system.* Retrieved on May 21, 2011, from http://www.icimod.org/?opg=949&document=1248

Kolodner, J. L. (1992). An introduction to case-based reasoning. *Artificial Intelligence Review, 6*, 3–34. doi:10.1007/BF00155578

Lee, J., Bharosa, N., Yang, J., Janssen, M., & Rao, H. R. (2011). Group value and intention to use — A study of multi-agency disaster management information systems for public safety. *Decision Support Systems, 50*, 404–414. doi:10.1016/j.dss.2010.10.002

Lu, Y., & Yang, D. (2011). Information exchange in virtual communities under extreme disaster conditions. *Decision Support Systems, 50*, 529–538. doi:10.1016/j.dss.2010.11.011

Maio, C. D., Fenza, G., Gaeta, M., Loia, V., & Orciuoli, F. (2011). A knowledge-based framework for emergency DSS. *Knowledge-Based Systems, 24*(8).

Marston, S., Li, Z., Bandyopadhyay, S., Zhang, J., & Ghalsasi, A. (2011). Cloud computing — The business perspective. *Decision Support Systems, 51*, 176–189. doi:10.1016/j.dss.2010.12.006

Michalowski, W., Rubin, S., Slowinski, R., & Wilk, S. (2003). Mobile clinical support system for pediatric emergencies. *Decision Support Systems, 36*(2), 161–176. doi:10.1016/S0167-9236(02)00140-9

Microsoft Azure Services. (n.d.). Retrieved on January 12, 2012, from http://www.microsoft.com/azure/default.mspx

Mirfenderesk, H. (2009). Flood emergency management decision support system on the Gold Coast, Australia. *Australian Journal of Emergency Management, 24*, 2.

Nurmi, D., Wolski, R., Grzegorczyk, C., Obertelli, G., Soman, S., Youseff, L., & Zagorodnow, D. (2010). *The eucalyptus open-source cloud-computing system.* The 9th IEEE/ACM International Symposium on Cluster Computing and the Grid. Retrieved April 22, 2011, from http://www.cca08.org/papers/Paper32-Daniel-Nurmi.pdf

Otten, J., Heijningen, B., & Lafortune, J. F. (2004). *The virtual crisis management centre. An ICT implementation to canalise information.* International Community on Information Systems for Crisis Response (ISCRAM2004) Conference, 3–4 May 2004, Brussels, Belgium.

Padmanabhan, N., Burstein, F., Churilov, L., Wassertheil, J., Hornblower, B., & Parker, N. (2006). A mobile emergency triage decision support system evaluation. *Proceedings of the 39th Hawaii International Conference on System Sciences* – 2006. Retrieved January 12, 2012, from http://www.computer.org/portal/web/csdl/doi/10.1109/HICSS.2006.17

Patel, V. C., McClendon, R. W., & Goodrum, J. W. (1998). Development and evaluation of an expert system for egg sorting. *Computers and Electronics in Agriculture*, *20*, 97–116. doi:10.1016/S0168-1699(98)00009-X

Peng, Y., Zhang, Y., Tang, Y., & Li, S. (2011). An incident information management framework based on data integration, data mining, and multi-criteria decision making. *Decision Support Systems*, *51*, 316–327. doi:10.1016/j.dss.2010.11.025

Rafea, A., Hassen, H., & Hazman, M. (2003). Automatic knowledge acquisition tools for irrigation and fertilization expert systems. *Expert Systems with Applications*, *24*, 49–57. doi:10.1016/S0957-4174(02)00082-9

Roussel, O., Cavelier, A., & van der Werf, H. M. G. (2000). Adaptation and use of a fuzzy expert system to assess the environmental effect of pesticides applied to field crops. *Agriculture Ecosystems & Environment*, *80*, 143–158. doi:10.1016/S0167-8809(00)00142-0

San Pedro, J., Burstein, F., Wassertheil, J., Arora, N., Churilov, L., & Zaslavsky, A. (2005). On the development and evaluation of prototype mobile decision support for hospital triage. *Proceedings of the 38th Hawaii International Conference on System Sciences*, 2005.

Santos, N., Gummadi, K. P., & Rodrigues, R. (2009). Towards trusted cloud computing. Retrieved April 22, 2011, from http://www.mpi-sws.org/~gummadi/papers/trusted_cloud.pdf

SoKNOS. (2011). *Service-oriented architectures supporting networks of public security sector.* Retrieved May 20, 2011, from http://www.soknos.de/index.php?id=197&L=0

Stair, R., & Reynolds, G. (2005). *Fundamentals of information systems* (3rd ed.). Thomson Course Technology.

United Nations. (2005). *Hyogo framework for action 2005-2015: Building the resilience of nations and communities to disasters.* World Conference on Disaster Reduction, January, Kobe, Hyogo, Japan.

Vouk, M. A. (2008). Cloud computing – Issues, research and implementations. *Journal of Computing and Information Technology – CIT, 16*(4), 235–246.

Wang, X., Qu, H., Liu, P., & Cheng, Y. (2004). A self-learning expert system for diagnosis in traditional Chinese medicine. *Expert Systems with Applications*, *26*, 557–566. doi:10.1016/j.eswa.2003.10.004

Yang, B., Lim, D., & Tan, A. C. C. (2005). VIBEX: An expert system for vibration fault diagnosis of rotating machinery using decision tree and decision table. *Expert Systems with Applications*, *28*, 735–742. doi:10.1016/j.eswa.2004.12.030

ENDNOTE

1 The term "cloud computing" has become popular mainly due to its comprehensiveness and flexibility for users' access. Cloud computing is growing extremely rapidly and numerous providers have became popular in this field, including the following recent examples:

- *Amazon.com (EC2)* is a web service that provides resizable computing resources on cloud. It offers designers the provision to make web-based applications more easily and effectively (Amazon EC2)
- *Google App Engine* offers a complete development stack that uses familiar technologies to build and host web applications (Google App Engine)
- *Microsoft Azure Services Platform (MASP)* provides a wide range of Internet services that can be consumed from either on-premises environments or the Internet (Microsoft Azure Services)

Chapter 5
Occlusion Handling in Object Detection

Farjana Z. Eishita
University of Saskatchewan, Canada

Ashfaqur Rahman
Central Queensland University Rockhampton, Australia

Salahuddin A. Azad
Central Queensland University Rockhampton, Australia

Akhlaqur Rahman
American International University, Bangladesh

ABSTRACT

Object tracking is a process that follows an object through consecutive frames of images to determine the object's movement relative other objects of those frames. In other words, tracking is the problem of estimating the trajectory of an object in the image plane as it moves around a scene. This chapter presents research that deals with the problem of tracking objects when they are occluded. An object can be partially or fully occluded. Depending on the tracking domain, a tracker can deal with partial and full object occlusions using features such as colour and texture. But sometimes it fails to detect the objects after occlusion. The shape feature of an individual object can provide additional information while combined with colour and texture features. It has been observed that with the same colour and texture if two object's shape information is taken then these two objects can be detected after the occlusion has occurred. From this observation, a new and a very simple algorithm is presented in this chapter, which is able to track objects after occlusion even if the colour and textures are the same. Some experimental results are shown along with several case studies to compare the effectiveness of the shape features against colour and texture features.

DOI: 10.4018/978-1-4666-1830-5.ch005

1. INTRODUCTION

Object tracking is the process of following moving objects across a video sequence (Trucco, & Plakas, 2006). In other words, object tracking is the problem of estimating the trajectory of an object in the image plane as it moves around a scene. Object tracking has many applications such as traffic monitoring, security & surveillance, human computer interaction, video annotation, video editing, medical imaging, robotics, augmented reality etc.

There are three major steps in video analysis – detection of the moving objects, tracking of moving objects from frame to frame and analysis of the object tracks to recognize their behavior (Yilmaz, Javed, & Shah, 2006). A tracker allocates unswerving labels to the tracked objects in different video frames. In addition, depending on the tracking field, a tracker can provide object-centric information, such as the area or shape of an object. Simple algorithms for video tracking rely on the selection of the region of interest in the first frame associated with the moving objects. Some of the demanding methods put constraints on the shape of the tracked object (Erdem, Tekalp, & Sankur, 2003, Shin, J., Kim, S., Kang, S., Lee, S., Paik, J., Abidi, B., & Abidi, M., 2005). In general, this type of algorithms includes apriori training on the possible shape of the object.

A typical video tracker has two components – *target representation & localization* and *filtering & data association*. The first process, which is mainly a bottom-up approach, deals with the appearance of the target. The second process, which is a top-down approach, deals with deals with dynamic of the tracked object, learning of scene priors and evaluation of hypothesis (Comaniciu, Ramesh, & Meer, 2003). Application of these two processes depends on the application and purpose of the tracking. Face tracking in cluttered scenario depends more on target representation than target dynamics (DeCarlo, & Metaxas, 2000), while in aerial video surveillance, target motion and target dynamics is more important than target representation. Target representation and localization algorithms can be classified into three groups – *blob tracking*, *kernel tracking* and *silhouette tracking*. Blob tracking algorithms localize the target object using blob detection, block based correlation or optical flow method. This sort of algorithms is suitable for tracking objects occupying a small region in the image (Yilmaz, Javed, & Shah, 2006). Kernel based algorithms localize the target objects through maximization of a similarity measure such as *Bhattacharyya coefficient*. Silhouette tracking localize the target objects by the detection of object boundary. This type of algorithms is suitable for tracking non rigid objects (Yilmaz, Javed, & Shah, 2006). Filtering and data association processes are used to deal with object dynamics, often by incorporating prior information about the scene and object. Kalman filter and particle filter are two well known filtering algorithms (Bradski, 1998, Comaniciu, & Meer, 2002, Han, & Davis, 2004). Kalman filter is an optimal recursive Bayesian filter for linear functions subjected to Gaussian noise. Particle Filter (PF) is a Monte Carlo (i.e. choosing randomly) method to monitor dynamic systems, which non-parametrically approximates probabilistic distribution using weighted samples (particles) (Arulampalam, Maskell, Gordon, & Clapp, 2002).

Occlusion can significantly undermine the performance of the object tracking algorithms. In many practical object tracking scenarios, a moving object can be entirely or partially occluded by other objects in the scene frequently. The object tracking algorithm must be able to detect the occlusion quickly and find the object once the occlusion is over.

In this chapter, a simple algorithm is introduced which works with the shape information of an object when occlusion occurs. The algorithm is computationally inexpensive and can be implemented in a straightforward way. In the proposed approach, we use a very simple shape identification method. Firstly, the shape information along is used with the other features. Secondly, the shape information alone is among different objects. In our experiment, two substances with the same colour and different sizes were taken. Applying the proposed approach, both the substances were successfully detected before and after the occlusion occurred in various movement situations. Experimental results demonstrate the effectiveness of the proposed method.

The chapter is organised as follows. Section 2 presents state-of-art methods for occlusion handling in object tracking processes. The proposed algorithm was discussed in section 3.

2. OCCLUSION – RELATED WORKS

A novel patch based model was proposed in (Deng, Yang, Lin, & Tang, 2007) for occlusion handling. While applying this model, they found that the performance near occlusion is not satisfactory because a segmented region in one image may often be visible only partially in the other image. As a solution to the problem, they proposed a model that first conducts colour segmentation on both images, and then a segment in one image is further cut into smaller patches corresponding to the boundaries of segments in the other when it is assigned with a disparity. The uniqueness constraint in a segment level is used to compute the occlusions. An energy minimization framework using graph-cuts was proposed to find a global optimal configuration including both disparities and occlusions. Yang et al. presented an algorithm that works with a global matching stereo model based on an energy-minimization framework (Yang, Wang, Yang, Stewe´nius, & Niste´r, 2009). The global energy contains two terms, the data term and the smoothness term. The data term is first approximated by a colour-weighted correlation, and then refined in occluded and low-texture areas with a repeated application of a hierarchical loopy belief propagation algorithm.

To improve the performance of the optical flow based methods, a new method has been proposed in (Parrilla, Ginestar, Hueso, Riera, & Torregrosa, 2008). Their research was based on the selection of landmark points representative of the moving objects in the first frame of the sequence to be analysed. A sparse optical-flow method has been used to estimate the movement of the points. To improve robustness of this approach, they proposed the use of adaptive filters and neural network to predict the expected instantaneous velocities of the objects using the predicted velocities as indicators of the performance of the tracking algorithm.

A weighted fragment based approach that handles partial occlusion was proposed in (Jeyakar, Babu, & Ramakrishnan, 2008). They derived the weight from the difference between the fragment and background colours. They also described a fast and stable model updating the method and demonstrated the process of merging edge information into the mean shift framework without using a joint histogram. With their proposed algorithm different shaped objects can be tracked. Wang et al. introduced a partial occlusion handler using histogram of oriented gradients and local binary patterns (Wang, Han, & Yan, 2009). Zhang et al. introduced a multi-object tracking with spices based particle swarm optimization (Zhang, Hu, Li, Qu, & Maybank, 2009). A hand tracking object is established in (Hamer, Schindler, Koller-Meier, & Gool, 2009) while interacting with an object. However, occlusion handling is not reliably handled by this approach.

For tracking objects, a scale invariant feature transform (SIFT) based mean shift algorithm is presented in (Zhou, Yuan, & Shi, 2008). SIFT features are used to correspond the region of interests across frames. In the intervening time, mean shift is applied to conduct similarity search through colour histograms. They evaluated the probability distributions from these two measurements in an expectation of maximizing scheme so that maximum likelihood estimation of similar regions can be achieved. By combining optical flow and stereo vision, an algorithm has been presented in (Parrilla, Riera, Torregrosa, & Hueso, 2008). for three dimensional object tracking in a stereo video sequence. To improve the performance of this method, adaptive filters and neural networks has been used to predict the expected instantaneous velocities of the objects. This method is not able to handle the occlusion of the moving objects when they disappear due to an obstacle.

3. PROPOSED ALGORITHM

The proposed algorithm considers three features – colour, texture, and shape information for tracking objects.

A. Colour

Colour is one of the most significant features for tracking objects. Several different object tracking systems have been established so far using the colour as one of the features of the object. The proposed approach also considers colour as one of the features. For example, if two objects have two different colours then they can be tracked readily. Conversely, if more than one object has exactly the same colour, the probability identification might be lower. In the proposed approach, colour histogram was used to reveal colour feature.

B. Texture

Object tracking based on colour feature is unreliable as mentioned in the previous section. However, using less responsive features such as image alterations can reduce this difficulty. Texture, which has not enjoyed major attention in tracking applications, provides a good option to enhance the power of colour descriptors. Hence, texture feature was used to avoid the difficulty with the colour feature. To reveal the texture of an object, co-occurrence matrix was used. The main characteristic of the co-occurrence matrix is – it keeps track of each of its consequent pixels (Parrilla, Riera, Torregrosa, Hueso (2008)). While the colour feature has the chance of failures to a great extent, the incorporation of texture feature can make the tracking method more reliable and reduce the probability of failure to some extent.

Figure 1. Centre and 8 significant points to determine the 8 distances from centre of an object

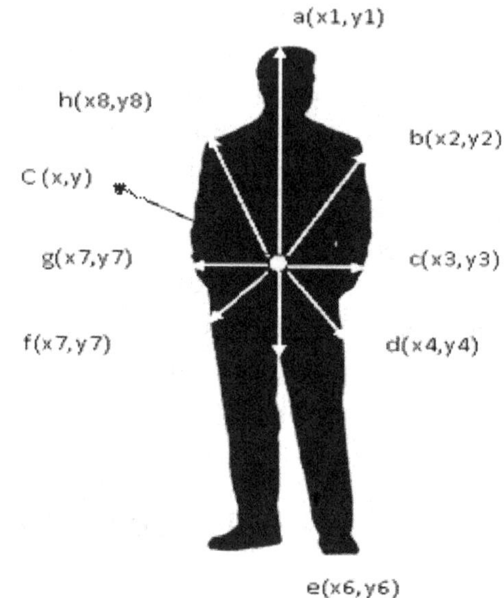

C. Shape

The proposed approach uses the shape information of the object in a very simple and easy way. First of all, the contour of the object is determined. Then the centre point of the contour area is derived. Next, eight significant distances were calculated from that centre point (Figure 1). Based on these eight distances, the object is tracked from frame to frame before and after the occlusion.

Given the centre $C(x,y)$, the eight distances are computed by Euclidian distance calculation formula as follows:

$$d_n = \sqrt{(x-x_n)^2+(y-y_n)^2} \text{ where } n = 1,2,3,\ldots,8 \quad (1)$$

The distances were normalized as

Figure 2. Graphical representation of the proposed algorithm

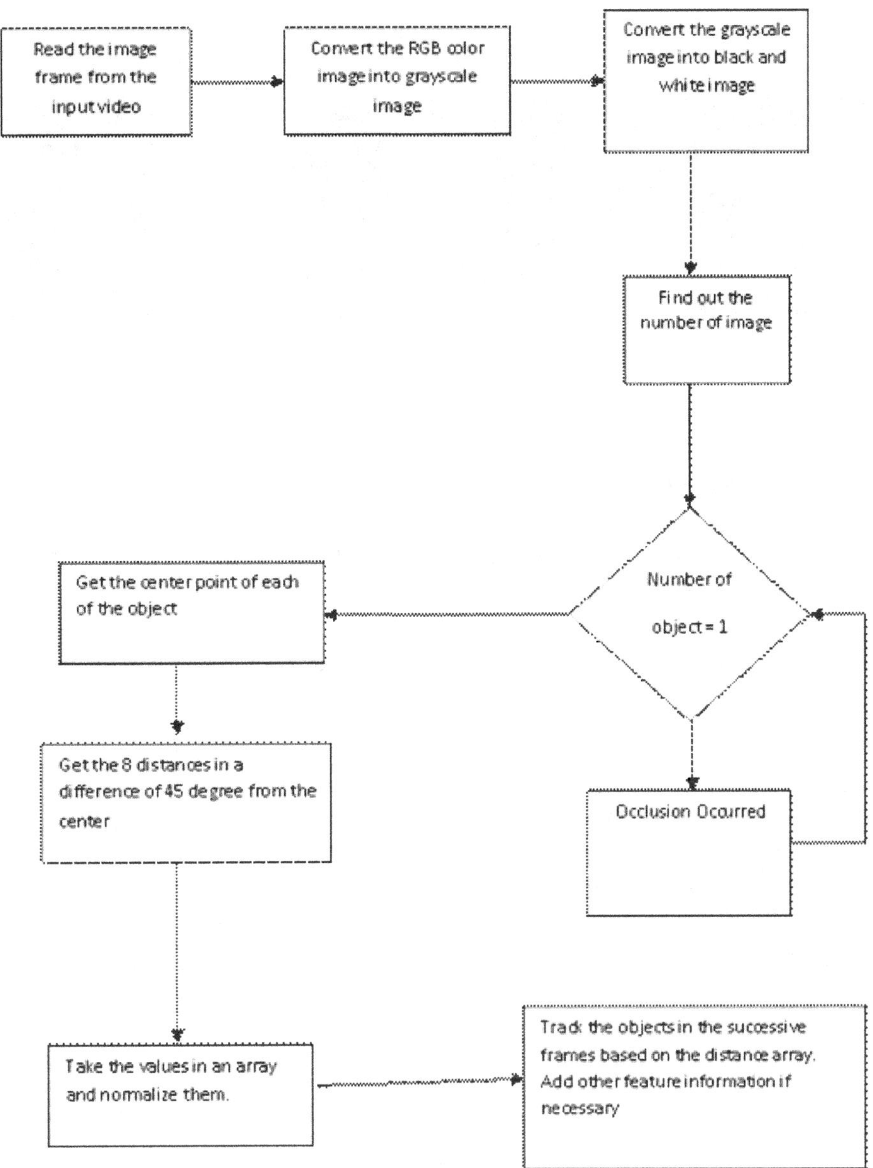

$$\text{DistanceArray} = \text{Normalize}[\text{DistanceArray}[d_1, d_2, d_3, d_4, d_5, d_6, d_7, d_8]] \quad (2)$$

The graphical representation of the algorithm is presented in Figure 2.

4. IMPLEMENTATION

A. Components and Tools

In our experiments two different cameras were used. First, we used Panasonic PV-GS300 Mini DV Camcorder for several of video sequences. Some more videos sequences were taken with Panasonic Lumix DMC-FX30. Both the cameras

Figure 3. (a) Two different objects O1 and O2 are being tracked; (b) O1 and O2 are under occlusion; (c) O1 and O2 are being tracked after the occlusion

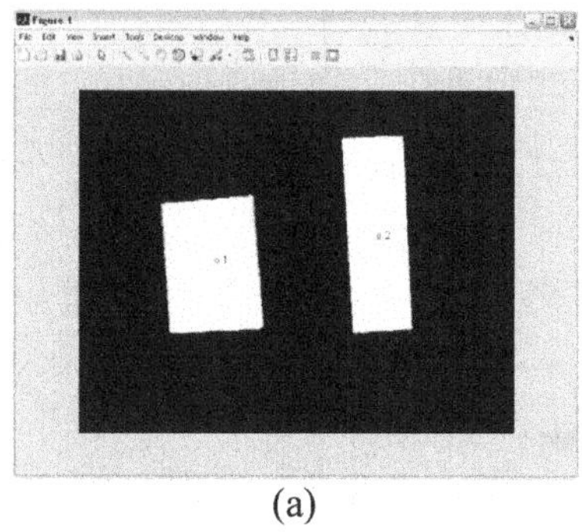

(a)

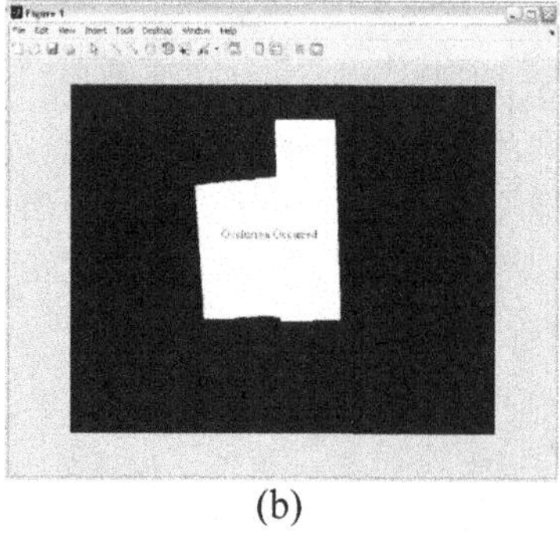

(b)

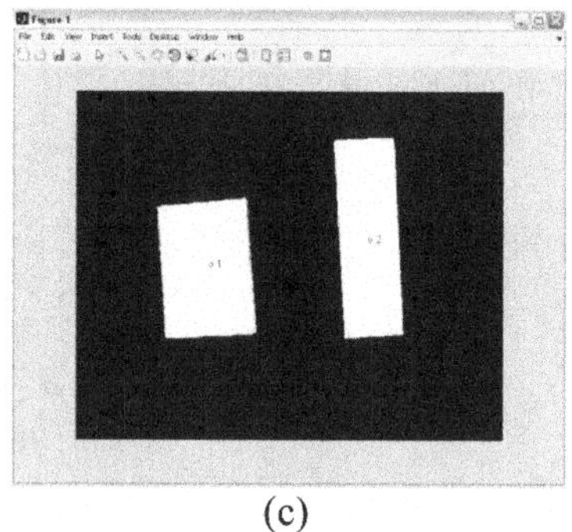

(c)

are of medium quality. The quality of the video was not refined but the quality was good enough to carry out the experiments. However, better results could be achieved if a better quality camera would have been used.

For executing the algorithm we used the image processing toolbox of MATLAB as it provides a complete set of reference-standard algorithms and graphical tools for image processing, analysis, visualization, and algorithm development. Most toolbox functions are written in the open MATLAB language, giving the ability to inspect the algorithms, modify the source code, and create user's own custom functions (Hamer, Schindler, Koller-Meier, & Gool, 2009).

B. Procedure

Firstly, the objects are detected in the video sequence. They are tracked through the frames before occlusion occurs. Figure 3(a) shows the tracking process. Whenever the occlusion occurs, it detects the occlusion as shown in Figure 3(b). After the occlusion is over, the two objects are tracked again. The direction of movement of the objects can be changed while in motion. Whatever the direction of the objects is, the proposed algorithm is able to track the objects before and after the occlusion has occurs as shown in Figure 3(c).

5. EXPERIMENTAL EVALUATION

A. Components and Tools

Several different cases have been presented based on the shape, size and moving directions of the objects. Based on these terms the result differs. The result of applying a histogram is also shown. After that a comparison table is presented.

Case 1

- **Number of objects:** 2
- **Object shapes:** Different
- **Object colour:** Same colour before and after occlusion
- **Object direction:**
  Before occlusion: O1 goes from left to right O2 goes from right to left
  After Occlusion: O1 goes from left to right O2 goes from right to left
- **Result:**
  - **Using Shape Information:** Successfully tracks the objects correctly before and after occlusion.
  - **Using Histogram:** Successfully tracks the objects correctly before and after occlusion.

Figure 4. (a) Two different objects O1 and O2 are being tracked before the occlusion; O1 is moving from left to right and O2 is moving from right to left; (b) Objects O1 and O2 are being tracked after the occlusion; O1 is moving from left to right and O2 is moving from right to left

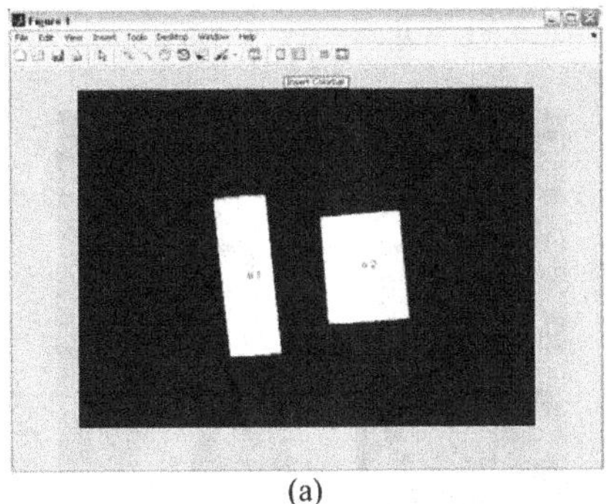

(a)

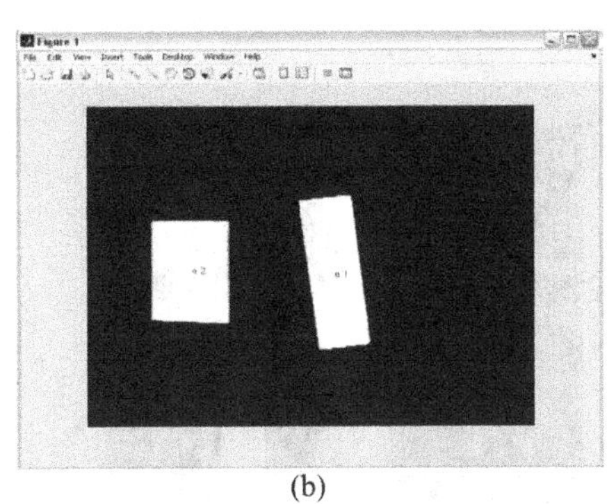

(b)

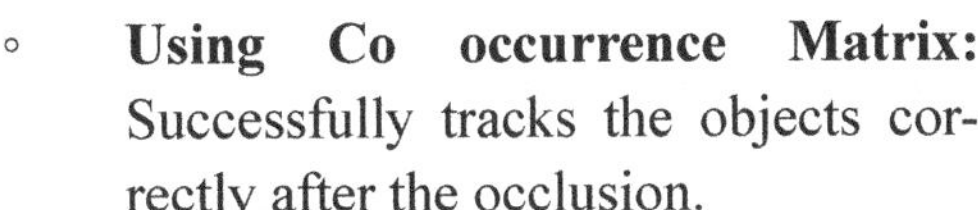

- ◦ **Using Co occurrence Matrix:** Successfully tracks the objects correctly after the occlusion.

The graphical representation of Case 1 is presented in Figure 4. While Figure 4(a) shows the condition before occlusion, Figure 4(b) shows the condition after the occlusion.

Case 2

- **Number of objects:** 2
- **Object shapes:** Different
- **Object colour:** Same colour before and after occlusion
- **Object direction:**
  Before occlusion: O1 goes from left to right O2 goes from right to left
  After Occlusion: O1 goes from right to left O2 goes from left to right
- **Result:**
  - ◦ **Using Shape Information:** Successfully tracks the objects correctly before and after occlusion.
  - ◦ **Using Histogram:** Successfully tracks thc objects correctly before and after occlusion.
  - ◦ **Using Co occurrence Matrix:** Successfully tracks the objects correctly after the occlusion.

The graphical representation is presented in Figure 5. While Figure 5(a) shows the condition before occlusion, Figure 5(b) shows the condition after the occlusion.

Case 3

- **Number of objects:** 2
- **Object shapes:** Almost similar
- **Object colour:** Same colour before and after occlusion
- **Object direction:**
  Before occlusion: O1 goes from left to right O2 goes from right to left
  After Occlusion: O1 goes from right to left O2 goes from left to right
- **Result:**
  - ◦ **Using Shape Information:** Successfully tracks the objects correctly before and after occlusion.
  - ◦ **Using Histogram:** Successfully tracks the objects correctly before and after occlusion.

Figure 5. **(a)** *Two different objects O1 and O2 are being tracked before the occlusion; O1 is moving from left to right and O2 is moving from right to left; (b) Objects O1 and O2 are being tracked after the occlusion has occurred; O1 is moving from right to left and O2 is moving from left to right*

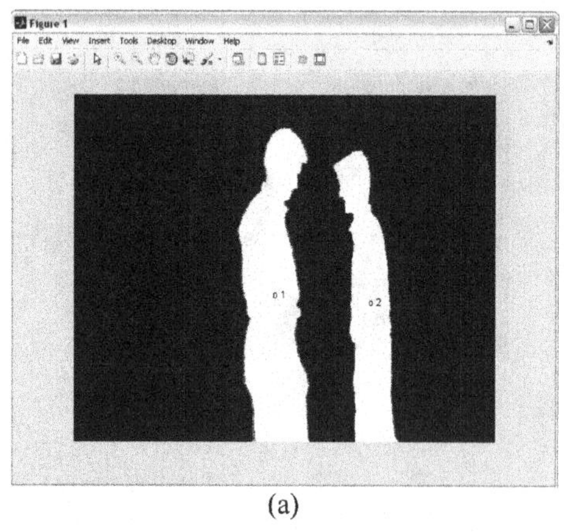

(a)

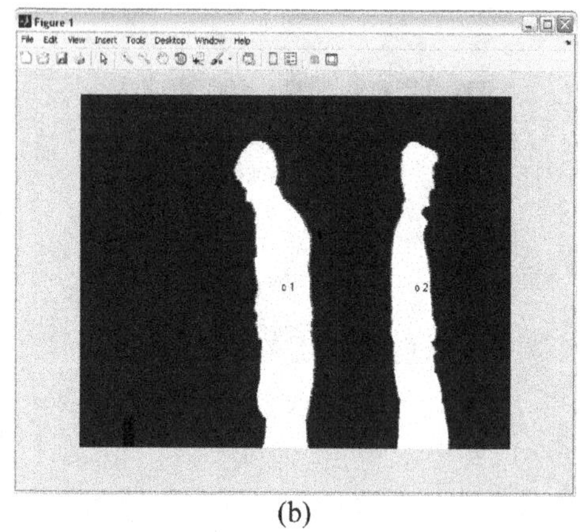

(b)

Figure 6. (a) Two different objects O1 and O2 are being tracked before the occlusion; O1 is moving from left to right and O2 is moving from right to left; (b) objects O1 and O2 are being tracked after the occlusion has occurred; O1 is moving from right to left and O2 is moving from left to right

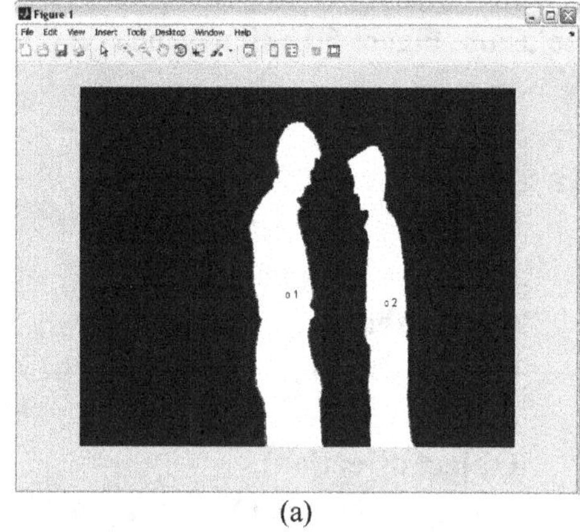

(a)

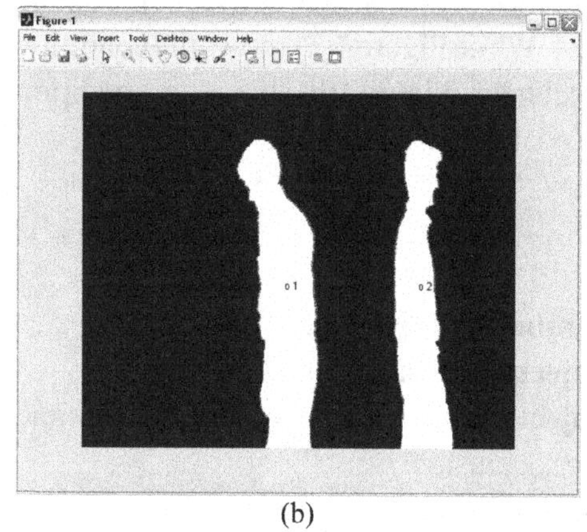

(b)

- ◦ **Using Co occurrence Matrix:** Successfully tracks the objects correctly after the occlusion.

The graphical representation is presented in Figure 6. While Figure 6(a) shows the condition before occlusion, Figure 6(b) shows the condition after the occlusion.

Case 4

- **Number of objects:** 2
- **Object shapes:** Almost similar
- **Object colour**: Same colour before and after occlusion
- **Object direction:**
  Before occlusion: O1 goes from left to right
  O2 goes from right to left
  After Occlusion: O1 goes from left to right

Figure 7. (a) Two different objects O1 and O2 are being tracked before the occlusion; O1 is moving from left to right and O2 is moving from right to left; (b) The tracker fails to track objects O1 and O2 after the occlusion; O1 is moving from left to right and O2 is moving from right to left

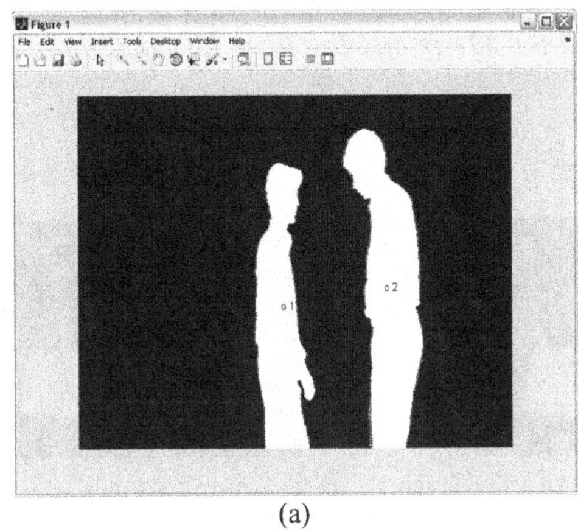

(a)

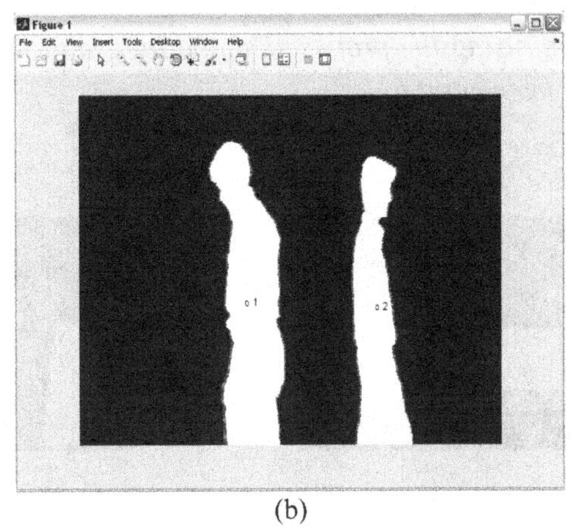

(b)

O2 goes from right to left

- **Result:**
  - **Using Shape Information:** Fails to track the objects correctly after occlusion.
  - **Using Histogram:** Fails to track the objects correctly after occlusion.
  - **Using Co occurrence Matrix:** Fails to track the objects correctly after the occlusion.

The graphical representation is presented in Figure 7. While Figure 7(a) shows the condition before occlusion, Figure 7(b) shows the condition after the occlusion.

Case 5

- **Number of objects:** 2
- **Object shapes:** Different
- **Object Colour:**
  Before occlusion: O1 Black, O2 Brown
  After Occlusion: O1 Black, O2 Black
- **Object direction:**
  Before occlusion: O1 goes from left to right
  O2 goes from right to left
  After Occlusion: O1 goes from left to right
  O2 goes from right to left
- **Result:**
  - **Using Shape Information:** Successfully track the objects correctly before and after occlusion.
  - **Using Histogram:** Fails to track the objects correctly after occlusion.
  - **Using Co occurrence Matrix:** Fails to track the objects correctly after the occlusion.

The graphical representation is presented in Figure 9. While Figure 8(a) shows the condition before occlusion and eventually Figure 8(b) and 8(c) show the condition after the occlusion.

B. Comparison

The proposed method is compared with other existing methods in this section. Moreover, graphical representations of the proposed algorithm using shape information as well other features are presented.

Let us consider Case 5 where the proposed algorithm using shape information successfully tracks the objects, while the other two features fail

Figure 8. (a) Two different objects O1 and O2 are being tracked before the occlusion; O1 is moving from left to right and O2 is moving from right to left; (b) The tracker fails to track objects O1 and O2 after the occlusion using histogram and co-occurrence matrix; O1 is moving from left to right and O2 is moving from right to left; (c) Two different objects O1 and O2 are successfully tracked after the occlusion using the proposed shape information algorithm; O1 is moving from left to right and O2 is moving from right to left

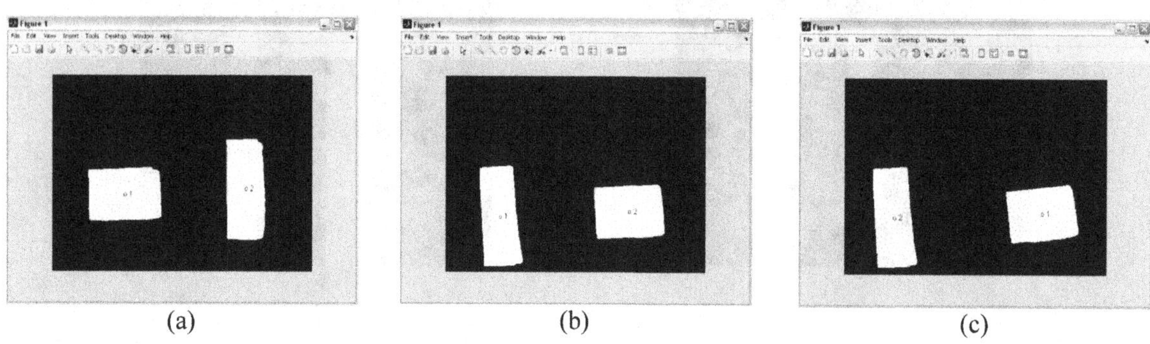

Figure 9. (a) Bar diagram of the O1 (left object) using co-occurrence matrix before occlusion; (b) Bar diagram of the O2 (right object) using co-occurrence matrix before occlusion; (c) Bar diagram of the O2 (left object) using co-occurrence matrix after occlusion. (d) Bar diagram of the O1 (right object) using co-occurrence matrix after occlusion.

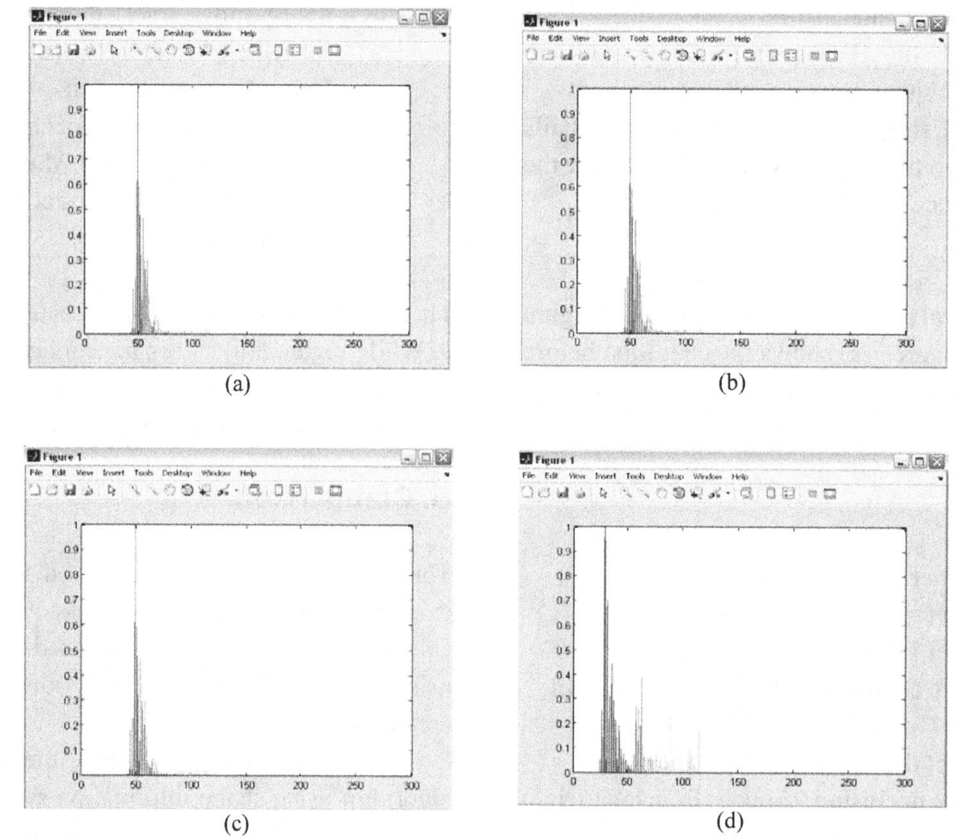

Figure 10. (a) Bar diagram of the O1 (left object) using colour histogram before occlusion; (b) Bar diagram of the O2 (right object) using colour histogram before occlusion; (c) Bar diagram of the O2 (left object) using colour histogram after occlusion; (d) Bar diagram of the O1 (right object) using colour histogram after occlusion

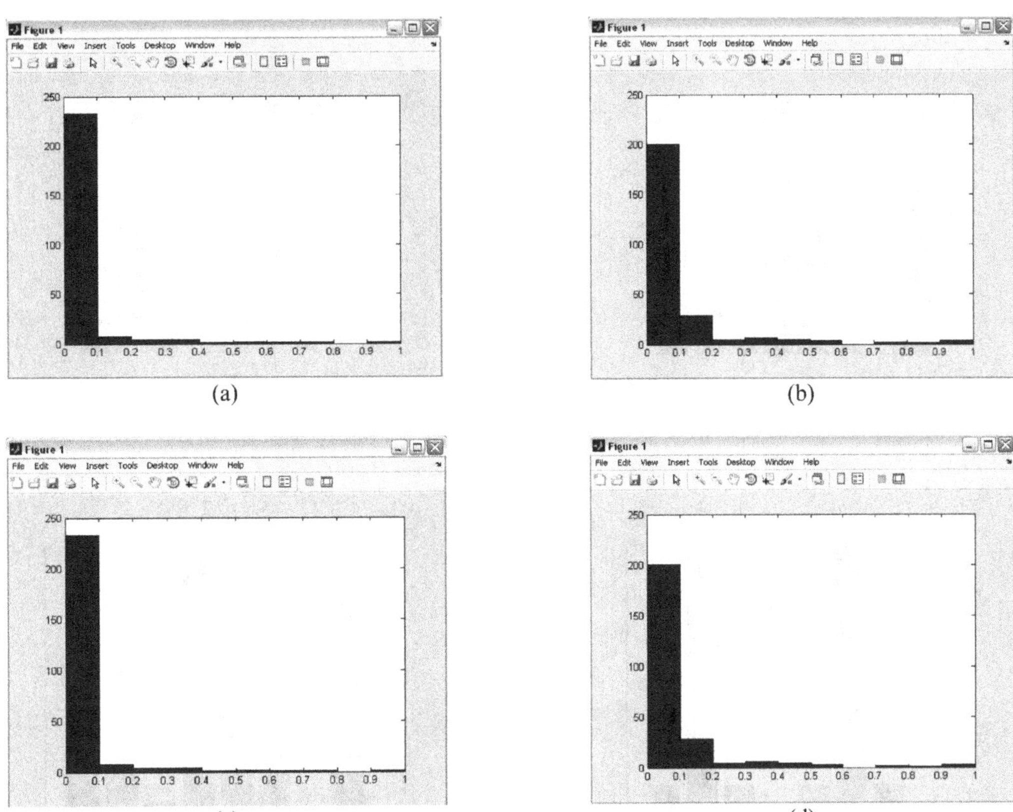

to track the objects. The Figure 9(a) – 9(d) illustrate the bar representation of the co-occurrence matrix for the objects in two frames prior to and after occlusion respectively. Since the objects do not change their direction after occlusion, Figure 9(a) and 9(d) should be similar. Likewise, Figure 9(b) and 9(c) should also be similar. But as the colours of the objects changes, the co-occurrence matrix fails to track the objects after occlusion.

When colour histogram is used, it also fails to track the objects. Figure 10(a)–10(d) illustrate the colour histogram representation of the two objects in two frames prior to and after occlusion respectively. Like the previous scenario, as the objects do not change their direction after occlusion, Figure 10(a) and 10(d) should be similar. Likewise, Figure 10(b) and 10(c) should be similar. But as the colours of the objects change, the colour fails to track the objects after occlusion.

Finally, if we consider the shape information, the proposed algorithm successfully tracks the objects before and after occlusion. Figure 11(a)–11(d) illustrate the bar diagram of shape information which represents the two objects in two frames before and after occlusion respectively. Although the colour of the objects is changed after occlusion, the proposed distance algorithm successfully tracks the objects before and after occlusion, whereas the co-occurrence matrix and histogram fail to after the objects after occlusion.

Figure 11. (a) Bar diagram of the O1 (left object) using shape information before occlusion; (b) Bar diagram of the O2 (right object) using shape information before occlusion; (c) Bar diagram of the O2 (left object) using shape information after occlusion; (d) Bar diagram of the O1 (right object) using shape information after occlusion

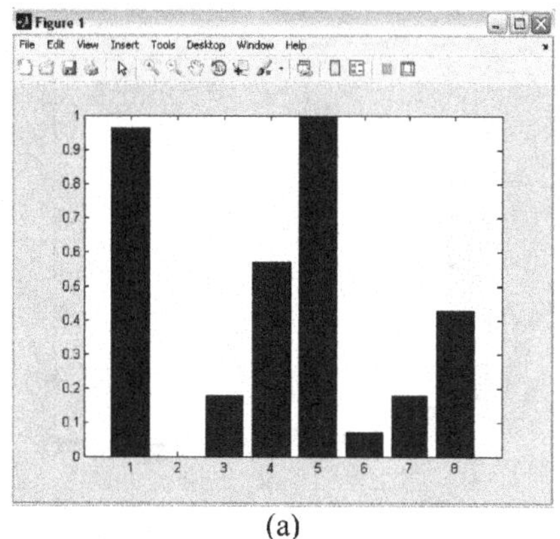

(a)

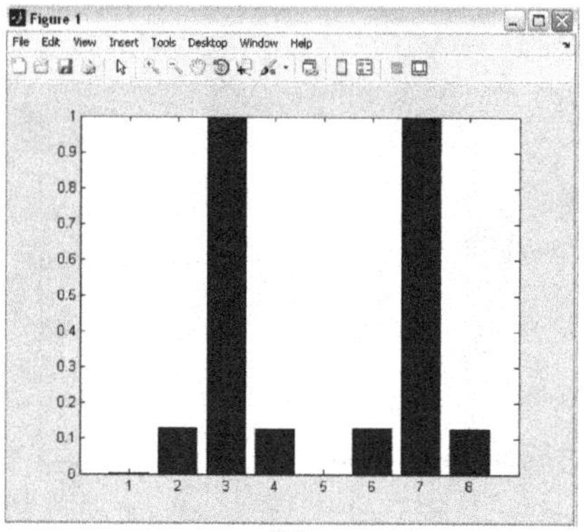

(b)

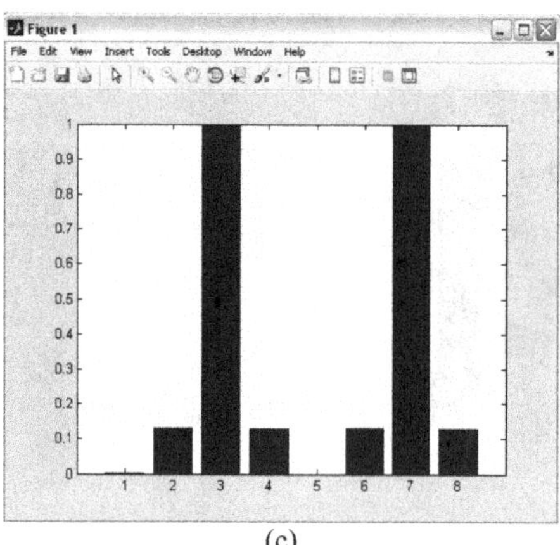

(c)

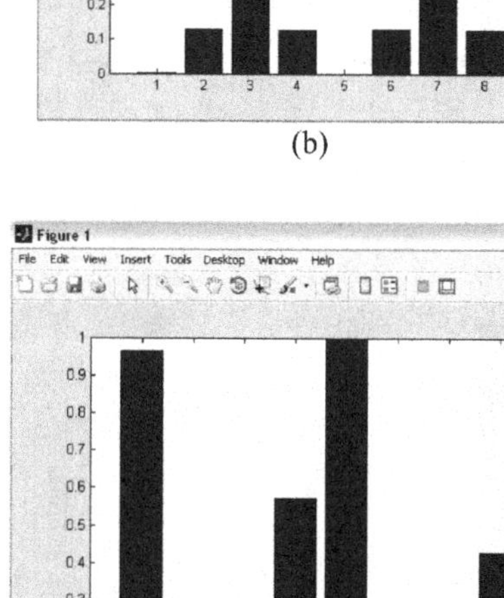

(d)

Although in some cases like case 4 our proposed algorithm fails to determine the objects but according to this section it can be established that in some cases where the colours of the objects are changed after occlusion, they cannot be tracked with the features like the co-occurrence matrix or histogram. In these kinds of cases, our proposed algorithm works successfully with the shape information feature. All these things are summarized in Table 1.

6. CONCLUSION AND FUTURE WORKS

In this chapter, we presented an algorithm that deals with the problem of occlusion handling during object tracking. In the proposed approach, we incorporated the shape information along with other factors and demonstrated that with the same colour, texture and motion, these two objects can be detected after the occlusion occurred using their shape information. Experimental results reveal that in most cases shape information works better than the other features. Although the proposed approach fails in some cases, it can be a very ef-

Table 1. Summary of the different cases considered in the experiments

Cases	Shape	Colours	Direction	Features Used	Result
Case 1	Different	Same colour before and after occlusion	Before occlusion: O1 L→R O2 R→L After Occlusion: O1 L→R O2 R→L	Histogram	Successful
				Co occurrence matrix	Successful
				Shape information	Successful
Case 2	Different	Same colour before and after occlusion	Before occlusion: O1 L→R O2 R→L After Occlusion: O1 R→L O2 L→R	Histogram	Successful
				Co occurrence matrix	Successful
				Shape information	Successful
Case 3	Almost Similar	Same colour before and after occlusion	Before occlusion: O1 L→R O2 R→L After Occlusion: O1 R→L O2 L→R	Histogram	Successful
				Co occurrence matrix	Successful
				Shape information	Successful
Case 4	Almost Similar	Same colour before and after occlusion	Before occlusion: O1 L→R O2 R→L After Occlusion: O1 L→R O2 R→L	Histogram	Fails
				Co occurrence matrix	Fails
				Shape information	Fails
Case 5	Different	Before occlusion: O1 Black O2 Brown After Occlusion: O1 Black O2 Black	Before occlusion: O1 L→R O2 R→L After Occlusion: O1 L→R O2 R→L	Histogram	Fails
				Co occurrence matrix	Fails
				Shape information	Successful

fective tracking method with one of the simplest algorithms.

The proposed system can be improved further. For example, the proposed algorithm takes eight significant distances for tracking a particular object. If there are similar types of objects, it can get confused after the occurrence of occlusion and tracking performance may degrade. To resolve the problem, the resolution of the shape information can be increased by taking more points along the contour. To make the algorithm more effective, additional features such as motion or silhouette can be considered.

REFERENCES

Arulampalam, M., Maskell, S., Gordon, N., & Clapp, T. (2002). A tutorial on particle filters for online nonlinear/non-Gaussian Bayesian tracking. *IEEE Transactions on Signal Processing, 2*(50), 174–188. doi:10.1109/78.978374

Bradski, G. R. (1998). Computer vision face tracking for use in a perceptual user interface. *Intel Technology Journal, Q2*, 15.

Collins, R., Liu, Y., & Leordeanu, M. (2005). Online selection of discriminative tracking features. *IEEE Transactions on Pattern Analysis and Machine Intelligence, 1*(27), 1631–1643. doi:10.1109/TPAMI.2005.205

Comaniciu, D., & Meer, P. (2002). Mean shift: A robust approach toward feature space analysis. *IEEE Transactions on Pattern Analysis and Machine Intelligence*, *5*(24), 603–619. doi:10.1109/34.1000236

Comaniciu, D., Ramesh, V., & Meer, P. (2003). Kernel-based object tracking. *IEEE Transactions on Pattern Analysis and Machine Intelligence*, *5*(25), 564–575. doi:10.1109/TPAMI.2003.1195991

DeCarlo, D., & Metaxas, D. (2000). Optical flow constraints on deformable models with applications to face tracking. *International Journal of Computer Vision*, *2*(38), 99–127. doi:10.1023/A:1008122917811

Deng, Y., Yang, Q., Lin, X., & Tang, X. (2007). Stereo correspondence with occlusion handling in a symmetric patch-based graph-cuts model. *IEEE Transactions on Pattern Analysis and Machine Intelligence*, *6*(29), 1086–1079.

Erdem, C. E., Tekalp, A. M., & Sankur, B. (2003). Video object tracking with feedback of performance measures. *IEEE Transactions on Circuits and Systems for Video Technology*, *4*(13), 310–324. doi:10.1109/TCSVT.2003.811361

Hamer, H., Schindler, K., Koller-Meier, E., & Van Gool, L. (2009). Tracking a hand manipulating an object. *12th International Conference Computer Vision*, (pp. 1475-1482).

Han, B., & Davis, L. (2004) Object tracking by adaptive feature extraction. *Proceedings International Conference on Image Processing (ICIP)*, (Vol. 3, pp. 638–644).

Jeyakar, J., Babu, R. V., & Ramakrishnan, K. R. (2008). Robust object tracking with background-weighted local kernels. *Journal of Computer Vision and Image Understanding*, *3*(112), 296–309. doi:10.1016/j.cviu.2008.05.005

Parrilla, E., Ginestar, D., Hueso, J. L., Riera, J., & Torregrosa, J. R. (2008). Handling occlusion in optical flow algorithms for object tracking. *Computers & Mathematics with Applications (Oxford, England)*, *3*(56), 733–742. doi:10.1016/j.camwa.2008.02.008

Parrilla, E., Riera, J., Torregrosa, J. R., & Hueso, J. L. (2008). Handling occlusion in object tracking in stereoscopic video sequences. *Journal of Mathematical and Computer Modelling*, *5-6*(50), 823–830.

Shin, J., Kim, S., Kang, S., Lee, S., Paik, J., Abidi, B., & Abidi, M. (2005). Optical flow-based real-time object tracking using non-prior training active feature model. *Real-Time Imaging*, *3*(11), 204–218. doi:10.1016/j.rti.2005.03.006

Trucco, E. L., & Plakas, K. (2006). Video tracking: A concise survey. *IEEE Journal of Oceanic Engineering*, *2*(31), 520–529. doi:10.1109/JOE.2004.839933

Wang, X., Han, T. X., & Yan, S. (2009). An HOG-LBP human detector with partial occlusion handling. In *IEEE 12th International Conference on Computer Vision*, (pp. 32–39).

Yang, Q., Wang, L., Yang, R., & Stewenius, H., & Nister. (2009). Stereo matching with colour-weighted correlation, hierarchical belief propagation, and occlusion handling. *IEEE Transactions on Pattern Analysis and Machine Intelligence*, *3*(31), 492–504. doi:10.1109/TPAMI.2008.99

Yilmaz, A., Javed, O., & Shah, M. (2006). Object tracking: A survey. *ACM Computing Surveys (CSUR)*, *4*(38). DOI=10.1145/1177352.1177355

Zhang, X., Hu, W., Li, W., Qu, W., & Maybank, S. (2009). Multi-object tracking via species based particle swarm optimization. *Computer Vision Workshops (ICCV Workshops) IEEE 12th International Conference*, *20*(11), 1105-1112.

Zhou, H., Yuan, Y., & Shi, C. (2008). Object tracking using SIFT features and mean shift. *Journal of Computer Vision and Image Understanding*, *3*(113), 345–352.

Chapter 6
Application of Multi-Objective Evolutionary Algorithms to Antenna and Microwave Design Problems

Sotirios K. Goudos
Aristotle University of Thessaloniki, Greece

ABSTRACT

Antenna and microwave design problems are, in general, multi-objective. Multi-objective Evolutionary Algorithms (MOEAs) are suitable optimization techniques for solving such problems. Particle Swarm Optimization (PSO) and Differential Evolution (DE) have received increased interest from the electromagnetics community. The fact that both algorithms can efficiently handle arbitrary optimization problems has made them popular for solving antenna and microwave design problems. This chapter presents three different state-of-the-art MOEAs based on PSO and DE, namely: the Multi-objective Particle Swarm Optimization (MOPSO), the Multi-objective Particle Swarm Optimization with fitness sharing (MOPSO-fs), and the Generalized Differential Evolution (GDE3). Their applications to different design cases from antenna and microwave problems are reported. These include microwave absorber, microwave filters and Yagi-uda antenna design. The algorithms are compared and evaluated against other evolutionary multi-objective algorithms like Nondominated Sorting Genetic Algorithm-II (NSGA-II). The results show the advantages of using each algorithm.

INTRODUCTION

Antenna and microwave design problems often require the optimization of several conflicting objectives. For example, objectives like gain maximization, sidelobe level (SLL) reduction and input impedance matching are common in antenna design problems. In addition, the microwave filter and absorber design problems are in general multi-objective. Multi-objective Evolutionary Algorithms (MOEAs) are suitable optimization techniques for solving such problems. The application of multi-objective evolutionary algorithms to such design problems provides the researcher with

DOI: 10.4018/978-1-4666-1830-5.ch006

a set of solutions. Then the most suitable design case for any given specifications can be selected.

Several evolutionary algorithms (EAs) have emerged in the past decade that mimic biological entities behavior and evolution. In this book chapter, we consider the Genetic Algorithms (GAs), the Particle Swarm Optimization (PSO) and the Differential evolution (DE). The GAs have been applied to a variety of microwave component and antenna design problems. In (Venkatarayalu, Ray, & Gan, 2005) a multi-objective EA is used for the generation of the Pareto front for the constraint dielectric filter design problem. In (Kuwahara, 2005) Pareto GA, a multi-objective GA, is used for the generation of the Pareto front for the Yagi-Uda design problem. Nondominated Sorting Genetic Algorithm-II (NSGA-II) (K. Deb, Pratap, Agarwal, & Meyarivan, 2002) is a popular and efficient multi-objective genetic algorithm, which has been used in several engineering design problems.

PSO (Kennedy & Eberhart, 1995) is an evolutionary algorithm based on the bird fly. PSO is an easy to implement algorithm with computational efficiency. PSO has been used successfully in constrained or unconstrained electromagnetic design problems. Multi-objective PSO algorithms include the Multi-objective Particle Swarm Optimization (MOPSO) (Coello Coello, Pulido, & Lechuga, 2004) and Multi-objective Particle Swarm Optimization with fitness sharing (MOPSO-fs) (Salazar-Lechuga & Rowe, 2005). MOPSO is utilized in (S. K. Goudos & Sahalos, 2006) for microwave absorber design while MOPSO-fs is applied to the filter design problem in (S. K. Goudos, Zaharis, Salazar-Lechuga, Lazaridis, & Gallion, 2007) and to antenna base station design in (S. K. Goudos, Zaharis, Kampitaki, Rekanos, & Hilas, 2009).

An evolutionary algorithm that has gained popularity recently is Differential evolution (DE), proposed by Price and Storn (Storn & Price, 1995; Storn & Price, 1997). Several DE variants or strategies exist. One of the DE advantages is the fact that very few parameters have to be adjusted in order to produce results. Several DE extensions for multi-objective optimization have been proposed so far. Generalized Differential Evolution (GDE3) (Kukkonen & Lampinen, 2005) is a multi-objective DE algorithm that has outperformed other multi-objective evolutionary algorithm for a given set of numerical problems (Kukkonen & Lampinen, 2007; Tan, 2008). An overview of both PSO and DE algorithms and the hybridizations of these algorithms with other soft computing tools can be found in (Das, Abraham, & Konar, 2008).

The main objective of this chapter is to introduce these state-of-art algorithms and present their application to antenna and microwave design problems. This chapter presents results from design cases using Multi-objective Particle Swarm Optimization and Multi-objective Differential Evolution. These include microwave absorber design, microwave filters and Yagi-uda antenna design. The chapter is supported with an adequate number of references.

This chapter is subdivided into four sections. Section 2 presents the definition of the general multi-objective optimization problem under constraints and the details of the algorithms. Section 3 describes the design cases and presents the numerical results. Finally, section 4 contains the discussion about the advantages of using a multi-objective approach and the conclusions.

MULTI-OBJECTIVE OPTIMIZATION ALGORITHMS

Multi-Objective Optimization with Constraints

The general constrained multi-objective optimization problem (MOOP) definition is (Marler & Arora, 2004):

Minimize $\mathrm{F}(\overline{x}) = [\mathrm{F}_1(\overline{x}), \mathrm{F}_2(\overline{x}), ..., \mathrm{F}_n(\overline{x})]$ (1)

Subject to $g_i(\overline{x}) \leq 0 \ i = 1, 2, ..., k$ (2)

$F(\overline{x})$ is the vector of the objective functions, g_i are the constraint functions, n is the number of objective functions and k is the number of constraint functions.

In principle, multi-objective optimization is different from single-objective optimization. In single-objective optimization one attempts to obtain the best solution, which is usually the global minimum or the global maximum depending on the optimization problem. In case of multiple objectives, there may not exist one solution, which is the best (global minimum or maximum) with respect to all objectives. In a typical MOOP, it is often necessary to determine a set of points that all fit a predetermined definition for an optimum. The predominant concept in defining an optimal point is that of Pareto optimality. Pareto-optimal solutions are those solutions (from the set of feasible solutions) that cannot be improved in any objective without causing degradation in at least one other objective.

Therefore, the above problem can be solved in two ways. The first way is to convert it to a single-objective optimization problem. This can be accomplished by using weights for different objective functions and penalty terms for the constraint functions. This method leads to a single solution. The second way is to use Pareto optimization, which means to optimize all the objectives simultaneously giving them equal importance. If none of the objective function values can be further improved without, impairing the value of at least one objective for a given solution then this solution is Pareto-optimal and belongs to the set of non-dominated solutions, which is called Pareto front. The main goal is to find some points (solutions) that belong to the Pareto front. From this set of non-dominated solutions, optimal filter designs that provide a suitable compromise between the objectives for the desired constraints can be realized. A multi-objective evolutionary algorithm can be used to solve this problem.

Multi-objective evolutionary algorithms have gained popularity and have been used extensively over the last years in several design problems in electromagnetics. The application areas among others include microwave absorbers (Chamaani, Mirtaheri, Teshnehlab, Shoorehdeli, & Seydi, 2008; Hosung, Hao, & Liang, 2008; Jiang, Cui, Shi, & Li, 2009), antenna arrays (Boeringer & Werner, 2006; Pal, Das, & Basak, 2011; Pal, Das, Basak, & Suganthan, 2011; Pal, Qu, Das, & Suganthan, 2010; Petko & Werner, 2008; Y. H. Lee, B. J. Cahill, S. J. Porter, & Marvin, 2004), wire (Choo, Rogers, & Ling, 2005; Kuwahara, 2005; Ramos, Saldanha, Takahashi, & Moreira, 2003; Venkatarayalu & Ray, 2004) and patch antennas (Chamaani, Mirtaheri, & Abrishamian, 2011; De Jong Van Coevorden, Garcia, Pantoja, Bretones, & Martin, 2005; Koulouridis, Psychoudakis, & Volakis, 2007; Petko & Werner, 2011; Yeung, Man, Luk, & Chan, 2008) .

An important issue regarding performance of multi-objective optimization is the so-called 'No Free Lunch' theorem (NFL) which is a class of theorems concerning the average behaviour of optimization algorithms over given spaces of optimization problems. It has been shown in (Wolpert & Macready, 1997) that when averaged over all possible optimization problems defined over some search space X, no algorithm has a performance advantage over any other. Similarly, the definition of the NFL theorem for multi-objective optimization is given in (David & Joshua, 2003). The NFL result concerning Pareto fronts essentially means that we ultimately learn nothing from the result that 'algorithm A outperforms algorithm B on a problem with Pareto front P'. This is because the NFL result guarantees that this will be counterbalanced by B outperforming A on some other problem or set of problems which share the same Pareto front P.

EAs use vectors to model the possible solutions. In order to distinguish the members of the non-dominated set from the population members we refer to the first as solutions and to the second ones as vectors. The definitions of dominance relations between two vectors (or individuals of the population) are given below. The weak dominance $\preceq$ relation between two vectors $\overline{x}_1, \overline{x}_2$ in the search space is defined as (Kukkonen & Lampinen, 2005):

$$\begin{aligned} &\overline{x}_1 \text{ weakly dominates } \overline{x}_2 \\ &\overline{x}_1 \preceq \overline{x}_2 \quad \text{iff } \forall i : F_i(\overline{x}_1) \leq F_i(\overline{x}_2) \end{aligned} \tag{3}$$

while the dominance $\prec$ relation is defined as:

$$\begin{aligned} &\overline{x}_1 \text{ dominates } \overline{x}_2 \\ &\overline{x}_1 \prec \overline{x}_2 \quad \text{iff } \overline{x}_1 \preceq \overline{x}_2 \wedge \exists i : F_i(\overline{x}_1) < F_i(\overline{x}_2) \end{aligned} \tag{4}$$

The above relations can be extended to include constraint dominance $\prec_c$ (Kukkonen & Lampinen, 2005):

$$\overline{x}_1 \text{ constraint-dominates } \overline{x}_2 \quad \overline{x}_1 \prec_c \overline{x}_2$$

when any of the following conditions are true:

1. $\overline{x}_1$ belongs to the feasible design space and $\overline{x}_2$ is infeasible.
2. $\overline{x}_1, \overline{x}_2$ are both infeasible but $\overline{x}_1$ dominates $\overline{x}_2$ in constraint function space.
3. $\overline{x}_1, \overline{x}_2$ both belong the feasible design space but $\overline{x}_1$ dominates $\overline{x}_2$ in objective function space.

Particle Swarm Optimization (PSO)

In PSO, the particles move in the search space, where each particle position is updated by two optimum values. The first one is the best solution (fitness) that has been achieved so far. This value is called pbest. The other one is the global best value obtained so far by any particle in the swarm. This best value is called gbest. After finding the pbest and gbest, the velocity update rule is an important factor in a PSO algorithm. The most commonly used algorithm defines that the velocity of each particle for every problem dimension is updated with the following equation:

$$\begin{aligned} u_{G+1,ni} &= wu_{G,ni} + c_1 rand_{1(0,1)}(pbest_{G+1,ni} - x_{G,ni}) + \\ &+ c_2 rand_{2(0,1)}(gbest_{G+1,ni} - x_{G,ni}) \end{aligned} \tag{5}$$

where $u_{G+1,ni}$ is the ith particle velocity in the nth dimension, G+1 denotes the current iteration and G the previous, $x_{G,ni}$ is the particle position in the nth dimension, $rand_{1(0,1)}, rand_{2(0,1)}$ are uniformly distributed random numbers in (0,1), w is a parameter known as the inertia weight, and c_1 and c_2 are the learning factors.

The parameter w (inertia weight) is a constant between 0 and 1. This parameter represents the particle's fly without any external influence. The higher the value of w, or the closer it is to one, the more the particle stays unaffected from pbest and gbest. The parameter c_1 represents the influence of the particle memory on its best position, while the parameter c_2 represents the influence of the swarm best position. Therefore, in the Inertia Weight PSO (IWPSO) algorithm the parameters to be determined are: the swarm size (or population size), usually 100 or less, the cognitive learning factor c_1 and the social learning factor c_2 (usually both are set to equal to 2.0), the inertia weight w, and the maximum number of iterations. It is common practice to decrease linearly the inertia weight starting from 0.9 or 0.95 to 0.4.

Clerc (Clerc, 1999) suggested the use of a different velocity update rule, which introduced a parameter K called constriction factor. The role of the constriction factor is to ensure convergence when all the particles have stopped their movement. The velocity update rule is then given by:

$$u_{G+1,ni} = K\left[u_{G,ni} + c_1 rand_{1(0,1)}(pbest_{G+1,ni} - x_{G,ni}) + \right. \\ \left. +c_2 rand_{2(0,1)}(gbest_{G+1,ni} - x_{G,ni})\right] \tag{6}$$

$$K = \frac{2}{\left|2 - \varphi - \sqrt{\varphi^2 - 4\varphi}\right|} \tag{7}$$

where $\varphi = c_1 + c_2$ and $\varphi > 4$. This PSO algorithm variant is known as Constriction Factor PSO (CFPSO).

One advantage of PSO when compared with a GA is the fact that the PSO algorithm is simpler. A typical GA consists of three operators: selection mutation and crossover. However, the PSO uses only one operator the velocity calculation. Also in the case of a GA several control parameters values have to be selected. Fewer control parameters have to be adjusted in the PSO algorithm.

Multi-Objective Particle Swarm Optimization (MOPSO)

PSO seems to be suitable for multi-objective optimization due to its speedy convergence in single objective problems. Over the last years, various researchers have proposed several Multi-Objective PSO algorithms. The MOPSO algorithm proposed by Coello Coello et al (Coello Coello, Pulido, & Lechuga, 2004) has been validated against highly competitive evolutionary multi-objective algorithms like NSGA-II (K. Deb, Pratap, Agarwal, & Meyarivan, 2002). The characteristics of this MOPSO algorithm are:

1. The historical record of best solutions found by a particle is used to store nondominated solutions generated in the past. Therefore, a Repository is introduced and the positions of the particles that represent nondominated solutions are stored. The parameter that has to be adjusted is the Repository Size.
2. A new mutation operator is also introduced. This operator intends to produce a highly explorative behaviour of the algorithm. The effect of mutation decreases as the number of iterations increase. The parameter of mutation probability is therefore used.
3. The idea of an adaptive grid is introduced. An external archive is used to store all the solutions that are nondominated with respect to the contents of the archive. Into the archive the objective function space is divided into regions. The adaptive grid is a space formed by hypercubes. Each hypercube can be interpreted as a geographical region that contains a number of particles. The adaptive grid is used to distribute in a uniform way the largest possible amount of hypercubes. It is necessary therefore to provide the parameter of grid subdivisions.

As reported in (Coello Coello, Pulido, & Lechuga, 2004) the MOPSO algorithm is relatively easy to implement. The exploratory capabilities of PSO are improved using the mutation operator. Additionally, the authors find in the test problems they have used that MOPSO requires low computational cost, which is a key issue in cases of electromagnetic optimization.

More details of the algorithm implementation can be found in (Coello Coello, Pulido, & Lechuga, 2004).

Multi-Objective Particle Swarm Optimization with Fitness Sharing (MOPSO-fs)

MOPSO-fs (Salazar-Lechuga & Rowe, 2005) utilizes not only the PSO technique to guide the search, but also the fitness sharing to spread the solutions along the Pareto front. Fitness sharing is used in the objective space and enables the algorithm to maintain diversity between solutions. This means that particles within highly populated areas in the objective space are less likely to be followed. An external repository is also used to store the nondominated particles found. At each iteration, the best particles found are inserted into this repository. The repository helps to guide the search for the next generations and maintains a set of non-dominated solutions until the end of the process. This set of solutions forms the Pareto front.

The structure of the MOPSO-fs algorithm is given below:

1. We consider an M-size population of N-dimensional vectors (particles) $\mathbf{x}^m, m = 1, 2, ..., M$, where N is actually the number of design parameters. In the first step, the algorithm initializes with random population from a uniform distribution. The external repository is filled with all the non-dominated particles. The fitness sharing value f_{sh}^m is calculated for each particle in the repository. According to the fitness sharing principle, particles that have more particles in their vicinity are less fit than those that have fewer particles surrounding their vicinity. The fitness sharing value for the mth particle is given by

$$f_{sh}^m = 10 / n_v^m \tag{8}$$

The denominator in (8) is given by:

$$n_v^m = \sum_{j=1}^{R} sharing^{m,j} \tag{9}$$

where R is the number of particles in the repository and $sharing^{m,j}$ is derived by:

$$sharing^{m,j} = \begin{cases} 1 - \left(d^{m,j} / \sigma_{share} \right)^2 & \text{if } d^{m,j} < \sigma_{share} \\ 0 & \text{otherwise} \end{cases} \tag{10}$$

where $d^{m,j}$ is the Euclidean distance between the mth and the jth particle, while σ_{share} is the radius of the vicinity area of a particle. A high value of f_{sh}^m suggests that the vicinity of mth particle is not highly populated.

2. Provided that a fitness sharing is assigned for each particle in the repository, some particles from the repository are chosen as leaders. These particles are going to be followed by the rest of the particles in the next iteration. The leaders are chosen according to roulette wheel selection, i.e., particles with higher levels of fitness are likely to be selected. This will allow them to explore places less explored in the search space. The velocity update rule for the mth particle is:

$$u_n^m = w \cdot u_n^m + c_1 \cdot r_1 \cdot (pbest_n^m - x_n^m) + c_2 \cdot r_2 \cdot (gbest_n^h - x_n^m) \tag{11}$$

where the subscript n denotes the dimension, while u_n^m and x_n^m are the nth component of the particle velocity and position, respectively. Furthermore, in (11), r1 and r2 are random numbers between (0,1), w is the inertia weight, c1 and c2 are the learning factors. Finally, $pbest_n^m$ is the best position found by the mth particle so far, and $gbest_n^h$ is the leader particle position along nth dimension. The position of each particle is updated using the expression:

$$\mathbf{x}^m = \mathbf{x}^m + \mathbf{u}^m \tag{12}$$

3. The repository is updated with the current solutions found by the particles. Two criteria are used: dominance and fitness sharing value. The particles that dominate those inside the repository will be inserted whereas all solutions dominated will be deleted. Thus, we maintain the repository as the Pareto front found so far. In the case where the repository is full of non-dominated particles and a particle non-dominated by any in the repository is found, their fitness sharing is compared. If it is better than the worst fitness sharing in the repository, then the new particle replaces the one with the worst fitness sharing. The fitness sharing of all particles is updated when a particle is inserted in the repository or deleted from the repository.
4. Finally, the memory of each particle is updated according to the criterion of dominance. Therefore, if the current particle position dominates the previous one, the current position replaces the previous one in the particle's memory.

MOPSO-fs has been shown to be highly compleptive with MOPSO and NSGA-II on numerical test problems in (Salazar-Lechuga & Rowe, 2005).

Differential Evolution

A population in DE consists of *NP* vectors $\overline{x}_{iG}, i = 1,2,......NP$, where *G* is the generation number and *NP* is the population size. The population is initialized randomly from a uniform distribution. Each D-dimensional vector represents a possible solution. The initial population evolves in each generation with the use of three operators: mutation, crossover and selection. Depending on the form of these operators several DE variants or strategies exist in the literature (Storn, 2008; Storn & Price, 1997). The choice of the best DE strategy depends on the problem type (Mezura-Montes, Velazquez-Reyes, & Coello Coello, 2006). The most popular is the one known as DE/rand/1/bin strategy. In this strategy, a mutant vector $\overline{v}$ for every target vector $\overline{x}_{iG}$ is computed by:

$$\overline{v}_{i,G+1} = \overline{x}_{r_1,G} + MP(\overline{x}_{r_2,G} - \overline{x}_{r_3,G}), \quad r_1 \neq r_2 \neq r_3 \tag{13}$$

where r_1, r_2, r_3 are randomly chosen indices from the population, and *MP* is a mutation control parameter. After mutation the crossover operator is applied to generate a trial vector $\overline{u}_{i,G+1} = \left(u_{1i,G+1}, u_{2i,G+1}, ...u_{Di,G+1}\right)$ whose coordinates are given by:

$$u_{ji,G+1} = \begin{cases} v_{ji,G+1}, & \text{if rand(j)} \leq CR \text{ or j=rn(i)} \\ x_{ji,G}, & \text{if rand(j)} > CR \text{ and j} \neq \text{rn(i)} \end{cases} \tag{14}$$

where $j = 1,2,......D$, rand(j) is a number from a uniform random distribution from the space [0,1], rn(i) a randomly chosen index from (1,2,......D) and *CR* the crossover constant from the space [0,1]. DE uses a greedy selection operator. According to this selection scheme for minimization problems:

$$\overline{x}_{i,G+1} = \begin{cases} \overline{u}_{i,G+1}, & \text{if } f(\overline{u}_{i,G+1}) < f(\overline{x}_{i,G}) \\ \overline{x}_{i,G}, & \text{otherwise} \end{cases} \tag{15}$$

where $f(\overline{u}_{i,G+1})$, $f(\overline{x}_{i,G})$ are the fitness values of the trial and the old vector respectively. Therefore, the newly found trial vector $\overline{u}_{i,G+1}$ replaces the old vector $\overline{x}_{i,G}$ only when it produces a lower objective function value than the old one. Otherwise, the old vector remains in the next generation. The stopping criterion for the DE is usually the generation number or the number of objective function evaluations. DE produced better results than PSO on numerical benchmark problems with low and medium dimensionality (30 and 100 dimensions) (Vesterstrom & Thomsen, 2004). However, on noisy test problems, DE was outperformed by PSO. In (S. K. Goudos, Zaharis, Baltzis, Hilas, & Sahalos, 2009) a comparative study between DE and PSO variants is presented for the design of radar absorbing materials (RAM). The number of problem dimensions was 10 and DE outperformed the PSO variants in terms of convergence speed and best values found. The shape reconstruction of a perfectly conducting 2-D scatterer using DE and PSO is presented in (Rekanos, 2007,, 2008). Also both algorithms have been applied to 1-D small-scale inverse scattering problems (Semnani, Kamyab, & Rekanos, Oct. 2009). In these cases, DE outperformed PSO. In (Panduro, Brizuela, Balderas, & Acosta, 2009) a comparison between DE, PSO and Genetic algorithms (GAs) for circular array design is presented. DE and PSO showed similar performances and both of them had better performance compared to GAs.

One of the DE advantages is that very few control parameters have to be adjusted in each algorithm run. However, the control parameters involved in DE are highly dependent on the optimization problem.

Generalized Differential Evolution (GDE3)

Multi-objective DE algorithms extend the classical DE algorithm for solving MOOP. Generalized Differential Evolution (GDE3) that introduced in (Kukkonen & Lampinen, 2005) can solve problems that have n objectives and k constraint functions. It can handle any number of objectives and any number of constraint functions including the cases n=0 (constraint satisfaction problem) and k=0 (unconstraint problem). In case of n=1 and k=0 the algorithm is the same as the original DE. The classical DE algorithm can be considered as a special case of GDE3. Therefore, one could change the current *DE/rand/1/bin* strategy to any other exciting DE strategy or to any method that a trial vector is compared against an old vector and the better one is preserved. GDE3 has outperformed other evolutionary algorithms in numerical benchmark problems (Kukkonen & Lampinen, 2007; Tan, 2008). It has been successfully applied to the molecular sequence alignment problem (Kukkonen, Jangam, & Chakraborti, 2007), to microwave filter design (S. K. Goudos & Sahalos, 2010) and Yagi antenna design (S. K. Goudos, Siakavara, Vafiadis, & Sahalos, 2010).

GDE3 modifies the selection rule of the basic DE. In the modified selection rule the trial vector is selected to replace the old vector in the next generation if it weakly constraint-dominates the old vector. The following selection rules apply to the GDE3 algorithm:

- If both vectors (trial and old) are infeasible, then the trial vector is selected only if it weakly dominates the old vector in constraint violation space, otherwise the old vector is preserved.
- If one vector is feasible and the other is unfeasible, then the feasible vector is selected.
- If both vectors (trial and old) are feasible, then the trial is selected only if it weakly dominates the old vector in the objective function space. If the old dominates then the old vector is selected. If neither vector dominates each other in the objective function space then both vectors are selected for the next generation.

Therefore, the population size may increase in the next generation. To decrease the population back to the original size a sorting technique is applied. This uses the concept of Crowding Distance (CD), which approximates the crowdedness of a vector in its non-dominated set like NSGA-II (K. Deb, Pratap, Agarwal, & Meyarivan, 2002). The vectors are sorted based on non-dominance and crowdedness. The worst population members are removed and the population size is set to the original size. The basic idea is to prune a non-dominated set to have a desired number of solutions in such a way that the remaining solutions have as good diversity as possible, meaning that the spread of extreme solutions is as high as possible, and the relative distance between solutions is as equal as possible. The pruning method of NSGA-II provides good diversity in the case of two objectives, but when the number of objectives is more than two, the obtained diversity declines drastically (Kalyanmoy Deb, Thiele, Laumanns, & Zitzler, 2005). The method used in GDE3 is based on a crowding estimation technique using nearest neighbors of solutions in Euclidean sense, and a technique for finding these nearest neighbors quickly. More details about the GDE3 pruning method can be found in (Kukkonen & Deb, 2006). Therefore, the selection based on Crowding Distance is improved over the original method of the NSGA-II to provide a better-distributed set of vectors.

A basic difference exists between NSGA-II and GDE3 regarding the population size after a generation. In NSGA-II the population size after a generation is increased to 2*NP*. Then non-dominated ranking is applied and *NP* non-dominated vectors are selected. In GDE3 after a generation the population size is *NP* +m, where $m \in \left[0, NP\right]$, because the population size is increased only when the trial $\overline{u}_{i,G+1}$ and the old vector $\overline{x}_{i,G}$ are feasible and do not dominate each other. Therefore non-dominated ranking is applied to *NP* +m population size, which can be less in general than 2*NP* thus resulting in less computational time than NSGA-II (Kukkonen & Lampinen, 2005). GDE3 can be implemented in such a way that fewer function evaluations are required because not always all the objectives and the constraints have to be evaluated, e.g. by inspecting constraint evaluations (even one constraint) can be enough to determine, which vector will be selected for the next generation. However, in case of feasible vectors all the function evaluations are required.

The GDE3 algorithm is outlined below:

1. Initialize random population of *NP* individuals. Set m=0.
2. Evaluate objective function and constraint function values for every vector of the population.
3. Apply the mutation and crossover operators according to (13) and (14) and create a trial vector $u_{i,G+1}$.
4. Evaluate objective function and constraint function values for the trial vector.
5. Apply the selection operator according to the following criterion:

$$\overline{x}_{i,G+1} = \begin{cases} \overline{u}_{i,G+1}, & \text{if } \overline{u}_{i,G+1} \preceq_c \overline{x}_{i,G} \\ \overline{x}_{i,G}, & \text{otherwise} \end{cases} \tag{16}$$

6. Set $m = m + 1, \overline{x}_{NP+m,G+1} = \overline{u}_{i,G+1}$ if

$$\forall j : g_j(\overline{u}_{i,G+1}) \leq 0 \ \wedge \ \overline{x}_{i,G+1} == \overline{x}_{i,G} \ \wedge \ \overline{x}_{i,G} \nprec \overline{u}_{i,G+1} \tag{17}$$

7. Apply non-dominated ranking to *NP* + *m* vectors. Select *NP* non-dominated vectors and set *m*=0.
8. Repeat step 3 until the maximum number of generations $G_{\max}$ is reached.

GDE3 variations with different DE strategies can be easily created simply by using different equations for crossover and mutation than (13) and (14). The advantage of the GDE3 is that it is designed for any number of objectives and constraints without adding new control parameters to that of the original DE strategy. GDE3 uses a constraint handling method that reduces the number of the objective functions evaluations. More details about the GDE3 algorithm can be found in (Kukkonen & Lampinen, 2005).

Control Parameter Selection

It must be pointed out that several PSO and DE variants exist in the literature. In order to select, the best algorithm for every problem one has to consider the problem characteristics. For example, micro-PSO performs very well for microwave image reconstruction (Huang & Sanagavarapu Mohan, Mar. 2007). Another key issue is the selection of the algorithm control parameters, which is also in most cases problem-dependent. The control parameters selected here for these algorithms are those that commonly perform well regardless of the characteristics of the problem to be solved.

A empirical rule in DE states that for single objective optimization if nothing is known about the problem then the initial values for control parameters could be $MP = 0.9$, $CR = 0.9$, $NP = 5 \cdot D.....30 \cdot D$, where D is the number of unknown variables. In case of multi-objective optimization and conflicting objectives lower values for control parameters than those in single objective optimization are used. This is due to the fact that conflicting objectives maintain diversity and restrain the search speed. The value of the mutation control parameter MP is a compromise between speed and robustness. It has been found that a value $MP = 0.5$ is suitable for most of the problems (Kukkonen & Lampinen, 2006,, 2007). The value of the crossover operator CR can be relatively low as has been shown in (Kukkonen & Lampinen, 2006). The population size can be selected the same way as in single objective optimization or according to the desired size of the Pareto front. Therefore the control parameters chosen for GDE3 are according to (Kukkonen & Lampinen, 2006,, 2007) $MP = 0.5$, $CR = 0.1$.

For NSGA-II (K. Deb, Pratap, Agarwal, & Meyarivan, 2002) usual values for control parameters are $p_c = 0.9$ for crossover probability and $p_m = 1 / D$ the mutation probability for real valued variables or $p_m = 1 / l$, where l is the string length for binary-coded variables.

The main characteristics of the MOPSO (Coello Coello, Pulido, & Lechuga, 2004) algorithm are; the repository size, the mutation operator and the grid subdivisions. The repository is the archive where the positions of the particles that represent non-dominated solutions are stored. Therefore the parameter that has to be adjusted is the repository size. This is usually set equal to the swarm size. MOPSO introduces a mutation operator that intends to produce a highly explorative behavior of the algorithm. The effect of mutation decreases as the number of iterations increase. A setting of 0.5 has been found suitable (Coello Coello, Pulido, & Lechuga, 2004) after experiments for mutation probability. Similarly, a value of 30 has been found suitable (Coello Coello, Pulido, & Lechuga, 2004) for the parameter of grid divisions. The above parameters are those selected for our problem given below for the MOPSO algorithm.

MOPSO-fs also uses a repository to store all the all the non-dominated solutions (Salazar-Lechuga & Rowe, 2005). As in MOPSO the repository size parameter is set equal to swarm size. Another parameter that has to be set in MOPSO-fs is the sigma share value. This is set empirically after several trials to 2.0.

It must be pointed out that several modifications were made to MOPSO and MOPSO-fs algorithms. Constraint handling was added to both algorithms. Furthermore in case of discrete valued variables like the material number the velocity update rules given by the Binary PSO were used (Kennedy & Eberhart, 1997). More details about these modifications can be found in (S. K. Goudos & Sahalos, 2006; S. K. Goudos, Zaharis, Kampitaki, Rekanos, & Hilas, 2009).

NUMERICAL EXAMPLES

Microwave Absorber Design Using MOPSO

The problem of a planar microwave absorber (Figure 1) design lies in minimizing of the reflection coefficient of an incident plane wave in a multilayer structure for a desired range of angles and frequencies. The reflection coefficient depends on the thickness and the electric and magnetic properties of each layer. Minimization of the reflection coefficient is a classical multi-objective optimization problem. In (S. K. Goudos & Sahalos, 2006) the MOPSO algorithm for solving absorber design problem is applied.

The absorber design is defined as the minimization problem of the reflection coefficient $R_1^{TE/TM}$ (expressed in dB) given below:

Figure 1. A multi-layer planar absorber

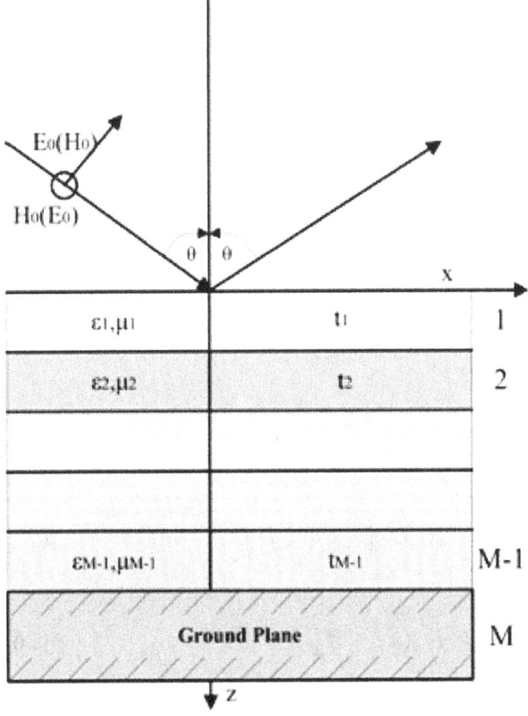

$$R_1^{TE/TM} = 20\log\left\{\max\left|R(f,\theta)\right| \quad f \in \mathrm{B}, \theta \in \mathrm{A}\right\} \tag{18}$$

where $\max\left|R(f,\theta)\right|$ is the maximum reflection coefficient at the first layer over the desired frequency and angle range for a given polarization. B is the desired set of frequencies and A is the desired set of angles. The total thickness of the absorber is the sum of the thicknesses of the layers:

$$T_{tot} = \sum_{i=1}^{M-1} t_i \tag{19}$$

It is obvious that for this type of multi-objective problem, there is not a single global solution and it is often necessary to determine a set of points that all fit a predetermined definition for an optimum. The main goal is to find some points that belong in the Pareto front. In this case, an optimal absorber for a desired total thickness can be realized. A multi-objective optimization algorithm method can be used to solve this problem. In (S. K. Goudos & Sahalos, 2006) a modification was made to MOPSO. The original MOPSO uses a constant value of 0.4 for inertia weight and sets $c_1=c_2=1$ in velocity equation. In order to increase the search space inertia weight is randomly chosen from the interval [0.4,0.9]. Also uniformly distributed random numbers are used for the constants c_1 and c_2 from the interval [1.49, 2.0]. Parametric studies using a trial and error method have shown that no optimum values for c_1 and c_2 really exist. The values c_1 and c_2 are in fact problem dependent in the range 1.00 to 3.5. An empirical rule states that their sum should not exceed 4.1.

Experimental results have shown that for the particular problem of absorber design the MOPSO algorithm performs better in finding the Pareto front. MOPSO in its new form is computationally more efficient than NSGA-II for the same population size.

Another modification made to the initial MOPSO algorithm was to include both binary and real coded variables. Therefore a hybrid real-binary PSO is used. The maximum layer thickness was set (as in (Michielssen, Sajer, Ranjithant, & Mittra, 1993)) equal to 2mm. A five-layer broad band absorber in the frequency range from 200MHz to 2GHz for normal incidence and TE polarization is selected.

MOPSO is validated against NSGA-II. The Pareto front for the five-layer structure is found. The parameters chosen for MOPSO were: 60 particle swarm size, 60 particles repository size, 3000 iterations, 30 grid divisions and a mutation probability of 0.5. For NSGA-II the population size was set equal to 100, crossover probability was set to 0.9 and mutation probability to 0.05. One may notice that for the MOPSO the total number of objective-function evaluations was set equal to 180,000 while for NSGA-II the total number of objective function evaluations was set to 300,000. Thus a smaller number of objective-function evaluations is used than the number required in (Weile, Michielssen, & Goldberg, 1996). The optimization goal was to find 100 points of the Pareto front. The average computational times in seconds required for each algorithm run are 29.51 and 58.59 for MOPSO and NSGA-II respectively. The Pareto front found is shown in Figure 2. One may notice that MOPSO slightly outperforms NSGA-II. The Pareto front found by MOPSO is almost identical with that found by NSGA-II with the exception of more points found in the 4-5mm region. It seems that MOPSO manages to find a larger dispersion of points in the front. Therefore, both MOPSO and NSGA-II can find feasible solutions and speed up convergence to the Pareto front.

Dielectric Filter Design Using MOPSO-fs

Microwave filter design is a common problem. Several design approaches exist in the literature. Multi-layer dielectric filter design under constraints has also been a favorite subject among researchers (Hoorfar, Zhu, & Nelatury, 2003; Venkatarayalu, Ray, & Gan, 2005). Such design constraints require that the reflection coefficient value in the passband or stopband region should not lie respectively above or below a predefined level. MOPSO-fs is used in (S. K. Goudos, Zaharis, Salazar-Lechuga, Lazaridis, & Gallion, 2007) for microwave filter design.

The structure of a multi-layer dielectric filter is shown in Figure 3. The unknown variables are the thickness and the electromagnetic characteristics of each layer. These characteristics are the frequency dependent (in general) complex permittivity and permeability.

The microwave filter design problem can be expressed by the minimization of the objective functions given below:

$$f_1(x) = \sum_p \left[\left| R_{TE}(x, f_p) \right|^2 + \left| R_{TM}(x, f_p) \right|^2 \right] \quad (20)$$

$$f_2(x) = \sum_s \left[\left(1 - \left| R_{TE}(x, f_s) \right|^2 \right) + \left(1 - \left| R_{TM}(x, f_s) \right|^2 \right) \right] \quad (21)$$

Moreover, the design problem is subject to the following constraints:

$$g_1(x) = 20 \log \left(R_{TE}(x, f_p^c) \right) < -10dB \quad (22)$$

$$g_2(x) = 20 \log \left(R_{TM}(x, f_p^c) \right) < -10dB \quad (23)$$

$$g_3(x) = 20 \log \left(R_{TE}(x, f_s^c) \right) > -5dB \quad (24)$$

$$g_4(x) = 20 \log \left(R_{TM}(x, f_s^c) \right) > -5dB \quad (25)$$

$$g_5(x) = T_{tot}(x) \le T_{des} \quad (26)$$

Figure 2. Pareto fronts found with MOPSO and NSGA-II for five-layer broad-band absorber optimized for normal incidence, TE polarization for f=0.2-2GHz

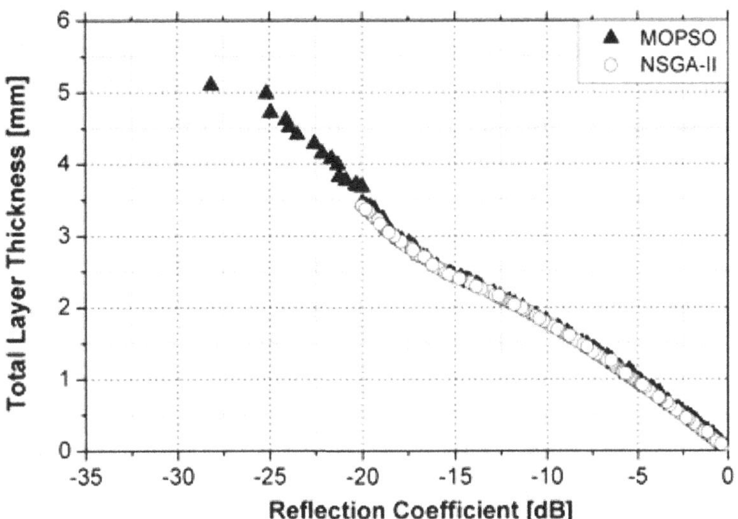

where R_{TE} and R_{TM} are the reflection coefficients of the filter structure respectively for the transverse electric (TE) and the transverse magnetic (TM) modes, T_{tot} is the total layer thickness of the design found and T_{des} is the desired total layer thickness.. In addition, f_p and f_s define correspondingly the passband and the stopband frequency ranges, while f_p^c and f_s^c define respectively the passband and the stopband frequencies where constrains must be satisfied. The main goal is to find a number of points that belong to the Pareto front. Then,

Figure 3. Multi-layer dielectric filter structure

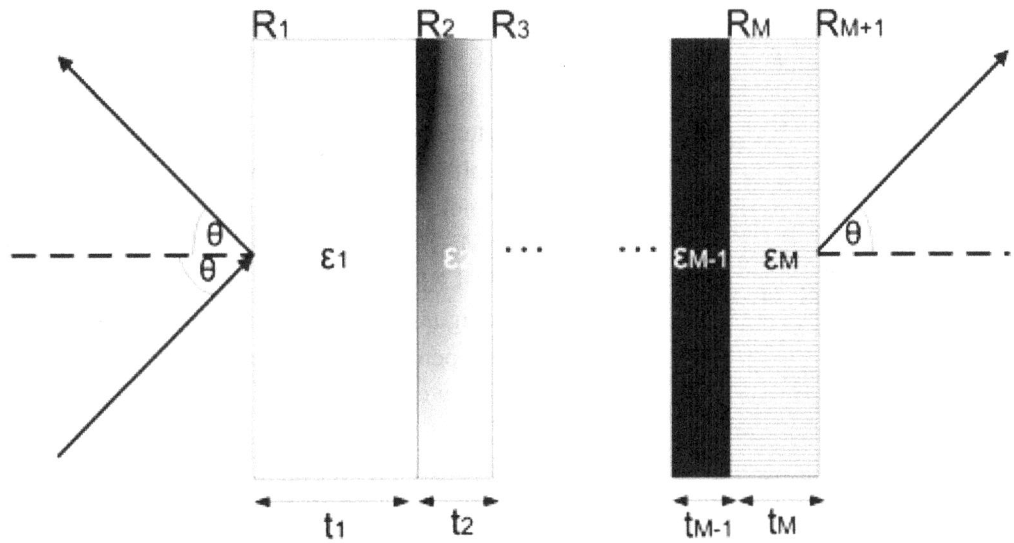

optimal filter designs can be selected from this Pareto front.

A seven-layer example filter design case is presented. As in (Venkatarayalu, Ray, & Gan, 2005) the angle of incidence is set to $\vartheta = 45^\circ$ The design frequency range is set from 24GHz to 36GHz. The same predefined material database as in (Hoorfar, Zhu, & Nelatury, 2003; Venkatarayalu, Ray, & Gan, 2005) was used. This database consists of 15 commercially available dielectric materials with real permittivity values of 1.01, 2.20, 2.33, 2.50, 2.94, 3.00, 3.02, 3.27, 3.38, 4.48, 4.50, 6.00, 6.15, 9.20, and 10.20. These values remain constant over the design frequency range. The lower and upper allowable limits of layer thickness are set to 1mm and 10mm respectively.

MOPSO-fs and NSGA-II are applied for a band-pass filter design case. The parameters chosen for MOPSO-fs were 100-particle swarm size, 100-particle repository size, 1000 iterations and a sigma share value of 2. For NSGA-II the population size was set equal to 100, 1000 generations were used, and finally the crossover and mutation probabilities were set respectively equal to 0.9 and 0.1 for both real and binary variables. Each algorithm runs for 10 times and the best results are compared. The filter design specifications are given below. The passband and stopband frequencies are set to

$$28GHz \le f_p < 32GHz \text{ and}$$

$$24GHz \le f_s < 28GHz,$$

$$32GHz \le f_s < 36GHz.$$

The range of constraints are set to

$$29GHz \le f_p^c < 31GHz \text{ and}$$

$$24GHz \le f_s^c < 26GHz,$$

$$34GHz \le f_s^c < 36GHz.$$

The total desired thickness is set to 20mm. Figure 4 presents a filter design case with 17.92mm total thickness. In (Venkatarayalu, Ray, & Gan, 2005) a band-pass filter with total thickness of 33.44mm is reported, which is found using a multi-objective evolutionary algorithm. For both TE and TM modes, the new design presents a similar or better behavior. The thicknesses of the layers are 4.719, 1.001, 4.921, 1.037, 1.018, 1.958 and 3.254mm, while the corresponding dielectric constants are 2.2, 1.01, 10.2, 2.2, 4.5, 2.94 and 3.02. Figure 5 shows the Pareto front for the band-pass filter case. Each point of the Pareto front represents a feasible filter design case, which fulfils all the constraints. MOPSO-fs manages to find a larger dispersion of points in the front and clearly outperforms NSGA-II. The position of the case of Figure 4 is shown in the Pareto front with an arrow. MOPSO-fs produces better results compared with NSGA-II.

Pareto Optimization of Open Loop Ring Resonator (OLRR) Filters Using Multi-Objective Differential Evolution

Another popular microwave filter design case is that of Open Loop Ring Resonator (OLRR) filters. These are comprised of two uniform microstrip lines and an open loop between them. Synthesis of OLRRs has been presented in (Chu-Yu & Cheng-Ying, 2006; Koziel & Bandler, 2008). In (Koziel & Bandler, 2008) the space mapping technique is used for filter design. This is accomplished in conjunction with FEKO (2003) a commercially available EM solver. FEKO is a hybrid MoM/FEM software, which is also used for the OLRR filter design. An OLRR filter is shown in Figure 6. The frequency response of such a filter depends on the filter dimensions and spacings between microstrip lines. The design parameters are the ones shown in Figure 6 $(W_1, W_2, L_1, L_2, L_3, L_4, S_1, S_2, S_3)$, all expressed in mm. It must be pointed out that in (Koziel &

Figure 4. Frequency response of the seven-layer band-pass filter

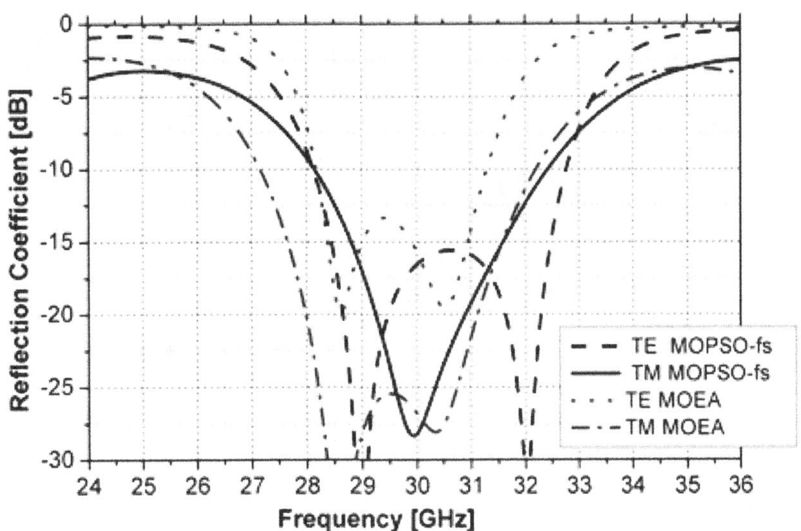

Bandler, 2008) W_1 and W_2 are considered to be constant and equal to 0.4mm. Therefore, two additional design variables are added to the problem. Such a filter design problem can be defined (Koziel & Bandler, 2008) by two objectives subject to two constraint functions. The first objective is to maximize the $|S_{21}|$ in the passband frequency range. The second objective is to minimize the $|S_{21}|$ in the stopband frequency range. Additionally constraints can be set for $|S_{21}|$ levels in both the passband and the stopband frequency range. This design problem is therefore defined by the minimization of the objective functions:

$$F_1(\overline{x}) = -20\log\left\{\min\left|S_{21}(\overline{x}, f)\right|, \quad f \in f_p\right\} \tag{27}$$

$$F_2(\overline{x}) = 20\log\left\{\max\left|S_{21}(\overline{x}, f)\right|, \quad f \in f_s\right\} \tag{28}$$

Subject to:

$$g_1(\overline{x}) = 20\log\left(\left|S_{21}(\overline{x}, f_p^c)\right|\right) > C_{dB}^P \tag{29}$$

$$g_2(\overline{x}) = 20\log\left(\left|S_{21}(\overline{x}, f_s^c)\right|\right) < C_{dB}^S \tag{30}$$

where $\overline{x} = (W_1, W_2, L_1, L_2, L_3, L_4, S_1, S_2, S_3)$ the vector of filter geometry, f_p and f_s define correspondingly the passband and the stopband frequency ranges, f_p^c and f_s^c define respectively the passband and the stopband frequencies where constrains must be satisfied. Also C_{dB}^P and C_{dB}^S define the minimum and maximum allowable values in the passband and stopband frequency ranges respectively where constrains are applied.

The OLRR filter was modeled in FEKO. The design specifications chosen are the same as in (Koziel & Bandler, 2008). The passband and stopband frequencies are set to

$2.7GHz \leq f_p < 3.3GHz$ and

$1.5GHz \leq f_s < 2.6GHz$,

$3.4GHz \leq f_s < 4.5GHz$ respectively.

The range of constraints are set to

Figure 5. Pareto front found with MOPSO-fs and NSGA-II for the band-pass design

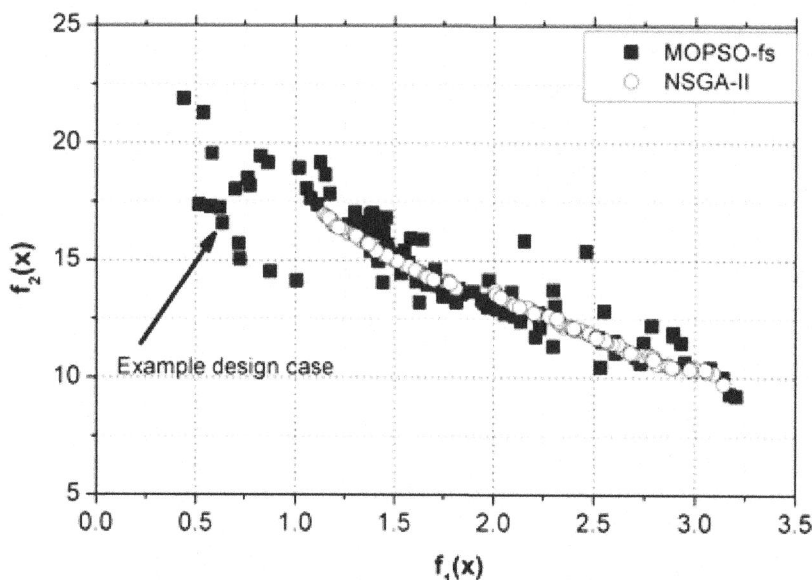

$2.8GHz \leq f_p^c < 3.2GHz$ and

$1.5GHz \leq f_s^c < 2.5GHz$,

$3.5GHz \leq f_s^c < 4.5GHz$

and we set

$C_{dB}^P = -3dB, C_{dB}^S = -20dB$.

For each FEKO run, 15 frequency sweeps are taken in the frequency range 1.5-4.5 GHz. This requires about a total time of 3.2 sec in a PC with Intel Core 2 Duo E8500 at 3.16GHz with 4GB RAM. In order to integrate the in-house source code of the multi-objective algorithms with FEKO, a wrapper program was created. FEKO, except of using a graphical user interface, offers the option to run the EM solver engine from command line. It requires an input file that defines the model geometry. This input file uses a script language that allows users to define variables and control options like the frequency range, the number of frequency points and the required data in the output file. The wrapper creates a FEKO input file for each random vector created by the algorithms and runs FEKO. The output file, which in our case is defined to contain the frequency and the S-parameters is read by the wrapper and the objective and constraint functions are evaluated.

The GDE3 algorithm is applied to the OLRR design problem (S. K. Goudos & Sahalos, 2010). GDE3 is compared against NSGA-II, MOPSO and MOPSO-fs. A population of 20 vectors is selected for all algorithms. The total number of generations is set to 1000. All algorithms are executed 20 times. The control parameters that were given in the previous section are used for all algorithms.

The frequency response of an example design is given in Figure 7. A finer mesh was used in FEKO model with 300 frequency points to provide a smooth response. One may notice that the filter has low magnitude values also out of the desired stopband frequency bands. It is evident that in the frequency bands between 1.0 and 1.5 GHz and 4.5 and 5.0 GHz the $|S_{21}|$ value lies below -50dB

Figure 6. Open loop ring resonator filter geometry

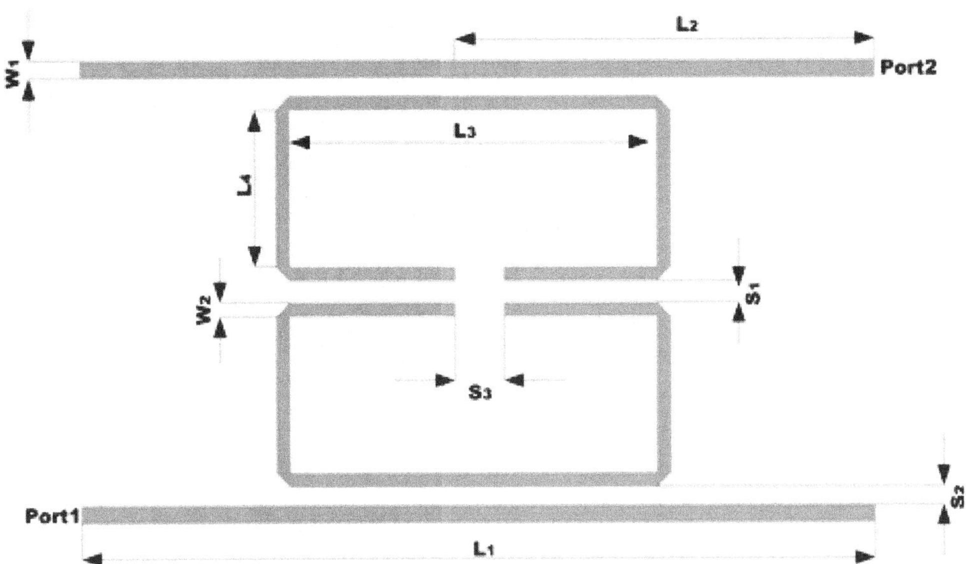

and -30dB respectively. The Pareto fronts produced are given in Figure 8. It is clear that the GDE3 algorithm outperforms the other algorithms. GDE3 solutions dominate most of the solutions found by NSGA-II. Both algorithms have found 20 points of the Pareto front. MOPSO-fs and MOPSO have found 15 and 11 points respectively. For this problem, these algorithms require a larger number of iterations. Their solutions are dominated by NSGA-II and GDE3 results.

Yagi-Uda Design Using Multi-Objective Differential Evolution

Antenna design problems are in general multi-objective. Common design objectives include gain maximization, sidelobe level reduction and input impedance matching. The above-mentioned objectives are often subject to constraints. The design of Yagi-Uda antennas that satisfy such objectives and constraints is a common problem, which has been addressed in the literature (Baskar, Alphones, Suganthan, & Liang, 2005; Bemani & Nikmehr, 2009; Chen & Cheng, 1975; D. K. Cheng, 1991; David K. Cheng & Chen, 1973; Chou, Hung, & Chen, 2009; Jones & Joines, 1997; Kuwahara, 2005; J. Y. Li & Guo, 2009; Misra, Chakrabarty, & Mangaraj, 2006; Rattan, Patterh, & Sohi, 2008; Sun, Zhou, Wei, & Liu, 2010; Teisbaek & Jakobsen, 2009; Venkatarayalu & Ray, 2003,, 2004). The optimization goal is to find the optimum element lengths and spacings that fulfill the design specifications.

Figure 9 shows an *N*-element Yagi-Uda antenna. This antenna consists of a single driven element, one reflector element and *N-2* director elements. Such an *N*-element Yagi-Uda antenna has *2N-1* antenna parameters that determine the antenna characteristics, apart from the elements' radius. The design parameters are $\overline{x} = \left(L_1, L_2, ..., L_k, ..., L_N, S_1, S_2, ..., S_k, ...S_{N-1}\right)$ where $2L_k$ is the length of the *kth* element, and S_k is the spacing between the *kth* and *(k+1)th* elements.

The Yagi-Uda antenna design goal is to find the optimum geometry that satisfies given performance specifications such as high gain, $Gain(\overline{x})$, low sidelobe level, $SLL(\overline{x})$, and input impedance close or equal to 50Ω. The last objec-

Figure 7. OLRR bandpass filter example case

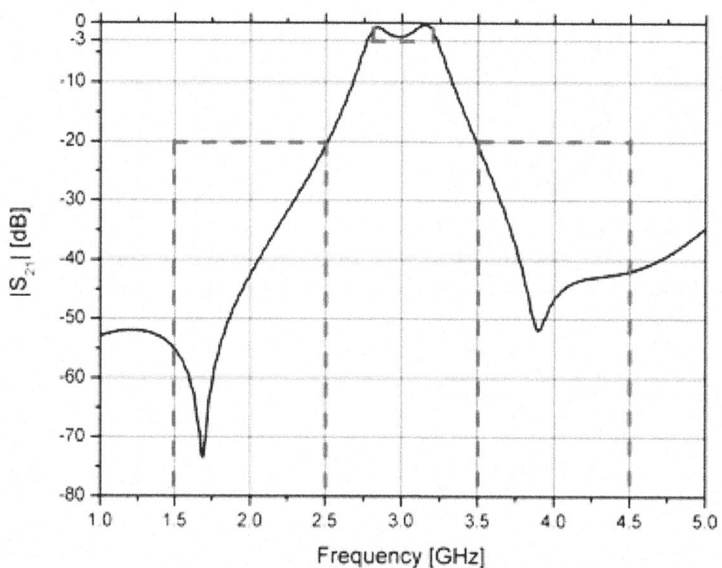

Figure 8. Pareto fronts for the OLRR bandpass filter design case found by all algorithms

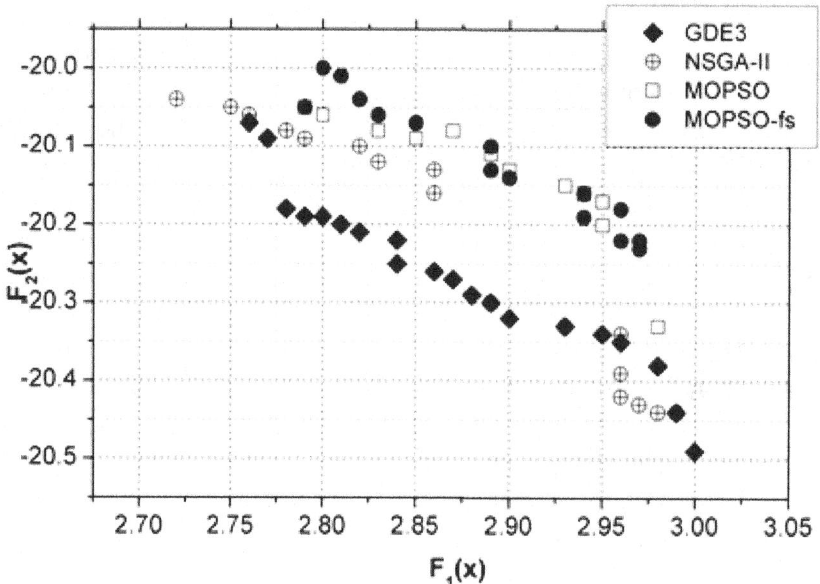

tive can also be defined as having a Voltage Standing Wave Ratio (VSWR), $VSWR(\overline{x})$, close to one. It is obvious that such a problem is multi-objective. In the literature the above objectives have been combined in a single objective function using different weight factors (Baskar, Alphones, Suganthan, & Liang, 2005; Jones & Joines, 1997; J. Y. Li & Guo, 2009; Rattan, Patterh, & Sohi, 2008).

In (S. K. Goudos, Siakavara, Vafiadis, & Sahalos, 2010) the Yagi-Uda antenna design problem

Figure 9. N-element Yagi-Uda antenna

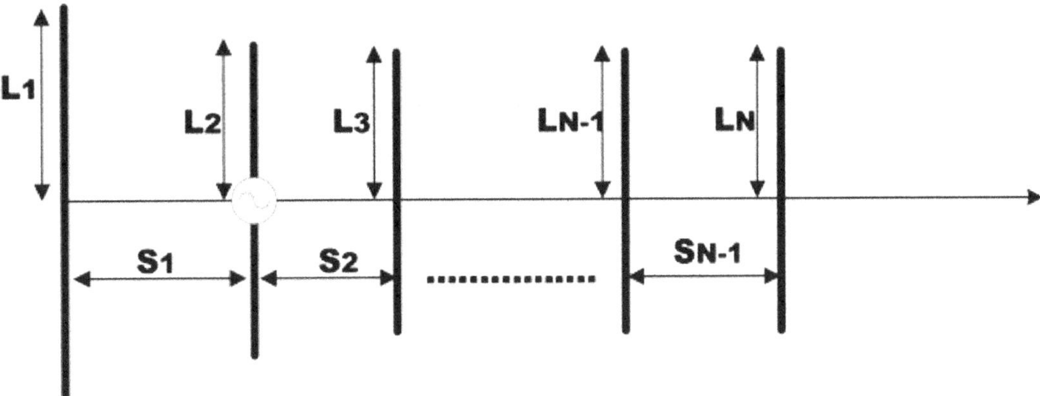

is expressed as the minimization of the following objective functions:

$$\begin{aligned} F_1(\overline{x}) &= -Gain(\overline{x}) \\ F_2(\overline{x}) &= SLL(\overline{x}) \\ F_3(\overline{x}) &= VSWR(\overline{x}) \end{aligned} \tag{31}$$

Moreover, the design problem is subject to the following constraints:

$$\begin{aligned} g_1(\overline{x}) &= Gain(\overline{x}) \geq Gain_L \\ g_2(\overline{x}) &= VSWR(\overline{x}) \leq VSWR_L \end{aligned} \tag{32}$$

where $Gain_L$, $VSWR_L$ are the minimum allowable gain and the maximum allowable VSWR respectively. The methods of moments-based numerical electromagnetics code (NEC-2) has been used in the analysis. In particular, SuperNEC a commercially available NEC-2 version with MATLAB interface is used.

The GDE3 and NSGA-II algorithms are applied to a six-element Yagi antenna. The population size is set to 40 for both algorithms in all cases. The iteration number is set to 1000. The control parameters chosen for GDE3 are according to (Kukkonen & Lampinen, 2006,, 2007) for solving problems with three objectives *F*= 0.2, *CR* = 0.2. These values have been verified with several trials.

In NSGA-II the crossover and mutation probabilities are set equal to 0.9 and 0.1, respectively.

This example is common in the literature (Baskar, Alphones, Suganthan, & Liang, 2005; Jones & Joines, 1997; Kuwahara, 2005). For this case we set $Gain_L = 11dBi$, $VSWR_L = 2$ and the dipole radius to 0.003369λ. The Pareto fronts for this case are shown in Figure 10 and 11 for GDE3 and NSGA-II, respectively. Three example cases that were found by GDE3 are reported in Table 1. Figure 12 depicts the corresponding radiation patterns. The results obtained by GDE3

Figure 10. Pareto front for six-element Yagi-Uda antenna found by GDE3

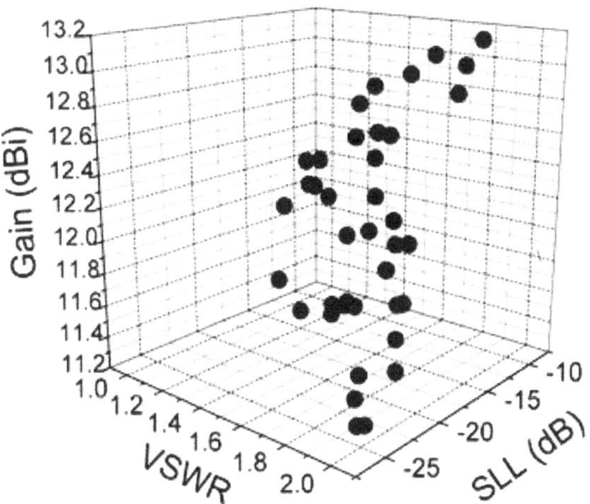

Table 1. Design parameters and results found by GDE3 for a six-element Yagi-Uda antenna

	1		2		3	
Element	L(λ)	s(λ)	L(λ)	s(λ)	L(λ)	s(λ)
1	0.241	-	0.240	-	0.238	-
2	0.222	0.128	0.225	0.329	0.230	0.295
3	0.221	0.104	0.219	0.292	0.221	0.238
4	0.217	0.268	0.215	0.303	0.214	0.307
5	0.213	0.361	0.208	0.383	0.206	0.383
6	0.215	0.342	0.213	0.386	0.208	0.393
Gain(dBi)	12.72		13.00		12.88	
Z(Ω)	49.67 - j5.49		30.99-j3.22		29.16 + j1.97	
VSWR	1.12		1.62		1.72	
SLL(dB)	-12.02		-12.09		-15.50	

have in average lower SLL values than the results found by NSGA-II. In terms of gain and VSWR both algorithms produce similar results. The three designs found by GDE3 have high gain values. Design 1 outperforms the designs from (Jones & Joines, 1997) and (Baskar, Alphones, Suganthan, & Liang, 2005) in terms of gain and sidelobe level values. Design 2 presents the higher gain than all (13dBi). For this case there is tradeoff between gain and VSWR value. Design 3 provides the lowest SLL (-15.50dB) of all but the VSWR deteriorates at the value of 1.72. The average execution time for GDE3 and NSGA-II is 1790.63 and 1804.62 seconds respectively. The total number of objective function evaluations is again 40,000. In (Kuwahara, 2005) for the six-element case a total number of 300,000 objective is required.

Figure 11. Pareto front for six-element Yagi-Uda antenna found by NSGA-II

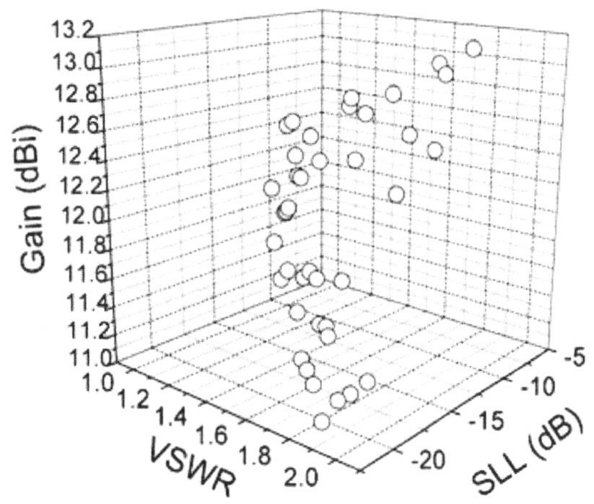

FUTURE RESEARCH DIRECTIONS

The research domain of multi-objective evolutionary algorithms is growing rapidly. The application of MOEAs to antenna and microwave design problems introduces new challenges regarding performance and computational cost. Therefore, new research directions have to be explored. A current and growing research trend in evolutionary algorithms is their hybridization with local optimizers. Such MOEAs and their application to electromagnetic design will be part of our future

Figure 12. Radiation patterns of six-element Yagi-Uda antenna design cases found by GDE3

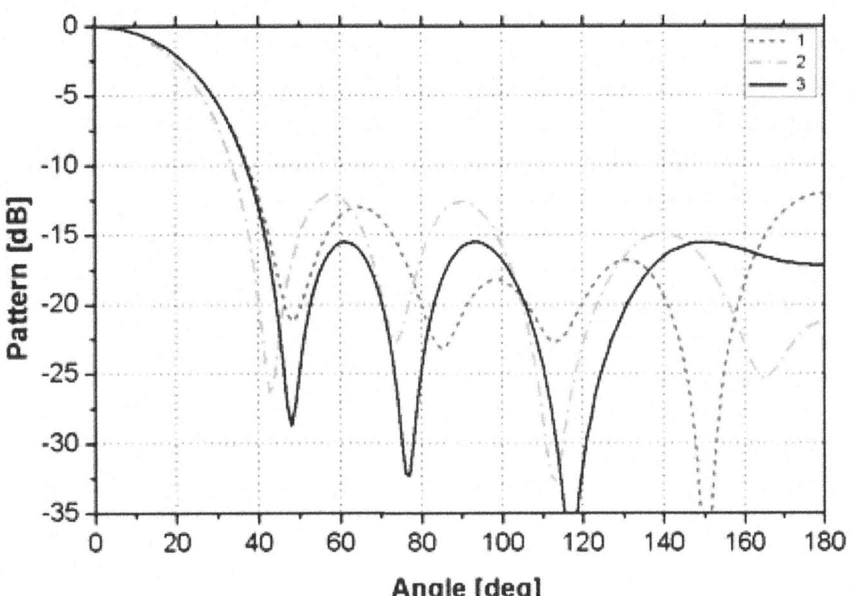

work. Parallelization techniques that use several CPUs or multicore programming can also be used in order to reduce computational cost.

Furthermore, we plan to explore the applicability of other state-of-the-art MOEAs to antenna and microwave design problems such as the MOEA/D (H. Li & Zhang, 2009), the multi-objective evolutionary algorithms based on summation of normalized objective values and diversified selection (SNOV-DS) (Qu & Suganthan, 2010) and the recently proposed new MOPSO (S. Z. Zhao & Suganthan, 2010).

CONCLUSION

Multi-objective evolutionary algorithms can be used successfully to solve antenna and microwave design problems. MOPSO and MOPSO-fs are multi-objective PSO algorithms, which have been compared against NSGA-II. MOPSO and MOPSO-fs are both quite efficient and may produce better results in general than NSGA-II. From the absorber design problem, it is evident that both MOPSO and NSGA-II can produce the Pareto front. MOPSO and MOPSO-fs compared with NSGA-II can find similar or slightly better results depending on the design case. The main advantage of the PSO algorithms is that both require for the same number of iterations and population size less computational time than NSGA-II.

GDE3 is a multi-objective DE algorithm that has proven to be very efficient. It is obvious from the OLRR filter design that GDE3 can produce better results for the same population size and for the same number of generations compared with NSGA-II. MOPSO and MOPSO-fs. One of the GDE3 advantages is the fact that requires less computational load than NSGA-II. This is due to the fact the population size that is ranked after a generation is usually less than the one required by NSGA-II. MOPSO and MOPSO-fs are both outperformed clearly by GDE3 for this case.

The antenna design cases found by the GDE3 outperform these reported in the literature. The biggest advantage of using GDE3 for Yagi-Uda antenna design is probably the fact that it can handle efficiently this tri-objective problem subject to any number of design constraints using a multi-objective approach. It must also be pointed out that GDE3 and NSGA-II require less number of objective function evaluations for the same Yagi-Uda design than the Pareto GA (Kuwahara, 2005).

The above presented examples have indicated the advantages of a multi-objective approach for solving complex antenna and microwave design problems. The practical designs subject to several constraints presented in this chapter show the applicability of using MOEAs to electromagnetics. All algorithms can be combined with a numerical method. In such cases where computational time plays an important role, fast convergence is an additional requirement. These algorithms can be easily expanded to other microwave and antenna design problems.

REFERENCES

Baskar, S., Alphones, A., Suganthan, P. M., & Liang, J. J. (2005). Design of Yagi-Uda antennas using comprehensive learning particle swarm optimisation. *IEE Proceedings. Microwaves, Antennas and Propagation*, *152*, 340–346. doi:10.1049/ip-map:20045087

Bemani, M., & Nikmehr, S. (2009). A novel wide-band microstrip Yagi-Uda array antenna for WLAN applications. *Progress in Electromagnetics Research B*, *16*, 389–406. doi:10.2528/PIERB09053101

Boeringer, D. W., & Werner, D. H. (2006). Bezier representations for the multiobjective optimization of conformal array amplitude weights. *IEEE Transactions on Antennas and Propagation*, *54*(7), 1964–1970. doi:10.1109/TAP.2006.877173

Chamaani, S., Mirtaheri, S. A., & Abrishamian, M. S. (2011). Improvement of time and frequency domain performance of antipodal Vivaldi antenna using multi-objective particle swarm optimization. *IEEE Transactions on Antennas and Propagation*, *59*(5), 1738–1742. doi:10.1109/TAP.2011.2122290

Chamaani, S., Mirtaheri, S. A., Teshnehlab, M., Shoorehdeli, M. A., & Seydi, V. (2008). Modified multi-objective particle swarm optimization for electromagnetic absorber design. *Progress in Electromagnetics Research-Pier*, *79*, 353–366. doi:10.2528/PIER07101702

Chen, C. A., & Cheng, D. K. (1975). Optimum element lengths for Yagi-Uda arrays. *IEEE Transactions on Antennas and Propagation*, *AP-23*(1), 8–15. doi:10.1109/TAP.1975.1141001

Cheng, D. K. (1991). Gain optimization for Yagi-Uda arrays. *IEEE Antennas and Propagation Magazine*, *33*(3), 42–45. doi:10.1109/74.88220

Cheng, D. K., & Chen, C. A. (1973). Optimum element spacings for Yagi-Uda arrays. *IEEE Transactions on Antennas and Propagation*, *AP-21*(5), 615–623. doi:10.1109/TAP.1973.1140551

Choo, H., Rogers, R. L., & Ling, H. (2005). Design of electrically small wire antennas using a Pareto genetic algorithm. *IEEE Transactions on Antennas and Propagation*, *53*(3), 1038–1046. doi:10.1109/TAP.2004.842404

Chou, H. T., Hung, K. L., & Chen, C. Y. (2009). Utilization of a yagi antenna director array to synthesize a shaped radiation pattern for optimum coverage in wireless communications. *Journal of Electromagnetic Waves and Applications*, *23*(7), 851–861. doi:10.1163/156939309788355298

Chu-Yu, C., & Cheng-Ying, H. (2006). A simple and effective method for microstrip dual-band filters design. *IEEE Microwave and Wireless Components Letters*, *16*(5), 246–248. doi:10.1109/LMWC.2006.873584

Clerc, M. (1999). *The swarm and the queen: towards a deterministic and adaptive particle swarm optimization.* Paper presented at the 1999 Congress on Evolutionary Computation, CEC 99 Washington, DC.

Coello Coello, C. A., Pulido, G. T., & Lechuga, M. S. (2004). Handling multiple objectives with particle swarm optimization. *IEEE Transactions on Evolutionary Computation*, *8*(3), 256–279. doi:10.1109/TEVC.2004.826067

Das, S., Abraham, A., & Konar, A. (2008). Particle swarm optimization and differential evolution algorithms: Technical analysis, applications and hybridization perspectives. In Liu, Y. L., Sun, A. S., Lim, E. P. L., Loh, H. T. L., & Lu, W. F. L. (Eds.), *Studies in computational intelligence* (*Vol. 116*, pp. 1–38). doi:10.1007/978-3-540-78297-1_1

David, W. C., & Joshua, D. K. (2003). *No free lunch and free leftovers theorems for multiobjective optimisation problems.* Paper presented at the 2nd International Conference on Evolutionary Multi-Criterion Optimization, EMO 03, Faro, Portugal.

De Jong Van Coevorden, C. M., Garcia, S. G., Pantoja, M. F., Bretones, A. R., & Martin, R. G. (2005). Microstrip-patch array design using a multiobjective GA. *IEEE Antennas and Wireless Propagation Letters*, *4*(1), 100–103. doi:10.1109/LAWP.2005.845907

Deb, K., Pratap, A., Agarwal, S., & Meyarivan, T. (2002). A fast and elitist multiobjective genetic algorithm: NSGA-II. *IEEE Transactions on Evolutionary Computation*, *6*(2), 182–197. doi:10.1109/4235.996017

Deb, K., Thiele, L., Laumanns, M., & Zitzler, E. (2005). Scalable test problems for evolutionary multiobjective optimization. In *Evolutionary Multiobjective Optimization* (pp. 105-145).

FEKO. (2003). *User's manunal, FEKO suite 5.2.* Retrieved from www.feko.info

Goudos, S. K., & Sahalos, J. N. (2006). Microwave absorber optimal design using multi-objective particle swarm optimization. *Microwave and Optical Technology Letters*, *48*(8), 1553–1558. doi:10.1002/mop.21727

Goudos, S. K., & Sahalos, J. N. (2010). Pareto optimal microwave filter design using multiobjective differential evolution. *IEEE Transactions on Antennas and Propagation*, *58*(1), 132–144. doi:10.1109/TAP.2009.2032100

Goudos, S. K., Siakavara, K., Vafiadis, E. E., & Sahalos, J. N. (2010). Pareto optimal Yagi-Uda antenna design using multi-objective differential evolution. *Progress in Electromagnetics Research*, *105*, 231–251. doi:10.2528/PIER10052302

Goudos, S. K., Zaharis, Z. D., Baltzis, K. B., Hilas, C. S., & Sahalos, J. N. (2009, June). *A comparative study of particle swarm optimization and differential evolution on radar absorbing materials design for EMC applications.* Paper presented at the International Symposium on Electromagnetic Compatibility - EMC Europe, 2009

Goudos, S. K., Zaharis, Z. D., Kampitaki, D. G., Rekanos, I. T., & Hilas, C. S. (2009). Pareto optimal design of dual-band base station antenna arrays using multi-objective particle swarm optimization with fitness sharing. *IEEE Transactions on Magnetics*, *45*(3), 1522–1525. doi:10.1109/TMAG.2009.2012695

Goudos, S. K., Zaharis, Z. D., Salazar-Lechuga, M., Lazaridis, P. I., & Gallion, P. B. (2007). Dielectric filter optimal design suitable for microwave communications by using multiobjective evolutionary algorithms. *Microwave and Optical Technology Letters*, *49*(10), 2324–2329. doi:10.1002/mop.22755

Hoorfar, A., Zhu, J., & Nelatury, S. (2003). Electromagnetic optimization using a mixed-parameter self-adaptive evolutionary algorithm. *Microwave and Optical Technology Letters*, *39*(4), 267–271. doi:10.1002/mop.11187

Hosung, C., Hao, L., & Liang, C. S. (2008). On a class of planar absorbers with periodic square resistive patches. *IEEE Transactions on Antennas and Propagation*, *56*(7), 2127–2130. doi:10.1109/TAP.2008.924766

Huang, T., & Sanagavarapu Mohan, A. (March 2007). A microparticle swarm optimizer for the reconstruction of microwave images. *IEEE Transactions on Antennas and Propagation*, *55*(3 I), 568-576.

Jiang, L., Cui, J., Shi, L., & Li, X. (2009). Pareto optimal design of multilayer microwave absorbers for wide-angle incidence using genetic algorithms. *IET Microwaves Antennas & Propagation*, *3*(4), 572–579. doi:10.1049/iet-map.2008.0059

Jones, E. A., & Joines, W. T. (1997). Design of yagi-uda antennas using genetic algorithms. *IEEE Transactions on Antennas and Propagation*, *45*(9), 1386–1392. doi:10.1109/8.623128

Kennedy, J., & Eberhart, R. (1995). *Particle swarm optimization.* Paper presented at the IEEE International Conference on Neural Networks, Piscataway, NJ.

Kennedy, J., & Eberhart, R. C. (1997). *Discrete binary version of the particle swarm algorithm.* Paper presented at the IEEE International Conference on Systems, Man and Cybernetics.

Koulouridis, S., Psychoudakis, D., & Volakis, J. L. (2007). Multiobjective optimal antenna design based on volumetric material optimization. *IEEE Transactions on Antennas and Propagation*, *55*(3), 594–603. doi:10.1109/TAP.2007.891551

Koziel, S., & Bandler, J. W. (2008). Space mapping with multiple coarse models for optimization of microwave components. *IEEE Microwave and Wireless Components Letters*, *18*(1), 1–3. doi:10.1109/LMWC.2007.911969

Kukkonen, S., & Deb, K. (2006). A fast and effective method for pruning of non-dominated solutions in many-objective problems. *Lecture Notes in Computer Science*, *4193*, 553–562. doi:10.1007/11844297_56

Kukkonen, S., Jangam, S. R., & Chakraborti, N. (2007). *Solving the molecular sequence alignment problem with generalized differential evolution 3 (GDE3).* Paper presented at the IEEE Symposium on Computational Intelligence in Multicriteria Decision Making.

Kukkonen, S., & Lampinen, J. (2005). *GDE3: The third evolution step of generalized differential evolution.* Paper presented at 2005 IEEE Congress on Evolutionary Computation, (CEC 2005).

Kukkonen, S., & Lampinen, J. (2006). *An empirical study of control parameters for the third version of generalized differential evolution (GDE3).* Paper presented at the IEEE Congress on Evolutionary Computation, CEC 2006.

Kukkonen, S., & Lampinen, J. (2007). *Performance assessment of generalized differential evolution 3 (GDE3) with a given set of problems.* Paper presented at the IEEE Congress on Evolutionary Computation, 2007. CEC 2007.

Kuwahara, Y. (2005). Multiobjective optimization design of Yagi-Uda antenna. *IEEE Transactions on Antennas and Propagation*, *53*(6), 1984–1992. doi:10.1109/TAP.2005.848501

Lee, Y. H., Cahill, B. J., Porter, S. J., & Marvin, A. C. (2004). A novel evolutionary learning technique for multi-objective array antenna optimization. *Progress in Electromagnetics Research-Pier*, *48*, 125–144. doi:10.2528/PIER04012202

Li, H., & Zhang, Q. (2009). Multiobjective optimization problems with complicated pareto sets, MOEA/ D and NSGA-II. *IEEE Transactions on Evolutionary Computation*, *13*(2), 284–302. doi:10.1109/TEVC.2008.925798

Li, J. Y., & Guo, J. L. (2009). Optimization technique using differential evolution for Yagi-Uda antennas. *Journal of Electromagnetic Waves and Applications*, *23*(4), 449–461. doi:10.1163/156939309787612356

Marler, R. T., & Arora, J. S. (2004). Survey of multi-objective optimization methods for engineering. *Structural and Multidisciplinary Optimization*, *26*(6), 369–395. doi:10.1007/s00158-003-0368-6

Mezura-Montes, E., Velazquez-Reyes, J., & Coello Coello, C. A. (2006). *A comparative study of differential evolution variants for global optimization.* Paper presented at the GECCO 2006 - Genetic and Evolutionary Computation Conference, Seattle, WA.

Michielssen, E., Sajer, J.-M., Ranjithant, S., & Mittra, R. (1993). Design of lightweight, broad-band microwave absorbers using genetic algorithms. *IEEE Transactions on Microwave Theory and Techniques*, *41*(6-7), 1024–1030. doi:10.1109/22.238519

Misra, I. S., Chakrabarty, R. S., & Mangaraj, B. B. (2006). Design, analysis and optimization of V-dipole and its three-element Yagi-Uda array. *Progress in Electromagnetics Research*, *66*, 137–156. doi:10.2528/PIER06102604

Pal, S., Das, S., & Basak, A. (2011). Design of time-modulated linear arrays with a multi-objective optimization approach. *Progress in Electromagnetics Research B*, *23*, 83–107. doi:10.2528/PIERB10052401

Pal, S., Das, S., Basak, A., & Suganthan, P. N. (2011). Synthesis of difference patterns for Monopulse antennas with optimal combination of array-size and number of subarrays - A multi-objective optimization approach. *Progress in Electromagnetics Research B*, *21*, 257–280.

Pal, S., Qu, B., Das, S., & Suganthan, P. N. (2010). Linear antenna array synthesis with constrained multi-objective differential evolution. *Progress in Electromagnetics Research B*, *21*, 87–111.

Panduro, M. A., Brizuela, C. A., Balderas, L. I., & Acosta, D. A. (2009). A comparison of genetic algorithms, particle swarm optimization and the differential evolution method for the design of scannable circular antenna arrays. *Progress in Electromagnetics Research B*, *13*, 171–186. doi:10.2528/PIERB09011308

Petko, J. S., & Werner, D. H. (2008). The pareto optimization of ultrawideband polyfractal arrays. *IEEE Transactions on Antennas and Propagation*, *56*(1), 97–107. doi:10.1109/TAP.2007.913147

Petko, J. S., & Werner, D. H. (2011). Pareto optimization of thinned planar arrays with elliptical mainbeams and low sidelobe levels. *IEEE Transactions on Antennas and Propagation*, *59*(5), 1748–1751. doi:10.1109/TAP.2011.2122212

Qu, B. Y., & Suganthan, P. N. (2010). Multi-objective evolutionary algorithms based on the summation of normalized objectives and diversified selection. *Information Sciences*, *180*(17), 3170–3181. doi:10.1016/j.ins.2010.05.013

Ramos, R. M., Saldanha, R. R., Takahashi, R. H. C., & Moreira, F. J. S. (2003). The real-biased multiobjective genetic algorithm and its application to the design of wire antennas. *IEEE Transactions on Magnetics, 39*(3 I), 1329-1332.

Rattan, M., Patterh, M. S., & Sohi, B. S. (2008). Optimization of Yagi-Uda antenna using simulated annealing. *Journal of Electromagnetic Waves and Applications*, *22*(2-3), 291–299. doi:10.1163/156939308784160749

Rekanos, I. T. (2007, March 19-23). *Conducting Scatterer reconstruction using differential evolution and particle swarm optimization.* Paper presented at the 23rd Annual Review of Progress in Applied Computational Electromagnetics (ACES), Verona, Italy.

Rekanos, I. T. (2008). Shape reconstruction of a perfectly conducting scatterer using differential evolution and particle swarm optimization. *IEEE Transactions on Geoscience and Remote Sensing*, *46*(7), 1967–1974. doi:10.1109/TGRS.2008.916635

Salazar-Lechuga, M., & Rowe, J. E. (2005). *Particle swarm optimization and fitness sharing to solve multi-objective optimization problems.* Paper presented at the Congress on Evolutionary Computation.

Semnani, A., Kamyab, M., & Rekanos, I. T. (2009, Oct.). Reconstruction of one-dimensional dielectric scatterers using differential evolution and particle swarm optimization. *IEEE Geoscience and Remote Sensing Letters*, *6*(4), 671–675. doi:10.1109/LGRS.2009.2023246

Storn, R. (2008). Differential evolution research - Trends and open questions. *Studies in Computational Intelligence*, *143*, 1–31. doi:10.1007/978-3-540-68830-3_1

Storn, R., & Price, K. (1995). *Differential evolution—A simple and efficient adaptive scheme for global optimization over continuous spaces*. Tech. Rep. TR-95-012, from http://citeseer.ist.psu.edu/article/storn95differential.html

Storn, R., & Price, K. (1997). Differential evolution - A simple and efficient heuristic for global optimization over continuous spaces. *Journal of Global Optimization*, *11*(4), 341–359. doi:10.1023/A:1008202821328

Sun, B. H., Zhou, S. G., Wei, Y. F., & Liu, Q. Z. (2010). Modified two-element Yagi-uda antenna with tunable beams. *Progress in Electromagnetics Research*, *100*, 175–187. doi:10.2528/PIER09111501

Tan, K. C. (2008). CEC 2007 Conference report. *IEEE Computational Intelligence Magazine*, *3*(2), 72-73.

Teisbaek, H. B., & Jakobsen, K. B. (2009). Koch-fractal Yagi-Uda antenna. *Journal of Electromagnetic Waves and Applications*, *23*(2-3), 149–160. doi:10.1163/156939309787604337

Venkatarayalu, N. V., & Ray, T. (2003). Single and multi-objective design of Yagi-Uda antennas using computational intelligence. *Congress on Evolutionary Computing, 2*, 1237-1242.

Venkatarayalu, N. V., & Ray, T. (2004). Optimum design of Yagi-Uda antennas using computational intelligence. *IEEE Transactions on Antennas and Propagation*, *52*(7), 1811–1818. doi:10.1109/TAP.2004.831338

Venkatarayalu, N. V., Ray, T., & Gan, Y. B. (2005). Multilayer dielectric filter design using a multiobjective evolutionary algorithm. *IEEE Transactions on Antennas and Propagation*, *53*(11), 3625–3632. doi:10.1109/TAP.2005.858565

Vesterstrom, J., & Thomsen, R. (2004). *A comparative study of differential evolution, particle swarm optimization, and evolutionary algorithms on numerical benchmark problems.* Paper presented at the Congress on Evolutionary Computation, CEC2004 Portland, USA.

Weile, D. S., Michielssen, E., & Goldberg, D. E. (1996). Genetic algorithm design of Pareto optimal broadband microwave absorbers. *IEEE Transactions on Electromagnetic Compatibility*, *38*(3), 518–525. doi:10.1109/15.536085

Wolpert, D. H., & Macready, W. G. (1997). No free lunch theorems for optimization. *IEEE Transactions on Evolutionary Computation*, *1*(1), 67–82. doi:10.1109/4235.585893

Yeung, S. H., Man, K. F., Luk, K. M., & Chan, C. H. (2008). A trapeizform u-slot folded patch feed antenna design optimized with jumping genes evolutionary algorithm. *IEEE Transactions on Antennas and Propagation*, *56*(2), 571–577. doi:10.1109/TAP.2007.915473

Zhao, S. Z., & Suganthan, P. N. (2010). Two-lbests based multi-objective particle swarm optimizer. *Engineering Optimization*, *43*(1).

KEY TERMS AND DEFINITIONS

Finite Element Method (FEM): is a numerical technique for finding approximate solutions of partial differential equations (PDE) as well as integral equations. In electromagnetics FEM is applicable to the modeling of electrically large or inhomogeneous dielectric bodies.

Genetic Algorithms: A stochastic population-based global optimization technique that mimics the process of natural evolution.

Hybrid MoM/FEM: A hybrid technique that features full coupling between metallic wires and surfaces in the MoM region and heterogeneous dielectric bodies in the FEM region.

Method of Moments (MoM): A method for solving electromagnetic field problems using a full wave solution of Maxwell's integral equations in the frequency domain. The MoM is applicable to problems involving currents on metallic and dielectric structures and radiation in free space.

Sidelobe Level (SLL): The ratio, usually expressed in decibels (dB), of the amplitude at the peak of the main lobe to the amplitude at the peak of a side lobe.

Chapter 7
Using Computational Intelligence for Improved Teleoperation over Wireless Network

Salman H. Khan
National University of Sciences & Technology (NUST), Pakistan

Arsalan H. Khan
Northwestern Polytechnical University (NPU), P.R. China

Zeashan H. Khan
Center for Emerging Sciences, Engineering and Technology (CESET), Pakistan

ABSTRACT

The role of computational intelligence techniques in applied sciences and engineering is becoming popular today. It is essential because the autonomous engineering applications require intelligent decision in real time in order to achieve the desired goal. This chapter discusses some of the approaches to demonstrate various applications of computational intelligence in dependable networked control systems and a case study of teleoperation over wireless network. The results have shown that computational intelligence algorithms can be successfully implemented on an embedded application to offer an improved online performance. The different approaches have been compared and could be chosen as per application requirements.

INTRODUCTION

Computational intelligence (CI) has its roots in close observation of the natural phenomenon and it combines a set of fuzzy, adaptive and evolutionary methods that are intelligent enough to learn from experience to effectively solve problems. CI is enabling new ways to develop intelligent systems that will one-day outclass humans in self learning, model development and prediction. The earlier methods of artificial intelligence, AI (or, GOFAI *i.e.,* Good Old-Fashioned Artificial Intelligence, as per the term introduced by John Haugeland, professor of philosophy at the University of

DOI: 10.4018/978-1-4666-1830-5.ch007

Figure 1. Unilateral teleoperation

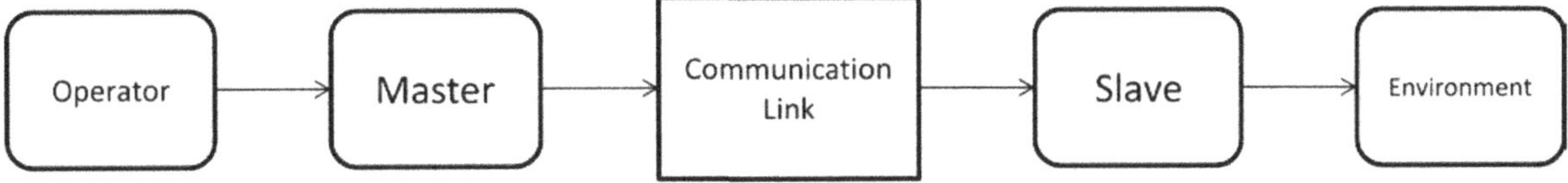

Figure 2. Bilateral teleoperation

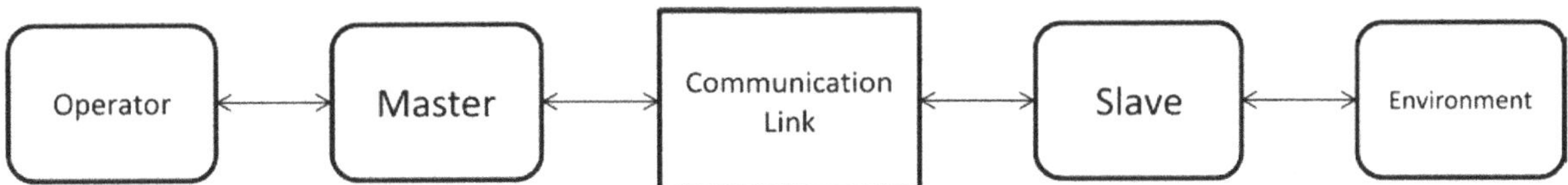

Chicago) were logic based approaches that have evolution from top to bottom (Guturu, 2008). In contrast, the modern CI methods generally have bottom-to-top where model is built from unstructured beginning. They use stochastic or heuristic optimization algorithms and strategies such as Fuzzy Systems, Neural Networks, Evolutionary Computation, Rough sets, Hybrid methods, Swarm Intelligence, Symbolic Machine learning, Statistical data mining, Artificial Immune Systems, etc.

Teleoperation includes Monitoring, Supervision, Control, Diagnosis and it deals with the interaction between Network/Communication and Control. It may be considered as a special case of network controlled systems (NCS) with specific terminology of master and slave subsystems sharing control information over a communication network. The network controlled systems (NCS) are those systems where at least one of the subsystem i.e. sensor, actuator and controller communicate over a network (Khan et al, 2010). For NCS, the quality of service (QoS) of the network is of utmost importance which is defined as the capability to differentiate between different traffic classes (or users) as compared to other traffic (or users) (Park, 2005). It also takes into account the parameters of data link e.g. signal to noise ratio (SNR), bit error rate (BER) and packet loss rate (PLR), jitter, and network utilization (throughput), which gives a measure of successful delivery of data packets. Some of the parameters of network QoS are shared with the objective QoS. Quality of control (QoC) in NCS is referred to as the desired performance delivered by the closed-loop control system (robot in our case). Various parameters of QoC include stability, response time, steady-state performance, etc. among which stability is of premier importance in QoC analysis (Mechraoui et al, 2009).

The network based teleoperation is known to be of several types. This includes unilateral teleoperation where the control information/command moves unidirectional as can be seen in Figure 1. The other possibility is to exchange some data between the master/slave stations as is the case of bilateral teleoperation. This may be a visual feedback via camera to assist operator at the master station as in Figure 2.

In the third type, force feedback is provided to the operator so that he can feel the environment. The force feedback is usually coupled with visual information as seen in Figure 3 below.

In networked communication, obtaining a model of network dynamics is a difficult task. Therefore, mostly supervised or unsupervised learning (or training) based techniques are considered for these measurement vectors to build a classifier or an estimator. Unsupervised learning is suitable for the large data sets and more complex models than with the supervised learning. Thus,

Figure 3. Bilateral teleoperation with force feedback

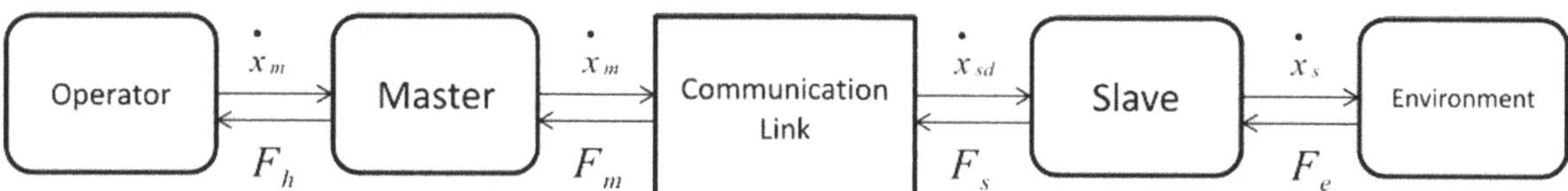

Figure 4. Hardware/software architecture of NeCS-Car benchmark

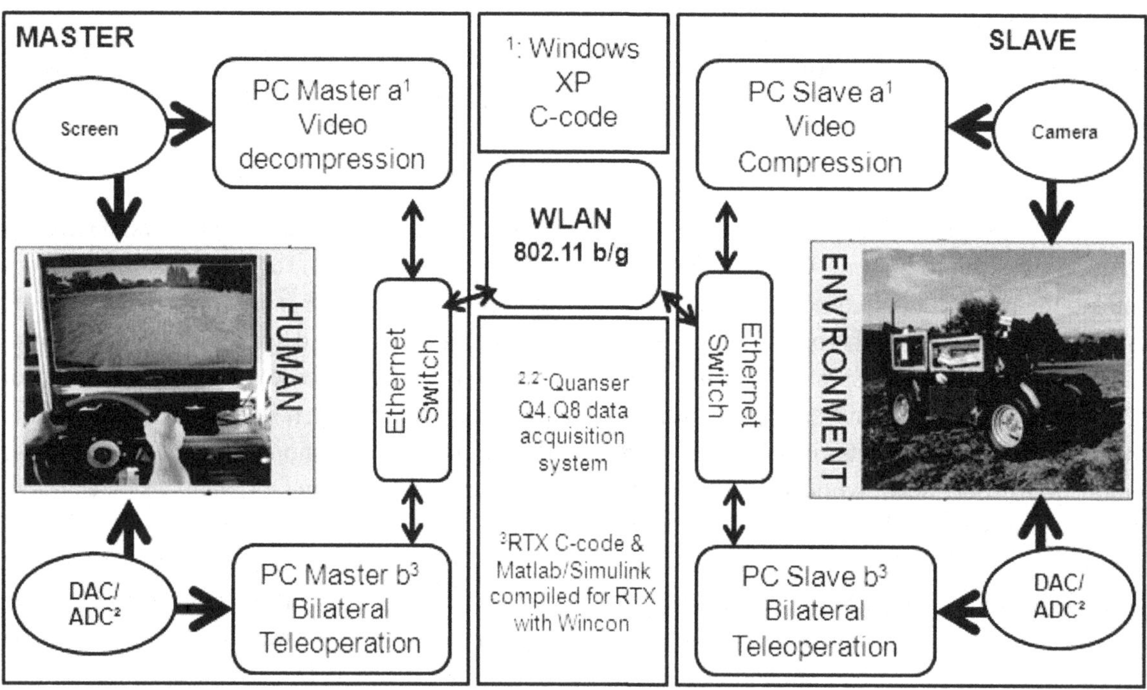

in the unsupervised learning, no classes are defined a priori, and the methodology can work for models with deep hierarchies, e.g. Independent component analysis (ICA), Principle component analysis (PCA) and clustering algorithms are unsupervised methods (Xu, 1994). In supervised learning, true class or parameter of the sample is used as opposed to the unsupervised learning (Cristianini et al. 2000). In addition, the supervised methods usually utilize off-line learning in order to develop a model. Some of the examples include fuzzy logic, neural networks, adaptive neural networks, support vector machines (SVM) etc (Dote, 1998), (Zhu, 2005). Since, the network QoS can be classified based on the classes defined by supervised training of off-line data, only supervised learning methods are discussed here for the classification of wireless network quality of service to be used for our adaptive scheme.

The current focus is the application of networked teleoperation (NT) of a drive-by-wireless benchmark where the teleoperation data is exchanged over the communication network. The overall system is shown in Figure 4. A remote driver takes control action based on the video received from the slave vehicle. The embedded PC hosts 2 operating systems, each having their own network card and can be considered as 2 separate PCs for video and the control system. There are two networks involve in the communication ar-

Figure 5. A typical profile of delay and packet loss over Ethernet

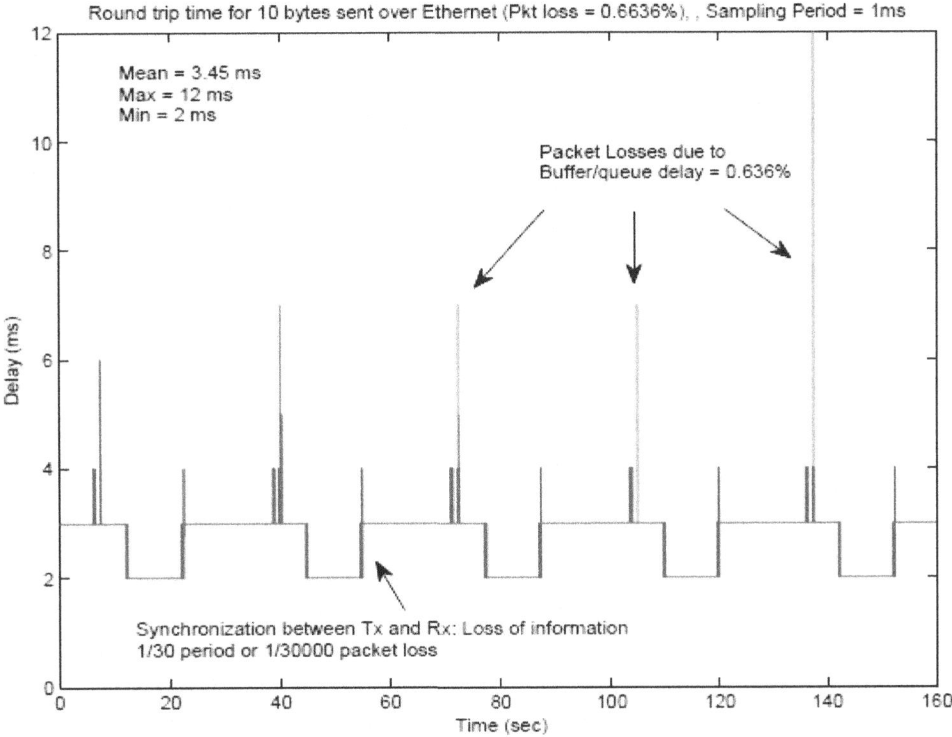

chitecture as indicated in the block diagram. The embedded wired network is Ethernet on each side which is connected to WLAN via a 100 Mbps switch for wireless communication which permits mobility in the teleoperation. There are two network flows, the control flow (for time critical date e.g. speed, position, brake, etc) is sent over UDP, implemented by RTX. While the other one is non-real time video flow over TCP. The packet size for control information is 83 bytes (125 bytes with header) of data sent with a sampling rate of 1000 Hz (1 Mbps). About 20% of the traffic sent over UDP is lost.

Figure 5 shows a typical profile of packet loss and delay over Ethernet, as captured during experimentation. The mean delay observed is 3.5 ms over the Ethernet. However, as the data is routed through Ethernet-WLAN-Ethernet loop, more delays will be introduced and packet loss rate will augment. For video data, both TCP/IP or UDP/IP protocols and different compression algorithms were tested. Two IP cameras with MPEG-4 compression for real-time video can also be connected to the slave Ethernet switch to generate traffic perturbations (data rate of 3.1 Mbps over TCP/IP measured while driving) over the network. For video data, TCP is used to ensure successful transmission of large packets as a little loss of an MPEG compressed stream sequence can result into a number of missing frames, which affects the video quality. The video data is about 40KB sent every 40ms i.e. approx 10 Mbps after compression at the mobile platform. For the on-board camera mounted on NeCS Car, we used UDP packets coded in bmp format for non-real-time video, where we can vary the video data rate (hence the quality of the frame where packet loss generates black bands in the received frames). The variation of frame rate (FPS) to degrade or improve the video quality is not addressed here for simplicity. For control data reconstruction due to packet loss, our approach is similar to (Hirche,

2005) where scattering transform energy is exchanged to continuously monitor the passivity condition in order to choose between the HLS and Zeroing.

It seems that the overall QoS in NT applications is rather a complex phenomenon which takes into account the hybrid parameters including systems dynamics, communication imperfections, human perception, haptics, environmental effects and nonlinearities of physical world in order to deliver certain quality of telepresence to the teleoperation supervisor. We need to take into account the control performance, i.e. quality of control (QoC) as well as network QoS. For teleoperation performance, weighted errors can be used as a measurement of tracking performance (Dede et al. 2007).

We have tested fuzzy, neural and SVM based QoS classifiers to compare the performance in real time. For fuzzy classifier, triangular and trapezoidal functions membership functions are used as these are the most suitable ones for the real time operation (Kasiolas et al. 1999). Also, the later implementation would be much easier with these functions. Since, the network conditions may change rapidly, we need to sample the input variables quite often, so the whole fuzzy block has to be computationally efficient (Li et al. 2009). Therefore, the Sugeno-Type Fuzzy Inference with constant membership functions for the output are used (Pirmez et al., 2007). Since some rules may be redundant it should be possible to reduce the rule base matrix with the singular value decomposition (SVD).

During the development of the QoS classifier module, some alternative designs were considered e.g. Adaptive Neuro-Fuzzy Inference System (ANFIS) wherein a simple neural network replaces the strict membership functions and rules. This approach works similar to that of the classic neural networks. Since, the ANFIS module has to be taught with quite large input/output data sets and the QoS output data can't be measured before hand, this method is highly dependent on the original fuzzy classifier and can be used to simplify the initial FIS (Munir et al. 2004). Thus, output data from the original QoS module (with classic FIS) is used during the learning and testing processes. Artificial Neural Network (ANN) simulates the learning process of human brain with an advantage of modeling the complex nonlinearities in the data series. ANN is mostly utilized to compare with the ANFIS in order to find the smallest network that could solve the QoS estimation problem (Din et al., 2008). The training data for the ANN is composed of the known input parameters and output/target values calculated with FIS, just like for the ANFIS. A feed forward network with a backward propagation is used in our case.

The support vector machines (SVM) classification is known as an optimal method as it transforms the input vector sequence into theoretically infinite feature space (Xie et al, 2009). The essential idea of SVM approximation is to map data into a high dimensional space by a nonlinear mapping and then performing linear regression in the feature space. In general, SVM gives better results than ANFIS as it minimizes the structural risk as compared to the empirical risk minimized by ANFIS (Feng et al., 2006).

BACKGROUND AND PREVIOUS WORK

Teleoperation has diversified application area including undersea, nuclear, metal processing, medicine, aerospace, education and entertainment industries. Some interesting examples are Puma paint project, Telerobotic system and Lunokhod, etc. Puma paint allows web users to virtually draw paintings on computer and the PUMA 750 robot draws them on real canvas (Stein et al. 2005). Telerobot is made by Telelabs, University of Western Australia, which allows students to perform experiments in far away labs through internet (Rae, 2004). Lunokhod was a soviet unmanned ground vehicle (UGV) that operated

Figure 6. Bilateral teleoperation based on scattering variables

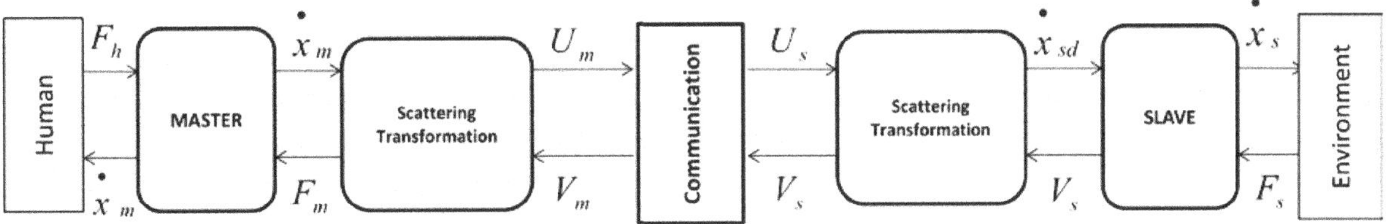

Figure 7. Bilateral teleoperation with position control

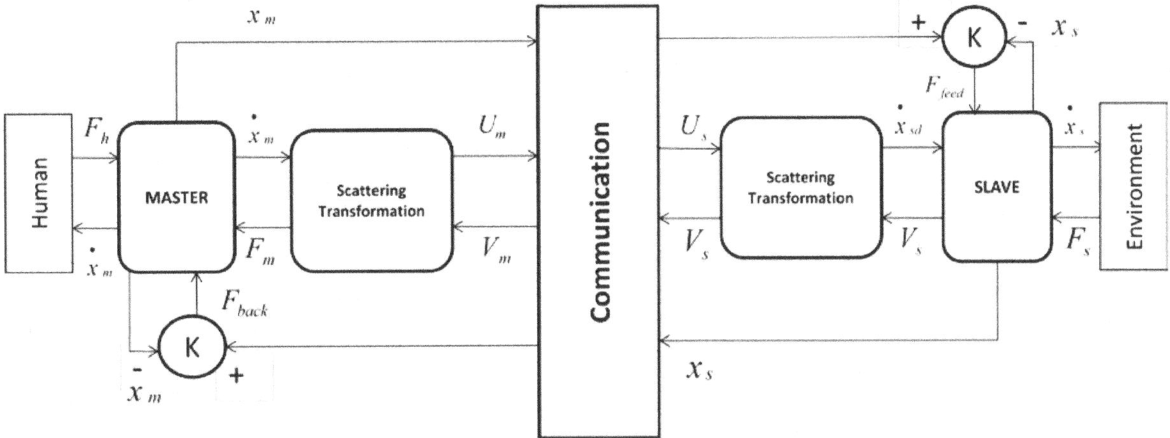

on moon and covered 10,540m in eleven months (Bleicher, 2010).

It is also important to understand the teleoperation terminology and various types as it is used in different applications with different objectives. In mini-invasive surgery, position control is needed with force feedback sensing to provide a relative feel to distant surgeon.

There are many approaches in teleoperation where different nonlinear, adaptive and robust controllers have been designed to address different types of application needs. We are considering the passivity based teleoperation controller as introduced by (Anderson et al., 1989) and shown in Figure 6 above. It is evident that the force and velocity commands are translated into scattering variables Um,Vm and Us,Vs. Where 'm' stands for master and 's' for slave variables. Later on, the position control is added by (Chopra et al., 2003) as shown in Figure 7. The position loop is added with a gain *K* on the position error. As the choice of controller is application dependent and the current focus is the application of computational intelligence methods to the networked teleoperation, we are deliberately restricting ourselves to this passivity based position control architecture for the stability and tracking of master commands.

The introduction of networked communication in remote teleoperation introduces a QoS dependent factor in closed-loop control performance. Hence, QoC is dependent on the quality of wireless network in wireless NCS. (Mechraoui et.al, 2010) tackled the co-design problem of wireless NCS with distributed Bayesian network approach. The Bayesian Network defines the QoS model and incorporates its effects on QoC. This Bayesian model diagnoses any QoS/QoC problems in wireless network (Horizontal Handoff) as well as on board controller is reconfigured so that the control performance is not compromised. As a result of this reconfiguration wireless network adapts itself to dynamic requirements as diagnosed by the Bayesian Net. Similar approaches will be discussed later so that a co-conception and co-design methodology can be established (Khan et al, 2011).

QoS Centric Intelligent Decisions

In multimedia communication, as employed in robotic teleoperation, call/connection admission control (CAC) is a mechanism to accept or reject the new call/connection request depending on whether the resources required for new calls can be reserved while maintaining the desired level of QoS of ongoing calls. Traditional approaches for CAC in multimedia applications were based on various parameters such as bandwidth requirement of various links, maximum allowable packet loss probability, network traffic load etc (Guturu, 2008). But these methods were unable to maintain acceptable levels of QoS under severe traffic and congestion problems. To solve this problem various CI based techniques are reported in literature. (Ahn et. al, 2004) proposed a dynamic connection admission control (CAC) algorithm that uses a Hopfield-type neural network for provisioning QoS in multimedia wireless networks. Algorithm finds the best possible QoS level for all multimedia connections that maximizes the resource utilization maintaining fairness in resource distribution, while minimizing the information loss probabilities.

The problem is treated like a multi-objective optimization problem and Hopfield neural network is used to calculate the QoS vector. (Barbancho et. al, 2007) studied the application of neural nets on every wireless sensor node. An algorithm named sensor intelligence routing (SIR) is presented as a QoS driven routing algorithm based on computational intelligence.

Swarm Intelligence

Swarm intelligence algorithms applied to mobile ad-hoc networks pose improved performance in QoS levels, routing, link bandwidth allocation and energy efficiency. Typical application of such algorithms in the network routing problem is demonstrated by (Arabshahi et.al, 2001) where swarm intelligence is used for adaptive routing in wireless communication networks. Intelligent network routing detects network bottlenecks and maintains a desired level of QoS.

Optimization Based Approaches and Genetic Algorithms

There are many multimedia applications of wireless mesh networks that require efficient data transfer from one base station to multiple distributed receivers, such as tele-robots working in collaboration. This feature can be supported by multicast tree with orthogonal channels assigned appropriately. However, the optimal multicast routing and channel assignment problem is proved to be Non-deterministic Polynomial time hard problem (NP-hard). (Cheng et.al) developed a unified framework for solving the Wireless Mesh Network (WMN) multicast problem using intelligent computational methods. The proposed frame work includes problem formulation, solution representation, fitness function and an effective channel assignment algorithm which works in a manner to avoid channel conflicts by efficiently assigning channels to each searched multicast tree. A heuristic algorithm approach is used because the minimum-interference channel assignment problem is NP-hard. Such an algorithm aims to reduce both the channel conflict and resource utilization.

Three QoS multicast routing algorithms are applied based on genetic algorithm (GA), simulated annealing (SA), and tabu search (TS), separately. These algorithms integrate the multicast tree construction and channel assignment and are used to search low cost routing trees which have least interference for channel assignment. The idea is that for each searched delay-bounded multicast tree, first the channels are assigned to its links by the proposed channel assignment algorithm, and then evaluated by the total channel conflict and tree cost. Hence, the strong search capability of GA, SA and TS can be well utilized to solve this problem.

Fuzzy and Hybrid Approaches

In (Munir et.al, 2007), a fuzzy logic based scheme is described that efficiently estimates network congestion and then acts accordingly in order to reduce it and to maintain QoS. The scheme employs QoS management and control module on each node and on the base station. Buffer size on wireless sensor nodes and the number of packets received or transmitted are used to decide congestion state and then need to take decision or not. In case of congestion, only high priority event driven information packets are transmitted. A fuzzy based approach is developed to evaluate the performance of wireless ad-hoc networks by considering QoS requirements as found in (Y. A. Alsbou et al.). First of all, the parameters affecting QoS, such as information delay, jitter and packet loss in multimedia wireless network (IEEE 802.11) are measured. These measured parameters are then used to decide the good, average or poor level of QoS, keeping in view the parameter requirements for each multimedia application. The computational intelligence approach makes possible a single output QoS without dealing with complex analytical and mathematical models with associated computational burden. (F. Xia et.al) discussed application of computational intelligence towards QoS management in interesting paradigm of Wireless Sensor/Actuator Networks (WSANs). A fuzzy logic control based QoS management is developed which is simple, general and scalable. Fuzzy logic controller is implemented inside each sensor node which adjusts its sampling period to the deadline miss ratio through feedback control. Deadline miss ratio associated with transmission from sensor to actuator is maintained at a desired level which ensures QoS in resource constrained, dynamic environments and dynamic channel capacity. The authors claimed to be the first to apply fuzzy logic control to QoS in WSANs, though fuzzy logic control has been previously applied to feedback scheduling/resource management.

In (Saraireh et.al), a Fuzzy Inference System (FIS) is used to assess the QoS provided by wireless network for three real time audio and video applications. Since the standard IEEE 802.11 does not meet the QoS requirements of real time multimedia application therefore Fuzzy and genetic-fuzzy hybrid approaches were applied to enhance QoS in wireless multimedia networks. Both approaches search for optimized value of minimum contention window (CW_{min}) in IEEE 802.11 MAC protocol. QoS is affected by CW_{min}, which decides the waiting time of wireless station before transmitting a packet and is dependent on packet collision/network congestion. It was found that there was not much difference in the performance of the FIS and hybrid-fuzzy system in improving the quality of service.

Bayesian Network Based Approach

In (Araujo et.al), a Bayesian framework is presented in which Bayesian network is used to plan and evaluate performance of wireless local area network (WLAN). Computational intelligence is used to categorize the environment as indoor or outdoor and to establish a correlation between the QoS parameters and distance. (Ruiz et.al) investigated the application of computational intelligence in real time multimedia networks that can adapt their various parameters like video size, audio and video codecs etc. in order to optimize QoS. A genetic algorithm was used to decide the triggering of the adaptation process based on network parameters conditions while the SLIPPER

Figure 8. Networked teleoperation over a hybrid/heterogeneous network

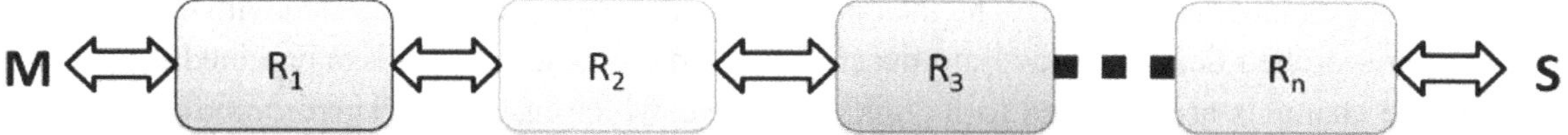

rule induction algorithm was used to select new set of parameters based on user perceived QoS.

INTELLIGENT CONTROL AND DECISION FOR NETWORKED TELEOPERATION

Issues, Controversies, Problems

The main focus in networked teleoperation is to ensure a certain level of teleoperation quality which ultimately depends on the QoC and network QoS. This requires understanding of multi domain phenomenon which can influence the performance. It is interesting to consider a situation where the teleoperation information passes through a hybrid/heterogeneous network. In the literature, a hybrid network is usually referred to a connection of different networks with more than one type of physical layer e.g. WLAN (wireless) connected to Ethernet (wired). While, the heterogeneous network is said to have same type of physical layer e.g. a combination of WLAN (wireless) with WiMAX (wireless) broadband network.

The challenge posed in multi network scenario is to maintain end-to-end QoS for teleoperation quality. This is illustrated in Figure 8. The teleoperation information travels from master (M) to slave (S) and on its way it passes through R_1, R_2 ... R_n networks with QoS_1, QoS_2 ... QoS_n as different available network policies. The individual network QoS strategies may be different including soft and hard real time support as well as best effort QoS with different constraints posed by the intermediate PHY and MAC layer. Due to non-convergence of these policies, the delay and variation in delay (jitter) as well as other QoS parameters cannot be globally optimized. This is the reason why IP based QoS control is more preferred and this feature is seriously addressed in IPv6. The extension of IPv6 is even available in sensor networks e.g. in the case of 6loWPAN, where IPv6 is stacked over 802.15.4.

Now, it is important to justify why a communication network should be used for teleoperation. Following are some of the advantages and tradeoffs:

1. NCS are a popular area in mobile teleoperated robotics. With the increase in efficiency of communication methods it is possible to decrease the on board computations in wireless network nodes. This not only reduces the overall cost but also gives energy efficient and low volume, less bulky network components. This approach has an advantage over embedded controllers which have limited computational, and energy resources. But the associated tradeoffs with wireless communication are the delays, band limited channels and packet dropouts and resulting information loss (Hespanha et al., 2007).
2. Good QoS is required for successful and efficient network teleoperation and maintaining acceptable QoC.
3. Furthermore, the mobility of the robot also adds some problems, e.g. increasing the distance between the control station and the robot increases the number of lost packets due to decreased signal strength and increased bit error rate (BER) (Zhu et al., 2005).

Therefore, an intelligent decision, based on communication and control bounds, is required to choose between an embedded controller and a WLAN Access Point (AP). There is also a possibility of performing a handover to other available nodes.

The communication architecture in mobile robotics may be centralized, in which case there is a fixed or mobile node, which communicates with all the other nodes, or decentralized, where individual mobile nodes will operate without any central controller (Schwager et al., 2007). In the decentralized control scheme, each component solves a part of the problem and shares memory without having a global view of the mission which means that there is less emphasis on computation than communication. In distributed control systems, communication is an important parameter and individual components don't need to share memory (Martinez et al., 2007). In related research work, many approaches have been used for distributed control of mobile robots. In (Fierro and Lewis, 1996) the dynamic model of the mobile robot is controlled by means of neural networks. In (Aicardi et al., 1995) and (Canudas-de-Wit and Sordalen, 1992), a nonlinear control approach has been introduced. Another research area, related to the hybrid architecture of control for autonomous navigation robots is studied in (Benzerrouk et al., 2008).

Solutions and Recommendations

As described above, we are interested to develop a co-design approach for networked teleoperation where control and communication shake hand in order to provide a minimum level of teleoperation quality as obtained in terms of quality of experience (QoE). The possibilities in adapting control/network parameters are discussed as follows.

Controller Adaptation

The control algorithm can be adapted by varying the sampling period of the off-board controller with in permissible stability/performance limits as per available QoS. In addition, several robust and adaptive control techniques are also available. Some QoS based diagnosis and fault tolerant control approaches may also be utilized where network faults can be isolated from dynamic system faults. In this way, the control can be switched to an embedded controller if low QoS is detected by the diagnostic block.

Network Adaptation

The parameters e.g. delay, packet loss rate, jitter and reliability are some of the QoS indicators. The minimum requirements assume that these parameters are bounded for QoS oriented end-to-end architecture. In adapting the network parameters for QoS control, several methods are available at different OSI layer. In general, the adaptation can be done by tuning communication channel, frequency, modulation, data rate adaptation (PHY layer) at the physical layer. Also, the packet size adaptation at MAC layer is also possible. QoS parameters at the Network layer include bandwidth allocation and priority assignment to some flows or network addresses. Intelligent routing algorithms are also a possibility to reduce network delay to some prioritized nodes. Admission control at Network/Session layer is also an option to allow or block new comers joining the network in order to optimize the available resources. Some QoS options at different OSI layers are indicated in Table 1.

In QoS estimation, a good model of network dynamics is not a practical solution. Instead model less techniques including optimal Estimation e.g. Kalman Filter, Artificial intelligence techniques e.g. Fuzzy Logic, Neural Networks and Machine learning techniques e.g. Supervised,

Table 1. Some QoS features in OSI model

OSI Layer	Example of QoS feature
Application Layer	RTP, DNS, FTP, HTTP etc.
Presentation Layer	Inter Application/Presentation: CASE/SASE ASCII, EDCDIC, X.25 DAR, NCP, NDR etc.
Session Layer	Session initiation Protocol (SIP), Proxy etc.
Transport Layer	UDP protocol (no Ctrl & re-Tx), TCP (Ctrl & re-Tx), SCTP (unicast, session oriented), DCCP, TFRC
Network Layer	IP (IntServ, DiffServ), MPLS
Data Link Layer	IEEE 802.1 p/q, ATM, Frame Relay
Physical Layer	Frequency hopping, Switching, TDMA

Unsupervised and Reinforcement Learning are used.

Artificial intelligence techniques have gained popularity and there are multiple applications found in literature where fuzzy decision is used in wireless networks e.g. handover/handoff decision, Admission Control, Congestion Control of traffic, Scheduling and Network Policing etc.

Two applications are discussed here which reflects the utility of computational intelligence for intelligent decision in networked robotics.

1. For intelligent handover decision (IHO), a QoS based *network rating function* (NRF) is evaluated for each of the candidate networks. In the literature, many researchers have proposed a horizontal hand off (HHO) strategy e.g. in (Wang et al., 2007) which treats the handover with in a multi station network utilizing the same wireless communication protocol. They proposed making a decision by taking into account the Received Signal Strength (RSS), the power consumption and the cost of communication (Chen et al., 2004). However, it is advantageous to add into these parameters, the influence of the QoS on the QoC of the mobile robot as found in (Mechraoui et al., 2009). The dependence between these parameters is formulated by using the graph approach. Whereas, the stochastic nature of the wireless network is exhibited by making use of the probability theory.
   Thus, Bayesian network approach is used in such application which is one of the powerful tools of artificial intelligence. Bayesian networks (Pearl, 1988) can be considered as a convenient tool which permits to handle two big problems commonly encountered in artificial intelligence, in applied mathematics and in engineering; i.e., the uncertainty and complexity (Mechraoui et al., 2009). They are used especially for diagnosis (Mechraoui et al., 2008) and prognosis (Muller et al., 2004) of the complex hybrid systems and also to make intelligent decision (Weber et al., 2008). However, Bayesian network requires 'a priori' conditional probability of each node which is used to quantify the QoC of the robot as a function of the QoS of the wireless network.
2. In drive-by-wireless teleoperation, a remote vehicle is controlled with a wireless connection in contrast with traditional electrical, hydraulic and mechanical methods. The control and video information is exchanged between the driver (master) and the vehicle (slave) bilaterally during teleoperation as shown in Figure 9. Long distance teleoperation employs hybrid/heterogeneous communication network to transport command and feedback data between the operator and the

Figure 9. Co-design scheme for networked teleoperation

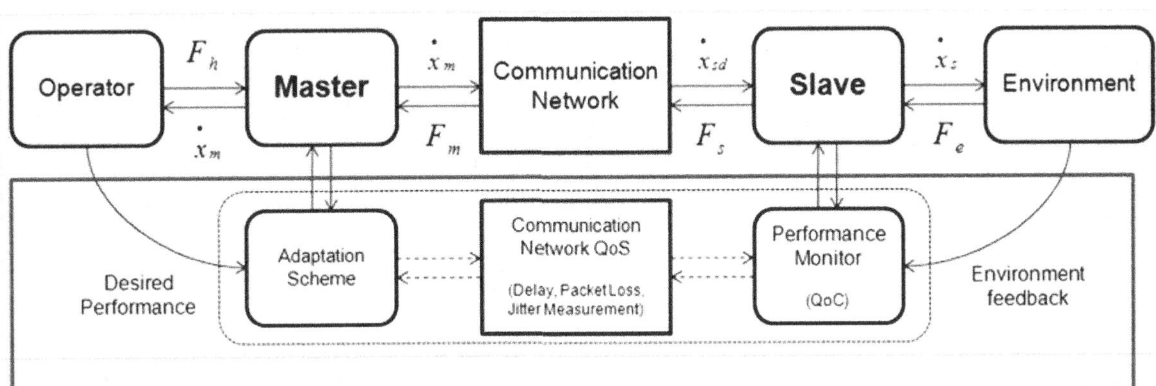

slave system as direct control is impossible in scenarios where the mobile teleoperator (slave) is located in hard to reach or dangerous remote areas. In addition to mobility, a wireless network eliminates hard connections between one or more control and sensor modules which results in simple design and lowered installation and maintenance costs. Moreover, for multi-vehicle case, a wireless network is more effective than point-to-point communication links. However, the wireless networks induce additional delays and information loss as they could be easily perturbed by the environmental effects and interference due to multipath effects or due to other communicating entities. The drive-by-wireless systems require multi domain knowledge including communication networks, vehicle dynamics and bilateral teleoperation with force feedback for better haptic sensation. In the literature, generally, bilateral teleoperation utilizes master-slave pair which communicates over a communication network.

Despite its interesting features, bilateral teleoperation has some limitations and performance dependencies over several factors. The number of task they can perform as compared to human are also limited, since the dexterity of teleoperator is poorer than the human dexterity. This even worsens and sometimes destabilize with the added time delays. In addition to stability, bilateral teleoperator are supposed to provide sufficient transparency despite the presence of mechanical nonlinearities and communication imperfections. We only consider passivity based architecture for bilateral teleoperation of drive-by-wireless applications, which utilize energy concepts and impose the passivity requirement for each individual sub-system. However, this approach is too conservative, in the sense that it does not guarantee good performance under all operating conditions. This justifies the intelligent adaptation of control gains with the operating conditions to maximize the performance and satisfy all control objectives as shown in Figure 9.

In modeling a communication channel only time delay is considered during analysis and full knowledge of communication protocol with its flexibilities, limitations and QoS aspects are rarely addressed by the control engineers. However, it is interesting to investigate that even if the wave variables are exchanged between master and slave, giving a notion of importance to this information or using some network based tactics can improve the quality of tracking and performance in bilateral teleoperation for drive-by-wireless application. The performance monitor evaluates the *control quality* while adaptation

Table 2. Comparison of different QoS estimation approaches

Criteria	FIS	ANFIS	ANN	SVM
MSE	$7.3x10^{-3}$	$9.04x10^{-3}$	$9.25x10^{-3}$	$53.3x10^{-3}$
Time (μs)	1.19	3.91	5.49	50.316
Monotonicity (%)	96	78	83	83.13
Flatness (%)	48	0	0	41.85
Implementation	Moderate	Moderate	Moderate	Difficult

scheme takes appropriate action as per network *quality of service* (QoS). This requires a co-design approach applied to robotic systems.

For QoS estimation, Comparison of different techniques is performed in order to justify its viability for our application. It is very difficult to objectively compare different approaches if there are no arbitral output values of the system. Therefore, five criteria are proposed include Execution time of the estimator per sample, flatness of the function, Monotonicity, Mean Square Error (MSE) and ease of Hardware Implementation.

It has been noticed from Table. 2 that the FIS, ANFIS and ANN have close values for MSE with FIS as more monotonic than others, while the ANFIS and ANN have zero flatness which is a positive aspect. The implementation complexity for the three is moderate. SVM has a greater value of MSE, however more training may converge the MSE value. The computation time is greater and implementation is more difficult than others. FIS is considered as the QoS classifier in our work due to easy implementation and smaller execution time. A three layer feed forward back propagation ANN block is shown in Figure 10.

Co-Design Approach

Following sub-blocks participate in the Co-design structure which was described in the last section. The complete block diagram is shown in Figure 11. All individual blocks are described here one by one:

1 Smoothing & Filtering

The wireless network exhibits stochastic behavior with random fluctuations. In order to further process the signal, a moving average filter is used to smooth out the variations. A buffer of $\tau = 50$ms is used to average out the measured signal.

2 QoS Estimation

Three parameters namely Delay, Packet loss and Signal to Noise ratio as a function of distance between Master and Slave are taken as input to QoS estimation block. Following computations are performed:

$$Delay = \frac{\sum_{i=0}^{n}(R_i - S_i)}{n} \quad (1)$$

Where,

R_i – Reception time of Packet *i*
S_i – Sent time of Packet *i*
n – Total number of Packets

$$Pkt\_loss = \frac{\sum_{i=0}^{n}(R_{k+1} - R_k) \succ Ts}{n} \quad (2)$$

Where,

R_{k+1} – Reception time of Packet at time k+1
R_k – Reception at time k

Figure 10. Architecture of 3 layers feed forward back propagation ANN

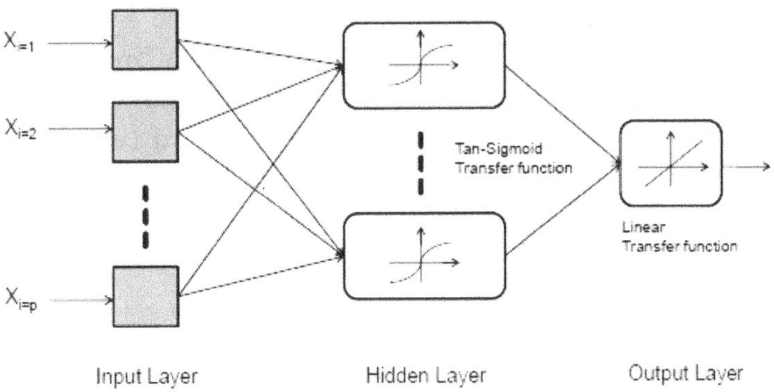

Figure 11. Network QoS based controller adaptation

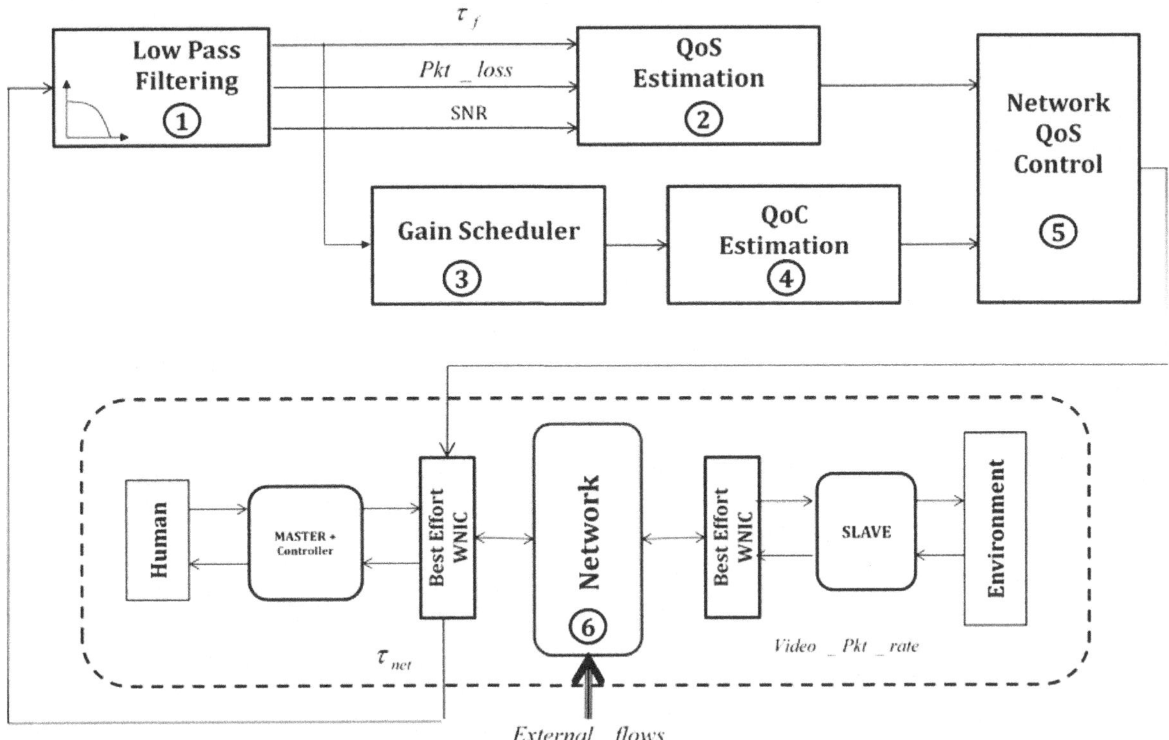

n – Total no of Packets

$$SNR = P_t + G_t + G_r - P_{loss} - N_{power} - A_{misc} \quad (3)$$

Where,

P_t – T_x Power

G_t – T_x gain

G_r – R_x gain

P_{loss} – Path loss

N_{power} – Noise Power

A_{misc} – Miscellaneous attenuation

Table 3. QoS FIS rule base

Rule	DL	PL	SNR	QoS	α
1	NE	LW	HH	EX	1
2	NE	HH	MD	GD	1
3	NE	VH	LW	BD	1
4	SL	NE	HH	EX	0.5
5	LG	NE	MD	GD	0.5
6	VL	NE	LW	BD	0.5

The membership functions are shown in Figure 12, 13 and 14 above. The delay has three membership functions (MFs) i.e. *short, long* and *very long*, packet loss has *normal, high* and *very high* MFs, while SNR has *high, medium* and *low* MFs. The resulting QoS has *good, bad* and *excellent* states. Table 3 shows the effect of each input variable on the QoS as weighed by α. The dependency of QoS on input functions is depicted in Figure 15 and 16 respectively.

3 Gain Scheduler

The third block in the co-design architecture is the gain scheduling. With increasing delay, the gain for the position control loop needs to be decreased in order to respect passivity and therefore stability. The gain is adapted from the relation between delay τ and gain K as shown in Figure 17. The outer most curve shows the values of gain where stability is lost as experienced in real time. Next, the inner curve gives the limit imposed by the passivity condition as per Equation 4. The inner most curve shows the practical values of K_{pass} applied on the system which takes into account the worst case value of B_{s1}. Worst case damping values are used in the passivity criteria to make sure that the passivity is respected at all operating conditions.

The variation in passivity condition is dependent on the time delay and varying values of master and slave damping B_m and B_{s1} respectively (Anderson & Spong, 1989). B_{s1} varies due to the non-linearities e.g. backlash (0.2328 rad approximately), dry friction etc in the Rack and Pinion Gearset (RPG) as well as due to wheels in contact with the environment. Whereas, B_m is different for different drivers. The worst case values for B_{s1} and B_m are practically estimated as 1.3123 N.m.s/rd (without wheels) and 0.0817 N.m.s/rd (free steering) respectively.

4 QoC Estimation

Passivity is given by respecting Equation 4 below. Large K implies small steady state error and thus good QoC is achieved due to better position tracking. It can be noted that higher gain shows better performance but as the delay increases; in order to preserve passivity, the gain allowed by the passivity criteria decreases. So there is a compromise on QoC when QoS decreases.

$$K_{pass} \prec \sqrt{\frac{B_m . B_{s1}}{T^2}} \tag{4}$$

5 Network QoS Control

The fifth block in the co-design architecture is the fuzzy QoS management block. The input variables include QoS (estimated above) and Control quality (QoC), while the output is the video packet rate as shown in Figure 18. All these input and output variables are normalized between 0 and 1. To control the delay experienced in the control loop, the video traffic can be varied.

This variation can be performed in the steps of 10 packets/sec to vary from 10 packets (121 kbps) to 1000 packets (12.1 Mbps). The round trip time (RTT) delay from 0 ms to 500 ms is taken into account for NeCS-Car ($\tau = \tau_{RTT}/2$). Delay exceeding 500 ms is considered as communication breakdown and therefore the NeCS-Car emergency system takes over to stop the car immediately.

6 Network

The sixth block represents the wireless network. Moxa 802.11 b/g WLAN router is used with

Figure 12. Time delay input variable with 3 membership functions

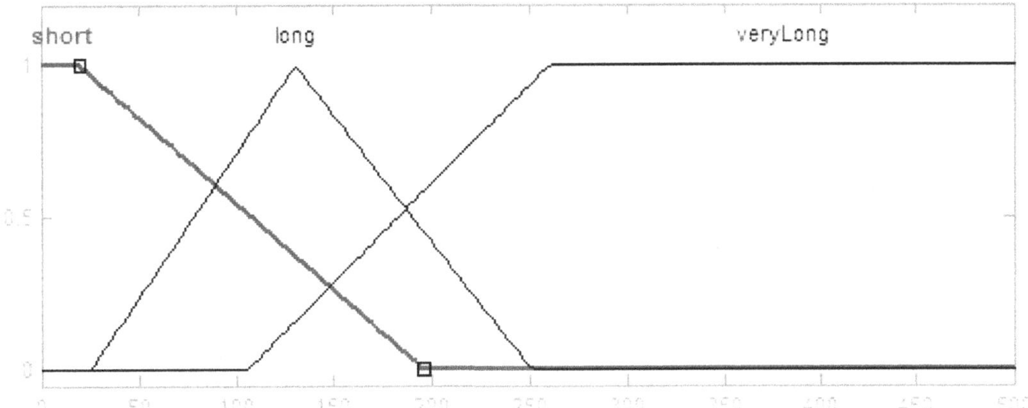

Figure 13. Packet loss input with 3 membership functions

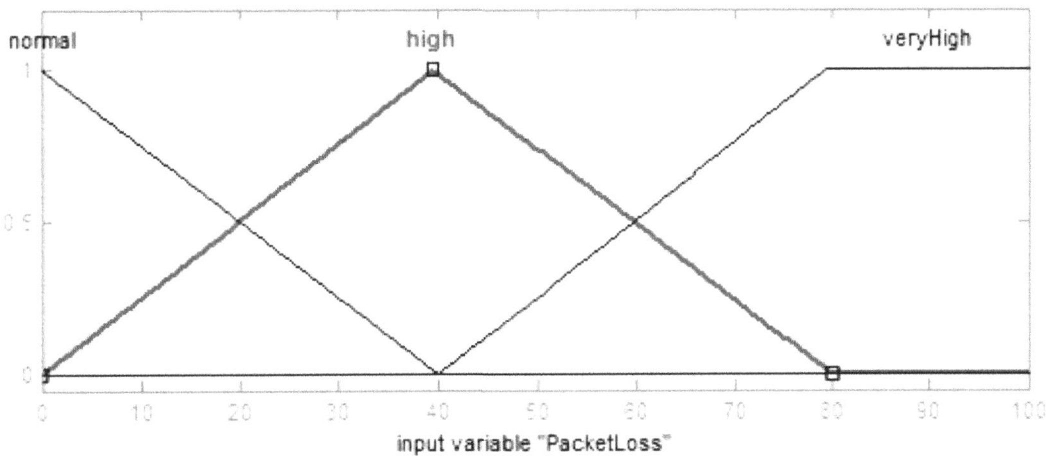

Figure 14. SNR input with 3 membership functions

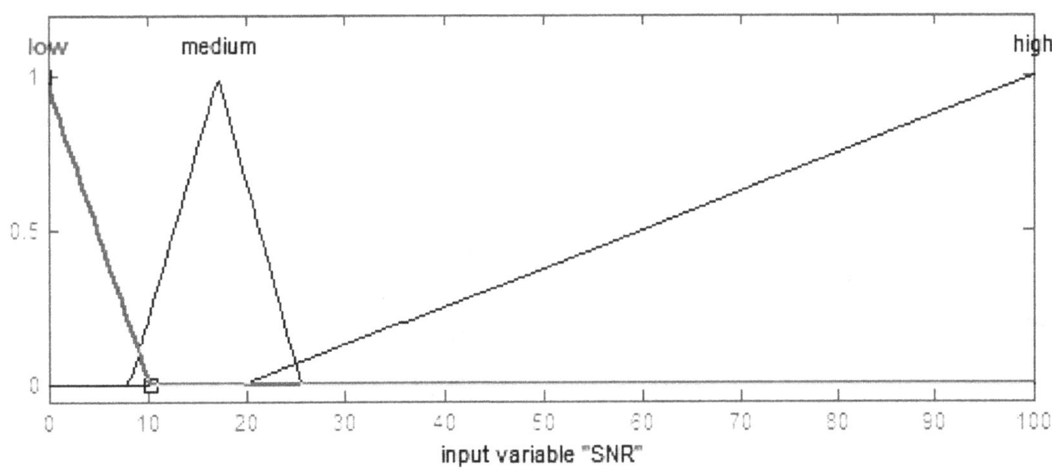

Figure 15. QoS as a function of packet loss and delay

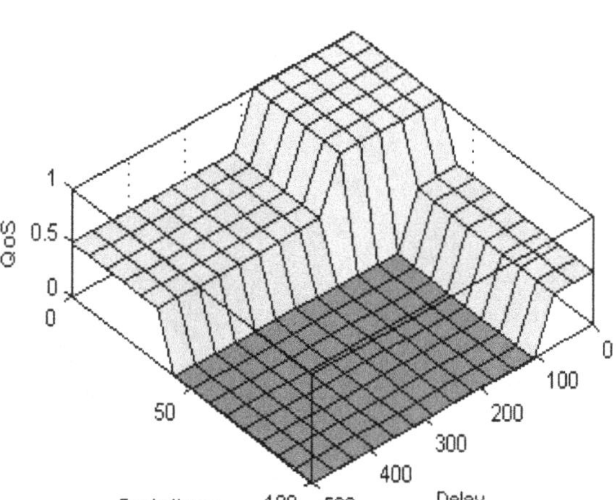

Figure 16. QoS as a function of SNR and delay

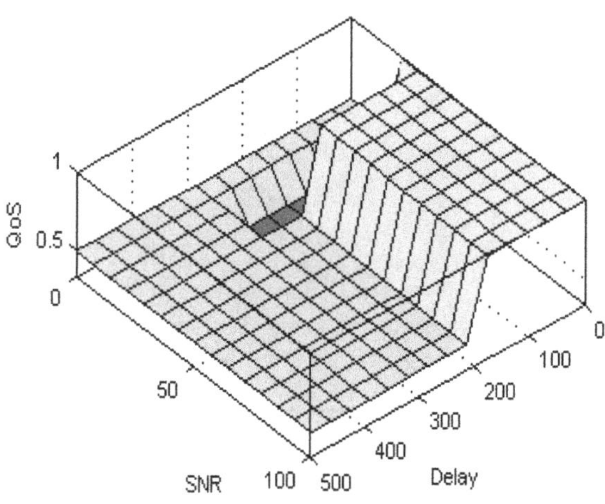

Figure 17. Variation of gain K with delay

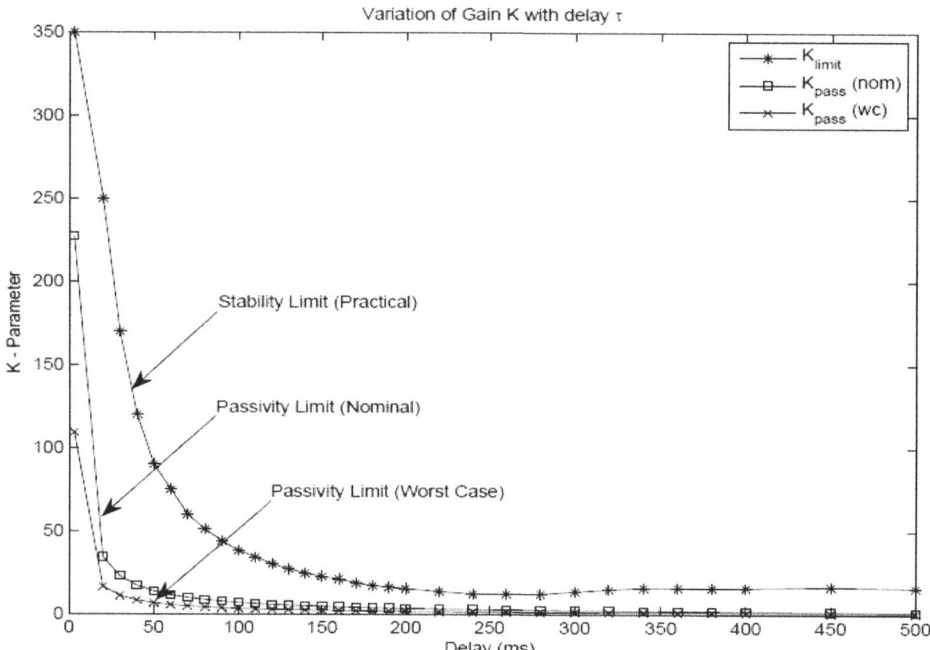

industrial temperature range. The Client/Server configuration is available with no QoS support. However, there is a possibility of adaptive modulation and coding as per SNR/RSS. Also, external antenna support is available. The packet size is approximately 1500 bytes with additional 200 bytes for WLAN overhead.

Figure 19 depicts the offline testing of co-design scheme by utilizing the real test data. It can be pointed out that the resulting QoS is scaled between 0 and 1 and it changes as per fuzzy inference depending on the variations of input variables. Figure 20 shows a real scenario in which no adaptation is used. In this case the QoC decreases

Table 4. Network QoS management

Rule	QoS	QoC	Distance	PR	α
1	NE	GD	NE	HH	1
2	NE	BD	NE	LW	1
3	NE	AV	NE	MD	1
4	GD	NE	NE	HH	0.5
5	BD	NE	NE	LW	0.5
6	AV	NE	NE	MD	0.5
7	NE	NE	VL	LW	1

Figure 18. Packet rate surface

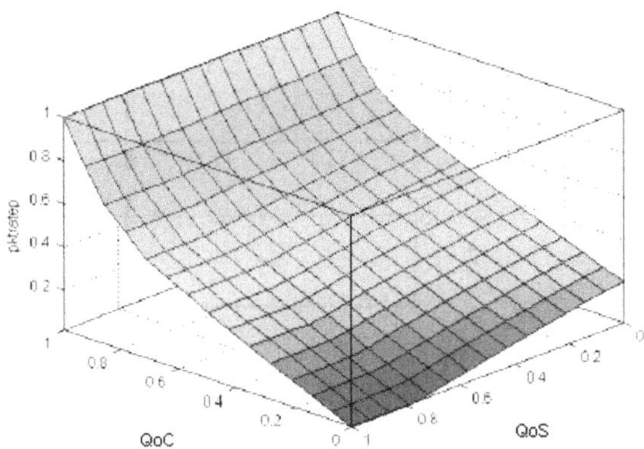

Figure 19. Offline testing of fuzzy QoS estimation

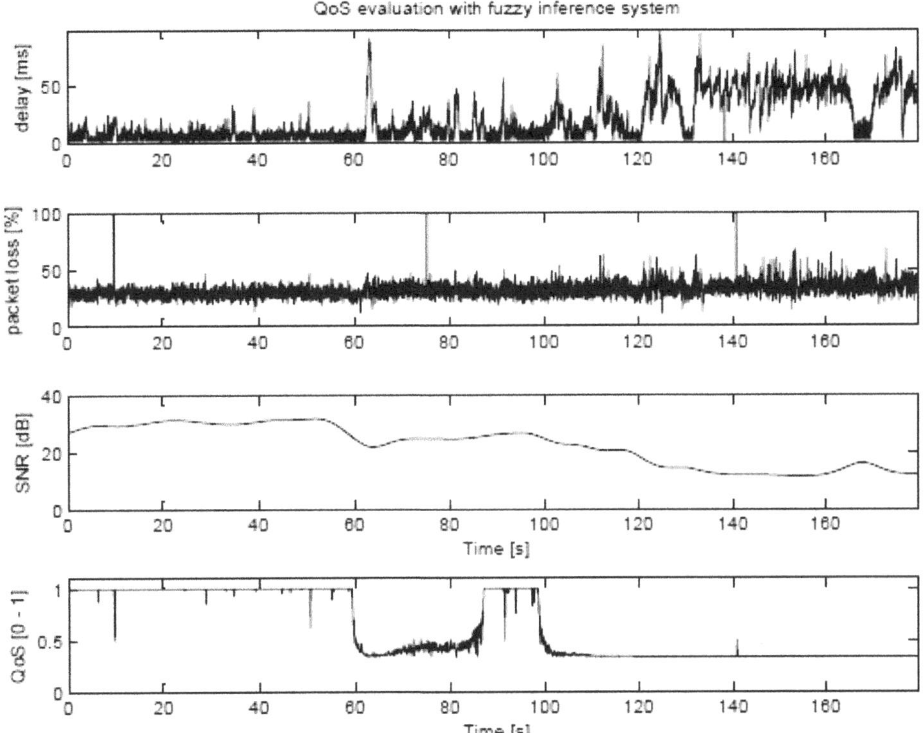

as the delay and packet loss increases. There is no improvement in QoS when the perturbation flows (ϕ_1, ϕ_2 = 3.1 Mbps) are added at 60 and 120 sec. However, in Figure 21 as the adaptation is enabled the QoC and QoS improves despite the same delay and packet loss scenario.

FUTURE RESEARCH DIRECTIONS

The co-design approach for networked teleoperation is presented in this chapter. For networked bilateral teleoperation, the quality of control as our objective could be imagined to translate into transparence quality. This raises a requirement

Figure 20. QoC with degraded network QoS - No adaptation

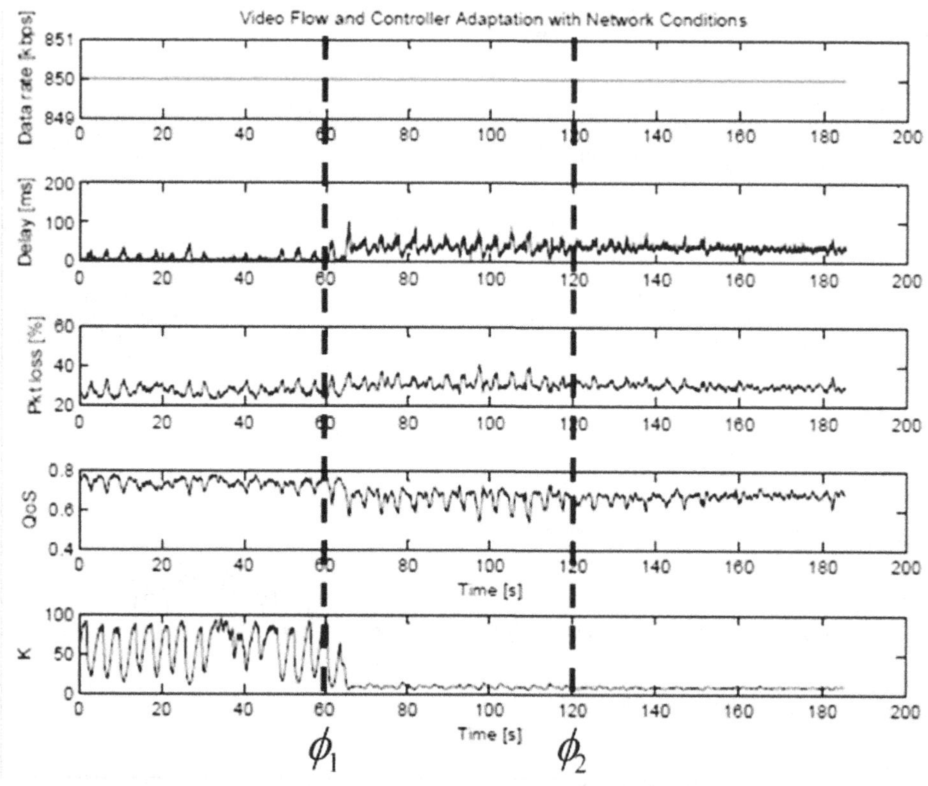

Figure 21. QoC with degraded QoC - with adaptation

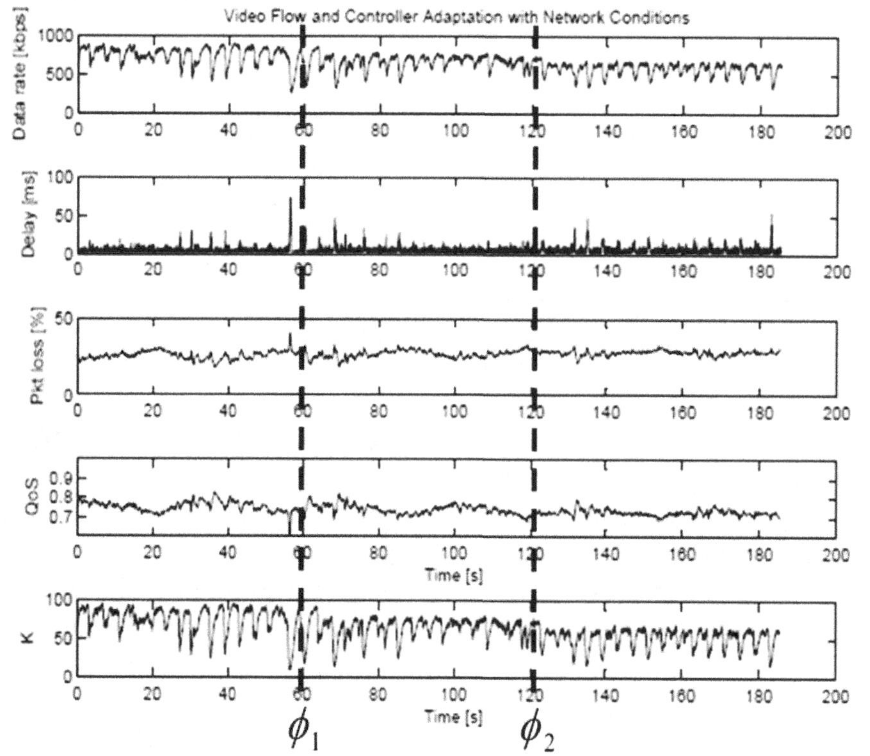

that how much haptic information is enough from the slave side. If degradation is necessary in the haptic quality due to lowered QoS, what should be its bounds so that it will remain acceptable to the operator while respecting the passivity conditions. Indeed, it is a promising area of technology and is conceptually very close to the fault detection and fault tolerant control (FDI/FTC) in engineering systems. The co-design approach emphasizes more rigorous testing to robustly perform at every operating point of the system in order to verify the adaptation in control/network parameters throughout operation. We have shown that QoS/link estimation using fuzzy/neural techniques is reasonably accurate, which can be improved. It can also be extended to multi link analysis to switch the network in case of low QoS or for handover purpose.

CONCLUSION

This chapter describes a co-design methodology in networked control systems with emphasis on bilateral teleoperation of a robotic vehicle. Various methods have been considered where QoC and QoS can be active or passive to respond the desired objectives. A fuzzy based adaptation scheme is described to quantify quality of service over network. The reconfiguration is performed when external flows degrade the QoS by introducing more delays and packet losses. This results in degraded QoC for control performance. The management of QoS may also include admission control and bandwidth allocation type mechanisms which restrict the external flows and manage them with respect to their priority. Two network architectures have been compared, one with the *best effort network* and the other with *QoS adaptation*. The results have shown that the QoS based approach provides better results as compared to the non-QoS network. However, the implementation of adaptive QoS support is a challenging issue in the wireless hardware available today.

REFERENCES

Ahn, C. W., & Ramakrishna, R. S. (2004, January). QoS provisioning dynamic connection- admission control for multimedia wireless networks using a Hopfield neural network. *IEEE Transactions on Vehicular Technology, 53*(1), 106–117. doi:10.1109/TVT.2003.822000

Al-Sbou, Y. A. (2010, December). Fuzzy logic estimation system of quality of service for multimedia transmission. *International Journal of QoS Issues in Networking, 1*(1).

Anderson, R. J., & Spong, M. W. (1989). Bilateral control of teleoperation with time delay. *IEEE Transactions on Automatic Control, 34*, 494–501. doi:10.1109/9.24201

Arabshahi, P., Gray, A., et al. (2001). Adaptive routing in wireless communication networks using swarm intelligence. In *9th AIAA Int. Communications Satellite Systems Conference*, (pp. 17-20).

Araujo, J., Rodrigues, J., Fraiha, S., Gomes, H., Cavalcante, G., & Frances, C. R. (2010). Strategy for WLAN planning and performance evaluation through Bayesian networks as computational intelligence approach. In Rebai, A. (Ed.), *Bayesian network*. doi:10.5772/10066

Barbancho, J., Leon, C., Molina, F. J., & Barbancho, A. (2007). Using artificial intelligence in routing scheme for wireless networks. *Computer Communications, 30*, 2802–2811. doi:10.1016/j.comcom.2007.05.023

Bleicher, A. (2010). Forgotten Soviet moon rover beams light back to Earth. *IEEE Spectrum*, August.

Chen, L. J., Sun, T., Chen, B., Rajendran, V., & Gerla, M. (2004). A smart decision model for vertical handoff. *Proceedings of the 4th International Workshop on Wireless Internet and Re-configurability*, Athens, Greece.

Cheng, H., & Yang, S. (2011). Joint multicast routing and channel assignment in multi radio multichannel wireless mesh networks using intelligent computational methods. *International Journal of Applied Soft Computing*, *34*(2).

Chopra, N., Spong, M. W., Ortega, R., & Barabanov, N. E. (2004). *Position and force tracking in bilateral teleoperation* (pp. 269–280). Advances in Communication Control Networks.

Cristianini, N., & Taylor, J. S. (2000). *An introduction to support vector machines and other kernel-based learning methods*. New York, NY: Cambridge University Press.

Dede, M. I. C., & Tosunoglu, S. (2007). *Parallel position/force controller for teleoperation systems*. 5th IFAC Workshop on Technology Transfer in Developing Countries: Automation in Infrastructure Creation, DECOM-TT, Izmir, Turkey.

Din, N. M., & Fisal, N. (2008). Fuzzy logic bandwidth prediction and policing in a DiffServ aware network. *Journal of Computers*, *3*, 18–23. doi:10.4304/jcp.3.5.18-23

Dote, Y. (1998). Soft computing (immune networks) in artificial intelligence. *Proceedings of IEEE International Symposium on Industrial Electronics*, ISIE'98, Vol. 1, (pp. 1 –7).

Feng, H., Shu, Y., Wang, S., & Ma, M. (2006). SVM-based models for predicting WLAN traffic. *IEEE International Conference on Communications* (pp. 597-602).

Guturu, P. (2007). *Computational intelligence in multimedia networking and communications-Trends and future directions. Computational Intelligence in Multimedia Processing: Recent Advances in the series 'Studies in Computational Intelligence*. Heidelberg, Germany: Springer Verlag.

Hirche, S. (2005). *Haptic telepresence in packet switched communication networks*. PhD thesis, TU-Munich, Germany.

Jaques, P. A., & Viccari, R. M. (2006). Considering student's emotions in computer-mediated learning environments. In Ma, Z. (Ed.), *Web-based intelligent-learning systems: Technologies and applications* (pp. 122–138). Hershey, PA: Information Science Publishing.

Kasiolas, A., & Makrakis, D. (1999). A fuzzy-based traffic controller for high-speed ATM networks using realistic traffic models. *IEEE Transactions on Multimedia Computing and Systems*, *2*, 389–394.

Khan, Z. H. Genon-Catalot, D., & Thiriet, J. M. (2011). Drive-by-wireless teleoperation with network QoS adaptation. *International Journal of Advanced Engineering Sciences and Technology*, *2*(2). ISSN: 2230-7818

Khan, Z. H., Genon-Catalot, D., & Thiriet, J. M. (2010). A co-design approach for bilateral teleoperation over hybrid networks. *18th Mediterranean Conference on Control and Automation (MED)*, Marakesh, Morroco

Li, Z., Wang, W., & Jiang, Y. (2009). Managing quality-of-control and requirement-of-bandwidth in networked control systems via fuzzy bandwidth scheduling. *International Journal of Control, Automation and Systems*, *7*(2), 289–296. doi:10.1007/s12555-009-0215-7

Mechraoui, A., Khan, Z. H., Thiriet, J.-M., & Gentil, S. (2009). *Co-design for wireless networked control of an intelligent mobile robot*. In International Conference on Informatics in Control, Automation and Robotics (ICINCO), Milan, Italy.

Mechraoui, A., Thiriet, J.-M., & Gentil, S. (2010). *Online distributed Bayesian decision and diagnosis of wireless networked mobile robots*. In 18th Mediterranean Conference on Control and Automation, Marrakech, Morocco.

Muller, A., Weber, P., & Salem, A. B. (2004). *Process model based dynamic Bayesian networks for prognostic.* Fourth International Conference on Intelligent Systems Design and Applications, ISDA 2004, Budapest, Hungary.

Munir, S. A., Bin, Y., Biao, R., & Jian, M. (2007). Fuzzy logic based congestion estimation for QoS in wireless sensor network. *IEEE International Symposium on Wireless Communications and Networking* (pp. 4336–4341).

Park, K. I. (2005). QoS in packet networks. *Springer*, 2005.

Pearl, J. (1988). *Probabilistic reasoning in intelligent systems: Networks of plausible inference*. Morgan Kaufman Publishers.

Pirmez, L., Delicato, F. C., Pires, P., Mostardinha, A., & de Rezende, N. (2007). Applying fuzzy logic for decision-making on wireless sensor networks. *IEEE International Symposium on Fuzzy Systems* (pp. 1-6).

Rae, S. (2004). *Using telerobotics for remote kinematics experiments.* Honors Thesis, School of Mechanical Engineering, University of Western Australia.

Ruiz, P. M., Botía, J. A., & Gómez-Skarmeta, A. (2004). Providing QoS through machine-learning-driven adaptive multimedia applications. *IEEE Transactions on Systems, Man, and Cybernetics B*, *33*(4), 1398–1411. doi:10.1109/TSMCB.2004.825912

Saraireh, M., Saatchi, R., Al-Khayatt, S., & Strachan, R. (2007). Assessment and improvement of quality of service in wireless networks using fuzzy and hybrid genetic fuzzy approaches. *Journal of Artificial Intelligence Research*, *27*(2-3), 95–111. doi:10.1007/s10462-008-9090-5

Stein, M. R., & Madden, C. P. (2005). *The Puma Paint Project: Long term usage trends and the move to three dimensions.* IEEE International Conference on Robotics and Automation, ICRA.

Weber, P., Theilliol, D., & Aubrun, C. (2008). Component reliability in fault diagnosis decision-making based on dynamic Bayesian networks. *Proceedings of the Institution of Mechanical Engineers Part O, Journal of Risk and Reliability*, (pp. 161-172).

Xia, F., Zhao, W. H., Sun, Y. X., & Tian, Y. C. (2007). Fuzzy logic control based QoS management in wireless sensor/actuator networks. *Sensors (Basel, Switzerland)*, *7*(12), 3179–3191. doi:10.3390/s7123179

Xie, J. (2009). Optimal control of chaotic system based on LS-SVM with mixed kernel. *Third International Symposium on Intelligent Information Technology Application*, Vol. 1, (pp. 622-625).

Xu, L. (1994). Theories for unsupervised learning: PCA and its nonlinear extensions. *Proceedings of IEEE International Conference on Neural Networks*, ICNN'94, Orlando, Florida, Vol. 2, (pp. 1252a, 1253 –1257).

Zhu, X. (2005). *Semi-supervised learning literature survey.* University of Wisconsin – Madison.

Chapter 8
Bangla Music Genre Classification

Ashfaqur Rahman
Centre for Intelligent and Networked Systems, Central Queensland University Rockhampton, Australia

ABSTRACT

Bangladesh is very rich in its musical history. Music documented the lives of the people from the ancient times. This chapter provides a guideline for classifying Bangla songs into different genres using a machine learning approach. Four different genres, namely Rabindrasangit, Folk song, Adhunik song, and Pop music, were used in the experiments. A set of second order features are used for representing the trend of change of primary features computed over the timeline of the song. The features are incorporated into a number of classification algorithms and a classification framework is developed. The uniqueness of the genres is clearly revealed by high classification accuracies achieved by the different classifiers.

1. INTRODUCTION

The sharing and use of audio-visual files over the web has become very popular over the last decade with the enormous growth of internet. There are popular websites like youtube, google video, etc. that share the audio/video files. From the user point of view an important issue is how to search for a song/music. There are different preferences among the users. From the search engine point of view a categorization of the songs helps in answering the queries in a more relevant and efficient manner. Popular search engines like Google offers separate tabs for multimedia search. Music genre classification finds significant applications in such areas.

The music genre classification process works in two steps – (i) Learning and (ii) Prediction. The learning process first divides the entire song into a set of non–overlapping contiguous windows. Characteristic audio features are extracted from each of these windows and a set of second order

DOI: 10.4018/978-1-4666-1830-5.ch008

features (e.g. mean, standard deviation, etc.) are computed from the primary features over all the windows. A classifier is trained on the second order feature set and target genres from a set of training songs. During prediction the second order features produced from the test songs are presented to the trained classifier to predict the genre.

The effectiveness of second order features to capture the trend of change of primary features depends on the number of windows and the length of the songs. With higher number of windows the second order features like mean, standard deviation, etc. are less effective. The second order features are still necessary for the sake of comparison as the number of equal length windows may vary among different songs of different length. It is thus necessary to efficiently capture the change pattern of primary features over the windows as it provides significant information for genre separation. The effectiveness however still depends on the different genres under consideration. For example, in Bangla songs there are genres including – (i) Rabindrasangit, (iii) Folk song, (iii) Adhunik, and (iv) Pop music. The instruments in use and the way they are played, the style of singing, etc. are significantly different among these genres. The change pattern of audio features varies significantly among these different genres of Bangla songs and needs to be captured more efficiently.

In this chapter we present a set of second order features representing change pattern of audio features and a classification framework using these features to characterize Bangla songs. To the best of our knowledge this is the first approach towards Bangla song classification into different genres. The research aims to investigate – (i) a novel set of second order features for tracking the change pattern of primary audio features over the windows, (ii) the impact of including the new second order features into the Bangla song classification process, and (iii) the use of various classifiers for assessing the strength of the second order features for Bangla song classification. We have conducted a number of experiments on a diverse set of Bangla songs with the state-of-the-art and the new second order features and the findings as presented in the results section.

The chapter is organized as follows. A review of the existing research work for the classification of music genre is presented in Section 2. The theoretical framework for obtaining the new features is explained in Section 3 and the Bangla song classification framework is presented in Section 4. Section 5 presents the experimental setup, results and analysis. Section 6 concludes the chapter.

2. RELATED WORK

This section presents some description of the music genres in Bangladesh and recent research work on music genre classification.

2.1 Bangla Music Genres

In this chapter we focussed on four genres in Bangla music: – (i) Rabindrasangit, (iii) Folk song, (iii) Adhunik song, and (iv) Pop music. A brief description (Wikipedia Contributors, 2012) of each genre is presented in this section.

Rabindra Sangit

Rabindra Sangit refers to the songs written by Rabindra Nath Tagore. Some people also refer to them as Tagore songs. These songs are considered as cultural treasures of Bangladesh. The Rabindrasangit deals with varied themes and are immensely popular. These songs form a foundation for the Bengali culture. It is said that his songs are the outcome of 500 years of literary & cultural churning that the Bengali community has gone through (Wikipedia Contributors, 2012). Rabindrasangit has become a distinctive discipline of music. Practitioners of this genre are protective of Bengali tradionalist practice. Rabindrasangit demands an educated, intelligent & cultured audience to appreciate the lyrical beauty of his compositions.

Folk Song

Bangla folk music has a long history. Folk songs are characterised by their simple musical structure and words. Once upon a time (before advent of radio) the stage performances of folk singers used to be the only entertainment for the vast rural population of Bangladesh. Several people contributed to what has become one of the most important musical influences in lives of Bangladeshis. Lalon Fokir, Hason Raja and Ramesh Shill are some of them. Later on Abbas Uddin played a key role to popularise folk music. Folk music can clearly be classified into several sub-genres: (a) Baul:, (b) Bhandari, (c) Bhatiali, (d) Bhawaiya, (e) Gajir geet, (f) Gombhira, (g) Hason Raja, (h) Jaari, (i) Jatra Pala, (j) Kirtan, (k) Pala, (l) Kobi gaan, (m) Lalon, (n) Mursiya, (o) Shaari, (p) Upojatiyo, (q) Letto's song:, (r) Wedding songs. The detail on the description of these classifications is available in [20].

Adhunik Song

After arrival of new communication and digital media, many of the folk songs were modernised and incorporated into Adhunik song. Adhunik song literally means modern songs. To outsiders this genre may seem an extremely ambiguous way of nomenclature. But it has particular motivations. Just before the Indian independence, several new minor musical groups emerged (mainly as playback songs for movies). These songs failed to fit into any particular genre. These songs seemed to be tied together by common theme of *music for the masses*. Most of these songs were far moved from the classical modes. Hence, a miscellaneous category called *Adhunik song* was created. Over time these so called modern songs have become fairly old. But they continue to be called by the same name.

Pop Music

Pop music initially started with the so-called band music. And as the name suggests, the music was heavily influenced by Western Music. The greatest contributors to pop or pop-rock music also included the following singers: Azam Khan and Fakir Alamgir. Artists of the Adhunik Song and Folk genre also contributed to the pop music from time to time. The popularity of the band music was started enormously with the music of some famous band groups which had some mixed flavor of our melody with Western pop-rock stream. Now–a–days there are hundreds of bands playing different types of pop songs in Bangladesh.

2.2 Music Genre Classification

The classification task depends on feature extraction. The feature extraction process used by all the existing techniques starts by dividing the entire song into a set of non-overlapping contiguous windows and computing features from the different windows. A summary of these features (the second order features) over all the windows or a subset of them is used for the classification purposes. The different approaches differ in terms of window size, features and classifiers used as described below.

A classification approach was presented in (Silla, Koerich, Kaestner, 2008) that uses multiple feature vectors and a pattern recognition ensemble approach, according to space and time decomposition schemes. A set of binary classifiers were used whose results were merged in order to produce the final music genre label (space decomposition). Music segments were also decomposed according to time segments obtained from the beginning, middle and end parts of the original music signal (time-decomposition). The final classification was obtained from the set of individual results, according to a combination procedure. The machine learning algorithms used were Naïve Bayes, Decision Trees, *k*–Nearest Neighbours, Support Vector Machines and Multi-Layer Perceptron Neural Nets. Experiments were carried out on a dataset of *Latin music* categorized into 10 musical genres. The approach used 30 musical features and a window size 30. The classification accuracy of 65.06% was achieved.

A Support Vector Machine based approach was adopted in (Annesi, Basili, Gitto, Moschitti, & Petitti, 2007) to design an automatic classifier of music genres. They used existing features in the current literature and engineered some new ones to capture the aspects of songs that had been neglected in previous studies. The classification results on two datasets suggest that the model on very simple features reaches the state-of-art accuracy (on the ISMIR dataset) and very high performance on a music corpus collected locally. The specific window size used for computing the features was not precisely mentioned. A total of five features were used in the experiment. The SVM classifier achieved an accuracy of 82.3% on 500 songs of *Italian music*.

Two statistical techniques namely Gaussian Mixture Modelling and a Vector Quantization scheme were investigated in (Pye, 2000) for music classification. The techniques provide useful tools in the management of a typical digital music library. The author used a window size of 25 ms. Two features were used for the investigation namely MFCC and MP3CEP. The database used a total of 175 Songs. The song types were blues, easy listening, classical, opera and dance (techno). The classification accuracy of as high as 96% was achieved.

An algorithm was described in (Guaus, & Herrera, 2007) that had been designed after different tests using different sets of descriptors and classifiers databases. The purpose of all these tests was to create a plain classifier capable of dealing with different environments and serving as a baseline for further improvements. They used five features and a window size of 30 sec in their experiment. The features were MFCC, Spectral Centroid, Spectral Flatness, Spectral Flux and Zero Crossing Rate. They used SVM as the classifier. The data set contained 400 songs including classical, dance, hiphop, jazz, pop, blues, and rock. They also used speech as data. They achieved a classification accuracy of 71.87%.

A technique was presented in (Barbedo, & Lopes, 2007) that divided the signals into 21.3 ms windows, from which four features were extracted. The values of each feature were treated over one–second analysis segments. Some statistical results of the features along each analysis segment were used to determine a vector of summary features that characterized the respective segment. Next, a classification procedure used those vectors to differentiate between genres. The classification procedure had two main characteristics: (1) a very wide and deep taxonomy, which allows a very meticulous comparison between different genres, and (2) a wide pair-wise comparison of genres, which allows emphasizing the differences between each pair of genres. The final classification of the signal was given by the genre that appears more times along all signal segments. Decision tree was used as a classifier. The data set used 2266 music excerpts of 29 genres. A classification accuracy of 87% was achieved.

A multiresolution algorithm was used in (Bergstra, Casagrande, & Eck, 2005) that compensates for the large discrepancy in temporal scale between feature extraction (47 ms) and song classification (3–5 minutes). Their solution is to aggregate and classify features at an intermediate scale. They divided an input song into contiguous, non-overlapping windows of 13.9 seconds, and computed the mean and variance in standard timbre features over each segment. They calculated a relatively large number of frame-level timbre features from 47ms frames of single-channel audio at 22050Hz using their own software Bergstra. This resulted in 402 frame-level features, so that their meta-feature vector had 804 dimensions. Adaboost (Schapire, 1990) was used for classification purposes. In their data set they used 1515 full length audio files organized into 10 genres. They achieved an accuracy of 86.92%.

A system for classifying audio files was described in (Burred, 2005) that was based on a hierarchical classifier and on automatic feature selection. The results of the contest evaluation were presented and compared with a previous evaluation performed by the authors. A window size of 30 seconds was used and a total of sixteen features were considered. The classifier used was GMM. The data set they used contained 1515 full-length audio files which were organized into 10 genres. A classification accuracy of 59.22% was achieved.

A content-based audio classification and retrieval method was proposed in (Li, & Guo, 2000). Given a feature set, which was composed of perceptual and cepstral feature, optimal class boundaries between classes, were learned from the training data by using SVMs. The experiments were conducted to compare various classification methods and feature sets. A window size of 32 ms was used in the experiments. The features used were – total power, sub-band powers, brightness, bandwidth and pitch, and mel–frequency cepstral coefficients (MFCCs). SVM was used as a classifier. In data set, the authors used 409 pieces of sound and achieved a classification accuracy of 86.81%.

A music genre classification was presented in (Ahrendt, Meng, & Larsen, 2004) with special emphasis on the decision time horizon and ranking of tapped delay-line short-time features. The fusion using majority voting was compared with techniques such as dynamic PCA (DPCA). The most frequently suggested features in the literature were employed including mel frequency cepstral coefficients (MFCC), linear prediction coefficients (LPC), zero-crossing rate (ZCR), and MPEG-7 features. To rank the importance of the short time features, a consensus sensitivity analysis was applied. They used a window size of 30 ms. Gaussian and neural network based classifiers were used. They achieved a classification accuracy of 80%.

In general the existing works focus on developing different features from the different songs and use different types of classifiers to differentiate between music genres. The entire song is divided into non-overlapping contiguous windows and primary audio features obtained from the different windows are converted into second order features or primary features from a certain number of windows (e.g. first, last and middle) are used. This is done to compute an equal number of features from all the songs for classification purposes. As the existing works do not explicitly track the change of primary audio features over the windows it leaves space for improvement. Moreover none of the above approaches are tested on Bangla music. This motivates us to explore a novel set of second order features and use them to classify Bangla music.

3. THEORETICAL FRAMEWORK

Considering a song as a time varying signal, it can is divided in into N non–overlapping contiguous time windows each of length Δt. A set of M characteristic audio features $f_1(w), f_2(w), \ldots, f_M(w)$ are computed from w–th window where $1 \leq w \leq N$. A set of second order features namely mean and standard deviation, as used in the current literature, are computed for each primary feature f_j over all the windows as:

$$\mu(f_j) = \frac{\sum_{w=1}^{N} f_j(w)}{N} \quad (1)$$

$$\sigma(f_j) = \sqrt{\frac{\sum_{w=1}^{N} [f_j(w) - \mu(f_j)]^2}{N}} \quad (2)$$

As can be observed from (1) and (2) the mean μ and standard deviation σ of a feature f_j are computed over all the windows in the entire song. The mean describes the central location of the data, and the standard deviation describes the variability. σ thus represents the average amount of change of a feature but does not take into consideration the trend of change. With a small number of windows it still represents the trend implicitly but fails to do so with higher number of windows *N*. Regression on samples is an efficient approach to represent trend. Considering the different values of a feature f_j over the windows $f_j(1), f_j(2), \ldots, f_j(N)$ we can use a second order polynomial function to represent the trend as

$$f_j^{'} = a_0 + a_1 w + a_2 w^2 \quad (3)$$

where w represents the window number. We can define an error function as

$$\xi = \frac{1}{2}\sum_{w=1}^{N}[f_j^{'} - a_0 - a_1 w - a_2 w^2]^2 \quad (4)$$

The objective is to obtain the parameters a_0, a_1, a_2 that represents the trend of change of feature f_j where $1 \leq j \leq M$. The best fitting values can be obtained by partial differentiation of (4) w.r.t. a_0, a_1, a_2 and equating to zero which gives,

$$a_0 N + a_1 \sum_{w=1}^{N} w + a_2 \sum_{w=1}^{N} w^2 = \sum_{w=1}^{N} f_j^{'} \quad (5)$$

$$a_0 \sum_{w=1}^{N} w + a_1 \sum_{w=1}^{N} w^2 + a_2 \sum_{w=1}^{N} w^3 = \sum_{w=1}^{N} w f_j^{'} \quad (6)$$

$$a_0 \sum_{w=1}^{N} w^2 + a_1 \sum_{w=1}^{N} w^3 + a_2 \sum_{w=1}^{N} w^4 = \sum_{w=1}^{N} w^2 f_j^{'} \quad (7)$$

The three linear Equations (5)–(7) can be solved to obtain values of the parameters a_0, a_1, a_2 for a feature f_j. These three parameters can be used as the second order features along with μ and σ. The process can be repeated for computing these five second order features for all the primary audio features.

4. CLASSIFICATION FRAMEWORK

The objective of the classification framework is to classify Bangla songs using a set of second order features. The classification framework is divided into two parts – (i) Learning and (ii) Prediction. In both of these phases the feature extraction plays an important role. The feature extraction phase is described in Section 4.1. The learning and prediction of Bangla genres using the second order features features are described in Section 4.2.

4.1 Feature Extraction

During the feature extraction process the Bangla song is divided into a set of *N* non–overlapping windows. A set of characteristic audio features are extracted from each of these windows. The set of primary audio features used in our experiments are compiled from the current literature that are representative of Bangla songs and presented in Table 1. The basic methods used for feature computation are RMS (Root Mean Square), FFT (Fast Fourier Transform), Beat, and Method of Moments. A set of five second order features namely *mean* (μ), *standard deviation* (σ), and three parameters a_0, a_1, a_2 of the best fitting second order polynomial are extracted for each primary feature as it changes over the windows. For *M* primary audio features, each song is represented by $5 \times M$ second order features.

4.2 Learning and Prediction

The training and test processes are presented in Figure 1. Second order features are computed from each of the Bangla songs (training set). These features obtained from the feature extraction stage and corresponding target genres are fed into the learning algorithm of a classifier. The classifier parameters are optimized to find the best mapping from the features to the target genres. For prediction, Bangla songs from test set are presented to the feature extractor and second order features as computed are presented to the classifier. The predictions are matched with the known genres to compute the classification accuracy.

5. RESULTS AND DISCUSSION

5.1 Experimental Setup

Bangla music in ancient times was mostly linked to prayer and due to this immense influence most folk songs are related to some sort of praise of the gods and their creation. Modernisation of Bangla music occurred at different times and most of these modernisation processes happened independently of western influence. Bangla songs of the following genres were used in our experiments – (i) Rabindrasangit, (iii) Folk song, (iii) Adhunik, and (iv) Pop music. All the songs are available in WAV format (CD Quality 44100 samples, 16 bit). We selected 1200 songs for our work and genre has 300 songs. We randomly selected 50 songs from each genre to form the test set and the remaining for the training set (Table 2).

We have used WEKA (Hall, Frank, Holmes, Pfahringer, & Reutemann, 2009) for machine learning classifiers. The classifiers used are Support Vector Machine (SVM), J48 (C4.5 Pruned / Unpruned Decision Tree), and Naïve Bayes classifiers (NB). We have used the following Java libraries for extracting the features from the songs: JAudio, jMIR, LibXtract, JSymbolic. From the literature review it can be noticed that researchers previously used different windows sizes which range from 3 ms to 30 s. In the experiments the window size was chosen by using all common window sizes, comparing the performance of each window size on the test songs. Experimenting different window sizes with the same test case – it was found that the best classification accuracy was achieved with a window size of 11 ms and the results reported in this chapter are based on that.

We have conducted two types of classifications – (a) pair–wise classification and (b) all–genre classification as presented next.

5.2 Pair Wise Classification

Bangla songs of only two genres were considered at a time for pair wise classification experiments. A total of six pairs were considered from the four genres of Bangla songs. The classification results obtained with different classifiers using the old and new features for each pair of genres are presented next. For each case two results are shown – (a) Classification results with mean and standard deviation of the primary features (Table 1) and (b) Classification results with mean, standard deviation, and polynomial coefficients.

5.2.1 Band and Rabindrasangit

The first pair of genres presented here are *Band* and *Rabindrasangit*. The songs of these two genres are very different in almost every audio aspect. The classification result with mean and standard deviation is presented in Table 3 and that with the addition of polynomial coefficients is presented in Table 4. SVM fetches 100% accuracy in both cases. J48 (Decision Tree) also perform well with 93% accuracy and that accuracy remains constant in both cases. The accuracy of Naïve Bayes classifier increases by 7% with the use of polynomial coefficients.

Table 1. List of audio features used in the experiments

Feature Name	Feature Description
2D Method of Moments	This feature gives a spectrograph description and its changes over a relatively short time frame (Mittra, & Varadarajan, 2007). The features are computed from a series of frames of spectral data analysed using two-dimensional method of moments.
Root Mean Square (RMS)	RMS defines the measure of the power of a signal over a window.
Beat Histogram	In acoustics, a beat is interference between two sounds of slightly different frequencies, perceived as periodic variations in volume whose rate is the difference between the two frequencies (Wikipedia, 2012). Beat Histogram represents the relative strength of rhythmic regularities (tempi) in a signal and is computed from the auto-correlation of the RMS (Tzanetakis, 2005).
Beat Sum	Beat sum is the sum of all bins in the beat histogram. This is a good measure of the importance of regular beats in a signal (Wikipedia, 2012).
Strongest Beat	The strongest beat in a signal, in beats per minute, found by finding the highest bin in the beat histogram (McKay, & Fujinaga, 2009, McEnnis, McKay, & Fujinaga, 2005, McKay, & Fujinaga, 2006, McKay, & Fujinaga, 2005).
Strength of Strongest Beat	Strength of strongest beat is defined by how strong the strongest beat in the beat histogram is compared to other potential beats (McKay, & Fujinaga, 2009, McEnnis, McKay, & Fujinaga, 2005, McKay, & Fujinaga, 2006, McKay, & Fujinaga, 2005).
Fraction of Low Energy Frames	This feature is defined as the fraction of previous windows whose RMS is less than the mean RMS. This gives an indication of the variability of the amplitude of windows (McKay, & Fujinaga, 2009, McEnnis, McKay, & Fujinaga, 2005, McKay, & Fujinaga, 2006, McKay, & Fujinaga, 2005).
FFT Bin Frequency Labels	This indicates the bin label (in Hz) of each power spectrum or magnitude spectrum bin obtained from FFT analysis of a signal (McKay, & Fujinaga, 2009, McEnnis, McKay, & Fujinaga, 2005, McKay, & Fujinaga, 2006, McKay, & Fujinaga, 2005).
Magnitude Spectrum	A measure of the strength of different frequency components. Derived directly from the FFT.
Power Spectrum	A measure of the power of different frequency components. Derived directly from the FFT.
Compactness	Compactness is closely related to Spectral Smoothness and sums over the frequency bins of an FFT. This provides an indication of the noisiness of the signal and is found by comparing the components of a window's magnitude spectrum with the magnitude spectrum of its neighbouring windows (Pachet, & Roy, 2009).
MFCC	Mel-Frequency Cepstral Coefficients (MFCCs) are useful for describing a spectrum window.
Spectral Centroid	Spectral Centroid stands for the centre of mass of the power spectrum.
Spectral Centroid Variability	The standard deviation of the spectral centroid over the last 100 windows.
Spectral Flux	Spectral Flux is defined as the spectral correlation between adjacent windows. It is a measure of the amount of spectral change in a signal. Found by calculating the change in the magnitude spectrum from frame to frame.
Spectral Rolloff Point	Spectral rolloff is defined as the frequency where 85% of the energy in the spectrum is below this point. This is a measure the right-skewedness of the power spectrum (McKay, & Fujinaga, 2009, McEnnis, McKay, & Fujinaga, 2005, McKay, & Fujinaga, 2006, McKay, & Fujinaga, 2005).
Strongest Frequency Via FFT Maximum	An estimate of the strongest frequency component of a signal (in Hz) and defined as the FFT bin with the highest power (McKay, & Fujinaga, 2009, McEnnis, McKay, & Fujinaga, 2005, McKay, & Fujinaga, 2006, McKay, & Fujinaga, 2005).
Zero Crossings	Zero Crossing is calculated by counting the number of times that the time domain signal crosses zero within a given window. It is an indication of frequency as well as noisiness.
Strongest Frequency Via Zero Crossings	An estimate of the strongest frequency component of a signal, in Hz, found via the number of zero-crossings (McKay, & Fujinaga, 2009, McEnnis, McKay, & Fujinaga, 2005, McKay, & Fujinaga, 2006, McKay, & Fujinaga, 2005).
Method of Moments	This feature consists of the first five statistical moments of the spectrograph. This includes the area (zero–th order), mean (first order), power spectrum density (second order), spectral skew (third order), and spectral kurtosis (fourth order). These features describe the shape of the spectrograph of a given window.

Figure 1. Learning and prediction in Bangla song classification

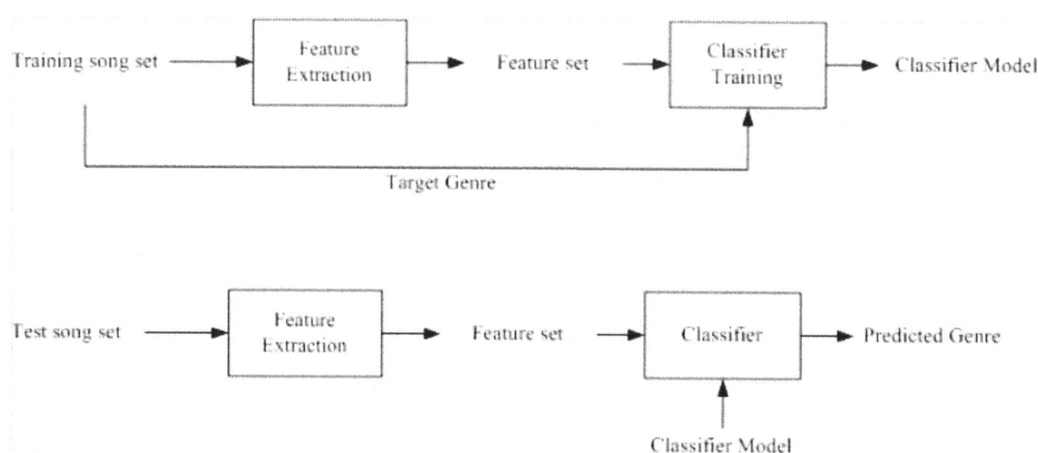

Table 2. Training and test set of Bangla songs

	Adhunik	**Band**	**Folk**	**Rabindrasangit**
Training	250	250	250	250
Test	50	50	50	50

Table 3. Band and Rabindrasangit binary classification with mean and standard deviation

Classifier	**J48**			**SVM**			**NB**		
Accuracy	93%			100%			86%		
Confusion Matrix		Band	Rabindra		Band	Rabindra		Band	Rabindra
	Band	46	4	Band	50	0	Band	43	7
	Rabindra	3	47	Rabindra	0	50	Rabindra	7	43

Table 4. Band and Rabindrasangit binary classification with mean, standard deviation, and polynomial coefficients

Classifier	**J48**			**SVM**			**NB**		
Accuracy	93%			100%			92%		
Confusion Matrix		Band	Rabindra		Band	Rabindra		Band	Rabindra
	Band	46	4	Band	50	0	Band	44	6
	Rabindra	3	47	Rabindra	0	50	Rabindra	2	48

5.2.2 Adhunik and Folk

The pair of genres presented here are *Adhunik* and *Folk* song and the classification results are reported in Table 5 and Table 6. Here all the classifiers show better performance with the use of mean, standard deviation, and polynomial coefficients. The accuracy increases from 84% to 85% for J48, from 91% to 92% for SVM and from 71% to 72% for Naïve Bayes.

Table 5. Adhunik and Folk binary classification with mean and standard deviation

Classifier	J48			SVM			NB		
Accuracy	84%			91%			71%		
Confusion Matrix		Adhunik	Folk		Adhunik	Folk		Adhunik	Folk
	Adhunik	43	7	Adhunik	45	5	Adhunik	43	7
	Folk	9	41	Folk	4	46	Folk	22	28

Table 6. Adhunik and Folk binary classification with mean, standard deviation, and polynomial coefficients

Classifier	J48			SVM			NB		
Accuracy	85%			92%			72%		
Confusion Matrix		Adhunik	Folk		Adhunik	Folk		Adhunik	Folk
	Adhunik	42	8	Adhunik	46	4	Adhunik	45	5
	Folk	7	43	Folk	4	46	Folk	23	27

Table 7. Band and Folk binary classification with mean and standard deviation

Classifier	J48			SVM			NB		
Accuracy	88%			95%			80%		
Confusion Matrix		Band	Folk		Band	Folk		Band	Folk
	Band	41	9	Band	49	1	Band	35	15
	Folk	3	47	Folk	4	46	Folk	5	45

Table 8. Band and Folk binary classification with mean, standard deviation, and polynomial coefficients

Classifier	J48			SVM			NB		
Accuracy	93%			96%			83%		
Confusion Matrix		Band	Folk		Band	Folk		Band	Folk
	Band	46	4	Band	49	1	Band	36	14
	Folk	3	47	Folk	3	47	Folk	3	47

Table 9. Band and Adhunik binary classification with mean and standard deviation

Classifier	J48			SVM			NB		
Accuracy	86%			96%			74%		
Confusion Matrix		Adhunik	Band		Adhunik	Band		Adhunik	Band
	Adhunik	43	7	Adhunik	48	2	Adhunik	35	15
	Band	7	43	Band	2	48	Band	11	39

Table 10. Band and Adhunik binary classification with mean, standard deviation, and polynomial coefficients

Classifier	J48			SVM			NB		
Accuracy	91%			96%			78%		
Confusion Matrix		Adhunik	Band		Adhunik	Band		Adhunik	Band
	Adhunik	46	4	Adhunik	49	1	Adhunik	35	15
	Band	5	45	Band	3	47	Band	7	43

Table 11. Folk and Rabindrasangit binary classification with mean and standard deviation

Classifier	J48			SVM			NB		
Accuracy	88%			93%			83%		
Confusion Matrix		Folk	Rabindra		Folk	Rabindra		Folk	Rabindra
	Folk	43	7	Folk	45	5	Folk	40	10
	Rabindra	5	45	Rabindra	2	48	Rabindra	7	43

Table 12. Folk and Rabindrasangit binary classification with mean, standard deviation, and polynomial coefficients

Classifier	J48			SVM			NB		
Accuracy	88%			95%			72%		
Confusion Matrix		Folk	Rabindra		Folk	Rabindra		Folk	Rabindra
	Folk	45	5	Folk	47	3	Folk	32	7
	Rabindra	7	43	Rabindra	2	48	Rabindra	10	40

5.2.3 Band and Folk

The classification results on *Band* and *Folk* songs are presented in Table 7 and Table 8. Even though the songs of these genres share some commonality in terms of rhythm and pitch, it can be noted that the classification accuracy achieved is better than the pair *Adhunik* and *Folk* in general. Here the use of mean, standard deviation, and polynomial coefficients is giving better performance with J48 (88% to 93%), SVM (95% to 96%) and Naïve Bayes classifier (80% to 83%).

5.2.4 Adhunik and Band

Adhunik and *Band* songs are the two candidates considered here with the classification results presented in Table 9 and Table 10. With the use of mean, standard deviation, and polynomial coefficients, J48 is showing better performance (91% to 86%) compared to using only mean and standard deviation. SVM is giving identical performance (96%) in both cases. Naïve Bayes also gives better performance (74% to 78%) with the use of mean, standard deviation, and polynomial coefficients.

5.2.5 Folk and Rabindrasangit

The classification results on *Folk* song and *Rabindrasangit* are reported in Table 11 and Table 12. It can be seen that with J48 the performance remains same (88%) with the use of new features. With SVM the performance improves (93% to 95%). But with Naïve Bayes classifier the performance decreases (83% to 72%) considerably using the new features.

5.2.6 Adhunik and Rabindrasangit

Adhunik and *Rabindrasangit* are the last pair experimented with classification results presented in Table 13 and Table 14. Here again J48 giving identical performance (87%) in both cases. SVM is showing an increase of classification accuracy from 90% to 94%. Here the Naïve Bayes showing very small decrease of performance (1%) using the mean, standard deviation, and polynomial coefficients.

Table 13. Adhunik and Rabindrasangit binary classification with mean and standard deviation

Classifier	**J48**			**SVM**			**NB**		
Accuracy	87%			90%			75%		
Confusion Matrix		Adhunik	Rabindra		Adhunik	Rabindra		Adhunik	Rabindra
	Adhunik	42	8	Adhunik	44	6	Adhunik	39	11
	Rabindra	5	45	Rabindra	2	48	Rabindra	14	36

Table 14. Adhunik and Rabindrasangit binary classification with mean, standard deviation, and polynomial coefficients features

Classifier	**J48**			**SVM**			**NB**		
Accuracy	87%			94%			74%		
Confusion Matrix		Adhunik	Rabindra		Adhunik	Rabindra		Adhunik	Rabindra
	Adhunik	47	3	Adhunik	46	4	Adhunik	37	13
	Rabindra	6	44	Rabindra	0	50	Rabindra	13	37

Table 15. All genre classification with mean and standard deviation. Here, **A** *– Adhunik,* **B** *– Band,* **F** *– Folk,* **R** *– Rabindrasangit.*

Classifier	**J48**					**SVM**					**NB**				
Accuracy	70.5%					85%					58%				
Confusion Matrix		**A**	**B**	**F**	**R**		**A**	**B**	**F**	**R**		**A**	**B**	**F**	**R**
	A	41	1	4	4	**A**	49	0	0	1	**A**	32	1	13	4
	B	1	33	10	6	**B**	0	42	5	3	**B**	0	39	9	2
	F	3	8	33	6	**F**	2	2	41	5	**F**	2	12	34	2
	R	6	6	4	34	**R**	3	7	2	38	**R**	5	18	16	11

Table 16. All genre classification with mean, standard deviation, and polynomial coefficients. Here, **A** *– Adhunik,* **B** *– Band,* **F** *– Folk,* **R** *– Rabindrasangit.*

Classifier	**J48**					**SVM**					**NB**				
Accuracy	72.5%					86%					51%				
Confusion Matrix		**A**	**B**	**F**	**R**		**A**	**B**	**F**	**R**		**A**	**B**	**F**	**R**
	A	44	1	5	0	**A**	49	0	0	1	**A**	32	3	11	4
	B	2	34	8	6	**B**	0	41	5	4	**B**	0	28	17	5
	F	5	4	34	7	**F**	4	1	42	3	**F**	3	7	35	5
	R	3	7	7	33	**R**	2	4	4	40	**R**	10	16	17	7

5.3 All Genre Classification

Table 15 and Table 16 represent the classification results over all the genres of Bangla songs considered together. Here it can be seen that J48 is performing better with the new features. It is showing an increase in classification accuracy (2.5%) with the use of mean, standard deviation, and polynomial coefficients (72.5% instead of 70.5%). Even with all genre classification – SVM is giving the best performance – here giving 86% accuracy with the new features compared to 85% with mean and standard deviation only. Here it should be also noted that Naïve Bayes's

Figure 2. Comparative classification accuracy using old features and combining old and new features with (a) J48, (b) SVM, and (c) Naïve Bayes classifiers on different mixtures of genres

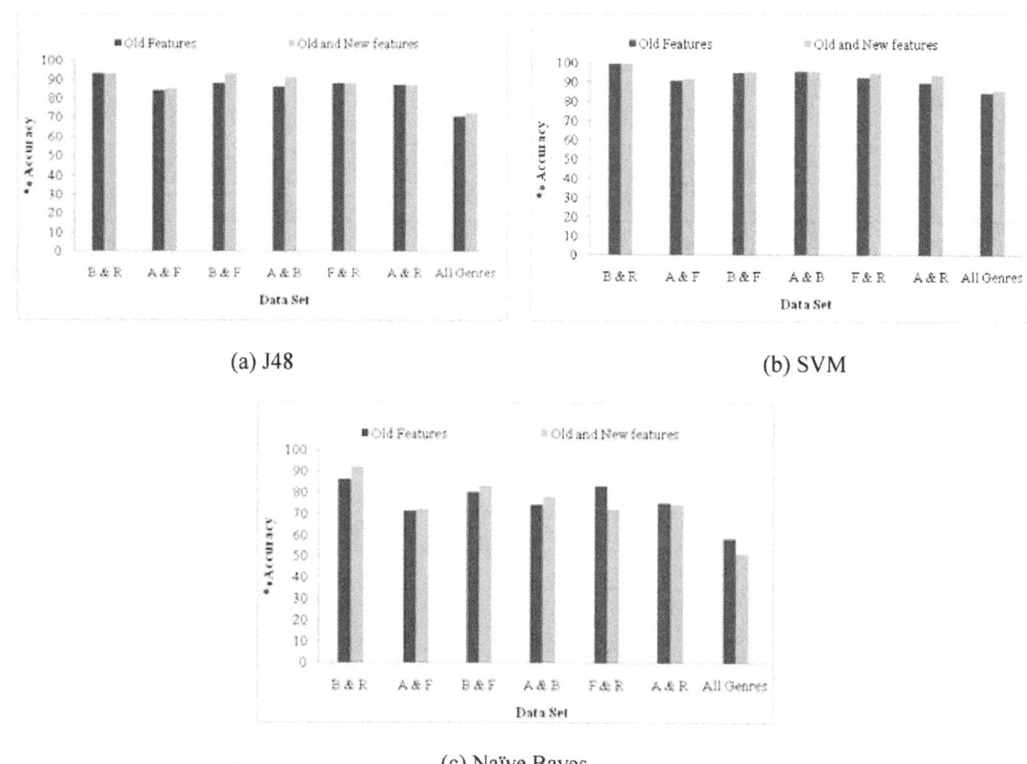

(a) J48

(b) SVM

(c) Naïve Bayes

performance falls about 7% with the use of mean, standard deviation, and polynomial coefficients. Inspecting the confusion matrix it can be noted that – Band and Folk are the mostly misclassified genre among each other.

5.4 Analysis of Classifier Performance

The Figure 2 summarizes the classification performance of the different classifiers on the Bangla songs with and without the use of new features. Out of the three classifiers, two classifiers namely J48 and SVM show better performance with the use of new features. Naïve Bayes classifier in general underperforms as compared to the other classifiers. This can be attributed to the fact that Naïve Bayes classifier is based on the principle of conditional independence among the features given their class. As all the used features are second order and computed from the same primary features they are not entirely independent and lead to lower classification results. Note that a comparison of only the performance of the old and new features on Bangla song classification for different classifiers is presented here. As this is the first research towards Bangla song classification, there are no published results available in the literature for a comparison.

6. CONCLUSION AND FUTURE RESEARCH DIRECTIONS

In this chapter we have presented the findings of investigating the impact of using second order features representing the change pattern of primary audio features for Bangla song classification. It is evidenced from the experimental results that the second order features improves the classification performance of Support Vector Machine in all cases of pair-wise and all-genre classification. The J48 classifier either performs better or similar with the use of new features. Out of seven cases (pair-wise and all-genre combined) Naïve Bayes classifier performs better in four cases and underperforms in three cases. Altogether the addition of second order features to explicitly track the change of primary features over the windows has significant impact on the classification of Bangla songs. In general the classification accuracy improves with the addition of new features. The higher classification accuracy also establishes the uniqueness of the different genres.

To the best of our knowledge automation of Bangla music classification is an unexplored research area. The research presented in this chapter is the first of its kind and can be explored further in a number of ways. We have analysed the trend of change of features over the song using second order polynomials only. Spline functions can also be explored in this regard. Some genres like folk songs have some sort of periodicity inherent in them and period analysis tools from signal analysis research can be explored in this regard. Finally the research is confined to only four types of genres. Each of these genres can be further classified and is also an unexplored research area. For example folk songs can be further classified into Baul,, Bhatiali, Bhawaiya, Gajir geet, Hason Raja, Jaari etc.

ACKNOWLEDGMENT

The author wishes to thank Mashuqur Rahman, Abhijit Bhowmik, Parves Kawser, and Nusrat Sultana from the American International University, Bangladesh for the valuable research contributions they provided during the concept experimentation for this chapter.

REFERENCES

Ahrendt, P., Meng, A., & Larsen, J. (2004). Decision time horizon for music genre classification using short time features. *European Signal Processing Conference (EUSIPCO),* (pp. 1293–1296).

Annesi, P., Basili, R., Gitto, R., Moschitti, A., & Petitti, R. (2007). Audio feature engineering for automatic music genre classification. In *Large Scale Semantic Access to Content (Text, Image, Video, and Sound) (RIAO '07)*, (pp. 702-711).

Barbedo, J. G. A., & Lopes, A. (2007). Automatic genre classification of musical signal. *EURASIP Journal on Applied Signal Processing, 1*, 157–169.

Bergstra, J., Casagrande, N., & Eck, D. (2005). *Two algorithms for timbre- and rhythm-based multi-resolution audio. Tech. Report, Music Information Retrieval Exchange*. MIREX.

Burred, J. J. (2005). *A hierarchical music genre classifier based on user-defined taxonomies. Proceedings of Music Information Retrieval Evaluation Exchange*. MIREX.

Guaus, E., & Herrera, P. (2007). *A basic system for music genre classification*. International Conference on Music Information Retrieval.

Hall, M., Frank, E., Holmes, G., Pfahringer, B., & Reutemann, I. (2009). The WEKA data mining software: An update. *SIGKDD Explorations, 11*(1). doi:10.1145/1656274.1656278

Li, S. Z., & Guo, G. (2000). *Content-based audio classification and retrieval using SVM learning*. IEEE Pacific-Rim Conf. on Multimedia.

McEnnis, D., McKay, C., & Fujinaga, I. (2005). jAudio: Additions and improvements. *Proceedings of the International Conference on Music Information Retrieval,* (pp. 385–386).

McKay, C., & Fujinaga, I. (2005). *Automatic music classification and similarity analysis*. International Conference on Music Information Retrieval.

McKay, C., & Fujinaga, I. (2006). jSymbolic: A feature extractor for MIDI files. *Proceedings of the International Computer Music Conference,* (pp. 302–305).

McKay, C., & Fujinaga, I. (2009). jMIR: Tools for automatic music classification. *Proceedings of the International Computer Music Conference.*

Mittra, R., & Varadarajan, V. (2007). A technique for solving 2D method-of-moments problems involving large scatterers. *Microwave and Optical Technology Letters*, *8*(3), 127–132. doi:10.1002/mop.4650080304

Pachet, F., & Roy, P. (2009). Analytical features: A knowledge-based approach to audio feature generation. *EURASIP Journal on Audio, Speech, and Music Processing.*

Pye, D. (2000). Content-based methods for the management of digital music. *IEEE International Conference on Acoustics, Speech, and Signal Processing (ICASSP), 4,* (pp. 2437–2440).

Schapire, R. E. (1990). The strength of weak learnability. *Machine Learning*, *5*(2), 197–227. doi:10.1007/BF00116037

Silla, C. N., Koerich, A. L., & Kaestner, C. A. A. (2008). A machine learning approach to automatic music genre classification. *Journal of the Brazilian Computer Society*, *14*(3), 7–18. doi:10.1007/BF03192561

Tzanetakis, G. (2005). *Tempo extraction using beat histograms. Music Information Retrieval Evaluation eXchange*. MIREX.

Wikipedia. (n.d.). *Beat (acoustics)*. Retrieved January 5, 2012, from http://en.wikipedia.org/wiki/Beat_(acoustics)

Wikipedia. (n.d.). *Music of Bangladesh*. Retrieved January 5, 2012, from http://en.wikipedia.org/wiki/Music_of_Bangladesh

Chapter 9
Automatic Recognition and Localization of Saudi License Plates

Lama Hamandi
American University of Beirut, Lebanon

Khaled M. Almustafa
Prince Sultan University, Kingdom of Saudi Arabia

Rached N. Zantout
Prince Sultan University, Kingdom of Saudi Arabia

Hasan R. Obeid
Zawya, Lebanon

ABSTRACT

In this chapter, localizing Saudi license plates in images and recognizing characters automatically in those plates are described. Three algorithms to recognize English and Arabic characters in Saudi license plates are presented. The three algorithms rely on processing information from lines strategically drawn vertically and horizontally through a character. In most of the cases, all letters and numbers were able to be recognized. Furthermore, two approaches for localization, "object adjacency" and "character recognition," are described in this chapter. The algorithms were successfully applied to images containing Saudi License plates as shown through the results presented. A hybrid approach is also presented in which vertical alignment was used to aid the recognition phase in correctly recognizing characters. The hybrid method is only applicable to new Saudi license plates since they contain redundant information in both Arabic and English sections.

DOI: 10.4018/978-1-4666-1830-5.ch009

INTRODUCTION

Recognizing characters automatically in license plates has become a necessity in this age. Law enforcement and surveillance using cameras has overwhelmed human operators with gigabytes of video and still pictures. Searching manually for a certain license plate in a video is time consuming and error prone for current human operators. Having a human in the loop compromises the security and integrity of the system. Human beings are susceptible to intentional or non-intentional data tampering. An automatic system that detects and recognizes license plates is a must in areas like surveillance, identification of vehicles through video footage, automatic traffic violation systems and access control. Automatic License Plate Recognition (ALPR) is usually divided into two major parts, localization and recognition. Localization locates the part of the image which contains the license plate, while recognition identifies the individual characters on the assumption that the image being identified is that of a license plate.

In this chapter, we present three algorithms to recognize characters in Saudi license plates. All algorithms rely on processing information from lines strategically drawn through a character. The first algorithm calculates the number of peaks for each line. A peak is a place in the line where the pixels' color changes from black to white. This algorithm is based on an earlier version (Obeid & Zantout, 2007; Obeid et. al, 2007) used to recognize characters in Lebanese plates. The second algorithm calculates the pixels density for a specific crossing line in a character. Pixel density is defined as the number of pixels having a specific intensity level to the total number of pixels in a line. The third algorithm calculates the position of the peaks introduced in the first algorithm rather than only their numbers. For each algorithm, the features were calculated for all possible letters and numbers. A study was then done on the best way to be able to differentiate between the letters and numbers based on the feature of the algorithm. Some of the methods had difficulty differentiating between a pair (or more) of characters. In general, methods that have high processing requirements were able to distinguish between characters while methods that were computationally simple had some difficulty with some pairs.

In this chapter, two simple but effective algorithms are also presented for locating plates in an image that contains Saudi license plates. The algorithms are adaptations of the algorithm presented in (Obeid et. al, 2007) for Lebanese license plates. In the first method, the image is segmented into labeled objects. Then the adjacency relationship between the different objects is studied to identify the part of the image which contains a license plate. The algorithm does not require recognizing the objects before locating the license plate. In the second method, instead of relying first on the alignment, the segmented objects are identified first by applying the three different recognition algorithms (Almustafa et.al, 2010; Zantout & Almustafa, 2011) to each object deemed possible to be a license plate component. A lot of ambiguity existed in the characters even after applying the recognition algorithms. This prompted the use of vertical alignment between objects to disambiguate between possibilities of characters. Although this method uses alignment between objects, however it only checks for vertical alignment between pairs of objects rather than horizontal alignment between up to six objects. This enables the method to be both simple and accurate. The major drawback of the method is that it is applicable only to new Saudi license plates. This was not considered a serious drawback since old Saudi license plates are due to be phased out totally by the end of year 2011.

In the next section, literature is reviewed for similar work done for license plates in general. Then, a description of Saudi license plates is given for readers unfamiliar with this kind of license plates. This information is imperative for understanding why certain decisions were made and thresholds were chosen. In the following section, three algorithms to recognize characters in Saudi license plates are presented along with results of applying these methods to actual Saudi license plates. Various thresholds used are presented along with a discussion of the results of applying the methods to actual license plates. Next, algorithms for plate localization are presented. The chapter concludes with a summary of achievements and suggestions for future research.

BACKGROUND

Although general Optical Character Recognition (OCR) methods can be used to recognize the characters in a license plate, ALPR systems usually do not have the processing power required to implement such algorithms. Furthermore, since the character set in license plates is limited and the font is unique, simpler algorithms are usually devised and implemented for ALPR specific purposes. Localization algorithms can be categorized into three approaches (Jia et.al, 2004). First, the color-based approach which uses the distinctive character colors to differentiate them from the background. Second, the edge-based approach which uses lines (edges) of characters and their boundaries. Third, the texture-based approach which searches for specific patterns or textures in the image to locate a license plate.

Character Recognition

Character recognition is a very important step in any ALPR system. Character recognition methods that currently exist in the literature can be classified into analytical and global approaches. In the analytical approach (Obeid & Zantout, 2007), individual characters are segmented from a license plate. Each character is recognized individually and the combination of the recognition results is used to produce a list of possible plates. The global approach (Agha et.al, 2004; Brad, 2001) recognizes a set of characters as a whole and does not rely on recognizing individual characters. The advantage of the global approach over the analytical is that in the global approach the segmentation phase is not necessary. All three methods presented in this chapter for character recognition fall under the analytical approach type.

In (Brad, 2001; Ponce et.al, 2001; Fang et.al, 2009; Ozbay & Ercelebi, 2005), template matching is used to recognize the characters in a license plate. Using templates has two main disadvantages. The first disadvantage is that matching requires having templates stored in the memory for correlation. The second disadvantage is the high sensitivity to noise and scale. Any change in the character's shape might mislead template matching into producing wrong results. In (Wang et.al, 2009), the image of a Chinese license plate character is treated first with a 3*3 element to produce what the authors label as "ALBP map". The ALBP map is then divided into 6*6 blocks. Each 6*6 block's histogram is concatenated into a vector which is then matched to vectors in a library. The authors report a 98.39% recognition rate with a 7.4 reduction in processing time. When Gabor filters are combined with their method, the authors report a recognition rate larger than 99% with a 10% increase in processing time over the method without Gabor filters. In (Fang et.al, 2009), template matching is used for character recognition. The authors admit that template matching is very sensitive to noise and is limited to one kind of font and one size. Poor quality license plate photos were not identified correctly. Errors due to lighting, movement and weather conditions affect the localization part which in turn affects the character recognition part. In (Sarfraz et.al, 2003) characters are extracted from license plates and then normalized to a 40*40 pixels size to make the method invariant to scaling. Then template matching is used by calculating the hamming distance between the unknown character and each of the possible characters in the database. The authors claim that template matching after normalization is more noise tolerant than structural analysis.

A 95.24% recognition rate is reported for ideal cases, cases where there was rotation, color errors or dirt and under various illumination conditions.

Others, (Broumandnia & Fathy, 2005; Kwasnicka & Wawrzyniak, 2002; Van Heerden & Botha, 2010; Turchenko et. al, 2003), use neural networks which are better for recognition. However Neural Network methods have their own disadvantages. The first main disadvantage is the high complexity of Neural Network methods which leads to large delays in processing. The second main disadvantage is that Neural Networks necessitate a phase of learning before they can be used. In our approach, no learning is needed and the algorithms are very simple relying on information available through minimal processing.

License Plate Localization

In order to locate a license plate in an image, researchers usually use either line detection (Kwasnicka & Wawrzyniak, 2002) (edge detection), histogram processing (Brad, 2001)and (Ozbay & Ercelebi, 2005) (gray value variation), blob analysis (Parker & Federl, 1996) and (Turchenko et. al, 2003) (study of regions), or a combination of these techniques. Line detection is usually done using Hough Transform to find lines that belong to characters. This is usually followed by grouping lines into closed boxes that represent the characters in the license plate. Hough Transform is superior in finding lines out of edges (Kwasnicka & Wawrzyniak, 2002); however it is sensitive to noise and computationally intensive. Histogram processing is the process of extracting lines from the image (usually, either vertically or horizontally) and studying the pixel values for each extracted line. In (Ozbay & Ercelebi, 2005) the numbers of white and black pixels in a line are used to extract text areas on a mixed image. If the number of white pixels, in a line, is less than a desired threshold or greater than another threshold, white pixels are converted to black. Other histogram processing methods use information about valleys and peaks to localize a license plate. Valleys correspond to dark areas in the histogram and peaks correspond to light areas. Fast variation between the dark and bright colors would indicate that such a line contains pixels that are part of a license plate (Brad, 2001) and (Kwasnicka & Wawrzyniak, 2002). Histogram processing is a considerably simple and fast technique since it only requires to extract lines and to study the values in each line. Histogram processing has at least one disadvantage which is that it is sensitive to the orientation of the license plate in the image. Blob analysis primarily works with regions instead of individual pixels. Plates are located according to characteristics determined by the bounding box surrounding the different regions. By thresholding regions according to the width, height, area, width to height ratio (Parker & Federl, 1996), and position on the x-axis and y-axis (Turchenko et. al, 2003), (Obeid & Zantout, 2007) of the bounding boxes, only possible license plate candidates are identified. Blob analysis requires a segmentation phase to precede it to extract the possible regions. Our approach can be considered to use a kind of histogram processing for character recognition and some kind of blob analysis for license plate localization.

SAUDI LICENSE PLATES

Figure 1 shows the different license plates that existed on the streets in Saudi Arabia as of year 2011. All license plates have sections which contain letters exclusively and sections which contain numbers exclusively.

In old plates letter and numeral sections are on the same horizontal level separated by the word Saudi. Both sections and the separating word only exist in Arabic. The number of letters and numerals in the old version is three each. In the new version of Saudi license plates, the letter and numeral sections are on the same horizontal level for each language. Letters and numerals

Figure 1. Saudi license plates

 New Long	 New Short
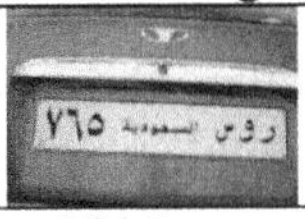 Old Long	 Old Short

exist in English and Arabic with a separating space. New Saudi license plates contain exactly three letters and up to four numerals for both languages. There is a one to one relationship between each character in the English section and the corresponding character in the Arabic section. The English character is always below its corresponding Arabic character. Both old and new Saudi license plates have two different layouts. One that is larger in width than the other, but in both cases the characteristics are the same. Furthermore, the distance between the letters in the letters section and the distance between the numerals in the numerals section is significantly smaller than the distance between letters on one hand and numbers on the other.

TableT1 shows the equivalence between English and Arabic characters in new license plates. Not all letters in the Arabic alphabet neither all characters in the English alphabet are in. However, all digits (0 through 9) are used.

In the new Saudi plates, each character, as well as each line dividing the regions is painted with the string "The Kingdom of Saudi Arabia" in both Arabic and English, for authentication reasons. This and the fact that usually images of license plates are noisy, necessitates some preprocessing of the image of a license plate before being able to localize it. Preprocessing starts by converting the colored image into a binary version. This reduces the information content without compromising the information necessary for localization. Then the algorithm uses binarization to label pixels in the image as "object pixels" and "background pixels." Currently, the threshold for binarization of an image is manually set by the user.

Table 1. Equivalence of English and Arabic characters

ا	A	ب	B	ح	J	د	D	ر	R	س	S	ص	X	ط	T	ع	E	ق	G
ك	K	ل	L	م	Z	ن	N	ه	H	و	U	ى	V						
٠	0	١	1	٢	2	٣	3	٤	4	٥	5	٦	6	٧	7	٨	8	٩	9

Figure 2. License plate, a- Before pre-processing; b, c, d- After pre-processing with different thresholds

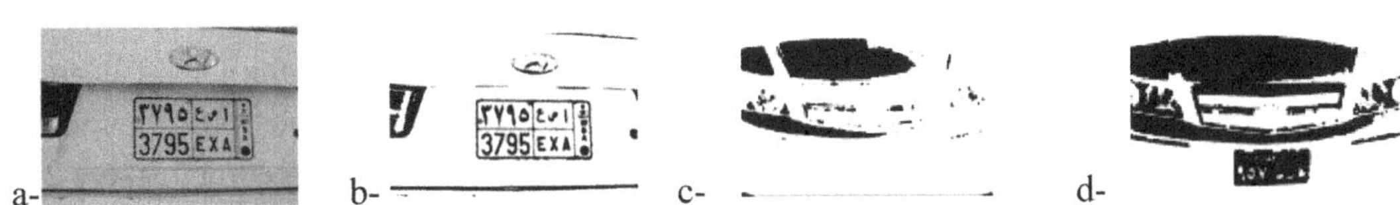

Figure 2 shows a license plate example before and after pre-processing.

The thresholding level is very important since it will affect whether the license plate is visible or not in the image. Figure 2 shows two binarized images, one with a bad thresholding level (F2c) and another with an appropriate one (F2d). related pixels will form regions that are visually distinct from other regions. Those regions will contain gaps, rough contours, small holes, or narrow breaks. The morphological operations of closing, majority, and thinning are then applied to the binarized image in order to enhance the quality of the objects. Region growing is then used to group all adjacent object pixels that are not adjacent to any other object pixels into one object. This step usually produces a large number of objects. The majority of those objects are small objects that are formed out of a small number of pixels. Such objects are considered noise and removed from the list of identified objects. Also large objects that are larger than the maximum possible size of a license plate character are filtered out of the list of objects.

CHARACTER RECOGNITION

In this section, three algorithms for recognizing characters in a Saudi license plate are described. All algorithms assume that the character has been identified as belonging to a Saudi license plate. The algorithm just tries to guess what the character is. All algorithms extract the information necessary to identify the character from lines taken at strategic locations across the bounding box of the character. The lines are taken horizontally and vertically in the middle and the extremities of the bounding box. The algorithms differ in the kind of information extracted from each line. One algorithm (peak position) relies on determining the positions where the pixels of a line change their color from dark to light. Another algorithm (peak number) relies on determining the number of color changes in a line without regards to their positions. The third algorithm (percentage) relies on calculating the percentage of pixels in a line that have the character color versus the total number of pixels in a line. In terms of computational complexity, the peak number algorithm is the most simple while the percentage algorithm is the most demanding. However, in terms of being able to recognize the most characters and accuracy, the percentage algorithm is the best while the peak numbers is the worst.

Character Recognition Algorithm Using the Number of Peaks Approach

In this algorithm the number of Peaks is calculated for a given factor. A Peak is defined as a crossing from a black pixel to a white pixel. A line starting with a white pixel is considered to have one peak at the beginning. The lines labeled in Figure 3 as 1 and 4 are always taken in the middle of the image horizontally and vertically respectively. Those lines will be referred to as (H) and (V) respectively. Lines 2, 3, 5 and 6 are taken at a distance from the boundaries of the bounding box of the character. This distance is always of a factor of the total length/width of the character. Lines 2, 3, 5 and 6 will be referred to as top (T), bottom (B), left (L) and right (R) respectively.

In Figure 3 line 1 which contains only one section where there is a transition from black pixels to white pixels this means that this line returns a value of 1. Line 3 returns a value of 2 since line 3 contains two transitions from black pixels to white pixels. On the other hand the line 4 starts with white pixels in the topmost section and contains two other sections of connected white pixels. This means it returns a value of 3.

The algorithm was run on all possible characters that are contained within a Saudi license plate using factors 1/3, 1/4 and 1/10. The number of peaks for each line was recorded. Table 2 shows the results of running the algorithm on the ten

Figure 3. Crossing lines of an image

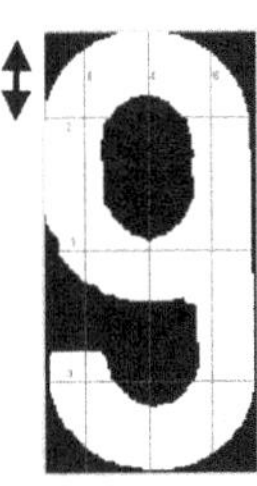

English numbers for a factor of 1/10 (Zantout & Almustafa, 2011).

The information for each set of characters (Arabic numbers, English numbers, Arabic numbers in old license plates, Arabic letters, English letters, Arabic letters in old license plates) was mined to find out the minimum number of lines that can be used. The only restriction was to use, as much as possible, the same factor for all sets of characters. At a minimum we tried to use the same factor for the same line throughout the character types. For each set, the first guideline was to start with the line that would divide the characters in this type into the maximum number of groups. For example, for the English numbers, the V line divided the numbers into three different groups, those that have a V line with 1 peak, those that have two peaks and those that have three. The second guideline was to use lines that would result in groups having an almost equal number of members.

Table 2. English numbers' number of peaks for specific line crossing for F=1/10

F=1/10 English	H	T	B	V	L	R
0	2	1	1	2	1	1
1	1	1	1	1	1	1
2	1	1	1	3	2	2
3	1	1	1	3	2	2
4	1	1	1	2	1	1
5	1	1	1	3	2	2
6	1	1	1	3	1	2
7	1	1	1	2	2	1
8	1	1	1	3	2	2
9	1	1	1	3	2	1

Figure 4 shows that to identify an English number, the L line should be first used to divide the English numbers into two groups. The first group consists of all numbers that would have 1 peak in their L line, namely the numbers 1, 4, 0 and 6. The second group consists of all numbers that would have two peaks in their L line, namely the numbers 7, 9, 3, 2, 8 and 5. For the first group, the V line is then used to break it up into three subgroups. Those that have 1 peak in their V line (the number 1), those that have two peaks (numbers 0 and 4) and those that have 3 peaks (number 6). So using this method, it is possible to recognize a 1 or a 6 using two lines only the L line and the V line. In order to differentiate between the 0 and the 4 the H line needs to be checked. If it contains 1 peak then this is the number 4 otherwise if it contains 2 peaks then this is the number 0. The same procedure is used to distinguish between the numbers in the second group. Using the R line, two subgroups are obtained, the numbers 7 and 9 which have 1 peak in their R line and the numbers 3, 2, 8 and 5 which have 2 peaks in their R lines. Distinguishing between the 7 and the 9 is done by counting the peaks in their V line. If two peaks are found then it is the number 7, otherwise if three peaks are found then it is the number 9. Differentiating between 2, 3, 5 and 8 is not possible using 1/10 factor. The L line with factor 1/3 is used to break the numbers up into two groups (2 and 3) and (5 and 8). Distinguishing between 2 and 3 is done by using the R line with a factor of 1/4. Distinguishing between 5 and 8 is done by using the L line with a factor of 1/4.

Figure 5 shows the flowchart for recognizing Arabic numbers (Hindi numerals) in a new Saudi license plate. The factor 1/4 was chosen here as the main factor. It was used to properly recognize numbers 3, 2, 5, 4, 7, 9 and 8. All factors could not distinguish between 0, 1 or 6 and

Figure 4. Flowchart for the English numbers based on the number of peaks algorithm

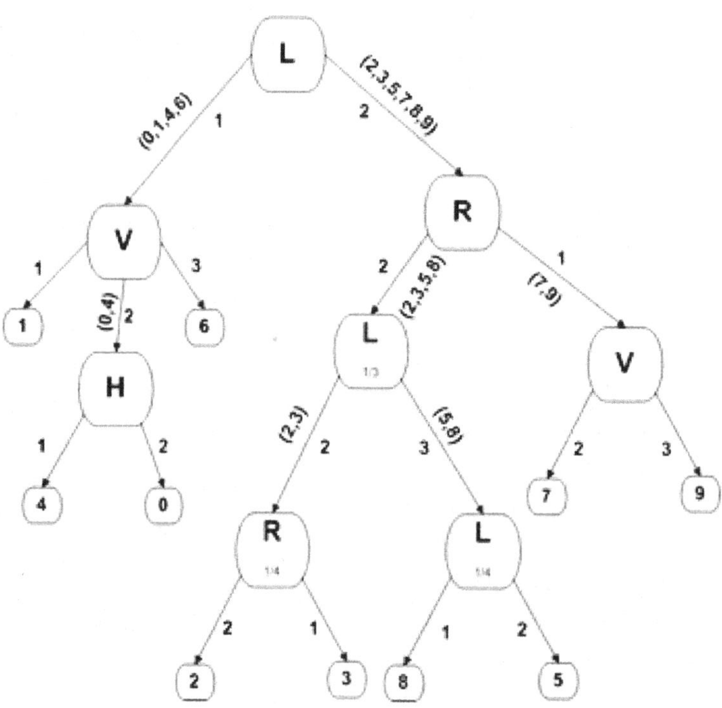

therefore this algorithm will not be able to distinguish between those numbers no matter which factor would be used. Another test should be found to distinguish between the 0, 1, or 6 numbers in new Saudi license plates. This was not considered as a major drawback for this method since in new license plates there is redundancy between the English and Arabic sections. The number of peaks method can recognize all numbers in the English section, this information can be used to corroborate the information from the Arabic section, even if we are not able to distinguish between 0, 1 and 6 in the Arabic section. Similarly, for Arabic numbers (Hindi numerals) in an old Saudi license plate, all factors could not distinguish between 0, 1 or 6. For English letters in a new Saudi license plate, a factor of 1/10 was used to properly recognize all the letters except for differentiating between the T and the L. All factors could not distinguish between T and L, in this case, it is also not a serious problem because in new Saudi license plates, there is a redundancy between the English sections and the Arabic sections. The equivalent Arabic letters ط and ل can be distinguished using this algorithm. As for Arabic characters in new Saudi license plate, Figure 12 shows that a factor 1/10 was also chosen here as the main factor. Only the letter ع is identified correctly when the V line returns 3. The L line with a factor of 1/3, the R line with a factor of 1/4, the B line with a factor of 1/3, the T line with a factor of 1/4, the R line with a factor of 1/4, the B line with a factor of 1/4, and the L line with a factor of 1/4 should all be used to be able to distinguish between all characters. Similarly, for Arabic letters in an old Saudi license plate, the factors 1/10, 1/3, 1/4 can be used to recognize all characters.

The "number of Peaks" algorithm was executed on images of license plates containing all possible characters shown in Figure 6. The algorithm was successful in recognizing all characters. Characters extracted from license plates were used to test the amount of noise that the algorithm can withstand before it will not be able to recognize any more characters. The number of peaks algorithm was successful in recognizing all characters whether preprocessed or taken directly from the license plates. Figure 6 shows the images produced by the algorithm for number 9. The upper leftmost image shows the original image used which is the number 9 extracted from the image of a real license plate. The image was first turned into its negative (shown in the upper middle image) since the algorithm assumes white pixels are background pixels and black pixels are character pixels. Noise was added to the number 9 that resulted in the upper rightmost image. The first phase of preprocessing results in the lower leftmost image and the second phase of preprocessing resulted in the lower middle image. Finally, the lower rightmost image shows the recovered image after morphological operations were done on the image output by the second phase of preprocessing.

Two types of error performance were considered, noisy images and images in which noise was artificially introduced. Both simulations showed very good results of recognizing the

Figure 5. Flowchart for the Arabic New Letters Based on the number of peaks Algorithm

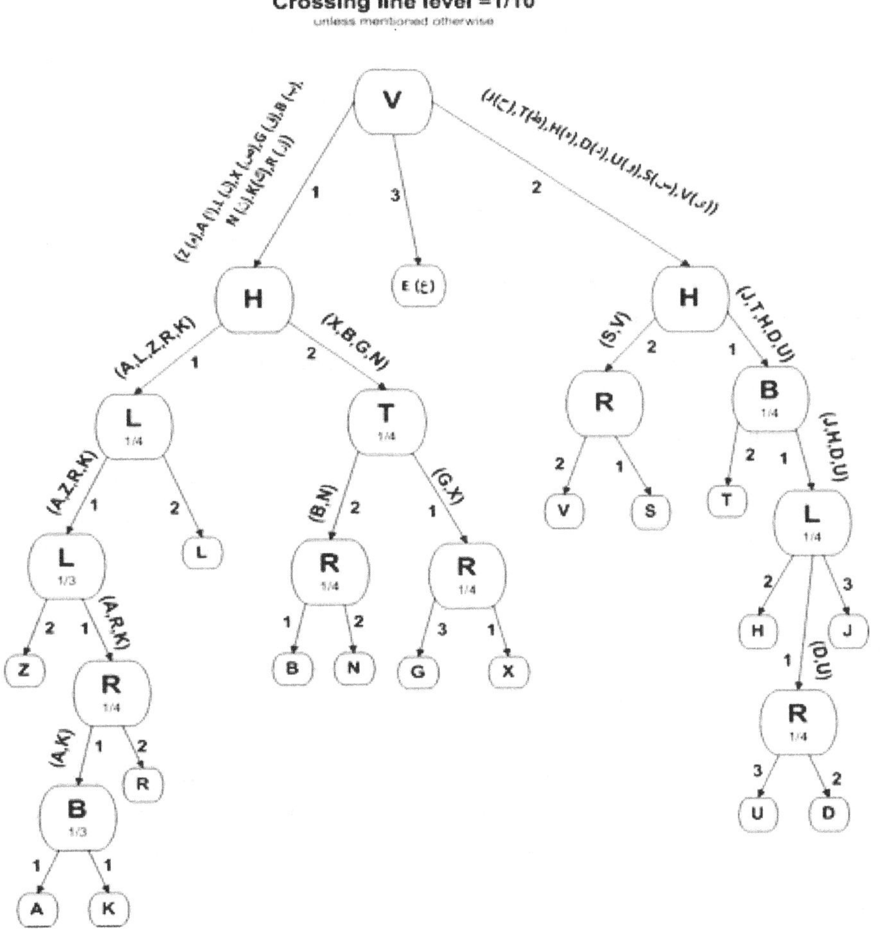

Figure 6. Simulation of the number of peaks algorithm from plate to recognition with introduced noise

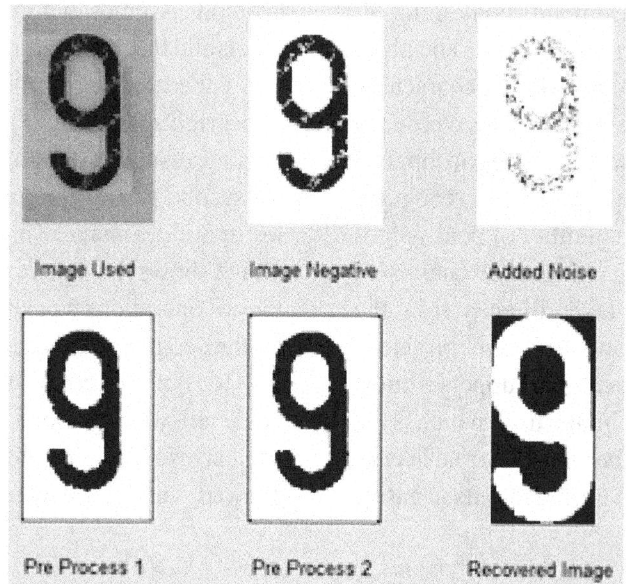

characters. Artificial noise was introduced using Equation (1)

$$P = Q + \mu n \tag{1}$$

Q is a matrix representation of the image. n is a matrix that has the same size as Q and consists of uniformly distributed pseudo-random numbers. μ is a constant which is used to control the amount of noise to introduce in the image. The performance is measured using the Frobenius norm of $(P-Q)$. The Frobenius norm of a $m\times n$ Matrix A is defined as the square root of the sum of the absolute squares of its elements and is given in Equation (2)

$$\|A_F\| = \sqrt{\sum_{i=1}^{m}\sum_{j=1}^{n} | a_{ij} |^2} \tag{2}$$

A plot of the Frobenius norm as a function of μ is shown in Figure 7. The solid vertical lines show the averaged threshold for the value of μ for different type of characters where the noisy image can be recognized by the algorithm. The dashed vertical line shows the averaged threshold for the value of μ beyond which the Human eye would not be able to recognize the character. The human eye threshold was determined empirically based on human responses to the noisy images. Figure 7 shows the results of running the algorithm on artificially induced noisy photos of English numerals, English Letters, Arabic Numbers and Arabic Letters using the number of peaks algorithm and simulating an average of 60 runs for each character. It turns out that the value of the threshold of recognition is equal to $\mu = 15.93$ for Arabic letters, $\mu = 6.57$ for English numbers, $\mu = 13.55$ for English letters and $\mu = 10.42$ for Arabic Numbers, while the human eye threshold was 17 in this case.

The performance of the algorithm was also tested when the images of the characters are rotated. The rotation of the image is only considered around the z-axis (perpendicular to the image plane) with an angle θ measured from the x-axis counter clockwise as seen in Figure 8. The solid lines in Figure 18 indicate the x and y axis, and

Figure 7. Performance of the Frobenius norm of (P-Q) as a function of for the number of peaks algorithm

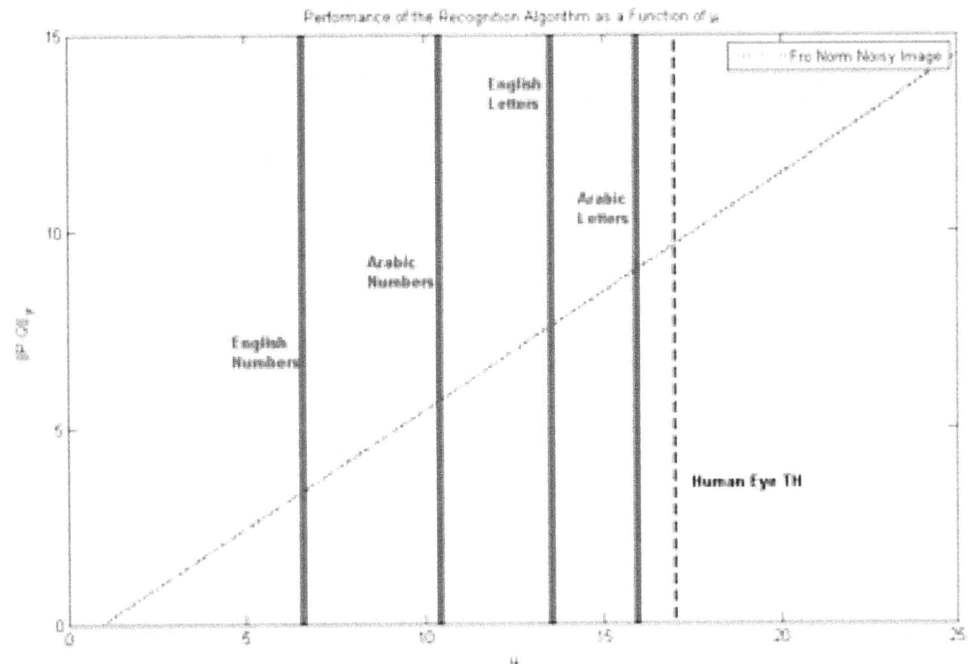

the broken lines show the axes after they were rotated by the angle of rotation θ.

The test was done on all possible characters in a Saudi license plate. The maximum rotational angle with which a given number can be correctly identified by the recognition algorithm is noted. Any degree of rotation greater than the given angle, for a specific image, would give incorrect results. Table 3 shows the results for English numbers in a Saudi license plate. It is clear that 0 is invariant under rotation since, no matter how it is rotated, it will always give two peaks. 5 is the least invariant number to rotation since a rotation of 1 degree will make it unrecognizable by the algorithm.

Character Recognition Algorithm using the Percentage Approach Algorithm

In this algorithm the percentage of character pixels to total number of pixels for a crossing is used to identify a character. The same crossing lines used in the algorithm for the number of peaks are used in this algorithm. In Figure 3, line number 1 crosses the middle of the bounding box of the character 9. Most of the pixels on line 1 belong to the character 9; this is why the percentage returned is 91%. he algorithm was run on all pos-

Figure 8. A sample of a rotated image

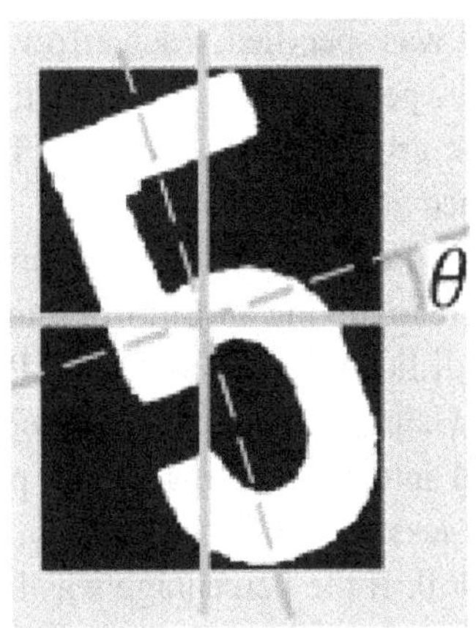

Table 3. Resulted rotational thresholds for the number of peaks algorithm for English numbers

English Number	Threshold Angle for Number of Peaks Algorithm	
	Positive Rotation	Negative Rotation
0	180°	-180 °
1	180°	-3 °
2	3°	-1 °
3	5°	-5 °
4	17°	-9 °
5	1°	-1 °
6	43°	-26 °
7	1°	-4 °
8	4°	-3 °
9	4°	-3 °

sible characters that are contained within a Saudi license plate using factors of 1/3, 1/4 and 1/10. The percentage returned for each specific line was recorded, for every character in the English and Arabic sections of old and new Saudi license plates, in tables (Zantout & Almustafa, 2011). Similar to what was done for the algorithm that uses the number of peaks; the tables were studied to determine the minimum number of lines that can be used to recognize characters in a Saudi License plate using percentages.

The flowchart shown in Figure 9 detail how to recognize a character given the percentages of the crossing lines. One main factor was used in the flowchart. Wherever needed, if a different factor was used it was specified. Each arrow is labeled with both the percentage returned for the specific line and the group of characters that have to be distinguished at that stage.

Figure 9 is a flowchart summarizing the procedure for recognizing an English number from a new Saudi license plate using the Percentage algorithm. Using the H line the English numbers are divided into two groups. If the percentage returned is less than 0.6 then the character is 4, 7, 2, 1, 3 or 0. If the percentage was larger than 0.0.6 then the character is 5, 6, 8 or 9. Distinguishing between 5, 6, 8 and 9 is done by using the T line. a 5 returns a percentage less than 0.4 while 6, 8 or 9 return a higher percentage. Distinguishing between 6, 8 or 9 is not possible using a factor of 1/4. Distinguishing between 4, 7, 2, 1, 3 and 0 is done by using first the R line. 4, 7 and 2 return a percentage lower than 0.7 while 0, 1 and 3 return a higher percentage. Distinguishing between 4, 7 and 2 is done using the T line. 2 returns a percentage larger than 0.4 while 4 or 7 return a lower percentage. The B line is then used to distinguish between 4 and 7. 4 returns a percentage larger than 0.5 while 7 returns a smaller percentage. Distinguishing between 1, 3 and 0 is done by first using the T line. If it returns a percentage larger than 0.6 the character is 1. Otherwise, the L line is used and if it returns a percentage larger than 0.6 the character is 0, otherwise it is 3. Using a factor of 1/3, the T line is used to recognize a 6 if the percentage is lower than 0.4, while 8 or 9 return a percentage higher than 0.4. Finally the B line returns an 8 if the percentage is higher than 0.4; it returns 9 if the percentage is lower.

Similar flowcharts were built to recognize English letters and Arabic letters in New and old plates (Zantout & Almustafa, 2011). Due to the different fonts used in new and old license plates, the lines, percentages and factors used for the recognition algorithm are different between old and new license plates for the same Arabic numbers.

It was shown that the percentage algorithm can correctly recognize all English and Arabic numbers and letters in new Saudi plates and Arabic numbers and letters in old Saudi plates.

The same error analysis that was done for the number of peaks algorithm was repeated for the percentage algorithm. It turns out that the percentage algorithm gives better results, on average, than the number of peaks approach. In Figure 10, the solid vertical lines show the averaged threshold for the value of μ beyond which the noisy image is so corrupted that the algorithm would not be able to recognize a character correctly.

Figure 9. Flowchart for the English numbers based on the percentage algorithm

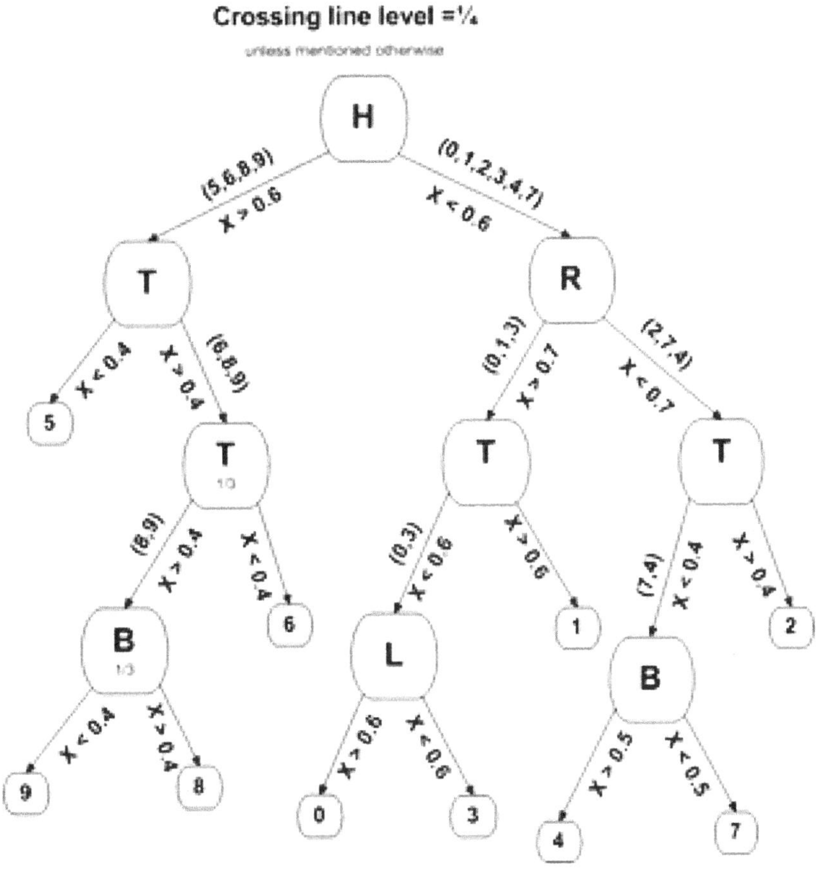

In the case of English numerals, the value of the threshold of recognition is μ = 21.48, for English Letters μ = 18.32, for Arabic numbers μ = 15.38 and for Arabic Letters μ = 15.37. All values for μ were calculated as an average of 60 runs for all possible characters. The dashed vertical line shows the human eye threshold to recognize the noisy images and it is μ = 17 in this case. The human eye threshold was determined empirically based on human responses to the noisy images. Figure 10 clearly shows that the algorithm, on average, can recognize characters to a threshold better than Humans in all cases except for Arabic letters. Performance of the algorithm due to image rotation was also tested. It was found that the percentage algorithm is more sensitive to rotation than the number of peaks algorithm.

Character Recognition Algorithm Using the Position Approach Algorithm

In this algorithm, the positions of the peaks for a given crossing line are considered. The algorithm calculates the position of the peak for a given factor instead of calculating the number of peaks or percentages. We have two types of crossing lines for this algorithm as seen in Figure 11, the solid lines with titles adjacent to them as H, T, B, V, L and R, and are associated with the factor F. The solid lines vary in locations based on the value of the factor used. The other crossing lines are the dashed lines and are fixed in the 1/3 and 2/3 locations for the horizontal and the vertical lines. The image is divided into nine different

Figure 10. Performance of the Frobenius norm of (P-Q) as a function of for the percentage algorithm

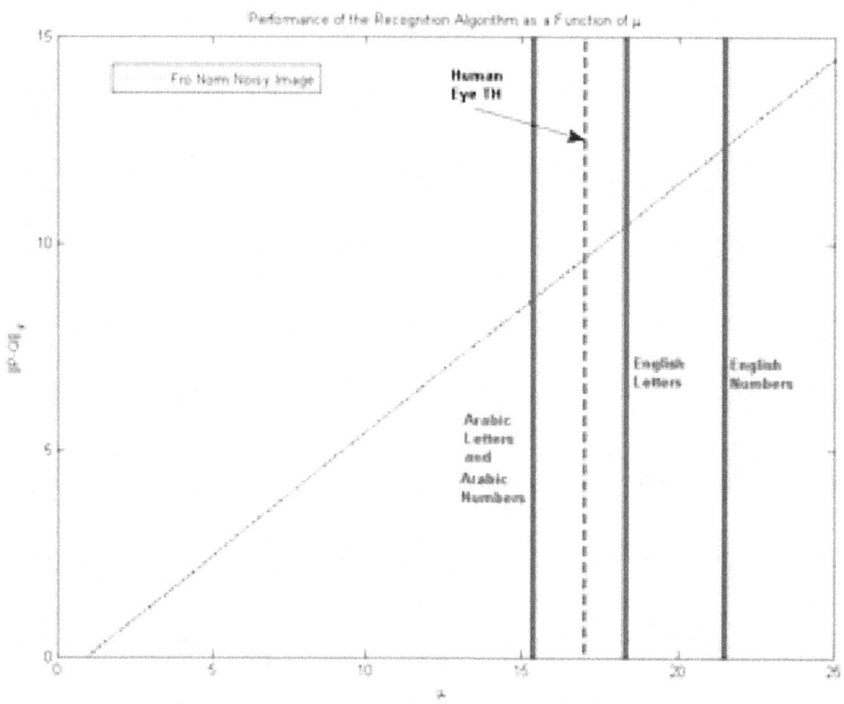

locations; three of those locations can contain peaks for every solid line. In Figure 11, the T line with F=1/4 has two peaks, one peak is left of the leftmost dashed line while the other is to the right of rightmost dashed line. This means that the positions of the peaks for the T line in Figure 11 is in the left (L) and right (R). No peak is available in the center (C) of the T line. The peak position algorithm would then return 1 for left, 0 for middle and 1 for right. Similarly, the L line has a peak above the topmost dashed line and another below the lowermost dashed line. Again here, no peak is available between the lines so the algorithm returns 1 for top (T), 0 for center (C) and 1 for below (B).

Table 4 gives the results for peak positions for English numbers of a Saudi license plate using a factor of 1/4. Each column in the table has two headings. The topmost heading indicates the line used H, T, B, V, L and R. The lower heading indicates the position on the line where the peak is. A 1 in a column means that there is a peak in that position for that line. A 0 indicates no peak is found in that position on that line.

Figure 12 summarizes the procedure of recognizing an English number in a Saudi license

Figure 11. Crossing line of an image for the position algorithm

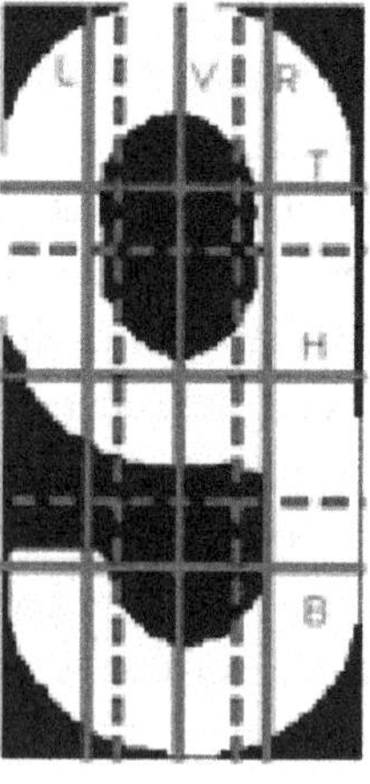

Table 4. English numbers' position of the peaks for specific line crossing for F=1/4

	H			T			B			V			L			R		
1/4	**L**	**C**	**R**	**L**	**C**	**R**	**L**	**C**	**R**	**T**	**C**	**B**	**T**	**C**	**B**	**T**	**C**	**B**
English Numbers																		
0	1	0	1	1	0	1	1	0	1	1	0	1	1	0	0	1	0	0
1	0	1	0	1	1	0	0	1	0	1	0	0	1	0	0	1	0	0
2	0	1	0	1	0	1	1	0	0	1	1	1	1	1	0	1	0	1
3	0	1	0	1	0	1	1	0	1	1	1	1	1	0	1	1	0	0
4	1	0	0	1	0	0	1	0	0	1	0	1	1	0	0	0	1	0
5	1	0	0	1	0	0	1	0	1	1	1	1	1	0	1	1	1	0
6	1	0	0	1	0	1	1	0	1	1	1	1	1	0	0	1	1	0
7	0	1	0	0	1	0	1	0	0	1	1	0	1	0	1	1	0	0
8	1	0	0	1	0	1	1	0	1	1	1	1	1	0	0	1	0	0
9	1	0	0	1	0	1	1	0	1	1	1	1	1	0	1	1	0	0

plate using the peak positions approach with a factor of 1/4.

Similar tables and flowcharts can be built for the remaining characters of Saudi license plates (Zantout & Almustafa, 2011). It was shown that the position of peaks algorithm can correctly recognize English and Arabic numbers and English letters in new Saudi plates. It can also recognize Arabic letters in old Saudi plates. However, it cannot distinguish between Arabic letters ا and م in new Saudi plates. This is not considered a problem since letters in the English section can be correctly recognized and therefore the Arabic letters can be deduced. Moreover, Arabic numbers 2 and 3 in old Saudi plates cannot be distinguished.

Error performance for this algorithm was done in a similar way to the first two approaches. In Figure 13, the solid vertical lines show the averaged threshold for the value of beyond which the noisy image is so corrupted that the algorithm would not be able to recognize a character correctly.

In the case of English numerals, the value of the threshold of recognition is $\mu = 19.30$, for the English Letters $\mu = 5.97$, for the Arabic numbers $\mu = 10.88$ and for Arabic Letters $\mu = 15.83$. The average was also taken over 60 runs for all possible characters, as was done for the previous algorithms. The dashed vertical line shows the human eye threshold to recognize the noisy images and it is $\mu = 17$ in this case also. The human eye threshold was determined empirically based on human responses to the noisy images in this case also.

The algorithm was run on rotated images of all possible characters in a Saudi license plate and ranges for the angles of rotation for which each character was correctly recognized are denoted in (Zantout & Almustafa, 2011). Any degree of rotation greater than the given angle, for a specific image, would give incorrect results.

The algorithm was run on noisy images where artificial noise was added to the clear image to simulate noise. The algorithm was successful in recognizing those cases.

PLATE LOCALIZATION

In this section, two algorithms that were developed for locating a Saudi license plate in an image are described. Both algorithms rely on two sources of information. The first source is the alignment between the different possible characters. As discussed previously, characters in a Saudi license

Figure 12. Flowchart for the English numbers based on the positions of peaks algorithm

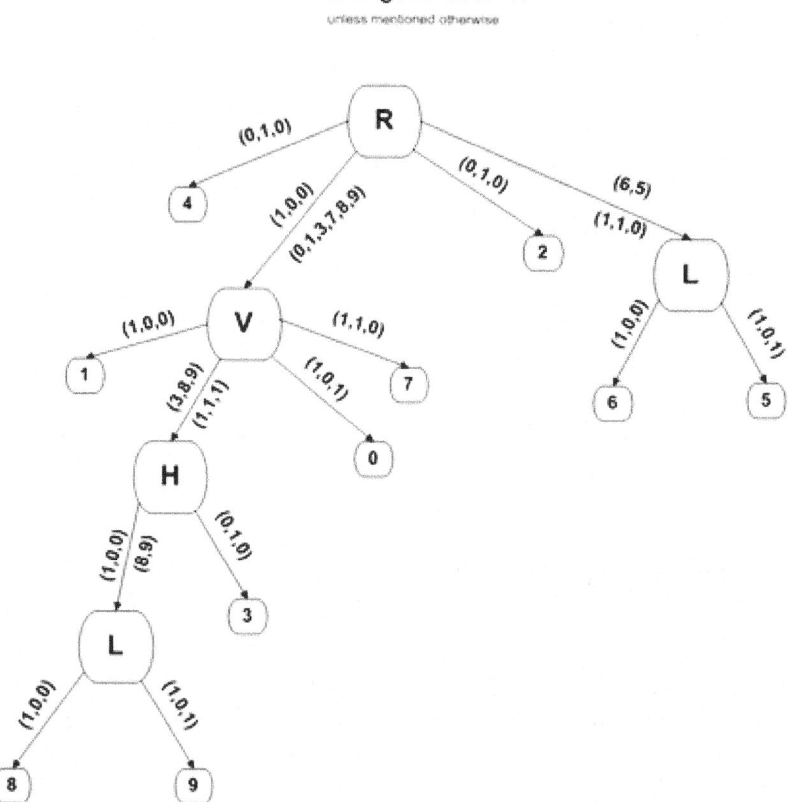

plate have horizontal alignment in that the license plate numbers are aligned horizontally. In case of new license plates, each Arabic character is aligned with its corresponding English character vertically. The Arabic character is always on top of the English character. The second information that the algorithms use is the actual estimate of the character. The difference between the two algorithms is the extent at which the algorithm relies on the alignment and the extent that it relies on character recognition. In the first algorithm, horizontal and vertical alignments are exploited first to locate a license plate. Then recognition is used to identify the characters. Recognition for each character is done after the character type is known (Arabic or English and Letter or number). In the second algorithm, only vertical alignment is exploited to restrict the choices for characters. However recognition does not assume any prior information about a character and therefore tries to recognize the type as well as value of the character. The advantage of the first method, compared to the second method, is its applicability to both old and new license plates while its disadvantage is that it will not work if a partial license plate is in the image.

Plate Localization Using Alignment Information First

The localization phase is subdivided into four steps. The first step determines which one of the objects identified in the preprocessing phase are possible candidates for characters from a Saudi license plate. The second step would form series out of objects by observing the adjacency between

Figure 13. Performance of the Frobenius norm of (P-Q) as a function of μ for the percentage algorithm

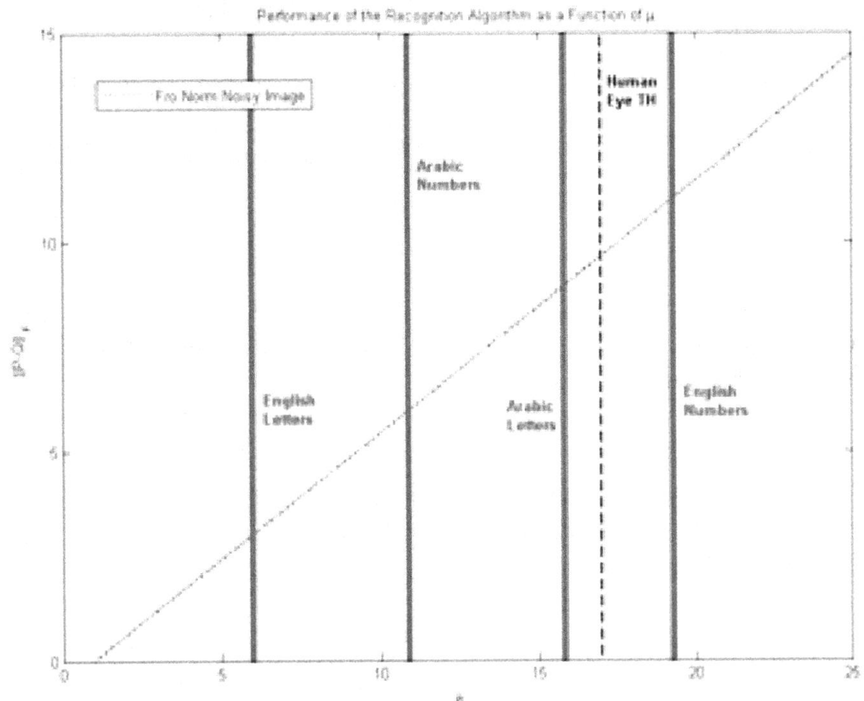

objects. The third step would determine the possibility of series belonging to a Saudi license plate by observing adjacency between series. The fourth step is required only in case of new license plates being in the image. In this step, the existence of four series adjacent horizontally and vertically is tested. If four adjacent series exist then we have a new license plate, otherwise we have an old license plate.

In all Saudi license plates, the characters (whether letters or numbers) have some common size characteristics. As shown in Figure 1, if we assume that the whole license plate is assumed to appear in the image, those characteristics are:

1. The width of the object should be less than 1/6 width of the image.
2. The height of the object should be less than half the height of the image.
3. A set of characters are considered adjacent if and only if they satisfy the X-axis constraint and the upper and low Y-Axis constraints.

The X-Axis constraint for a Saudi license plate depends on both characters being tested for adjacency. If the width to height ratio of the first character is greater than .9 and the ratio of background pixels to object pixels in the bounding box of the character is greater than .8 then the character is most likely an Arabic 0. The character to the right of the Arabic 0 would be adjacent to the Arabic 0 only if it satisfies Equation (3).

$$X_1 - X_2 < W * 5 \quad (3)$$

Where, as shown in Figure 14,

- X_1 is the x-coordinate of the upper-right corner of the bounding box of the Arabic 0.

Figure 14. X-axis adjacency constraint

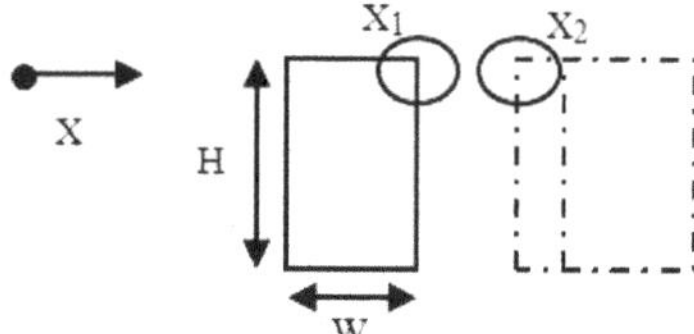

- X_2 is the x-coordinate of the upper-left corner of the bounding box of the character to the right of the Arabic 0.
- W is the width of the bounding box of the Arabic 0.

The multiplier 5 in Equation (3) was used because of the small size of the character in height relative to other numbers. The equation takes 5 times the width of the Arabic 0 to find adjacency.

If the character under consideration is not the Arabic 0, then the character to its right is considered adjacent if and only if X satisfies Equation (4).

$$X_1 - X_2 < H * 1.5 \tag{4}$$

One and a half times the height of the character would be the threshold to find adjacent characters. The height was used because the rest of the characters are taller than wider, and characters in Saudi plates are more than a width of a character in space.

The Y-Axis constraints also depend on both characters being considered for adjacency. In order for two characters to be adjacent, they should also satisfy the y-axis constraints expressed mathematically in Equations (5) and (6).

$$Y_1 - (H * 0.2) <= Y_2 <= Y_1 + (H * 0.5) \tag{5}$$

Where, as shown in Figure 15,

- Y_1 is the y-coordinate of the upper right corner of the leftmost character.
- Y_2 is the y-coordinate of the upper left corner of the rightmost character.
- H is the height of the bounding box of the leftmost character.

$$Y_3 - (H * .5) <= Y_4 <= Y_3 + (H * .2) \tag{6}$$

Where, as shown in Figure 16,

- Y_3 is the y-coordinate of the lower right corner of the leftmost character.
- Y_4 is the y-coordinate of the lower left corner of the rightmost character.
- H is the height of the bounding box of the leftmost character.
- 0.2 and 0.5 were determined by calibration done on several images of Saudi license plates.

All Saudi license plates have two series of equally spaced characters. One series consists exclusively of alphabetic characters (letters) and the other consists exclusively of digits (numbers). However, in short layout license plates, the characters series and the numbers series are very close to each other. This leads to the series being mistaken as one series rather than two. This is why, in the second step of the localization phase,

Figure 15. Upper Y-axis adjacency constraint

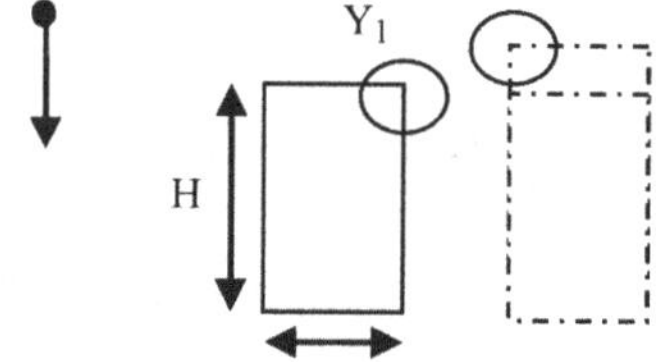

Figure 16. Lower Y-axis adjacency constraint

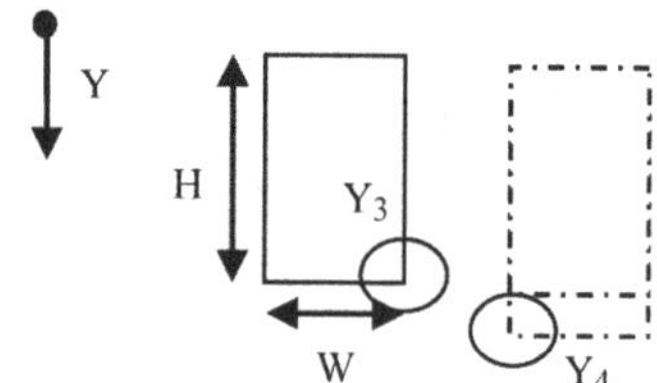

the objects that passed the test in the first step are considered as potential license plate candidates. The distance between each object and its adjacent objects is calculated. Looking at all distances between adjacent objects, there will be one distance (y) which is different from all other distances (x) as shown in Figure 17. Then the objects that are around "x" near each other are part of the same series. The objects that are at a distance of "y" from each other would belong to different series.

All Saudi license plates have two series of characters that are horizontally adjacent. The left series will always contain numbers (whether in Arabic or English) and the right series will always contain exactly three objects that are alphabetic characters (whether English or Arabic). In the third localization step, horizontally adjacent series that satisfy the series adjacency conditions are grouped into one region. The series adjacency conditions are:

1. The number of objects in the rightmost series is 3.

2. X -coordinates that satisfy Equation (7):

$$X_1 < X_2 < X_1 + W \quad (7)$$

Where, as shown in Figure 18,

- X_1 is the x-coordinate of the upper right corner of the leftmost series' bounding box.
- X_2 is the x-coordinate of the upper left corner of the rightmost series' bounding box.
- W is the width of the leftmost series.

3. The upper boundaries of the bounding boxes of the two series that form the region should not be off by more than 10% of the height. So should be the case for the lower boundaries.
4. The average spacing in one series should not be off from the average spacing in the other series by more than 50%.

For old Saudi license plates, at the end of the third localization step, the license plate is identified. However new license plates have two, vertically adjacent, regions. So the fourth step of the localization algorithm would be to check whether there are two regions that are vertically adjacent, as shown in Figure 19. Two regions are considered to be adjacent vertically if the vertical boundaries of their bounding boxes are not off horizontally by more than 10% of the width. This means that the X-coordinates of the upper left corners of the bounding boxes of both regions should satisfy Equation (8).

$$X_1 - (5\% * W) < X_2 < X_1 + (5\% * W) \quad (8)$$

Where, as shown in Figure 19,

- X_1 is the x-coordinate of the upper left corner of the upper region's bounding box.
- X_2 is the x-coordinate of the upper left corner of the lower region's bounding box.
- W is the average width of the both regions.

The algorithm was tested on 13 images. In 11 of the 13 images, license plates were recognized properly and no other objects were mistaken for license plates. In 2 images, license plates were

Figure 17. Characters to series

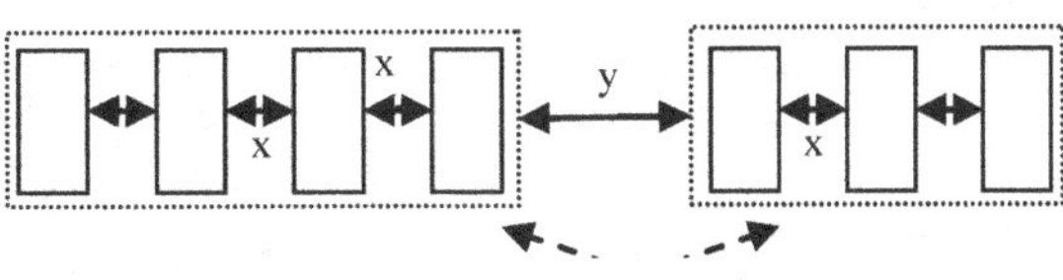

Figure 18. Series horizontal adjacency

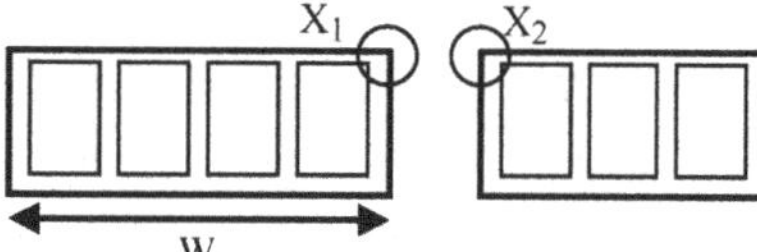

incorrectly recognized. This was due mainly to incorrect preprocessing of the images. In these 2 images, there were missing characters that are required to determine whether a series is English or Arabic series and characters that were connected to other large objects. In one of the images, the correct license plate was recognized but an extra candidate was also identified as a possible license plate.

As an example consider the license plate shown in Figure 20 before and after preprocessing with a threshold of 100.

Step 1 – Check adjacency: The X and Y coordinates vary between a character and another. The X coordinate should follow the following equation X1 - X2 < H * 1.5. Consider Figure 21 on which 4 points are shown that will be used to check for adjacency.

Consider the leftmost character ٨ and the Arabic zero ٠. The coordinates of points 1 and 2 on these characters are shown in Figure 21. Checking the conditions, we find that those two characters are adjacent.

Figure 19. Series vertical adjacency

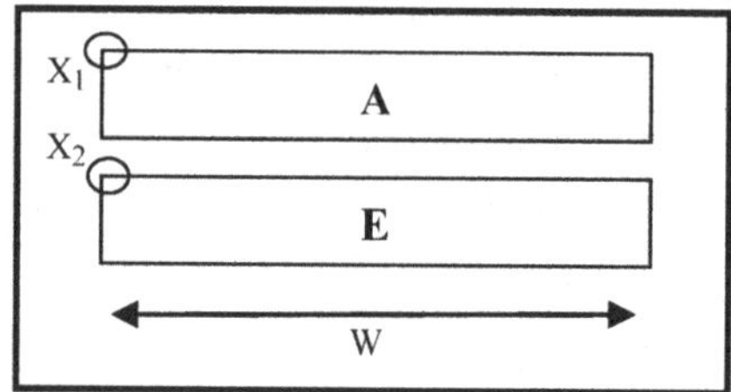

$X_2 - X_1 < H * 1.5$, $X_2 - X_1 = 211 - 184 = 27$, $H * 1.5 = 80 * 1.5 = 120$, $27 < 120$

Condition 1:

$Y_1 - (H * 0.2) <= Y_2 <= Y_1 + (H * 0.5)$

$Y_1 - (H * 0.2) = 245 - (80 * 0.2) <= Y_2 <= 245 + (80 * 0.5)$

$229 <= Y_2 <= 285$

Condition 2:

$Y_3 - (H * 0.5) <= Y_4 <= Y_3 + (H * 0.2)$

$325 - 40 <= 296 <= 325 + 16$

$285 <= 296 <= 341$

Therefore these two characters are adjacent.

Consider now the Arabic zero and the rightmost ٨. Figure 21 shows the coordinates of points 1 and 2 considered for adjacency.

Checking the conditions, we find:

Figure 20. a- Original image of a license plate; b- Processed image

a-  b- 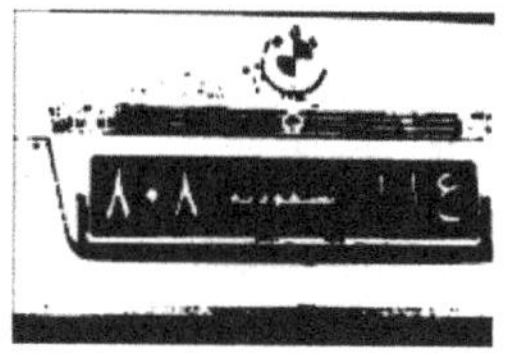

Figure 21. Coordinates of points used to check for adjacency of leftmost ٨ and the Arabic zero ٠

$X_2 - X_1 = 259 - 231 = 28 < 20 * 5 = 100$

$= 28 < 100$

Condition 1:

$Y_1 - (H * 0.2) <= Y_2 <= Y_1 + (H * 0.5)$

$Y_1 - (H * 0.2) = 277 - (19 * 0.2) <= Y_2 <= 277 + (19 * 0.5)$

$273 <= Y_2 <= 286$ Condition 1 is not valid

No need to check condition 2, since condition 1 is not valid. So these two characters are not adjacent.

But since the system looks backward and forward for adjacency, the system now checks if the rightmost ٨ is adjacent to the Arabic zero on its left. The following computations show that the rightmost ٨ is adjacent to Arabic zero.

$X_2 - X_1 < H * 1.5$ and H is the height of the current character under testing which is ٨

$X_2 - X_1 = 259 - 231 = 28 < 76 * 1.5 = 114$

$= 28 < 114$

Condition 1:

$Y_2 - (H * 0.2) <= Y_1 <= Y_2 + (H * 0.5)$

$Y_2 - (H * 0.2) = 246 - (76 * 0.2) <= Y_2 <= 246 + (76 * 0.5)$

$231 <= Y_1 <= 284$ and $Y_1 = 277$

Condition 2:

$Y_3 - (H * 0.5) <= Y_4 <= Y_3 + (H * 0.2)$

$322 - 38 <= 296 <= 322 + 15$

Figure 22. Coordinates of points used to check for adjacency of rightmost ٨ and the Arabic zero

Figure 23. Adjacent characters found by the algorithm

$284 <= 296 <= 337$ and $Y_4 = 296$

٨ and Arabic zero are adjacent.

By the end of Step 1, all of the characters in the image of Figure 23 are adjacent to each other.

Step 2: Searching for a potential license plate: Not all adjacent characters have the same separating distance. At the end of this step, the only section that was a potential license plate candidate is shown in Figure 23. Figure 24 shows the separating distances between the characters. Taking the most common distance between each character and its adjacent one, the system can split the character candidates into two separate adjacent sections (Figure 25).

Step 3: The rightmost section has 3 characters and the X coordinates does not satisfy the following equation:

$X_1 < X_2 < X_1 + W$

$292 < 582 < (292 + 144)$ this equation is not valid

Step 4: In case the above equation could not find adjacent sections, then we are dealing with an old plate. Similar procedure can be followed to localize a new Saudi plate. Figure 26 shows an image containing a Saudi license plate.

Figure 27 shows the image for the English letter "E" after successfully locating the plate of Figure 26. Figure 28 and F29 show all the resulting characters in their bounding boxes after successfully locating the plate in the Figure 26 for the numbers sections (Arabic (top) and English (bottom)), and the letters sections (Arabic (top) and English (bottom)) respectively.

The only difficulty faced was the need for human setting of the threshold of binarization for images taken under different lighting conditions. The threshold needed to be changed when a plate was not localized in an image. Once the correct threshold was used, the algorithm located the license plate and extracted the characters of the license plate correctly.

Plate Localization Using the Hybrid Method

Like the algorithm detailed in the previous section, after preprocessing, the algorithm determines all

Figure 24. Adjacent characters with the separating distance shown

Figure 25. Two adjacent sections extracted from license plate of Figure 38

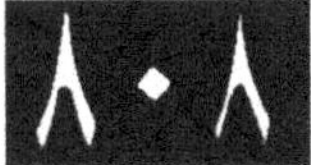

blobs in the image under consideration. Then the objects are filtered based on their size. Objects that are too small or too large are discarded from being possible Saudi license plate characters. Such small or large objects are considered as not being of interest. As an example the rear light in Figure 26 will be filtered as a large object. The trunk key hole will also be filtered as a small object. The objects, from Figure 26, that made it through the filter can be seen in Figures F30, F31 and F32. The algorithm then computes the x-coordinates of the center points for each possible object. Two objects having close x-coordinates are vertically aligned. This means they are possible candidates for letters or numbers in a new Saudi license plate (Arabic on top of English). However, they might be the letters K.S.A as well as the palm tree symbol in the plate, as seen in the rightmost part of the plate in Figure 26. For example, the x coordinates of two objects (that correspond to the number 3 in Arabic and English) are almost equal (290.5 vs. 291.5) as seen in Table 6. This means that the corresponding objects are vertically aligned.

Figure 26. An image with Saudi license plate

First we check to see if the object is a number, so we run all three algorithms associated with recognizing numbers on it for English and Arabic. The results are shown in Table 5. The number 999 is used for cases when the object was not recognized as a correct number. The total number of objects for the plate of Figure 26 is 22 objects. Each row contains the results of tests for one object. For example, the second cell in the row corresponding to object 1 indicates that the pixel-density algorithm when applied to object 1 resulted in recognizing it as the number 8. The results of applying the Position of Peak algorithm are shown in the third column of Table 5. The results of applying the Number of Peaks algorithm are shown in the fourth column. For object 1, both algorithms recognized it as the number 1. Looking at Table 6, we can see that objects 2 and 3 are vertically aligned. Also Table 6 shows that objects 4 and 5 are vertically aligned as well as objects 6 and 7, objects 9 and 10 and objects 12 and 13. Object 3 is also determined from Table 6 to be above object 2, this means that object 3 is an Arabic character and object 2 is an English characters. Looking at the results of object 3 as an Arabic number, we conclude that it must be the number 3 since all three algorithms recognized an Arabic 3. Looking at the results of object 2 as an English number, we cannot conclude that it also must be the number 3.

One method recognized an English 3 while the other two methods recognized an English 5 and an English 2. However, we have already determined, through vertical alignment, that ob-

Figure 27. The letter "E" after locating the plate

Figure 28. Numbers in bounding boxes

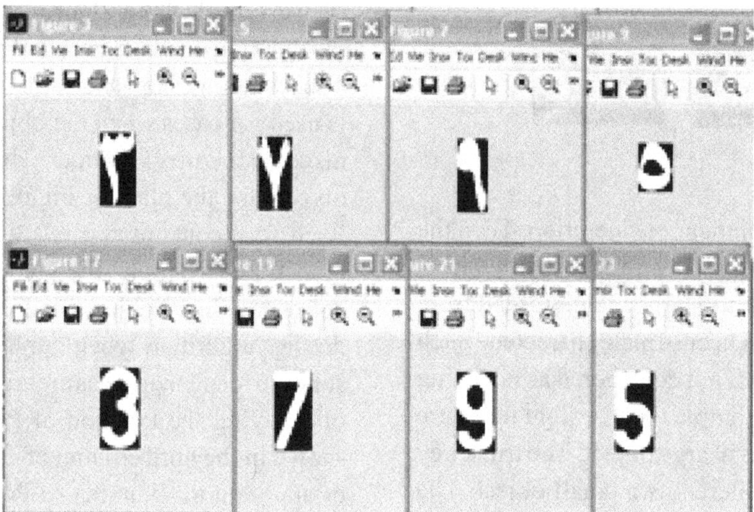

Figure 29. Letters in bounding boxes

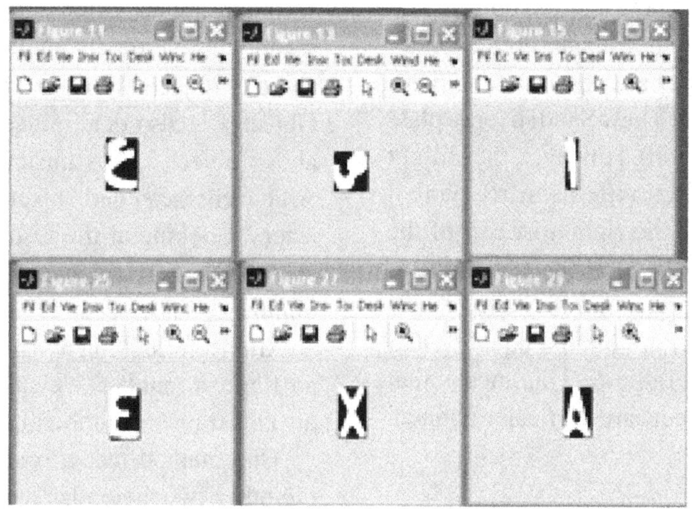

jects 2 and 3 are the same number, object 2 in Arabic and object 3 in English. This leads us to affirm that objects 2 and 3 are the number 3 in Arabic and English respectively. Objects 4 and 5 are vertically aligned and they both agree on being the number 7. In this case all six methods (three assuming object 4 is an English number and three assuming object 5 as an Arabic number) agree that the number is 7. In the case of objects 6 and 7 only one method (Position of Peak) was not able to recognize object 6 as an English number. All other methods agree that objects 7 and 6 are the number 9 in Arabic and English respectively. Objects 9 and 10 are also aligned vertically as evident from Table 6. Looking at Table 5, we conclude that all methods agree that objects 9 and 10 are the number 5 in Arabic and English respectively. Objects 12 and 13 are also vertically aligned. In this case two methods out of three return the number 2 in both cases. In case

Figure 30. Objects to be considered as numbers

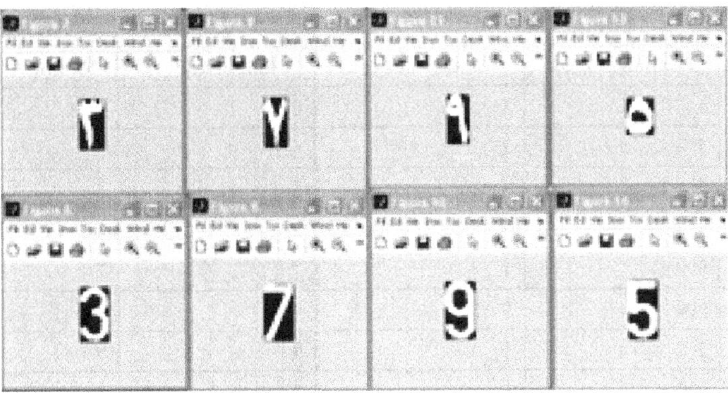

of object 12, it is recognized by one method as an English 9. In case of object 13, one method recognizes it as the Arabic number 4. However the majority of the methods (four out of six) agree that objects 12 and 13 are the number 2 in English and Arabic respectively. All other vertically aligned objects do not agree on one number. For example, objects 14 and 15 are vertically aligned with object 14 being below object 15. This means that object 14 is an English number and object 15 is an Arabic number. Looking at the first three columns of Table 5, in the row corresponding to object 14, two out of three methods agree that object 14 is the English number 1. Compare this result with the last three columns in Table 5 in the row corresponding to object 15. Two out of three methods agree that object 15 is the Arabic number 5. However, since objects 14 and 15 are vertically aligned and the English result does not agree with the Arabic result, then objects 14 and 15 are not considered to be numbers belonging to a Saudi license plate. However, we are not yet in a position to rule out objects 14 and 15 as being part of a Saudi license plate. Objects 14 and 15 can still be letters rather than numbers. The same analysis was done to objects 20 and 21 which are vertically aligned. Object 20 can be recognized as the English number 1 while object 21 can be recognized as the Arabic number 2. This means that the Arabic results do not agree with the English results and therefore we cannot conclude that objects 20 and 21 are not numbers in a Saudi license plate. They can still be letters in the Saudi license plate. Objects 16 and 17 are also vertically aligned. Object 16 is recognized as Arabic 0 while object 17 is recognized as English 4. So English and Arabic results do not agree and therefore objects 16 and 17 are not numbers in the Saudi License plate. Table 7 shows the final resulting number portion of the simulated plate.

Similarly, the objects are checked to see if they are possible letters. All three algorithms associated with recognizing letters in English and Arabic are run on each object. Tables T7 and T8 show the corresponding results. The fifth cell in Table 8 shows the grouping of rows 12 and 13 from Table 7. In this case, the most repeated letter is E, which is the first letter of the plate of Figure 26. Tables T6 and T8 agree that there are 7 characters that could possibly be in a new Saudi license plate. Since in Saudi license plates we have exactly three letters to the right of up to four numbers, this means that the first four characters in Tables T6 and T8 are numbers and the next three characters are letters. Table 10 shows the final resulting number and letter portions of the plate under consideration.

The algorithm was run on images of 22 plates for a total number of 308 Arabic and English characters. Results show 83.9% accuracy for

Table 5. Results of checking which filtered objects are numbers

	English			Arabic		
Object	**Pixels Density**	**Position of Peak**	**Number of Peaks**	**Position of Peak**	**Number of Peaks**	**Pixels Density**
1	8	1	1	0	999	0
2	3	5	2	5	4	999
3	2	7	4	3	3	3
4	7	7	7	3	5	6
5	2	999	1	7	7	7
6	9	999	9	999	4	0
7	3	1	1	9	9	9
8	4	999	1	4	8	8
9	1	999	0	5	5	5
10	5	5	5	5	4	2
11	9	1	1	999	8	6
12	2	2	9	2	4	3
13	5	2	6	2	4	2
14	8	1	1	0	999	7
15	1	999	999	5	7	5
16	8	1	1	0	999	0
17	8	4	4	6	3	2
18	8	1	1	0	999	1
19	2	999	1	999	999	7
20	8	1	1	0	999	0
21	8	2	0	2	2	0
22	8	1	1	1	999	0

Table 6. X-coordinates for all filtered objects

271.5	290.5	291.5	329.5	330.5	367.5	368.5	382.5
406.5	407.5	423.5	459.5	461.5	495.5	499.5	519.5
538.5	543.5	589.5	591.5	594.5	663.5		

identifying the license plates when the size of the plate is small compared to the size of the image as shown in Figure 33a. The accuracy rises to 87.75% when the size of the plate is comparable to the size of the image as shown in Figure 33b.

Two main issues degraded the accuracy of the method. The first issue is the existence of large screws, used to mount the plate onto the car, that sometimes overlap with some characters in the plate. The second issue is the rotation of the image of the plate about the z-axis (axis perpendicular to the image) makes it hard for the recognition algorithm to recognize the characters.

Table 7. Resulting numbers for the plate

All Resulting Numbers							
3	7	9	5	2	?	?	?

Figure 31. Objects to be considered as letters

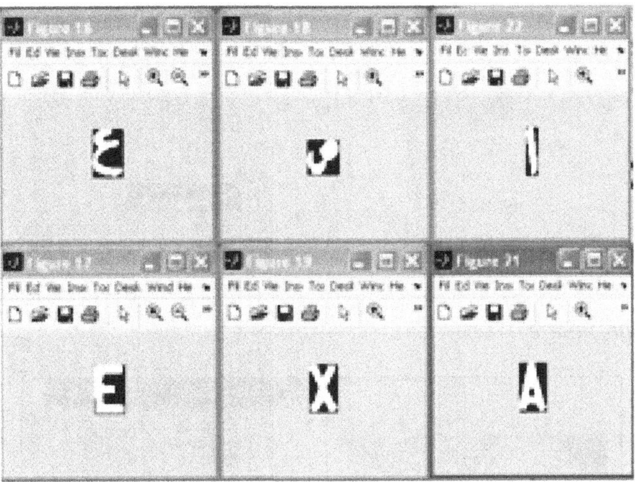

FUTURE RESEARCH DIRECTIONS

Throughout the chapter, many values were used in the recognition of characters. In all three methods, factors were limited to 1/3, 1/4, and 1/10. In the percentage method, percentages were compared to different values ranging from 0.3 to about 0.7. In the peak positions method the areas for middle, left and right or middle, top and bottom were taken at a 1/3 boundary from the edges of the bounding box. All of those numbers were determined empirically in the current research. It would be beneficial to conduct a study to show whether those are the optimal numbers or whether there exist some alternative numbers that would give better results. In the process of localizing a license plate in an image, there are three types of thresholds used. The first type of thresholds is used, in the pre-processing stage, when labeling pixels as background or object pixels. The second type of thresholds is used to remove large or small objects that are not possible characters in a Saudi license plate. The third type of thresholds is used in checking the alignment of objects to decide whether two objects are vertically aligned or not. Currently all thresholds are determined empirically and manually. Future research should focus on automating the thresholds so that they would be function of the image properties rather than fixed for every image. Future research should also focus on making the RGB-level threshold for binarization an adaptive function of the overall RGB level distribution. A second possible area of enhancement is to make adaptive the determining of the threshold for the area of an object for noise removal. A third enhancement would be adapting the algorithms to be able to deal with images of partial license plates rather than requiring the complete license plate in the image. In case a part of the license plate is corrupted by noise, the algorithm should be able to extract whatever information is present in the image and extrapolate. For example, the area in which a character was not correctly recognized could be a candidate for reprocessing with different

Figure 32. Unwanted objects

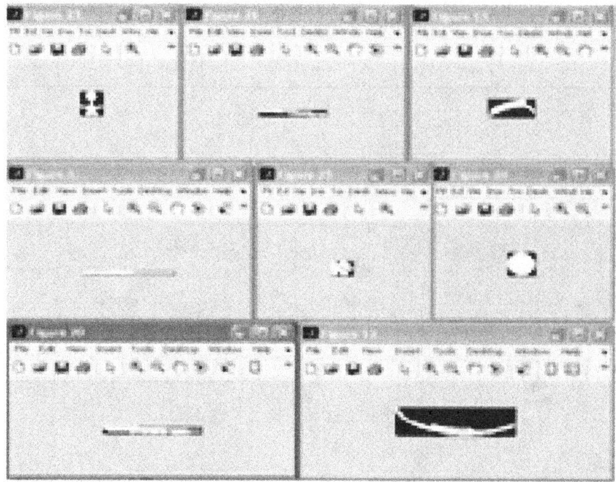

Figure 33. Plate size in an image

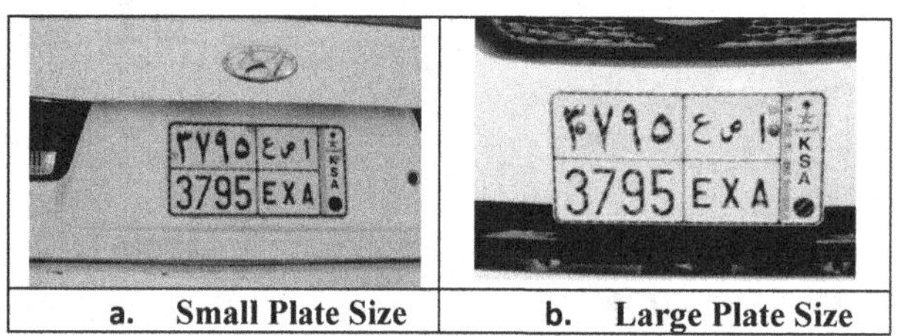

a. **Small Plate Size** b. **Large Plate Size**

thresholds. In particular, for new license plates, even when both regions have incorrectly identified characters, the redundancy between English and Arabic regions can be explored to ameliorate the recognition. Both algorithms may be adapted to work on non-Saudi license plates since they rely on geometric relationships between objects and the actual shapes of the characters in a license plate. In fact, the first algorithm was adapted from an earlier one which was used to locate Lebanese license plates in images. Also the second algorithm can be adapted to work on old Saudi license plates, if needed, by exploiting the horizontal alignment of characters in Saudi license plates rather than only their vertical alignment relationship.

Currently the developed methods run on a PC using MATLAB. Future research should also concentrate on optimizing the current MATLAB code to support real-time video. Currently, it would take around 15 seconds on the average to process all characters in a Saudi license plate. Such a response time is acceptable only for cases where the vehicle stops in front of the camera. If optimization of the MATLAB code does not reduce the response time to an acceptable level, then parallelism should be explored. The algorithms are highly parallelizable. First, the lines can be independently processed and we do not need to wait for one line to be processed to be able to process another. Even the processing of the lines can be parallelized since the information resulted from a line is local and does not depend on global features. Another optimization can be explored which is to find out whether we can minimize the number of lines to be processed by looking at lines differently from what was suggested in this chapter. Another area of optimization would be to explore the alternative lines that can be used to

Table 8. Results of letters for all filtered objects

	English			Arabic		
Row	Pixels Density	Position of Peak	Number of Peaks	Position of Peak	Number of Peaks	Pixels Density
1	K	X	T	A	A	H
2	J	B	S	U	E	Z
3	D	R	A	A	U	E
4	J	R	A	F	H	K
5	T	F	T	A	A	S
6	V	B	S	V	E	V
7	J	T	T	Z	L	S
8	J	J	U	K	X	K
9	X	R	D	N	S	D
10	V	E	Z	F	E	V
11	J	F	U	A	X	V
12	D	D	S	E	E	E
13	E	E	E	F	E	X
14	T	X	V	F	X	X
15	X	X	X	F	L	E
16	K	X	F	A	A	H
17	A	A	A	B	U	H
18	T	X	T	A	A	U
19	F	X	T	V	F	S
20	B	X	T	A	A	H
21	B	R	G	F	V	H
22	F	T	H	A	A	F

Table 9. Resulting possible letters for the plate

?	A	?	?	E	X	A	A

Table 10. Final license plate results

3	7	9	5	E	X	A

recognize a character. This is especially important if we want to parallelize the work since an alternative line might be required for another set of characters and thus would have been processed for those characters. Finally, optimization can also be achieved by trying to see whether mixing between processing of lines using different methods can give better results. For example, starting with the number of peaks method and then switching to the positions of peaks or percentages. Future work should also focus on checking whether the methods are valid for other license plates within the Gulf Cooperation Council (GCC), Middle East and North Africa (MENA) region or the world. The methods are independent of the language used. They explore the differences between shapes of the characters being used and therefore should be applicable to any license plate. Furthermore, it would be interesting to see whether the methods (or an extension) can be used for recognition of other than license plate characters. Road signs, passport information, indoor direction signs are all valid areas to test the methods since they involve a limited set of characters that have unique differences.

CONCLUSION

In this chapter, we presented three methods for recognizing characters in Saudi license plates. All methods rely on analyzing information about pixels in six lines. Three lines are taken vertically across the bounding box of the character to be recognized while the other three lines are taken horizontally. The first method, number of peaks, counts the number of times there is a difference (peak) between pixels along the line from black to white. The second method, pixel percentage method, calculates the percentage of character pixels to total number of pixels on a line. The third method, peak positions method, relies on the positions of the peaks of the first method rather than their number.

The percentages method is the most resistant to noise with performance near or better compared to human performance. Number of peaks is the worst method in terms of resistance to noise. Percentages method is the most resistant to rotation errors while the peak positions method gives the worst results when characters are rotated.

The "number of Peaks" algorithm can successfully recognize English numbers in new Saudi license plates; however, it cannot distinguish between Arabic numbers 0, 1 and 6 in old and new Saudi license plates. The algorithm can successfully recognize old and new Arabic letters, but it cannot distinguish between English letters T and L.

The percentage algorithm can correctly recognize all English and Arabic numbers and letters in new Saudi plates and Arabic numbers and letters in old Saudi plates.

Also in this chapter, algorithms to locate and identify Saudi license plates in images were presented. The first algorithm depends on studying the positions of individual objects on one hand and the positions of whole series on the other. The algorithm has shown good results in locating plates with the current pre-processing method. The only drawback is that the fixed threshold needs to be changed in order to correctly locate plates. Notwithstanding the threshold issue, the algorithm was able to localize all plates in all images tested except in one case where a false positive was reported along with the true positive. The second algorithm depends on locating and recognizing characters. Localization of the plate is done by first determining all objects in the image that can possibly be characters in the license plate. Then all large or small objects are discarded and this method concentrates on the objects that have appropriate size. The coordinates of the center point of the bounding box for all remaining objects are found and then possible vertical alignment between these objects are checked. After finding the vertically aligned objects, the recognition algorithms are applied to recognize those objects and to differentiate the numbers from the letters in the plate. The second algorithm has shown good results also. Errors in locating license plates occurred mainly in two cases. The first case was when the license plate had large screws that were considered as part of nearby characters. The second case was when the license plate was rotated in the image thereby rendering characters unrecognizable.

REFERENCES

Agha, B., Yehya, M., Jerman, M., Hattab, T., & Sidawi, K. (2004). *2005). Arabic optical character recognition system* (pp. 5–19). Beirut Arab University.

Almustafa, K., Zantout, R., & Obeid, H. (2010, November, December). *Pixel density: Recognizing characters in a Saudi license plate*. The 2010 International Conference on Intelligent Systems Design and Applications Cairo, Egypt.

Brad, R. (2001). *License plate recognition system*. Computer Science Department, Lucian Blaga University, Sibiu, Romania. Retrieved from http://remus.ulbsibiu.ro/publications/papers/icics2001.pdf

Broumandnia, A., & Fathy, M. (2005, January). Application of pattern recognition for Farsi license plate recognition. *International Journal on Graphics, Vision and Image Processing*, *5*(2), 25–31.

Fang, L., Song-Yu, Z., & Lin-Jing, H. (2009, December). *Image extraction and segment arithmetic of license plate recognition.* 2nd International Conference on Power Electronics and Intelligent Transportation System, Shenzhen, China.

Jia, W., He, X., & Piccardi, M. (2004). Automatic license plate recognition: A review. *Proceedings of International Conference on Imaging Science, Systems and Technology* (pp. 43-49). Las Vegas, Nevada.

Kwasnicka, H., & Wawrzyniak, B. (2002, November). *License plate localization and recognition in camera pictures.* Artificial Intelligence Methods Conference, Gliwice, Poland.

Obeid, H., & Zantout, R. (2007, May). *Line processing: An approach to ALPR character recognition.* ACS/IEEE International Conference on Computer Systems and Applications. Amman, Jordan

Obeid, H., Zantout, R., & Sibai, F. (2007, November). *License plate localization in ALPR systems.* 4th International Conference on Innovations in Information Technology Dubai, United Arab Emirates.

Ozbay, S., & Ercelebi, E. (2005, November). Automatic vehicle identification by plate recognition. *Transactions on Engineering, Computing and Technology, 9.*

Parker, J. R., & Federl, P. (1996). *An approach to license plate recognition.* University of Calgary. Retrieved from http://pages.cpsc.ucalgary.ca/~federl/Publications/LicencePlate1996/licence-plate-1996.pdf

Ponce, P., Wang, S. S., & Wang, D. L. (2001). *License plate recognition.* Report, Department of Electrical and Computer Engineering, Carnegie Mellon University. Retrieved from http://www.ece.cmu.edu/~ee551/Final_Reports/Gr18.551.S00.pdf

Sarfraz, M., Ahmed, M. J., & Ghazi, S. A. (2003, July). *Saudi Arabian license plate recognition system.* International Conference on Geometric Modeling and Graphics. International Conference on Geometric Modeling and Graphics, London, England.

Turchenko, V. Kochan, V., Koval, V., Sachenko, A., & Markowsky, G. (2003, May). Smart vehicle screening system using artificial intelligence methods. *Proceedings of 2003 Spring IEEE Conference on Technologies for Homeland Security*, Cambridge, Massachusetts (pp. 182-185).

Van Heerden, R. P., & Botha, E. C. (2010, November). *Optimization of vehicle license plate segmentation and symbol recognition*. The 21st Annual International Symposium of the Pattern Recognition Association of South Africa, Stellenbosch, South Africa.

Wang, Y., Zhang, H., Fang, X., & Guo, J. (2009, February). *Low-resolution Chinese character recognition of vehicle license plate based on ALBP and Gabor filters*. Seventh International Conference on Advances in Pattern Recognition, Kolkata, India.

Zantout, R., & Almustafa, K. (2011, November). *Automatic recognition of Saudi license plates*. Technical Report, Prince Sultan University, Kingdom of Saudi Arabia.

ADDITIONAL READING

Al-Hmouz, R., & Challa, S. (2010). License plate localization based on a probabilistic model. *Machine Vision and Applications*, *21*, 319–330. doi:10.1007/s00138-008-0164-9

Almustafa, K., Zantout, R., & Obeid, H. (2011, April). *Recognizing characters in Saudi license plates using character boundaries*. The Seventh International Conference on Innovations in Information Technology, Abu Dhabi, United Arab Emirates.

Almustafa, K., Zantout, R., & Obeid, H. (2011, February). *Peak position, recognizing characters in Saudi license plates*. IEEE GCC Conference and Exhibition for Sustainable Ubiquitous Technology, Dubai, United Arab Emirates.

Gonzalez, R. C., & Woods, R. E. (2002). *Digital image processing* (2nd ed., pp. 523–532). Upper Saddle River, NJ: Prentice Hall.

Guo, J. M., & Liu, Y. F. (2008, May). License plate localization and character segmentation with feedback self-learning and hybrid binarization techniques. *IEEE Transactions on Vehicular Technology*, *57*(3).

Suresh, K. V., Mahesh Kumar, G., & Rajagopalan, A. N. (2007, June). Superresolution of license plates in real traffic videos. *IEEE Transactions on Intelligent Transportation Systems*, *8*(2). doi:10.1109/TITS.2007.895291

Yuan, J., Du, S. D., & Zhu, X. (2008, December). Fast super-resolution for license plate image reconstruction. *19th International Conference on Pattern Recognition* (pp. 1-4).

Chapter 10
Numerical Integration Using Swarm Intelligence Techniques

Naceur Khelil
Laboratory of Applied Mathematics, Universite Mohamed Khider de Biskra, Algeria

Leila Djerou
LESIA Laboratory, Universite Mohamed Khider de Biskra, Algeria

Mohamed Batouche
CCIS-King Saud University, Saudi Arabia

ABSTRACT

This chapter proposes quadrature methods (PSOQF) for approximate calculation of integrals within Particle Swarm Optimization (PSO). PSO is a technique based on the cooperation between particles. The exchange of information between these particles allows to resolve difficult problems. Riemann quadrature formula (RQF) will be discussed first, followed by Trapezoidal quadrature Formula (TQF). Finally, a comparison of these methods presented is given.

INTRODUCTION

The primary purpose of numerical integration (or quadrature) is the evaluation of integrals $(I = \int_a^b f(x)dx)$ which are either impossible or else very difficult to evaluate analytically. Numerical integration is also essential for the evaluation of integrals of functions available only at discrete points. Such functions often arise in the numerical solution of differential equations or from experimental data taken at discrete intervals.

In calculus the integrals are (signed) areas and can be approximated by sums of smaller areas, such as the areas of rectangles. We begin by choosing a partition X that subdivides $[a.b]$:

$$X = \{a \le x_0 < x_1 < \ldots < x_{N-1} < x_N \le b\}$$

The subintervals $[x_{i-1}, x_i]$ determine the width of each of the approximating rectangles. For the height, we can choose any height of the function $f(x_i^*)$ where $x_i^* \in [x_{i-1}, x_i]$.

DOI: 10.4018/978-1-4666-1830-5.ch010

The resulting approximation is:

$$\int_a^b f(x)\,dx \simeq \sum_{i=1}^{N} f(x_i^*)(x_i - x_{i-1}) \qquad (1)$$

In this chapter we propose a choice (of $x_i^* \in [x_{i-1}, x_i]$) using Particle Swarm Optimization.

This chapter is organized as follows. The second section recalls methods of integration the more used. In the third section, a formulation adapted to the strategy of particle swarm optimization and the construction of an algorithm to generate the different agents in a swarm. The fourth section exposes an illustrated example to show how the PSO algorithm can lead to a satisfactory result for numerical integration. In the fifth section, we discuss the future research directions, finally the comments and conclusion are made in sixth section.

BACKGROUND

To use (1) in order to approximate integrals in with actual numbers, we need to have a specific x_i^* in each interval $[x_{i-1}, x_i]$. Several ways to choose x_i^* are (for example):

1. Approximation with Riemann Quadrature Formula (RQF): if we choose x_i^* the right-hand point, then the resulting approximation is: $\int_a^b f(x)\,dx \simeq \sum_{i=1}^{N} f(x_{i-1})(x_i - x_{i-1})$

2. Approximation with Riemann Quadrature Formula (RQF): if we choose x_i^* the left-hand point, then the resulting approximation is: $\int_a^b f(x)\,dx \simeq \sum_{i=1}^{N} f(x_i)(x_i - x_{i-1})$

3. Approximation with Trapezoidal Quadrature Formula (TQF): if we choose x_i^* to take an average of the right-hand and left-hand, then the resulting approximation is:

$$\int_a^b f(x)\,dx \simeq \sum_{i=1}^{N} \frac{f(x_{i-1}) + f(x_i)}{2}(x_i - x_{i-1})$$

THE PROPOSED METHOD

As is well known, that for a function $f : x \in [a,b] \to R$, bounded on the interval $[a,b]$, is integrable if and only if $\forall \varepsilon > 0\ \exists X$ (partition) over $[a,b]$ s.t. $\sum_{i=1}^{N} (L_i - l_i)(x_i - x_{i-1}) < \varepsilon$, (Figure 4), where $L_i = \sup_{[x_{i-1}, x_i]} f(x)$ and $l_i = \inf_{[x_{i-1}, x_i]} f(x)$. Therefore, the purpose of this problem is to find $x_i^* \in [x_{i-1}, x_i]$ that returns the quantity $\sum_{i=1}^{N} (L_i - l_i)(x_i - x_{i-1})$ the smallest possible. The quality of the result depends on the choice of $x_i^* \in [x_{i-1}, x_i]$. How to choose the $x_i^* \in [x_{i-1}, x_i]$? To do this, conceptually we would like to select them using particle swarm optimization.

OVERALL DESCRIPTION STRATEGY OF PARTICLE SWARM OPTIMIZATION

In the mid 1995, a new stochastic algorithm has appeared, namely 'particle swarm optimization' PSO. The term 'particle' means any natural agent that describes the `swarm' behavior. The PSO model is a particle simulation concept, and was first proposed by Eberhart and Kennedy (Eberhart and Kennedy, 1995). Based upon a mathematical description of the social behavior of swarms, it has been shown that this algorithm can be efficiently generated to find good solutions to a

Figure 1. The left sums, RQF

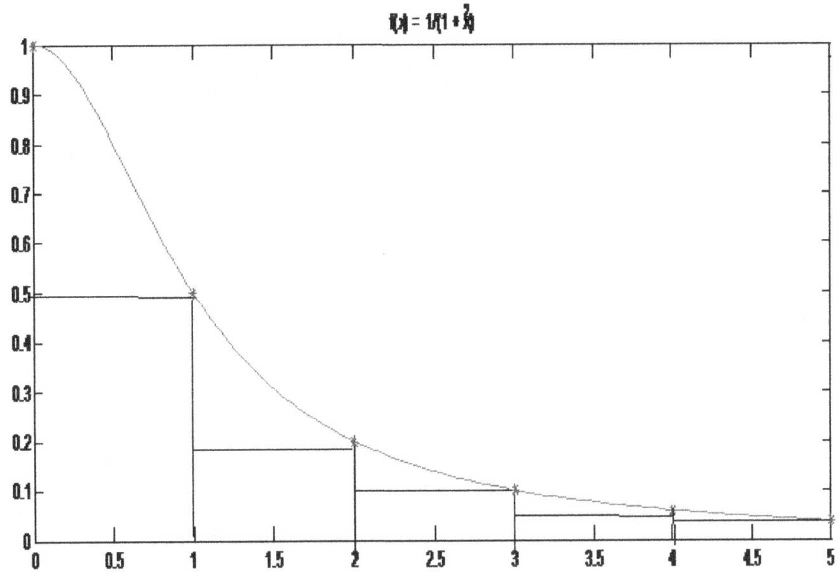

Figure 2. The right sums, RQF

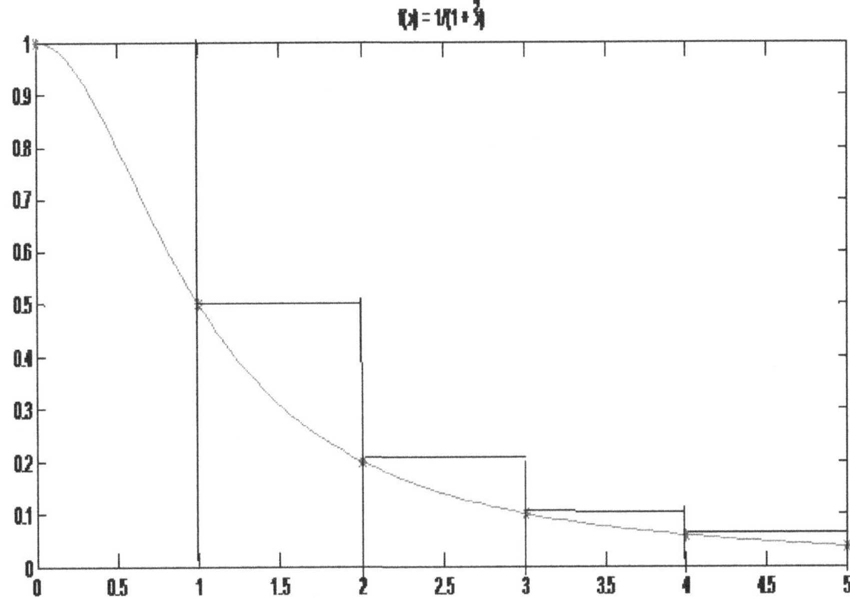

certain number of complicated situations such as, for instance, the static optimization problems, the topological optimization and others (Parsopoulos et al., 2001a, 2001b; Fourie and Groenwold, 2000, 2001). Since then, several variants of the PSO have been developed (Eberhart et al., 1996; Kennedy, 1998; Kennedy and Eberhart, 2001; Shi and Eberhart, 2001; Kennedy and Spears, 1998; Shi and Eberhart, 1998a, 1998b; Clerc, 1999). It has been shown that the question of convergence

Figure 3. The trapezoid quadrature formula, TQF

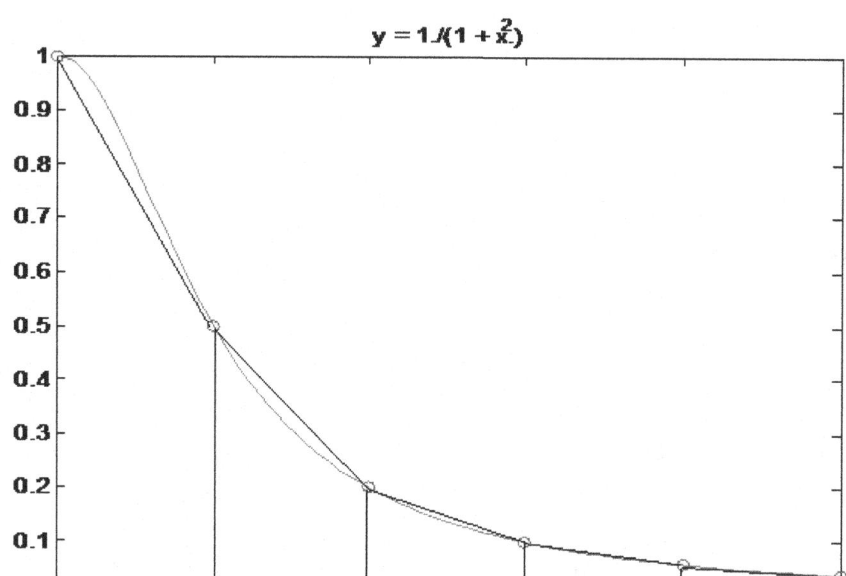

Figure 4. The error sums, 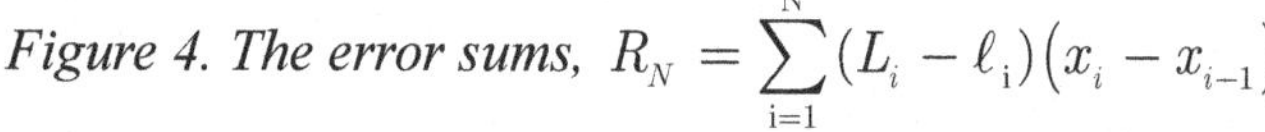 $R_N = \sum_{i=1}^{N} (L_i - \ell_i)(x_i - x_{i-1})$

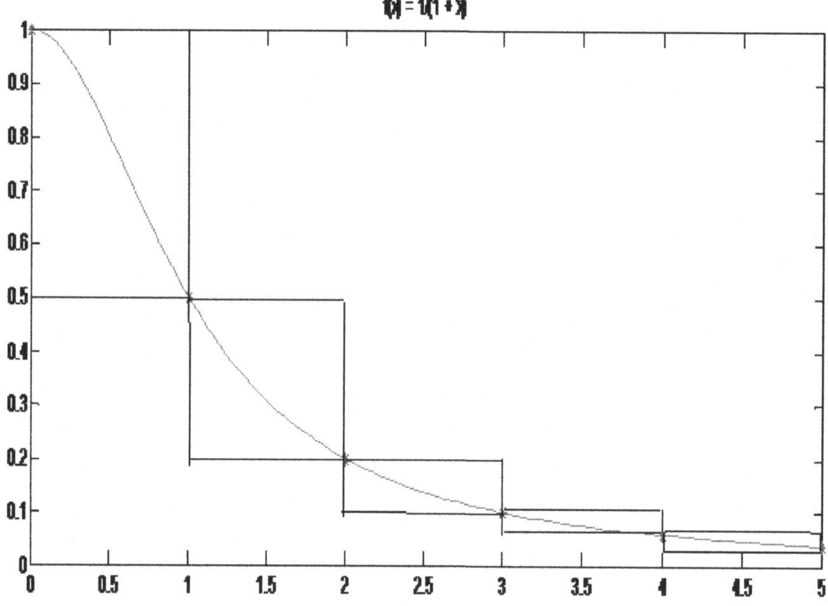

of the PSO algorithm is implicitly guaranteed if the parameters are adequately selected (Eberhart and Shi, 1998; Cristian, 2003). Several kinds of problems solving start with computer simulations in order to find and analyze the solutions which do not exist analytically or specifically have been proven to be theoretically intractable.

The particle swarm treatment supposes a population of individuals designed as real valued vectors - particles, and some iterative sequences of their domain of adaptation must be established. It is assumed that these individuals have a social behavior, which implies that the ability of social conditions, for instance, the interaction with the neighborhood, is an important process in successfully finding good solutions to a given problem.

The strategy of the PSO algorithm is summarized as follows: We assume that each agent (particle) *i* can be represented in a *N* dimension space by its current position $X_i = (x_{i1}, x_{i2}, ...x_{iN})$ and its corresponding velocity. Also a memory of its personal (previous) best position is represented by, $p_i = (p_{i1}, p_{i2}, ...p_{iN})$ called (pbest), the subscript i range from 1 to *s*, where *s* indicates the size of the swarm. Commonly, each particle localizes its best value so far (pbest) and its position and consequently identifies its best value in the group (swarm), called also (sbest) among the set of values (pbest).

$$v_{ij}^{k+1} = w_{ij}v_{ij}^{k} + c_1 r_1^k \left[(pbest)_{ij}^k - x_{ij}^k\right] + c_2 r_2^k \left[(sbest)_{ij}^k - x_{ij}^k\right] \tag{2}$$

The velocity and position are updated as

$$x_{ij}^{k+1} = v_{ij}^{k+1} + x_{ij}^{k} \tag{3}$$

where are the position and the velocity vector of particle i respectively at iteration *k + 1*, c_1 et c_2 are acceleration coefficients for each term exclusively situated in the range of *2--4*, w_{ij} is the inertia weight with its value that ranges from *0.9* to *1.2*, whereas r_1, r_2 are uniform random numbers between zero and one. For more details, the double subscript in the relations (2) and (3) means that the first subscript is for the particle i and the second one is for the dimension *j*. The role of a suitable choice of the inertia weight w_{ij} is important in the success of the PSO. In the general case, it can be initially set equal to its maximum value, and progressively we decrease it if the better solution is not reached. Too often, in the relation (2), w_{ij} is replaced by w_{ij} / σ, where σ denotes the constriction factor that controls the velocity of the particles. This algorithm is successively accomplished with the following steps (Khelil, N. et al. 2009; Djerou L. et al 2011):

1. Set the values of the dimension space *N* and the size *s* of the swarm (s can be taken randomly).
2. Initialize the iteration number *k* (in the general case is set equal to zero).
3. Place every agent between *a* and *b*; arrange them in ascending sequence respectively. There are *N+2* nodal points and *N+1* segments, then calculate the fitness values at the *N+1* segments. The fitness is defined as:

$$f(i) = \sum_{j=1}^{N} \left(L_{ij} - l_{ij}\right)\left(x_{ij} - x_{ij-1}\right) \tag{4}$$

where

$$L_i = \sup_{[x_{i-1}, x_i]} f(x) \text{ and } l_i = \inf_{[x_{i-1}, x_i]} f(x).$$

If the termination condition is met, then stop (The termination condition is defined as: choose a ε which is very close to 0, if the minimum fitness value is less than ε, then stop), choose the optimum solution $X_* \left(a \le x^*_0 < x^*_1 < .... < x^*_N \le b\right)$ and then $\int_a^b f(x)\,dx \simeq \sum_{j=1}^{N} f\left(x_j^*\right)\left(x_j - x_{j-1}\right)$. Otherwise, continue.

4. Each agent must be updated by applying its velocity vector and its previous position using Equation (3).
5. Repeat the above step (3, 4 and 5) until convergence criterion is reached.

The PSO algorithm is applied, with parameter setting (Table 1).

To validate the feasibility and validity of the algorithm for numerical integration, here is a simulation example.

EXAMPLE

This example can be viewed as typical cases which provide a good illustration. We note that, the accuracy of results depends manifestly to success of particles in the swarm to locate the best points. For easy interpretation, the numerical results evaluated by PSO algorithm, those obtained by the Riemann quadrature formula and Trapezoidal quadrature formula have been compared (Table 2).

Let's estimate the integral $\int_0^1 400x(1-x)e^{-2x}dx$ whose exact value is 27.0671

Approximation with Riemann Quadrature Formula (RQF)

Approximating the integral by the Riemann sum with N = 5. If we divide [0,1] into five equal intervals and we choose the sample point to be the upper right of each interval $[x_{i-1}, x_i]$, then $x_1^* = 0.2,\ x_2^* = 0.4,\ x_3^* = 0.6,\ x_4^* = 0.8, x_5^* = 1.0,$ we have:

$$\int_0^1 400x(1-x)e^{-2x}dx$$
$$= \sum_{i=1}^{5}\left(x_i - x_{i-1}\right)f(x_i^*)$$
$$= (0.2)\left[(f(0.2)+f(0.4)+f(0.6)+f(0.8)+f(1)\right]$$
$$= 25.5744,$$

with an error = 1.4927

Table 1. Parameters setting to generate the PSO algorithm for this study

Population Size	21
Number of Iterations	500
Acceleration coefficients: c_1 and c_2	0.5
Inertial weight	1.2 to 0.4
Desired accuracy	10^{-5}

Approximation with Trapezoidal Quadrature Formula (TQF)

Approximating the integral by the Trapezoidal sum with N= 5. If we divide [0,1] into five equal intervals, then

$x_1^* = 0.2,\ x_2^* = 0.4,\ x_3^* = 0.6,\ x_4^* = 0.8, x_5^* = 1.0,$

we have:

$$\int_0^1 400x(1-x)e^{-2x}dx$$
$$= \sum_{i=1}^{5}\left(x_i - x_{i-1}\right)f(x_i^*)$$
$$= (0.2/2)\left[(f(0.2)+2*f(0.4)+2*f(0.6)+2*f(0.8)+f(1)\right]$$
$$= 21.2844,$$

with an error = 5.7827

Approximation with PSO Quadrature Formula (PSOQF)

Approximating the integral by the PSO sum with N = 5. If we divide [0,1] into five equal intervals and we choose the sample point that minimize the quantity $f(i) = \sum_{j=1}^{5}\left(L_{ij} - l_{ij}\right)\left(x_{ij} - x_{ij-1}\right)$ by PSO (Algorithm PSO section 2), then $x_1^* = 0.2,\ x_2^* = 0.4,\ x_3^* = 0.6,\ x_4^* = 0.8, x_5^* = 0.877,$ we have:

Table 2. The integral results of the three methods

Segment numbers	Integration methods	h(step)	X^*	Value	Error
5	RQF	h = 0.2	[0.2 0.4 0.6 0.8 1] '	25.5744	1.4927
5	TQF	h/2	[0.2 0.4 0.6 0.8 1] '	21.2844	5.7827
5	PSOQF	h	[0.2 0.4 0.6 0.8 0.877] '	27.0680	0.0009

Figure 5. The RQF

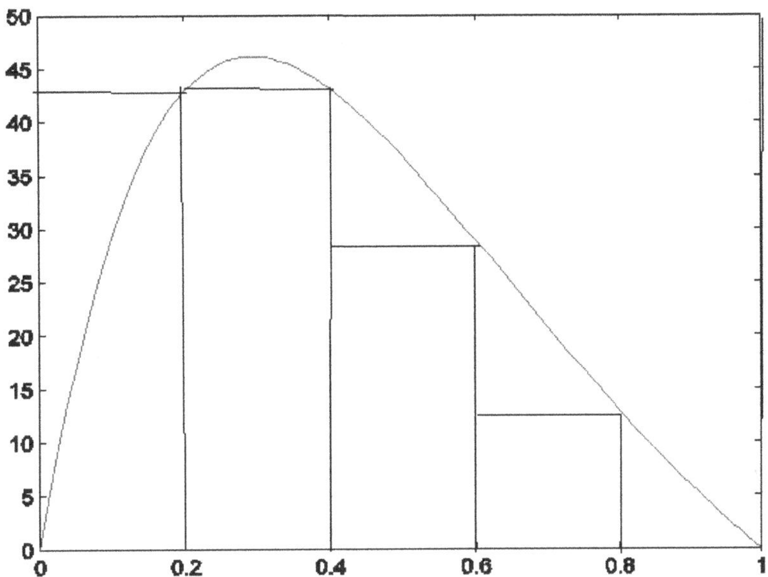

$$\int_0^1 400x(1-x)e^{-2x}dx$$
$$= \sum_{i=1}^{5}(x_i - x_{i-1})f(x_i^*)$$
$$= (0.2)[(f(0.2)+f(0.4)+f(0.6)+f(0.8)+f(0.877)]$$
$$= 27.0680,$$

with an error = 9.4405e-004

Diagnostic of the Error

The computational complexity (CC) is based on the number of segments, in the example, for a number of segments equals to 5 the PSOQF algorithm is superior to conventional methods (Table 2).

FUTURE AND EMERGING TRENDS

The use of particle swarm optimization (PSO) for 1D numerical integration has been discussed and examined in this chapter. However, questions on multiple integration, in the numerical computation generally (Interpolation, differential equation, eigenvalues and eigenvectors,...) remain again.

This idea is especially expandable for double (and triple) integrals of functions of two (or three) variables. Indeed, in a similar manner we consider a function f of two variables defined on a closed rectangle

$$D = [a,b]\times[c,d] = \{(x,y) \in R^2 \,|a \le x \le b, c \le y \le d\}$$

Figure 6. The TQF

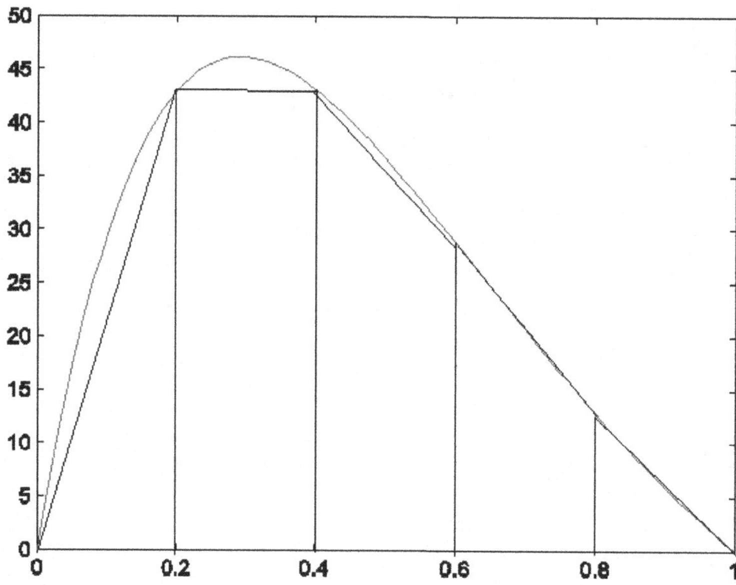

Figure 7. The PSOQF

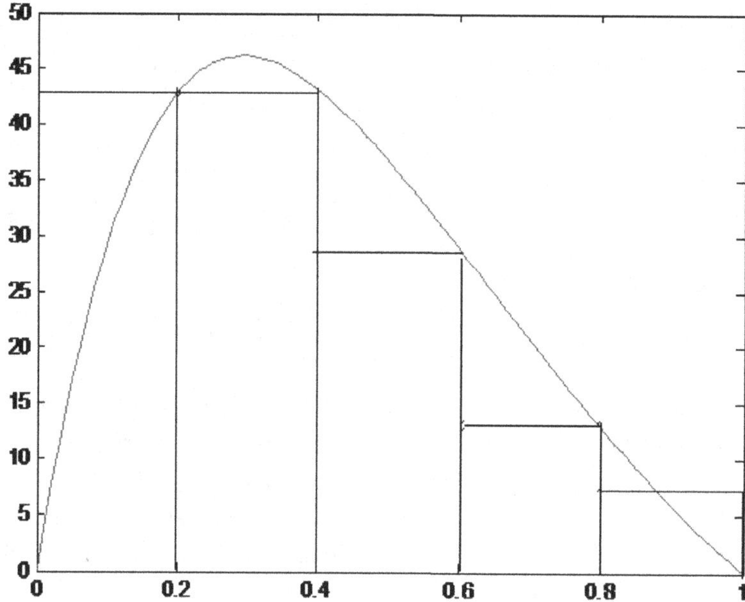

The first step is to divide the rectangle D into subrectangles. We accomplish this by dividing the interval $[a,b]$ into M subintervals $\left[x_{i-1}, x_i\right]$ and dividing $[c,d]$ into N subintervals $\left[y_{j-1}, y_j\right]$.

We form the subrectangles

$$\begin{aligned} D_{ij} &= \left[x_{i-1}, x_i\right] \times \left[y_{j-1}, y_j\right] \\ &= \left\{(x,y) \middle| x_{i-1} \le x \le x_i, y_{j-1} \le y \le y_j\right\} \end{aligned}$$

If we choose a sample point $\left(x_{ij}^{*}, y_{ij}^{*}\right)$ in each D_{ij}, then we can approximate

$$\iint_{D} f(x,y)\,dxdy \simeq \sum_{i=1}^{M}\sum_{j=1}^{N} f\left(x_{ij}^{*}, y_{ij}^{*}\right)\left(x_{i} - x_{i-1}\right)\left(y_{j} - y_{j-1}\right)$$

And we can demonstrate that it is equivalent to, for a function f from $[a,b]\times[c,d]$ in D, is integrable, if and only if, for $\varepsilon \succ 0$, there exist a partition D_{ij} of $[a,b]\times[c,d]$ $\sum_{i=1}^{M}\sum_{j=1}^{N}\left(L_{ij} - l_{ij}\right)\left(x_{i} - x_{i-1}\right)\left(y_{j} - y_{j-1}\right) \prec \varepsilon$ where $L_{ij} = \sup_{D_{ij}} f(x,y)$ and $\ell_{ij} = \inf_{D_{ij}} f(x,y)$

Therefore, the purpose of this problem is to find $\left(x_{i}^{*}, y_{j}^{*}\right) \in D_{ij}$ that returns (in a certain manner) the quantity

$$\sum_{i=1}^{m}\sum_{j=1}^{n}(L_{ij} - l_{ij})(x_{i} - x_{i-1})(y_{j} - y_{j-1})$$

the smallest possible. How to choose the $\left(x_{i}^{*}, y_{j}^{*}\right) \in D_{ij}$? To do this, we would like to select them using particle swarm optimization.

CONCLUSION

The particle swarm optimization is used to investigate the best integrating points (points at which the function is to be evaluated), since the PSO scheme is powerful, and easier to apply specially for this type of problems. Also, the PSO method can be used directly and in a straight forward manner. The experimental results show that our proposed method performs even better than the traditional numerical integration and out performs the state-of-the-art methods.

ACKNOWLEDGMENT

The authors wish to thank the referees for their careful reading of the manuscript and their comments and suggestions. This work was sponsored, in part, by the ANDRU (L'Agence Nationale pour le Développement de la Recherche Universitaire): Under the contract N⁰ 8u07907.

REFERENCES

Clerc, M. (1999). The swarm and the queen: Towards a deterministic and adaptive particle swarm optimization. In *Proceedings of the 1999 IEEE Congress on Evolutionary Computation*, Washington DC, (pp. 1951–1957).

Cristian, T. I. (2003). The particle swarm optimization algorithm: Convergence analysis and parameter selection. *Information Processing Letters*, *85*(6), 317–325. doi:10.1016/S0020-0190(02)00447-7

Djerou, L., Khelil, N., & Batouche, M. (2011). Numerical integration method based on particle swarm optimization. In Tan, Y. (Eds.), *Part I, LNCS 6728* (pp. 221–226). Berlin, Germany: Springer-Verlag. doi:10.1007/978-3-642-21515-5_26

Eberhart, R. C. (1996). *Computational intelligence PC tools*. Boston, MA: Academic Press Professional.

Eberhart, R. C., & Kennedy, J. (1995). A new optimizer using particles swarm theory. In *Sixth International Symposium on Micro Machine and Human Science*, Nagoya, Japan, (pp. 39–43).

Eberhart, R. C., & Shi, Y. (1998). *Parameter selection in particle swarm optimization.*

Fourie, P. C., & Groenwold, A. A. (2000). Particle swarms in size and shape optimization. In *Proceedings of the International Workshop on Multi-disciplinary Design Optimization*, Pretoria, South Africa, August 7-10, (pp. 97–106).

Fourie, P. C., & Groenwold, A. A. (2001). Particle swarms in topology optimization. In *Extended Abstracts of the Fourth World Congress of Structural and Multidisciplinary Optimization*, Dalian, China, June 4-8, (pp. 52–53).

Kennedy, J. (1998). The behaviour of particles. *Proceedings of the 7th Annual Conference on Evolutionary Programming,* (pp.581–587).

Kennedy, J., & Eberhart, R. C. (Eds.). (2001). *Swarm intelligence*. San Francisco, CA: Morgan Kaufmann Publishers.

Khelil N., & al. (2009). Improvement of Gregory's formula using particle swarm optimization. In *The Proceeding of International Conference on Computer and Applied Mathematics,* Vol. 58, (pp. 940–942).

Parsopoulos, K. E., et al. (2001a). Stretching technique for obtaining global minimizers through particle swarm optimization. In *Proceedings of the PSO Workshop*, Indianapolis, USA, (pp. 22–29).

Parsopoulos, K. E., et al. (2001b). Objective function stretching to alleviate convergence to local minima. *Non linear Analysis TMA, 47*, 3419–3424.

Parsopoulos, K. E., & Vrahatis, M. N. (2001). Modification of the particle swarm optimizer for locating all the global minima. In Kurkova, V. (Eds.), *Artificial Neural Networks and Genetic Algorithms* (pp. 324–327). New York, NY: Springer.

Shi, Y. H., & Eberhart, R. C. (1998a). A modified particle swarm optimizer. In *Proceedings of the 1998 IEEE International Conference on Evolutionary Computation*, Anchorage, Alaska, May 4-9.

Shi, Y. H., & Eberhart, R. C. (1998b). Parameter selection in particle swarm optimization. In Porto, V. W., & Waagen, D. (Eds.), *EP 1998, LNCS* (*Vol. 1447*, pp. 591–600). Heidelberg, Germany: Springer.

Shi, Y. H., & Eberhart, R. C. (2001). Fuzzy adaptive particle swarm optimization. In *IEEE International Conference on Evolutionary Computation*, (pp. 101–106).

Wang, X.-H. (2004). Numerical integration study based on triangle basis neural network algorithm. *Journal of Electronics and Information Technology*, *26*(3), 394–399.

Zerarka, A., & Khelil, N. (2006). A generalized integral quadratic method: improvement of the solution for one dimensional Volterra integral equation using particle swarm optimization. *International Journal of Simulation and Process Modelling*, *2*(1-2), 152–163.

Zerarka, A., Soukeur, A., & Khelil, N. (2009). The particle swarm optimization against the Runge's phenomenon: Application to the generalized integral quadrature method. *International Journal of Mathematical and Statistical Sciences*, *1*(3), 171–176.

ADDITIONAL READING

Davis, P. J., & Rabinowitz, P. (1984). *Methods of numerical integration*. New York, NY: Academic Press.

Djerou, L., Khelil, N., & Batouche, M. (2011). Numerical integration method based on particle swarm optimization. In Tan, Y. (Eds.), *Part I, LNCS 6728* (pp. 221–226). Berlin, Germany: Springer-Verlag. doi:10.1007/978-3-642-21515-5_26

Engels, H. (1980). *Numerical quadrature and cubature*. New York, NY: Academic Press.

Evans, G. (1993). *Practical numerical integration*. New York, NY: Wiley.

Evans, M., & Swartz, T. (1995). Methods for approximating integrals in statistics with special emphasis on Bayesian integration problems. *Statistical Science*, *10*, 254–272. doi:10.1214/ss/1177009938

Van den Bergh, F. (2001). *An analysis of particle swarm optimizers*. Ph.D thesis, University of Pretoria.

Zerarka, A., Soukeur, A., & Khelil, N. (2009). The particle swarm optimization against the Runge's phenomenon: Application to the generalized integral quadrature method. *International Journal of Mathematical and Statistical Sciences*, *1*(3), 171–176.

Chapter 11
A Multilevel Thresholding Method Based on Multiobjective Optimization for Non-Supervised Image Segmentation

Leila Djerou
LESIA Laboratory, Universite Mohamed Khider de Biskra, Algeria

Naceur Khelil
Laboratory of Applied Mathematics, Universite Mohamed Khider de Biskra, Algeria

Nour El Houda Dehimi
L.B.M. University, Algeria

Mohamed Batouche
University Mentouri–Constantine, Algeria

ABSTRACT

The aim of this work is to provide a comprehensive review of multiobjective optimization in the image segmentation problem based on image thresholding. The authors show that the inclusion of several criteria in the thresholding segmentation process helps to overcome the weaknesses of these criteria when used separately. In this context, they give a recent literature review, and present a new multi-level image thresholding technique, called Automatic Threshold, based on Multiobjective Optimization (ATMO). That combines the flexibility of multiobjective fitness functions with the power of a Binary Particle Swarm Optimization algorithm (BPSO), for searching the "optimum" number of the thresholds and simultaneously the optimal thresholds of three criteria: the between-class variances criterion, the minimum error criterion and the entropy criterion. Some examples of test images are presented to compare with this segmentation method, based on the multiobjective optimization approach with Otsu's, Kapur's, and Kittler's methods. Experimental results show that the thresholding method based on multiobjective optimization is more efficient than the classical Otsu's, Kapur's, and Kittler's methods.

DOI: 10.4018/978-1-4666-1830-5.ch011

INTRODUCTION

Image segmentation is a low level image processing task that aims at partitioning an image into regions in order that each region groups contiguous pixels sharing similar attributes (intensity, color, etc.). It is a very important process because it is the first step of the image understanding process, and all others steps, such as feature extraction, classification and recognition, depend heavily on its results.

Image segmentation has been the subject of intensive research; the number of published works treating this problem is difficult to value. It is a consequence of several factors:

- The diversity of images and the increase of their use.
- The evolution of computation machines that allows the exploration of news approaches and techniques and also it facilitates the evaluation of empiric results.
- The complexity of the segmentation problem; the uniqueness of segmentation of an image doesn't exist in most cases; a good method of segmentation is therefore, the one that will permit to arrive to a better interpretation of the image segmentation.

A wide variety of image segmentation techniques have been reported in the literature. A good review of these methods can be found in (Pal, 1993). In general, these techniques can be categorized into thresholding, edge-based, region growing and clustering techniques.

Image thresholding is an important technique for image processing and pattern recognition that can be classified as bi-level thresholding and multilevel thresholding. Bi-level thresholding classifies the pixels of an image into two classes, one including those pixels with gray levels above a certain threshold, the other including the rest. Multilevel thresholding divides the pixels into several classes. The pixels belonging to the same class have gray levels within a specific range defined by several thresholds.

Edge-based segmentation algorithms are the most common methods for identifying meaningful image discontinuities. The gray-level discontinuity focuses on abrupt changes in gray level, color or texture. The edge information is very useful for segmentation since it can be used to obtain other image properties such as area and shape.

In region growing techniques, the regions start from a set of seed points. From these points, the regions grow by appending to each seed those neighbouring pixels that have similar properties. The selection of the seed points and of similarity criteria depends on the problem under consideration and the type of image data that is available depends on the problem.

Clustering in image segmentation is defined as the process of identifying groups of similar image primitives. These image primitives can be pixels, regions, line elements and so on, depending on the problem encountered. This is accomplished by a predefined list of quality criteria such as spatial coherence and feature homogeneity.

In spite of the abundance of works in this domain, the problem of image segmentation remains the subject of several research efforts, which have shown that the segmentation techniques based on the combination of some criteria give a good segmentation result and increase the ability to apply the same technique to a wide variety of images. They have also shown that combining criteria helps to overcome the weaknesses of these criteria when used separately. A new trend of problem formulation for image segmentation is to use multiobjective optimization approach in its decision making process.

Multiobjective optimization (MO) (also known as multicriterion) extends the optimization theory by permitting several design objectives to be optimized simultaneously (Nakib and al., 2007). A MO problem is solved in a way similar to the conventional single-objective (SO) problem. The goal is to find a set of values for the design variables that simultaneously optimizes several objectives (or cost) functions. In general, the solution obtained through a separate optimization of each objective (i.e. SO optimization) does not represent a feasible solution of the multiobjective problem.

The use of MO approaches has been found in image segmentation methods with clustering (Handl and Knowles, 2007), (Matake and al., 2007), (Saha and Bandyopadhyay,2008), histogram thresholding methods. There is also an attempt of using multiobjective approach for evaluation of image segmentation methods (Saha and Bandyopadhyay, 2010), (Bong and Mandava, 2010).

Many applications such as document image analysis, map processing, scene processing, computer vision, pattern recognition and quality inspection of materials consider the image thresholding technique a crucial operation because it is straight forward to implement and further process steps have to rely on the segmentation results. For this reason, we insist in this chapter, on thresholding segmentation technique. We provide a comprehensive review of multiobjective optimization in image shreholding problem. We present some existing methods, in this arena, and propose a new non-supervised thresholding approach based on non-Pareto multiobjective optimization and Particle Swarm Optimization (BPSO) (Kennedy and Eberhart, 1997), this approach enables to determinate the "optimum" number of the thresholds and simultaneously the optimal thresholds of three criteria: the between-class variances criterion, the minimum error criterion and the entropy criterion.

This chapter contains seven sections that permit to understand the objective of work and to present its importance. We expose in section 2 and section 3, the multilevel thresholding problem and its formulation as a multiobjective problem. In the section 4 and section 5, we describe the formulation of the multiobjective Optimization and its use in image segmentation with thresholding techniques, in this context, we present a new multi-level image thresholding technique, called Automatic Threshold based on Multiobjective Optimization (ATMO) that combines the flexibility of multiobjective fitness functions with the power of a Binary Particle Swarm Optimization algorithm (BPSO). The section 6 and section7 outlines the discusses future work directions and the conclusions derived from this work.

2. MULTILEVEL THRESHOLDING PROBLEM

Image thresholding is widely used as a preliminary step, to separate object(s) and background. For an image with clear objects in the background, its histogram is usually assumed to have one valley between two peaks, representing the background and the objects respectively. The bi-level thresholding divides the object pixels at one gray level while the background pixels at another, is widely used. For rather complex images, on the other hand, the multilevel thresholding segments the pixels into several distinct groups in which the pixels of the same group have gray levels within a specific range.

For example, for an image I of N pixels, with gray levels range over $[0..L]$, the multilevel image thresholding is the task of separating the pixels of the image I in classes $(C_0, C_2, .., C_n, ..., C_K)$, by setting the thresholds $\{t_1, t_2, ..., t_k\}$ such that $t_1 < t_2 < ... < t_K$. With k denoting the number of selected thresholds $(1 \leq k \leq L-1)$, the image is then partitioned into $k+1$ classes:

$$C_0 = \{0, 1, ..., t_1 - 1\}, ...,$$
$$C_n = \{t_n, t_n + 1, ..., t_{n+1} - 1\}, ...,$$
$$C_k = \{t_k, t_k + 1, ..., L\}.$$

For the placement of the thresholds most of the thresholding algorithms employ the histogram $h(g)$. The histogram is a statistic of the image and $h(i)$, $i=0, ..., L$, shows the occurrence of gray level i, where:

$$\sum_{i=0}^{L} h(i) = N \tag{1}$$

The normalized probability at level i is defined as:

$$p(i) = \frac{h(i)}{N}, \sum_{i=1}^{L} p(i) = 1 \tag{2}$$

The problem of multilevel thresholding consists in selecting the set of thresholds $(t_1^*, t_2^*, ..., t_k^*)$ in such a way that a criterion (an objective function) $F(t_1, t_2, ..., t_k)$ is optimized (minimized or maximized), such that:

$$(t_1^*, t_2^*, ..., t_k^*) = \arg\max F(t_1, t_2, ..., t_k) \tag{3}$$

Various parametric and non-parametric thresholding methods and criteria have been proposed in order to perform bi-level thresholding (Sezgin and Sankur, 2004), (Sahoo and Soltani,1988). They are extendable to multilevel thresholding as well, However, for optimal multilevel thresholding, existing algorithms are being trapped by an exhaustive search of all possible threshold subsets, then the objective function is evaluated of every possible placement of the thresholds and take the positions for which the objective function is optimal, thus implies to evaluate $\binom{n}{k}$ possibilities, which can be shown as:

$$\binom{n}{k} = \frac{n!}{k!(n-k)!} = \frac{n(n-1)(n-2)...(n-k+1)}{k(k-1)...1} \geq \left(\frac{n}{k}\right)^k \tag{4}$$

As an example, for an image has $L = 256$ gray levels and the number of classes is $M = 5$ (the number of thresholds is M-1=4), the thresholds can only be placed in the interval [1 . . 255]. The number of possibilities times the objective function has to be calculated is $\binom{255}{4} = 17200610505$. For real time implementations the exhaustive search is therefore not a solution and faster algorithms, which find the optimal thresholds without checking every possible placement, are needed.

To overcome this problem, several techniques have been proposed (Hammouche and al., 2010). Some of them are designed especially for computation acceleration of a specific objective function, such as the Otsu's function (Liao and al., 2001; Lin 2001), while other techniques are designed to be used with a general purpose. Among the last category, we can find dichotomization techniques (Yen and al., 1995; Sezgin and al.,2000), iterative schemes (Yin and Chen,1997), reduction strategies (Kim and al.,2003), and the meta-heuristic techniques (Hammouche and al.,2010; Djerou and al.,2009).

In dichotomization techniques, the histogram is dichotomized into two distributions by using a bi-level thresholding and the distribution with the largest variance is further dichotomized in two more distributions by applying the same bi-level thresholding. This dichotomization process is repeated until as topping criterion is satisfied. The dichotomization techniques are faster algorithms. Unfortunately, they are suboptimal techniques and they do not provide the optimal threshold values.

The iterative scheme starts with initial thresholds. Then, these thresholds are adjusted iteratively to improve the value of the objective function. This improvement process stops when the value of the objective function does not increase between two consecutive iterations. However, the iterative schemes are sensitive to initial values of thresholds and can converge to the local optimum.

In reduction strategy, the solution of the histogram is reduced using the wavelet transform (Kim and al.,2003). From the reduced histogram, the optimal thresholds are determined faster by optimizing the objective function based on an exhaustive search. The selected threshold values are then expanded to the original scale.

Several metaheuristics have been used for fast multilevel thresholding, including, particle swarm optimization (Djerou and al.,2009; Yourui and Shuang, 2008; Zahara and al., 2005), genetic algorithm (Tao and al., 2003, Hammouche and al.,2008), bacterial foraging algorithm (Kayalvizhi and Sathya, 2011), honey bee algorithm (Horng, 2009), ant colony optimization (Liang and al., 2006; Chang and Yan, 2003), simulated annealing (Nakib and al.,2008) and many others, a description of some of them can be found in (Hammouche and al.,2010).

3. FORMULATION OF MULTI-LEVEL IMAGE THRESHOLDING AS A M.O. PROBLEM

The segmentation problem can be formulated as a multiobjective optimization problem. In most cases this problem is NP-hard (Nakib, and al., 2010).

The segmentation of an image *I*, using, for example, a homogeneity criterion *A*, is defined as a partition

$P = R_1, \ldots, R_n$ of *I* where *n* is the number of regions.

$I = \cup R_i$, $i \in [1, n]$

R_i connected region; $\forall i \in [1, n]$

$A(R_i) = True$, $\forall i \in [1, n]$

$A(R_i \cup R_j) = \text{False}, \forall i \in [1, n]$, for all connect regions (R_i, R_j).

We note that the uniqueness of the segmentation result is not guaranteed by the conditions above. The results of segmentation do not only depend on the information contained in the image, but also on the used method to find the optimal solution.

Generally, to force the uniqueness of the solution, regularization is obtained by constraining the problem. This constraint consists in optimizing a function *F*, characterizing the quality of a good segmentation. Then, the last condition is:

$$F(T^*) = \underset{P \in P(A)}{Min}\, F(P) \quad (5)$$

where *F* is a decreasing function and $P_A(I)$ is the set of all possible partitions of *I*.

It is clear that this condition does not entirely solve the problem of uniqueness of the segmentation. Indeed, some segmentation may have the same optimal solution *P**. This explains the need for using metaheuristics to solve the optimization problem.

In the literature several criteria to regularize the segmentation problem are presented (Sezgin and Sankur, 2004). However, there is no single criterion able to regularize the segmentation problem for all kinds of images. Then, in order to have a good segmentation on more kinds of images, we use simultaneously some criteria. To optimize simultaneously these criteria, we use MO techniques. Consequently, the segmentation problem can be formulated as an MO problem.

Minimize/Maximize $f_m(t_1, \ldots, t_{N-1})$; $m = 1, 2, \ldots, M$ (6)

Subject to $0 < t_1 < t_2 < \ldots < t_{N-1} < L$

where *M* is the number of criteria used for the segmentation, $(t_1, \ldots, t_{N-1})$ the segmentation thresholds, and *L* the number of gray levels.

4. MULTIOBJECTIVE OPTIMIZATION

In many real world situations, there may be several objectives that must be optimized simultaneously in order to solve a certain problem.

The main problem considering Multiobjective Optimization "MO" is that there is no accepted definition of optimum in this case, and therefore it is difficult to compare one solution with another one. In general, these methods produce multiple solutions, each of which is considered acceptable and equivalent when the relative importance of the objectives is unknown. The best solution is subjective and depends on the need of the designer or decision maker.

The multiobjective optimization can be formally stated as (Coello Coello,1999):

Find the vector $x^* = \left[x_1^*, x_2^*, ..., x_n^*\right]^T$ of decision variables which will satisfy the m inequality constraints:

$$g_i(x) \geq 0, \qquad i = 1, 2, ..., m \tag{7}$$

The p equality constraints

$$h_i(x) = 0, \qquad i = 1, 2, ..., p \tag{8}$$

and optimizes the vector function

$$f(x) = \left[f_1(x), f_2(x), ..., f_k(x)\right]^T \tag{9}$$

The constraints given in Equations (7) and (8) define the feasible region F which contains all the admissible solutions. Any solution outside this region is inadmissible since it violates one or more constraints. The vector x*denotes an optimal solution in F.

The notion of optimality was originally introduced by F. Edgeworth in 1881 and later generalized by V. Pareto in 1896. It is called Pareto optimum, use of this concept almost always doesn't give a single solution but a set of them, which is called the Pareto optimal set. The vectors of the decision variables corresponding to the solutions included in the Pareto optimal set are called nondominated. The plot of the objective functions whose nondominated vectors are in the Pareto optimal set is called the Pareto front (Coello Coello, 2006).

There are three classes of approaches for solving multiobjective optimization problems (Deb, 2001): transformation in a single-objective problem, non-pareto and pareto approaches. In the first class, the transformation the multiple objectives into a single-objective function is typically done by assigning a numerical weight to each objective (evaluation criterion) and then combining the values of the weighted criteria into a single value by either adding or multiplying all the weighted criteria. Among methods that use this approach, we can mention aggregating method, ε-constraint method and min-max goal programming method.

The second is non aggregated approach. Generally, the methods in this class, treat objectives separately. Two groups of methods exist in the literature: lexicographical selection and parallel selection.

In the last class "Pareto approach", the evaluation methods is not simply to aggregate the multiple objectives into an objective function with a weighted formula. The evaluation of possible (intermediate) solutions is based on dominancy relation. This approach considers the interrelationship between objectives in evaluating intermediate solution before an algorithm settles to approximately Pareto-optimal solutions (Bong, 2006).

Several metaheuristics have been developed for MO problems (Nakib and al.,2010), including particle swarm optimization, ant colony optimization, genetical algorithms, simulated annealing.

The most research of the possible application of the metaheuristics approaches in solving Multiobjective Optimization Problems "MOP" was with evolutionary algorithm (Coello Coello, 1999). David Schaffer is normally considered to be the first to have designed a multiobjective optimization evolutionary algorithm during the mid-1980s (Schaffer, 1985). Schaffer's approach, called Vector Evaluated Genetic Algorithm

"VEGA" consists of a simple genetic algorithm with a modified selection mechanism. At each generation, a number of sub-populations were generated by performing proportional selection according to each objective function in turn. These sub-populations would then be shuffled together to obtain a new population, on which the Genetic Algorithm (GA) would apply the crossover and mutation operators in the usual way.

As compared to GA multiobjective, there is limited research endeavour of using PSO in for solving MOP (Reyes-Sierra, et al., 2006). The research in this context is divided in two classes: non-Pareto approach PSO and Pareto approach.

Generally, the developed algorithms, in PSO non-Pareto approach, are inspired by AG. The Vector Evaluated Particle Swarm Optimization (VEPSO) is a derived algorithm from the VEGA algorithm (Schaffer, 1985), that uses an approach called multi-swarms, or each swarm is valued by using one of functions objectives of the problem and the different swarms exchange information of their better positions (Reyes-Sierra, et al., 2006).

In PSO Pareto approach, the leader selection methods based on Pareto dominance are generally used. The most straightforward approach is simply to consider every particle that presented the nondominated solution, as a leader. Several schemes of leader selection are possible (Reyes-Sierra and al., 2006).

5. MO IN IMAGE SEGMENTATION WITH THRESHOLDING TECHNIQUES

The use of MO in image segmentation with thresholding techniques has been found dominated by Nakid et al. (Nakib and al.,2007; 2008;2009;2010). They have proposed to find the optimal thresholds that allow to optimize a set of criteria as the objective functions. The aim is to increase the information on the position of the optimal threshold to obtain the correct segmentation.

5.1. Thresholding Method Based on Pareto Multi-Objective Optimization (TPMO)

Nakib et al. (Nakib and al.,2010) have proposed a thresholding method based on Pareto multi-objective optimization (*TPMO*) by adapting the evolutionary algorithm *NSGA-II* (elitist non-dominated sorting genetic algorithm) (Deb and al.,2002). It is supervised method; it is based on the assumption that the number of segmentation classes is known.

The proposed algorithm consists in the optimization simultaneously of the three functions (criteria): the biased intraclass variance criterion, Shannon entropy criterion and the two-dimensional entropy criterion. The final solution or Pareto solution corresponds to that allowing a compromise between the different segmentation criteria, with out favouring any one.

5.2. Combination of Segmentation Objectives (CSO)

Nakib et al. (Nakib and al.,2008) have proposed a non-supervised image segmentation method based on non-Pareto multiobjective optimization, called Combination of Segmentation Objectives (CSO). To find the optimal thresholds of two criteria: the within-class criterion and the overall probability of error criterion, they have used the plain aggregating approach, that consists in converting the problem into a single-objective optimization problem by aggregating the objectives.

$$f_{eq}(x) = \sum_{i=1} w_i f_i(x) \tag{10}$$

where:

f_{eq}: the new objective function (criterion)

$f_1, \ldots, f_k$: the original objective functions to be minimized

x: parameters vector ;

w_i: weighting parameters that satisfy the following relations:

$$\begin{cases} 0 \le w_i \le 1 \\ \sum_{i=1}^{k} w_i = 1 \end{cases}$$

To optimize the multiobjective function they have used Simulated Annealing because of the unknown variations of the objective function that depend on the characteristics of the images. But before searching for the thresholds, a peak-finding algorithm is used to identify the most significant peaks in the histogram.

5.3. Automatic Threshold based on Multiobjective Optimization (ATMO)

The proposed *ATMO* method *(AutomaticThreshold based on Multiobjective Optimization*) combines the flexibility of multiobjective fitness functions with the power of a Binary Particle Swarm Optimization algorithm (BPSO) (Kennedy and Eberhart, 1997) for searching vast combinatorial state spaces.

The idea was inspired from the segmentation problematic:

- There does not exist any thresholding criterion that is capable to produce an optimal thresholding result for all images. The use non-Pareto multiobjective optimization aims to obtain good thresholding results independently of the image.
- Finding the "optimum" number of thresholds, in a whole gray-level range, is usually a challenge since it requires a priori knowledge. However, despite the amount of research in this area, the outcome is still unsatisfactory (Wu and al.,2004; Yen and al., 1995; Hammouche and al.,2008; Nakib and al.,2008). The use the BPSO aims to optimize the number of classes.

Binary Particle Swarm Optimization "BPSO" (Kennedy and Eberhart, 1997) is a variant of PSO, which was adapted to search in binary space. In BPSO, the component values of particle's position are restricted to the set $\{0, 1\}$. The velocity is interpreted as a probability to change a bit from 0 to 1, or from 1 to 0 when updating the position of particles. This can be done using a sigmoid function, defined as:

$$sig(x) = \frac{1}{1+e^{-x}} \tag{11}$$

Hence, the equation for updating positions is the probabilistic update equation, namely (Kennedy and Eberhart, 1997),

$$x_{i,j}(t+1) = \begin{cases} 0 & if \quad r_j(t) \ge sig(v_{i,j}(t+1)) \\ 1 & if \quad r_j(t) < sig(v_{i,j}(t+1)) \end{cases} \tag{12}$$

where: $r_j(t) \sim U(0,1)$ is a random number between 0 and 1, $x_{i,j}$ is a component value of particle's position i and $v_{i,j}$ is a component value of particle's velocity i, that is updated as using the following equation:

$$v_{i,j}(t+1) = \omega v_{i,j}(t) + c_1 r_{1,j}(t)(y_{i,j}(t) - x_{i,j}(t)) + c_2 r_{2,j}(t)(\hat{y}_j(t) - x_{i,j}(i)) \tag{13}$$

Here, $x_i(t)$ is the current position of the particle. $v_i(t)$ is the current velocity of the particle. $y_i(t)$ is the personal best position of the particle; the best position visited so far by the particle i. $\hat{y}_i(t)$ is the global best position of the swarm; the best position visited so far by the entire swarm. ω is the inertia weight which serves as a memory of previous velocities; the inertia weight controls the impact of the previous velocity (Van den Bergh, 2002). The cognitive component $y_i(t) - x_i(t)$ represents the particle's own experience as to where the best solution is. The social component $\hat{y}(t) - x_i(t)$ represents the belief of the entire swarm as to where the best solution is. c_1 and c_2 are acceleration constants and $r_1(t), r_2(t) \sim U(0,1)$, where $U(0,1)$ is a random number between 0 and 1 (Van den Bergh, 2002).

Velocity updates can also be clamped through a user defined maximum velocity, *Vmax*, which would prevent them from exploding, thereby causing premature convergence (Van den Bergh, 2002).

To solve our multiobjective problem, we adapt the VEPSO (Reyes-Sierra and al., 2006) method that consists in using a set of sub-swarms $\boldsymbol{S} = \{Ss_1, \ldots, Ss_p, \ldots, Ss_{Nc}\}$; Ss_p is the sub-swarm *p*, and *Nc* is the number of sub-swarm and it represents the number of criteria used f_p; $p = 1..Nc$. Each sub-swarm Ss_p is valued by using an algorithm *BPSO that* searches the optimal thresholds, by optimizing one of objective functions of the problem f_p, which uses the gray level thresholds as parameters. It starts with large number initial thresholds (gray levels range of pixels in giving image), then, these thresholds are dynamically refined to improve the value of the objective function. The different sub-swarms communicate between them through the exchange of their better position by using the uniformity measure *U* (Sahoo and al., 1988; Yin, 1997).

In this approach, we use three threshold criteria and a selection operator of the best thresholds. The threshold criteria can be described as follows:

Let there be *N* pixels in a given image, with gray levels range over *[0..L]* and n_i denote the occurrence of gray level *i*, giving a probability of gray level *i* as:

$$p_i = \frac{n_i}{N} \tag{14}$$

Entropy Criterion

The Kapur's method (Kapur and all.,1985) is based on the entropy theory. It consists in the maximization of the sum of entropies for each class, as follows:

$$f(t_1, t_2, \ldots, t_k) = H_0 + H_1 + \ldots + H_k \tag{15}$$

where:

Figure 1. Principe of proposed ATMO method

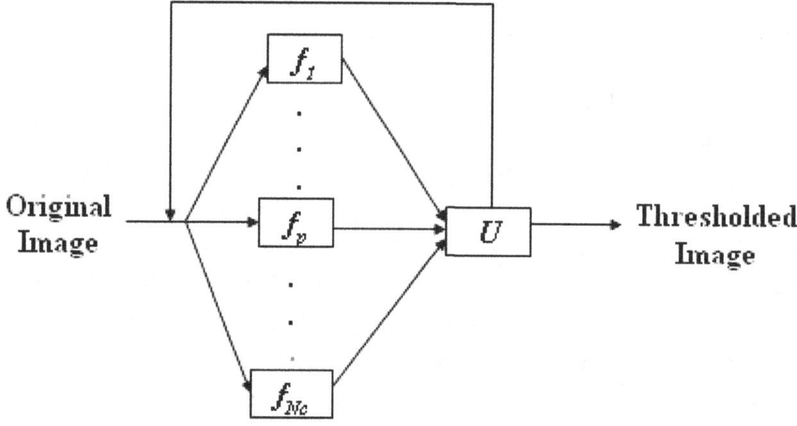

$$H_0 = -\sum_{i=0}^{t_1-1} \frac{p_i}{\omega_0} \ln \frac{p_i}{\omega_0},\ \omega_0 = \sum_{i=0}^{t_1-1} p_i$$

$$H_1 = -\sum_{i=t_1}^{t_2-1} \frac{p_i}{\omega_1} \ln \frac{p_i}{\omega_1},\ \omega_1 = \sum_{i=t_1}^{t_2-1} p_i$$

$$H_2 = -\sum_{i=t_2}^{t_3-1} \frac{p_i}{\omega_2} \ln \frac{p_i}{\omega_2},\ \omega_2 = \sum_{i=t_2}^{t_3-1} p_i$$

$$H_k = -\sum_{i=t_k}^{L} \frac{p_i}{\omega_k} \ln \frac{p_i}{\omega_k},\ \omega_k = \sum_{i=t_k}^{L} p_i$$

The optimal segmentation threshold vector $(t_1^*, t_2^*, ..., t_k^*)$ is that maximizing the total entropy:

$$(t_1^*, t_2^*, ..., t_k^*) = Arg \max_{0<t_1<t_2<...<L} f(t_1, t_2, ..., t_k)$$

Between-Class Variance Criterion

The Otsu's method (Otsu, 1979) is based on the discriminant analysis. It consists in the maximization of the between-class variance of the thresholded image as:

$$f(t_1, t_2, ..., t_k) = \omega_0\omega_1(\mu_0 - \mu_1)^2 + \omega_0\omega_2(\mu_0 - \mu_2)^2 + \omega_0\omega_3(\mu_0 - \mu_3)^2 + ... +$$

$$\omega_0\omega_k(\mu_0 - \mu_k)^2 + \omega_1\omega_2(\mu_1 - \mu_2)^2 + \omega_1\omega_3(\mu_1 - \mu_3)^2 + ... +$$

$$\omega_1\omega_k(\mu_1 - \mu_k)^2 + ... + \omega_{k-1}\omega_k(\mu_{k-1} - \mu_k)^2 \quad (16)$$

where:

$$\omega_n = \sum_{i=t_n}^{t_{n+1}-1} p_i,\ \mu_n = \sum_{i=t_n}^{t_{n+1}-1} \frac{i \times p_i}{\omega_n} \text{ and}$$
$$0 \le n \le k$$

The optimal segmentation threshold vector $(t_1^*, t_2^*, ..., t_k^*)$ makes the total variance maximum:

$$(t_1^*, t_2^*, ..., t_k^*) = Arg \max_{0<t_1<t_2<...<L} f(t_1, t_2, ..., t_k)$$

Minimum Error Criterion

Kittler and Illingworth proposed a method (Kittler and Illingworth, 1986) that assumes a parametric form of the histogram, which is fit to a mixture of Gaussians, aiming at minimizing the error between that parametric distribution and the actual histogram as follows:

$$f(t_1, t_2, ..., t_k) = 1 + 2 \times \sum_{i=0}^{k} \left(\omega_i \left(\ln \sigma_i - \ln \omega_i\right)\right) \quad (17)$$

where:

$$\omega_n = \sum_{i=t_n}^{t_{n+1}-1} p(i)$$

$$\sigma^2_n = \sum_{i=t_n}^{t_{n+1}-1} \frac{p(i) \times (i - \mu_n)^2}{\omega_n} \text{ and}$$

$$\mu_n = \sum_{i=t_n}^{t_{n+1}-1} \frac{p(i) \times i}{\omega_n},\ 0 \le n \le k$$

The optimal segmentation threshold vector $(t_1^*, t_2^*, ..., t_k^*)$ is given by:

$$(t_1^*, t_2^*, ..., t_k^*) = Arg \min_{0<t_1<t_2<...<L} f(t_1, t_2, ..., t_k)$$

Selection Criterion

The uniformity measure U is used for evaluating the quality of thresholded image and eventually to select the best thresholds. The uniformity measure

U is widely mentioned in the literature (Sahoo and al., 1988; Yin, 1997):

$$U = 1 - 2k \frac{\sum_{j=0}^{k} \sum_{i \in C_j} (g_i - m_j)^2}{N(g_{\max} - g_{\min})^2} \tag{18}$$

where: k is the number of thresholds, C_j is the segmented Class j, g_i is the gray level of pixel i, m_j is the mean of the gray levels of those pixels in segmented region j, N is the number of total pixels in the given image, $g_{\max}$ is the maximal gray level of the pixels in the given image, g_{min} is the minimal gray level of the pixels in the given image.

The value of the uniformity measure is between 0 and 1. A higher value of uniformity means that the quality of the thresholded image is better.

Proposed Algorithm

For the ease of describing the proposed algorithm, let us first define the following symbols:

- A is an image contains N pixels with gray levels from 0 to L-1.
- Nt is the maximum number of thresholds, $Nt=L-1$.
- $T=\{t_k, k=1...Nt\}$ is the set of Nt thresholds.
- Nc is the number of thresholding criteria used.
- $S=\{Ss_1, ..., Ss_p, ..., Ss_{Nc}\}$ is the swarm of Nc sub-swarms of the same size s, such that $Ss_p = \{X_1^p, ..., X_i^p, ..., X_s^p\}$ is the sub-swarm p ; $p = 1..Nc$,
- $X_i^p = (x_{i,1}^p, ..., x_{i,j}^p, ..., x_{i,Nt}^p)$ indicates the particle i of sub-swarm p, with $x_{i,k}^p \in \{0,1\}$, for $j = 1,..., Nt$ such that, if $x_{i,k}^p = 1$ then the corresponding t_k in T has been chosen to be part of the solution proposed by X_i^p. Otherwise, if $x_{i,k}^p = 0$ then the corresponding t_k in T is not part of the solution proposed by X_i^p.
- n_i^p is the number of thresholds represented by particle X_i^p of sub-swarm Ss_p, such that:

$$n_i^p = \sum_{k=1}^{Nt} x_{i,k}^p \text{ with } n_i^p \leq Nt$$

- T_i^p is the multi-threshold solution represented by particle X_i^p of sub-swarm Ss_p, such that:

$$T_i^p = (t_k) \forall k : x_{i,k}^p = 1, \text{ with } T_i^p \subseteq T$$

- n_{gbest}^p : the number of thresholds represented by the global best particle X_{gbest}^p of sub-swarm Ss_p; $X_{gbest}^p = (x_{gbest,1}^p, ..., x_{gbest,j}^p, ..., x_{gbest,Nt}^p)$, such that:

$$n_{gbest}^p = \sum_{k=1}^{N_t} x_{gbest,k}^p, \quad \text{with } n_{gbest}^p \leq Nt$$

- T_{gbest}^p : the multi-threshold solution represented by global best particle X_{gbest}^p of sub-swarm Ss_p, such that:

$$T_{gbest}^p = (t_k) \forall k : x_{gbest,k}^p = 1, \text{ with } T_{gbest}^p \subseteq T$$

- *Tgbest* is the threshold best combination, in the swarm S that maximizes the uniformity measure U.
- *Ngbest* is the number of thresholds in the threshold best combination *Tgbest* in the swarm.

p_{ini} is a user-specified probability defined in (Omran and al., 2006), (Kuncheva and Bezdek, 1998), which is used to initialize a particle position, $\boldsymbol{x}_i$, as follows:

$$x_{i,k}^{p} = \begin{cases} 0 & if\ r_k(t) \geq p_{ini} \\ 1 & if\ r_k(t) < p_{ini} \end{cases} \quad (19)$$

where: $r_k(t) \sim U(0,1)$

Obviously a large value for p_{ini} results in selecting most of the thresholds in T.

The algorithm works as follows: T is a set of thresholds, initialised by the integer values from 1 to L-1, L is the maximum gray level in image A. The sub-swarm Ss_p of particles is then randomly initialized. The *BPSO* algorithm is then applied to find the "best" set of thresholds, T^{p}_{gbest}, from T, which optimizes the objective function f_p according to T^{p}_{gbest}. The different sub-swarms Ss_p communicate between them, through the exchange of their better position $(T^{p}_{gbest}, n^{p}_{gbest})$ to decide whether the threshold best combination *Tgbest*, in the swarm, that maximizes the uniformity measure U. The algorithm is then repeated using the new T= *Tgbest* and the new *Nt*=*Ngbest*. When the particles of sub-swarm are then re-initialized; the first *Nt* elements of a particle are initialized according to Equation (19), and rests are initialized by 0. When the termination criteria are met, T=*Tgbest* will be the resulting "optimum" set of the threshold best combination, in the whole gray level range.

The *ATMO* algorithm is summarized below:

1. Initialize $T = \{t_k, t_k = 1 \ldots L\text{-}1\}$ is the set of *N*t thresholds, *Nt*= *L-1*, for *a*n image with gray levels from *0* to *L*.
2. For each sub-swarm Ss_p in *S*, *p*=1…,Nc
   a. Initialize the particle X^{p}_{i}, with $x^{p}_{i,k} \sim U\{0,1\}$; i = 1,…, s and k = 1,…, *Nt* using Equation19
   b. Randomly initialize the velocity V^{p}_{i} of each particle X^{p}_{i} in Ss_p, such that $v^{p}_{i,k} \in [-5,5]$, i= 1,…, s and k = 1,…, *Nt*. The range of [-5,5] was set empirically.
3. For each particle X^{p}_{i} in Ss_p ; i= 1,…, s and p = 1,…, *Nc*
   a. Calculate the objective function according f_p.
4. Apply the binary PSO velocity and position update equations (Equations 12 and 13) to find the *lbest* solution (n^{p}_{i}, T^{p}_{i}) and the *gbest* solution $(n^{p}_{gbest}, T^{p}_{gbest})$.
5. Repeat steps 3) until the termination criteria are met.
6. Calculate the uniformity measure $U(T^{p}_{gbest})$, *p*=*1*…*Nc*, using Equation 18.
7. *Tgbest*= T^{p}_{gbest}, *Ngbest* = n^{p}_{gbest} / $U(T^{p}_{gbest}) = \underset{h=1\ldots NC}{Max}(U(T^{h}_{gbest}))$
8. *Nt*= *Ngbest*;
9. Re-initialize the particle X^{p}_{i} of sub-swarm Ss_p, with $x^{p}_{i,k} \sim U\{0,1\}$ i = 1,…, s and k = 1,…, *Nt* using Equation 19, and $x^{p}_{i,k} = 0$, for k = *Nt*+1…, L-1.
10. Repeat steps 3 through 8 until termination criteria are met.

The Termination Criteria (*TC*) can be a user-defined maximum number of iterations or a lack of progress in improving the best solution found so far for a user-specified consecutive number of iterations.

Evaluation of the Performance

To evaluate the performance of the proposed *ATMO* algorithm, we present some experiments, with various images (Figure 2). These images are: one synthetic image (Square image) where the actual number of classes was known in advance, one known natural image (Lenna), one MRI and one satellite image of Lake Tahoe. The optimal range for number of classes for Lenna image is taken from (Turi, 2001) which was based on a visual analysis survey conducted by a group of ten people. Similarly, the optimal range for the MRI and Lake Tahoe images are taken from (Omran

Figure 2. Test images: (a) Square, (b) Lenna, (c) Lake Tahoe, and (d) MRI

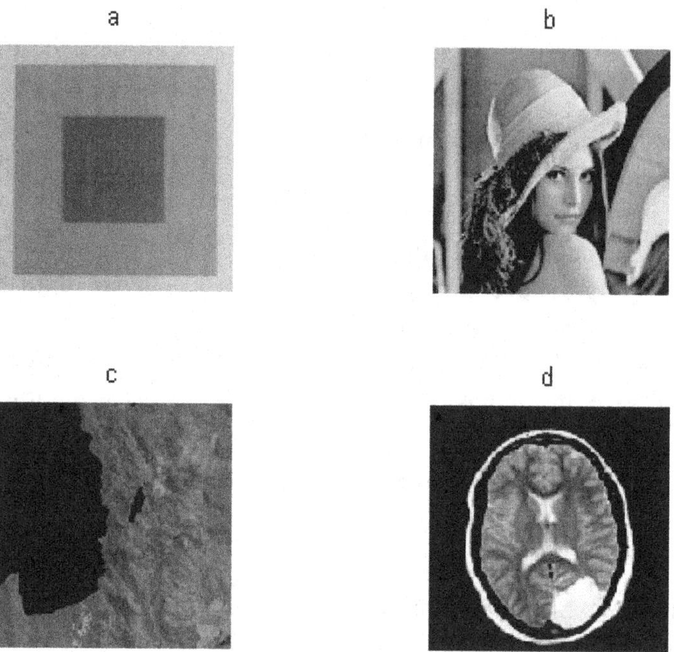

and al., 2006), they were estimated by a group of three people.

Our experiments are performed on a computer having Intel Core 2 Duo processor (3 GHZ) and 2 GB memory. The *ATMO* parameters were empirically set; Table 1 summarizes values of parameters of *ATMO* with which we got good results. These values are applied for the segmentation of all test images.

In order to measure the performance of the segmentation, we used the criterion of Peak Signal to Noise Ratio (PSNR), which is used as a quality measurement between the original image and the thresholded image, the value is normally expressed in decibels (dB). The higher the *PSNR*, the better the quality of the thresholded, or reconstructed image. The *PSNR* is defined as.

$$PSNR = 20\log_{10}\left(\frac{255}{RMSE}\right) \quad (20)$$

Where *RMSE* is the root mean-squared error, which is defined as:

$$RMSE = \sqrt{\frac{1}{M \times N}\sum_{i=1}^{M}\sum_{j=1}^{N}\left(I(i,j) - \hat{I}(i,j)\right)^2}$$

where I and $\hat{I}$ are the original and the thresholded images, and $M \times N$ are the dimensions of the image.

Since the proposed algorithm is of stochastic type, its performance cannot be judged by the result of a single run. 50 different runs have been carried out, for each image, to reach valid conclusion about the performance of the algorithm. The dynamic behavior of the proposed method is also studied by calculating the mean and standard deviation concerning: the number of classes (C_{ATMO}), the uniformity measure U and the *PSNR* value. The higher standard deviation shows that the results of the experiment are unstable.

From these results (Table 2), it is clear that:

Table 1. ATMO parameters

Parameters	Designation	values
p_{ini}	User-specified probability	0.75
Nc	Number of sub-swarm	3
s	Number of Particles in each sub-swarm	50
$NI1$	Number of Iterations; for step 4 of algorithm	50
$NI2$	Number of Iterations; for step 9 of algorithm	10
ω	Inertia weight	0.72
c_1	Acceleration constant	1.8
c_2	Acceleration constant	1.4
$Vmax$	Maximum velocity	255

- The proposed *ATMO* method has small standard deviation values (for the C_{ATMO}, U and *PSNR*), for all test images, showing the stability of the proposed algorithm.
- The proposed *ATMO* algorithm found a correct number of classes, for the synthetic image, and a solution within the optimal range, for the real images.

In order to show the quality of the thresholded results in segmentation based on the simultaneous optimization of some criteria and their results when these criteria used separately, a comparison of *PSNR* values for the proposed ATMO method and Otsu's, Kapur's and Kittler's methods with exhaustive search is presented in Table 3. The proposed approach automatically determines the "optimum" number of the thresholds as well as the adequate threshold values. However, the automatic determination of the threshold number still leaves a problem of the Otsu's, Kapur's and Kittler's methods, For this reason, the Otsu's, Kapur's and Kittler's methods are applied by varying the number of thresholds, then the optimal threshold number, which makes the objective function optimal (maximum for Otsu's or Kapur's functions and minimum for Kittler's), is determined. The optimal threshold values obtained by these methods are shown in Table 4.

From the results presented in Table 3, it can be seen that, for almost all the images, the proposed *ATMO* algorithm gives the highest value of PSNR value. This performance is due to the inclusion of several criteria in the segmentation process.

For a visual understanding of the thresholding in the segmentation by the ATMO algorithm, the test images are thresholded and are shown in Figure 3. The gray level histograms of these images with threshold values are illustrated in Figure 4.

6. FUTURE RESEARCH DIRECTIONS

There are many difficult problems in the field of pattern recognition and image processing, most these problems result of image segmentation step, because all others steps, such as feature extraction, classification and recognition, depend heavily on its results. These problems are the focus of much active research in order to find efficient approaches to address them. Indeed, the presented techniques are generally specific to a particular domain, sensitive to noise in the data. From where, the idea is of looking for new

Table 2. Computational results of ATMO

Images	$C_{Optimal}$	C_{ATMO}	U	$PSNR$
Square	3	3±0	0.851±0.041	18.79±0.08
Lenna	[5,10]	6.64 ±0.05	0.953±0.140	21.76 ±0.12
Tahoe	[3,7]	4.89 ±0.02	0.945±0.362	19.23 ±0.41
IRM	[4,8]	5.18 ±0.287	0.896±0.251	16.53±0.15

Figure 3. Thresholded images: (a) Square, (b) Lenna, (c) Lake Tahoe, and (d) MRI

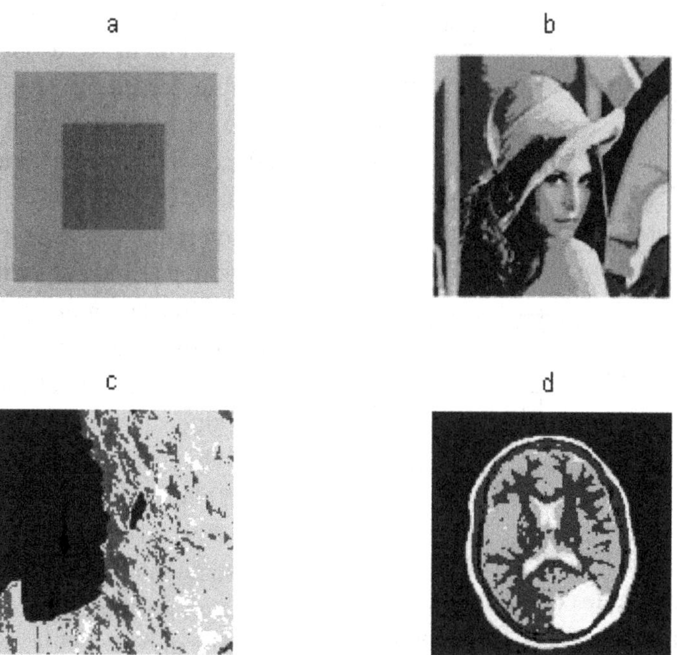

approaches based on the auto-organization and the emergence which are the possibility to treat the imprecise and incomplete data that are two inherent features to the image data.

A set of meta-heuristic optimization techniques based on the concept of auto-organization and emergence has proved their mettle in solving multilevel thresholding problem. There are encouraging us to continue research in this direction by improving the existing approaches in the aim of treating image sequences, by adding other segmentation criteria, or developing other methods based on multiobjective optimization for image thresholding, by using the recent meta-heuristic optimization techniques that are not well exploited in image segmentation such as artificial bee algorithms, Bacterial foraging algorithms and Immune-based algorithms.

7. CONCLUSION

This chapter has presented a comprehensive review of the directions and challenges of multiobjective optimization approaches in image segmentation. We have provided a recent literature review in this arena and we present a non-supervised thresholding approach based on non-Pareto multiobjective optimization and Particle Swarm Optimization, this approach enables to determinate the "optimum" number of the thresholds and simultaneously the optimal thresholds of three criteria: the between-class variances criterion, the

Table 3. Optimal comparison of PSNR values for the methods under evaluation

Images	Otsu	Kapur	Kittler	ATMO
Square	19.02	18.48	18.72	19.05
Lenna	21.84	20.83	20.55	21.97
Tahoe	19.89	20.01	19.16	20.04
IRM	15.93	16.62	15.84	16.76

Table 4. Optimal threshold values obtained by various methods

Images	Otsu	Kapur	Kittler	*ATMO*
Square	100- 141	100- 141	99- 138	100- 141
Lenna	43-79-104-144-177	43-80-104-141-177	35-74-100-152-186	69-110-135-166-197
Tahoe	70-89-113	70-89-113	72- 96-131	70-100-130
IRM	23-70-90-173	23-71-103-181	25-70-110-176	23-70-101-176

Figure 4. Gray level histograms with threshold values: (a) Square, (b) Lenna, (c) Lake Tahoe. and (d) MRI

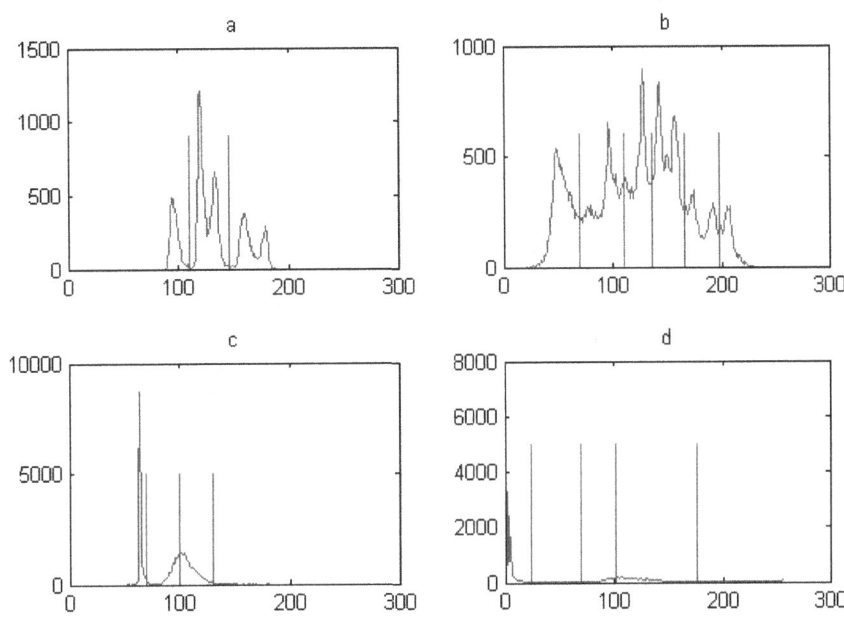

minimum error criterion and the entropy criterion. The proposed method is validated by illustrative examples; comparison with the exhaustive search Otsu's, Kapur's and Kittler's methods shows the robustness of the proposed method, and its non dependence towards the kind of the image to be segmented, and also shows that image segmentation based on the simultaneous optimization of some criteria gives satisfactory results and increases the ability to apply one same technique to a wide variety of images.

ACKNOWLEDGMENT

The authors wish to thank the referees for their careful reading of the manuscript and their comments and suggestions. This work was sponsored, in part, by the ANDRU (L'Agence Nationale pour le Développement de la Recherche Universitaire): Under the contract N^0 8u07907.

REFERENCES

Bong, C. W. (2006). *Multiple objectives hybrid metaheuristic for spatial-based redistricting: The framework and algorithms*. Ph.D. Thesis, University Malaysia Sarawak.

Bong, C. W., & Mandava, R. (2010). Multiobjective optimization approaches in image segmentation – The directions and challenges. *International Journal of Advances in Soft Computnig Applications*, *2*(1), 40–64.

Chang, Y., & Yan, H. (2003). An effective multilevel thresholding approach using conditional probability entropy and genetic algorithm. In Jin, J. S., Eaqdes, P., Feng, D. D., & Yan, H. (Eds.), *Conferences in Research and Practice in Information Technology* (*Vol. 22*, p. 21).

Coello Coello, C. A. (1999). A comprehensive survey of evolutionary-based multiobjective optimization techniques. *Knowledge and Information Systems*, *1*(3), 129–156.

Coello Coello, C. A. (2006). Evolutionary multiobjective optimization: A historical view of the field. *IEEE Computational Intelligence Magazine*, February, 28-36.

Deb, K. (2001). *Multi-objective optimization using evolutionary algorithms*. England: John Wiley and Sons, Ltd.

Deb, K. (2002). A fast elitist non-dominated sorting genetic algorithm for multiobjective optimization: NSGA II. *IEEE Transactions on Evolutionary Computation*, *5*(3), 115–148.

Djerou, L., Dehimi, H., Khelil, N., & Batouche, M. (2009). Automatic multilevel thresholding using binary particle swarm optimization for image segmentation. In the *Proceeding of the International Conference of Soft Computing and Pattern Recognition*, (pp. 67-71).

Faceli, K., De-Carvalho, A. C. P. L. F., & De-Souto, M. C. P. (2007). Multi-objective clustering ensemble with prior knowledge. *Lecture Notes in Computer Science*, ▪▪▪, 4643.

Hammouche, K., Diaf, M., & Siarry, P. (2008). A multilevel automatic thresholding method based on a genetic algorithm for a fast image segmentation. *Journal of Computer Vision and Image Understanding*, *109*(2), 163–175. doi:10.1016/j.cviu.2007.09.001

Hammouche, K., Diaf, M., & Siarry, P. (2010). A comparative study of various meta-heuristic techniques applied to the multilevel thresholding problem. *Journal of Engineering Applications of Artificial Intelligence*, *23*(5), 676–688. doi:10.1016/j.engappai.2009.09.011

Handl, J., & Knowles, J. (2007). An evolutionary approach to multiobjective clustering. *IEEE Transactions on Evolutionary Computation*, *11*, 56–76. doi:10.1109/TEVC.2006.877146

Horng, M. H. (2009). A multilevel image thresholding using the honey bee mating optimization. *Journal of Applied Mathematics and Computation*, *215*(9), 3302–3310. doi:10.1016/j.amc.2009.10.018

Kapur, J. N., Sahoo, P. K., & Wong, A. K. C. (1985). A new method for gray-level picture thresholding using the entropy of the histogram. *Journal of Computer Vision Graphics Image Processing*, *29*, 273–285. doi:10.1016/0734-189X(85)90125-2

Kayalvizhi, R., & Sathya, P. D. (2011). Optimal segmentation of brain MRI based on adaptive bacterial foraging algorithm. *Journal of Neurocomputing*, *74*, 2299–2313. doi:10.1016/j.neucom.2011.03.010

Kennedy, J., & Eberhart, R. (1995). Particle swarm optimization. *Proceedings of IEEE International Conference on Neural Networks*, Perth, Australia, Vol. 4, (pp. 1942-1948).

Kennedy, J., & Eberhart, R. (1997). A discrete binary version of the particle swarm algorithm. *Proceedings of the Conference on Systems, Man, and Cybernetics*, (pp. 4104-4109).

Kim, B. G., Shim, J. I., & Park, D. J. (2003). Fast image segmentation based on multi-resolution analysis and wavelets. *Pattern Recognition Letters, 24*, 2995–3006. doi:10.1016/S0167-8655(03)00160-0

Kittler, J., & Illingworth, J. (1986). Minimum error thresholding. *Pattern Recognition, 19*(1), 41–47. doi:10.1016/0031-3203(86)90030-0

Kuncheva, L., & Bezdek, J. (1998). Nearest prototype classification: Clustering, genetic algorithms, or random search? *IEEE Transactions on Systems, Man and Cybernetics. Part C, Applications and Reviews, 28*(1), 160–164. doi:10.1109/5326.661099

Liang, Y. C., Chen, A. L., & Chyu, C. C. (2006). Application of a hybrid ant colony optimization for the multilevel thresholding in image processing. *Lecture Notes in Computer Science, 4233.* ISSN 0302-9743

Liao, P. S., Chen, T. S., & Chung, P. C. (2001). A fast algorithm for multilevel thresholding. *Journal of Information Science Engineering, 17*, 713–727.

Lin, K. C. (2001). Fast thresholding computation by searching for zero derivates of images between-class variance. In *27th Annual Conference on IEEE Industrial Electronics Society* (pp. 393–397).

Matake, N., Hiroyasu, T., Miki, M., & Senda, T. (2007). Multiobjective clustering with automatic k-determination for large-scale data. *Genetic and Evolutionary Computation Conference*, London, England, (pp. 861-868).

Nakib, A., Oulhadj, H., & Siarry, P. (2007). Image histogram thresholding based on multiobjective optimization. *Signal Processing, 87*, 2516–2534. doi:10.1016/j.sigpro.2007.04.001

Nakib, A., Oulhadj, H., & Siarry, P. (2008). Non-supervised image segmentation based on multiobjective optimization. *Pattern Recognition Letters, 29*, 161–172. doi:10.1016/j.patrec.2007.09.008

Nakib, A., Oulhadj, H., & Siarry, P. (2009). Fractional differentiation and non-Pareto multiobjective optimization for image thresholding. *Engineering Applications of Artificial Intelligence, 22*, 236–249. doi:10.1016/j.engappai.2008.07.005

Nakib, A., Oulhadj, H., & Siarry, P. (2010). Image thresholding based on Pareto multiobjective optimization. *Engineering Applications of Artificial Intelligence, 23*, 313–320. doi:10.1016/j.engappai.2009.09.002

Omran, M., Salman, A., & Engelbrecht, A. (2006). Dynamic clustering using particle swarm optimization with application in image segmentation. *Pattern Analysis and Applications Journal, 8*(4).

Otsu, N. (1979). A threshold selection method from gray-level histograms. *IEEE Transactions on Systems, Man, and Cybernetics, 9*(1), 62–66. doi:10.1109/TSMC.1979.4310076

Pal, N. R., & Pal, S. K. (1993). A review on image segmentation techniques. *Pattern Recognition, 9*(26), 1277–1294. doi:10.1016/0031-3203(93)90135-J

Reyes-Sierra, M., & Coello, C. A. C. (2006). Multi-objective particle swarm optimizers: A survey of the state-of-the-art. *International Journal of Computer Intelligence Research, 2*(3), 287–308.

Saha, S., & Bandyopadhyay, S. (2008). *Unsupervised pixel classification in satellite imagery using a new multiobjective symmetry based clustering approach.* IEEE Region 10 Annual International Conference.

Saha, S., & Bandyopadhyay, S. (2010). A new symmetry based multiobjective clustering technique for automatic evolution of clusters. *Pattern Recognition, 43*(3). doi:10.1016/j.patcog.2009.07.004

Sahoo, P. K., Soltani, S., & Wong, A. K. C. (1988). A survey of thresholding techniques. *Computer Vision Graphics and Image Processing*, *41*, 233–260. doi:10.1016/0734-189X(88)90022-9

Schaffer, J. D. (1985). Multiple objective optimization with vector evaluated genetic algorithm. In the *Proceedings of the First International Conference on Genetic Algorithms*, (pp. 93-100). July, Pittsburgh (USA).

Sezgin, M., & Sankur, B. (2004). Survey over image thresholding techniques and quantitative performance evaluation. *Journal of Electronic Imaging*, *13*(1), 146–165. doi:10.1117/1.1631315

Sezgin, M., & Tasaltin, R. (2000). A new dichotomization technique to multilevel thresholding devoted to inspection applications. *Pattern Recognition Letters*, *21*, 151–161. doi:10.1016/S0167-8655(99)00142-7

Srinivas, N., & Deb, K. (1995). Multiobjective optimization using non-dominated sorting in genetic algorithms. *Evolutionary Computation*, *2*(8), 221–248.

Tao, W. B., Tian, J. W., & Liu, J. (2003). Image segmentation by three level thresholding based on maximum fuzzy entropy and genetic algorithm. *Pattern Recognition Letters*, *24*, 3069–3078. doi:10.1016/S0167-8655(03)00166-1

Tao, W. B., Tian, J. W., & Liu, J. (2003). Image segmentation by three level thresholding based on maximum fuzzy entropy and genetic algorithm. *Pattern Recognition Letters*, *24*, 3069–3078. doi:10.1016/S0167-8655(03)00166-1

Turi, R. H. (2001). *Clustering-based color image segmentation*. Ph.D Thesis, Monash University, Australia.

Van den Bergh, F. (2002). *An analysis of particle swarm optimizers*. PhD Thesis, Department of Computer Science, University of Pretoria.

Wu, B. F., Chen, Y. L., & Chiu, C. C. (2004). Recursive algorithms for image segmentation based on a discriminant criterion. *International Journal of Signal Processing*, *1*, 55–60.

Xu, R., & Wunsch, D. (2005). Survey of clustering algorithms. *IEEE Transactions on Neural Networks*, *16*, 645–678. doi:10.1109/TNN.2005.845141

Yen, C., Chang, F. J., & Chang, S. (1995). A new criterion for automatic multilevel thresholding. *IEEE Transactions on Image Processing*, *4*, 370–378. doi:10.1109/83.366472

Yin, P. Y., & Chen, L. H. (1997). A fast iterative scheme for multilevel thresholding methods. *Journal Signal Process*, *60*, 305–313. doi:10.1016/S0165-1684(97)00080-7

Yourui, H., & Shuang, W. (2008). Multilevel thresholding methods for image segmentation with Otsu based on QPSO. *Congress on Image and Signal Processing*, (pp. 701-705).

Zahara, E., Fan, S. K. S., & Tsai, D. M. (2005). Optimal multi-thresholding using a hybrid optimization approach. *Pattern Recognition Letters*, *26*(8), 1082–1095. doi:10.1016/j.patrec.2004.10.003

ADDITIONAL READING

Abraham, A., Hassanien, A. E., Siarry, P., & Engelbrecht, A. (2009). *Foundations of computational intelligence, Volume 3, global optimization: Theoretical foundations and applications, 203*. Springer Studies in Computational Intelligence.

Biswas, A., Dasgupta, S., Das, S., & Abraham, A. (2007). Synergy of PSO and bacterial foraging optimization - A comparative study on numerical benchmarks. *Innovations in Hybrid Intelligent Systems*, *44*, 255–263. doi:10.1007/978-3-540-74972-1_34

Coello Coello, C. A., & Cruz Cortes, N. (2005). Solving multiobjective optimization problems using an artificial immune system. *Genetic Programming and Evolvable Machines*, *2*, 163–190. doi:10.1007/s10710-005-6164-x

Dréo, J., Pétrowski, A., Siarry, P., & Taillard, E. (2005). *Metaheuristics for hard optimization*. Springer. Holland, J. H. (2006). Studying complex adaptive systems. *Journal of Systems Science and Complexity*, *19*(1), 1–8.

Horng, M. H., & Jiang, T. W. (2011). Multilevel image thresholding selection based on firefly algorithm. *ICIC Express Letters*, *5*(2), 557–562.

Jin, Y., & Sendhoff, B. (2004). Constructing dynamic optimization test problems using the multi-objective optimization concept. In *Applications of Evolutionary Computing* (*Vol. 3005*, pp. 525–536). Lecture Notes in Computer Science Springer. doi:10.1007/978-3-540-24653-4_53

Ma, Z., Tavares, J. M. R. S., Jorge, R. N., & Mascarenhas, T. (2010). A review of algorithms for medical image segmentation and their applications to the female pelvic cavity. *Computer Methods in Biomechanics and Biomedical Engineering*, *13*(2), 235–246. doi:10.1080/10255840903131878

Miller, J. H., & Page, S. E. (2007). *Complex adaptive systems: An introduction to computational models of social life*. Princeton University Press.

Passino, K. M. (2002). Biomimicry of bacterial foraging for distributed optimization and control. *IEEE Control Systems Magazine*, *22*(3), 52–67. doi:10.1109/MCS.2002.1004010

Rogowska, J. (2008). Overview and fundamentals of medical image segmentation. In Bankman, I. (Ed.), *Handbook of medical image processing and analysis*. Elsevier. doi:10.1016/B978-012077790-7/50009-6

Shukla, P. K., & Deb, K. (2007). On finding multiple Pareto-optimal solutions using classical and evolutionary generating methods. *European Journal of Operational Research*, *81*, 1630–1652. doi:10.1016/j.ejor.2006.08.002

Siarry, P. (2009). *Optimization in signal and image processing*. John Wiley & Sons, Digital Signal and Image Processing Series Edition ISTE.

Trojanowski, K., & Wierzchon, S. T. (2009). Immune-based algorithms for dynamic optimization. *Information Sciences*, *179*, 1495–1515. doi:10.1016/j.ins.2008.11.014

Zhang, Y. J. (1996). A survey on evaluation methods for image segmentation. *Pattern Recognition*, *29*, 1335–1346. doi:10.1016/0031-3203(95)00169-7

Chapter 12
On the Use of Particle Swarm Optimization Techniques for Channel Assignments in Cognitive Radio Networks

Hisham M. Abdelsalam
Cairo University, Egypt

Haitham S. Hamza
Cairo University, Egypt

Abdoulraham M. Al-Shaar
Cairo University, Egypt

Abdelbaset S. Hamza
University of Nebraska-Lincoln, USA

ABSTRACT

Efficient utilization of open spectrum in cognitive radio networks requires appropriate allocation of idle spectrum frequency bands (not used by licensed users) among coexisting cognitive radios (secondary users) while minimizing interference among all users. This problem is referred to as the spectrum allocation or the channel assignment problem in cognitive radio networks, and is shown to be NP-hard. Accordingly, different optimization techniques based on evolutionary algorithms were needed in order to solve the channel assignment problem. This chapter investigates the use of particular swarm optimization (PSO) techniques to solve the channel assignment problem in cognitive radio networks. In particular, the authors study the definitiveness of using the native PSO algorithm and the Improved Binary PSO (IBPSO) algorithm to solve the assignment problem. In addition, the performance of these algorithms is compared to that of a fine-tuned genetic algorithm (GA) for this particular problem. Three utilization functions, namely, Mean-Reward, Max-Min-Reward, and Max-Proportional-Fair, are used to evaluate the effectiveness of three optimization algorithms. Extensive simulation results show that PSO and IBPSO algorithms outperform that fine-tuned GA. More interestingly, the native PSO algorithm outperforms both the GA and the IBPSO algorithms in terms of solution speed and quality.

DOI: 10.4018/978-1-4666-1830-5.ch012

INTRODUCTION

Administrative spectrum management approach is the currently used approach by the regulators to allocate spectrum to different wireless services. Efficient utilization of open spectrum in cognitive radio networks requires appropriate allocation of idle channels (spectrum frequency bands not used by licensed users) among coexisting cognitive radios (secondary unlicensed users) while minimizing interference (Zhao, Peng, Zheng, & Shang, 2009). In this approach, secondary users access the spectrum opportunistically by identifying spectrum availability (spectrum white holes) instantaneously and without interfering with the primary users. For a secondary user, to be capable of overlaying its transmission successfully, cognition capabilities are needed, such as being aware for the surrounding, learning and understanding the variations and activities, and accordingly, adjusts operating parameters to operate efficiently.

The problem of assigning channels (frequency bands) among primary and secondary users while minimizing interference among all users is known as the resource allocation or the channel assignment problem in cognitive radio networks. This problem is shown to be NP-hard in the literature (Peng, Zheng, & Zhao, 2006). Accordingly, several heuristics were proposed to solve the channel assignment problem using game theory (Nie & Comaniciu, 2006), pricing and auction mechanisms (Huang, Berry, & Honig, 2006; Kloeck, Jaekel, & Jondral, 2005), local bargaining (Cao & Zheng, 2005), and vertex labeling (Peng, etl al, 2006;Zheng & Peng, 2005).Recently, evolutionary algorithms are used to address the resource allocation problem. In particular, in (Zhao, Peng, Zheng, & Shang, 2009), three evolutionary algorithms were performed including genetic algorithm (GA), quantum genetic algorithm (QGA), and particle swarm optimization (PSO) techniques.

This chapter investigates the quality of the PSO techniques, in terms of solution speed and quality, in solving the channel assignment problem in cognitive radio networks. In particular, the chapter studies the definitiveness of using the native PSO algorithm proposed by Kennedy et al. (Kennedy & Eberhart, 1997) and the Improved Binary PSO (IBPSO) algorithm (Yuan, Nie, Su, Wang, & Yuan, 2009) to solve the assignment problem. In addition, the performance of these algorithms is compared to that of a fine-tuned genetic algorithm (GA) for this particular problem. Three utilization functions, namely, Mean-Reward, Max-Min-Reward, and Max-Proportional-Fair, are used to evaluate the effectiveness of three optimization algorithms. Extensive simulation results show that, PSO and IBPSO algorithms outperform that fine-tuned GA. More interestingly, the native PSO algorithm outperforms both the GA and the IBPSO algorithms in terms of solution speed and quality.

The remainder of this chapter is organized as follows. The following section presents the system model and defines the problem statement. The PSO and the IBPSO algorithms are then presented, followed by simulation results and analysis. Finally, future research and conclusions are given.

SYSTEM MODEL AND PROBLEM STATEMENT

To better understand the problem addressed in this paper, we consider the first commercial application of CR in TV white space (interleaved spectrum).

Figure 1 shows a sample setup for a cognitive radio network. A typical cognitive network consists of a set of primary users X each is assigned a channel selected from a pool of M orthogonal, non-overlapping spectrum bands that differ in bandwidth and transmission range. Each channel of them is associated with a protection area with protection radius dP(x,m). However, it is assumed here that dP (x,m) is the same for all channels for simplicity in analysis. There are N coexisting secondary users that are planned to utilize these idle channels occupied by primary users in order to provide their services. A secondary can be a wireless access point (or transmission link). It is assumed that each secondary user can utilize multiple channels at one time, but limited to the radio interface constraint.

Each secondary user keeps a list of available channels that it can use without interfering with neighboring primary users (Figure 1). The spectrum access problem becomes a channel allocation problem. A secondary user's transmission is bounded by a minimal, and maximal transmission powers that are user-specific. These boundaries have corresponding transmission ranges of and, respectively. Also, the transmission of secondary user can not overlap with the transmission of the primary user who uses the same channel. Therefore, each secondary user can adjust its transmission range by tuning its transmit power on channels to avoid interference with primary users.

Different secondary users are assigned different available spectrum based on its location, radio interface, and requirements. Each secondary user should be aware of its position with respect to the surrounding primary users, three different scenarios exist (Figure 2):

a. The secondary user exists within the protection range of the primary user, then it cannot use the channel occupied by this primary user.
b. The secondary user is located outside the protection range of the primary user, but its dS dmin, it still cannot use the channel occupied by this primary user.
c. The secondary user exists outside the protection range of the primary user, and dS, dmin, then this secondary user can operate on this channel, with a transmission range of dS (n,m) as long as it is less than the dmax.

The following are the key components in the used model (Peng, Zheng, & Zhao, 2006):

Figure 1. Structure of a simple cognitive radio network

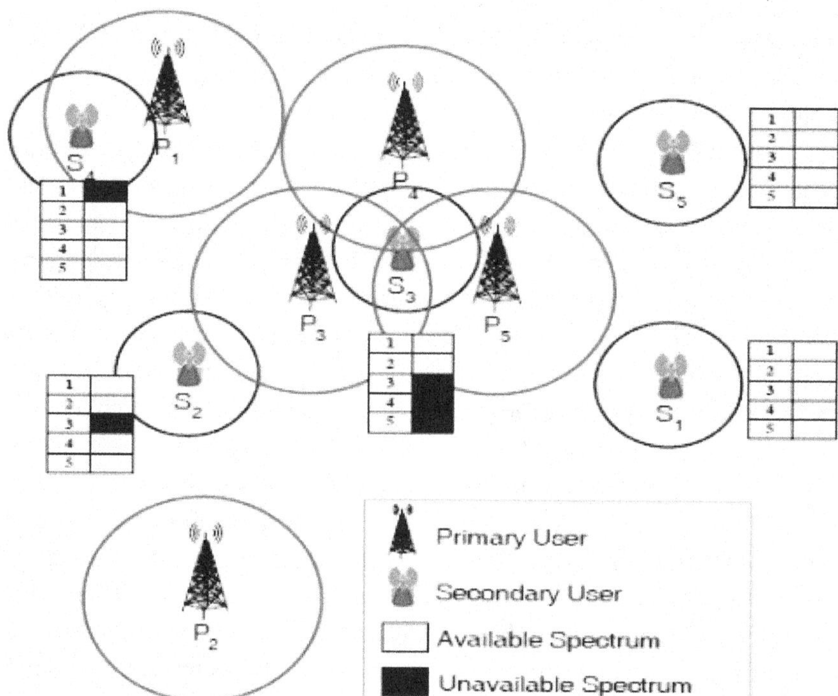

Figure 2. Secondary-primary position's scenarios

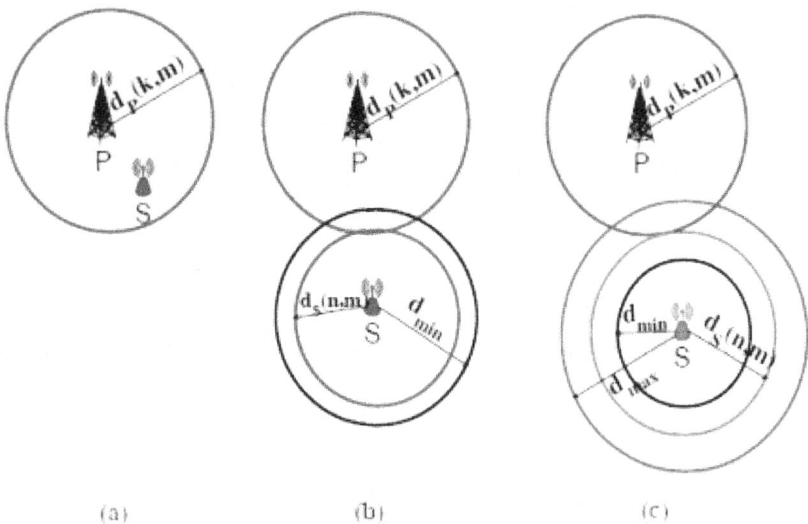

- **Channel availability:** $L=\left\{l_{n,m} \mid l_{n,m} \int 0,1\right\}_{N\times M}$ is a matrix representing per user available spectrum: $l_{n,m}$ = 1 if and only if channel *m* is available to user *n*.
- **Channel reward:** B $=\{bn,m\}N^*M$, a matrix representing the channel reward: Bn,m represents the maximum reward that can be acquired by user n using channel m.
- **Interference constraint:** Let $C=\left\{C_{n,k,m,} \mid C_{n,k,m,} \int \{0,1\}\right\}_{N\times N\times M}$,a matrix represents the interference constraints among secondary users. Cn,k,m =1, if users n and k would interfere if they use channel m simultaneously. Cn,k,m = 1 – ln,m.
- **Conflict free channel assignment:** Let $A=\left\{a_{n,m} \mid a_{n,m} \int (0,1)\right\}_{N\times M}$, a matrix that represents the assignment: $a_{n,m}$ = 1 if channel m is assigned to user n.
- **User Reward:** R $=\left\{B_n=\sum_{m=0}^{M-1} a_{n,m} \cdot b_{n,m}\right\}_{N\times 1}$ represents the reward vector that each user gets for a given channel assignment. In our context, the reward is the coverage area of the secondary user which is proportional to d_S^2 (n,m).

The objective of the spectrum allocation problem in open spectrum systems is to find a channel allocation that maximizes a utilization function U(R).

To define U(R), two spectrum design factors can be considered, namely, spectrum utilization and fairness. Different combinations of these two factors result in different definitions for the U(R) function. We consider three utilization functions, namely, Mean-Reward (MR), Max-Min-Reward (MMR), and Max-Proportional-Fair (MPF). The following equations reproduced from (Peng, Zheng, & Zhao, 2006)to describe these three utilization functions:

$$U_{MSR}=\frac{1}{N}\sum_{n=0}^{N-1} B_n=\frac{1}{N}\sum_{n=0}^{N-1}\sum_{m=0}^{M-1} a_{n,m} \cdot b_{n,m} \quad (1)$$

$$U_{MMR}=\min_{0\le n\le N} B_n=\min_{0\le n\le N}\sum_{m=0}^{M-1} a_{n,m} \cdot b_{n,m} \quad (2)$$

$$U_{MPF} = \left[\prod_{n=0}^{N-1} \left(\sum_{m=1}^{M-1} a_{n,m} \cdot b_{n,m} + 1E - 4 \right) \right]^{\frac{1}{N}} \quad (3)$$

A baseline reward of 1E - 4 is used in order to prevent the case of having auser with no channels (user starvation).

OPTIMIZATION ALGORITHMS FOR CHANNEL ASSIGNMENT

This section gives the formulation of the GA, PSO, and the IBPSO algorithms for solving the channel assignment problem under interference constraints in cognitive radio networks.

Genetic Algorithm (GA)

In this study, the genetic algorithm (GA) reported in (Zhao, Peng, Zheng, & Shang, 2009)is implemented in order to solve the problem under the three utilization functions. However, according to a previous study (Hamza & Elghoneimy, 2010) the selection of the GA parameters considerably affects the quality of the presented solution. Thus, we conclude that, in order to study the impact of the network parameters, we need to fine-tune the GA for each utilization function to ensure that the used GA will yield the best possible solution for each utilization function. The result of this study is summarized in Table 1. Algorithm 1 shows the procedures of solving the spectrum allocation problem in cognitive radio networks employing the genetic algorithm.

Particle Swarm Optimization (PSO) Algorithm

In (Kennedy & Eberhart, 1997), a discrete binary version of the PSO was introduced. This algorithm uses the concept of the velocity as a probability that a bit takes either logical 010, or 000. In this algorithm, a particle's velocity is continuous. The update function of particle's velocity is given in Equation 4:

$$v_{ij}^{t+1} = wv_i + \alpha_1 C_1 \left(pb_i^t \right) + \alpha_1 C_1 \left(gb^t - x_i^t \right) \quad (4)$$

where w is an inertia weight, α_1 and α_2 are random numbers uniformly distributed between 0 and 1, C1 and C2 are cognitive and social parameters, pb_{ti} local best at iteration t, gbt global best at iteration t and x_{ti} is position for variable i at iteration t.

A special sigmoid function $(sig\ (vi(t)))$ is used in order to calculate the vusing the velocity calculated above.

$$\overline{v}_i^{t+1} = sig\left(v_i\left(t\right)\right) = \frac{1}{1 + e^{-v_i(t)}} \quad (5)$$

Finally, a particle's position is updated according to:

Table 1. GA fine-tuned parameters under different utilization functions

Literature	Selection (Zhao, et. al, 2009)	MR	MMR	MPF
Population Size	20	20	200	500
Crossover Probability	0.80	0.85	0.85	0.85
Mutation Probability	0.01	0.1	0.1	0.1
Crossover Method	Two-points	Uniform	Single point	Single point
Selection Scheme	Roulette Wheel	Tournament(Size=5)	Random	Random

Algorithm 1.

1: **begin**
2: Define utilization function *U*(*R*).
3: Given the matrices *L, B, and C*, set the solution length as $d = \sum_{n=0}^{N-1} \sum_{m=0}^{M=0} l_{n,m}$
and set $L1 = \{(n, m) | l_{n,m} = 1\}$ such that elements in $L1$ are arranged increasingly in *n* and *m*.
4: Generate an initial population with random chromosomes.
5: Define parameters based on Table 1.
6: **while** (t <max number of iterations) **do**
7: For all chromosomes, map the *jth* element in $L1$ for $1<j<L1$. For all *m*, search all (*n, k*)that satisfies $C_{n,k,m} = 1$, and check if
$a_{n,m} = a_{k,m} = 1$, randomly set one of them to 0.
8: Evaluate each chromosome according to the objective function *U*(*R*).
9: Perform the desired selection and crossover scheme.
10: **end while**
11: Find the current best solution.
12: **end**

$$x_i^{t+1} \begin{cases} 1 & if\ r_{ij} < \bar{v}_i^{t+1}, \\ 0 & otherwise. \end{cases} \quad (6)$$

where r_{ij} are uniformly random numbers between 0 and 1. The following algorithm shows the procedures of solving the spectrum allocation problem in cognitive radio networks employing particle swarm optimization technique.

Algorithm 2 shows the generic procedures of solving the spectrum allocation problem in cognitive radio networks using the Binary Particle Swarm Optimization algorithm.

Improved Binary PSO (IBPSO) Algorithm

The Improved Binary PSO (IBPSO) (Yuan, Nie, Su, Wang, & Yuan, 2009) relies on the basic idea of local best position and global best position that is originally proposed by J. Kennedy and R. Eberhart in (Kennedy & Eberhart, 1997). In IBPSO algorithm, an individual is a bit string which starts it strip from a random point in the search space and tries to become nearer to the global best position and previous best position of itself. However, unlike the original PSO, IBPSO employs logical operators in the equations used to update both, velocity and position according to Equation (4) and (5), respectively.

$$v_{id}^{t+1} = \omega_1 \otimes \left(pbest_{id}^t \oplus x_{id}^t\right) + \omega_2 \otimes \left(gbest_d^t \oplus x_{id}^t\right) \quad (7)$$

$$x_i^{t+1} = x_i^t \oplus v_i^t \quad (8)$$

where i, t, and d represents the particle's number, number of iteration, and solution dimension (number of variables), respectively. w1 and w2 are two random binary integer numbers uniformly distributed in the range of [0, 1].

The IBPSO relies on bitwise logical operators where the solution is guided to local best and global best values with uniform probability to keep the stochastic nature of the algorithm. Through finding the solution x matched with local best and global best. New x depends on improving the old x with the velocity that depends on local and global best solutions. Analyzing the operation of this algorithm, we find that the solution stuck in local optimal with low probability ofgetting out of this local optimal solution.

Algorithm 2.

begin
Define utilization function $U(R)$.
Given the matrices *L, B, and C*, set the solution length as $d=\sum_{n=0}^{N-1}\sum_{m=0}^{M=0} l_{n,m}$ and set $L1 = \{(n,m)| l_{n,m} = 1\}$ such that elements in $L1$ are arranged increasingly in *n* and *m*.
Generate an initial population with random particles.
Define parameters (number of particles, maximum number of iterations, and *Pmut*).
while (t <max number of iterations) **do**
For all particles, map the *jth* element in $L1$ for $1 < j < L1$. For all *m*, search all (*n; k*) that satisfies $C_{n,k,m}= 1$, and check if $a_{n,m} = a_{k,m} = 1$, randomly set one of them to 0.
Evaluate each particle's position according to the objective function $U(R)$.
If a particle's current position is better than its previous best position, update it.
Determine the best particle (according to the particle's previous best positions).
Update particles' velocities according to Equation 4.
Calculate v_i^{t+1} for particle *i* using Equation 5.
Move particles to their new positions according to Equation 6.
end while
Find the current best solution.
end

Algorithm 3 shows the generic procedures of solving the spectrum allocation problem in cognitive radio networks using the IBPSO algorithm.

SIMULATION RESULTS AND ANALYSIS

This section presents and analyzes the simulation results of the performance of the GA, PSO, and the IBPSO algorithms with respect to the MR, MMR, and MPF utility functions under consideration. In order to ensure consistency and stability, the results reported in this study represent the average of 50 experiments. Experimental simulation reported in this paper is performed using MATLAB (running on a 2:66 GHz Core 2 Duo processor PC with 2 GB RAM with a 32 bits register). Figures 3, 4, and 5 show box plots that demonstrate the performance of the three algorithms under investigation under MR, MMR, and MPF utility functions, respectively.

Figure 3 depicts the box plot of the time elapsed to reach the optimum solution using different three algorithms under the MR utilization function. As we can see, GA present the worst performance compared to other algorithms where it possesses the largest median. Moreover, its median is larger than the max of other algorithms. On the other hand, the original PSO outperforms all algorithms as its median is less than the medians of all other algorithms (0:052sec). Numerical results of the three algorithms under the MR utilization function are tabulated in Table 2.

Although the solution space of the problem is small, the IBPSO algorithm using small number of particles stuck in local optima and fails to find the optimum solution found by other algorithms even with large number of iterations. Therefore, a large number of particles (20000 particles) is used while in other PSO algorithms the number of particles is only, 20 particles.

The proposed enhanced PSO solves this problem by using the mutation operation which expands the exploration of the search space, and therefore outperformed the IBPSO.

The box plots of the time elapsed to reach the optimum solution using different three algorithms under the MMR, and MPF utilization functions are shown in Figure 4 and Figure 5, respectively. Table 3 and Table 4 contain results of MMR and MPF utilization functions, respectively. Again,

Algorithm 3.

begin
Define utilization function $U(R)$.
Given the matrices L, B, *and* C, set the solution length as $d=\sum_{n=0}^{N-1}\sum_{m=0}^{M=0} l_{n,m}$ and set $L1 = \{(n,m) | l_{n,m} = 1\}$ such that elements in $L1$ are arranged increasingly in n and m.
Generate an initial population with random chromosomes.
Define parameters based on Table 1.
while (t <max number of iterations) **do**
For all chromosomes, map the jth element in $L1$ for $1 < j < L1$. For all m, search all (n, k) that satisfies $C_{n,k,m} = 1$, and check if $a_{n,m} = a_{k,m} = 1$, randomly set one of them to 0.
Evaluate each chromosome according to the objective function $U(R)$.
If a particle's current position is better than its previous best position, update it.
Determine the best particle (according to the particle's previous best positions).
Update particles' velocities.
Move particles to their new positions.
end while
Find the current best solution.
end

the GA presents the worst performance among other algorithms. For the IBPSO, the interquartile Distance is significantly reduced since the algorithm employs a large number of particles (20000), however it is median is larger than both original PSO and the proposed enhanced PSO.

A common observation from these three figures is that the GA presents the worst performance among all algorithms. The reason of this performance is that in GA, several operations are performed such as: selection, mutation, and crossover. Also, several parameters are involved in the GA and hence, it takes long time per iteration.

What also worth note is that the proposed enhanced PSO performance improves as the solution space gets more complicated where its performance becomes comparable to the original PSO. Comparing the original and the proposed enhanced PSO algorithms, the interquartile dis-

Figure 3. Comparison of the GA, PSO, and IBPSO algorithms under the MR

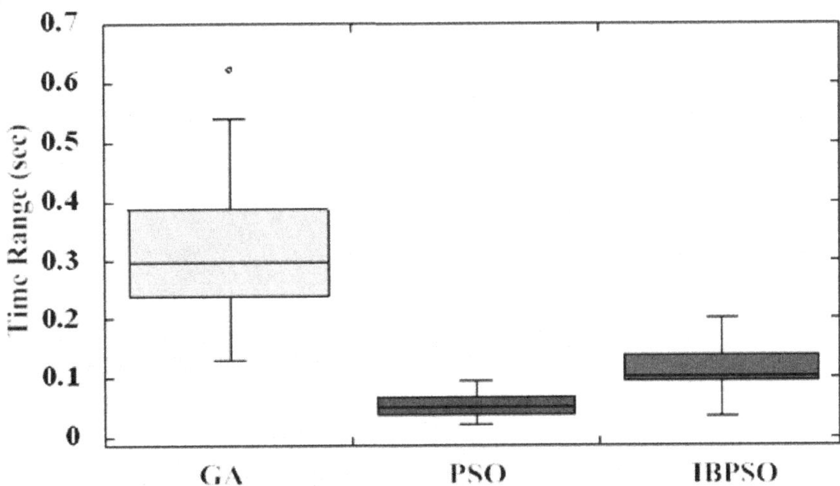

Figure 4. Comparison of the GA, PSO, and IBPSO algorithms under the MMR

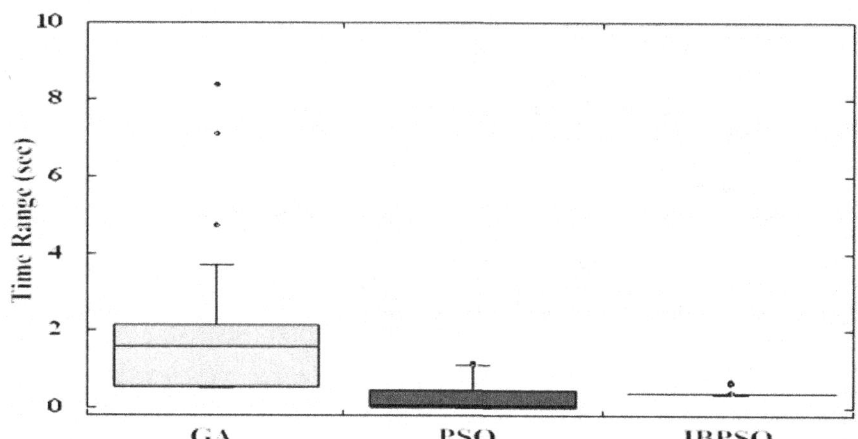

tance of the proposed algorithm is less than the one of the original PSO.

Another aspect that can be used in order to evaluate the effectiveness of the investigated algorithms, is the reward obtained by users, versus the iterations. For this purpose, the objective value versus the iterations is plotted for different algorithms, under different utilization functions. For this study, a fixed number iterations and populations (2000, and 20, respectively) are used for the comparison purpose.

Figure 6 depicts the performance of three algorithms under the MR utilization function. Due to the simplicity of the objective function, the three algorithms present comparable performance.

From the figure, PSO and GA algorithms, are almost identical, and outperform other algorithms. On the other hand, the enhanced IBPSO, maintained a steady increasing rate, however, it requires a larger number of iterations, compared to the GA and the PSO algorithms, in order to find the best achievable solution.

Figure 5. Comparison of the GA, PSO, and IBPSO algorithms under the MPF

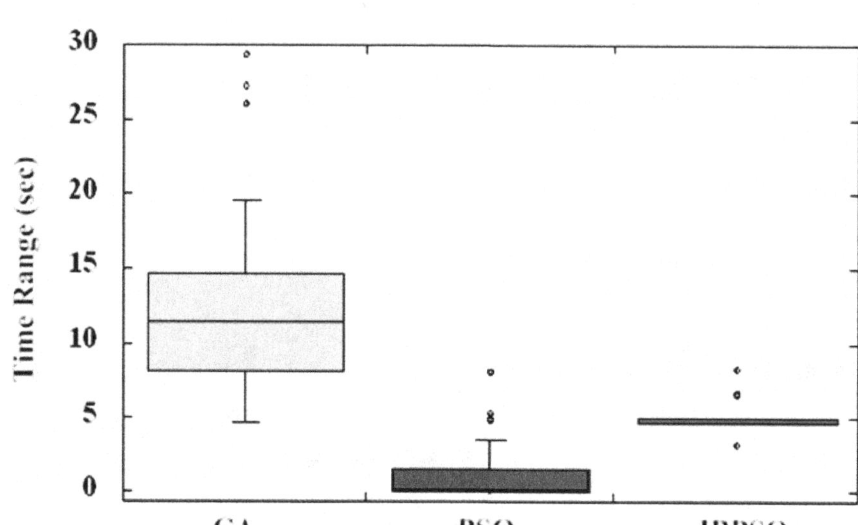

Table 2. Results of different algorithms under the MR function

	GA	PSO	IBPSO
Minimum	0.13	0.022	0.036
Maximum	0.623	0.095	0.199
Mean	0.316	0.055	0.111
Median	0.296	0.052	0.102
Std Deviation	0.11	0.018	0.036
Variance	0.012	0	0.001

Table 3. Results of different algorithms under the MMR function

	GA	PSO	IBPSO
Minimum	0.525	0.007	0.375
Maximum	8.385	1.163	0.704
Mean	1.891	0.26	0.447
Median	1.609	0.076	0.387
Std Deviation	1.569	0.309	0.12
Variance	2.462	0.096	0.014

In spite of the simplicity of this objective function, it can be noticed that the IBPSO presents the worst solution among the three algorithms. For the IBPSO, the lack of the searching diversity, mentioned before, reflects on the solution found as it stuck at a certain, suboptimal, solution with no improvement noticed along the iterations.

Figure 6 plots the objective value versus iterations of the three algorithms under the MMR utilization function. It is shown that both PSO and enhanced IBPSO reached the best possible value, and hence, outperforming other two algorithms.

For the PSO, and the enhanced IBPSO, a steady increasing rate towards the best solution is maintained. However, the enhanced IBPSO outperforms the PSO, since it achieves the best possible solution in a less number of iterations. For the GA, a steady increasing rate is observed, but a much more worse solution is found compared to the PSO, and the enhanced IBPSO. It also can be seen that, the IBPSO presents the worst performance among the three algorithms.

Similar to the MMR performance, both PSO, and enhanced PSO out performs the GA and the IBPSO algorithm in the study under MPF utilization function (Figure 8). For the PSO, it achieves a better solution at early phases (since it is a fully directed search), however, at late phases the solution is improved with a small rate. On the other hand, for the enhanced IBPSO it presents a stable increasing rate towards the best achievable value compared to the PSO. This performance is due to the fact that the enhanced IBPSO possesses a higher searching diversity due to the mutation capability.

For the GA, a similar performance to the enhanced IBSPO, with respect to the increasing rate, is noticed. However, the GA finds a worse solution compared to the PSO and the enhanced IBPSO.

FUTURE RESEARCH DIRECTIONS

This chapter discussed how Computational Intelligence Techniques (namely; Genetic Algorithms and Particle Swarm Optimization) are used to tackle a problem that received attention in recent years from both the practical point of view and the computational point of view.

With the rapid expansion of wireless devices in the last decade, efficient spectrum utilization of the limited spectrum resources became the

Table 4. Results of different algorithms under the MPF function

	GA	PSO	IBPSO
Minimum	4.717	0.014	3.186
Maximum	29.352	8.092	8.236
Mean	12.226	1.119	4.657
Median	11.402	0.155	4.909
Std Deviation	5.629	1.722	1.026
Variance	31.696	2.968	1.054

Figure 6. Reward versus iterations under MSR utilization function

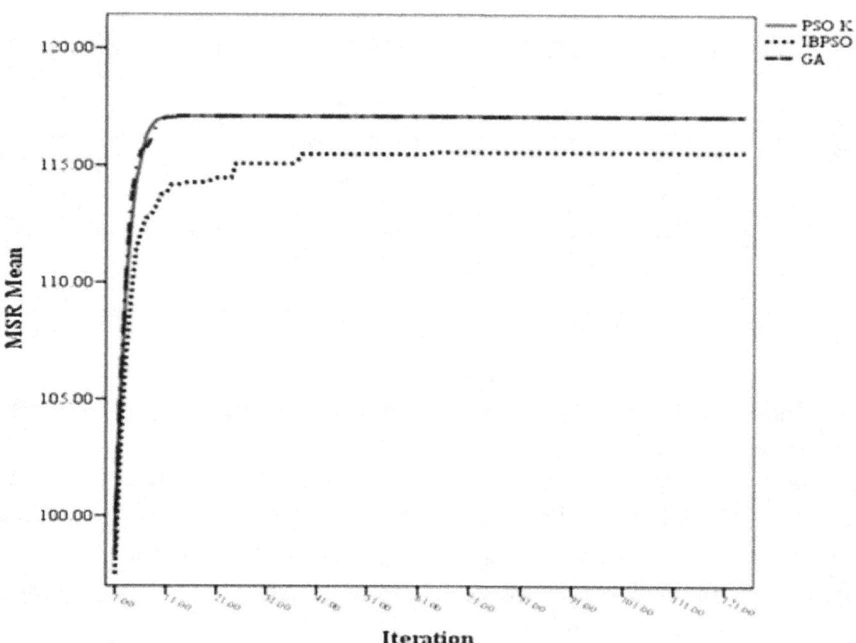

Figure 7. Reward versus iterations under MMR utilization function

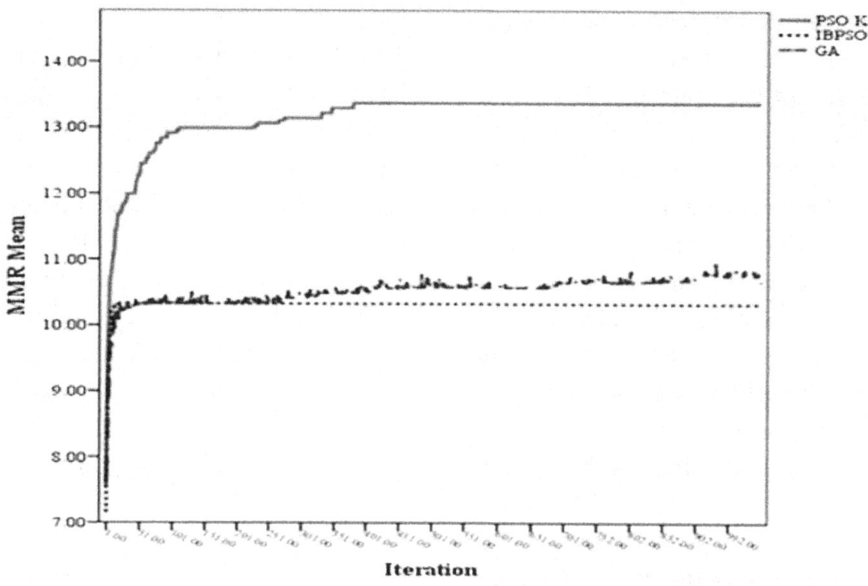

focus of network management practitioners. The concept of cognitive radio (focus of this chapter) was proposed to deal with this issue, more specifically; the spectrum allocation or the channel assignment problem in cognitive radio networks. This problem was shown to be NP-hard. Extensive simulation results presented in the chapter show that, in general, Particle Swarm Optimization Algorithms outperform fine-tuned Genetic Algorithms.

Figure 8. Reward versus iterations under MPF utilization function

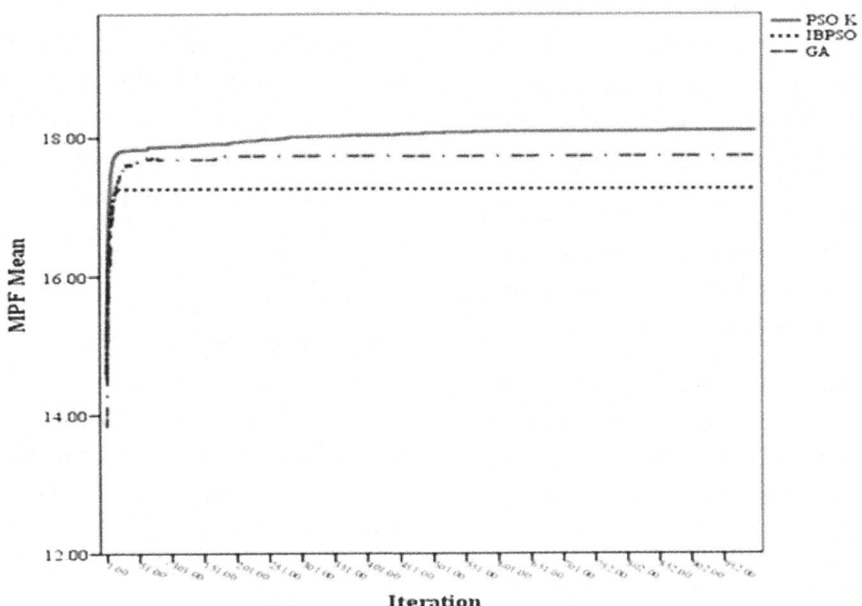

This study can be extended on two main axes: (1) to include other key parameters of cognitive radio networks and a judicious selection of parameters is performed in order to better utilize the spectrum of the cognitive networks; and (2) to investigate and fine-tune PSO algorithms for more efficient and effective solutions.

CONCLUSION

In this paper, we investigate the spectrum allocation problem in cognitive radio networks under varying network parameters. A fine-tuned generic algorithm (GA) is used to solve two utilization functions, namely, the Mean-Reward (MR), and the Max-Proportional-Fair (MPF), under different values for the primary user's protection range. Extensive simulation results show that a network with primary users of large protection areas degrades the utilization of the spectrum under both MR and MPF utility functions.

REFERENCES

Cao, L., & Zheng, H. (2005). Distributed spectrum allocation via local bargaining. In *IEEE SECON 2005 Proceedings* (*Vol. 5*, pp. 119–127). China: IEEE Communications.

Hamza, A., & Elghoneimy, M. (2010). On the effectiveness of using genetic algorithm for spectrum allocation in cognitive radio networks. In *High-Capacity Optical Networks and Enabling Technologies (HONET), 2010* (pp. 183–189). Cairo, Egypt: IEEE. doi:10.1109/HONET.2010.5715770

Huang, J., Berry, R., & Honig, M. (2006). Auction-based spectrum sharing. *Mobile Networks and Applications*, *11*(3), 405–418. doi:10.1007/s11036-006-5192-y

Kennedy, J., & Eberhart, R. (1997). A discrete binary version of the particle swarm algorithm. In *1997 IEEE International Conference on Systems, Man, and Cybernetics, Computational Cybernetics and Simulation* (Vol. 5, pp. 4104-4108). Orlando, FL: IEEE.

Kloeck, C., Jaekel, H., & Jondral, F. (2005). Dynamic and local combined pricing, allocation and billing system with cognitive radios. In *2005 First IEEE International Symposium on New Frontiers in Dynamic Spectrum Access Networks, DySPAN 2005* (pp. 73-81). Baltimore, MD: IEEE.

Nie, N., & Comaniciu, C. (2006). Adaptive channel allocation spectrum etiquette for cognitive radio networks. *Mobile Networks and Applications*, *11*(6), 779–797. doi:10.1007/s11036-006-0049-y

Peng, C., Zheng, H., & Zhao, B. (2006). Utilization and fairness in spectrum assignment for opportunistic spectrum access. *Mobile Networks and Applications*, *11*(4), 555–576. doi:10.1007/s11036-006-7322-y

Settles, M. (2005). *An introduction to particle swarm optimization* (pp. 1–8). Moscow, Idaho: University of Idaho.

Umarani, R., & Selvi, V. (2010). Particle swarm optimization-evolution, overview and applications. *International Journal of Engineering Science*, *2*(7), 2802–2806.

Yuan, X., Nie, H., Su, A., Wang, L., & Yuan, Y. (2009). An improved binary particle swarm optimization for unit commitment problem. *Expert Systems with Applications*, *36*(4), 8049–8055. doi:10.1016/j.eswa.2008.10.047

Zhao, Z., Peng, Z., Zheng, S., & Shang, J. (2009). Cognitive radio spectrum allocation using evolutionary algorithms. *IEEE Transactions on Wireless Communications*, *8*(9), 4421–4425. doi:10.1109/TWC.2009.080939

Zheng, H., & Peng, C. (2005). Collaboration and fairness in opportunistic spectrum access. In *2005 IEEE International Conference on Communications, ICC 2005* (Vol. 5, pp. 3132-3136). Beijing, China: IEEE.

KEY TERMS AND DEFINITIONS

Channel Allocation: A radio resource management process for allocating bandwidth and communication channels to base stations, access points and terminal equipments.

Cognitive Radio (CR): A form of wireless communication in which a transceiver can intelligently detect which communication channels are in use and which are not, and automatically changes itstransmission or reception parameters to communicate efficiently, while avoiding interference with licensed or licensed exempt users.

Evolutionary Algorithm (EA): A subset of evolutionary computation, a generic population-based meta-heuristic optimization algorithm. An EA uses some mechanisms inspired by biological evolution: reproduction, mutation, recombination, and selection.

Genetic Algorithm (GA): A search heuristic that mimics the process of natural evolution. This heuristic is routinely used to generate useful solutions to optimization and search problems.

Particle Swarm Optimization (PSO): A computational method that optimizes a problem byiteratively trying to improve a candidate solution (particles) with regard to a given measure of quality by having a population of particles and moving these particles around in the search-space according to simple mathematical formulae over the particle's position and velocity.

Radio Frequency (RF): A rate of oscillation in the range of about 3 kHz to 300 GHz, which corresponds to the frequency of radio waves, and the alternating currents which carry radio signals

Unlicensed Band Cognitive Radio: A form of CR that can only utilize unlicensed parts of radio frequency spectrum.

Chapter 13
Optimisation of Radiation Beam in Linear Nodes Array of Wireless Sensor Network for Improved Performance

N. N. N. Abd. Malik
Universiti Teknologi Malaysia, Malaysia

M. Esa
Universiti Teknologi Malaysia, Malaysia

S. K. S. Yusof
Universiti Teknologi Malaysia, Malaysia

S. A. Hamzah
Universiti Teknologi Malaysia, Malaysia

M. K. H. Ismail
Universiti Teknologi Malaysia, Malaysia

ABSTRACT

This chapter presents an intelligent method of optimising the radiation beam of wireless sensor nodes in Wireless Sensor Network (WSN). Each node has the feature of a monopole antenna. The optimisation involves selection of nodes to be organised as close as possible to a uniform linear array (ULA) in order to minimise the position errors, which will improve the radiation beam reconfiguring performance. Instead of utilising random beamforming, which needs a large number of sensor nodes to interact with each other and form a narrow radiation beam, the developed optimisation algorithm is emphasized to only a selected number of sensor nodes which can construct a linear array. Thus, the method utilises radiation beam reconfiguration technique to intelligently establish a communication link in a WSN.

DOI: 10.4018/978-1-4666-1830-5.ch013

INTRODUCTION

Wireless sensor networks (WSN) is a new monitoring and control capability for applications such as precision agricultural (to monitor the pesticides level in the drinking water; to check the air pollution in real time); industrial (transportation; health care; managing inventory; monitoring product quality) (Akylidiz, et al., 2002) and in military for surveillance, reconnaissance, and combat scenarios (Chen, et al., 2002). A representation of sensor network communication architecture is depicted in Figure 1.

WSN is a compact system that combines microsensor technology and low-power signal processing, computation, and low-cost wireless networking. It represents a significant improvement over traditional sensors, networks and wireless communications. There are large numbers of small sensor nodes being deployed over an area. The sensor nodes are small, with limited processing and computing resources, and inexpensive devices. The nodes can sense various physical attributes such as temperature, light, humidity, velocity, and magnetic field. The nodes then measure, and collect desired information from the area of interest. Based on some local analyzing and processing, they will establish communication and transmit the sensed data to the end user for further analysis as shown in Figure 1.

The sensor nodes in WSN are low power devices equipped with one or more sensors, a processor, a transceiver and a power supply that typically use the battery as the power source. Since the sensor nodes have limited memory and usually deployed in hazardous areas, a transceiver is implemented for wireless communication to transfer the data to the base station. The battery is the main power source in the sensor node. It has very restricted lifetime thus contributes to the issues of restricted communication limited memory and computing capabilities (Chen, et al., 2002). Consequently, the sensors should be designed to be smaller, cheaper, intelligent and highly energy efficient. At the same time, the sensors should be efficient in terms of transmitted power and

Figure 1. Sensor networks communication architecture (Akylidiz, et al., 2002)

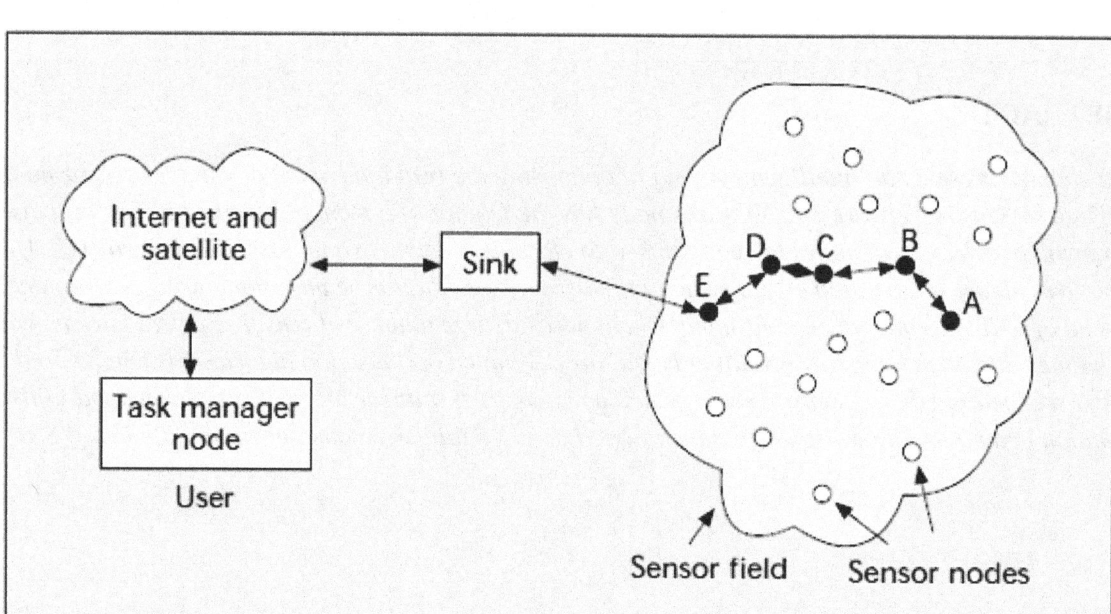

coding in order to reduce any unnecessary extra transmission power and to improve the overall system performance.

WSN has its own design and resource constraints. Resource constraints include a limited amount of energy, short communication range, low bandwidth, and limited processing and storage in each node (Culler, et al., 2004). Obstruction in the environment can also limit communication between nodes, which in turn affects the network connectivity or topology (Yick, et al., 2008).

In order to improve the WSN's performance, beamforming capability is integrated in all sensor nodes (Elmusrati & Hasu, 2007; Yao, et al., 1998). The sensor nodes can intelligently organise themselves to cooperate with each other, and perform a radiation beam optimisation. The radiation beam reconfiguring technology has a potential to intelligently coordinate the radiation transmission of the sensor nodes into a narrow beam, thus increases the desired transmission range.

BEAMFORMING IN WIRELESS SENSOR NETWORKS

Beamforming is a process of joining the signal from different antenna elements in order to come out with single output of the antenna array. It has been discussed that antenna array can improve the channel capacity and expand the range of signal's coverage (Van Veen, & Buckley, 1988; Litva, et al., 1996). Besides, an antenna array also can overcome the multipath fading problem and then decrease the bit error rate (Godara, 1997).

In WSN, beamforming is a combination of radio signals from each sensor node which acts as a set of small non-directional antennas to simulate a large directional antenna. Furthermore, beamforming can adaptively steer the antenna beam towards the desired angle thus suppressing interference signals from another directions. The antenna gain is proportional to the number of antenna elements (Godara, 1997). Therefore, it has been proved that by using several sensor nodes, the main beam peak power density can be of several orders of magnitude higher compared to a single sensor node. Hence, beamforming can be used to intelligently improve communication quality in WSN technology.

Currently, there has been increasing attention in using advanced beamforming technologies in WSN. Due to severe power consumption constraint and long distance requirement in communication range of sensor nodes, one way to overcome the problem without significantly increase the complexity of the sensor nodes is by introducing beamforming.

Implementation of beamforming algorithms in WSN environment is available in the literatures (Yao, et al., 1998; Xu, et al., 2002; Tummala, et al., 2005, Tummala et al., 2008). Some use signal processing techniques. These mostly analyse the performance of beamforming using the theory of random arrays. In order to realise the beamforming algorithm in WSN, some factors need to be considered, because, unlike conventional arrays, WSNs are usually randomly deployed. Hence, this will generate phase errors and affect the performance of the antenna array. Thus, resulting in degraded beamformer performance, compared to that of an array of equally spaced fixed elements.

One solution to the problems created from the random placement of sensor nodes is to develop an optimisation algorithm for the radiation beam of the nodes (Tummala, et al., 2008) which utilises linear array. In this chapter, the objective of the work is to determine the optimum radiation beam that is reconfigured for linear sensor nodes array, by given a random deployment of sensor nodes. The radiation beam of the actual linear sensor nodes array is intelligently optimised so that it is comparable with the ULA.

THE RADIATION PATTERN OF THE ANTENNA ARRAY

It is assumed that a linear array of K omnidirectional elements as in Figure 2 is located at a distance far enough from the signal source s(t), such that the arriving signal wavefront s(t) is a plane wave. The signal s(t) arrives at the array at an angle $\theta_{\alpha o}$ with respect to the x-axis (i.e., $z = 0$). If d_K is the distance between the Kth node and the reference node at the origin, then s(t) arrives at the Kth node earlier by t_k seconds with respect to the reference sensor node (Litva, et al., 1996), as in

$$t_k = \frac{d_k \cos\theta_{\alpha 0}}{c} \tag{1}$$

where c is the speed of light and d_k is the x-coordinate of the kth element or kth node.

Each array element is weighted by a complex weight w_k for $k = 0, 1, 2, \ldots.\ k, K$ which multiplies the incoming signal,

$$w_k = I_k e^{j\omega t_m \theta_{\alpha 0}} \tag{2}$$

The amplitude of each element response, I_k is assumed to be unity. Adding all the elements' weighted inputs results in the radiation pattern (the spatial response) of the array or the array factor (Litva, et al., 1996), $F(\theta_\alpha)$ for any arbitrary angle θ_α, as:

$$F(\theta_\alpha) = \sum_{k=1}^{K} w_k^{\,*} e^{j\beta d_k \cos\theta_\alpha} \tag{3}$$

By using Equation (1) and wavenumber $\beta = 2\pi/\lambda$, the maximum value of $F(\theta_\alpha)$ at $\theta_\alpha = \theta_{\alpha o}$ which is the main lobe of the radiation pattern that points towards $\theta_{\alpha o}$. The normalised power gain G is given by

$$G(\theta_\alpha) = \frac{|F(\theta_\alpha)|^2}{\max |F_{\theta\alpha}(\theta_\alpha)|^2} \tag{4}$$

Figure 2. A Kx1 linear array of equally spaced isotropic elements

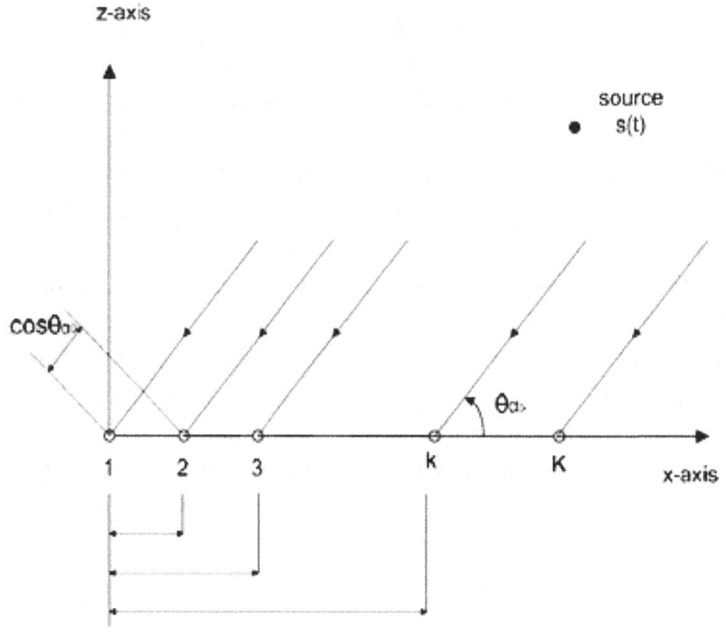

SIMULATION PROCESS OF THE RADIATION BEAM OPTIMISATION

The process of intelligently optimising the radiation beam is shown as a flow chart of the simulation model given in Figure 3.

An example is considered for a 9-node linear array that is implemented in MATLAB environment. Initially, 150 sensor nodes in random distribution are plotted inside a region of 100 m^2 as shown in Figure 4. Each sensor node will communicate with nearby nodes (i.e., the neighbour node) which are only within the communication radius. The algorithm starts by selecting the centre node which has the most neighbour nodes within its communication radius. Then, the active cluster is determined by referring to the centre node as the centre of a cluster.

Initially, the radiation beam pattern of the 9-element ULA is simulated by referring to the centre node as the centre element. ULA is assumed with internode spacing of $\lambda/2$; having isotropic antenna elements as in Figure 6. The algorithm will then optimise the beam radiation pattern of the actual linear sensor nodes by computing the array factor as in Figure 5. The node organisation best approximates the ULA. The optimisation of the radiation beam is accomplished for 20 iterations. The process is repeated for different sensor nodes organisation in order to select for the best performance of the optimum radiation beam.

Figure 3. Simulation models for the evaluation of actual linear sensor nodes array in random deployment of sensor nodes

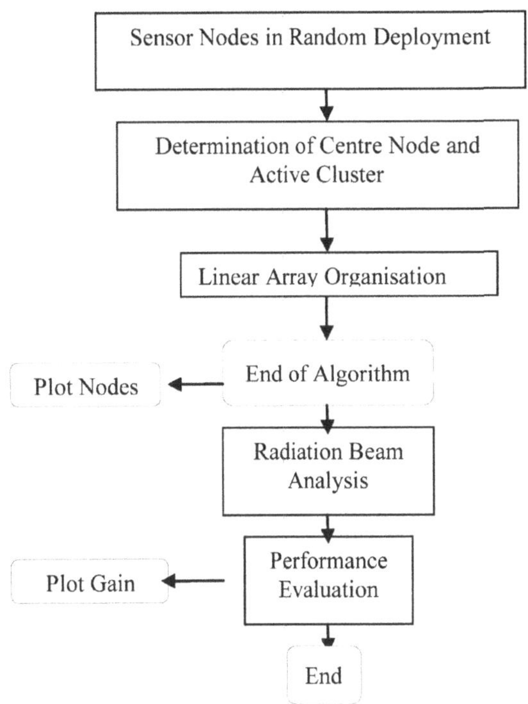

RESULTS AND DISCUSSION

Radiation beam analysis is implemented in the simulation algorithm, hence, it is able to compare the radiation beam of the actual 9-sensor node linear array with the ULA. Different iterations in different node organisations are simulated in order to optimise different radiation beam performance. The performances are plotted as shown in Figures 7 to 10 for the 1st, 2nd, 3rd and 4th iterations, respectively. Therefore, the optimum radiation beam pattern that is the most similar to the ULA can be selected. The narrow main beam is also steered to the desired angle of 30°.

For each of the iterations, a similar centre node is chosen to be optimised. However, the other sensor nodes that are optimised to construct a linear sensor nodes array are different whenever the iterations are varied. It depends on the minimum distance range from the ULA elements and the arrangement of sensor nodes which is comparable to the ULA.

From the analysis, the effect of different node organisations in a 9-sensor node linear array can be shown. The actual linear nodes array with the position errors causes a severe impact on the increment of the sidelobe levels, but only minimal reduction for the main lobe gain. However, by using Least Square (LS) method, the radiation beam analysis result demonstrates excellent agreement

Figure 4. Sensor nodes in random deployment within an area of 100 m². An active cluster is shown.

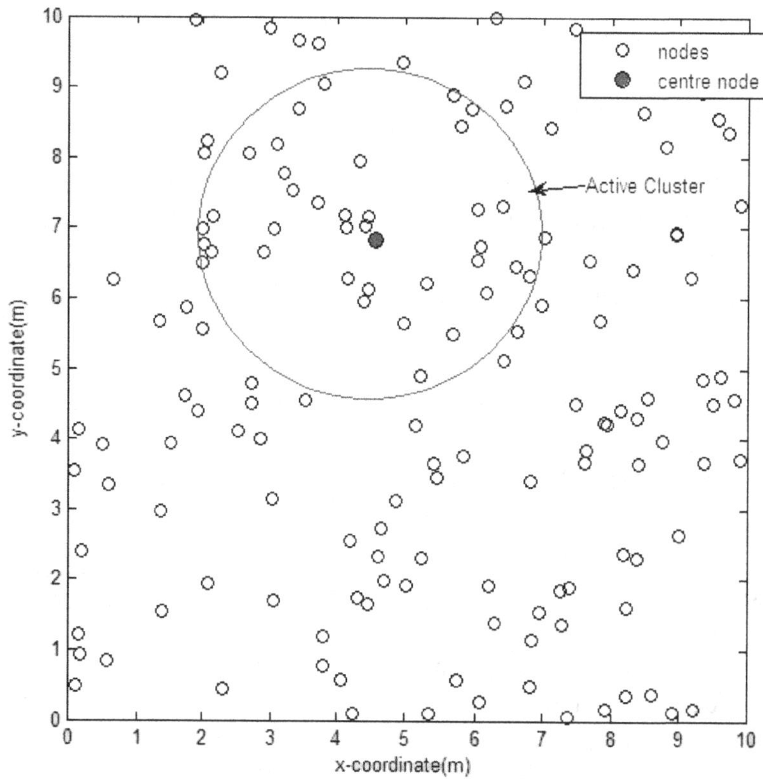

Figure 5. Simulation model of the radiation beam

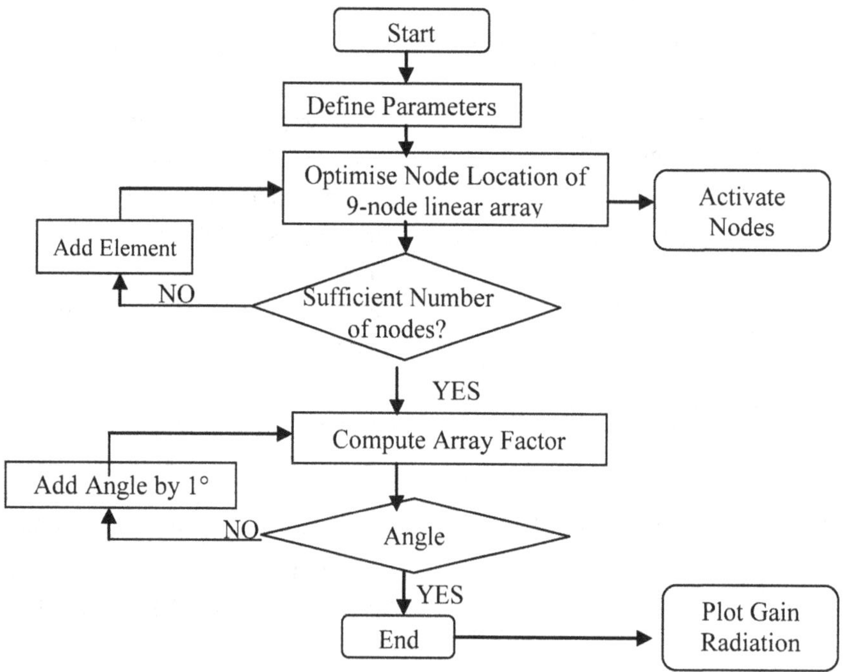

Figure 6. Intelligent optimising of sensor node organisation (actual linear nodes array vs. ULA)

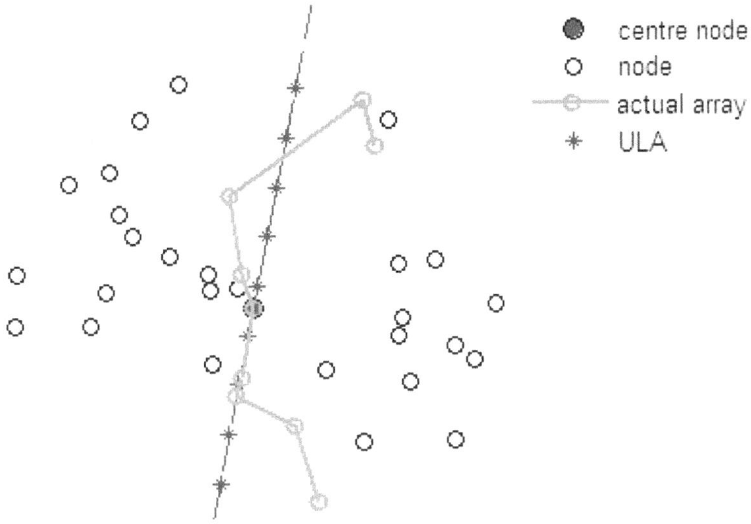

Figure 7. Power gain of the 1st iteration of intelligent sensor node organisation

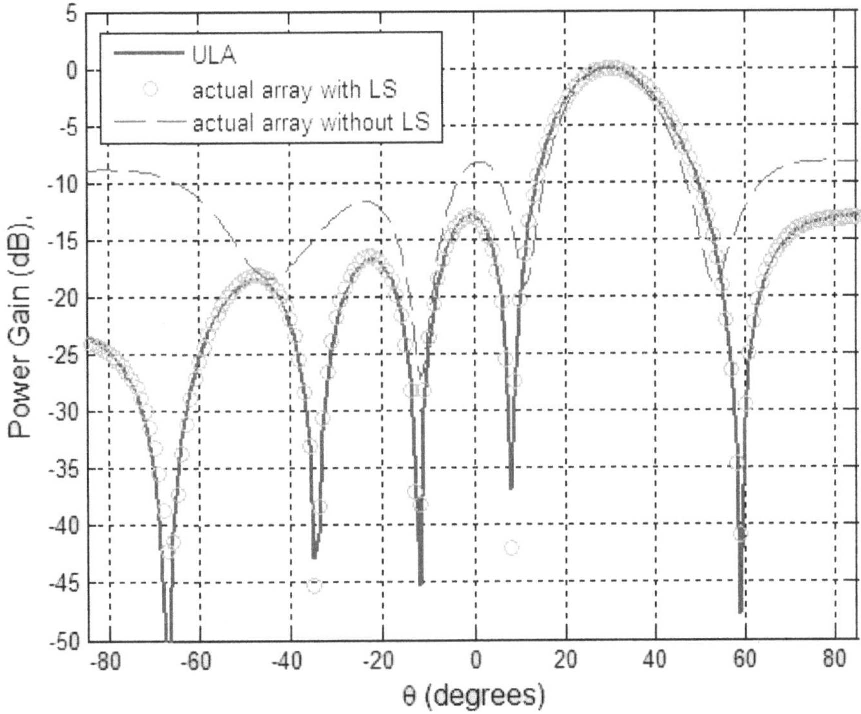

with the performance of the ULA. From the 1st iteration as in Figure 7.0, the maximum normalised power gain of the actual linear nodes array with LS remains unchanged although with the presence of position errors in the node organisation. The sidelobe levels also show similar performances as the sidelobes from the ULA.

The simulated results also demonstrate the different effects on the radiation beam performance with the alteration of the node organisation. Fig-

Figure 8. Power gain of the 2nd iteration of intelligent sensor node organisation

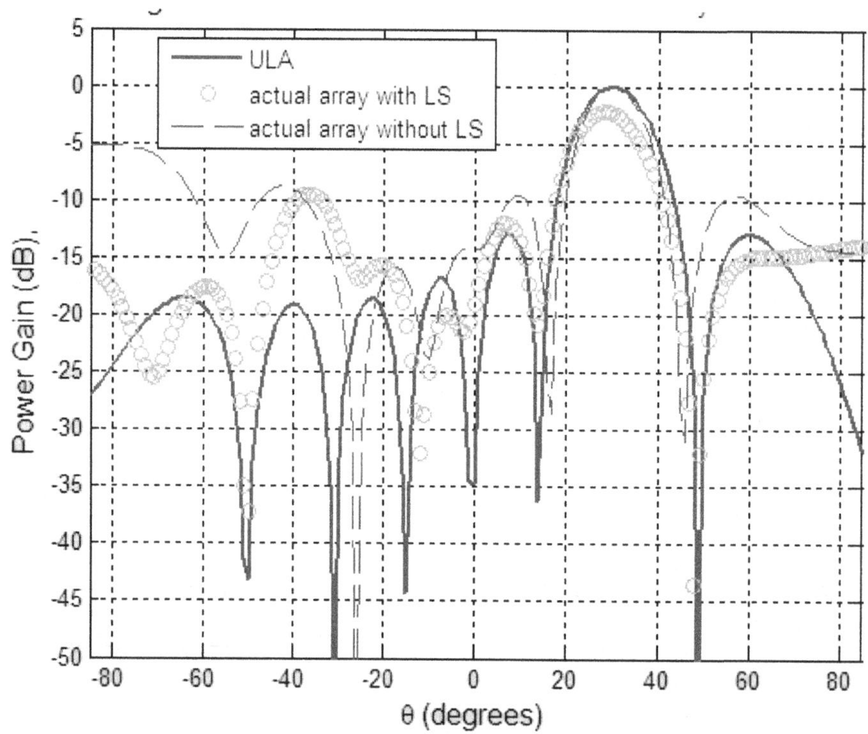

Figure 9. Power gain of the 3rd iteration of intelligent sensor node organisation

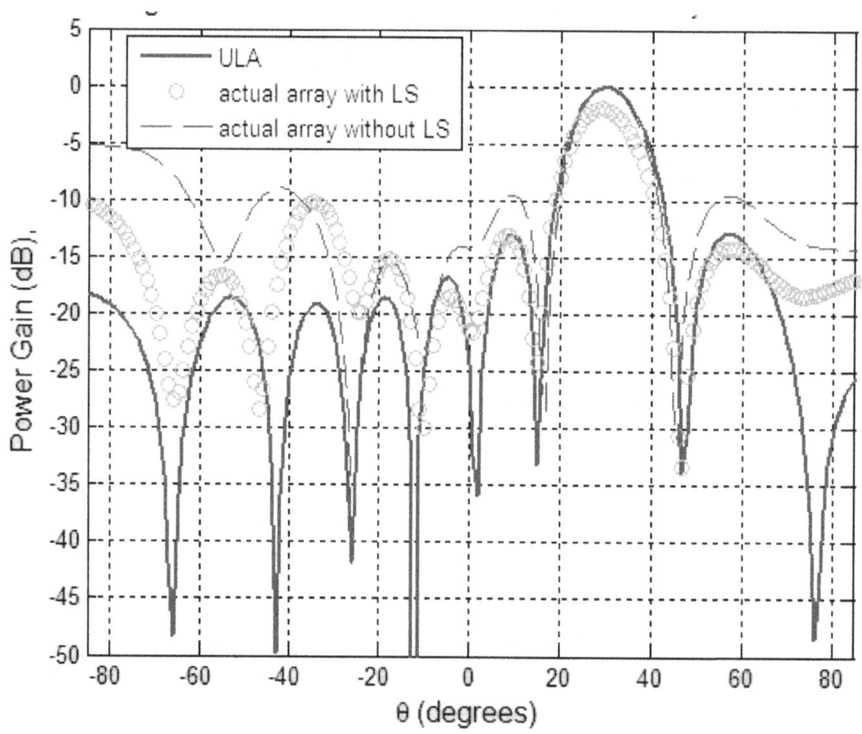

Figure 10. Power gain of the 4th iteration of intelligent sensor node organisation

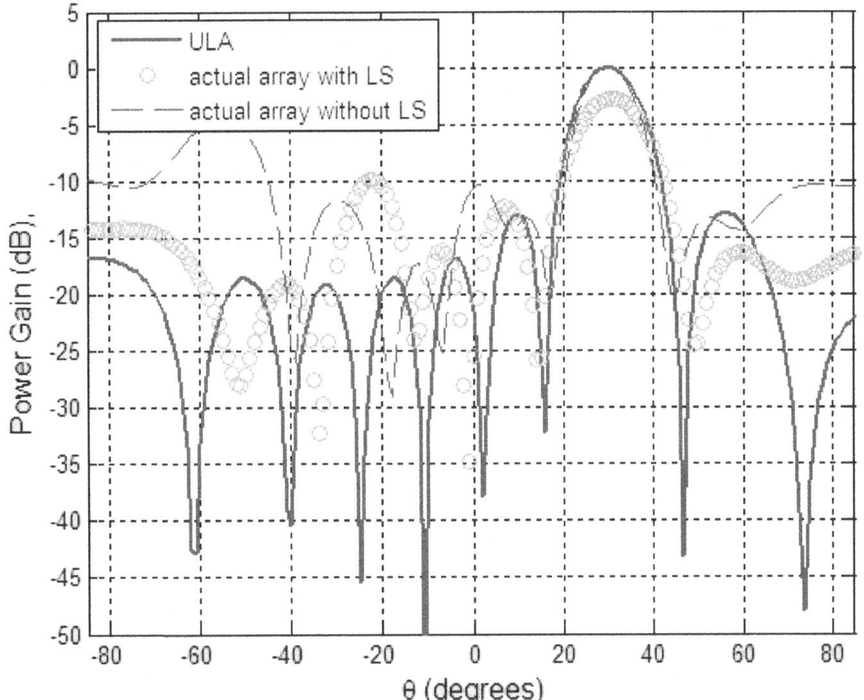

ures 8 and 9 illustrate narrower 3-dB beamwidths compared to the 3-dB beamwidth of Figure 7. However, the main beam or the maximum power gain shows an insignificant small decrement.

At the 4th iteration, there is a slight reduction at the main beam peak power for the actual array with LS compared to the ULA. In addition, a slight increment of the sidelobe levels is observed.

Although in the random deployment of WSN, the algorithm can optimise the actual 9-sensor node linear array in order to search for the optimum radiation beam performance. The analysis result demonstrates excellent agreement with the radiation beam of ULA. The desired beam performance can be selected by using the radiation beam analysis in order to meet the desired transmission signal.

FUTURE RESEARCH DIRECTIONS

The intelligent node coordination can be implemented in a physical WSN test-bed or real WSN environment. Extensive digital signal processing algorithm can thus be developed in order to complement the work. Otherwise, implementing within a commercially available WSN set-up or system would be of less hassle. However, this will incur unavoidable high costs that can be a problem, unless strong support is received from respective communication network provider or organisation.

Other geometrical forms of node organisations can be considered, such as circular and planar. It would be interesting to compare their performances with the selected linear arrangement. In addition, it is worthwhile to consider adaptive radiation beampattern of narrow radiation beam. Furthermore, significant work on multiobjective design by using optimisation technique is possible for optimal intelligent overall performance. Such design aims for simultaneous objectives such as sidelobe levels suppression, controllable beam-width, and null placements of the array's radiation beam. Recently, a successful preliminary work has been shown (N. N. N. Abd. Malik, et al., 2010), that promises intelligence as a reality.

CONCLUSION

Each sensor node has the behaviour of an omni-directional antenna with limited transmission capabilities. Combination of multiple sensor nodes is expected to provide greater transmission distances. The intelligent node organisation has been successfully optimised to identify the most excellent node organisation in order to participate in the linear node array. Simulation results illustrate that the intelligent construction of the linear node array organisation from random deployment offers superior performance to closely approximate the ULA.

ACKNOWLEDGMENT

The authors acknowledge the support given by Universiti Teknologi Malaysia, and Ministry of Higher Education for supporting PhD studies of N. N. N. Abd. Malik.

REFERENCES

Abd. Malik, N. N. N., Esa, M., Yusof, S. K., & Hamzah, S. A. (2010). Evaluation on optimum geometrical of linear node array for self-organization in a wireless sensor network. *Proceedings of IEEE Asia-Pacific Conf. on Applied Electromagnetics (APACE 2010),* IEEE Computer Soc., 2010, (pp. 1 – 4).

Akyildiz, I. F., Su, W., Sankarasubramaniam, Y., & Cayirci, E. (2002). Wireless sensor networks: A survey. *IEEE Communications Magazine,* 102–114. doi:10.1109/MCOM.2002.1024422

Chen, J. C., Yao, K., & Hudson, R. E. (2002). Source localization and beamforming. *IEEE Signal Processing Magazine*.

Culler, D., Estrin, D., & Srivastava, M. (2004). Overview of sensor networks. *Computer, 37*(8). doi:10.1109/MC.2004.93

Elmusrati, M., & Hasu, V. (2007). Random switched beamforming for uplink wireless sensor Networks. *IEEE 65th Vehicular Technology Conference VTC2007-Spring,* 22-25 April 2007 (pp. 3150 – 3154).

Godara, L. C. (1997). Application of antenna arrays to mobile communications, Part II: Beamforming and directional-of–arrival considerations. *Proceedings of the IEEE, 85*(8), 1195–1245. doi:10.1109/5.622504

Litva, J., & Kwok-Yeung Lo, T. (1996). *Digital beamforming in wireless communications*. Boston, MA: Artech House, Inc.

Papalexidis, N., Walker, T. O., Gkionis, C., Tummala, M., & McEachen, J. (2007). *A distributed approach to beamforming in a wireless sensor network*. Forty-First Asilomar Conference on Signals, Systems and Computers, IEEE, 4-7 Nov. 2007.

Quanquan, L., Dongfeng, Y., Yong, W., & Ruihua, Z. (2006). A new sensor antenna-array selecting method in wireless sensor networks. *Proceedings 2006 International Conference on Communications, Circuits and Systems,* Vol. 3, 25-28 June (pp. 1523 – 1529).

Tummala, M., Wai, C. C., & Vincent, P. (2005). Distributed beamforming in wireless sensor networks. *Conference Record of the Thirty-Ninth Asilomar Conference on Signals, Systems and Computers,* October 28 - November 1, 2005 (pp. 793 – 797).

Van Veen, B. D., & Buckley, K. M. (1988). Beamforming: A versatile approach to spatial filtering. *IEEE ASSP Magazine*.

Vincent, P., Tummala, M., & McEachen, J. (2008). A new method for distributing power usage across a sensor network. *Ad Hoc Networks*, *6*(8), 1258–1280. Retrieved from http://www.sciencedirect.com/science/journal/15708705 doi:10.1016/j.adhoc.2007.11.014

Yao, K., Hudson, R. E., Reed, C. W., Chen, D., & Lorenzelli, F. (1998). Blind beamforming on a randomly distributed sensor array system. *IEEE Journal on Selected Areas in Communications*, *16*(8), 1555–1567. doi:10.1109/49.730461

Yick, J., Mukherjee, B., & Ghodal, D. (2008). Wireless sensor network survey. *Computer Networks*, *52*(12). doi:10.1016/j.comnet.2008.04.002

KEY TERMS AND DEFINITIONS

Active Cluster: The centre node as the centre of a cluster.

Beamforming: A process of joining the signal from different antenna elements in order to come out with single output of the antenna array. In WSN, beamforming is a combination of radio signals from each sensor node which acts as a set of small non-directional antennas to simulate a large directional antenna.

Linear Array: Assumed as a number of omni-directional elements that are located at a distance far enough from a signal source, such that the arriving signal wavefront is a plane wave.

Omni-Directional: Radiation in all directions.

Radiation Pattern: Is the spatial response of the array or the array factor (Litva, et al., 1996), $F(\theta_\alpha)$ for any arbitrary angle θ_α.

Sensor Nodes: In WSN, these are low power devices equipped with one or more sensors, a processor, a transceiver and a power supply that typically use the battery as the power source.

Sidelobe: Any lobe other than the main radiation lobe of the antenna.

Wireless Sensor Networks (WSN): A new monitoring and control capability for applications such as precision agricultural (to monitor the pesticides level in the drinking water; to check the air pollution in real time); industrial (transportation; health care; managing inventory; monitoring product quality) (Akylidiz, et al., 2002) and in military for surveillance, reconnaissance, and combat scenarios (Chen, et al., 2002).

Chapter 14
ACPSO:
A Novel Swarm Automatic Clustering Algorithm Based Image Segmentation

Salima Ouadfel
University Mentouri – Constantine, Algeria

Mohamed Batouche
University Mentouri – Constantine, Algeria

Abdlemalik Ahmed-Taleb
Universite Valenciennes, France

ABSTRACT

In order to implement clustering under the condition that the number of clusters is not known a priori, the authors propose a novel automatic clustering algorithm in this chapter, based on particle swarm optimization algorithm. ACPSO can partition images into compact and well separated clusters without any knowledge on the real number of clusters. ACPSO used a novel representation scheme for the search variables in order to determine the optimal number of clusters. The partition of each particle of the swarm evolves using evolving operators which aim to reduce dynamically the number of naturally occurring clusters in the image as well as to refine the cluster centers. Experimental results on real images demonstrate the effectiveness of the proposed approach.

INTRODUCTION

Image segmentation is the first important process in numerous applications of computer vision. It can be viewed as a clustering process that aims to partition the image into different meaningful clusters with homogeneous characteristics using discontinuities or similarities of image components (Monga & Wrobel, 1987). Several clustering methods are provided in the literature (Jain, Murty, & Flynn, 1999). They fall into two categories: hierarchical and partitioning methods. Hierarchical methods proceed by stages producing a sequence of partitions, where each partition corresponds to a different number of clusters. A hierarchical algorithm yields a tree representing the nested

DOI: 10.4018/978-1-4666-1830-5.ch014

grouping of patterns. Partitioning methods obtain a single partition of the pixels by moving pixels iteratively from one group to another, starting from an initial partition. An extensive survey of various clustering techniques can be found in (Jain, Murty, & Flynn, 1999). The focus of this paper is on the partitional clustering algorithms.

Hard or crisp partitional clustering (Duda, & Hart, 1973) and fuzzy partitional clustering (Bezdek, Keller, Krishnampuram, & Pal, 1999) are two partitioning clustering algorithms such that hard clustering assigns each data point to only one cluster while fuzzy clustering assigns each data point to several clusters with varying degrees of memberships. The most widely used hard partitioning algorithm is the iterative K-means approach (Al-Sultan, & Khan, 1996; Forgy, 1965; Hartigan, 1975). In the K-means algorithm, pixels with similar features like gray levels or colors are grouped in the same cluster. The clustering is obtained by iteratively minimizing a cost function that is dependent on the distance of the pixels to the cluster centers. The major problem with this algorithm like most of the existing clustering algorithms is that its result is sensitive to the selection of the initial partition, it may converge to local optima and it requires the a priori specification of the number of clusters *K*.

To deal with the limitations existing in the traditional partition clustering methods, a number of new clustering algorithms have been proposed with the inspiration coming from observations of natural processes (Theodoridis & Koutroumbas, 2003).

In order to remedy the drawbacks of K-means, this chapter proposes a new dynamic image clustering algorithm based on a modified version of particle swarm optimization The proposed algorithm, called by us the ACPSO (Automatic Clustering with PSO) effectively search for both the optimal cluster centers positions and the number of effective clusters, and this with minimal user interference. ACPSO has the following characteristics: (1) particles can contain different cluster number in a range defined by minimum and maximum cluster number, (2) Particles are initialized randomly to process different cluster numbers in a specified range, (3) The goal of each particle is to search the optimum number of clusters and the optimum cluster centers, (4) Three new evolving operators are introduced to evolve dynamically the partitions encoded in the particles.

BACKGROUND

Problem Definition

The clustering problem can be formally defined as follows. Given a data set $Z = \left\{z_1, z_2, ...z_n\right\}$ where z_i is a data item and n is the number of data items in *Z*. The clustering aims to partitioning *Z* into *K* compacts and well separated clusters.

Compactness means that members of a cluster are all similar and close together. One measure of compactness of a cluster is the average distance of the cluster instances compared to the cluster center.

$$compactness(c_j) = \frac{1}{n_j} \sum_{z_i \in C_j} \left(z_i - m_j\right)^2 \quad (1)$$

where m_j is the center of the *j*th cluster and n_j is its cardinal. Lower value of *compactness* (c_j) is better.

Thus, the overall compactness of a particular grouping of *K* clusters is just the sum of the compactness of the individual clusters

$$compactness = \frac{1}{n} \sum_{j=1}^{K} \sum_{z_i \in C_j} (z_i - m_j)^2 \quad (2)$$

Separability means that members of one cluster are sufficiently different from members of another cluster (cluster dissimilarity). One measure of the separability of two clusters is their squared distance.

$$separability(c_i, c_j) = \left\| m_i - m_j \right\| \tag{3}$$

where m_i and m_j are the center of the *i*th and *j*th cluster respectively.

The separability of the partition of *K* clusters could be defined as following:

$$Separability = \sum_{i=1}^{K} \min_{j} separability(c_i, c_j) \tag{4}$$

The bigger the distance, the better the separability, so we would like to find groupings where separability is maximized.

Unsupervised Clustering Algorithms

Clustering can be formally considered as a particular kind of NP-hard grouping problem (Hruschka, Campello, Freitas, & de Carvalho, 2009). This assumption has stimulated much research and use of efficient approximation algorithms.

One of the most frequently used clustering algorithms is the iterative K-means algorithm (MacQueen, 1967; Selim & Ismail, 1984). The K-means algorithm starts with K cluster centers randomly selected using some heuristics. Each data item in the data set is then assigned to the closest cluster center according to a distance measure. The centers are updated by using the mean of the associated items. The process is repeated until some stopping criterion is verified. Although the k-means algorithm has been widely used due to its easy implementation, it has two major drawbacks: it is too sensitive to the initial clusters centers and it needs to specify the number of clusters in advance. However, in many practical cases, it is impossible to determine the exact cluster number in advance. Under these circumstances, the k-means algorithm often leads to a poor clustering performance.

In the literature, many approaches to finding dynamically the number of clusters has been proposed. In (Ball, & Hall, 1967), the ISODATA (Iterative Self-Organizing data Analysis technique) was proposed. Like the K-means algorithm, ISODATA assigns each item to the closest cluster center; however, it adds division of a cluster c_i into two clusters if the cluster standard deviation of c_i exceeds a user-specified threshold th_{div}, and processing of fusion of two clusters if the distance between their centers is smaller than another user-specified threshold th_{merg}. Using this variant, the optimal partition starting from any arbitrary initial partition can be obtained. However, it requires many parameters to be specified by the user. (Huang, 2002) proposed SYNERACT, which combines K-means with hierarchical descending approaches. (Rosenberger, & Chehdi, 2000) introduced a new improvement to the K-means algorithm. During each step of the clustering process, from a set of K clusters, a cluster with the higher intra_cluster distance is chosen for splitting into two clusters. Next, the K-means algorithm is applied to the (K+1) clusters. The iterative procedure is repeated until a valid partition of the data items is obtained. Pelleg and Moore (Pelleg, & Moore, 2000) proposed X-means algorithm which is based on the classical K-means algorithm with the model selection. Hamerly (Hamerly, 2003) proposed G-means algorithm which splits clusters that not fit a Gaussian distribution.

Since the problem of data clustering can be easily viewed as a complex optimization problem (Halkidi, Batistakis, & Vazirgiannis, 2001), several optimization algorithms have been used for optimizing the cost function and to find the optimal number of clusters. For example, in (Bandyopadhyay, & Maulik, 2002), the authors proposed a nonparametric Variable string length genetic algorithm (VGA), with real encoding of the cluster centers in the chromosome. In (Venkatesh, Satapathy, Murthy & Reddy, 2007). Hybrid a novel variable length GA (VLIGA) algorithm which is an improvement version of VGA was proposed with a modified mutation function. In (Das, & Konar,

2009), authors proposed an evolutionary-fuzzy clustering algorithm for automatically grouping the pixels of an image into different homogeneous regions. The algorithm does not require a prior knowledge of the number of clusters. The fuzzy clustering task in the intensity space of an image is formulated as an optimization problem. An improved variant of the differential evolution (DE) algorithm has been used to determine the number of naturally occurring clusters in the image as well as to refine the cluster centers. Bandyopadhyay proposed in (Bandyopadhyay, 2003) a Variable String Length Simulated Annealing (VFC-SA) algorithm, which applied a simulated annealing algorithm to the fuzzy c-means clustering technique and used a cluster validity index measure as the energy function. Tseng and Yang (Tseng, & Yang, 2001) proposed a genetic algorithm based approach for the clustering problem. The proposed method can search for a proper number of clusters and classify non overlapping objects into these clusters. Lin et al. (Lin, Yang, & Kao, 2005) presented an automatic genetic clustering algorithm based on a binary chromosome representation. Lai (Lai, 2005) adopted the hierarchical genetic algorithm to solve the clustering problem. In the proposed method, the chromosome consists of two types of genes, control genes and parametric genes. The control genes are coded as binary digits. The parametric genes are coded as real numbers to represent the coordinates of the cluster centers. The total number of "1" represents the number of clusters. In (Lukashin, & Fuchs, 2001). authors proposed an algorithm to determine the optimal number of clusters by applying SA to cluster microarray data. In their method, first the fuzzy k-means algorithm is used to minimize the sum of within-cluster distance, then, the optimal number of clusters is obtained from the SA algorithm. In (Das, Abraham, & Konar 2008), authors proposed a dynamic clustering algorithm based on a modified version of classical Particle Swarm Optimization (PSO) algorithm, known as the Multi-Elitist PSO (MEPSO) model. A new particle representation scheme has been adopted for selecting the optimal number of clusters from several possible choices. It also employs a kernel-induced similarity measure instead of the conventional sum-of-squares distance. In (Liu, Chih, Kuo, & Tommy, 2008) a new fuzzy clustering algorithm is proposed by combining the possibility clustering and ISODATA clustering algorithm. This new algorithm not only can determine the number of clusters dynamically with the degree of possibility of each date point, but also can reduce the number of input parameters of ISODATA algorithm. In (Othman, Deris, Illias, Zakaria, & Mohamad, 2006) an approach for solving the automatic clustering of the Gene Ontology is proposed by incorporating cohesion-and-coupling metric into a hybrid algorithm consisting of a genetic algorithm and a split-and-merge algorithm. In (Markus, & Grani, 2009) authors address the problem of cluster number selection by using a k-means approach that exploits local changes of internal validity indices to split or merge clusters. The split and merge k-means issues criterion functions to select clusters to be split or merged and fitness assessments on cluster structure changes. In (Das, Chowdhury, & Abraham, 2009) authors propose a Bacterial Evolutionary clustering algorithm, which can partition a given dataset automatically into the optimal number of groups. Experiments were done with several synthetic as well as real life data sets including a remote sensing satellite image data. The results establish the superiority of the proposed approach in terms of final accuracy. In (Omran, Salman & Engelbrecht, 2006). Omran et al. presented dynamic clustering PSO (DCPSO), which is, in fact, a hybrid clustering algorithm where binary PSO is used to determine the number of clusters while the traditional K-means method performs the clustering operation with this number of clusters. In (Abraham, Das, & Roy, 2007)., Abraham et al. combined the Fuzzy clustering algorithm with the multielitist PSO (MEPSO) to find automatically the number of clusters. In (Alam, Dobbie, & Riddle, 2008) authors proposed an evolutionary particle swarm optimization for data clustering. The proposed algorithm is based on the evolution of swarm generations. After each generation, the swarm dynamically adjusts itself in order to reach optimal position.

Particle Swarm Optimization

Particle swarm optimization (PSO) is a population-based evolutionary computation method first proposed by Kennedy and Eberhart (Kennedy, & Eberhart, 1995).. It originated from the computer simulation of the individuals in a bird flock or fish school, which basically show a natural behavior when they search for some target (e.g., food). The PSO algorithm is initialized with a swarm of n particles randomly distributed over the search area with a random velocity and a random position. Each particle encodes a potential solution to the optimization problem. Particles flies through the search space and aims to converge to the global optimum of a function attached to the problem.

Each particle x_1 in the swarm is represented by the following characteristics: the current position of the particle (p_i) and the current velocity of the particle (v_i). Its movement through the search space is influenced dynamically according to its personal best position *Pbest*, which is the best solution that it has so far achieved and its neighbors' best position P_g. At each iteration t, the particle's new position and its velocity are updated as follows:

$$p_i(t) = p_i(t-1) + v_i(t) \quad (5)$$

$$v_i(t) = wv_i(t-1) + c_1 \times rand_1(p_{best} - p_i(t-1)) + c_2 \times rand_2(p_g - p_i(t-1)) \quad (6)$$

The parameter w is an inertia weight and it is equivalent to a temperature schedule in the simulated annealing algorithm and controls the influence of the previous velocity: a large value of w favors exploration, while a small value of w favors exploitation (Shi, & Eberhart, 1998). As originally introduced, w decreases linearly during the run from w_{min} to w_{max}. c_1 and c_2 are two constants which control the influence of the social and cognitive components such that $c_1 + c_2 = 4$. $rand_1$ and $rand_2$ are random values in the range [0,1].

Two topologies of neighborhoods exist in the literature: the *gbest* model and the *lbest* model. The *gbest* model maintains only a single best solution, called the global best particle, across all the particles in the swarm. This particle acts as an attractor, pulling all the particles towards it. The *gbest* offers a faster rate of convergence at the expense of robustness. The *lbest* model tries to prevent premature convergence by maintaining multiple attractors. In fact, *gbest* model is actually a special case of the *lbest* model. Experiments have shown that *lbest* algorithm converges somewhat more slowly than the *gbest* version, but it is less likely to become trapped in an inferior local minimum.

MAIN FOCUS OF THE CHAPTER

In this section, we describe an automatic image clustering algorithm based on a new version of particle swarm optimization algorithm, called ACPSO.

Let $Z = \{z_1, z_2, ...z_n\}$ be the image with n number of pixels. The ACPSO maintains a swarm of particles, where each particle represents a potential solution to the clustering problem. Each particle encodes an entire partition of the image Z. ACPSO tries to find an optimal partition $C = \{c_1, c_2, ...c_k\}$ of K optimal number of compactness and well separated clusters. In ACPSO, both the numbers of clusters as well as the appropriate clustering of the data are evolved simultaneously using the search capability of particle swarm optimization algorithm.

Particle Representation

The initial population $P = \{X_1, X_2, X_3, ...X_{NP}\}$ is made up of *NP* possible particles (solutions). For a user-defined maximum cluster number K_{max}, a single particle x_i is a vector of K_{max} binary numbers 0 and 1 (flags) and K_{max} real numbers that represents the K_{max} cluster centers.

For a particle x_i, each probably cluster center m_{ij} (j=1...K_{max}) is associated with a binary flag $\gamma_{ij}(j = 1....K_{max})$. The cluster center m_{ij} is valid and so selected to clustering the image pixels, if the corresponding flag $\gamma_{ij} = 1$ and invalid if $\gamma_{ij} = 0$. The total number of "1" implicitly represents the number of clusters encoded in a particle.

If it is found that no flag could be set to one in a particle (all cluster centers are invalid and so no selected), two random flags are selected and we re-initialize them to 1. Thus the minimum number of possible clusters is always 2.

Two examples of the particle structure in the proposed approach are shown in Figure 1.

Population Initialization

To generate the initial population of particles, we use in this paper the random generation strategy until all particles in a population are created. For a particular particle x_i, K_i cluster centers are randomly selected points from the given data set and K_i flags are randomly generated. Note that if the number of valid centers contained in a particle is less than two, then its flags are reinitialized.

Fitness Evaluation

The fitness of a particle indicates the degree of goodness of the solution it represents. In this work, the fitness function of a particle is based on the Ray and Turi's validity criterion (Turi, 2001) proposed to color image segmentation using the $\frac{\text{intra}}{\text{inter}}$ ratio with a multiplier function to avoid the selection of low cluster numbers. The criterion is defined as:

$$V(K) = (c \times N(2,1) + 1) \times \frac{\text{intra}}{\text{inter}} \tag{7}$$

where c=25 is a constant multiplier, *K* is the number of clusters found by the clustering algorithm and *N(2,1)* is a Gaussian function with mean 2 and standard deviation of 1. The intra and inter cluster distances represent respectively the compactness and the separability measures of clusters and are defined by Equation (2) and Equation (4).

A lower value of *V(K)* indicates a better quality of the clustering.

Figure 1. Two examples of the particle structure in the ACPSO algorithm

actvation-clusters-part — cluster-centers-part

[0,0,1,1,0 , 12.5, 45.7, 36.5, 22.5, 66.3]

Particle *i* represents 2 clusters, and the associated cluster centers are 36.5 and 22.5. Cluster centers 12.5, 45.7 and 66.3 are invalid and not used to clustering the image.

actvation-clusters-part — cluster-centroids-part

[1,0,1,0,1 , 39.5, 45.7, 26.5, 40.3, 33.3]

Particle *i* represents 3 clusters, and the associated cluster centers are 39.5, 26.5 and 33.3. Cluster centers 45.7, 26.5 and 40.3 are invalid.

The Ray and Turi's measure based fitness function (to be maximized) for the particle x_i encoding K_i valid clusters is given by:

$$Fitness_i = \frac{1}{V(K_i) + eps} \tag{8}$$

where *eps* is a small bias term equal to 2×10^{-4} and prevents the denominator of Equation (8) from being equal to zero. When the algorithm converges, the particle that has the maximum Fitness value will be the optimal particle.

Evolving Operators

The evolving operators are specifically designed to allow the number of the clusters of the particles to be changed dynamically. In the following, we describe each evolving operator.

Perturb Operator

A valid cluster c_{ij} of the configuration encoded in a particle x_i is chosen randomly to be perturbed. The centre m_{ij} of the selected cluster c_{ij} is then modified as follows:

$$m_{ij}^{new} = m_{ij}^{old} + \delta * m_{ij}^{old} \tag{9}$$

where m_{ij}^{new} and m_{ij}^{old} represent the new and the old cluster centre of the cluster c_{ij}. δ is a random number between [-1, 1].

Thus the cluster encoded by the particle is reconfigured, although the number of clusters belonging to it remains unaltered.

Split Operator

For a particle x_i, we compute the compactness measure for each valid cluster according to Equation (1). Let *S* the set of clusters c_{ij} $(j = 1...k_i)$ with the compactness measure higher than a threshold th_{split}. The threshold th_{split} is defined as the global compactness measure (see Equation (2)) divided by the number of clusters of the particle x_i.

A cluster c_{ij} from the set *S* is selected for splitting into two new valid clusters, with the probability P_{split} defined as follows:

$$P_{split}(c_{ij}) = \frac{\frac{1}{n_j} \sum_{z_k \in c_{ij}} \left\| z_k - m_{ij} \right\|^2}{\sum_{s=1}^{K_i} \frac{1}{n_s} \sum_{z_k \in c_{is}} \left\| z_k - m_{is} \right\|^2} \tag{10}$$

That is, the *sparser* cluster c_{ij}, the more possibly it is selected as the cluster for the split operator and vice versa.

The resulting number of clusters is $K_i + 1$ and must be lower than K_{max}, otherwise, the split operator terminates.

Merge Operator

For a particle x_i, first the pairwise separation distances D_{jl} between all distinct pairs of valid cluster (c_{ij}, c_{il}) are calculated according to Equation (3). Let *S* the set of pairs of valid cluster with the distance D_{jl} lower than a threshold th_{merge}. The threshold th_{merge} is defined as the average distance of D_{jl} for all distinct pairs of valid clusters.

A pair of distinct valid cluster (c_{ij}, c_{il}) of *S* is selected for the merge operator with the probability P_{merge} defined as follows:

$$P_{merge}(c_{ij}, c_{il}) = 1 - \frac{D_{jl}}{\max(D_{jl})} \tag{11}$$

where $\max(D_{jl})$ is the maximum pairwise separation distance between all distinct pairs of valid cluster centers from the set *S*.

The final number of clusters must be greater than 2, otherwise, the merge operator terminates.

Any one of the above-described evolving operators is applied for a particle if it is selected. The particle is selected with an adaptive probability P_e as in (Srinivas, & Patnaik, 1994). Let *gbest* the global best fitness of the current iteration; $\overline{Pbest}$ be the average fitness value of the population and $Pbest_i$ be the fitness value of the solution (particle) to be evolved. The expression for probability, P_e is given below:

$$P_e = \begin{cases} k_2 \times \dfrac{(gbest - Pbest_i)}{(gbest - \overline{Pbest})} & if\ Pbest_i > \overline{Pbest} \\ k_4 & if\ Pbest_i \le \overline{Pbest} \end{cases}$$

Here, values of k_2 and k_4 are kept equal to 0.5 (Srinivas, & Patnaik, 1994). This adaptive probability helps PSO to avoid getting stuck at local optimum.

The value of P_e increases when the fitness of the particle is quite poor. In contrast when the fitness of the particle is a good solution, P_e will be low so as to reduce the likelihood of disrupting good solution by evolving operators.

The framework of the ACPSO algorithm is given as follows:

1. Initialize the maximum cluster number K_{max} and all the constant parameters;
2. Initialize each particle x_i with random k randomly selected cluster centers and flags; initialize velocities.
3. Initialize for each particle x_i the $Pbest_i$
4. Initialize the *gbest*
5. For each particle x_i
    - For each pixel z_p calculate its distance from all valid cluster centers
    - Assign zp to the closest cluster center
    - Calculate the fitness value $Fitness_i$ using Equation 7.
    - Set $Pbest_i = Fitness_i$.
    - If ($Pbest_i$ > *gbest*) then set *gbest* = $Pbest_i$.
6. Update the position and the velocity of each particle according to Equations (5) and (6)
7. Apply randomly the evolving operators to alter the clusters centers of selected particles.
8. If termination criterion is satisfied go to step 9 else go to step 5
9. Segment the image using the optimal number of clusters and the optimal clusters centers given by the best global particle.

Figure 2. Test images

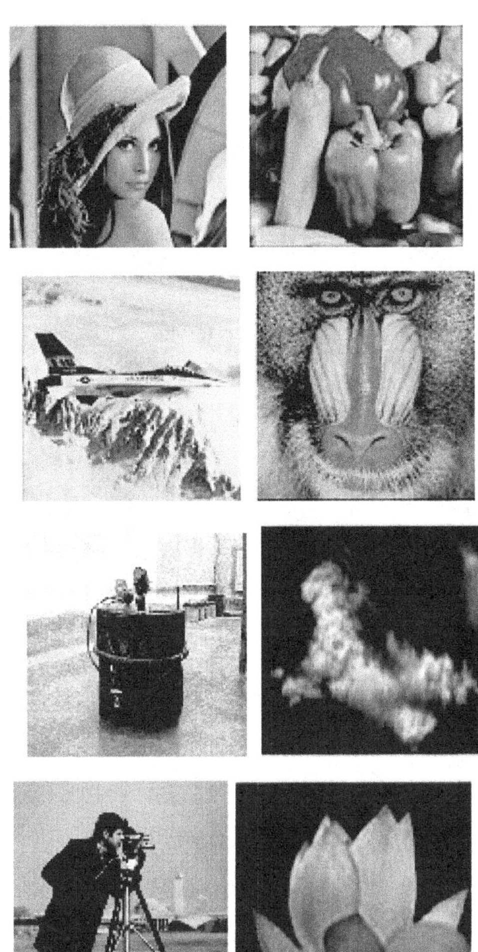

Figure 3. Samples of segmented images resulting from ACPSO

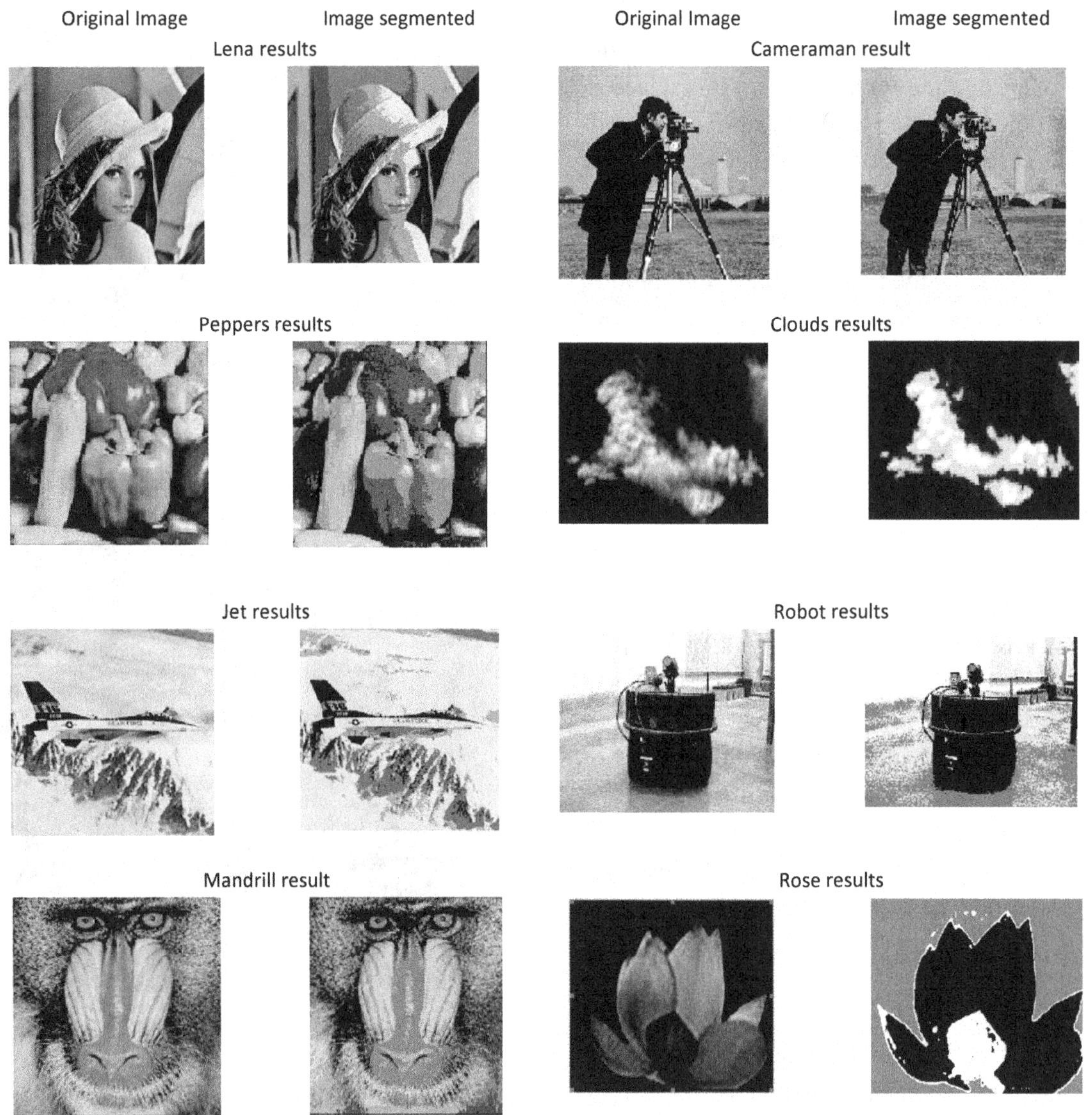

Table 1. Parameter setup of the clustering algorithms for the image segmentation problem

DCPSO		ACPSO		ISODATA	
parameter	**value**	**parameter**	**value**	**Parameter**	**value**
Pop size	100	Pop size	50		
Inertia	0.72	W_{min} W_{max}	0.4 0.9	Threshold for split clusters	10
C_1,C_2 P_{ini}	1.494 0.75			Threshold for merge clusters	1
K_{max} K_{min}	20 2	K_{max} K_{min}	20 2	K_{max} K_{min}	*20* *2*

Table 2. Number of clusters found by the clustering algorithms for real grayscale images

Image	Optimal number of clusters	ISODATA	DCPSO	ACPSO
LENA	7	6.79±0034	6.65±0.134	7.02± 0.234
MANDRILL	6	6.95±0.004	6.25±0.345	6.05±0.456
CAMERAMAN	5	6 ±0.010	5.3±0.082	5.06±0.0767
PEPPERS	7	6.686±0.536	6.87±0.054	7.20±0.250
CLOUDS	4	3.237±0.310	4.53±0.112	4.30±0.116
ROSE	3	4.50±0.007	3.70±0.637	3.25±0.024
ROBOT	3	4.849±1.920	2.35±0.015	3.51±0.120
JET	5	5.40±0.967	5.6±0.043	5.05±0.023

Solutions and Recommendations

In order to evaluate the ability of our algorithm ACPSO to find the optimal clusters, we have tested it using natural images with varying range of complexity. Figure 2 shows some 256x256 gray scale images. The performance of three dynamic clustering algorithms (DCPSO, ACPSO and ISODATA) to the segmentation of these images was compared.

The parameter settings of DCPSO and ISODATA algorithm were determined by both referring to original papers and performing empirical studies. For ACPSO, we carried out a thorough experiment with different parameter settings of the clustering algorithm. In Table 1, we report an optimal set-up of the parameters that gives the best results for the test images

The clustering algorithms used in the experimental tests have been run several times for each test image. The optimal number of clusters has not been provided to any of the three optimization algorithm. Table 2 and Table 3 report the experimental results obtained over tested grayscale images in terms of the mean values and standard deviations of the number of classes found and the final Turi measure reached by the three clustering algorithms over runs. The results have been stated over 40 independent runs in each case.

From Tables 2-3 we can see that the proposed algorithm ACPSO outperforms the state of-the-art DCPSO and ISODATA algorithms for the present images related problems. The proposed algorithm is able to find the optimal number of clusters with better clustering result in term of the Turi cluster validity index.

Figure 3 shows the original images and their segmented counterparts obtained using the ACPSO algorithm.

Table 3. Automatic clustering result over real grayscale images using the Turi based fitness function over 40 independent runs

	$(\text{Turi index})^{-1}$		
Image	**ISODATA**	**DCPSO**	**ACPSO**
LENA	0.19	0.16	**0.12**
MANDRILL	0.14	0.12	**0.10**
CAMERAMAN	0.097	0.089	**0.086**
PEPPERS	0.16	0.12	**0.10**
CLOUDS	0.094	0.074	**0.070**
ROSE	0.107	0.097	**0.084**
ROBOT	0.19	0.067	**0.052**
JET	0.098	0.070	**0.067**

FUTURE WORK

As future work, there are many ways to improve the performance of the proposed algorithm. First the development of a method for the selection of optimal parameters is an interesting venue in the future research. Secondly the hybridization of ACPSO algorithm with others heuristic operators is also an interesting path for future research, that can give us more insights regarding the behaviour and potential advantages and disadvantages of different metaheuristics. Finally, the use of quantum behaved particle swarm optimisation is also considered in the future work for a better exploration of the search space.

CONCLUSION

In this chapter we have presented a new particle swarm optimization based method for automatic image clustering. ACPSO, in contrast to most of the existing clustering techniques, requires no prior knowledge of the data to be classified. ACPSO used a modified version of the particle swarm optimization (PSO) algorithm to determine the number of naturally occurring clusters in the image as well as to refine the cluster centers. Each particle encoded a partition of the image with a number of clusters chosen randomly from the set of the maximum number of clusters. The partition of each particle of the swarm evolves using evolving operators which aim to reduce dynamically the number of clusters centers. Superiority of the new method has been demonstrated by comparing it with ISODATA algorithm and a recently developed partitional clustering technique based on Particle Swarm Optimization (PSO) algorithm.

REFERENCES

Abraham, A., Das, S., & Roy, S. (2007). Swarm intelligence algorithms for data clustering. In Maimon, O. Z., & Rokach, L. (Eds.), *Soft computing for knowledge discovery and data mining* (pp. 279–313). New York, NY: Springer-Verlag.

Al-Sultan, K. S., & Khan, M. M. (1996). Computational experience on four algorithms for the hard clustering problem. *Pattern Recognition Letters*, *17*(3), 295–308. doi:10.1016/0167-8655(95)00122-0

Alam, S., Dobbie, G., & Riddle, P. (2008). An evolutionary particle swarm optimization algorithm for data clustering. In *Swarm Intelligence Symposium*, (pp. 1-6).

Ball, G., & Hall, D. (1967). A clustering technique for summarizing multivariate data. *Behavioral Science*, *12*, 153–155. doi:10.1002/bs.3830120210

Bandyopadhyay, S. (2003). *Simulated annealing for fuzzy clustering: Variable representation, evolution of the number of clusters and remote sensing applications.* unpublished, private communication.

Bandyopadhyay, S., & Maulik, U. (2002). Genetic clustering for automatic evolution of clusters and application to image classification. *Pattern Recognition*, *35*, 1197–1208. doi:10.1016/S0031-3203(01)00108-X

Bezdek, J. C., Keller, J., Krishnampuram, R., & Pal, N. R. (1999). *Fuzzy models and algorithms for pattern recognition and image processing.* Dordercht, The Netherlands: Kluwer Academic Publishers.

Das, S., Abraham, A., & Konar, A. (2008). Automatic kernel clustering with multi-elitist particle swarm optimization algorithm. *Pattern Recognition Letters*, *29*, 688–699. doi:10.1016/j.patrec.2007.12.002

Das, S., Chowdhury, A., & Abraham, A. (2009). A bacterial evolutionary algorithm for automatic data clustering. *IEEE Congress on Evolutionary Computation, CEC 09*, (pp. 2403-2410).

Das, S., & Konar, A. (2009). Automatic image pixel clustering with an improved differential evolution. *Applied Soft Computing*, *1*, 226–236. doi:10.1016/j.asoc.2007.12.008

Duda, R. O., & Hart, P. E. (1973). *Pattern classification and scene analysis*. Chichester, UK: John Wiley and Sons.

Forgy, E. W. (1965). Cluster analysis of multivariate data: Efficiency versus interpretability of classification. *Biometrics*, *21*, 768–769.

Halkidi, M., Batistakis, Y., & Vazirgiannis, M. (2001). On clustering validation techniques. *Journal of Intelligent Information Systems*, *17*(2-3), 107–145. doi:10.1023/A:1012801612483

Hamerly, G. (2003). *Learning structure and concepts in data using data clustering*. Unpublished doctoral dissertation, University of California, San Diego.

Hartigan, J. A. (1975). *Clustering algorithms*. New York, NY: John Wiley and Sons.

Hruschka, E. R., Campello, R. J. G. B., Freitas, A. A., & de Carvalho, A. C. P. L. F. (2009). A survey of evolutionary algorithms for clustering. *IEEE Transactions on Systems, Man, and Cybernetics, Part C: Applications and Reviews*, *39*(2), 133-155. ISSN 1094-6977

Huang, K. (2002). A synergistic automatic clustering technique (Syneract) for multispectral image analysis. *Photogrammetric Engineering and Remote Sensing*, *1*(1), 33–40.

Jain, A. K., Murty, M. N., & Flynn, P. J. (1999). Data clustering: A review. *ACM Computing Surveys*, *31*(3), 264–323. doi:10.1145/331499.331504

Katari, V., Satapathy, S. C., Murthy, J., & Reddy, P. P. (2007). Hybridized improved genetic algorithm with variable length chromosome for image clustering. In *International Journal of Computer Science and Network Security*, *7*(11), 21–131.

Kennedy, J., & Eberhart, R. C. (1995). Particle swarm optimization. In *Proceedings of the IEEE International Conference on Neural Networks*, Piscataway, NJ, (pp. 1942–1948).

Lai, C. C. (2005). A novel clustering approach using hierarchical genetic algorithms. *Intelligent Automation and Soft Computing*, *11*(3), 143–153.

Lin, H. J., Yang, F. W., & Kao, Y. T. (2005). An efficient GA-based clustering technique. *Tamkang Journal of Science and Engineering*, *8*(2), 113–122.

Liu, W., Chih, C. H., Kuo, B. C., & Coleman, T. (2008). An adaptive clustering algorithms based on the possibility clustering and ISODATA for multispectral image classification. *Proceedings of the International Society for Photogrammetry and Remote Sensing (ISPRS – XXI Congress)*, Beijing, China, July 3 – 11.

Lukashin, A. V., & Fuchs, R. (2001). Analysis of temporal gene expression profiles: Clustering by simulated annealing and determining the optimal number of clusters. *Bioinformatics (Oxford, England)*, *17*(5), 405–414. doi:10.1093/bioinformatics/17.5.405

MacQueen, J. (1967). Some methods for classification and analysis of multivariate observations. In *Proceedings of the Fifth Berkely Symposium on Mathematical Statistics and Probability*, (pp. 281–297).

Markus, M., & Grani, M. (2009). Automatic cluster number selection using a split and merge k-means approach. *20th International Workshop on Database and Expert Systems Application*, (pp. 363-367).

Monga, O., & Wrobel, B. (1987). Segmentation d'images: Vers une méthodologie. *Traitement du Signal*, *4*(3), 169–193.

Omran, M. G., Salman, A., & Engelbrecht, A. (2006). Dynamic clustering using particle swarm optimization with application in image segmentation. *Pattern Analysis and Applications Journal*, *8*(4), 332–344. doi:10.1007/s10044-005-0015-5

Othman, R. M., Deris, S., Illias, R. M., Zakaria, Z., & Mohamad, S. M. (2006). Automatic clustering of gene ontology by genetic algorithm. *International Journal of Information Technology*, *3*(1), 37–46.

Pelleg, D., & Moore, A. (2000). X-means extending K-means with efficient estimation of the number of clusters. In *Proceedings of the 17th International Conference on Machine Learning*, 2000, (pp. 727–734).

Rosenberger, C., & Chehdi, K. (2000). Unsupervised clustering method with optimal estimation of the number of clusters: Application to image segmentation. In *Proceedings IEEE International Conference on Pattern Recognition (ICPR)*, Vol. 1, Barcelona, (pp. 1656– 1659).

Selim, S. Z., & Ismail, M. A. (1984). K-means type algorithms: a generalized convergence theorem and characterization of local optimality. *IEEE Transactions on Pattern Analysis and Machine Intelligence*, 81–87. doi:10.1109/TPAMI.1984.4767478

Shi, Y., & Eberhart, R. C. (1998). A modified particle swarm optimizer. In *Proceedings of IEEE Congress on Evolutionary Computing*, (pp. 69–73).

Srinivas, M., & Patnaik, L. M. (1994). Adaptive probabilities of crossover and mutation in genetic algorithms. *IEEE Transactions on Systems, Man, and Cybernetics*, *24*(4). doi:10.1109/21.286385

Theodoridis, S., & Koutroumbas, K. (2003). *Pattern recognition* (2nd ed.). Amsterdam, the Netherlands: Elsevier Academic Press.

Tseng, L. Y., & Yang, S. B. (2001). A genetic approach to the automatic clustering algorithm. *Pattern Recognition*, *34*(2), 415–424. doi:10.1016/S0031-3203(00)00005-4

Turi, R. (2001). *Clustering-based colour image segmentation*. Unpublished Doctoral dissertation, Monash University, Australia.

Chapter 15
A Survey of Semantic Web Based Architectures for Adaptive Intelligent Tutoring System

Suraiya Jabin
Jamia Millia Islamia Central University, India

K. Mustafa
Jamia Millia Islamia Central University, India

ABSTRACT

Most recently, IT-enabled education has become a very important branch of educational technology. Education is becoming more dynamic, networked, and increasingly electronic. Today's is a world of Internet social networks, blogs, digital audio and video content, et cetera. A few clear advantages of Web-based education are classroom independence and availability of authoring tools for developing Web-based courseware, cheap and efficient storage and distribution of course materials, hyperlinks to suggested readings, and digital libraries. However, there are several challenges in improving Web-based education, such as providing for more adaptivity and intelligence. The main idea is to incorporate Semantic Web technologies and resources to the design of artificial intelligence in education (AIED) systems aiming to update their architectures to provide more adaptability, robustness, and richer learning environments. The construction of such systems is highly complex and faces several challenges in terms of software engineering and artificial intelligence aspects. This chapter addresses state of the art Semantic Web methods and tools used for modeling and designing intelligent tutoring systems (ITS). Also it draws attention of Semantic Web users towards e-learning systems with a hope that the use of Semantic Web technologies in educational systems can help the accomplishment of anytime, anywhere, anybody learning, where most of the web resources are reusable learning objects supported by standard technologies and learning is facilitated by intelligent pedagogical agents, that may be adding the essential instructional ingredients implicitly.

DOI: 10.4018/978-1-4666-1830-5.ch015

INTRODUCTION

Intelligent tutoring systems (ITS) appeared during the 1970s, driven by the success of knowledge-based systems and expert systems. These essentially instruct learners largely without the intervention of human beings. They introduce a set of ideas, like the use of computational models of domains, allowing the possibility of reasoning and explaining domain problems automatically. Developments were made in trainees' models, instructional and pedagogical planning, and user interfaces. In the 1990s, with the Web boom, some ITS ideas were incorporated in new computer-aided instruction paradigms, like e-learning and distributed learning. However, there is a clear difference in the level of interactions and types of skills addressed by ITS and other generic e-learning systems.

The use of artificial intelligence techniques to educational software design influenced the evolution from Computer Assisted Instruction (CAI) to Intelligent Tutoring Systems (ITS) or Intelligent Computer Assisted Instruction (ICAI). Computer-based Instruction (CBI) and Web-based Instruction (WBI) are the two primary instructional products with the understanding that CBI utilizes CDROM (or non-Web-based) technology to deliver its courseware, and WBI utilizes Internet (or Web-based) technologies. The type of delivery medium has played an important role in determining what typical instructional designs are possible.

The system consists of several core modules, which are relatively independent of each other to allow easy upgradability and portability to other teaching domains (Bittencourt et al., 2009). These modules are:

1. Personalized **Student/Learner Model**, which monitors the progress of every individual student. Learner modeling module is composed of mechanisms that acquire and represent the learner's knowledge about a specific subject domain.

Figure 1. A general schematic of ITS

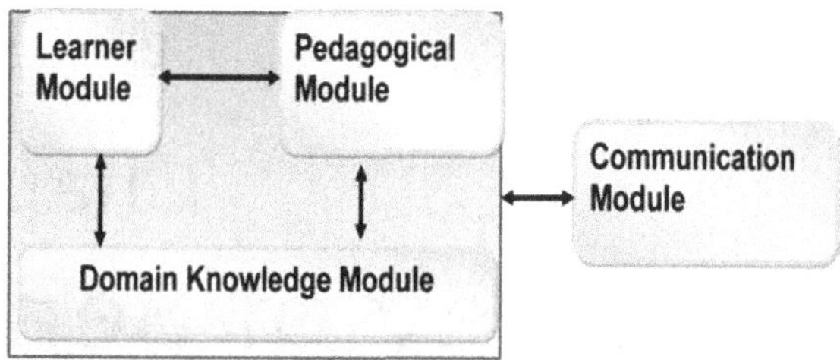

2. An **Expert/Domain Knowledge Model**, basically contains a domain knowledge base and some mechanisms to reason about this knowledge. Generally, this module is responsible for problem solving tasks, using some resources from AI such as logic, production rules, semantic network, frames and bayesian networks.
3. **Pedagogical/Teacher module** is responsible for selecting resources from a domain as well as deciding about the pedagogical action to be accomplished during the interaction process with the learner.
4. **Communication /Interface module** is responsible for directly managing the interactions with the learners.

One of the hottest research topics in recent years among the AI and WWW community, has been the Semantic Web. The World Wide Web is a collection of electronic documents linked together like a spider web. These documents are stored on servers located around the world. Web contains virtually boundless information in the form of documents. The semantic web (SW) extends the classical web in the sense that it allows a semantic structure of web pages, giving support to humans as well as artificial agents to understand the content inside the web applications. As a result, Semantic Web provides an environment that allows software agents to navigate through web documents and execute sophisticated tasks. SW itself offers numerous improvements in the context of Web-based educational systems contributing to upgrade the learning quality. Tim Berners-Lee (Berners-Lee et al., 2001), inventor of the Web, proposed the term Semantic Web, and defined it as follows: *the Semantic Web is not a separate Web but extension of the current one, in which information is given well-defined meaning, better enabling computers and people to work in cooperation. This is a web of data that can be processed by machines directly and indirectly.*

An adaptive web-based educational system (AWBES) is a system that changes its configuration in order to improve the students learning. In other words, its goal is to provide adaptive interactions to the learners aiming to improve the quality of services (Vouk et al., 1999). The adaptation types are described as follows (Santos et al., 2003):

- **Instructional Model Adaptation:** It allows the student to have a variety of content, activities and services according to the specifications made by the course author. At project time, the author may only specify which attributes a user may have, aiming to receive certain content, activity or access to a service. At execution time, the student model has to be checked for specified conditions agreements in order to decide which content, activities and services will be provided to the student. The referred content, activities and services shall be properly modeled to apply this adaptation at execution time;
- **Adaptive Interactions:** It supports the students whilst they interact in a certain course. This support is addressed to the student and the tutor, possessing several services, contents and activities to work in the interaction. Besides, user support is given by considering the information stored in different models, especially the user, group and service models;
- **Presentation Adaptation:** It presents an individualized user interface for each student according to his or her model. It does not refer only to what the user has customized, but also to what the system has learned from previous interactions of that and other users. This is one of the most efficient ways of building the presentation for certain user learning.

This chapter presents a survey of different architectures used to combine Semantic Web techniques with ITSs, explaining its elements, relationships, challenges, and the different design criterions, offering some guidelines to make decisions when different implementation solutions are possible.

SEMANTIC WEB TECHNOLOGIES

The Semantic Web (Matthews, 2005) initiative of the World-Wide Web Consortium (W3C) has been active for the last few years and has attracted interest and skepticism in equal measure. The initiative was inspired by the vision of its founder, Tim Berners-Lee, of a more flexible, integrated, automatic and self-adapting Web, providing a richer and more interactive experience for users. The W3C has developed a set of standards and tools to support this vision, and after several years of research and development, these are now usable and could make a real impact. However, people are still asking how they can be used in practical situations to solve real problems.

The impact of the Semantic Web is likely to be particularly strong in distance learning, libraries and information management as well as in collaborative research. The UK is particularly strong in these areas.

Discernment

The semantic web or Web 2.0 are terms used to describe Internet applications and features which enable user interaction, as opposed to the former

'Web 1.0' style of static, information resource-style web pages. These include blogs, wikis, discussion boards, instant messaging, document or image sharing sites and myriad other user-interactive applications.

Many staff members in education are now investigating the use of Web2.0 technologies (interactive and collaborative tools supporting activities such as group authorship of documents or mind maps or adding audio and video into the learning process) in assessment, learning and teaching, libraries, and other areas of the student experience.

"The Semantic Web provides a common framework that allows data to be shared and reused across application, enterprise, and community boundaries. It is a collaborative effort led by W3C. It is based on the Resource Description Framework (RDF)." W3C, http://www.w3.org/2001/sw/

That is, providing meaningful ways to describe the resources available on the Web and, perhaps more importantly, why there are links connecting them together (Koivunen et al., 2001). Thus the notion arises of semantics being part of the Web, capturing the reason things are there. Once the Web has a mechanism for defining semantics about resources and links, then the possibility arises for automatic processing of the Web by software agents, rather than mediation by people.

A simple example used to motivate the Semantic Web is the need to discover documents on the Web, not only from their textual content, as conventional search engines do, but also from a description. The problem is exemplified by the frustration in finding articles written by a particular author, rather than those which include the author's name. In response to the query 'Tim Berners-Lee' a search engine will respond with all the papers including that phrase, some of which will be by Tim Berners-Lee, but most of which will cite or refer to him – as this paper does. The Semantic Web can allow each document on the Web to be annotated stating who its author was, when it was created, and what content it has; then only those with the appropriate author will be returned.

To add these descriptions or annotations, it is necessary to state what this additional description, sometimes known as 'metadata', should be, and how it should be interpreted.

History

The Semantic Web initiative was started as the Web Metadata Working Group in 1998, and subsequently became the Semantic Web Activity (Semantic Web Activity link) which has taken the view that the Semantic Web:

provides a common framework that allows data to be shared and reused across application, enterprise, and community boundaries. It is a collaborative effort led by W3C with participation from a large number of researchers and industrial partners. It is based on the Resource Description Framework, which integrates a variety of applications using XML for syntax and URIs for naming.

Some of the works produced two influential proposals including the Resource Description Framework Model and Syntax Specification (Lassila et al., 1999) and the Resource Description Framework Schema Specification (Brickley et al., 2000). However, at that stage activity was on a small scale and there was confusion on its scope and usefulness, so work shaped into a more exploratory phase. The DAML programme, a DARPA-sponsored initiative in the US, was set up and proposed several influential approaches to the problems posed by the Semantic Web.

Within the last two to three years, work has moved on within W3C with increased vigour. Two major working groups of the W3C, the RDF Core Working Group and the Web Ontology Working Group have produced major sets of recommendations. Exploratory activities within W3C have also been extensive under the Semantic Web Advanced Development programme and the

Figure 2. Berners-Lee's layered architecture of the Semantic Web

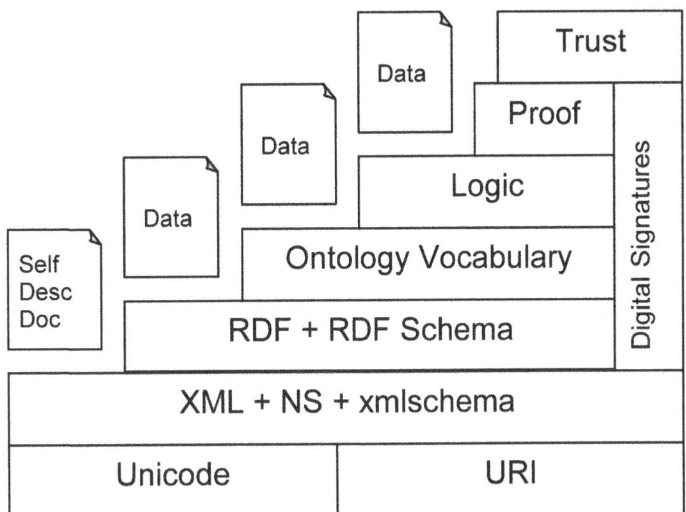

Semantic Web Advanced Development in Europe project sponsored by the European Commission.

The Layered Architecture

The common use of the term Semantic Web is to identify a set of technologies, tools and standards that form the basic building blocks of a system to support the vision of a Web imbued with meaning. The Semantic Web has been developing into a layered architecture, which is often represented using a diagram first proposed by Tim Berners-Lee, with many variations since. Figure 2 gives a typical representation of this diagram.

While necessarily a simplification which has to be used with some caution, it nevertheless gives a reasonable conceptualisation of the various components of the Semantic Web. We describe briefly these layers.

- **Unicode and URI**: Unicode, the standard for computer character representation, and URIs, the standard for identifying and locating resources (such as pages on the Web), provide a baseline for representing characters used in most of the languages in the world, and for identifying resources.
- **XML:** XML and its related standards, such as Namespaces, and Schemas, form a common means for structuring data on the Web but without communicating the meaning of the data. These are well established within the Web already.
- **Resource Description Framework:** RDF is the first layer of the Semantic Web proper. RDF is a simple metadata representation framework, using URIs to identify Web-based resources and a graph model for describing relationships between resources. Several syntactic representations are available, including a standard XML format.
- **RDF Schema:** Its a simple type modelling language for describing classes of resources and properties between them in the basic RDF model. It provides a simple reasoning framework for inferring types of resources.
- **Ontologies:** a richer language for providing more complex constraints on the types of resources and their properties.
- **Logic and Proof:** It refers to an automatic reasoning system provided on top of the ontology structure to make new inferences. Thus, using such a system, a software

agent can make deductions as to whether a particular resource satisfies its requirements (and vice versa).
- **Trust:** The final layer of the stack addresses issues of trust that the Semantic Web can support. This component has not progressed far beyond a vision of allowing people to ask questions of the trustworthiness of the information on the Web, in order to provide an assurance of its quality.

Further details of these languages are introduced in guideline materials such as [(Manola et al., 2004); (Smith et al., 2004)], and [(Antoniou et al., 2004); (Passin, 2004)]. Moreover, the basic layers of the Semantic Web are in place, and the following notable recommendations were released by the W3C on 10th February 2004, covering the RDF, RDF Schema and Ontology layers.

- RDF/XML Syntax Specification (Revised) (Beckett, 2004)
- RDF Vocabulary Description Language 1.0: RDF Schema (Brickley et al., 2004)
- RDF Primer (Manola et al., 2004)
- Resource Description Framework (RDF): Concepts and Abstract Syntax (Klyne et al., 2004)
- RDF Semantics (Hayes, 2004)
- RDF Test Cases (Grant et al., 2004)
- Web Ontology Language (OWL) Use Cases and Requirements (Heflin, 2004)
- OWL Web Ontology Language Reference (Dean et al., 2004)

Progress on the rule and reasoning layer of the Semantic Web has been slower, with many proposals varying from simple queries to modal logic theorem provers. This is still an active research area.

Languages for the Semantic Web

The Semantic Web aims for machine understandable web resources, whose information can then be shared and processed both by automated tools such as search engines, and by human users. OWL is intended to be used when the information contained in documents needs to be processed by applications, as opposed to situations where the content only needs to be presented to humans. OWL can be used to explicitly represent the meaning of terms in vocabularies and the relationships between those terms. This representation of terms and their interrelationships is called ontology. OWL has more facilities for expressing meaning and semantics than XML, RDF, and RDF-S, and thus OWL goes beyond these languages in its ability to represent machine interpretable content on the Web.

Figure 3 shows an example of representing the same piece of information in HTML and in XML. While HTML is layout-oriented, XML is more structure-oriented. Web resources are usually only human understandable: HTML only provides rendering information for textual and graphical information intended for human consumption. It is based on a fixed set of tags to format text; in XML, tags are arbitrary (user-defined) and bear some semantic information themselves. XML Schema provides the necessary framework for creating XML documents by specifying the valid structure, constraints, the number of occurrences of specific elements, default values, and data types to be used in the corresponding XML documents. The encoding syntax of XML Schema is XML, and just like XML itself XML Schema documents use *namespaces* that are declared using the *xmlns* attribute. Namespaces define contexts within which the corresponding tags and names apply (Devedzic, 2004).

By using XML, OWL information can easily be exchanged between different types of computers using different types of operating system and application languages. OWL became a W3C

Figure 3. a) A piece of HTML code; b) The same information in XML code

```
<UL>
<LI> George F. Luger, <EM> Artificial Intelligence: Structures and Strategies for
Complex Problem Solving </EM>, Pearson Education Publishing Company.
</UL>
```

```
<BOOK>
   <AUTHOR> George F. Luger </AUTHOR>
   <TITLE> Artificial Intelligence: Structures and Strategies for Complex Problem
Solving </TITLE>
   <PUBLISHER> Pearson Education Publishing Company </PUBLISHER>
   <YEAR> 2004 </YEAR>
</BOOK>
```

(World Wide Web Consortium) Recommendation in February 2004. A W3C Recommendation is understood by the industry and the web community as a web standard. Also it is a stable specification developed by a W3C Working Group and reviewed by the W3C Membership.

RDF is a framework for describing Web resources, such as the title, author, modification date, content, and copyright information of a Web page. Regardless of the representation syntax, RDF models use traditional knowledge representation techniques in order to provide better semantic interoperability (traditionally, Object-Attribute-Value triplets are natural semantic units for representing a domain). Still, an RDF model just provides a domain-neutral mechanism to describe metadata, but does not define (a priori) the semantics of any application domain. It is used to represent data about data (metadata), and a model for representing data about "things on the Web" (resources) by using O-A-V triplets or statements. Each statement is essentially a relation between an object (a resource), an attribute (a property), a value (a resource or free text). Alternatively, each RDF model can be represented as a directed labeled graph, or in an XML-based encoding.

SEMANTIC WEB AND EDUCATION

It is difficult to predict where the Semantic Web will affect the Higher and Further Education sector as it is not yet clear where the major impact of the Semantic Web will be in general. However, there are four clear areas where there could be major implications for both teaching and research (Matthews, 2005):

1. **Information Management:** the Semantic Web enhances the capabilities of those tools which form a familiar part of the current Web so that they can become useful information management tools in their own right. The Web is already an information source of choice for many learners and researchers. A more structured and directed approach to managing this information space, both within institutions and across the whole community, can make this information more useful, with less wasted effort, and more capacity to measure the quality of information. By making the annotation machine readable, it becomes accessible to automatic processing, carrying out many routine tasks which consume people's time. A further impact is likely to be in the business of running education, allowing more efficient information flow around institutions.

2. **Digital Libraries:** the impact on digital libraries, combined with the Open Access Initiative and the rise of open archiving is likely to be quite profound. Libraries become 'value-added' information annotators and collators rather than the archivists of externally published literature and the holders of the published output of institutions. The Semantic Web, although not a prerequisite or a motivator for this change is nevertheless likely to smooth its development. The tools are in place for sharing classification schemes and to allow the community to develop, deepen and share such schemes. The information infrastructure tools discussed above will have particular impact on the way students and researchers find information, so these tools may typically be provided and adapted by libraries who will tailor them to the needs of their own users. The Semantic Web, like the current Web, has the capacity of being an overwhelming place; libraries are well-placed to make sense of this for the HE and FE community.
3. **Building communities and collaborations:** a major impact is likely to occur in the way that academic communities work together. The tools for forming virtual communities and sharing information across that community are simple and lightweight, and, if the development of blogs and the use of RSS is an indication, it can enhance the interaction of an interested community drastically. Providing a richer annotation structure to these can enhance their usefulness, bringing them into the information infrastructure as well as providing a means of communication to people across the world.
   Support for virtual collaborations is a much larger issue, as it requires tighter control over resources and security. This is largely taking place in the Grid community and efforts to construct a Semantic Grid are already well underway, bringing the machine readable annotation to automate the discovery and negotiation of services onto the Grid.
4. **E-Learning:** all of the above influence e-learning. However, we should also consider specifically, support for the presentation and delivery of course materials and for assisting and assessing students. Again, the impact of the Semantic Web is likely to mean that these can be more closely tailored to the needs of the user, with a choice of learning objects mediated through selection mechanisms. The Semantic Web can provide context and co-ordination, with workflow tools providing a supporting infrastructure. Also this is the main focus of this chapter.

VIRTUAL LEARNING ENVIRONMENT

Most of the Universities or Educational Institutes use VLE (Virtual Learning Environment portal) to deliver online courses. Some well-known LMSes are Moodle, Blackboard and Sakai. Moodle is an Open Source Course Management System (CMS), also known as a Learning Management System (LMS) or a Virtual Learning Environment (VLE). It has become very popular among educators around the world as a tool for creating online dynamic web sites for their students. To work, it needs to be installed on a web server somewhere, either on one of your own computers or one at a web hosting company. Moodle [http://moodle.org/] is one of the best VLE as it is well appreciated by educational sector. The focus of the Moodle project is always on giving educators the best tools to manage and promote learning, but there are many ways to use Moodle:

1. Moodle has features that allow it to scale to very large deployments and hundreds of thousands of students, yet it can also be used for a primary school or an education hobbyist.

2. Many institutions use it as their platform to conduct fully online courses, while some use it simply to augment face-to-face courses (known as blended learning).
3. Many of our users love to use the activity modules (such as forums, databases and wikis) to build richly collaborative communities of learning around their subject matter (in the social constructionist tradition), while others prefer to use Moodle as a way to deliver content to students (such as standard SCORM packages) and assess learning using assignments or quizzes.

SCORM is the "Shareable Content Object Reference Model". It is a set of standard specifications that are designed to help us share learning materials between different systems. It is primarily used by, and in, Learning Management Systems (LMSes, also known as VLEs). The basic idea of SCORM is that, if you create a piece of learning material such as a multiple-choice exercise, you should be able to upload that material into any LMS system, and it should work: the LMS should be able to display it, and the exercise should be able to report its information (student scores etc.) back to the LMS system. There are two major versions of SCORM: SCORM 1.2, which is older and more widely-supported, and SCORM 2004, which is newer, and possibly better, but not so widely-supported at the moment. Hot Potatoes 6 supports SCORM 1.2.

Learning management systems (LMS) are powerful integrated systems that support a number of activities performed by teachers and students during the E-Learning process. Teachers use an LMS to develop Web-based course notes and quizzes, to communicate with students and to monitor and grade student progress. Students use it for learning, communication and collaboration. As is the case for a number of other classes of modern Web-based systems, LMS offer their users "one size fits all" service. But adaptation is essentially LOCAL – "ONE SIZE FITS ALL" approach won't work. The adaptive mechanism aims at extending Moodle in order to enable it to provide courses that fit the different students' learning styles. Moodle provides teachers with many different types of learning objects or activities, ranging from simply presenting learning material or examples to more advanced features such as quizzes, glossaries, surveys, wikis, chat, and many more. The adaptive mechanism is developed in a generic way, giving teachers and administrators the possibility to add whatever kind of learning object they want to use in their adaptive courses. As a result, teachers can continue using the learning management system, while taking full advantages of its enhanced features. Additionally, the adaptive mechanism facilitates the provision of courses that more closely fit students' different learning styles and therefore promotes learning.

Ubiquitous learning (Graf et al., 2009) allows students to learn at any time and any place. Adaptivity plays an important role in ubiquitous learning, aiming at providing students with adaptive and personalized learning material, activities, and information at the right place and the right time. However, for providing rich adaptivity, the student model needs to be able to gather a variety of information about the students. In this paper, Graf has introduced an automatic, global, and dynamic student modeling approach, which frequently updating information about students' progress, learning styles, interests and knowledge level, problem solving abilities, preferences for using the system, social connectivity, and current location. This information is gathered in an automatic way, using students' behavior and actions in different learning situations provided by different components/services of the ubiquitous learning environment. By providing a comprehensive student model, students can be supported by rich adaptivity in every component/service of the learning environment. The learning environment uses the multi-agent system paradigm, consisting of different servers and databases, and provides several services for the students. The services cover different areas of the educational process and support students in different situations. In order to provide students with learning material and activities for learning the basic elements of the course, the ubiquitous learning environment is combined with the learning management system Moodle (2008). It is with more than 45,000 registered sites world wide (Moodle Site, 2008) and an evaluation showed that it is one of the most appropriate environments to be extended with respect to adaptivity (Graf & List, 2005). The progress of students includes information about three variables. First, information about viewed learning objects (LO) and learning activities (LA) are stored, allowing seeing which LOs and LAs were visited or conducted last. Second, the students' state in the course is stored, indicating how many percentage of LOs and LAs a student has already conducted in each service and overall. Third, the questions asked in the discussion forum (including the extension of the question and answer service) are stored, indicating how many questions a student has posted and what he/she has posted so far. All three variables include not only information about the current progress of students but store also the past data.

ONTOLOGY AND LEARNING OBJECT REPOSITORIES

Ontology provides an explicit conceptualization that describes data semantics. Ontology defines a common vocabulary, interpretable by machines, for researches who need to share information about a domain, including definitions about a basic concept of a domain and their relationships (Noy et al., 2001). This way, Ontology is the backbone of Semantic Web. In the structure of ITS, the use of ontology focuses mainly on learning objects (LO) aspects. Besides, that does not facilitate the definition and communication of components of the system's architecture (Adriana et al., 2008). An architecture for ITS supported by Semantic Web extends the use of ontology, in where the representation of each component is made by a specific ontology.

Conceptual structures that define an underlying ontology are germane to the idea of machine processable data on the SemanticWeb. Ontologies are (meta) data schemas, providing a controlled vocabulary of concepts, each with an explicitly defined and machine processable semantics. By defining shared and common domain theories, ontologies help both people and machines to communicate concisely, supporting the exchange of semantics and not only syntax. Hence, the cheap and fast construction of domain-specific ontologies is crucial for the success and the proliferation of the Semantic Web.

A learning object is defined and described as follows by the Institute of Electrical and Electronics Engineers, Inc. (IEEE) Learning Technology Standards Committee (LTSC):

A Learning Object is any entity, digital or non-digital, which can be used, re-used or referenced during technology supported learning. Examples of technology supported learning include computer-based training systems, interactive learning environments, intelligent computer-aided instruction systems, distance learning systems, and collaborative learning environments. Examples of Learning Objects include multimedia content, instructional content, learning objectives, instructional software and software tools, and persons, organizations, or events referenced during technology supported learning.

Some of the main things that the LOM is designed to help you achieve are:

- Creation of well structured descriptions of learning resources. These descriptions should help facilitate the discovery, location, evaluation and acquisition of learning resources by students, teachers or automated software processes.
- Sharing of descriptions of learning resources between resource discovery sys-

tems. This should lead to a reduction in the cost of providing services based on high quality resource descriptions.

- Tailoring of the resource descriptions to suit the specialised needs of a community. This may include choosing suitable controlled vocabularies for classification, reducing the number of elements that are described or adding new ones from other resource description schemas.
- Creators and publishers may use the LOM along with other specifications to "tag" learning resources with a description that can be associated with the resource. This will provide information in a standard format similar to that found on the cover and fly-page of a text book.

Although the term, "learning object" originated from the notion of "object-oriented" computing and programming, which suggests that ideal way to build a computer program or anything digital is to assemble it from standardized, small, interchangeable chunks of code, the approach is somewhat different in an e-learning setting. In this case, learning management systems (LMS), of which popular commercial ones are BlackBoard, WebCT, and Desire2Learn, could be considered large meta-objects, that contain spaces for the incorporation of granular objects. The analogy that is often used to describe this is that of LEGO™ building blocks. The building blocks have a standard shape and configuration, but they can be used and put together in many ways, to create unique entities, limited only by the imagination (and good planning).

A few of the larger learning object repositories that encourage downloading and sharing of resources include the following:

- **Campus Alberta Repository of Educational Objects (CAREO).** Comprised of 5,000 multidisciplinary teaching materials, the database is searchable, and the collection is web-based. This Canadian project has been recognized as a leader in the LOR initiative. http://www.careo.org
- **Federal Government Resources for Educational Excellence (FREE).** This contains numerous educational resources, which include teaching ideas, instructional activities, photographs, maps, audio files, digitized paintings, lesson plans. http://www.ed.gov/free
- **FreeFoto.com** This is one of several repositories that contain high-quality photographs for educational as well as commercial use. http://www.freefoto.com
- **Maricopa Learning Exchange**. This is a digital repository that contains more than 700 learning "packages" which include plans, ideas, samples, and resources. http://www.mcli.dist.maricopa.edu/mlx
- **Merlot**. Supported by a consortium of colleges, universities, and state systems, the digital resources are free and open to any users. Designed for higher education, the database includes links to more than 10,000 online learning materials, many with peer reviews, assignments, and ratings. http://www.merlot.org
- **Wisconsin Online Resource Center**. This digital repository contains more than 1,000 learning objects which are categorized for uses within certain higher education curricula. The image categories include business, general education, English as a Second Language, health, professional development, adult basic education, technical courseware. http://www.wisc-online.com

APPLYING SEMANTIC WEB TO E-LEARNING

The Semantic Web clearly has large application to e-learning, supporting both distance and local education. The notion of a 'learning object' as a separable unit of educational material which can be reused and combined with other learning objects has been a central feature of e-learning systems. This concept has been criticized for being too inflexible and not taking into account the particular learning needs of individuals or the requirements of context and emphasis of educators. However, used properly, it is a useful and powerful concept and one which the Semantic Web has much to offer.

Learning objects can be organised into repositories, and shared across peer-to-peer (P2P) networks. The Edutella project is seeking to provide an RDF-based P2P network for sharing learning objects. Individuals can publish learning objects to the network, providing rich metadata that is 'descriptive information about learning resources for the purposes of finding, managing, and using these learning resources more effectively'. Then the shared repository of learning objects can be searched and objects can be retrieved based on their semantic annotations.

Rich semantic annotation languages for learning objects are appearing. For example, the Educational Modelling Language (EML); the IMS Global Learning Consortium's proposed set of integrated standards for e-Learning subjects, including a Metadata Specification; and the Learning Object Metadata (LOM), a standard defined by the Learning Technology Standardization Committee (LTSC) of IEEE. All these are currently defined in XML but are adaptable into RDF for use in the Semantic Web. This will allow a richer interaction with the learning material, with ontology-based brokers for negotiating the requirements of learners to the available learning materials. Again, we are likely to see, in the next two to three years, the introduction of Semantic Web technology into Virtual Learning Environments, firstly at an experimental stage, and then more deeply embedded.

Beyond the search and discovery of learning objects, the development of learning plans and courses can be controlled via workflow languages. Explanatory context and insight into the development of knowledge can be provided by 'knowledge charts', defined by Stutt and Motta as 'pathways through controversies and narratives and other structures such as analogies and expositions of scientific principles' (Stutt et al., 2004). Again, RDF and other Semantic Web technologies provide the natural medium for representing and delivering such charts.

Intelligence of a Web-based educational system means the capability of demonstrating some form of knowledge-based reasoning in curriculum sequencing, in analysis of the student's solutions, and in providing interactive problem-solving support (possibly example-based) to the student, all adapted to the Web technology (Brusilovsky & Miller, 2001). Adaptivity can take different forms, such as (Brusilovsky, 1999):

- Collecting some data about the student working with the system and creating the student model;
- Adapting the presentation of the course material, navigation through it, its sequencing, and its annotation, to the student;
- Using models of different students to form a matching group of students for different kinds of collaboration;
- Identifying the students who have learning records essentially different from those of their peers (e.g., the students progressing too slow or too fast) and acting accordingly (e.g., show additional explanations, or present more advanced material).

There has been considerable success in building and using intelligent and adaptive Web-based educational applications. However, much more can and should be done. In the context of the

Semantic Web, intelligent Web-based education takes on new dimensions.

CASE STUDIES: SEMANTIC WEB BASED ADAPTIVE INTELLIGENT TUTORING SYSTEMS

Education is a very fertile soil for applying Web technologies anyway, and the Semantic Web opens a number of new doors and multiplies the prospects of Web based education. Some of the existing systems using ontology are analyzed below in this section:

1. **ITS based on InfoMap (Lu et al., 2004):** This ITS uses ontology InfoMap, which is based on declarative knowledge. This ITS has a module called tutor of curricula. In this system, the benefits of the use of ontology were minimized because it was restricted to describe a few modules of the system.
2. **Adaptive Instructional Planning using Ontologies (Karampiperis and Sampson, 2004):** The system described in the paper aims at solving the problem of how to put in sequence a set of learning objects. The architecture of this system shows a Pedagogical Module but does not present a clear representation of its concerns. There is not a description of how a course is organized.
3. **RDF Description Model for Manipulating Learning Objects (Bouzeghoub et al., 2004):** The paper presents a system based on three models: domain, knowledge, user and learning object. For each model is proposed a RDF Schema. There is not any intention of building a pedagogical model. This system focuses on the reuse of learning objects and each one has its own learning strategy. It is important to note that the OWL would be better than RDF Schema to describe each proposed model in that system.
4. **MathTutor (Frigo et al., 2005):** MathTutor is a multi-agent system tutor. The architecture includes the Student, Domain and Pedagogical Models. It is interesting to note that the ontology for Domain Model presents classes like Curriculum, Pedagogical_Unit, Problem and Interaction_Unit which seem to facilitate the interaction among the components of the system but that makes difficult to identify what are the concepts of domain.
5. **Going to the Moon (Ibrahim et al., 2005):** Going to the Moon implements the agent SAIC (Schema Activation and Interpersonal Communication) in a learning system for teaching children basic Astronomy. Figure 5 shows how the integration inside the system occurs. An important component of this system is the representation of the application domain by means of a domain ontology.
6. **An ontology-based architecture for Intelligent Tutoring System (Adriana, 2008):** This architecture extends the use of Semantic Web concepts, where the representation of each component is made by a specific ontology, making possible a clear separation of concerns of the components of ITS and explicit the communication among the components. This approach makes it easier to understand the concerns of each component and, consequently, to promote interoperability among the models of the architecture. The ontologies were built in Protégé 3.1.1 (Protégé, 2006), using OWL. The OWL, Web Ontology Language (W3C, 2004), emerges as a new standard that is supported by W3C for defining ontologies in the Semantic Web. The W3C recommendation presents three versions of OWL, depending on the degree of expressive power required. In this work, the OWL – DL version is used. Using graphs in Protégé, each OWL class can be represented with black colors, relationship between two classes can be

represented by blue arcs and the instances of each OWL class can appear in red color. Each instance represents a resource and each relationship represents a property. When there is a statement related to a resource and to a property, then there is a RDF (Resource Description Framework). RDF provides a simple but powerful triple-based representation language for Universal Resource Identifiers (URIs). The tasks performed by the Presentation Model: to read a decision from the Adaptation Model, to look for a learning object into LO Repository and to generate an interface view to the learner. The Presentation Model is the final stage of communication among the components of the architecture. Similarly they (Adriana, et al) suggest ontologies for each component and also successful method of communication among architecture's component. Analyzing the Semantic Web layers, this work contemplates URI layer when the LO Repository and the Presentation Model are accessed, providing means for identifying the learning objects. With RDF layer it is possible to make statements about resources within every RDF models of the architecture, giving types to resources and links. The Ontology layer supports the evolution of vocabularies as it can define relations between the different concepts. Representing the Ontology layer, there are the ontologies of each component of the architecture. The Logic layer enables the writing of rules but it needs many improvements. Though only one application of the proposed architecture has been shown, it is expected that it can be used in the development of other ITS. To accomplish that, it would be necessary some changes into the presentation layer and some RDF instances would be different. The elaborated ontologies would be the same or could be expanded in order to incorporate new characteristics. It would not be wrong to say that the modularity obtained offers facility of reuse and expansion of components.

7. **A computational model for developing semantic web-based educational systems (Bittencourt, 2009):** This paper presents a computational model for developing SWBES focusing on the problem of how to make the development easier and more useful for both developers and authors. This computational model is characterized by offering low development costs, scalability, extensibility, interoperability, and low maintenance costs. Moreover, with this approach it is also possible to deal with the development of artificial intelligence, interactive tools, difficulty of educational resource sharing, distribution of services, and use of domain ontologies. The case study shows positive results concerning the facilities and effectiveness for building particular educational applications. The use of agents, semantic web services and ontologies technologies ensure the construction of semantic web-based systems.
8. **Peter Reimann, Kalina Yacef and Judy Kayin (Reimann et al., 2011):** attempt to relate types of change processes that are prevalent in groups to types of models that might be employed to represent these processes. Following McGrath's analysis of the nature of change processes in groups and teams, they distinguish between development, adaptation, group activity, and learning. Two types of event-based process analysis are discussed in more depth: the first one works with the view of a process as a sequence pattern, and the second one see a process as an even more holistic and designed structure: a discrete event model. For both cases, they provide examples for event-based computational methods that proved useful in analyzing typical CSCL log files, such as those resulting from asynchronous interac-

tions (focus on wikis), those resulting from synchronous interactions (focus on chats).

SUMMARY OF ANALYSIS

ITS are still seen with skepticism due to the fact that they have not been extensively used in real educational settings. Once constructed, an ITS for a specific domain can not be reused for different domains without expending much time and effort. An approach to simplifying the ITS construction is to develop ITS authoring tools that can be used by a wider range of people to easily develop cost-effective ITS.

In computer environment, ITS should consider relationships between emotion, cognition and action in order to improve the interaction with the learner. ITSs that provide adaptation based on affective state of the learner, observational cues such as gesture, posture, conversation etc. are used. According to Cocea, it is very difficult for adaptive systems to process these kinds of observational cues. That is why most research attention is shifting towards ITSs that automatically process motivation/emotion cues as a means to assess affective states (Cocea, 2006).

Most of the analyzed system focuses on reusing learning objects, like the systems RDF Description Model for Manipulating Learning Objects and ELENA Smart Space for Learning (Simon et al., 2004). In general, each learning object has its own and different learning strategy that can compromise the uniformity of the system. There are systems that have a pedagogical model but do not show a clear representation of this model nor the relationship among the components.

Current trends in *Web technology* suggest that appropriate representation languages include *XML*, *XML* Schema, RDF, and RDF Schema languages, all developed under the auspices of WWW Consortium (http://www.w3.org/XML; http://www.w3.org/RDF). For developing domain ontologies, higher-level languages and graphical tools built on top of those four are a good choice (Brickley et al., 2000)

CONCLUSION AND FUTURE RESEARCH DIRECTIONS

A list of the technologies used in the implementation of semantic web-based e-learning system include PHP Platform, Apache Web Server, MySQL database, and RAP Semantic Web Toolkit. As a future work these may also be explored in order to come up with a robust model of adaptive ITS based on semantic web. Some computer scientists are now striving for simple-minded intelligence that would be easier to develop and perhaps only marginally inferior to full-fledged intelligent tutors. Further advances in information technologies may open other new possibilities.

Now days the recent trend is to design e-learning systems that can be made available in various languages (multilingual) it has become much easier to convert the applications/programmes in different languages. India is a multicultural/multilingual country; if the programme can be available in other languages it will benefit lots of learners from various parts of India/World.

Another recent trend in e-learning are making learning simple, easy and flexible for the learners, making the system easily navigable for the learners, course must be engaging with formative tests and small exercises in between. Tracking the learner is the most important thing so that we can see how they are doing or how much time they are giving to the online course.

REFERENCES

W3C. (2000). *Semantic Web advanced development*. Retrieved from http://www.w3.org/2000/01/sw/

W3C. (2001). *Semantic Web activity*. Retrieved from http://www.w3.org/2001/sw/

W3C. (2001). *Semantic Web advanced development in Europe*. Retrieved from http://www.w3.org/2001/sw/Europe/

W3C. (2001). *Web Ontology Working Group*. Retrieved from http://www.w3.org/2001/sw/WebOnt/

Adriana, D. S. J., & José Maria, P. (2008). An ontology-based architecture for intelligent tutoring system. *Interdisciplinary Studies in Computer Science,* (pp. 25-35). Retrieved from http://www.unisinos.br/publicacoes_cientificas/images/stories/Publicacoes / scientiavol19n1/25a35_art03_jacinto% 5Brev_ok%5D.pdf

Agent Markup Language, D. A. R. P. A. (DAML). (n.d.). *Homepage*. Retrieved from http://www.daml.org

Antoniou, G., & van Harmelen, F. (2004). *A Semantic Web primer*. MIT Press.

Barros, H. (2011). Steps, techniques, and technologies for the development of intelligent applications based on Semantic Web Services: A case study in e-learning systems. *Engineering Applications of Artificial Intelligence*, *24*(8). doi:10.1016/j.engappai.2011.05.007

Beckett, D. (2004). *RDF/XML syntax specification (revised).* W3C Recommendation 10th February 2004. Retrieved from http://www.w3.org/TR/rdf-syntax-grammar/

Berners-Lee, T., Hendler, J., & Lassila, O. (2001, May 17). The Semantic Web. *Scientific American*.

Bittencourt, E. C., Silva, M., & Soares, E. (2009). A computational model for developing semantic web-based educational systems. *Knowledge-Based Systems*, *22*, 302–315. doi:10.1016/j.knosys.2009.02.012

Bouzeghoub, A., Defude, B., Ammour, S., Duitama, J. F., & Lecocq, C. (2004). A RDF description model for manipulating learning objects. *Proceedings International Conference on Advanced Learning Technologies, IV,* Joensuu, ICALT, (pp. 81-85).

Brickley, D., & Guha, R. V. (2004). *RDF vocabulary description language 1.0: RDF schema*. W3C Recommendation 10th February 2004. Retrieved from http://www.w3.org/TR/rdf-schema/

Brusilovsky, P. (1999). Adaptive and intelligent technologies for web-based education. In C. Rollinger & C. Peylo (Eds.) *Künstliche Intelligenz Special Issue on Intelligent Systems and Teleteaching, 4*, 19-25.

Brusilovsky, P., & Miller, P. (2001). Course delivery systems for the virtual university. In Tschang, F. T., & Della Senta, T. (Eds.), *Access to knowledge: New information technologies and the emergence of the virtual university* (pp. 167–206). Amsterdam, The Netherlands: Elsevier Science and International Association of Universities.

Chen, N.-S., Kinshuk, Wei, C.-W., & Yang, S.J.H. (2008). Designing a self-contained group area network for ubiquitous learning. *Journal of Educational Technology & Society*, *11*(2), 16–26.

Cocea, M. (2006). *Assessment of motivation in online learning environments. Adaptive Hypermedia and Adaptive Web-based Systems, LNCS 4018*. Berlin, Germany: Springer-Verlag.

Dean, M., Schreiber, G., van Harmelen, F., Hendler, J., Horrocks, I., & McGuinness, D. L. … Stein, D. L. (2004). *OWL Web ontology language reference*. W3C Recommendation 10th February 2004. Retrieved from http://www.w3.org/TR/owl-ref/

Devedzic, V. (2004). Education and the Semantic Web. *International Journal of Artificial Intelligence in Education*, *14*(2), 39–65.

Devedzic, V. (2006). *IASTED International Conference on Artificial Intelligence and Applications, part of the 24th Multi-Conference on Applied Informatics*, Innsbruck, Austria, February 13-16, 2006 IASTED/ACTA Press 2006.

Educational Modelling Language (EML). (n.d.). *Homepage*. Retrieved from http://eml.ou.nl/eml-ou-nl.htm

Edutella Project. (n.d.). *Homepage*. Retrieved from http://edutella.jxta.org/

Fayed, G. (2006). E-learning model based on Semantic Web technology. *International Journal of Computing & Information Sciences*, *4*(2), 63–71.

Frigo, L. B., Cardoso, J., & Bittencourt, G. (2005). *Adaptive interaction in intelligent tutoring systems. Proceedings Methods/ Techniques in Web Based Education Systems, XXVI* (pp. 33–38). Salzburg: CIAH.

Graf, S., & List, B. (2005). An evaluation of open source e-learning platforms stressing adaptation issues. In P. Goodyear, D. G. Sampson, D. J.-T. Yang, Kinshuk, T. Okamoto, R. Hartley & N.-S. Chen (Eds.), *Proceedings of the 5th International Conference on Advanced Learning Technologies* (pp. 163-165). Los Alamitos, NM: IEEE Computer Science.

Graf, S., Yang, G., & Liu, T. C., & Kinshuk. (2009). Automatic, global and dynamic student modeling in a ubiquitous learning environment. *International Journal on Knowledge Management and E-Learning*, *1*(1), 18–35.

Grant, J., & Beckett, D. (2004). *RDF test cases*. W3C Recommendation 10th February 2004. Retrieved from http://www.w3.org/TR/rdf-testcases/

Hayes, P. (2004). *RDF semantics*. W3C Recommendation 10th February 2004. Retrieved from http://www.w3.org/TR/rdf-mt/

Heflin, J. (2004). *Web ontology language (OWL) use cases and requirements*. W3C Recommendation 10th February 2004. Retrieved from http://www.w3.org/TR/webont-req/

Ibrahim, Z., Dimitrova, V., & Boyle, R. (2005). A schema- based pedagogical agent to support children's conceptual understanding. *Proceedings International Conference on Artificial Intelligence in Education,* V, Amsterdam, AIED, (pp. 51-58).

IMS Global Learning Consortium. (n.d.). *Homepage*. Retrieved from http://www.imsglobal.org/

Karampiperis, P., & Sampson, D. (2004). Adaptive instructional planning using ontologies. In *Proceedings International Conference on Advanced Learning Technologies, IV*, Joensuu, ICALT, (pp. 126-130).

Klyne, G., & Carroll, J. (2004). *Resource description framework (RDF): Concepts and abstract syntax.* W3C Recommendation 10th February 2004. Retrieved from http://www.w3.org/TR/rdf-concepts/

Koivunen, M.-R., & Miller, E. (2001). W3C Semantic Web activity. *Proceedings of the Semantic Web Kick-off Seminar in Finland.* Retrieved from http://www.w3.org/2001/12/semweb-fin/w3csw

Lassila, O., & Swick, R. (1999). *Resource description framework (RDF) model and syntax specification*. W3C Recommendation, 22nd February 1999. Retrieved from http://www.w3.org/TR/1999/REC-rdf-syntax-19990222

Learning Object Metadata (LOM). (n.d.). *Homepage*. Retrieved from http://ltsc.ieee.org/wg12/

Lu, C. H., Wu, S. H., Tu, L. Y., & Hsu, W. L. (2004). The design of an intelligent tutoring system based on the ontology of procedural knowledge. In *Proceedings International Conference on Advanced Learning Technologies, IV,* Joensuu, ICALT, (pp. 525-530).

Manola, F., & Miller, E. (2004). *RDF primer*. W3C Recommendation 10th February 2004. Retrieved from http://www.w3.org/TR/rdf-primer/

Matthews, B. (2005). *Semantic Web technologies*. CCLRC Rutherford Appleton Laboratory, JISC Technology and Standards Watch. Retrieved from http://www.jisc.ac.uk/uploaded_documents/jisctsw_05_02bpdf.pdf

Noy, N. F., & Mcguinness, D. L. (2001). *Ontology development 101: A guide to creating your first ontology.* Retrieved from http://protege.stanford.edu/publications/ ontology_development/ ontology101.pdf

Passin, T. B. (2004). *Explorer's guide to the Semantic Web*. USA: Manning Publications Co.

Protégé. (2006). *The Protégé ontology editor and knowledge acquisition system*. Retrieved from http://Protege.Stanford.Edu

RDF Core Working Group. (n.d.). *Homepage*. Retrieved from http://www.w3.org/2001/sw/RDFCore/

Reimann, P., Yacef, K., & Kay, J. (2011). Analyzing collaborative interactions with data mining methods for the benefit of learning. In Puntambekar, S., Hmelo-Silver, C., & Erkens, G. (Eds.), *Analyzing interactions in CSCL: Methodology, approaches and issues* (pp. 161–185). Springer. doi:10.1007/978-1-4419-7710-6_8

Santos, O. C., Gaudioso, E., Barrera, C., & Boticario, J. G. (2003). An adaptive elearning platform. In *Proceedings of mICTE Multimedia, Information and Communication Technologies*. Badajoz, Spain: ALFANET.

Simon, B., Dolog, P., Miklos, Z., Olmeda, D., & Sintek, M. (2004). Conceptualizing smart spaces for learning. *Journal of Interactive Media in Education, Special Issue on the Educational Semantic Web*. Retrieved from http://www-jime.open.ac.uk/jime/article/viewArticle/78

Smith, M. K., McGuinness, D., Volz, R., & Welty, C. (2004). *OWL Web ontology language guide*. W3C Recommendation 10th February 2004. Retrieved from http://www.w3.org/TR/owl-guide/

Stutt, A., & Motta, E. (2004). Semantic Webs for learning: A vision and its realization. *Proceedings of EKAW 2004, LNCS 3257*, (pp.132-143). Springer-Verlag.

Vouk, M. A., Bitzer, D., & Klevans, R. (1999). Workflow and end-user quality of service issues in web-based education. *IEEE Transactions on Knowledge and Data Engineering*, *11*(4). doi:10.1109/69.790839

Chapter 16
Outlier Detection in Logistic Regression

A. A. M. Nurunnabi
SLG, University of Rajshahi, Bangladesh

A. B. M. S. Ali
CQUniversity, Australia

A. H. M. Rahmatullah Imon
Ball State University, USA

Mohammed Nasser
University of Rajshahi, Bangladesh

ABSTRACT

The use of logistic regression, its modelling and decision making from the estimated model and subsequent analysis has been drawn a great deal of attention since its inception. The current use of logistic regression methods includes epidemiology, biomedical research, criminology, ecology, engineering, pattern recognition, machine learning, wildlife biology, linguistics, business and finance, et cetera. Logistic regression diagnostics have attracted both theoreticians and practitioners in recent years. Detection and handling of outliers is considered as an important task in the data modelling domain, because the presence of outliers often misleads the modelling performances. Traditionally logistic regression models were used to fit data obtained under experimental conditions. But in recent years, it is an important issue to measure the outliers scale before putting the data as a logistic model input. It requires a higher mathematical level than most of the other material that steps backward to its study and application in spite of its inevitability. This chapter presents several diagnostic aspects and methods in logistic regression. Like linear regression, estimates of the logistic regression are sensitive to the unusual observations: outliers, high leverage, and influential observations. Numerical examples and analysis are presented to demonstrate the most recent outlier diagnostic methods using data sets from medical domain.

DOI: 10.4018/978-1-4666-1830-5.ch016

INTRODUCTION

The logistic regression model has found wide range of usage in various fields. Over the last few years, use of logistic regression has been exploded. Naturally, its use spurs the need to have diagnostic tools to justify the appropriateness of the model. Hosmer and Lemeshow (2000) pointed, "In recent years diagnostics has become an essential part of logistic regression". When analysing a data set some observations are often occurred that are somehow different from the majority, simply such observations are treated as the outliers. Sometimes the outlying observations are not incorrect rather they are made under exceptional circumstances, or they belong to other population(s). We often observe that outliers greatly affect the covariate pattern and consequently their presence can mislead our interpretation. So we need to identify such observations and study their impact on the model (Imon and Hadi, 2008). Although a rich pool of literature (Pregibon, 1981; Hosmer and Lemeshow, 2000; Ryan, 1997) exists for studying outlier diagnostics, the use of the logistic regression modelling especially for the detection of multiple outliers is still a major concern to the researchers and in need to the practitioners. It is now evident that most of the popular diagnostic methods based on single-case deletion approach can mislead the analysis in the presence of multiple outliers and /or influential cases because of the well-known masking and/or swamping problem (see Atkinson, 1986). As remedy to masking and swamping effects, the group-deletion approach is used in regression diagnostics. Group-deletion technique helps us to reduce the maximum disturbance by deleting the suspect group of influential cases at a time (see Hadi and Simonoff, 1993). It helps to make the data more homogeneous after the group-deletion (Nurunnabi *et al.*, 2011). Since most of the existing diagnostics approaches are originated from the ideas in linear regression, this chapter states the basic ideas in linear regression as well as logistic regression where it is relevant, and for the benefit of the reader.

In this chapter, we introduce logistic regression, the nature and general ideas of outliers and how we can find out outliers, without getting into the deep of the subject from the mathematical and/ or statistical point of view. We concentrate here to give the general understanding and to show the importance of outlier detection prior decision making and model building for the researchers in different fields. The rest of the chapter is structured as follows. Section 2 makes a basic discussion about logistic regression and different types of outliers. In Section 3, we introduce several recent and effective outlier detection methods followed by the numerical examples and analysis in section 4. Section 5 concludes the chapter with findings and some future issues of outlier detection in Logistic regression.

LOGISTIC REGRESSION MODEL FORMULATION

Regression analysis deals how the values of the response (dependent variable) change with the change of one or more explanatory (independent) variables. It is appealing because it provides a conceptually simple method for investigating functional relationship among variables (Chatterjee and Hadi, 2006). In any regression problem the key quantity is the mean value of the outcome (dependent or response) variable, given the value of the explanatory (independent) variable(s), $E(Y|X)$. In linear regression, we assume that this mean is expressed as an equation linear in X (or some transformations of X or Y) such as

$$E(Y / X) = \beta_0 + \beta_1 X_1 + \dots + \beta_p X_p . \quad (1)$$

Hence $Y = \beta_0 + \beta_1 X_1 + \dots + \beta_p X_p + \varepsilon$, (2)

$$= X\beta + \varepsilon = E(Y / X) + \varepsilon , \quad (3)$$

where X is an $n \times k$ matrix containing the data for each case with $k = p + 1$, Y is an $n \times 1$ vector of response, $\beta^T = (\beta_0, \beta_1, ..., \beta_p)$ is the vector of regression parameters and ε is the error vector. Main difference between linear regression and logistic regression is that the outcome (response) variable is categorical (binary, ordinal or nominal). In case of logistic regression, we use the quantity $\pi(X) = E(Y / X)$ to represent the conditional mean of Y given X. The specific form of the logistic regression model is

$$\pi(X) = \frac{e^{\beta_0 + \beta_1 X_1 + ... + \beta_p X_p}}{1 + e^{\beta_0 + \beta_1 X_1 + ... + \beta_p X_p}} \; ; \; 0 \leq \pi(X) \leq 1 \tag{4}$$

$$= \frac{\exp(Z)}{1 + \exp(Z)}, \tag{5}$$

where $Z = X\beta$. This form gives an *S*-curve configuration. The well-known 'Logit' transformation in terms of $\pi(X)$ is

$$g(X) = \ln\left[\frac{\pi(X)}{1 - \pi(X)}\right] = \beta_0 + \beta_1 X_1 + ... + \beta_p X_p \tag{6}$$

Hence, in logistic regression, the model in Equation (3) stands as

$$Y = \pi(X) + \varepsilon. \tag{7}$$

The unobserved error term

$$\varepsilon = \begin{cases} 1 - \pi(X) & w.p. \quad \pi(X); if \quad y = 1 \\ -\pi(X) & w.p. \quad 1 - \pi(X); if \quad y = 0 \end{cases} \tag{8}$$

has a distribution with mean zero and variance equal to $\pi(X)[1 - \pi(X)]$. Here ε violates most of the least squares assumptions and hence the Maximum Likelihood Estimation (MLE) method based on Iterative Reweighed Least Squares (IRLS) is used to estimate the parameters and fit the model (see Ryan, 1997). Here, we would logically let $y_i = 0$ if the *i*-th unit does not have the characteristic and $y_i = 1$ if the *i*-th unit does possess the characteristic. The quantity $\pi(x_i) = \pi_i$ is known as the probability for the *i*-th factor/covariate. The model in Equation (5) satisfies the requirement $0 \leq \pi_i \leq 1$. The fitted values for the logistic regression models are $\widehat{\pi}(x_i)$, the value of that is computed using $\widehat{\beta}$ from the MLE method.

Assumptions in Logistic Regression

The following assumptions are considered for performing logistic regression:

1. The model is correctly specified, *i.e.,*
    a. The true conditional probabilities are logistic functions of the independent variables.
    b. No important variable is omitted.
    c. No extraneous variable is included, and
    d. The independent variables are measured without errors.
2. Cases are independent.
3. The independent variables are not linear combination of each other. Perfect multicolinearity makes estimation impossible, while strong multicolinearity makes estimation imprecise.

Notion of Outliers

In general outliers are surprising or unusual observations in statistics. Observations are unusual or outliers in the sense that they are exceptional, they have extra role on model building process, or they may come from different population(s) and do not follow the pattern of the majority of the data. There are numerous definitions of outlier in statistics, machine learning and data mining literatures (Angiulli *et al.*, 2006; Breiman *et al.*, 1977; Beuning *et al.*, 2000; Knorr *et al.*, 2000; Terrell and Scott, 1992). What are outliers and what are the problems of outliers? A good answer is found in (Barnett and Lewis, 1995), "In almost every true series of observations, some are found, which differ so much from the others as to indicate some abnormal source of error not contemplated in the theoretical discussions, and the introduction of which into the investigations can only serve … to perplex and mislead the inquirer". In the context of scale parameter, we mean outlier is that is much larger than the bulk of the observations that it stands out, and that there is doubt about it being from the proposed model. In regression analysis, outlying observations are categorized into three: outliers, high leverage points and influential observations and are found by (i) the deviation in the space of explanatory variable(s); deviated points in *X*-direction called leverage points, (ii) the change in the direction of response (*Y*) variable (outlier in *Y*-direction but not a leverage point is called vertical outlier) (iii) the other is deviated in both the directions (*X* and *Y*). Influential observation is one which either individual or together with several other observations has a demonstrably larger impact on the calculated values of various estimates (coefficients, standard errors, *t*-values, etc) than is the case for most of the other observations (Belsley *et al.*, 1980). In case of binomial logistic regression, we observe outlier, high-leverage point or influential observation may occur mostly a) as the altercation (misclassification) between the binary (0, 1) responses, b) by meaningful deviations (we see also low leverage) in explanatory variables, and c) as the disagreement in response and explanatory variables together. All those cause the break of the normal pattern (*S*-curve configuration) of the majority data.

LOGISTIC REGRESSION DIAGNOSTICS

Accoding to Fox (1993), "Regression diagnostics are techniques for exploring problems that compromise a regression analysis and for determining whether certain assumptions appear reasonable". We use the term 'regression diagnostics' to serve the purpose for outlier detection in a dataset. Stahel and Weisberg (1991) pointed, 'Rather than modifying the fitting method, diagnostics condition on the fit using standard methods to attempt to diagnose incorrect assumptions, allowing the analyst to modify them and refit under the new set of assumptions'. Regression diagnostics is a combination of graphical and numerical methods. It is designed to detect and delete/refit (if necessary) the outliers first and then to fit the good data by classical methods. One of the most important issues of studying a logistic regression model is the estimation of parameters in presence of unusual observations (Nurunnabi *et al.*, 2010). Pregibon (1981) mentioned, "The most usual method for estimating the parameters in logistic regression is MLE, though the method has good optimality properties in ideal settings, but is extremely sensitive to 'bad' (bad from the point of view of outlying response (*Y*) and from the point of view of extreme points in the design space (*X*)) data". Two main causes for logistic regression diagnostics are: MLE estimation method for parameter estimation in logistic regression is very sensitive to unusual observations and in presence of influential observations, implicit assumption (all observations are equally reliable and should have an equal role in determining the regression equation and the subsequent conclusions (Chatterjee and Hadi, 1988)) is broken down as like as in linear regression.

A large body of literature is available (Belsley *et al.*, 1980; Cook and Weisberg, 1982; Chatterjee and Hadi, 1988; Hosmer and Lemeshow, 2000; Nurunnabi *et al.*, 2010; Nurunnabi *et al.*, 2011; Pregibon, 1981; Rousseeuw and Leroy,

2003; Ryan, 1997) for the identification of outliers. Pregibon (1981) provided the foundation of the theoretical works on logistic regression diagnostics that was extended from the idea of linear regression. Besides the formal diagnostic procedures, a number of different types of plotting procedures have been suggested for use of diagnostics in logistic regression (Hosmer and Lemeshow, 2000).

Likewise the linear regression, detection techniques for unusual observations in logistic regression are classified into three categories:

1. Outliers identification,
2. High leverage points identification, and
3. Influential observations identification.

Pregibon mentioned (1981), "For the logistic regression, the basic building blocks for the identification of outlying and influential points will again be a residual vector and a projection matrix". Hosmer and lemeshow (2000) pointed out that the key quantities for the logistic regression diagnostics, as in linear regression, are the components of the 'residual sum-of-squares' and the deviance for logistic regression. Both of them play the same role that the residual sum of squares plays in linear regression.

Identification of Outliers

Generally, outliers are identified by using residuals or some functions of the residuals. In linear regression, the *i*-th residual is defined as the difference between the observed and fitted value $(y_i - \hat{y}_i)$. Similarly, in logistic regression, the *i*-th residual is defined as

$$\hat{\varepsilon}_i = y_i - \hat{\pi}_i,\ i = 1,2,...,n. \tag{9}$$

Sometimes we also suppose that there are *j* distinct values of observed *x*. We denote the number of cases $x = x_j$ by m_j $(j = 1,2,...,j)$. In this situation, we define the *j*-th residual as

$$\hat{\varepsilon}_j = y_j - m_j\hat{\pi}_j,\ j = 1,2,...,n. \tag{10}$$

For the simplicity, we assume in this chapter, $m_j = 1$ and we get back the Equation (9). The observations possessing large residuals are suspect outliers. It is known that the un-scaled residuals are not readily applicable in detecting outliers. Some scaled residuals that are commonly used in diagnostics for the identification of outliers are introduced here. In logistic regression model, residuals can be defined on several scales. The two most useful are the components of chi-square (Pearson's residual) and the components of deviance. In logistic regression, we have Bernoulli errors and as a result the error variance is a function of the conditional mean, *i.e.*,

$$Var(y_i / x_i) = v_i = \hat{\pi}_i(1 - \hat{\pi}_i),\ i = 1,2,...,n. \tag{11}$$

Now, the Pearson residual for the *i*-th factor can be defined as

$$r_i = \frac{y_i - \hat{\pi}_i}{\sqrt{v_i}},\ i = 1, 2, \ldots, n. \tag{12}$$

According to Ryan (1997), we call an observation as an outlier if the corresponding $|r_i| \geq 3$. Pregibon (1981) derived a linear approximation to the fitted values, which yields a hat matrix for logistic regression

$$H = V^{1/2}X(X^TVX)^{-1}X^TV^{1/2}, \tag{13}$$

where V is the diagonal matrix with general elements v_i. Now, the above Equation (9) holds

$$\hat{\varepsilon}_i = y_i - \hat{\pi}_i \approx (1 - h_{ii})y_i,\ i = 1, 2, \ldots, n, \tag{14}$$

and the variance of the residual is

$$V(\hat{\varepsilon}_i) = v_i(1 - h_{ii}),\ i = 1, 2, \ldots, n, \tag{15}$$

which suggests that the Pearson residuals do not have variance equal to 1. For this reason we could use the standardized Pearson residual given by

$$r_{si} = \frac{y_i - \hat{\pi}_i}{\sqrt{v_i\left(1 - h_{ii}\right)}},\ i = 1, 2, \ldots, n. \tag{16}$$

The quantities r_i, r_{si} and h_{ii} (*i*-th diagonal element of leverage/projection matrix) are useful for detecting extreme points. Standardized Pearson's residual is suggested to use of single outlier identification and the *i*-th observation is termed as outlier if $\left|r_{si}\right| \geq 3$ in Equation (16). But the reality is; no guarantee that the data set will contain just a single outlier. Hampel *et al.* (1986) mentioned, "A routine data set may contain about 10% outliers in it". A group of outliers may cause of masking and swamping and as a result distort the fitting of a model in such a way that outliers may have artificially very small residuals so that they may appear as inliers. Hadi and Simonoff, (1993) mentioned that masking occurs when an outlying subset goes undetected because of the presence of another, usually adjacent, subset. Swamping occurs when good observations are incorrectly identified as outliers because of the presence of another, usually remote, subset of observations. A good number of diagnostic procedures have been suggested to identify multiple outliers in linear regression, but this issue is not as much addressed in logistic regression. A successful multiple outlier detection approach is group-deletion approach (Hadi and Simonoff, 1993). The basic principle of group-deletion diagnostic technique is to delete the group of suspect unusual cases (outliers, high-leverage points and influential observations) first, and then estimate the parameters of the regression model based on the remaining set of observations and later use these parameters to prepare the appropriate diagnostic measures. Sometimes graphical display like index plot, scatter plot, and character plot of explanatory and response variables could give us some ideas about the suspect unusual observations, but these plots are not useful for higher dimension of regressors. Some researchers suggest using robust regression techniques (e.g., the Least Median of Squares (LMS) or Least Trimmed of Squares (LTS), Reweighted Least Squares (RLS) (see Rousseeuw and Leroy, 2003) and some suggest to use Block Adaptive Computationally-effective Outlier Nominator (BACON) (Billor *et al.*, 2000) or Best Omitted from the Ordinary Least Squares (BOFOLS) (Davies *et al.*, 2004) for finding the group of suspect unusual observations. Assume that the number of suspect cases in a data set is *d* and a set of suspect cases that should be deleted is *D* and a set of cases 'remaining' in the analysis is *R*. Hence *R* contains (*n-d*) cases after the *d* cases are deleted. Without loss of generality, we can arrange the suspect cases as the last *d* rows of *X*, *Y* and *V* (variance-covariance matrix) matrices

$$X = \begin{bmatrix} X_R \\ X_D \end{bmatrix} Y = \begin{bmatrix} Y_R \\ Y_D \end{bmatrix} V = \begin{bmatrix} V_R & 0 \\ 0 & V_D \end{bmatrix}.$$

It is now possible to calculate the $\hat{\beta}_{(R)}$ based on the remaining set of observation. The estimates $h_{ii(R)}$, $v_{i(R)}$ and $\hat{\pi}_{i(R)}$ and are calculated according to the Equations (18), (19) and (20) respectively.

We mention here one of the recent group-deletion outlier detection methods, the Generalized Standardized Pearson Residual (GSPR) suggested by Imon and Hadi (2008), defined as

$$r_{si(R)} = \begin{cases} \dfrac{y_i - \hat{\pi}_{i(R)}}{v_{i(R)}(1 - h_{ii(R)})} & for \quad i \in R, \\ \dfrac{y_i - \hat{\pi}_{i(R)}}{v_{i(R)}(1 + h_{ii(R)})} & for \quad i \in D, \end{cases} \tag{17}$$

where

$$h_{ii(R)} = \hat{\pi}_{i(R)}(1 - \hat{\pi}_{i(R)})x_i^T \left(X_R^T V_R X_R\right)^{-1} x_i, \quad i = 1, 2, \ldots, n, \tag{18}$$

and

$$\hat{v}_{i(R)} = \hat{\pi}_{i(R)}(1 - \hat{\pi}_{i(R)}). \tag{19}$$

To get the *i*-th estimated value $\hat{\pi}_{i(R)}$ of the response variable a group of observations D is omitted using a group deletion approach (see Imon and Hadi, 2008), and the fitted values for the entire logistic regression model based on R (group of remaining observations) set are defined as

$$\hat{\pi}_{i(R)} = \frac{\exp\left(x_i^T \hat{\beta}_{(R)}\right)}{1 + \exp\left(x_i^T \hat{\beta}_{(R)}\right)}, \quad i = 1, 2, \ldots, n, \tag{20}$$

where $\hat{\beta}_{(R)}$ is the vector of estimated parameters based on the remaining set (R) of observations. Observations corresponding to the cases $\left|r_{si(R)}\right| > 3$ are considered as outliers.

Identification of High Leverage Points

We have mentioned that the set observations that are influential in the design space-X is known as high-leverage points. These are the quantities that provide the fitted values as the projection of the outcome variable into the covariate space. So it is really important to know which observations in the X-space are exerting too much influence on covariates and we call these observations high leverage points. According to Hocking and Pendleton (1983), "High-leverage points... are those for which the input vector x_i is, in some sense, far from the rest of the data". Hadi (1992) pointed that in the presence of a high-leverage point the information matrix may break down and hence the observations may not have the appropriate leverages. Much work has been done to identify high-leverage points in linear regression (e.g., Hoaglin and Welsh, 1978; Vellman and Welsch, 1981; Huber, 1981; Hadi, 1992).

For linear regression the well-known measure of leverage is given by the diagonal elements of the weight (or hat or leverage) matrix

$$W = X\left(X^T X\right)^{-1} X^T \tag{21}$$

For a perfect balanced design, the ith diagonal element of W can be written as

$$w_i = \frac{1}{n} + \frac{\left(x_{i1} - \bar{x}_{.1}\right)^2}{\sum\left(x_{i1} - \bar{x}_{.1}\right)^2} + \frac{\left(x_{i2} - \bar{x}_{.2}\right)^2}{\sum\left(x_{i2} - \bar{x}_{.2}\right)^2} + \ldots + \frac{\left(x_{ip} - \bar{x}_{.p}\right)^2}{\sum\left(x_{ip} - \bar{x}_{.p}\right)^2} \tag{22}$$

Here w_i is the Euclidean distance between the *i*th vector and the center of gravity ($1/n$, $\bar{x}_{.1}$, $\bar{x}_{.2}$, ..., $\bar{x}_{.p}$) for all vectors. Thus w_i's indicate how much the corresponding vector deviate from the bulk of the values of the explanatory variable. The larger the value of w_i the more extreme is the corresponding vector of observations of the explanatory variable. We have already seen in Equation (13) that a linear approximation to the fitted values suggested by Pregibon (1981) helps us to obtain a hat matrix H for a logistic regression model as

$$H = V^{1/2} X\left(X^T V X\right)^{-1} X^T V^{1/2}$$

Now whatever be the choice of the leverage matrix

$$\sum_{i=1}^{n} w_i = \text{Trace}(W) = k = \text{Trace}(H) = \sum_{i=1}^{n} h_i \tag{23}$$

where $k = p + 1$. Since the average value of h_i is k/n, Hoaglin and Welsch (1978) consider observations unusual when h_i exceeds $2k/n$ which is also known as *twice-the-mean* (2M) rule. Vellman and Welsch (1981) suggest considering the *thrice-the-mean* (3M) rule where h_i is considered as large when it exceeds $3k/n$. Other popular methods for the detection of high leverage points are the method suggested by Huber (1981), the method based on Mahalanobis distance (see Rousseeuw and Leroy, 1987) and the method based on potentials as suggested by Hadi (1992).

Although the h_i values as defined in (13) are very popular measures of leverages and observations possessing large h_i values are known as high leverage points, but they have potential disadvantages as well. In linear regression the leverage value is a monotonic increasing function of the distance of a covariance pattern from the mean. But Hosmer and Lemeshow (2000) pointed out that in logistic regression the most extreme points in the covariate space may not necessarily have high leverage if its weight is very small. For a logistic regression model the i-th leverage value is

$$h_i = \hat{\pi}_i(1 - \hat{\pi}_i)x_i^T(X^T VX)^{-1}x_i = v_i b_i, \quad i = 1, 2, \ldots, n \tag{24}$$

where

$$b_i = x_i^T \left(X^T VX\right)^{-1} x_i, \; i = 1, 2, \ldots, n. \tag{25}$$

If we look at the leverage value as defined in Equation (24), we will observe that a quantity that does increase with the distance from the mean (DM) is b_i as defined in Equation (25). But to compute the leverage value this quantity is multiplied by another quantity $\hat{\pi}_i(1-\hat{\pi}_i)$. For an extreme data point in the X-space it is expected that the quantity $\hat{\pi}_i$ should be very close to 0 or 1 which automatically implies that the product $\hat{\pi}_i(1-\hat{\pi}_i)$ should be very close to 0. Hence even if the quantity b_i is large, its corresponding h_i could be very small making the procedure of identifying high leverage points on the magnitude of h_i very cumbersome. Hosmer and Lemeshow (2000) suggest focusing on b_i if we are only interested in measuring the distance, however, they did not suggest any identification method based on these quantities. Imon (2006) suggested that it is not easy to derive a theoretical distribution of b_i, but it does not make any problem to obtain a suitable confidence bound type cut-off point for them. He considers b_i to be large if

$$b_i > \text{Median}(b_i) + 3\,\text{MAD}(b_i) \tag{26}$$

This type of form, analogous to a confidence bound for a location parameter, which was first introduced by Hadi (1992) in regression diagnostics and then used by many others. Since the above measures are based on single-case deletion approach, it is highly likely that they might be affected by masking and/or swamping phenomena and a group deletion version of leverage measure is required for logistic regression.

Identification of Influential Observations

Draper and John (1981) pointed out that observation with the largest residual was not the most influential, however, deletion of observation possessing a small residual, had a marked effect on the parameter estimates. Pregibon (1981) mentioned, "Residuals, standardized residuals, and leverage values are useful for detecting extreme points, but not for assessing their impact on various aspects of the fit ". To assess the impacts on the fit, we draw our attention to the identification of influential cases. Welsh (1982) pointed out that neither the leverage nor the Studentized residual alone will usually be sufficient to identify the influential cases. Andrews and Pregibon (1978) presented some examples where outlying observations have little influence on the estimates and the existence of outliers that do not matter. High-leverage points likely to be influential but it is also observed that as with outliers, high-leverage points need not be influential, and influential observations are not necessarily high-leverage points (see Chatterjee and Hadi, 1986).

Among a good number of diagnostic statistics in linear regression, Cook's distance (Cook 1977, 1979), and Difference in Fits (DFFITS) (Belsley *et al*, 1980), are the most popular two influence statistics to the practitioners. We may define the above statistics for logistic regression as follows. The *i*-th Cook's distance is

$$CD_i = \frac{\left(\hat{\beta}^{(-i)} - \hat{\beta}\right)^T (X^T V X)\left(\hat{\beta}^{(-i)} - \hat{\beta}\right)}{k v_i}, \quad i = 1,2,\ldots,n, \tag{27}$$

where $\hat{\beta}^{(-i)}$ is the estimated parameter of β with the *i*-th observation deleted. The *i*-th Cook's distance can be re-expressed in terms of the *i*-th standardized Pearson residual and leverage value as

$$CD_i = \frac{1}{k} r_{si}^2 \left(\frac{h_{ii}}{1 - h_{ii}}\right), \quad i = 1,2,\ldots,n. \tag{28}$$

Difference in fits is defined for logistic regression as

$$DFFITS_i = \frac{\hat{y}_i - \hat{y}_i^{(-i)}}{v_i^{(-i)} \sqrt{(1 - h_{ii})}}, \quad i = 1,2,\ldots,n, \tag{29}$$

where $\hat{y}_i^{(-i)}$ and $v_i^{(-i)}$ the *i*-th fitted response and the estimated standard error are respectively with the *i*-th observation deleted. Difference in fits values can be expressed in terms of standardized Pearson residuals and leverage values as

$$DFFITS_i = r_{si} \sqrt{\frac{h_{ii}}{(1 - h_{ii})} \frac{v_i}{v_i^{(-i)}}}, \quad i = 1,2,\ldots,n. \tag{30}$$

Observation possessing *DFFITS* value grater than $3\sqrt{k / n}$ is termed as an influential observation. Using Equations (28) and (30), it is easy to show the relationship between CD and DFFITS

$$\mathrm{CD}_i = \frac{v_i^{(-i)^2}}{k v_i^2} \mathrm{DFFITS}_i^2, \quad i = 1,2,\ldots,n. \tag{31}$$

Difference in fits is considered as a better choice (Imon, 2005) because; it is more informative about variance term than CD and it calculates simultaneous effect on both the parameter estimates and the estimate of variance. The above two well-known influence statistics are based on the single-case deletion approach and are inefficient when masking and/or swamping occur. Therefore, we need influence diagnostic measure that is free from these phenomena. Cook and Weisberg (1982) suggested generalized Cook's distance in this regard. This measure is defined only for the deletion of an influential group and consequently can not be applied for the identification of the influential cases for the entire data set.

Nurunnabi *et al.* (2010) introduced a group-deletion influence measure in logistic regression to cope with the problem of masking and swamping, and applied for the whole data set. They used group-deletion version of the residuals (Imon and Hadi, 2008) and leverage values (Nurunnabi *et al.*, 2010) both together to get their influence statistic. They developed Generalized Difference in Fits (GDFFITS) in logistic regression for the identification of influential cases. Developed statistic is used for the entire data set and defined as

$$GDFFITS_i = \begin{cases} \dfrac{\hat{y}_{i(R)} - \hat{y}_{i(R\text{-}i)}}{\sqrt{v_{i(R)} h_{ii(R)}}} & for \quad i\hat{I}R, \\ \dfrac{\hat{y}_{i(R+i)} - \hat{y}_{i(R)}}{\sqrt{v_{ii(R)} h_{ii(R+i)}}} & for \quad i\hat{I}D, \end{cases} \tag{32}$$

where $h_{ii(R)}$ and $v_{i(R)}$ are in Equations (18) and (19) respectively, and

$$h_{ii(R+i)} = \frac{h_{ii(R)}}{1 + h_{ii(R)}}. \tag{33}$$

Using Equations (17) and (32) our proposed GDFFITS quantities can be re-expressed in terms of GSPR and Generalized Weight (GW) as

$$GDFFITS_i = r_{si(R)} \sqrt{h^*_{ii(R)}}, \; i = 1, 2, \ldots, n, \tag{34}$$

where GW (Nurunnabi et al., 2010) was developed as a group-deleted version of weights, denoted by $h^*_{ii(R)}$ and defined as

$$h^*_{ii(R)} = \begin{cases} \dfrac{h_{ii(R)}}{1 - h_{ii(R)}} & \text{for} \quad i \in R, \\ \dfrac{h_{ii(R)}}{1 + h_{ii(R)}} & \text{for} \quad i \in D. \end{cases} \tag{35}$$

Here $h_{ii(R)}$ is similar as the quantities defined in Equation (18) and is derived after the deletion of the suspect cases. We suggest the *i*-th observations to be influential if

$$|\text{GDFFITS}_i| \geq c\sqrt{k / (n - d)}, \; i = 1, 2, \ldots, n. \tag{36}$$

We choose the value of *c*, a suitable constant between 2 and 3 (Hadi, 1992; Imon, 2005). Nurunnabi *et al.*, (2010) pointed out that aalthough the expressions for the above diagnostics are available for any arbitrary set of deleted cases, *D*, the choice of such a set is very important since the omission of this group determines the GDFFITS diagnostics for the whole set. For the identification of influential observations we can use the rule in Equation (36) and finally select 3 for the value of *c*, i. e., the *i*-th observation having

$$|\text{GDFFITS}_i| \geq 3\sqrt{k / (n - d)}, \; i = 1, 2, \ldots, n \tag{37}$$

to be declared as an influential observation.

EXAMPLES

In this section we consider few examples from medical domain to investigate the usefulness of the outlier diagnostic methods for the identification of single and multiple outlying and influential observations in logistic regression.

Brown Data

We first consider the Brown data set given in (Brown, 1980). The original objective of the author was to see whether an elevated level of acid phosphates (A.P.) in the blood serum would be of value for predicting whether or not prostate cancer patients also had lymph node involvement (L.N.I). The data set additionally contains data on the four more commonly used regressors, but we use here only A.P. in illustrating simple logistic regression with 53 cases. The observations from 53 patients are given in Table 1. The response variable is L.N.I. with indications of its presence as 1 and 0 indicates the absence of L.N.I. Although the scatter plot (*X*-*Y*) in simple logistic regression is of limited value in terms of visualization, sometimes such a plot can carry useful prior knowledge. Figure 1 (a) shows meaningful deviation of the 24th observation from the rest of the data. There is clearly an outlier (AP=187) among the patients without nodal involvement. And the data clearly overlap with the observation. The first study (Brown, 1980) showed that the 24th observation is an outlier.

We apply all single-case diagnostic measures for the identification of unusual cases if any. Table 2 presents standardized Pearson residual, leverage value (bi), and CD and DFFITS for this data and the results show that observation number 24 is an outlier, high-leverage and influential observation respectively. It is observed that the leverage measure swamps three more cases as high-leverage points. We observe the same thing from the Index plots in Figure 1.

Imon and Hadi's Modified Brown Data

It is reported from first example that the original Brown data contain 53 patients with one unusual (outlying) observation (case 24). This data set was modified by (Imon and Hadi, 2008) who put two more outliers (cases 54 and 55) with potentially high leverages (*X* = 200 and 220) so that they may be considered as influential observations. This modified data is presented also in Table 1 just by adding the last two cases with the same characteristics and variables.

The scatter plot of L.N.I. against acid phosphates (Figure 2) clearly shows that observations 24, 54 and 55 may severely distort the covariate pattern and consequently the S-curve configuration. They may be considered as outliers and high leverage points at the same time and thus should produce very high influences. Table 3 presents diagnostics for the Imon and Hadi's modified

Table 1. Data (1-53) from Brown (1980)

Index	LNI	AP	Index	LNI	AP	Index	LNI	AP	Index	LNI	AP
1	0	48	15	0	47	29	0	50	43	1	81
2	0	56	16	0	49	30	0	40	44	1	76
3	0	50	17	0	50	31	0	55	45	1	70
4	0	52	18	0	78	32	0	59	46	1	78
5	0	50	19	0	83	33	1	48	47	1	70
6	0	49	20	0	98	34	1	51	48	1	67
7	0	46	21	0	52	35	1	49	49	1	82
8	0	62	22	0	75	36	0	48	50	1	67
9	1	56	23	1	99	37	0	63	51	1	72
10	0	55	**24**	**0**	**187**	38	0	102	52	1	89
11	0	62	25	1	136	39	0	76	53	1	126
12	0	71	26	1	82	40	0	95	**54**	**0**	**200**
13	0	65	27	0	40	41	0	66	**55**	**0**	**220**
14	1	67	28	0	50	42	1	84			

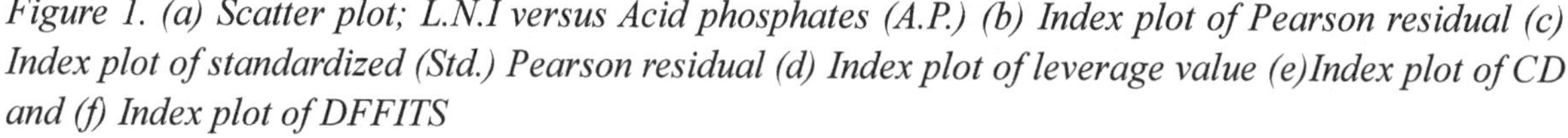

Figure 1. (a) Scatter plot; L.N.I versus Acid phosphates (A.P.) (b) Index plot of Pearson residual (c) Index plot of standardized (Std.) Pearson residual (d) Index plot of leverage value (e)Index plot of CD and (f) Index plot of DFFITS

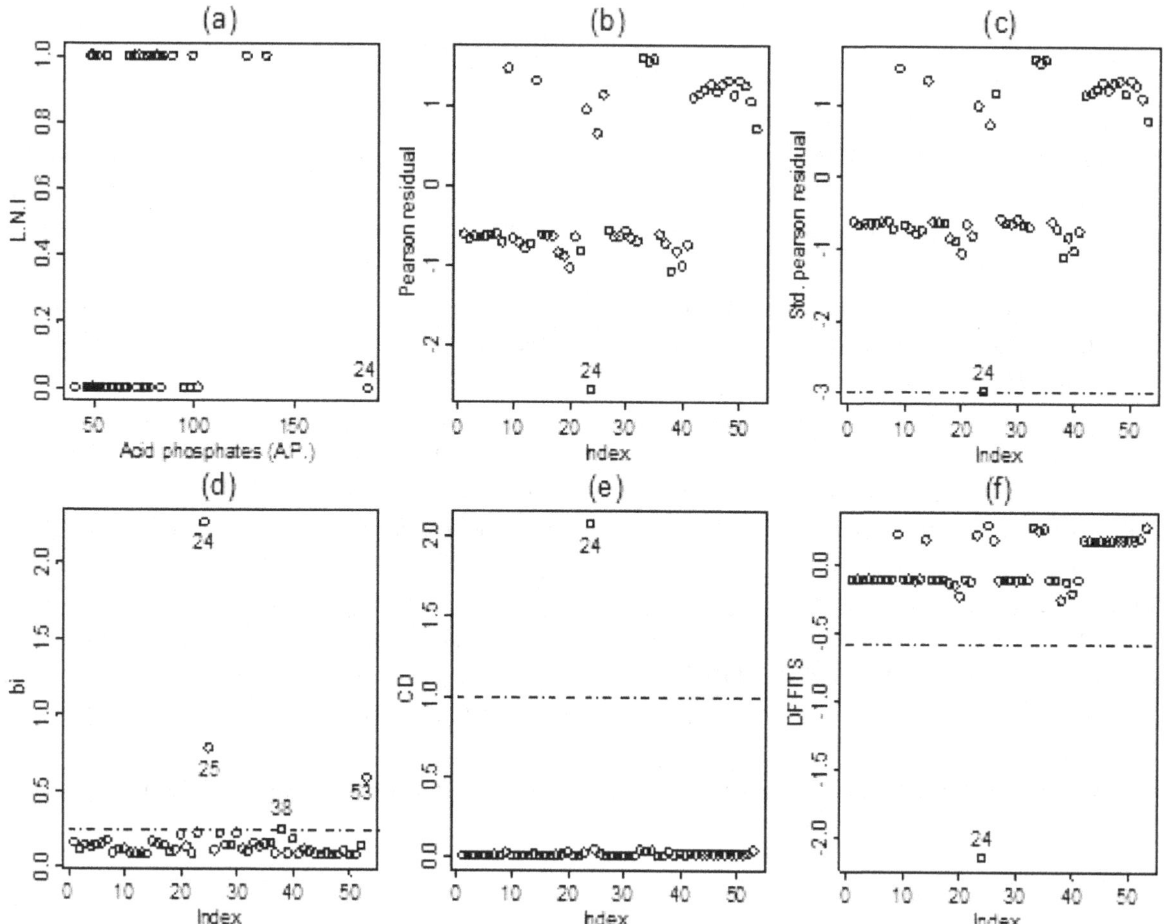

Brown data. We observe from this table that the most commonly used single-case deletion diagnostic methods fail to identify the unusual cases properly. Pearson and standardized Pearson residual both totally fail to identify any of the outlying cases. The Cook's distance, using 1 as the cut-off value, fails to identify even a single influential observation although the values for the cases 24, 54 and 55 are substantially larger than other cases. DFFITS identifies cases 54 and 55 correctly but masks case 24 (Figure 3 (d)). Table 3 and Figure 3 show that single-case deletion diagnostics are not sufficient for the identification of multiple outliers and multiple influential observations. Now we employ the group-deletion measures GSPR and GDFFTS to identify outliers and influential observations for this data set. We use the BACON algorithm to identify the suspect unusual observations and to form the deletion set D with the suspect cases and BACON identifies the cases 24, 54 and 55 as three suspect cases. We compute GSPR and GDFFITS for the whole set based on R (without the suspect cases) and results are presented in Table 4.

We observe from this table that the GSPR identifies all the three cases (24, 54 and 55) as

Table 2. Single-case deletion diagnostic measures for Brown (1980) data

Index	|ri| (3.00)	|rsi| (3.00)	b_i (0.247)	CD (1.00)	|DFFITS| (0.583)	Index	|ri| (3.00)	|rsi| (3.00)	b_i (0.247)	CD (1.00)	|DFFITS| (0.583)
1	-0.62	-0.63	0.158	0.006	-0.107	28	-0.64	-0.65	0.145	0.006	-0.106
2	-0.68	-0.68	0.114	0.005	-0.104	29	-0.64	-0.65	0.145	0.006	-0.106
3	-0.64	-0.65	0.145	0.006	-0.106	30	-0.57	-0.59	0.223	0.006	-0.110
4	-0.65	-0.66	0.134	0.006	-0.105	31	-0.67	-0.68	0.119	0.005	-0.104
5	-0.64	-0.65	0.145	0.006	-0.106	32	-0.70	-0.70	0.103	0.005	-0.104
6	-0.63	-0.64	0.152	0.006	-0.106	33	1.61	1.63	0.158	0.038	0.280
7	-0.61	-0.62	0.173	0.006	-0.108	34	1.56	1.58	0.139	0.033	0.259
8	-0.72	-0.73	0.094	0.005	-0.104	35	1.59	1.62	0.152	0.036	0.272
9	1.48	1.50	0.114	0.025	0.228	36	-0.62	-0.63	0.158	0.006	-0.107
10	-0.67	-0.68	0.119	0.005	-0.104	37	-0.73	-0.73	0.092	0.006	-0.104
11	-0.72	-0.73	0.094	0.005	-0.104	38	-1.08	-1.12	**0.252**	0.032	-0.254
12	-0.79	-0.80	0.086	0.006	-0.112	39	-0.83	-0.84	0.092	0.008	-0.123
13	-0.74	-0.75	0.089	0.006	-0.105	40	-1.01	-1.03	0.188	0.021	-0.206
14	1.32	1.34	0.086	0.017	0.187	41	-0.75	-0.76	0.087	0.006	-0.106
15	-0.62	-0.63	0.165	0.006	-0.107	42	1.11	1.13	0.118	0.018	0.188
16	-0.63	-0.64	0.152	0.006	-0.106	43	1.15	1.16	0.106	0.017	0.184
17	-0.64	-0.65	0.145	0.006	-0.106	44	1.21	1.22	0.092	0.016	0.180
18	-0.85	-0.86	0.097	0.008	-0.128	45	1.28	1.30	0.085	0.016	0.182
19	-0.89	-0.90	0.114	0.011	-0.145	46	1.18	1.20	0.097	0.016	0.181
20	-1.04	-1.07	0.213	0.025	-0.226	47	1.28	1.30	0.085	0.016	0.182
21	-0.65	-0.66	0.134	0.006	-0.105	48	1.32	1.34	0.086	0.017	0.187
22	-0.82	-0.83	0.090	0.007	-0.120	49	1.14	1.15	0.110	0.017	0.185
23	0.95	0.98	0.223	0.025	0.222	50	1.32	1.34	0.086	0.017	0.187
24	-2.57	**-2.98**	**2.265**	**2.075**	**-2.149**	51	1.26	1.27	0.086	0.016	0.181
25	0.65	0.72	**0.783**	0.044	0.294	52	1.06	1.08	0.145	0.020	0.198
26	1.14	1.15	0.110	0.017	0.185	53	0.72	0.78	**0.589**	0.040	0.281
27	-0.57	-0.59	0.223	0.006	-0.110						

outliers and we observe that the GDFFITS values for the suspected case are much larger than the rest and all of them exceed the cut-off value 0.588. Similar conclusions may be drawn from the index plot of GSPR and GDFFITS as shown in Figure 4 (a, b). All these three suspected cases are clearly separated from the others and are correctly identified as outliers and influential observations at the same time.

Modified Finney (1947) Data

We now consider another data set as an example of multiple logistic regression from Finney (1947). Three subjects were involved in the study. The data set was obtained to study the effect of the rate and volume of air inspired on a transient vaso-constriction in the skin of the digits. The nature of the measurement process was such that only the occurrence and nonoccurrence of vaso-

Figure 2. Scatter plot of L.N.I versus Acid Phosphates (A.P.)

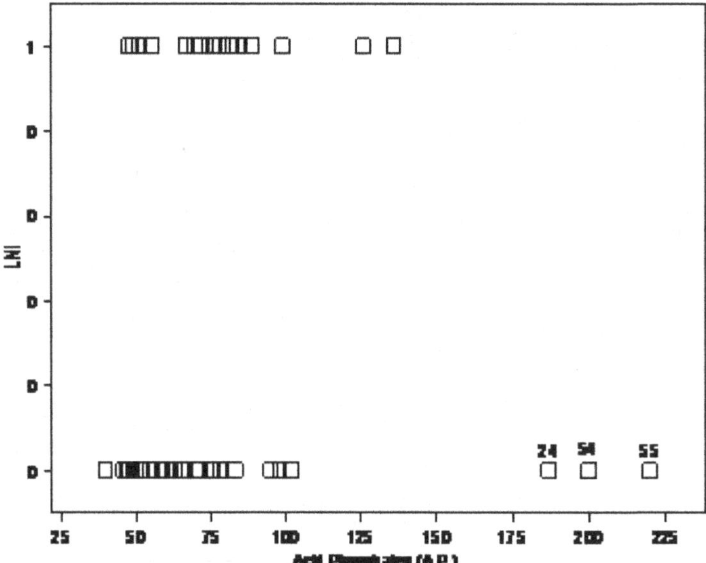

constriction could be reliably measured. This data set was analyzed extensively by Pregibon (1981). Looking at the pattern of occurrence and nonoccurrence with 25% and 75% contours in relation to rate and volume of the original data, it has been reported in his paper that this data set might contain two outliers (cases 4 and 18). We modify the data by putting two more outliers (cases 10 and 11) deliberately where occurrence (1) and nonoccurrence (0) are replaced with each other. The modified data set is presented in table 5 where the suspect cases are indicated by boldfaces. Character plot (Volume versus rate and response variable is indicated as 1 and 0) in Figure 5 gives the pattern indication in the data set.

We have shown that the single-case deletion diagnostics can not identify multiple unusual cases properly (see also Imon and Hadi, 2008; Nurunnabi *et al*., 2010). Now we apply the GSPR and GDFFITS algorithms for the identification of multiple outliers and multiple influential observations. Here we consider that the deletion set *D* contains 4 cases (4, 10, 11, 18), suggested by Figure 5 and Pregibon (1981). We reestimate the logistic model without the 4 cases and compute GSPR and GDFFITS values for the whole data set. Table 6 presents multiple influence diagnostics for the modified Finney data. We see from this table that the GSPR identifies all the 4 cases (4, 10, 11, 18) as outliers. On the contrary, GDFFITS successfully identifies all 4 influential cases and 3 more cases (13, 32 and 39) that were masked before the reestimation. Nurunnabi *et al.* (2010) showed that those three (13, 32, 39) cases are also influential for the data set. Figure 6 shows the same evidence as the graphical point of view.

FUTURE RESEARCH DIRECTIONS AND POTENTIAL USE IN OTHER FIELDS

Research for outlier diagnostics in logistic regression is not complete; it is extremely needed to find out easily compatible, generic and robust method in large and high dimensional data in presence of a large portion of outliers. The diagnostic techniques have potential research opportunity in multivariate

Table 3. Single-case deletion diagnostic measures for Imon and Hadi's modified Brown data

Index	|ri | (3.00)	|rsi| (3.00)	CD (1.00)	|DFFITS| (0.572)	Index	|ri|(3.00)	|rsi| (3.00)	CD (1.00)	|DFFITS| (0.572)
1	-0.72	-0.73	0.01	-0.119	29	-0.72	-0.73	0.01	-0.117
2	-0.73	-0.74	0.01	-0.110	30	-0.71	-0.72	0.01	-0.131
3	-0.72	-0.73	0.01	-0.117	31	-0.73	-0.74	0.01	-0.111
4	-0.73	-0.74	0.01	-0.114	32	-0.74	-0.74	0.01	-0.107
5	-0.72	-0.73	0.01	-0.117	33	1.38	1.40	0.03	0.232
6	-0.72	-0.73	0.01	-0.118	34	1.38	1.40	0.02	0.222
7	-0.72	-0.73	0.01	-0.122	35	1.38	1.40	0.03	0.229
8	-0.74	-0.75	0.01	-0.105	36	-0.72	-0.73	0.01	-0.119
9	1.37	1.38	0.02	0.207	37	-0.74	-0.75	0.01	-0.104
10	-0.73	-0.74	0.01	-0.111	38	-0.79	-0.80	0.01	-0.136
11	-0.74	-0.75	0.01	-0.105	39	-0.76	-0.76	0.01	-0.102
12	-0.75	-0.76	0.01	-0.101	40	-0.78	-0.79	0.01	-0.122
13	-0.74	-0.75	0.01	-0.103	41	-0.74	-0.75	0.01	-0.103
14	1.34	1.35	0.02	0.186	42	1.30	1.32	0.02	0.184
15	-0.72	-0.73	0.01	-0.121	43	1.31	1.32	0.02	0.181
16	-0.72	-0.73	0.01	-0.118	44	1.32	1.33	0.02	0.180
17	-0.72	-0.73	0.01	-0.117	45	1.33	1.35	0.02	0.182
18	-0.76	-0.77	0.01	-0.103	46	1.32	1.33	0.02	0.180
19	-0.77	-0.77	0.01	-0.106	47	1.33	1.35	0.02	0.182
20	-0.79	-0.80	0.01	-0.128	48	1.34	1.35	0.02	0.186
21	-0.73	-0.74	0.01	-0.114	49	1.31	1.32	0.02	0.182
22	-0.76	-0.76	0.01	-0.102	50	1.34	1.35	0.02	0.186
23	1.27	1.29	0.02	0.211	51	1.33	1.34	0.02	0.181
24	-0.91	-1.02	0.12	-0.498	52	1.29	1.31	0.02	0.190
25	1.19	1.24	0.06	0.341	53	1.21	1.25	0.04	0.300
26	1.31	1.32	0.02	0.182	54	-0.93	-1.07	0.18	**-0.594**
27	-0.71	-0.72	0.01	-0.131	55	-0.97	-1.16	0.30	**-0.782**
28	-0.72	-0.73	0.01	-0.117					

non-linear regression and in generalized linear model. Future research may be extended for multinomial logistic regression. It has great opportunity to direct the outlier detection techniques in logistic regression for the classification tasks in data mining, pattern recognition and machine learning.

Since, at the age of computer technology datasets are often with large volume so a careful inspection about outlier is as much necessary as the whole analysis, modelling and decision making. It has significance for reliable knowledge discovery in data mining context. Logistic regression diagnostics and modelling has great research potential and use in fields like marketing research (e.g., prediction of a customer's tendency to purchase a specific product), engineering (e.g., model specification and production design) and

Figure 3. (a) Index plot of Pearson residual (b) Index plot of standardized (Std.) Pearson residual (c) Index plot of CD and (d) Index plot of DFFITS

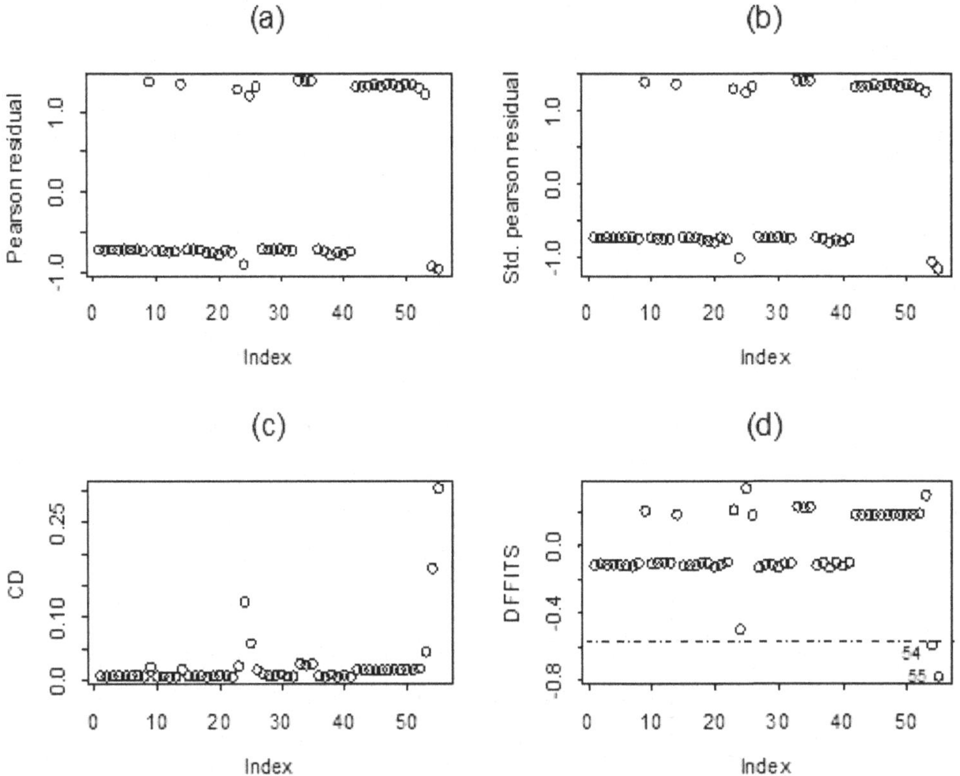

Figure 4. Imon and Hadi's modified Brown (1980) data; (a) Index plot of GSPR and (b) Index plot of GDFFITS

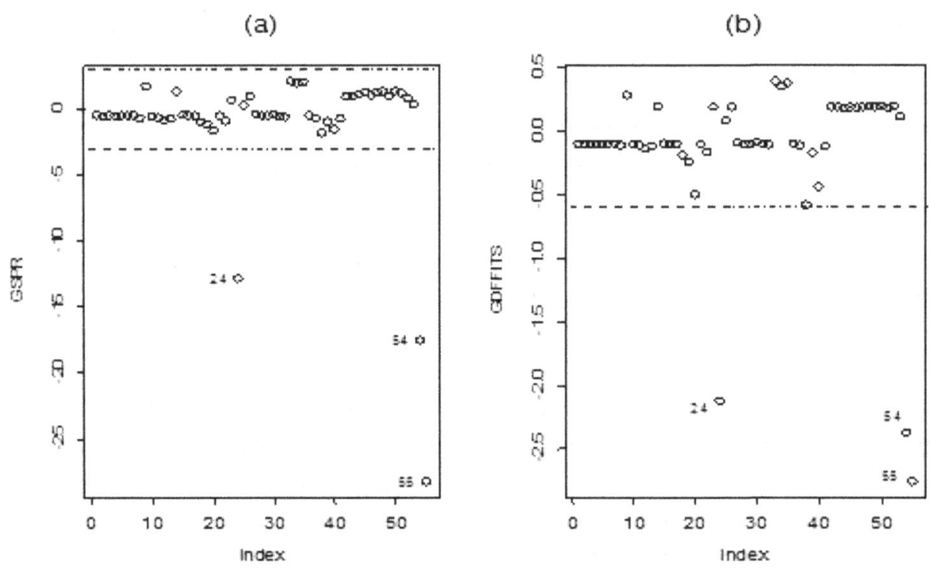

Table 4. Multiple-case deletion diagnostic measures for Imon and Hadi's modified Brown data

Index	|GSPR| (3.00)	|GDFFITS| (0.588)	Index	|GSPR| (3.00)	|GDFFITS| (0.588)	Index	|GSPR| (3.00)	|GDFFITS| (0.588)	Index	|GSPR| (3.00)	|GDFFITS| (0.588)
1	-0.505	-0.097	15	-0.493	-0.096	29	-0.529	-0.098	43	0.947	0.190
2	-0.607	-0.102	16	-0.517	-0.098	30	-0.420	-0.089	44	1.060	0.186
3	-0.529	-0.098	17	-0.529	-0.098	31	-0.593	-0.101	45	1.217	0.190
4	-0.553	-0.100	18	-1.021	-0.189	32	-0.650	-0.105	46	1.013	0.188
5	-0.529	-0.098	19	-1.155	-0.245	33	2.054	0.394	47	1.217	0.190
6	-0.517	-0.098	20	-1.677	-0.498	34	1.911	0.350	48	1.305	0.199
7	-0.482	-0.095	21	-0.553	-0.100	35	2.005	0.379	49	0.926	0.191
8	-0.697	-0.108	22	-0.949	-0.163	36	-0.505	-0.097	50	1.305	0.199
9	1.694	0.285	23	0.635	0.191	37	-0.714	-0.110	51	1.162	0.187
10	-0.593	-0.101	24	**-12.870**	**-2.121**	38	-1.851	-0.581	52	0.792	0.196
11	-0.697	-0.108	25	0.267	0.086	39	-0.973	-0.171	53	0.340	0.116
12	-0.862	-0.137	26	0.926	0.191	40	-1.556	-0.439	54	**-17.553**	**-2.376**
13	-0.748	-0.114	27	-0.420	-0.089	41	-0.766	-0.117	55	**-28.226**	**-2.759**
14	1.305	0.199	28	-0.529	-0.098	42	0.885	0.193			

Table 5. Modified Finney (1947) data

Index	Response	Volume	Rate	Index	Response	Volume	Rate
1	1	3.70	0.825	21	0	0.40	2.000
2	1	3.50	1.090	22	0	0.95	1.360
3	1	1.25	2.500	23	0	1.35	1.350
4	**1**	0.75	1.500	24	0	1.50	1.360
5	1	0.80	3.200	25	1	1.60	1.780
6	1	0.70	3.500	26	0	0.60	1.500
7	0	0.60	0.750	27	1	1.80	1.500
8	0	1.10	1.700	28	0	0.95	1.900
9	0	0.90	0.750	29	1	1.90	0.950
10	**0(1)**	0.90	0.450	30	0	1.60	0.400
11	**0(1)**	0.80	0.570	31	1	2.70	0.750
12	0	0.55	2.750	32	0	2.35	0.030
13	0	0.60	3.000	33	0	1.10	1.830
14	1	1.40	2.330	34	1	1.10	2.200
15	1	0.75	3.750	35	1	1.20	2.000
16	1	2.30	1.640	36	1	0.80	3.330
17	1	3.20	1.600	37	0	0.95	1.900
18	**1**	0.85	1.415	38	0	0.75	1.900
19	0	1.70	1.060	39	1	1.30	1.625
20	1	1.80	1.800				

Figure 5. Character plot of modified Finney (1947) data

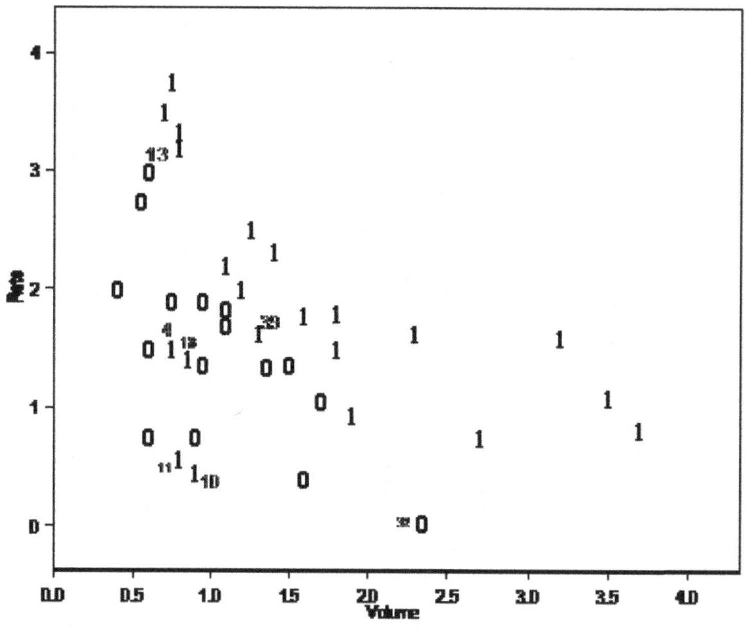

Table 6. Multiple-case deletion diagnostic measures for modified Finney (1947) data

Index	Response	|GSPR| (3.00)	|GDFFITS| (0.878)	Index	Response	|GSPR| (3.00)	|GDFFITS| (0.878)
1	1	0.000	0.000	21	0	-0.001	0.000
2	1	0.000	0.000	22	0	-0.005	0.000
3	1	0.035	0.005	23	0	-0.151	-0.046
4	**1**	**587.164**	**6.735**	24	0	-0.615	-0.257
5	1	0.041	0.006	25	1	0.079	0.018
6	1	0.020	0.002	26	0	0.000	0.000
7	0	0.000	0.000	27	1	0.061	0.012
8	0	-0.110	-0.029	28	0	-0.086	-0.020
9	0	0.000	0.000	29	1	0.576	0.376
10	**1**	**44522.925**	**11.236**	30	0	-0.008	0.000
11	**1**	**56039.735**	**11.493**	31	1	0.001	0.000
12	0	-0.276	-0.144	**32**	0	-1.144	**-1.295**
13	0	-1.997	**-1.895**	33	0	-0.229	-0.088
14	1	0.023	0.002	34	1	0.731	0.403
15	1	0.003	0.000	35	1	0.870	0.426
16	1	0.000	0.000	36	1	0.020	0.002
17	1	0.000	0.000	37	0	-0.086	-0.020
18	**1**	**386.514**	**6.276**	38	0	-0.015	-0.001
19	0	-0.718	-0.333	**39**	1	2.658	**1.140**
20	1	0.012	0.001				

Figure 6. Modified Finney (1947) data; (a) Index plot of GSPR and (b) Index plot of GDFFITS

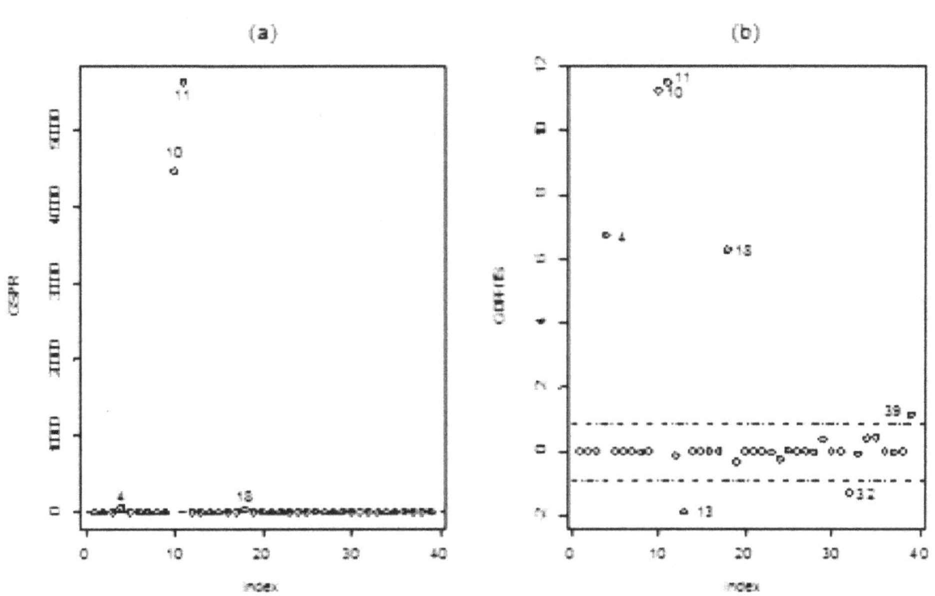

health science (such as genetic testing for susceptible diseases).

CONCLUSION

In this book chapter we have presented several popular and efficient diagnostic measures for the identification of different types of outliers (outliers, high-leverage points and influential observations) in logistic regression. In diagnostics, graphical methods exist but are not well suited, especially in multiple logistic regressions, because scatter plot is not even effective for more than one explanatory variable. For numerical measures, single case deletion techniques are not appropriate for the detection of multiple unusual cases as they are frequently affected by masking and swamping phenomena. We observe that the group deletion diagnostic methods perform efficiently for identifying multiple outliers and influential cases in logistic regression. But it is known that multiple case (group) deletion techniques are sometimes impossible for combinatorial problems, especially for massive (high-dimensional and large) data sets. Literature shows most of the times specific one diagnostic measure is not good enough for every situation. There is no single universally applicable or generic outlying observations detection technique. That is why it is problematic for practitioners to use the diagnostic measures efficiently. Practice and knowledge of data analysis can make the user perfect.

REFERENCES

Andrews, D. F., & Pregibon, D. (1978). Finding the outliers that matter. *Journal of the Royal Statistical Society. Series-B*, *40*, 85–93.

Angiulli, F., Basta, S., & Pizzuti, C. (2006). Distance-based detection and prediction of outliers. *IEEE Transactions on Knowledge and Data Engineering*, *18*(2), 145–160. doi:10.1109/TKDE.2006.29

Atkinson, A. C. (1986). Masking unmasked. *Biometrika*, *73*, 533–541. doi:10.1093/biomet/73.3.533

Barnett, V., & Lewis, T. B. (1995). *Outliers in statistical data*. New York, NY: Wiley.

Belsley, D. A., Kuh, E., & Welsch, R. E. (1980). *Regression diagnostics: Identifying influential data and sources of collinearity*. New York, NY: Wiley.

Billor, N., Hadi, A. S., & Velleman, F. (2000). BACON: Blocked adaptive computationally efficient outlier nominator. *Computational Statistics & Data Analysis*, *34*, 279–298. doi:10.1016/S0167-9473(99)00101-2

Breiman, L., Meisel, W., & Purcell, E. (1977). Variable kernel estimates of multivariate densities. *Technometrics*, *19*(2), 135–144.

Breunig, M., Kriegel, H. P., Ng, R., & Sander, J. L. O. F. (2000). Identifying density-based local outliers. In *Proceedings of the 2000 ACM SIGMOD International Conference on Management of Data* (pp. 93–104). New York, NY: ACM Press.

Chatterjee, S., & Hadi, A. S. (1986). Influential observations, high leverage points, and outliers in regression. *Statistical Science*, *1*, 379–416. doi:10.1214/ss/1177013622

Chatterjee, S., & Hadi, A. S. (1988). *Sensitivity analysis in linear regression*. New York, NY: Wiley.

Chatterjee, S., & Hadi, A. S. (2006). *Regression analysis by examples*. New York, NY: Wiley.

Cook, R. D. (1977). Detection of influential observations in linear regression. *Technometrics*, *19*, 15–18. doi:10.2307/1268249

Cook, R. D. (1979). Influential observations in regression. *Journal of the American Statistical Association*, *74*, 169–174.

Cook, R. D., & Weisberg, S. (1982). *Residuals and influence in regression*. London, UK: Chapman and Hall.

Davies, P., Imon, A. H. M. R., & Ali, M. M. (2004). A conditional expectation method for improved residual estimation and outlier identification in linear regression. *International Journal of Statistical Sciences, Special issue*, 191 – 208.

Draper, N. R., & John, J. A. (1981). Influential observations and outliers in regression. *Technometrics*, *32*, 21–26.

Fox, J. (1993). Regression diagnostics. In Beck, M. S. L. (Ed.), *Regression analysis* (pp. 245–334). London, UK: Sage Publications.

Hadi, A. S. (1992). A new measure of overall potential influence in linear regression. *Computational Statistics & Data Analysis*, *14*, 1–27. doi:10.1016/0167-9473(92)90078-T

Hadi, A. S., & Simonoff, J. S. (1993). Procedures for the identification of outliers. *Journal of the American Statistical Association*, *88*, 1264–1272.

Hampel, F. R., Ronchetti, E. M., Rousseeuw, P. J., & Stahel, W. A. (1986). *Robust statistics: The approach based on influence function*. New York, NY: Wiley.

Hoaglin, D. C., & Welsch, R. E. (1978). The hat matrix in regression and ANOVA. *The American Statistician*, *32*, 17–22.

Hocking, R. R., & Pendleton, O. J. (1983). The regression dilemma. *Communications in Statistics Theory and Methods*, *12*, 497–527. doi:10.1080/03610928308828477

Hosmer, D. W., & Lemeshow, S. (2000). *Applied logistic regression*. New York, NY: Wiley. doi:10.1002/0471722146

Huber, P. J. (1981). *Robust statistics*. New York, NY: Wiley.

Imon, A. H. M. R. (2005). Identifying multiple influential observations in linear regression. *Journal of Applied Statistics*, *32*, 73–90.

Imon, A. H. M. R. (2006). Identification of high leverage points in logistic regression. *Pakistan Journal of Statistics*, *22*, 147–156.

Imon, A. H. M. R., & Hadi, A. S. (2008). Identification of multiple outliers in logistic regression. *Communications in Statistics Theory and Methods*, *37*, 1967–1709. doi:10.1080/03610920701826161

Knorr, M. E., Ng, T. R., & Tucakov, V. (2000). Distance-based outlier: Algorithms and applications. *The VLDB Journal*, *8*(3-4), 237–253. doi:10.1007/s007780050006

Nurunnabi, A. A. M., Imon, A. H. M. R., & Nasser, M. (2010). Identification of multiple influential observations in logistic regression. *Journal of Applied Statistics*, *37*(10), 1605–1624. doi:10.1080/02664760903104307

Nurunnabi, A. A. M., Imon, A. H. M. R., & Nasser, M. (2011). A diagnostic measure for influential observations in linear regression. *Communications in Statistics Theory and Methods*, *40*(7), 1169–1183. doi:10.1080/03610920903564727

Nurunnabi, A. A. M., Imon, A. H. M. R., Shawkat, A. B. M., & Nasser, M. (2011). Outlier detection in linear regression. In Igelnik, B. (Ed.), *Computational modelling and simulation of intellect: Current state and future perspectives* (pp. 510–550). Hershey, PA: IGI Global. doi:10.4018/978-1-60960-551-3.ch020

Pregibon, D. (1981). Logistic regression diagnostics. *Annals of Statistics*, *9*, 977–986. doi:10.1214/aos/1176345513

Rousseeuw, P. J., & Leroy, A. M. (1987). *Robust regression and outlier detection*. New York, NY: Wiley.

Ryan, T. P. (1997). *Modern regression methods*. New York, NY: Wiley.

Stahel, W., & Weisberg, S. (1991). *Direction in robust statistics and diagnostics, (Preface)*. New York, NY: Springer-Verlag.

Terrell, G. R., & Scott, D. W. (1992). Variable kernel density estimation. *Annals of Statistics*, *20*(3), 1236–1265. doi:10.1214/aos/1176348768

Velleman, P. F., & Welsch, R. E. (1981). Efficient computing in regression diagnostics. *The American Statistician*, *35*, 234–242.

Welsch, R. E. (1982). Influence functions and regression diagnostics. In Launar, R. L., & Siegel, A. F. (Eds.), *Modern data analysis*. New York, NY: Academic Press.

Chapter 17
Quantum Computing Approach for Alignment-Free Sequence Search and Classification

Rao M. Kotamarti
Southern Methodist University, USA

Mitchell A. Thornton
Southern Methodist University, USA

Margaret H. Dunham
Southern Methodist University, USA

ABSTRACT

Many classes of algorithms that suffer from large complexities when implemented on conventional computers may be reformulated resulting in greatly reduced complexity when implemented on quantum computers. The dramatic reductions in complexity for certain types of quantum algorithms coupled with the computationally challenging problems in some bioinformatics problems motivates researchers to devise efficient quantum algorithms for sequence (DNA, RNA, protein) analysis. This chapter shows that the important sequence classification problem in bioinformatics is suitable for formulation as a quantum algorithm. This chapter leverages earlier research for sequence classification based on Extensible Markov Model (EMM) and proposes a quantum computing alternative. The authors utilize sequence family profiles built using EMM methodology which is based on using pre-counted word data for each sequence. Then a new method termed quantum seeding is proposed for generating a key based on high frequency words. The key is applied in a quantum search based on Grover algorithm to determine a candidate set of models resulting in a significantly reduced search space. Given Z as a function of M models of size N, the quantum version of the seeding algorithm has a time complexity in the order of $O(\sqrt{Z})$ *as opposed to O(Z) for the standard classic version for large values of Z.*

DOI: 10.4018/978-1-4666-1830-5.ch017

INTRODUCTION

Reformulation of algorithms with large complexities from conventional computers could result in greatly reduced complexity when implemented on quantum computers (Nielsen & Chuang, 2000)(Marinescu & Marinescu, 2005)(Yanofsky & Mannucci, 2008). The resulting reduction in complexity is due to the underlying quantum computational model that is no longer constrained by the limitations of a Turing machine model of the present day computing. While commercially available quantum computers are not yet available, important algorithms have been formulated and run on experimental quantum computers. As new quantum devices and manufacturing technologies mature, the availability of commercial quantum computers continues to increase.

The dramatic reductions in complexity for quantum algorithms coupled with the computationally challenging problems in some bioinformatics problems motivates us to devise efficient quantum algorithms for sequence (DNA, RNA, protein) analysis. This class of problems results in large complexities with respect to Turing machine computational models due to the long lengths and potentially large number of sequences involved. Additionally, in contrast to the traditional and generic string matching problem, sequence matching problems tend to be fuzzy in nature. These classes of problems are particularly appropriate for reformulation into quantum computer algorithms.

One bioinformatics sequence application is that of classifying a sequence, such as a string of nucleotides, based on similarity to known classes of sequences. Basic Local Alignment Search known as BLAST (Karlin & Altschul, 1990) and BLAST PSI (Altschul, 1997) are in popular use for searching across genomic databases. BLAST PSI builds a characteristic profile from an initial set of search results. The results are used to fine tune the initial profile of the related sequences and the search is retried thus successively improving the relevance and diversity of related sequences. The process is repeated until the researcher is convinced with the resulting profile and the improved set of related sequences. Another approach - Profile Hidden Markov Model, also referred to as ProfileHMM (Eddy, 1998) uses a probabilistic profile for search across a growing database of profileHMMs representing characteristic domains (small stretches of significance) such as protein families (PFAM) (Finn, et al., 2008). Though BLAST is by far more used due to its ability to work with raw sequence formats of the genomic data, ProfileHMM is steadily gaining recognition among researchers for its probabilistic basis as more and more profileHMMs are built and added. To improve performance further, in order to handle the steadily increasing sizes of genomic databases, parallel processing versions have been proposed for BLAST and profileHMM. Specialized hardware solutions have also been proposed for the latter (Oliver, Yeow, & Schmidt, 2008). Much of the growth in genomic databases is due to the advent of the next generation sequencing technology. Much more is expected, thus resulting in a significant data overload in the future as reported by several studies (Eddy, 1998)(Benson, Karsch-Mizrachi, Lipman, Ostell, & Wheeler, 2006).

The promise of quantum computing allows for drastically reduced complexities for certain classes of algorithms. Some of the more well-known quantum algorithms are a) the searching problem of Grover that offers a quadratic reduction of temporal complexity (Grover, 1996) and b) the large integer prime factoring algorithm of Shor that reduces the factoring algorithm complexity to $O(N)$ where N is the number of digits comprising the integer. The integer factoring quantum algorithm garnered a significant amount of public attention since the large Turing model complexity of large integer factoring is responsible for the security of the widely used public key cryptography system known as RSA encryption (Rivest, Shamir, & Adleman, 1978). The formulation of a quantum algorithm is not merely the recompilation of a Turing algorithm as it requires some knowledge of the theory of the quantum nature of particles and no standard engineering approaches have been yet been satisfactorily devised. This is one of the primary reasons that there are only a small number of quantum algorithms implemented at present. Furthermore, only a subset of all algorithms is conjectured to achieve significant complexity reductions when formulated for the quantum computational model (Bennett, Bernstein, Brassard, & Vazirani, 1997). The important sequence classification problem in bioinformatics is suitable for formulation as a quantum algorithm and results in a significant complexity reduction. The same algorithm if implemented on conventional computer architecture results in a complexity of $O(MN)$ as opposed to $O(\sqrt{KMN} + M'\frac{N}{K})$, where M is the number models, N is the length of a sequence, K is the number of equal size segments in a sequence and M' is the number of candidate models, if implementable on a quantum computing architecture.

The chapter is organized as follows. In the following subsection an overview of several background research areas is presented that provides the basis for understanding authors' approach. In particular, authors propose to use sequence models based on Extensible Markov Model (EMM) as opposed to Hidden Markov Model or BLAST PSI. The background briefly presents the EMM as much of EMM based Bioinformatics is already available as published research (Kotamarti R. M., Hahsler, Raiford, McGee, & Dunham, 2010). In the main focus section, the authors describe their technique for solving the sequence classification problem using quantum computing followed by an overview of the implementation. The implementation discussion summarizes the EMM based sequence models and methods as modified to incorporate quantum algorithmic extensions. Finally a conclusion is presented.

BACKGROUND

To successfully propose an implementation of quantum computing, we first need to be able to view the sequence classification in an appropriate framework. We do this by viewing sequence classification algorithms within the context of a dynamic Markov model called Extensible Markov Model. The last major subsection provides an overview of quantum computing within the framework described in the computational model of Deutsch (Deutsch, 1985) and Grover's algorithm (Grover, 1996) which is used in our proposed solution.

Sequence Analysis in Bioinformatics

Analysis and comparison of bioinformatics sequences is often based on the alignment of the sequences. This means that two or more sequences are initially positioned so that large sections of identical (or nearly identical) values (letters or symbols) are aligned together. There are several types of alignment algorithms, but they all suffer from large computational overhead. The similarity of different sequences is then determined based upon a scoring technique. For example, profileHMMs score alignments using the probabilistic occurrence of letters in consensus columns of multiple sequence alignments, whereas the BLAST method uses pre-developed score matrices such as the BLOSUM (Henikoff & Henikoff, 1992)and PAM (Dayhoff, Schwartz, & Orcutt, 1978) methods. However, alignment by itself is not sufficient for all types of sequence analyses as explained by Vinga et. al in(Vinga & Almeida, 2003) since some stretches of a sequence can relocate elsewhere due to chromosomal crossover in genetic recombination. Similarly, longer range relationships, such as complementarity between small stretches separated by variable length sequence fragments forming loops, may exist along the sequences. Such relationships are hard to capture in a strict alignment based analysis. A complementary technique for such situations utilizes frequency summaries of word patterns which produces a statistical signature for a sequence. This is the domain of alignment-free sequence analysis. In case of DNA or RNA sequences, a word summary captures the base composition along the whole of the sequence. Various techniques have been proposed in the literature such as the use of statistical signatures for clustering, classification etc. to arrive at reasonable phylogenetic trees and taxonomies (Blaisdell B., 1989) (Kotamarti, Raiford, Hahsler, Wang, McGee, & Dunham, Nov 2009).

Extensible Markov Model

An Extensible Markov Model (EMM) is a time varying Markov model (Dunham, Meng, & Huang, 2004). At any point in time an EMM can be viewed as a Markov model. The original applications for EMM were for river flood forecasting and rare event detection for traffic (automobile and VoIP). In these cases the input data is a stream of values from multiple sensors. Each input state is viewed as a vector of numeric values, one value from each sensor, at a point in time. The nodes in the Markov model graph represent clusters of similar input vectors. The arcs in the graph represent transitions between the events found in the associated cluster nodes. Thus an EMM provides a synopsis of the sequence of real world events. It achieves a reduction in the problem complexity due to the clustering. In the seven years since the first EMM paper, many algorithms have been created to manipulate the EMM model and apply it to different applications.

As of recent, Extensible Markov Model has been introduced as a sequence analysis tool with reduction in space and time complexity for modeling and classification. EMM of a sequence or a group of sequences summarizes sequence segments of equal sizes by organizing them into a Markov model framework. The nodes of such Markov model (EMM) represent clusters of similar sequence segments and the arcs represent the transition probabilities observed. EMM sequence applications have a time complexity of $O(N\frac{M}{K})$, where N, M and K represent the length of a sequence, number of sequences and the number of equal sized segments respectively. The EMMs are built from related sequences; the EMMs are used for subsequent classification and search analyses (Kotamarti, Raiford, Hahsler, Wang, McGee, & Dunham, Nov 2009)(Kotamarti R., Hahsler, Raiford, & Dunham, 2010)(Kotamarti R. M., Hahsler, Raiford, McGee, & Dunham, 2010). In this chapter, the authors use the EMM based statistical-signature representations to search and classify using quantum computing algorithms.

Quantum Computing

Quantum computers rely upon the quantum mechanical properties of elementary particles rather than the propagation and manipulation of electronic signals. Because quantum mechanical properties are modeled as being inherently probabilistic, the fundamental unit of information is different from that used in conventional computers; instead of bits, quantum-bits, or qubits are used. Qubits are modeled as probabilistic values that assume deterministic basis state values only when observed or measured. This behavior is a direct consequence of the theory of wave-particle duality and uncertainty in quantum physics. From an information processing point of view, a qubit is modeled as a complex value that can exist in a superposition or linear combination of its basis states. There are two basis states for a qubit and they represent the Boolean values 0 and 1. As an example, Equation 1 expresses the qubit $|\psi\rangle$ as a superposition of the basis values $|0\rangle$ and $|1\rangle$ using the so-called 'ket' notation for column vectors. The ket-notation is explained in more detail in the following section and the scalar vector coefficients α and β are complex values.

$$|\psi\rangle = \alpha|0\rangle + \beta|1\rangle \quad (1)$$

This mathematical qubit model is the key factor responsible for the complexity reductions offered by quantum computation since it allows for a unit of information to take on the conventional Boolean values of 0 and 1 simultaneously. In this manner, quantum computation can be qualitatively viewed as a method for exploiting parallelism of information as contrasted to parallel computation in conventional electronic computers where parallelism is achieved spatially by duplication of physical resources, such as multi-core processors, or temporal parallelism can be achieved by methods such as instruction-level pipelining.

There have been various different formulations of quantum computational models proposed. One of the first and most commonly used model is that of Deutsch (Deutsch, 1985) consisting of the following steps:

- Initialize a collection of particles (called a quantum register) to be in a basis state
- Apply a sequence of elementary operations (called a quantum program) to the particles while they remain in a state of superposition
- Measure or observe the quantum particles after the last quantum program instruction has been applied.

As an example of such a quantum computer, the quantum register could consist of a collection of trapped ions that are irradiated with a sequence of electromagnetic pulses of varying duration and polarity that cause the energy states of the ions to change. Changing the energy states in a predetermined way and also considering the interaction of the particles with one another (i.e. entanglement) represents the quantum computer algorithm. It is crucial that during the operations, or execution of the quantum program instructions, the trapped ions remain unobserved or in a state of superposition allowing for them to behave as both a Boolean 0 and 1 value. After the program execution is complete, an observation or measurement is performed that forces them to collapse into basis states representing a deterministic binary string. If the sequence of operations, or quantum program, is properly devised, the resulting deterministic string will be one of the desired solutions to the problem being computed and the fact that during the intermediate computations, each qubit represents both a 0 and 1, allows for all solutions to be computed in a single program execution.

Notation and Properties

Because qubits are modeled as being in both basis states simultaneously, the natural mathematical representation is that of a vector rather than the scalar 0 and 1 values used in binary computing. It is possible to formulate a quantum digit as that can take on any finite number of logic values; however, qubits are modeled as a superposition of only two basis vectors, $|0\rangle$ and $|1\rangle$. In general, qubits are not in a state of equal superposition and the complex-valued scalar coefficients α and β dictate the superposition at any given instant in time. When a qubit is measured or observed, it collapses into one of the basis states $|0\rangle$ or $|1\rangle$. The probability that the qubit collapses into state $|0\rangle$ is the square of the magnitude $|\alpha^2|$ and for $|1\rangle$ is $|\beta^2|$. This necessarily imposes the constraint that $|\alpha^2| + |\beta^2| = 1$ which is a consequence of the physical property of conservation of energy.

The Nobel Prize winning physicist Paul Dirac made many fundamental contributions to the field of quantum physics and in one of his well-known papers, he introduced a notation for quantum mechanical calculations that continues to be widely used today in both the physics and quantum computation literature (Dirac, 1939). This notation, sometimes called 'bra-ket' notation is used to describe the state of a quantum system. Because the state of a quantum system is mathematically represented as a column vector, bra-ket notation may also be used to denote vectors. In particular, a column vector is a 'ket' and is represented as $|\psi\rangle$ for a vector named ψ. A row vector named φ would be represented as a 'bra' denoted by $\langle\varphi|$.

Elementary operations performed on collections of qubits are referred to as quantum programming instructions, or in the context of quantum circuits, quantum logic gates. Because the state of a qubit is represented as a vector, a quantum instruction can be represented as a linear transformation of the representative vector and is hence specified by a particular transformation matrix, G. Certain quantum instructions are frequently used in quantum programs and are given names, analogously to conventional computer assembly language instructions such as the logical AND. Each of these commonly used quantum instructions has an associated transformation matrix. As an example, an operation evolves a qubit from a basis state to a state of equal superposition is the Hadamard operation represented by a 2×2 Hadamard transformation matrix. Equation (2) shows how a qubit $|\alpha(t)\rangle$ can be evolved from basis state $|0\rangle$ to a state of equal superposition of $|0\rangle$ and $|1\rangle$ by application of the Hadamard operation specified by the transformation matrix H2. The resulting state, $|\alpha(t + \tau)\rangle$ results after the application of the Hadamard operation that requires τ units of time to apply.

$$| \alpha(t+\tau)\rangle = H_2 \, | \alpha(t)\rangle = \frac{1}{\sqrt{2}}\begin{bmatrix}1 & 1\\ 1 & -1\end{bmatrix} | \alpha(t)\rangle = \frac{|0\rangle + |1\rangle}{\sqrt{2}} \tag{2}$$

The Hadamard operation as illustrated in Equation (2) is a very important and commonly used operation in quantum computing algorithms since it is necessary to evolve qubits that are initialized as basis values into states of superposition so that the algorithm can exploit the information-level parallelism.

Furthermore, the Hadamard operation is usually easily realized physically. As an example, a quantum computation that is being performed using photons and lenses can implement a Hadamard operation through use of a beam-splitter. Many other elementary quantum operations are known and have been implemented. The act of writing a quantum computing algorithm is then the choice and arrangement of a sequence of quantum instructions or operations to be applied to a quantum register.

Grover's Quantum Search

In the sequence classification problem being considered in this work, we make use of a particular quantum algorithm that was first reported by Grover in (Grover, 1996) where it was devised to find a particular object that is inserted into some unknown position in a set of N objects. Given a search problem of searching for a single object within a large unsorted list of N items, the Grover algorithm results in a complexity of $O(\sqrt{N})$ (Figure 1) which is both remarkable and non-intuitive; this is because in terms of conventional computation, it would require N comparisons in the worst case to find the desired object among an unsorted and unorganized collection. Although there are methods to quickly find a particular object among a set, such as organizing the set in a hash table, this conventional approach requires that the items be stored or organized in a particular method prior to invoking the search. Grover's search method places no constraint among the organization of the objects. In using the analogy to a hash table further, we note that in addition to requiring the objects in a set to be organized according to a particular hash function, there must also be a means to compute the hash value of the object being searched for. In Grover's implementation, a computation over properties of the object being searched for is also required; however, instead of a hash key, an artifact known as an oracle must be formed.

Grover search (Grover, 1996) can find the target item in $\sqrt{N}$ iterations as opposed to a clas-

Figure 1. Block diagram of one stage Grover iteration

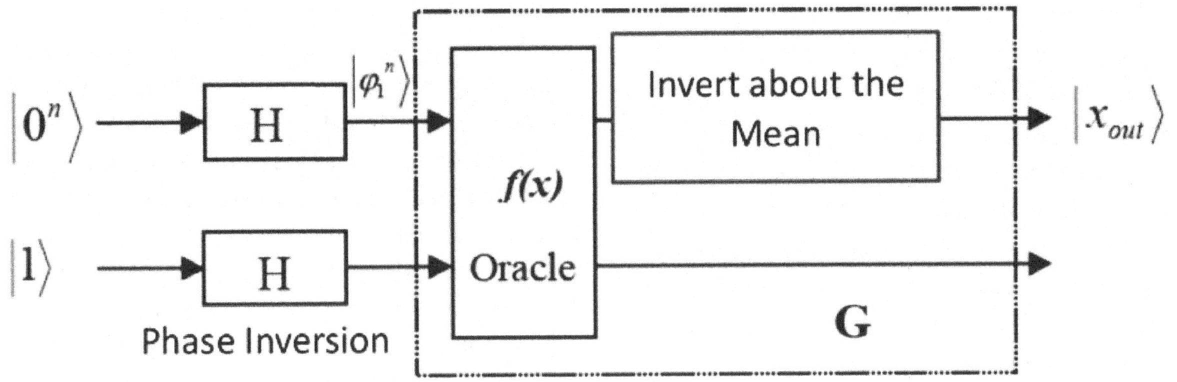

sic exhaustive search with N iterations where there are N number of items from which an item of interest is to be located. Grover algorithm makes use of the superposition of n bits where $N = 2^n$ when searching a particular state vector which is one of the N items. Once found, the algorithm marks it by shifting its phase and then applies successive amplitude boost iterations $\sqrt{N}$ times by when the desired state vector's probability of being found reaches a 1.

The oracle is actually a subset of quantum instructions that encapsulate properties of the item being searched for and can be thought of as a binary valued function, f, whose domain is all possible objects among a collection and whose range is {0, 1}. The oracle function then has value f = 1 when the argument is a copy of the value be searched foe and f =0 when the function argument is not the value being searched for. Grover devised an algorithm that made use of such an oracle and two other methods easily implemented as a sequence of quantum operations known as 'phase inversion' and 'inversion about the mean'. The combination of these techniques resulted in the search algorithm that achieved the non-intuitive O($\sqrt{N}$) complexity.

The chief difficulty in implementing Grover's method for general searching problems is that of formulating the oracle in such a manner that it can be efficiently and easily represented as a sequence of quantum computer instructions. One of the contributions of this paper is that the methods of exhaustive search and the sequence classification problem as described in the previous section can be mapped into a quantum algorithm based on the principles of Grover's search method.

The oracle, which generates a 1 or 0 depending on whether or not the desired item is found, marks the target state vector by applying a phase shift in the complex plane. The oracle is able to evaluate all 2^n state vectors in a single stage due to the quantum mechanical property of superposition. When the oracle function generates a 1, it marks the desired item's state vector. However, the first stage merely marks the desired target, if a measurement or observation was made after marking, the result would probabilistically result in any of the objects in the collection. This occurs because the marking is accomplished mathematically as a sign change in the quantum state, however, such sign information is lost since the probablity values are computed based on the amplitude of the quantum state vectors. What is desired is to somehow increase the probability that, upon a measurement, the marked object would result. In order to accomplish this, the probability amplitudes must be increased for the marked or desired value, and decreased for the objects that are not matches. To improve the probability of observation for the marked element, the corresponding amplitude is boosted using flip around the mean. The amplitude boost is performed several times and, in fact, after the $\sqrt{N}$ times, the probability of the desired item's state vector becomes close to 1. Thus, what is found and marked in a single first stage takes a total of $\sqrt{N}$ iterations called Grover iterations to evolve the system state to allow successful measurement of the intended state. Once measured, the corresponding amplitude, is used as an index to locate the desired target database entry.

MAIN FOCUS: SEQUENCE ANALYSIS

Modeling Sequence Classification

Before we attempt a quantum computing solution, we will first introduce the problem being addressed and present some solutions using the classic computing paradigm. For this, we assume that sequences are first organized into models instead of retaining them in their native raw sequence representations in the Genome databases. This allows us to leverage the multi-sequence alignments and the probabilistic extensions in the form of profileHMM methods subsequently. Once models are created and saved in libraries, they can be searched using a query of a new sequence. This turns the classification problem into a search problem which is then suitable for Grover's quantum algorithm.

For building sequence models, an HMM or EMM may be considered. For building HMMs, in particular the profileHMMs, multiple sequence alignment (MSA) is performed first using well known tools such as ClustalW (Thompson, Higgins, & Gibson, 1994). An MSA captures the best similarity possible by simply aligning the columns across all sequences in the set under study in such a way that the quality of alignment is maximized. Reader is advised to refer to the abundant literature available on understanding multiple sequence alignments. The MSA is input to build profileHMMs which takes the form as shown in Figure 2. In profileHMMs, consensus columns are mapped into Match states M and additional states such as Insert I and Delete D states are also used. These additional states account for patches of letters in the sequences that appear to have been somehow inserted or deleted due to random acts of nature (mutations, crossover etc.). Since a consensus column may use different symbols (different codons may code for same amino-acid), a probability distribution is specified representing the emission probabilities, so called in the HMM nomenclature. Furthermore, since insertion regions can be of different lengths and occur between consensus columns, they too are associated with a probability distribution for the residues that occur in those regions as shown in figure 2.

This is an example of profile Hidden Markov Model representing three consensus columns. The probability distributions for insertion and match states are shown. A multiple sequence alignment is used as input. The resulting profileHMM consists of three states for each (consensus) position in the alignment along with the emission probabilities for the match and insertion states. The arcs among states represent the transition probabilities.

The transition probabilities are associated with transitions among the three states though typically transitions between *insertion and deletion* in either direction are rare. Each consensus position within a sequence community uses three states and two lists of distribution probabilities. The time complexity for building profileHMMs including the pre-requisite multiple sequence alignment is $O(N + MN + M^2 + N^2 LogN)$ where M is the number of sequences and N is the size of a sequence.

In case of EMMs, building them does not require multiple sequence alignment, but does require counting the occurrences of words or

Figure 2. The profile HMM

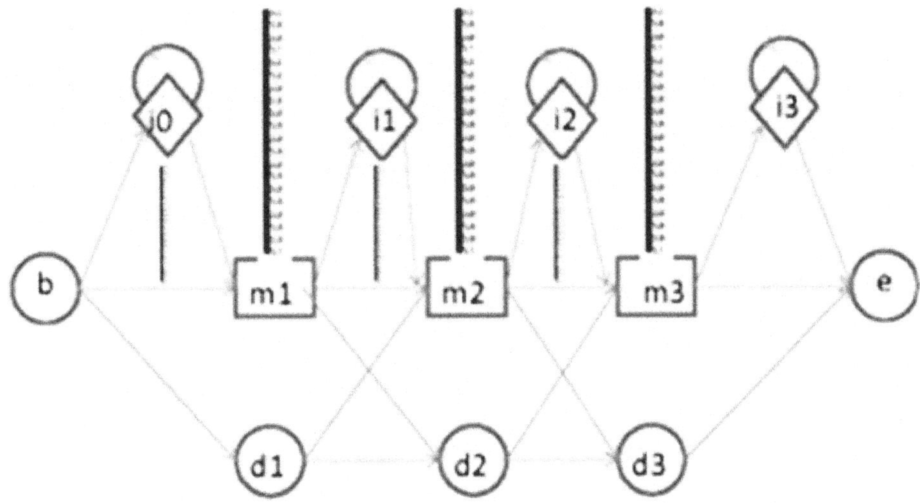

p-mers (subsequence of length p) where p is typically 2 or 3.

Counting *p-mers* involves sliding a p-mer window over the sequence and counting the corresponding p-mer letter pattern. If p=3 is selected, there would be 4^3 = 64 different combinations for a DNA sequence where the alphabet consists of 4 letters A,C,G and G. Actually for an EMM, a sequence is first divided into equal segments of size k and the count vector of occurrences is created for each segment. Such vectors are called Numerical Summarization Vectors (NSVs) in EMM nomenclature (Kotamarti, Raiford, Hahsler, Wang, McGee, & Dunham, Nov 2009). The NSVs thus prepared for each sequence in a group of sequences are organized into a markov model as shown in Figure 3. The nodes of an EMM represent clusters of related segments in NSV form. As such, each new NSV is first compared to each node's cluster to determine its placement. In case such placement is not possible, i.e, no cluster is a reasonable choice based on a squared Euclidean distance threshold, a new node is created starting yet another cluster. During the building process, transitions are counted between nodes which will be used for scoring subsequently. Since clustering is employed, the number of states and therefore the space used by an EMM tends to be a lot smaller than for profileHMMs. The time complexity for building the EMMs for sequence analysis is *O(NM/K)* where *M* is the number of sequences, *N* is the size of a sequence and *K* is the number of equal sized segments in a sequence.

Numerical Summary Vectors (NSV) constitute the numerical representations of equal sized segments along a molecular sequence which are used in building an EMM signature. Signature building starts with a start state; as each NSV is processed, it is compared to the existing states of the model. If the NSV is not found to be close enough (per a Squared Euclidean threshold) as in the case of NSV 1, a new state (1) is created with the new NSV as its □cli cluster member; otherwise, the new NSV (as in the case of NSV 3) is simply added to the matching cluster state node (state 1). When all NSVs are processed, the model building process is finished.

Search and Classification

Once models are created using HMM or EMM, they are available for search for a given sequence of interest (*query*). Typically, a query sequence is first converted into a model and then searched

Figure 3. The EMM building process

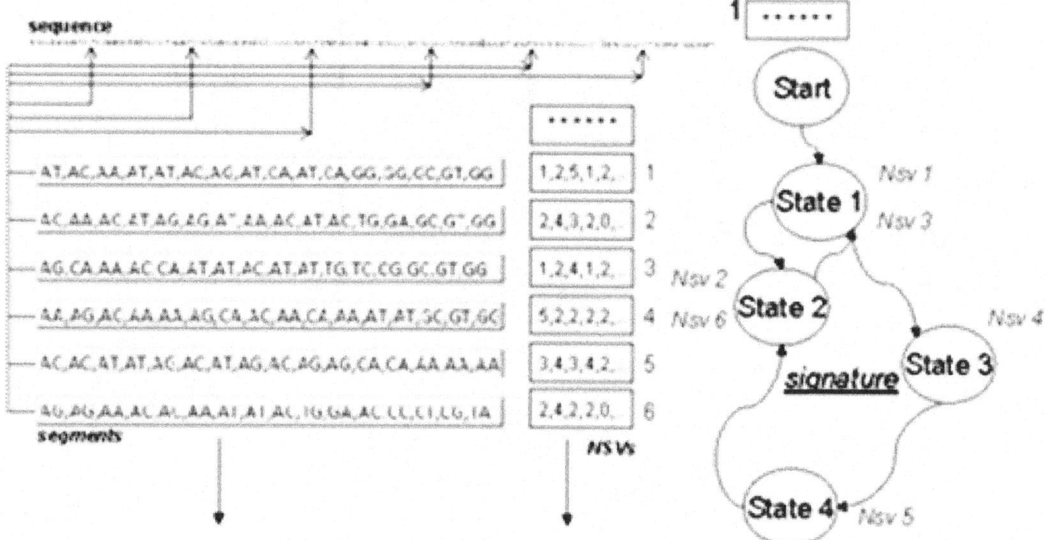

against the model database for retrieving the similar sequence communities also represented as models. In the output of such searches, the highest scoring model from the database is presented first as the most likely classification for the input sequence. These searches can take quite some time considering the algorithms in use and the exhaustive nature of such search. Unlike BLAST in a raw sequence database search, no heuristic is used for reducing the search space to the best of our knowledge. Each model in the library is considered, scored, ranked amongst others and then the output is generated. Since the database sizes are not as large as raw sequence databases, this is not yet a serious concern though some hardware and parallel solution are known to exist at least for the HMMs (Oliver, Yeow, & Schmidt, 2008).

To the best of our knowledge, the existing profileHMM literature or the current implementations are not published to the level of detail to perform a careful analysis. But, the basic algorithms used for evaluating a single model against a query are well understood to be based on Viterbi and the forward algorithm based on dynamic programming (Durbin, 1998). The book by Sean Eddy et. al (Durbin, 1998) describes these algorithms and various facets of them in great detail. The time complexity for a single model evaluation is given as $O(NM_s^2)$ where N is length of a sequence, but M_s is number of states which can be three times the number of consensus positions. In case of a search of a single query against a large database of models, this can be extrapolated with a multiplication factor equivalent to the size of the database in terms of models.

Due to the fact that EMM based models avoid alignment and are thus more efficient than HMM models (Kotamarti & Dunham, 2010), we use the profileEMM approach as the basis for quantum computing implementation of the sequence search (classification) solution. Since no dynamic programming based algorithm is used for evaluating a query sequence against an EMM, the time complexity is much smaller at $O(NM_s)$ where N is length of sequence and M_s is the number of model states which is typically a couple of orders of magnitude smaller than N. For example, an EMM for a sequence of 1500 bps (16S rRNA) would only take up 20 states at a segment length of 80. This is much smaller than an HMM where the number of states adding to the processing can take up to 1500 * 3 = 4800. However, since each model is evaluated one at a time against the query sequence, the time complexity for overall search through database requires extrapolation same as done for profileHMM. This implies that a single query sequence search or classification requires exhaustive consideration of all states of all the models in the database regardless of which modeling framework is used. This is the problem we will address using quantum solution in this paper.

From this point onwards, the analysis of comparative techniques for sequence analysis switches to comparing the methods of sequence search used in particular with EMMs. Of those available, the most suitable is further considered for quantum computing. In using the EMM method of model evaluation for a query, there are two approaches 1) standard method 2) seeding method. Recall that NSV is a p-mer count vector for a segment of a sequence and that there are 64 different types of counts for a p of 3.

Standard Method

This is the approach as described in the original publication (Kotamarti, Raiford, Hahsler, Wang, McGee, & Dunham, Nov 2009). Salient points are captured here for completeness. For each EMM in the model database,

1. For each NSV $\mathbf{s}_i$ (which is a count vector for a segment) of the query sequence,
    a. Find the nearest match state $\mathbf{s}_i$ of the model referred to as quasi alignment.
    b. Score the quasi alignment as $\mathbf{Q}_i$.
    c. Apply a weight $\mathbf{w}_i$ of **1** or a penalty **E** if the transition between the previously matched state and the current matched state is not present in the model.
2. Once all the NSVs of the query sequence are thus processed, generate the overall score $\mathbf{M}_j$ where **j** is the model number which ranges over all the available models in the database by taking the reciprocal of $\mathbf{1+ w_iQ_i}$.

Thus the *standard method* generates a score for each model against a query sequence and then selects the model with the best score. In this process, every model is considered in its entirety where as the *Seeding method* finds a way to eliminate the unlikely models using a only a partial evaluation as described next.

Seeding Method

Instead of exhaustively searching by cross comparing all nodes (or EMM states) of a query against all those of all models, a smaller candidate set is only evaluated in this method. Determining the candidate set requires some method by which candidate models are deduced. As observed in biological sequences, certain p-mers tend to occur more frequently than others. The more frequent they are, the more contributory they become for scoring. This is an information theoretic fact (Blaisdell B. E., 1986) and it is used in generating score matrices for EMM based sequence analysis (Kotamarti R., Hahsler, Raiford, & Dunham, 2010). Recall that each EMM state is essentially a representative count vector (NSV) with all possible elements. So, there would be 64 elements for each EMM state if we stay with the example of p=3. Fewer than the maximum possible number of p-mers ($<< \mathbf{4^{(p=3)}}$ $= \mathbf{64}$ in case of a 3-mer basis) is required to pick the most likely models. For example, if there are **x** number of elements, where $x << 4^p$, it is necessary to cross compare only x elements between the query states and the model states as opposed to considering all against all. In other words, we could think of **x** as a form of key for identifying the states or the models containing them. Choosing the correct value for **x** and the exact p-mers that make up the **x** elements is important in the design of a key. The Figure 4 describes how the database of models may be mapped to a set of keys designed from high usage p-mers and then searched to determine candidate models for final isolation of the best matched model. The seeding method is summarized as follows:

The model building process of the original approach (Kotamarti, Raiford, Hahsler, Wang, McGee, & Dunham, Nov 2009) is slightly modified to generate two needed pieces of information – a) p-mer occurrence statistics used subsequently to derive the high usage words and b) a p-mer composition for a representative key. The first three steps accomplish this as follows:

1. Maintain a word frequency table that is updated as models are built and stored in a model database.
2. Since model states are consolidated NSVs with all possible p-mer counts, establish a key of sufficient length to map and identify all the states of all the models.
3. Develop an index database of key mapped to model <name and state num> as follows:
    a. For each model, for each state, extract the key word and generate the key value.
    b. Update the corresponding index record by adding the model number.

    This means that at this point, given M models of N states, there would be MN entries with entry pointing to the corresponding model and

Figure 4. Model search with seeding method

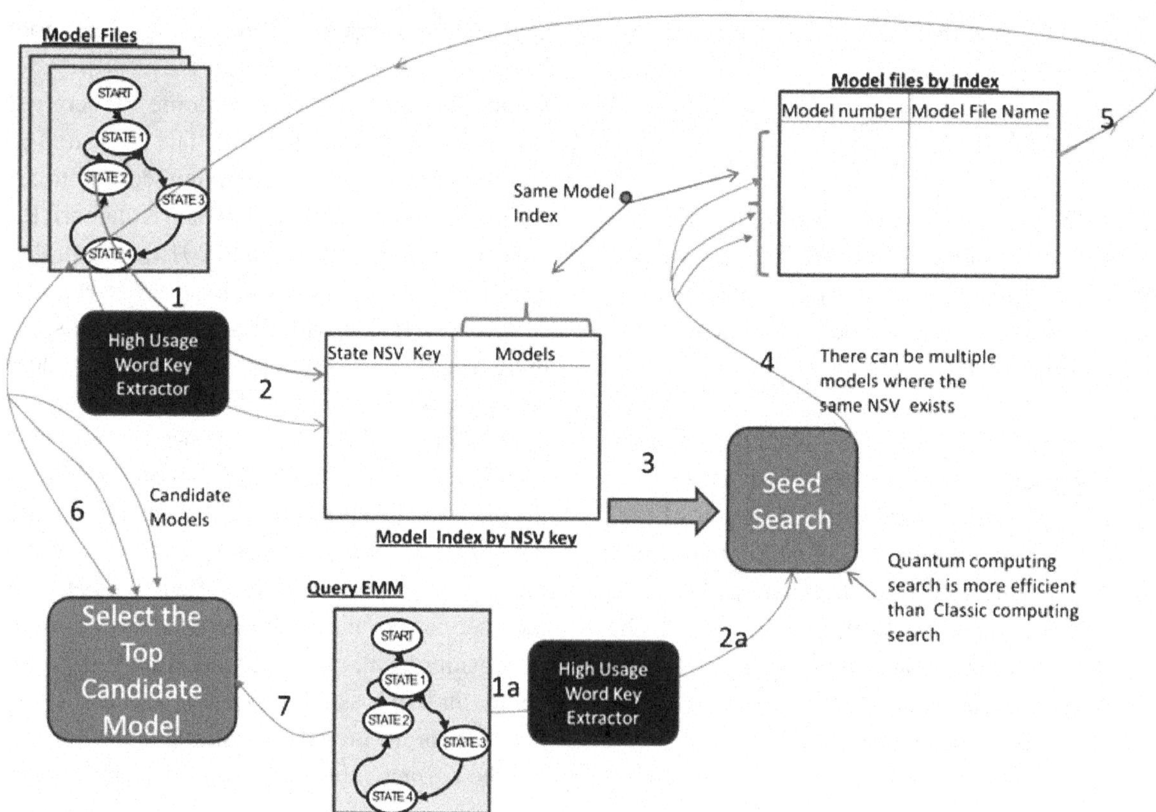

an index generated from select subset p-mer composition.

4. For each Query,
   a. Derive the EMM states (each state is associated with a consolidated p-mer count vector)
   b. For each EMM state,
      i. Extract the high usage words and create a key.
      ii. Search the key in the index database and extract the preliminary candidate models.
5. Rank the models found according to the number of hits. Apply threshold to derive candidate models.
6. Assess the query against the candidate models.
7. Generate rank order and select the highest ranking model.

Thus, once all models in the database are evaluated for a query using either method, the highest scoring model is chosen as the preferred classification for the query sequence. In case, there is more than one such model or if there are other high scoring models, they are listed for further subjective evaluation by the researcher.

The time complexity of the standard method is O(MN) and the same for seeding method is O(MN + M'N/K) where M is the number models, N is the length of a sequence, K is the number of equal size segments in a sequence and M' is the number of candidate models. The second term in the latter complexity formula accounts for handling the candidate models and the approach is more suited for quantum computing where the first term is reduced to a square root.

As can be seen, the mapping of model states (consolidated NSVs) against a model and searching across a database of models states are exhaustive and fairly sequential though EMM based methods (basic or improved key-mapped search) generally perform better than the dynamic programming based HMM methods. The Figure 4 also refers to the point of search where quantum computing offers parallelism more efficiently than any other method. Now we will consider the quantum computing paradigm to parallelize sequence search and classification.

SOLUTIONS AND RECOMMENDATIONS

Applying Grover's Algorithm

Since EMM based model representation and search are more efficient than the HMM counter parts (Kotamarti & Dunham, 2010), we will explore the quantum complement for the EMM approach.

The Figure shows the various components involved in searching for the right model given a query sequence and sequence communities in their EMM form. First, high usage p-mers are derived and tabulated as <key, model> data. Then a search is performed using the much smaller key data to arrive at a smaller candidate set of models that contain the best possible classification. The iterative exhaustive search in Classic Computing can be improved using the parallel computing based on quantum principle of superposition. This results in a significant improvement in processing time as quantum search based on Grover algorithm can complete exhaustive search in $\sqrt{N}$ where N is the aggregate number of model states. Finally, the candidate set is evaluated reasonably quickly even using the exhaustive search since the volume of data is much smaller.

Quantum Complement

For a given query, the classic version evaluates each model, one state at a time. An EMM node is a consolidation of similar sequence segments. In fact, it is necessary to search every member of every node of every EMM in the database for an NSV (recall NSV is a count vector of a sequence segment) of the query sequence. To realize parallelism, the search space is to be transformed into a single qubit register capable of representing all available database entries. The quantum complement of the classic version of the seeding method presented earlier is as follows:

1. For each NSV s_i (which is a count vector for a segment) of the query sequence,
   a. Find all occurrences of the matching states from the models database that are within a small threshold of distance.
2. Select the models with the most number of matched states as candidate models.
3. For each candidate model,
   a. Find all quasi alignments, i.e., find the nearest state for each NSV of the query sequence.
   b. Assign a weight W_i of 1 for each supported transition and a penalty $W_i = \varepsilon$ for the unsupported transitions.
   c. Score each candidate model by taking reciprocal of $1+\sum W_i Q_i$.
4. Select the model with the highest score as the preferred classification for the query sequence.
5. Retrieve other high scoring models to generate the search output.

The above algorithm has a time complexity of $O(\sqrt{KMN} + M'\frac{N}{K})$ where M is the number models, N is the length of a sequence, K is the number of equal size segments in a sequence and M' is the number of candidate models. The quantum paradigm reduces the serial comparisons $\boldsymbol{T}$ of all states of all models for a single query NSV, i.e, *1 out of* K, ($\boldsymbol{T} = \frac{MN}{K}$) against an NSV (count vector of a single segment in a query sequence) to one quantum step equivalent to the square root of total comparisons i.e. $\sqrt{T}$. For example, in case of a 1000 model database of 25 EMM states with an average cluster size of 10 per state, the number of serial comparisons required is $T = 25*1000*10 = 250{,}000$ in a classic computing system where as the same in a quantum system can be achieved in $\sqrt{T} = \sqrt{250{,}000} = 500$ Grover iterations. This marked improvement is possible by restructuring the algorithm to consider all models at once and then working only with the candidate models for further narrowing down the search.

Figure 5 shows how the quantum search is used in reducing the search space for determining the correct classification for a query sequence.

Quantum Representation

The classic computing algorithm for EMMs generally uses a centroid to represent the cluster of members (NSVs) in a state. This is not only adequate accuracy but also a way to reduce the space usage in model states. The subsequent query evaluations simply consider the state's centroid vector for match assessments. But, the centroid is not always the best representation of the underlying data especially in strain level models where the sequences are very similar except for a few small stretches. For example, if 16S rRNA sequences are used to model microbial strains consisting of multiple similar copies, several sequence segments would be nearly identical and therefore are clustered into the same state. If we realize that these are simple variations of a bit pattern, they can be thought of as superpositions of a qubit register of adequate length. Note that superposition is simply a term used to describe all possible permutations of a bit pattern.

Thus a single qubit register can represent the entire cluster of sequences due to superposition. Since all NSVs are of equal size, a single qubit register can in fact represent all NSV variations used in all states and in all of models. This allows for direct computation of distance between a query NSV and an NSV representation in each state quite efficiently and hence no need for centroid representation. Furthermore, by not using a centroid abstraction, the match accuracy is greatly enhanced due to elimination of averaging effects of centroid computations.

The Figure shows how the quantum search is used in reducing the search space for determining the correct classification for a query sequence. The darker blue is used for building the database of models while the lighter gray is used to represent the query processing. At first, all raw sequences are converted into numerical summarization vectors which are then transformed into compact EMMs with each node representing a cluster of similar NSVs. Next, a unique key is derived based on high usage counts in all NSVs which is then used to identify the model(s) corresponding to the key(s). With model database thus mapped with keys, it is now available for efficient quantum search as follows. First, a given query sequence is also converted to NSVs, then transformed into an EMM and a search key is derived. Next, the key is used to quantum search through the key-model database to find the candidate set of approximately matching models which are then evaluated one at a time to determine the most likely classification. Please note that Quantum algorithm can locate the matching key(s) within some DELTA threshold more quickly than any method known today as it uses superposition

Figure 5. Realizing sequence classification using quantum computing

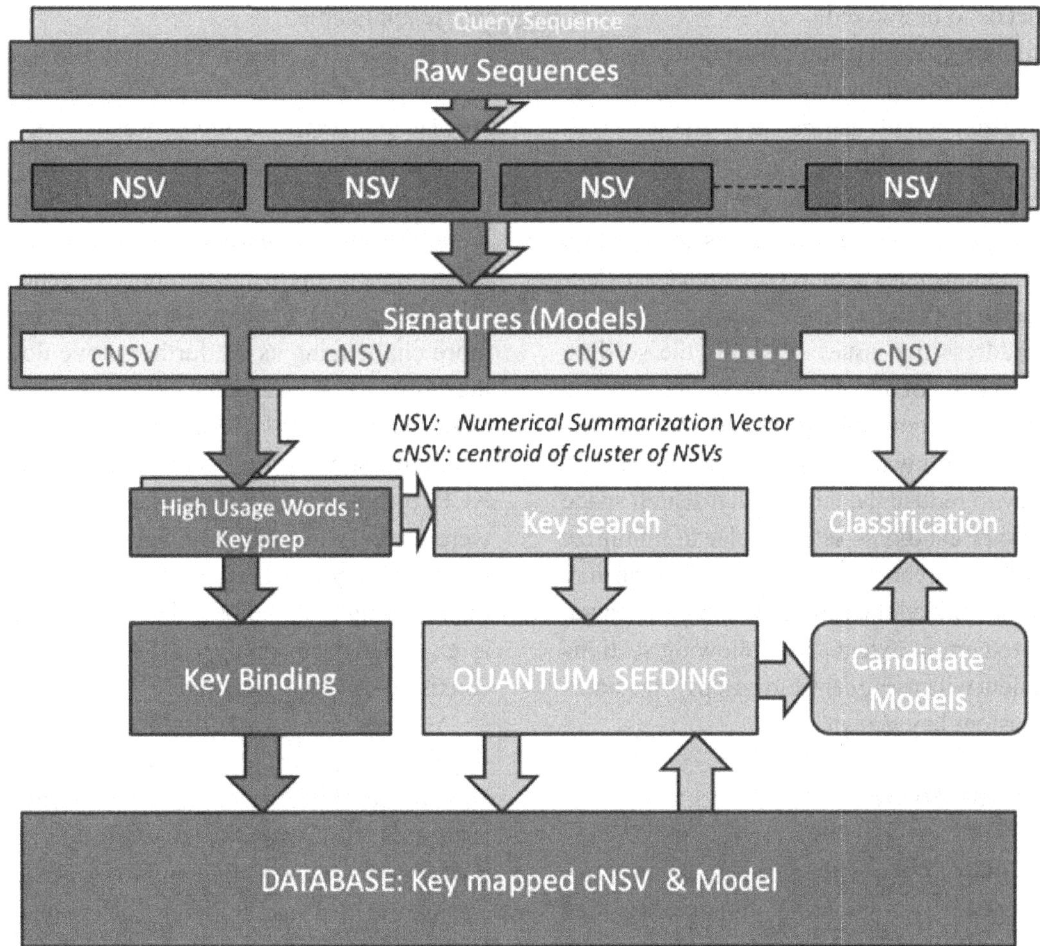

of 1 and 0. This becomes quite considerable when the number of entries to search is large which is the case with sequence analysis. Trader may note that the key mapped model database essentially is a key-model: index database.

A qubit register representation includes all possible states as indicated by 2^l where l is the length of a qubit register. But, not all combinations may represent a valid occurrence. For example, a qubit register of 8 can represent $2^8=256$ data items though the real database size may be smaller than 256, but greater than 128. In such cases, a query for a non-occurring combination would still produce a match. Similarly, in cases where a particular combination has no corresponding data in the database, a poorly framed query can still result in a match. As such, care must be taken to filter the results of a quantum search or the query itself needs to be filtered.

Alternately, application specific key may be generated, mapped to real data items and the qubit register length can be set to the length of the key only. Such practice will prevent unused combinations to be handled more efficiently. We will refer to this domain of issues in quantum representation and search as *Quantum Over Representation* (QOR).

To address the issues of QOR, the seeding method version of query evaluation is considered for quantum computing because the seeding process uses a few high usage p-mers to create a filter key to reduce the large model search space to a smaller candidate set. In order to minimize the QOR issues, centroid based consolidation may need to be utilized thus compromising match accuracy to certain extent. The following sections experiment with using centroid based EMM states and a custom key design.

Implementation

For our analysis, we will consider using the 16S rRNA sequences of microbial organisms as they were also used in the original publications on EMM based sequence analysis (Kotamarti, Raiford, Hahsler, Wang, McGee, & Dunham, Nov 2009). 16S rRNA, a part of ribosomal RNA, is an essential and ubiquitous gene sequence and it is commonly collected and used for microbial identification (Clarridge, 2004) and classification (W. G. Weisburg, jan. 1991).

The 16S rRNA Database utilized in this analysis is derived from the NCBI Microbial Complete Genome Database at http://www.ncbi.nlm.nih.gov/genomes/lproks.cgi. The sequences were extracted from the annotated whole genome sequence files using keyword searches. From this data, a new database was built that consists of individual files, one per microbial organism, in FASTA format. The original dataset was derived from the NCBI as of August 2009 and consists of 782 organisms each with multiple 16S sequences where applicable.

The FASTA header for each file contains five pieces of information: *phylum, class, genus, species* and *organism name*. Reader with some background on Microbiology will quickly note that the information is simply the classification hierarchy with *phylum* at the top. *Class* and *genus* are the next levels in the hierarchy. In general, the classification of an unknown sequence becomes more challenging as we further move down the hierarchy. For example, efficient *sub-genus* classification is still a research area. The authors found that some of the header information in the NCBI database was missing in some cases. There were several cases of missing genus or even class information. Since this type of information is used for verifying the topological accuracy, such data is excluded from analysis. The final database consisted of 676 organisms.

As stated, *Sub-genus* classification of microbial sequences is unavailable today to the best of our knowledge. However, using EMM addresses this issue quite efficiently (Kotamarti R. M., Hahsler, Raiford, McGee, & Dunham, 2010). First, a *species* (lower than *genus*) library is created in the form of EMMs. Recall that EMMs efficiently capture the sequence information in a dynamic markov model framework. Next, classification for all strains is generated using the 16S rRNA sequence information available for each strain. Each confirmed classification is further qualified with a declaration of statistical significance which is derived using extended Karlin-Altschul statistics (Kotamarti, Raiford, Hahsler, Wang, McGee, & Dunham, Nov 2009)(Kotamarti R. M., Hahsler, Raiford, McGee, & Dunham, 2010). Ambiguous classifications where more than one species matched a strain are reported with a more involved analysis using markers other than the 16S rRNA. But the percentage of these was found to be less than 2% by the authors and the problem is a well known issue due to the heterogeneity of the 16S rRNA.

It is important to note that each classification of a strain required evaluation of 455 species models of 18 states. This required a total of *18*455*18 = 147,420* NSV comparisons where a pattern *p* of 3 and NSV size of $4^3=64$ are used. Once again, recall that an NSV of p=3 has sixty four 3-mer variations and corresponding counts. While this is still a marked improvement over the prevailing methods and actually provides a missing sub-genus classifier, this can be further significantly improved using quantum computing.

Before we present the quantum solution, it may be noted that quantum computing is not yet a commercial reality to the extent that any quantum algorithm can be verified. As such, the authors are unable to include any such test results here.

Quantum Seeding

Using quantum search based on partial matching with *high usage p-mer keys* to identify a reduced set of candidate models is referred to as Quantum Seeding in this chapter.

The classic EMM Sequence Analysis(Kotamarti, Raiford, Hahsler, Wang, McGee, & Dunham, Nov 2009) solution used a segment size of 80, pattern width of 3, i.e. $p=3$ which resulted in NSV length of 64 with each element value ranging theoretically between a *0* and *78*. This would typically require 7-bits to represent each element and thus the NSV length in bits would be *7*64 =448*. But, many elements in an NSV would be zeroes and the sum of all elements is always equal to $\frac{N}{K}-(p-1)$ or $80-(3-1)=78$ where N is the sequence length, K is the number of equal sized segments and $\boldsymbol{p}$ is the pattern width used for p-mer counting. This implies that much of the NSV's elements are filled with zeroes. Instead of addressing the entire 2^{448} superpositions which is unrealistically larger than the actual search space, we will derive a key wide enough to represent the actual data.

For the dataset used, high usage p-mers of interest are determined to be as shown in the Table 1. To make sure that key length is adequate to map all available NSVs in the model database, we recall that there are *147,420* model states. If we retain centroid representation to consolidate all similar sequence segments clustered in the node (EMM state), one vector per state is sufficient. This means that we need a key to be at least 18 bits wide.

Table 1. Using high usage words as the key for quantum seeding

3-mer	Pos	M.F	LOD
AGU	11	0.13	20
AUG	14	0.13	20
GAU	35	0.13	20
GUA	44	0.13	20
UAG	50	0.13	20
UGA	56	0.13	20

For the microbial 16S rRNA database consisting of 455 species, there are 6 high usage 3-mers (words) out of a total of 64. The table lists the position within the NSV, the normalized mean frequency M.F and the Log Odds score (LOD) assigned. LOD score is defined as the log of ratio between joint frequency and product of individual frequencies. For example, LOD score for a 3-mer such as AGU involves counting the number of times the joint pattern AGU and the individual symbol i.e. A, G and U occur. Though all the six appear to have the same values, this is not necessarily the case for all datasets. All or some of these are used to generate the key for each 64-element NSV present in the model data base. The same key composition is also used in framing a query prior to quantum seeding. Note each model state has a cluster of NSVs.

Next we need to determine how many high usage 3-mers we can include in the key. Since the largest element (one out of 64 p-mer combinations) value is *0.13*, converting to an integral value by multiplying with *100* gives *13* which requires 4 bits to represent. Since we have *six* 3-mers to choose from, we choose any five as the key and simply mask most significant bits we do not use. Once model state database is mapped using such 18-bit key, it is ready for quantum search. Of course, the same key generation would also be required for the query sequence. Once Query key and the database are set up, we can use the algorithm mentioned earlier except that possibly larger number of preliminary candidate models would first be generated. This is because we are using only five out of 64 elements leading to a coarse search. The preliminary candidates are then evaluated one by one to find the most likely one along with the other most probable matching models.

This is a block diagram for finding a single model state that is within a threshold distance from the query NSV. The single 18-bit qubit register includes all binary combinations as superpositions which are simultaneously evaluated by the quantum logic. QDIST is a quantum circuit for computing distance between two vectors of length 18. QBSC is a Quantum bit string comparator (Oliveira & R, 2007) that generates two output lines to indicate if the distance is same, above or below the threshold T. The Q? consolidates the 2-line output and generates a trigger |1> which the Grover quantum circuit (Grover, 1996) } uses to isolate the state vector corresponding to the matched model NSV.

Quantum Oracle Function

Quantum computing relies on a core function that initially works with the superpositions. In our case, this function computes distance and flags all that meet the minimum distance criteria. The quantum circuit here has two components 1) distance computation and 2) comparator circuit to trigger when a state vector with minimum distance is found. The overall quantum solution would have to also involve Grover iterations (Grover, 1996) which come in play only after a state vector that satisfies the minimum threshold distance criterion is found. The distance function computes the Manhattan distance between two strings of 18 qubits. The Figure 6 shows the block diagram of such oracle along with a trigger/driver circuit for Grover. The transfer functions are given as appendix for a 2-qubit realization.

FUTURE RESEARCH DIRECTIONS

Precise identification of strains without depending on time consuming wet lab techniques or multi-marker analyses is an area of future research. Emergence of cloud computing facilitates large centralized genomic databases which rely on innovative search techniques. Setting up databases to be amenable for quantum computing is a direction promoted by the authors. The newly retrieved sequence data will find a convenient place in the emerging mobile devices while the

Figure 6. Finding the candidate models using quantum search

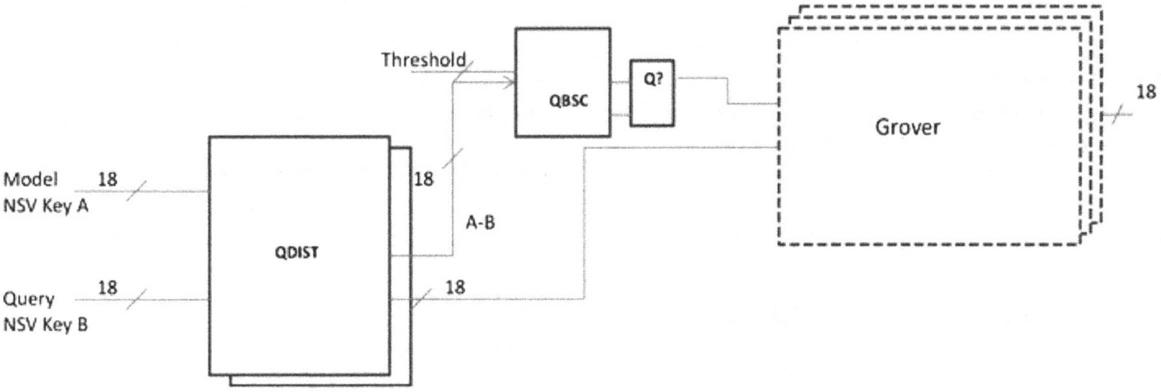

classification of them will be better performed in the cloud using parallel search techniques initially based on classic computing evolving to a quantum computing paradigm. Such trends reduce costs of strain identification and diagnosis in future clinics that leverage genomic tools.

CONCLUSION

Sequence analysis has extended from statistical BLAST based query of sequence database to probabilistic profileHMM based familial modeling (Figure 2) and analysis. With models as proven and useful representations, as their library sizes too start increasing, faster and better search methods become necessary. In anticipation toward a much larger model database with search issues due to increased data from the next generation sequencing, we proposed two methods 1) using Extensible Markov Models (Figure 3 instead of Hidden Markov Models and 2) evolving toward a quantum algorithm (Figures 1 and 6) for improving the search and classification.

Using the 16S rRNA sequences for 455 species, a classifier that was originally developed based on EMM methodology was utilizedand found to work accurately for 98% of the strains tested. The 2% error rate corresponds to the fact that the 16S rRNA is a multi-copy marker and as such using it alone is not sufficient in all cases. Since there is no known sub-genus classifier available today, to the best of our knowledge, the classifier's performance at 98% is reasonable. Using this data set and computation complexity as examples, we investigated how quantum computing could improve the time complexity.

Since parallel processing is possible with Quantum computing, we showed that a query sequence can be searched against a model data base very efficiently if candidate models are first determined based on results found from a quantum search on partial, but high usage p-mer counts. While such seeding of a search is not uncommon since introduction of BLAST, using quantum computing and in an alignment-free paradigm has not been attempted earlier to this point. As expected, candidate models can easily be isolated to a much smaller subset which can then be processed using classic computing.

As genomic databases continue to grow in the native form or the model form, faster heuristics and better representations will be required. Generating keys for quantum search and supplement classic computing with quantum assisted search space reduction using high usage words can be very useful even for databases in native or HMM form. Using multi-valued logic to represent the 4 bases of DNA/RNA or the 20 amino acids can be very powerful and calls for future research.

REFERENCES

Altschul, K. (1997). Gapped BLAST and PSI-BLAST: A new generation of protein database search programs. *Nucleic Acids Research*, *25*, 3389–3402. doi:10.1093/nar/25.17.3389

Bateman, A., Birney, E., Durbin, R., Eddy, S. R., Howe, K. L., & Sonnhammer, E. L. (2000). The Pfam protein families database. *Nucleic Acids Research*, *28*, 263–266. doi:10.1093/nar/28.1.263

Bennett, C., Bernstein, E., Brassard, G., & Vazirani, U. (1997). Strengths and weaknesses of quantum computing. *SIAM Journal on Computing*, *26*, 1510–1523. doi:10.1137/S0097539796300933

Benson, D. A., Karsch-Mizrachi, I., Lipman, D. J., Ostell, J., & Wheeler, D. L. (2006). GenBank. *Nucleic Acids Research*, *34*, D16–D20. doi:10.1093/nar/gkj157

Blaisdell, B. (1989). Average values of a dissimilarity measure not requiring sequence alignment are twice the averages of conventional mismatch counts requiring sequence alignment for a computer-generated model system. *Journal of Molecular Evolution*, *29*, 538–547. doi:10.1007/BF02602925

Blaisdell, B. E. (1986). A measure of the similarity of sets of sequences not requiring sequence alignment. *Proceedings of the National Acdemy of Sciences USA*, *83*, 5155–5159. doi:10.1073/pnas.83.14.5155

Clarridge, J. E. (2004). Impact of 16S rRNA gene sequence analysis for identification of bacteria on clinical microbiology and infectious diseases. *Clinical Microbiology Reviews*, *17*, 840–862. doi:10.1128/CMR.17.4.840-862.2004

Dayhoff, M. O., Schwartz, R. M., & Orcutt, B. C. (1978). A model of evolutionary change in proteins. *Atlas of protein sequence and structure*, Vol. 5, (pp. 345-351).

Deutsch, D. (1985). Quantum theory, the Church-Turing principle and the universal quantum computer. *Proceedings of the Royal Society of London. Series A: Mathematical and Physical Sciences*, *400*, 97–117. doi:10.1098/rspa.1985.0070

Dirac, P. (1939). A new notation for quantum mechanics. *Proceedings of the Cambridge Philosophical Society*, *35*, (p. 416).

Dunham, M. H., Meng, Y., & Huang, J. (2004). *Extensible Markov model* (pp. 371–374).

Durbin, R. (1998). *Biological sequence analysis: Probabilistic models of proteins and nucleic acids*. Cambridge University Press. doi:10.1017/CBO9780511790492

Eddy, S. R. (1998). Profile hidden Markov models. *Bioinformatics (Oxford, England)*, *14*, 755–763. doi:10.1093/bioinformatics/14.9.755

Finn, R. D., Tate, J., Mistry, J., Coggill, P. C., Sammut, S. J., & Hotz, H.-R. (2008). The Pfam protein families database. *Nucleic Acids Research*, *36*, D281–D288. doi:10.1093/nar/gkm960

Grover, L. K. (1996). A fast quantum mechanical algorithm for database search. *Proceedings of the ACM Symposium on the Theory of Computing*, (pp. 212-219).

Henikoff, S., & Henikoff, J. G. (1992). Amino acid substitution matrices from protein blocks. *Proceedings of the National Academy of Sciences of the United States of America*, *89*, 10915–10919. doi:10.1073/pnas.89.22.10915

Karlin, S., & Altschul, S. F. (1990). Methods for assessing the statistical significance of molecular sequence features by using general scoring schemes. *Proceedings of the National Academy of Sciences of the United States of America*, *87*, 2264–2268. doi:10.1073/pnas.87.6.2264

Kotamarti, R., Hahsler, M., Raiford, D., & Dunham, M. (2010). Sequence transformation to a complex signature form for consistent phylogenetic tree using extensible Markov model. *Computational Intelligence in Bioinformatics and Computational Biology (CIBCB)* (pp. 1 - 8). Montreal: ieeexplore.ieee.org.

Kotamarti, R. M., & Dunham, M. H. (2010). *Alignment-free sequence analysis using extensible Markov models.* Presented paper at 9th International Workshop on Data Mining in Bioinformatics (BIOKDD).

Kotamarti, R. M., Hahsler, M., Raiford, D., McGee, M., & Dunham, M. H. (2010). Analyzing taxonomic classification using extensible Markov models. *Bioinformatics (Oxford, England)*, *26*(18), 2235–2241. doi:10.1093/bioinformatics/btq349

Kotamarti, R. M., Raiford, D. W., Hahsler, M., Wang, Y., McGee, M., & Dunham, M. H. (Nov 2009). *Targeted genomic signature profiling with quasi-alignment statistics*. COBRA Preprint Series, Article 63.

Marinescu, D. C., & Marinescu, G. M. (2005). *Approaching quantum computing*. France: Pearson Prentice-Hall.

Nielsen, M. A., & Chuang, I. L. (2000). *Quantum computation and quantum information*. Cambridge University Press.

Oliveira, D., & Ramos, R. (2007). Quantum bit string comparator: Circuits and applications. *Quantum Computers and Computing*, *7*(1), 17–26.

Oliver, T., Yeow, L. Y., & Schmidt, B. (2008). Integrating FPGA acceleration into HMMer. *Parallel Computing*, *34*, 681–691. doi:10.1016/j.parco.2008.08.003

Rivest, R. L., Shamir, A., & Adleman, L. (1978). A method for obtaining digital signatures and public-key cryptosystems. *Communications of the ACM*, *21*, 120–126. doi:10.1145/359340.359342

Thompson, J. D., Higgins, D. G., & Gibson, T. J. (1994). CLUSTAL W: Improving the sensitivity of progressive multiple sequence alignment through sequence weighting, position-specific gap penalties and weight matrix choice. *Nucleic Acids Research*, *22*, 4673–4680. doi:10.1093/nar/22.22.4673

Vinga, S., & Almeida, J. (2003). Alignment-free sequence comparison-a review. *Bioinformatics (Oxford, England)*, *19*, 513–523. doi:10.1093/bioinformatics/btg005

Weisburg, W. G., Barns, S. M., Pelletier, D. A., & Lane, D. J. (1991). 16S ribosomal DNA amplification for phylogenetic study. *Journal of Bacteriology*, *173*(2), 697–703.

Yanofsky, N. S., & Mannucci, M. A. (2008). *Quantum computing for computer scientists*. Cambridge University Press.

APPENDIX: COMPLEXITY ANALYSIS

The quantum version of the seeding algorithm has a time complexity of $O(\sqrt{KMN} + K\frac{M'N}{K})$ which is much smaller than *O(MN)* for the standard classic version especially as the number of models grows. The term *KMN* comes from the fact that *M* models of $\frac{N}{K}$ states are searched *K* times for *K* segments of the query sequence. Since Grover algorithm searches MN / K states in $\sqrt{MN / K}$ the overall complexity accounting for *K* segments of query is $O(\sqrt{KMN})$.

APPENDIX: SYNTHESIS: TRANSFER FUNCTIONS

Quantum transfer functions operate on the input state vectors and evolve them to their target representations. The first is a 2-qubit function that computes the manhattan distance between two 2-qubit strings which can be easily extended to n-qubits. The second is a 2-qubit function that compares the 2-qubit string to a threshold and evolves to the result in two output qubits. The third evolves the two output qubits from the QBSC to generate a 1-qubit trigger for the Grover circuit.

Transfer function for the QDIST, QBSC and Q? functions are given in Figure 7 for a 2-qubit implementation which can easily be extended to the n-qubit.

Figure 7. Transfer functions for the quantum circuits

2-QDIST

a	a1	a2	b1	b2	d1	d2	g1	g2	g3	Projectors
0	0	0	0	0	0	0	0	0	0	|0><0|+
0	0	0	0	1	0	1	0	0	1	|9><1|+
0	0	0	1	0	1	0	0	1	0	|18><2|+
0	0	0	1	1	1	1	0	1	1	|27><3|+
0	0	1	0	0	0	1	1	0	0	|12><4|+
0	0	1	0	1	0	0	1	0	1	|5><5|+
0	0	1	1	0	0	1	1	1	0	|14><6|+
0	0	1	1	1	1	0	1	1	1	|23><7|+
0	1	0	0	0	1	0	0	0	0	|16><8|+
0	1	0	0	1	0	1	0	1	0	|10><9|+
0	1	0	1	0	0	0	0	1	1	|3><10|+
0	1	0	1	1	0	1	1	0	1	|13><11|+
0	1	1	0	0	1	1	1	0	1	|29><12|+
0	1	1	0	1	1	0	1	1	0	|22><13|+
0	1	1	1	0	0	1	1	1	1	|15><14|+
0	1	1	1	1	0	0	0	0	1	|1><15|

2-QBSC

O1	O2	g1	g2	g3	Projectors
0	0	0	0	0	|0><0|+
0	1	0	0	1	|9><1|+
0	1	0	1	0	|10><2|+
0	1	0	1	1	|11><3|+
1	0	0	0	0	|16><4|+
0	0	1	0	1	|5><5|+
0	1	1	1	0	|14><6|+
0	1	1	1	1	|15><7|+
1	0	0	0	1	|17><8|+
1	0	0	1	0	|18><9|+
0	0	0	1	0	|2><10|+
0	1	1	0	0	|12><11|+
1	0	1	0	1	|21><12|+
1	0	1	1	0	|22><13|+
1	0	1	0	0	|20><14|+
0	0	1	1	1	|7><15|

2-Q?

O1	O2	y	g	Projectors
0	0	1	0	|1><0|
0	1	0	1	|1><1|
1	0	1	1	|3><2|
1	1	0	0	|0><3|

G_{qdist} = |0><0|+|9><1|+|18><2|+|27><3|+|12><4|+|5><5|+|14><6|+|23><7|+|16><8|+|10><9|+|3><10|+|13><11|+|29><12|+|22><13|+|15><14|+|1><15|

G_{qbsc} = |0><0|+|9><1|+|10><2|+|11><3|+|16><4|+|5><5|+|14><6|+|15><7|+|17><8|+|18><9|+|2><10|+|12><11|+|21><12|+|22><13|+|20><14|+|7><15|

$G_{q?}$ = |1><0|+|1><1|+|3><2|+|0><3|

Chapter 18
Improving the Efficiency of Large-Scale Agent-Based Models Using Compression Techniques

Mitchell Welch
University of New England, Australia

Paul Kwan
University of New England, Australia

A.S.M. Sajeev
University of New England, Australia

Graeme Garner
Office of the Chief Veterinary Officer, Department of Agriculture, Fisheries and Forestry Australia, Australia

ABSTRACT

Agent-based modelling is becoming a widely used approach for simulating complex phenomena. By making use of emergent behaviour, agent based models can simulate systems right down to the most minute interactions that affect a system's behaviour. In order to capture the level of detail desired by users, many agent based models now contain hundreds of thousands and even millions of interacting agents. The scale of these models makes them computationally expensive to operate in terms of memory and CPU time, limiting their practicality and use. This chapter details the techniques for applying Dynamic Hierarchical Agent Compression to agent based modelling systems, with the aim of reducing the amount of memory and number of CPU cycles required to manage a set of agents within a model. The scheme outlined extracts the state data stored within a model's agents and takes advantage of redundancy in this data to reduce the memory required to represent this information. The techniques show how a hierarchical data structure can be used to achieve compression of this data and the techniques for implementing this type of structure within an existing modelling system. The chapter includes a case study that outlines the practical considerations related to the application of this scheme to Australia's National Model for Emerging Livestock Disease Threats that is currently being developed.

DOI: 10.4018/978-1-4666-1830-5.ch018

INTRODUCTION

In recent years, *Agent-based modelling* (ABM) has emerged as a robust technique for modelling complex, real-world phenomena. ABMs have been developed to simulate a broad range of natural and man-made systems including pedestrian movement, traffic movement, agricultural land use, social interactions, human and animal disease threats, and flocking behaviour in animals just to name a few (Berger, 2001; Busing & Mailly, 2004; D'Souza, Marino, & Kirschner, 2009; Elliston & Beare, 2006; Funk, Gerber, Lind, & Schillo, 1998; Miron, Garner, Donald, & Dyall, 2009; Perumalla & Aaby, 2008; Schelhorn, O'Sullivan, Haklay, & Thurstain-Goodwin, 1999; Strippgen & Nagel, 2009). Agent-based modelling has its origin in artificial intelligence applications where intelligent systems are designed around *intelligent agents* which are elements that perceive their environment through *sensors* and act upon their environment through *actuators*. The agent's behaviour is defined by an *agent function* that takes its input from the agent's sensors and calculates an action to be carried out using the actuators. This concept has been applied to the application of modelling by replicating entire complex phenomena as a system of multiple interacting agents. The agent-based modelling approach allows scientists to develop rich simulations capable of supporting experimentation at different conceptual levels within a complex system. This capability has led to the use of ABMs in a decision-support role for governments and industry, and fostered a demand for models with higher levels of detail within the individual agents and their interactions that provide an even greater scope for experimentation. In addition to this, ABMs are being applied to larger scale systems, modelling increasingly more complex phenomena.

An excellent example of this trend can be seen in Australia where agent-based simulation is being used to help protect the livestock industries from foreign animal diseases through the development of a national modelling capability to study disease threats. The *National Model for Emerging Livestock Disease Threats* (NMELDT), developed by Miron et al. in (Miron, et al., 2009), simulates the spread of important livestock diseases, such as foot and mouth disease (FMD), on a national scale by taking into account regional and seasonal factors, different species and production sectors, and marketing systems. The simulation uses a range of inputs such as geography, climatic data, disease life-cycle parameters, and livestock movement data through the National Livestock Identification System (NLIS). The NLIS is Australia's system for identifying and tracking beef and dairy cattle (Australia, 2009). It is a permanent, whole-of-life identification system which aims to ensure that individual animals can be tracked from property of birth to slaughter for bio-security, food safety, product integrity and market access purposes. The NLIS uses individual electronic devices —machine-readable, radio frequency identification devices (RFIDs) — that enable cattle to be permanently identified throughout their lifetime. Each device contains a microchip encoded with a unique number linked to a farm identifier. The animal movement data available in the NLIS database is an important input into the simulation platform.

Agent-based modelling is a very versatile computational technique for conducting simulation studies. However, as the modelling gets complex in terms of number of agents and their interactions, the simulations could become unacceptably slow. In order to apply agent-based modelling to more complex phenomena or produce more highly detailed simulations, techniques for efficiently managing the available processing power and system memory are required. This insures that ABMs can be executed within an operationally feasible time limit, using affordable/obtainable hardware. In this chapter, we survey the literature on agent-based disease modelling and their performance characteristics. We then elaborate a promising approach to address the performance issues. The approach we have used is a centralised, hierarchical technique for compressing an agent's state data that takes advantage of redundancy in the state data at different levels amongst simulation agents. The scheme, called *Dynamic Agent Compression* (DAC), allows agents to move into and out of a compressed state as they change over the course of the simulation. The DAC scheme presented in this chapter builds upon the work presented by Wendel and Dibble in (Wendel & Dibble, 2007). The scheme compresses the data stored within each agent in the model using a hierarchical scheme that allows agents to be compressed and de-compressed as they change within the simulation. The principles covered in this chapter can theoretically be applied to any agent-based model (or system), using any general purpose programming or scripting language. In order to give the work in this chapter practical basis, the national scale model developed by Miron et al. in (Miron, et al., 2009) and updated by Happold et al. (Happold et al., 2010) will be outlined in detail as an example of a large-scale ABM. It will then be presented as a test-bed for the implemented techniques outlined within this chapter.

The remainder of this chapter includes a general introduction to agents and agent-based simulation, a case study of the (Australian) National Model for Emerging Livestock Disease Threats (Miron, et al., 2009), a review of relevant literature, a conceptual outline of the dynamic agent compression scheme developed and an outline of a sample implementation of the scheme using the model developed in (Miron, et al., 2009).

BACKGROUND

Agents and Agent-based Modelling

As mentioned in section one, agent-based modelling draws its basis from the intelligent agent systems applied in artificial intelligence applications. They are designed around the principle of conceptually breaking complex systems down into individual components referred to as *Agents.* Although there is no strict definition for what actually constitutes an agent within an ABM, the models and artificial intelligence (AI) systems outlined in literature (Russell & Norvig, 2003) contain agents that are self-contained, autonomous, who are responsible for managing their own interactions, states and data. These agents interact and update their state in discrete time steps within the simulation and perceive the environment in which they exist. Agents can be heterogeneous in nature within a simulation; a single model can contain limitless 'types' or classes of agents. The systems developed in (Grecu & Gonsalves, 2000; Higgins & Richardson, 1995; Luke, Cioffi-Revilla, Panait, & Sullivan, 2004; Minar, Burkhart, Langton, & Askenazi, 1996; Richmond, Coakley, & Romano, 2009; Sonnessa, 2003) all specify multiple types of agents that interact to simulate phenomena. Agents can be conceptually mobile or static within a simulation. The STREETS simulation outlined in (Schelhorn, et al., 1999) provides an example of agents with different levels of mobility. The model simulates the movement of pedestrians through urban areas by the interaction of mobile 'pedestrian' agents with static 'environment' agents that represent the streets and pathways.

Agent-based models simulate the behaviour of complex systems from the bottom up through the state changes, actions and interactions of individual agents that make up the systems. This is referred to as *Emergent behaviour;* the combined behaviours of the systems component-agents define the behaviour of the system as a whole. A good way to describe emergent behaviour is with the analogy of the cells within organisms. An organism is made up of cells and the behaviour of these cells determines the behaviour of the whole organism in the same way as the behaviour of agents in an ABM determines its overall behaviour. An example of another computational system that demonstrates emergent behaviour is

Figure 1. Emergent behaviour in a complex system

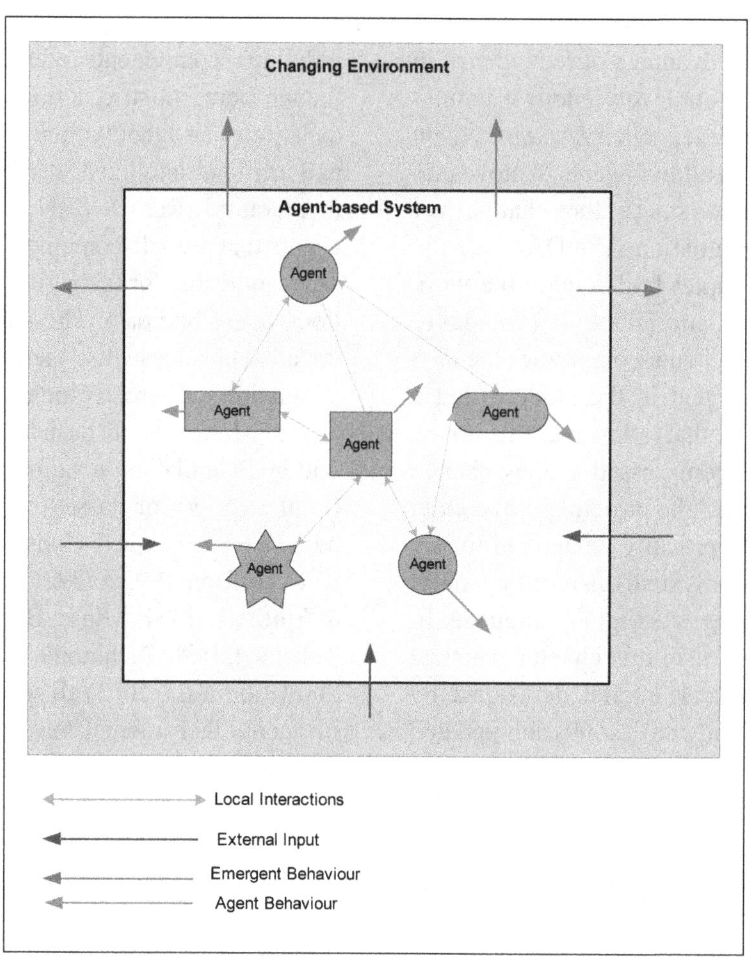

neural network (Russell & Norvig, 2003) used in many artificial intelligence applications. In a neural network, the combined action of all the nodes determines the output of the network. Figure 1 outlines the general principle of emergent behaviour. In this schematic figure, a heterogeneous set of agents interact amongst themselves while reacting to input from a changing environment. The agents produce individual behaviours within the agent-based system and the system as a whole exhibits the combined emergent behaviour of the external environment. An excellent example of the power of emergent behaviour at different levels can be seen in the SWARM simulation tool kit developed by Minar et al. (Minar, et al., 1996) where agents can be organised into groups (or swarms). These swarms can then be treated as a single agent in the simulation with behaviour defined by the constituent agents.

The key advantages of the agent-based modelling approach centre around the flexibility to model systems at different levels of detail through the emergent behaviour of the agents. By modelling with different levels of detail, scientists can develop rich modelling environments that are suited to decision support and experimentation. Decision makers can use ABMs to experiment with individual-level parameter values and see the effects of their changes on the whole system through emergent behaviour. Agent-based modelling provides a natural way to simulate many real world systems. It is far easier to break a problem down into its component parts and concentrate on modelling each component, rather than develop systems of equations for modelling a phenomenon as a whole. Another aspect of this mapping to real world concepts is the implementation within programming languages. Agents-based models can be efficiently and easily implemented within object oriented programming languages like Java or C++ without the need for complex mappings of conceptual agents to program procedures and sets of variables.

The main disadvantage with this type of modelling, as summarised by Crooks et al. (Minar, et al., 1996), also lies within the high level of details possible within the simulation. Because ABMs use a bottom-up modelling paradigm, the behaviour exhibited by an ABM is only as accurate as the behaviour exhibited by the individual agents within the ABM. Consequently, if the actions of the agents at the lowest level of the simulation are not realistic, then the emergent behaviour exhibited by the system as a whole will not be realistic. Obtaining accurate data related to the interactions and states of individual agents within a simulation can be an extremely large undertaking and in some situations impossible. This can make agent-based models expensive to produce and in situations where data is unavailable or difficult to quantify, the accuracy of an ABM can be significantly limited.

In addition to the data constraints, agent-based models can be expensive in terms of both memory usage and computational operations. This is due to the autonomous nature of each agent in the simulation and the state information they contain. In simple terms, as the complexity of the individual agent's processing and/or the number of agents in a simulation increases, the number of computational operations performed in each iteration of the simulation increases. A simulation's memory requirements increase as the amount of state information stored within each agent and the number of agents increases. There have been two general approaches to improve the performance of ABMs that are conceptually complex outlined in the available literature. The first approach involves the application of parallel programming techniques, such as cluster computing and technologies such as Nvidia's *Compute Unified Device Architecture* (CUDA) (NVIDIA, 2010) to provide systems capable of performing larger numbers of operations in each simulation iteration. This can be coupled with large banks of main memory, or memory swapping techniques that manage the large amount of state data. A second, less developed, approach for improving simulation performance involves the use of compression schemes to reduce the physical space required to store each individual agent and the number of operations required in each iteration to update the state of the simulation's agent. The work in this chapter builds upon this idea with the development of a hierarchical compression scheme that takes advantage of redundancy within the state data amongst the different agents.

Related Work

Over the last two decades a significant amount of research has gone into the development of agent-based modelling in the form of both domain-specific simulations (i.e. models developed for a specific phenomenon) and general ABM tool kits that provide scientists with ready-made software platforms which can be used to create customised simulations. Depending on the level of customisation required, such tasks require varying levels of programming skill. Some notable examples of ABM toolkits that have been widely referenced include the SWARM simulation system (Minar, et al., 1996), The NetLogo modelling environment (Tisue & Wilensky, 2004), The MASON toolkit (Luke, et al., 2004), the JAS agent-based simulation (Sonnessa, 2003), the RePast modelling package (Collier, 2004) and the Social Interaction Framework, *SIF*, with its associated Java toolbox presented in (Funk, et al., 1998). These toolkits produce discrete event, cycle based, and state update models that can be applied to a wide range of problems. Each toolkit offers different features and follows different agent paradigms, which are aimed at providing different capabilities for modellers. For example, NetLogo provides a 'Logo' style scripting language instead of using a general purpose language while the MASON toolkit uses a layered structure that allows the developer to break the simulation's agent data and event logic into different conceptual locations. These systems also allow for *geographical information system* (GIS) software packages to be integrated into their simulations, allowing for the development of spatial simulations. An example of this can be seen in the RePast (Collier, 2004) system that uses the OpenMap (LLC, 2005) GIS package.

A significant shortcoming that is present in all of these toolkits is their lack of scalability when dealing with large numbers of agents. These simulation systems are capable of simulating *thousands* of complex agents but are not designed to efficiently handle the *millions* of agents that can be present in simulations systems such as the NMELDT. Work in this area has explored two main solutions to the problem of modelling massive numbers of agents:

- The development of systems that allow agent-based models to take advantage of parallel processing technologies such as the effective use of multi-core processors, *cluster computers* and *graphics processing unit's* general parallel processing techniques. This research is based around the idea that the agent processing can be carried out with at least some degree of parallelism and, in turn, decreases the execution time.
- The implementation of compression and aggregation schemes that improve efficiency by representing the conceptual agents in the model with a smaller number of physical agents within the simulation system. This increases efficiency by reducing the number of update operations required per cycle to update the agents and the amount of memory occupied by the pool of agents.

A *cluster computer* consists of an interconnected network of heterogeneous computers or servers that communicate and solve large computational problems efficiently by dividing up the problem amongst the machines that process each part in parallel. There are a number of programming libraries such as the *Message Passing Interface(MPI)* (Gropp, Lusk, & Skjellum, 1999) and *the Parallel Virtual Machine* (PVM) (Sunderam, 1990) library that provide ready-made environments for creating distributed applications. Other customised systems have been developed for use in agent based modelling system applications. Because this topic is not the focus of this chapter, the specific details of these systems will not be covered but some examples of these include the ZASE (*Zillions of Agents-based Simulation Environment*) (Yamamoto, Tai, & Mizuta, 2007), the AGlobeX modelling environment (Sislak, Volf, Jakob, & Pechoucek, 2009) and systems outlined in (Sislak, et al., 2009) and (Rao, Jain, & Karlapalem, 2007). These all outline schemes to allow massive agent-based simulations, which can contain millions of agents, to be implemented and executed on one or across multiple standard desktop computer systems.

Another approach for applying parallel processing techniques to ABMs covered in current literature involves the making use of *graphics processing units* (GPU) found within desktop computers. Within an actual GPU, a large proportion of transistors are devoted to arithmetic processing. This differs from general purpose CPUs in which most of the transistors are used for cache and program flow control centres. The result of this design is that a GPU is suited to *data-parallel* programs where multiple instances of the same program are executed on multiple data elements in parallel. This can be achieved by using the functions provided by the OpenGL and Direct3D graphics card libraries or Nvidia's *Compute Unified Device Architecture* (CUDA) (NVIDIA, 2010), for the general processing tasks within agent-based models. The first approach, involving the OpenGL and Direct3D libraries, is referred to as *General Purpose Graphics Processing Unit* (GPGPU) programming (Goddeke, 2005). The work in (Lysenko & D'Souza, 2008), (D'Souza, et al., 2009) and (Perumalla & Aaby, 2008) provide solid examples of this technologies application to agent based modelling.

The second way to improve the performance of massive agent-based models is to compress and aggregate agents to different levels of granularity within the simulation. Compression is commonly used to improve the efficiency of applications in other areas of Computer Science such as in video and audio software. Compression essentially involves finding similarities within the data and applying efficient representations of the data (Li & Drew, 2004). This can either be done in a static fashion before the simulation begins or dynamically as the simulation progresses. The work in (Stage, Crookson, & Monserud, 1993) presents a system whereby multiple agents are represented by an aggregate agent. The algorithm works by treating each agent as a point in a multi-dimensional space. Each dimension in the agent's space represents one of the attributes that the agents possess. Examples of these could include age, location co-ordinates, disease life cycle parameters etc. Clustering algorithms are used to partition all the agents in the space into groups (i.e. clusters) of agents that possess similar attribute values. From here, the centroid of each cluster is calculated and the attribute values of this centroid are used to define a single agent that represents all agents in the cluster. In addition to this, the aggregate agent stores an *expansion factor* which indicates the number of agents that the aggregate agent represents. This is a one-off static process carried out at the start of the simulation. There is no alteration done to the clusters and the aggregate agents over the course of the simulation.

Wendel and Dibble (Wendel & Dibble, 2007) builds upon this idea presenting a system for dynamically compressing agents, allowing them to move in and out of their compressed state as their internal states change during the course of a simulation. The system works in either a *lossless* mode, where no information from each agent is lost during compression, or a *lossy* mode, which provides a higher level of compression but results in some information loss due to the compression process. The simulation system consists of two components: a set of agent containers that represent the clusters of agents in simulation and a compression manager, which acts as a 'wrapper' around the set of agents by coordinating model interactions with the agent containers. The agent containers contain a count of the number of agents that they represent, just as the system outlined in (Stage, et al., 1993). At the start of the simulation, the compression manager groups agents that are similar into containers. The agents that are particularly unique are left un-grouped. The agent containers behave exactly like the agents that they contain. The compression manager manages the queries to the agents by directing the queries to the appropriate containers or unique agents. The containers respond to the queries as if they were individual agents. As the internal states of some agents change, causing them to differentiate themselves from their groups, the compression manager removes them from their respective containers and instantiates them as unique agents. If a unique agent's attributes change to match those of the agents present within an existing container, the agent is added to that container.

The method used to group the agents into the containers determines whether the compression is lossy or lossless. If the agents that are grouped into a container are *identical*, that is all of their attributes have identical values, then the compression will be lossless. For agents that are *similar*, that is their attributes values are similar, they are grouped into the same containers and the compression will be lossy. The degree of information loss will depend upon the heterogeneity of the agents that are grouped into the same containers. Attributes of the agents stored within a container are categorised in one of three ways. The attribute may be *compressible*, *storable* or *state-dependent compressible*. Compressible attributes are those that can be compressed (i.e. one copy controlled by the container for all agents). Storable attributes are those attributes of each individual agent that cannot be compressed. An example of an attribute that could not be compressed is a serial number as they are unique to each agent. State-dependent compressible variables are those variables that have certain values that can change frequently and other values that do not change frequently. Therefore, the variable is only compressed when it contains a value flagged as not frequently changing. This is domain dependent and needs to be specified by the developer.

An implementation of this compression system in Java showed significant performance improvements when large numbers of agents were present in the simulation. In the sample model, up to 5% of the agents were heterogeneous and un-compressed. Agents transitioned frequently from compressed to un-compressed states resulting in an average turnover of 15 times during the course of the simulation. The experimental results showed that when the simulation contained low numbers (i.e. 100-500) of agents, the execution time was slightly higher than the benchmark that did not use the compression. This is due to the processing overhead of the compression manager. With larger numbers of agents, the execution times for the implementation using the compression system were significantly less. A detailed analysis of the results in (Wendel & Dibble, 2007) show that the potential benefits of the scheme can be even greater with specific agent based models.

METHODS

A High Level Overview

The architecture of the system uses a centralised approach where the core simulation modules update and interact with the agent set via an agent management interface. The interface decouples the agent data from the individual agents, as it is no longer encapsulated within each individual agent. For example, instead of an agent storing its own set of data, the agent manager stores the agent's data (along with the data of other agents) in a single, optimised structure that implements the compression system. The individual agent simply contains a pointer to the location of its data within the central manager. This allows for the system to take advantage of data redundancy across the entire set of agents and in addition to this, access to the data via the individual agents is still a simple operation. The interface can be implemented using parallel processing technologies (such as multithreading and distributed computing) depending upon the nature of the simulation and assets available to the simulation system. The use of these technologies means that this agent manager does not become a bottle-neck within the simulation. Figure 2 outlines the general architecture that the agent compression system uses. It is important to note that this is a general outline. Individual simulation systems can make modifications, depending upon the nature of the agents, their interactions and the way they connect to the other components of the simulation system (for example, GIS and database systems). Figure 2 also shows the flow of information (indicated by the arrows) between the components of an example modelling system. The *Simulation system* components are representative of a typical agent-based model where the simulation logic is implemented in a general purpose programming language and interfaces with database systems and possible GIS packages. The key component within this scheme is the *Central Agent Manager* which is responsible for managing the interactions with the agent set and the dynamic compression of the agents. The agent set itself consists of a set of custom objects that can, in turn, contains a set of sub-objects, forming a hierarchy of agent data.

Agents and Agent Data

The system proposed in this section is a form of loss-less compression that takes advantage of the inherent data-redundancy that is present amongst agents. The agents in ABMs can be viewed as containers that hold state information. This information can be of any type imaginable and be of any size feasible, depending upon the requirements of the model and the phenomena being simulated. In the case study covered in the following section on NMELDT, the Disease Natural History (DNH) and physical state integers are examples of complex numeric data structures, however other examples common in ABMs include co-ordinates for positions, numbers of individuals and distances to neighbours etc. Strictly speaking, the state data stored within agents can be classified as *continuous* or *discrete* and within these categories it can be *dynamic* or *static*. Continuous state data can take any value within a range (for example, a temperature measurement), whereas discrete data can only take on a value from a finite set of values (for example, a count of individuals). Dynamic information changes over the course of time where static information stays constant as time progresses. These properties determine the level of redundancy and, in turn, how efficiently the data can be compressed. The diagram (Figure 3) illustrates the relationship across the level of redundancy, the nature of the data (static or dynamic) and the effect of lossless compression will have on the data.

Data redundancy is a key concept when compressing data across multiple agents. In this context, redundant data refers to state data that is

Figure 2. The high-level organisation of the components that make up the compression scheme

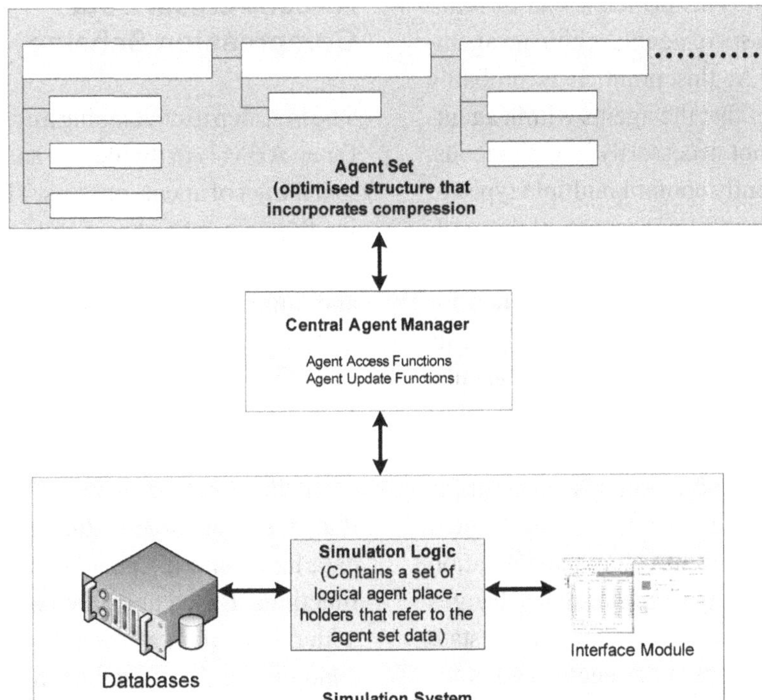

Figure 3. The efficiency of data compression techniques on data with different properties

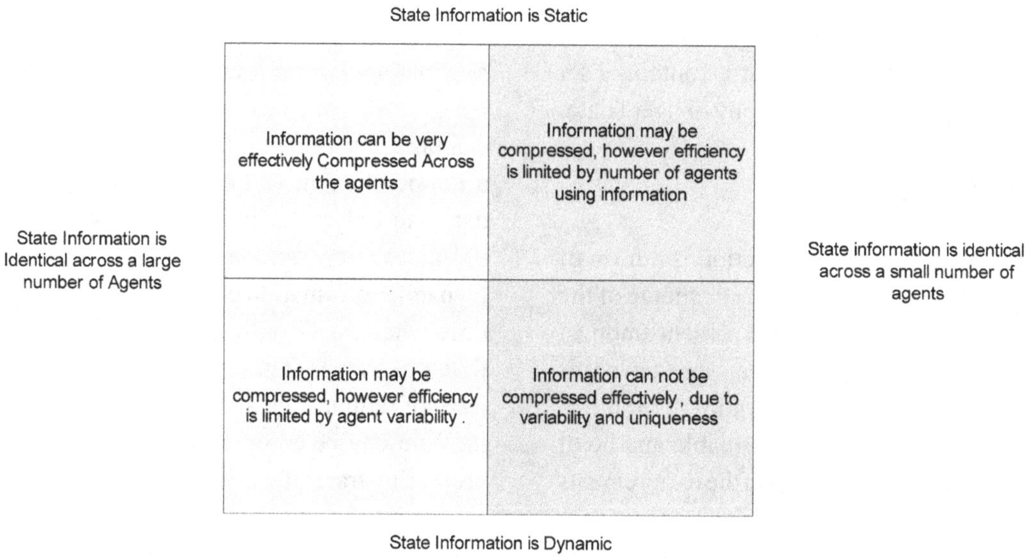

State Information is Static

State Information is Identical across a large number of Agents

Information can be very effectively Compressed Across the agents

Information may be compressed, however efficiency is limited by number of agents using information

State information is identical across a small number of agents

Information may be compressed, however efficiency is limited by agent variability.

Information can not be compressed effectively, due to variability and uniqueness

State Information is Dynamic

identical or similar (depending on the type of compression) across two or more agents. Compression schemes take advantage of redundancy by using an optimised representation of the redundant data within the structure or application that makes use of it. This principle can be readily applied across a set of agents within an agent-based simulation. At this point, it is probably prudent to point out that the agents within agent-based models are not necessarily homogeneous. Simulations frequently contain multiple types of agents, representing different aspects of the modelling domain. Each of these agents can have different sets of agent state data. The system for compressing state data in this chapter only deals with compressing a set of homogeneous agents, however the system can be implemented separately for each 'type' of agent in an ABM.

One key property of an agent's state data is its dynamic nature. In a typical ABM, each agent updates its state during each cycle of the simulation which, in turn, implies that the state data changes in each cycle. In addition to this, the agent's state data is often accessed by other agents and modules in the ABM. This poses a challenge to any compression system as the gains obtained from the compression of the data could very easily be out-weighted by the overhead of decompressing and re-compressing the data to allow it to be used.

A Hierarchical Data Compression Scheme

The first step to developing a compression scheme for an ABM is to divide and analyse the state data that the set of agents possess. This involves dividing the state data into separate items, determining which of these items are independent of others and ranking the data in terms of:

- Dynamic to static
- Redundant to unique

In this context, a state data is independent if it does not directly link to the agent's other data items and is updated according to separate functions. Based upon the properties of the data, a hierarchical data structure can be defined that contains the data based upon the combination of values present in each agent. The hierarchy is constructed by placing the least dynamic, most redundant data items at the top and moving down to the most dynamic, least redundant items at the bottom. The hierarchical structure has one level for each data item present within the agent type being compressed. By following the structure from the top layer to the bottom layer, the combination of values for each individual agent can be represented. Coupled with a *factor* value which stores the number of agents that the branch in the structure represents, this hierarchical structure can encapsulate the complete set of agents within the simulation. The representation and positioning of the agent data within the structure is completely independent of the events simulated within the model. Figure 4 displays the structure of the data within an example ABM based on this technique. In this figure, a simple hierarchy that represents a set of agents that have three data items is presented. These three items are:

1. *Movement distance*, which is a discrete numeric value in the range of 0 to 9 set at the time the agent is created.
2. *x coordinate*, which is an integer representing an x coordinate in a grid. This value is updated in each cycle according to an update function.
3. *y coordinate*, which is an integer representing a y coordinate in a grid. This value is updated in each cycle according to an update function.

Each logical agent in the simulation is represented by the combination of a top level data item (Movement Dist), one of its corresponding mid level items (x coordinate) and the corresponding bottom level item (y coordinate), with the factor storing the number of items represented by the branch. This hierarchy has been developed by applying the mentioned technique; the movement distance is the most static, and due to its discrete nature and limited range, it is also the most redundant. The x and y coordinate values are placed below this in the hierarchy (their order is arbitrary as they are identical in nature) as they are more dynamic and have a greater range.

Figure 4. The hierarchical data structure adopted to compress data in a sample agent set that contain three data items (movement distance, x coordinate, y coordinate)

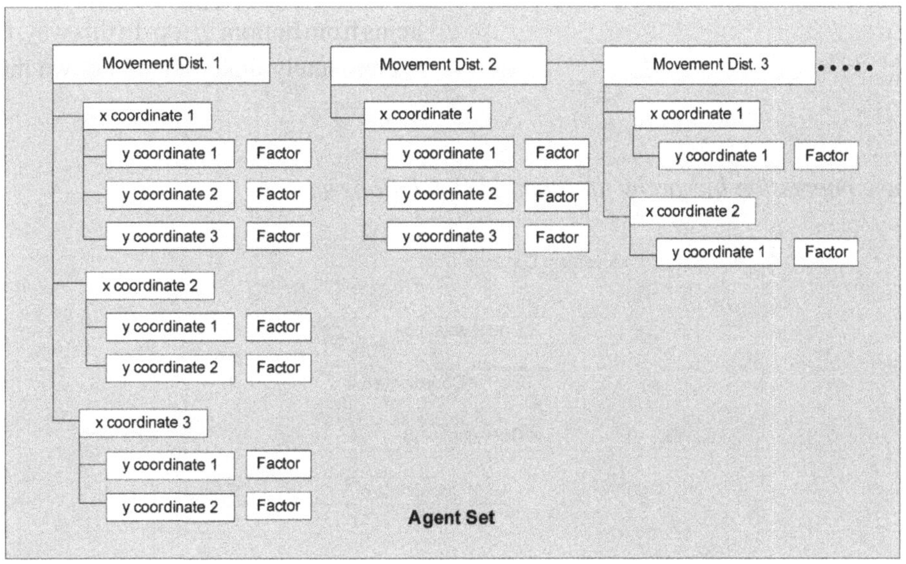

This hierarchical scheme provides compression by taking advantage of redundancy amongst the agent set at each level (by each data item) in the scheme. For example, if two agents are identical then they will be represented by the same branch in the scheme and the factor variable is simply set to 2. The storage saving is made by the scheme because it only requires one set of information to represent the two agents. In this situation, two agents have been compressed into one representation. Similarly, if two agents only differ by one value, for example the y coordinate value, then the same *movement distance* and *x coordinate* data items will be used to represent that agent, with only the unique *y coordinate* values being required to represent the two. The scheme results in the maximum amount of compression for each state data item present in the agents.

To show how compression is achieved, consider an example simulation with three agents of the type outlined above. The list below summarises the values stored in each agent:

1. Movement Distance = 5, x coordinate = 4.5, y coordinate = 6.7
2. Movement Distance = 5, x coordinate = 3.5, y coordinate = 6.8
3. Movement Distance = 5, x coordinate = 4.5, y coordinate = 6.7

You will notice that agents 1 and 3 are identical and only the *x* and *y* coordinates differ in agent 2. Figure 5 illustrates the compression hierarchy that will store the set of agents in this state. This diagram shows how the hierarchy makes use of redundancy to reduce the amount of storage space required. Instead of storing 3 copies of the movement distance (all with value 5), one is stored at the top of the hierarchy. Furthermore, agents 1 and 3 are represented by the same sub-branch, requiring only one set of the *x* and *y* values to be stored. Assuming that the movement distance is represented by a 32-bit integer and the coordinates are represented by a 64-bit Double Precision type, without compression these 3 agents would require 60 bytes to store the state information. Using the compression hierarchy, only 36 bytes are required (the space required for the factor storage is left out of these calculations as it is negligible when large numbers of agents are stored.)

The hierarchical structure is implemented using references to ordered sets of data items. The data sets are ordered as it allows for efficient access. The top layer consists of an ordered set of the top level data items. Each of these data items maintains a reference to the set of data items under it in the hierarchy and this continues down to the lowest level in the scheme. In addition to this, item sets maintain references to their parent items from bottom to top. In this way, the structure is completely linked up and down the hierarchy.

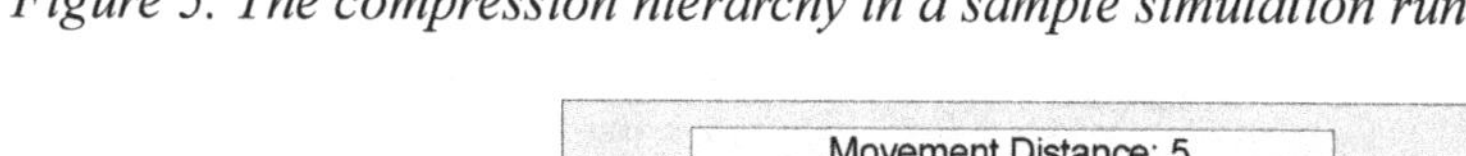

Figure 5. The compression hierarchy in a sample simulation run

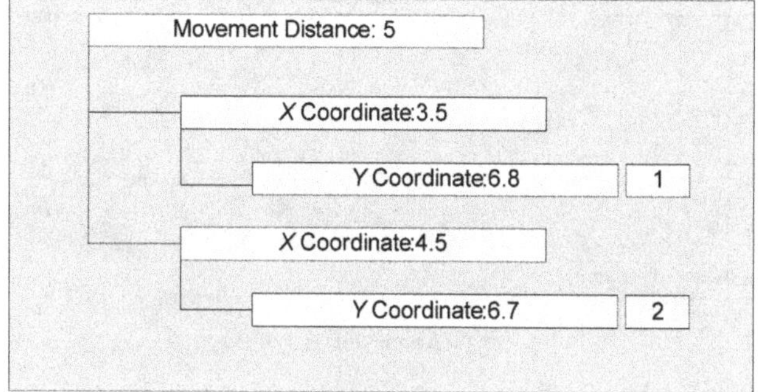

The hierarchical agent storage system integrates into the simulation's logic through the use of *place holders* that operate within the simulation where, normally, the standard agents would have existed with their complete set of data. These place holder agents simply contain references to the bottom level items within the compression hierarchy. This allows agent-wise access to the data stored within the compression scheme. Figure 6 outlines this integration, with the triangles representing the agents and the arrows representing the references to the agent data within the compression system.

Agent Access and Updates

The scheme that has been described provides an efficient way to represent the data contained within a set of agents, no matter how often agents change their state (and their state data) constantly through the progression of a simulation. In addition to this, the agent state data needs to be accessible from other modules via the place-holder agents in the simulation. This means that the compression scheme must be able to provide efficient access to the agent data and the ability for agent data to be updated within each cycle of the simulation. These requirements are addressed by a combination of the operations provided by the *Central Agent Manager* and the references to the agent data that are maintained by the logical place holder agents in the system. As mentioned in the previous section, the individual agent place holders can access their data via the references to the bottom level items in the storage structure. By following the set of references that are maintained within the data structure, the complete set of data items for each individual agent can be accessed by the place holder. This allows for agents to read and present their data to other modules and agents within the simulation. This deals with accessing data in an agent-wise fashion, but update operations are controlled by the *Central Agent Manager*. When an agent is updated, the values of its state information can change and the positioning within the compressed data structure must be altered. The exact details of the actual update operation performed on the individual agents will be different for each individual simulation and hence will not be covered in this chapter, but algorithm for updating the compression structure is relatively consistent for all simulations. The basic steps for updating an agent's state and compressing this state within the hierarchical structure are captured

Figure 6. Place-holder agents within the simulation logic (represent by the red triangles). These place-holders maintain references to the lowest data item belonging to them in the agent data hierarchy. This allows agent-wise access to the agent data contained in the compression hierarchy.

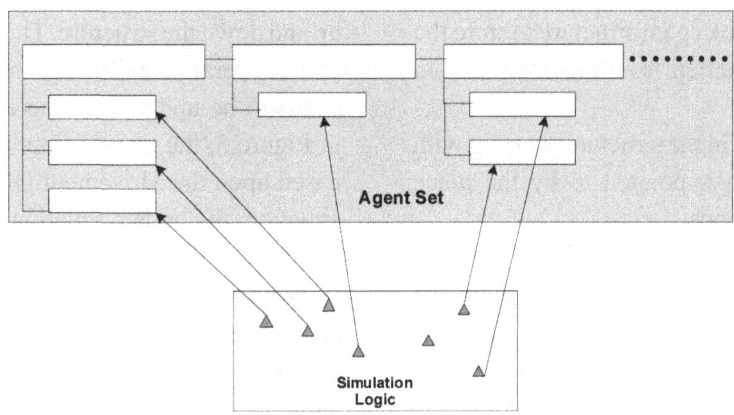

in the following algorithm which is repeated for each agent in the system:

1. Retrieve the agent's state information from the compression structure, decrementing the factor value wherever necessary. Using the state update algorithm, update the agent's state information to the next state.
2. For each layer in the compression structure, staring with the top data items, search for a matching data item to the corresponding updated layer in the agent.
   a. If a match is found, move down to the next layer in the hierarchy or increment the factor value if this is the bottom level agent.
   b. If a match is not found on this layer, create a new branch in the hierarchy for this value, generating all branches below this layer and setting the factor value to 1 on the bottom layer item.
3. Repeat for the next agent.

This algorithm essentially involves decompressing the agent, updating its state, then re-compressing the updated agent back into the hierarchy. The algorithm for decompressing agents data (used in step 1 of the access/update algorithm) involves reading the hierarchy from the bottom upward, following the references maintained within the structure. This procedure is summarised in the following algorithm:

1. Generate a blank agent structure to store the agents' information from the compression structure.
2. For each layer in the structure, starting with the bottom layer pointed to by the place holder's reference.
   a. Read the data item at the current layer to the correct location and copy the blank agent structure.
   b. If not the bottom layer, check for other branches from the current item.
      i. If there are no other branches, delete the item from the structure
   c. Update the current reference to the parent of the current reference.

This algorithm effectively removes the agent from the compressed structure and saves it in an uncompressed state.

Optimising the Agent Update Process

The update algorithm outlined in the previous section adds a significant amount of additional processing overhead, as each individual agent is de-compressed, updated and re-compressed. This process can be streamlined by updating agents in their compressed state, based upon the characteristics of the simulation. There are many situations where deterministic update operations that do not require cross-agent interactions are performed to the whole set of agents. For example, there may be a state update operation that determines the next state in a static manner based solely on the current state of each individual agent. This type of operation can be carried out on the complete set of agents without the need to de-compress each individual agent because each logical agent within the simulation will have an identical operation performed upon its state data. The process of updating the compressed data involves iterating through the hierarchy in a top-down fashion, updating data items by making use of the references up and down the structure. The exact nature of the update operation will be dependent on the data that needs to be updated. In the example developed in Figure 5, the x and y coordinates are updated based upon the Movement Distance data. In this situation, the update function can simply update the values directly in the compression hierarchy (leaving the factor untouched) in order to update all agents in the simulation. This reduces the number of CPU clock cycles required when compared to the algorithm outlined in the previous section. Similar reduction can be achieved when compared to an identical simulation that does not use this scheme as each data item updated in the compression hierarchy is used by multiple agents. A more solid example of this optimisation will be covered in the following section in the case study of the NMELDT.

Case Study: Applying Data Compression to the National Model for Emerging Livestock Disease Threats

The (Australian) National Model for Emerging Livestock Disease Threats, outlined in (Miron, et al., 2009), is a large scale, agent-based model designed to simulate the spread of infectious diseases amongst cattle, sheep and pigs within Australia. The model has been developed in the Java programming language and integrates a suite of Java modules, a PostgreSQL database and an open source mapping package called OpenMap [reference] to deliver a simulation system with a complete geographical information system (GIS) interface. The simulation software is designed to execute on a standard desktop PC; however the simulation data (provided by the PostgreSQL Database) can be hosted on a separate system and accessed via a network link. Figure 7 summarizes the high level architecture of the complete simulation system, with the arrows representing the flow of data between the major components. Figure 8, below, summarises the organisation of agent within the model. The basic agents within the simulation are *livestock* agents which represent individual sheep, cows or pigs in the model. The simulation can be required to model hundreds of thousands of these agents, so efficiency is essential for acceptable execution times. These agents are organised into groups that represent herds of animals. The agents within each group are homogeneous, representing that a herd can only consist of one type of animals. Premises including farms, saleyards and feedlots are represented by another class of agents that contain and manage the group agents. In Australia, every premise involved with the production of livestock has a *Property Identification Code* (PIC). The PIC is an eight character number identifying the location and ownership of a farming property.

In order to accurately simulate the spread of diseases and pests that effect livestock spatially, the movement of the actual livestock must be simulated. This principle is based around the idea that if an animal is infected with a disease or infested with pests is moved from one location to another, the disease or pests may be passed to uninfected/un-infested animals in the new location (thus spreading the disease/pest to the new location). This is achieved by modelling the movements at the individual agent's level, using sets of movement and geographical data. The agents that represent the premises have geographical point information associated within them which allows us to simulate the movement of livestock through the country by using the data obtained from the *NLIS* for cattle and artificially generated movement data for sheep and pigs. Cattle identified with the NLIS devices are electronically scanned as they move through the livestock chain. At the time of scanning, each owner's PIC can be recorded and linked to the NLIS device. This transaction information is then stored in a secure, central NLIS database. Thus the NLIS database contains a complete record of all the locations an individual animal has been throughout the course of its lifetime. Movement information for other species is less readily available and for this project relies on artificial movement data generated from expert's opinion and industry reports that outline management and selling behaviours. The details of the process by which this data is produced will be excluded for brevity. By cross referencing the movement data with the location information of each premise, the movement of individual animals (represented as the livestock agents) can be simulated throughout the country.

Figure 7. High-level overview of the National Emerging Livestock Disease Threats simulation system

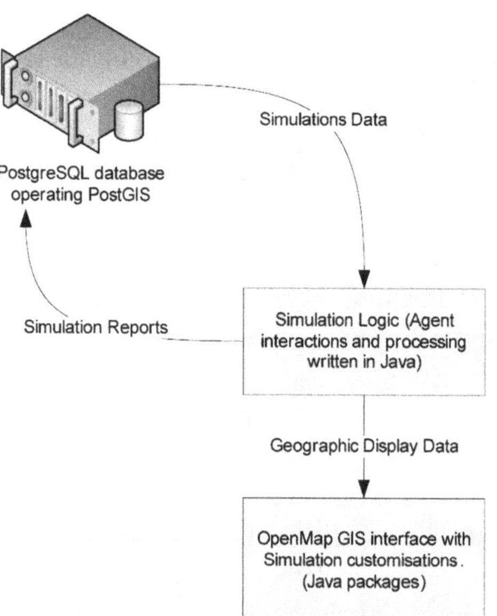

Figure 8. The agent hierarchy within the simulation. The premise agent can contain 0 or more group of agents and these group agents can contain 1 or more livestock agents. In this example, the facility agent contains two groups of livestock agents.

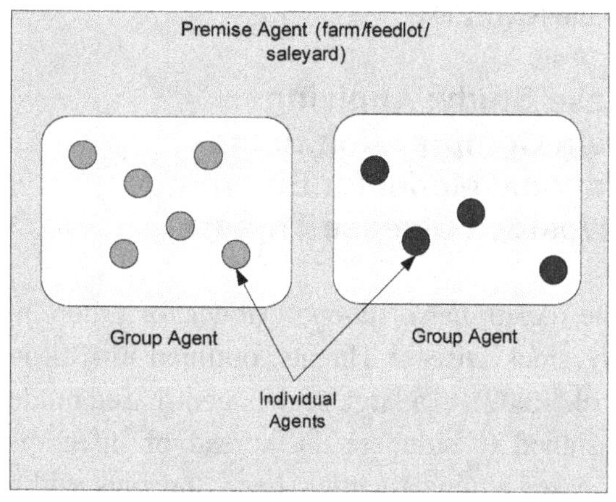

The application models disease transmission within herds and between premises through epidemiologically important 'pathways'. The initial focus of the work has been to simulate outbreaks of foot and mouth disease (FMD). FMD is a highly contagious disease of livestock affecting cattle, sheep and goats, and pigs that would have a major economic impact were it to be introduced into Australia (Commission, 2002). For FMD, in addition to simulating animal-to-animal spread within a herd, four pathways for spreading disease between premises have been included. In brief, the four pathways are:

- **Direct contact spread:** This pathway represents the spread of disease associated with movements of infected animals.
- **Local Spread:** This pathway refers to the spread of infection to neighbours and premises in close proximity to an infected premise where the actual source of the infection is not known and more than one possible mechanism can be identified. It has been recognised as particularly important for spread of diseases like FMD (Gibbens et al., 2001). By definition, it could involve various methods including local aerosol spread across fences, movement of stock, vehicles, people, straying stock, run off, sharing of equipment between neighbours, etc.
- **Windborne Spread:** This pathway represents the disease being spread by airborne dispersal of the infectious agent by the wind. This is simulated using a range of climatic and biological data fed into a complex geospatial algorithm.
- **Indirect Spread:** This pathway incorporates a range of mechanisms by which diseases could be spread between premises, not involving live animals. It includes spread associated with contaminated products, equipment and inanimate objects as well as people and vehicles.

The NMELDT conceptually simulates the spread of disease based upon a *Susceptible (S), Exposed(E), Infectious(I), Recovered (or removed) (R)* (SEIR) disease lifecycle model, where an agent (livestock animal) progresses through the lifecycle of disease states outlined in (1):

Susceptible→Exposed→Infectious→ Recovered (1)

In addition to the disease life cycle, a symptom life cycle is simulated that models the presence of clinical symptoms. This is separate, but related to the disease life cycle. The agent (livestock animal) progresses through the states of the symptom life cycle as outlined in (2):

Infected Without Symptom s→ Infected Showing Symptoms →After Symptoms (2)

The diseases states are:

1. *Susceptible*, where an animal is not infected with a disease but may become infected
2. *Exposed*, where the animal is infected but not yet infectious i.e. cannot pass the disease to others
3. *Infectious*, where the animal is infected and can pass the disease to other animals
4. *Recovered*, where the animal has recovered from the disease and is immune or is removed (e.g. if it dies of the disease or is culled). A recovered animal cannot be re-infected.

The symptom states are:

1. *Before symptoms*, where the animal may be infected but not showing symptoms
2. *Showing symptoms*, where the animal is infected and showing symptoms. Under some circumstances, a recovered animal may continue to show clinical evidence of the infection for a time.
3. *After Symptoms* where the animal has recovered and is no longer showing symptoms. Some infected animals may not show symptoms.

The agents maintain their own internal state information and update this information during discrete time cycles. A single simulation cycle represents a single day and each time cycle is broken down into four different stages. In each of these stages, different state update operations are carried out by agents. The simulation cycle consists of an early morning phase (00:00-06:00), a morning phase (06:00-12:00), an afternoon phase (12:00-18:00) and a night phase (18:00-24:00).The early morning phase is not used in the default setup. In the morning phase, livestock movements to saleyards are processed and a disease spread stage is carried out after the movements to represent the spread of disease within saleyards. In the afternoon phase, the movements away from saleyards and farm-to-farm direct (animal movements), indirect contacts and local spread pathways are processed. Finally, in the evening phase, a disease spread stage within the herd is carried out to represent the spread of disease between animals within an infected premise and windborne spread between different premises is simulated. Figure 9 outlines the simulation cycle.

The individual livestock agents store 64 bits of state information that consists of a *disease natural history (DNH)* information and the agent's current state within this DNH. The disease natural history specifies the number of days that the animal spends in each stage of the Disease Lifecycle and the Symptom lifecycle. This scheme of states is represented using two 32 bit Java integers (totalling 64 bits per agent). One integer holds two indicators that store the current disease and symptom states and two counters that keep track of the number of cycles that the agent has spent in the current disease and symptomatic states. The second integer stores the numbers of days spent in each of the disease and symptom states (along with vaccination and disease carrier information). Figure 10, below, outlines this scheme.

In Figure 11, the allocation of storage for the state information can be seen. The life cycle information is generated stochastically from a set

Figure 9. The conceptual simulation cycle used in the national model. This outlines the order of events within a single cycle of the model.

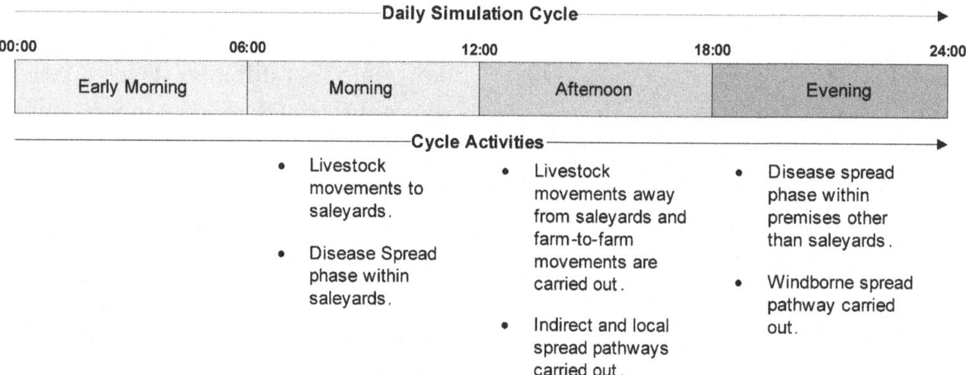

of distributions when the agent is created. When an agent is created, it is in the susceptible state and it remains static in this state until it becomes infected. Once infected, the agent transitions through its disease and symptomatic lifecycles using the counters in the physical status integer. Figures 11 and 12 show the main interface of the model while running a sample scenario.

The principles discussed in this chapter can be easily applied to the NMELDT, by treating the DNH and the physical status integers as separate data items that can be compressed across the whole agent set. The individual data items within these integers are not extracted and compressed individually. These components are left grouped together and the integers storing these are treated as individual pieces of data for the purposes of the compression scheme. The result of this is that each agent effectively has two pieces of state information for compression. The first of these is the Disease Natural History (DNH). The data contained within this integer is static across the lifetime of the simulation, after the contents have been calculated when the agent that the data belongs to is initialised. Because the lifecycle information stored in the DNH is sampled from a set of distributions, there are a finite number of different combinations that can be stored in the

Figure 10. The agent state information storage scheme

Physical Status Integer

Current Disease State	Current Symptom State	Counter: Symptom State	Counter: Disease State
8 Bits	8 Bits	8 Bits	8 Bits

Bit: 31 … 15 … 0

Lifecycle Integer

V	C	Days Before Symptoms	Days Of Symptoms	Recovered	Infectious	Exposed
		6 Bits	6 Bits	6 Bits	6 Bits	6 Bits

Bit: 31 … 0

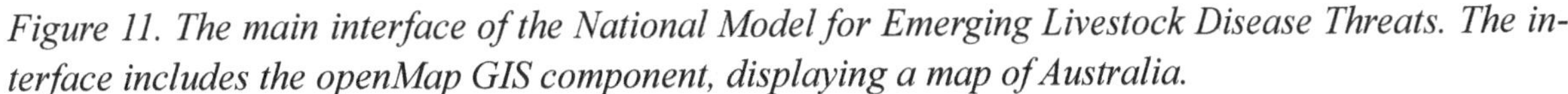

Figure 11. The main interface of the National Model for Emerging Livestock Disease Threats. The interface includes the openMap GIS component, displaying a map of Australia.

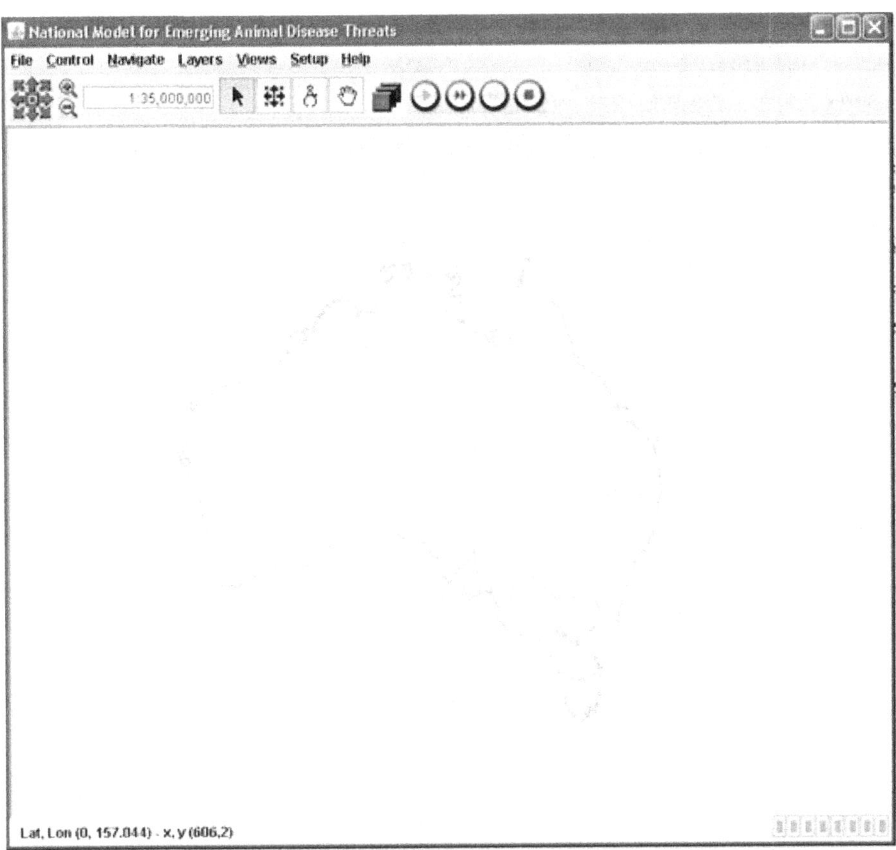

set of components. As a result, there is significant redundancy of this data across the set of agents. This data is highly suitable for compression. The second data item contains the current physical and disease states. This data is dynamic, changing during each cycle of the simulation. There is still a significant level of data redundancy as agents transitioning into the same disease state during the same cycle will have the same values stored in each counter. Based on these properties, the hierarchical scheme can be applied to compress this state information. Figure 13 gives a high level overview of the agent data hierarchy applied. The scheme uses two levels of abstraction to group agents that have identical information in the DNH integer and then within these groups, identical physical status are combined and a counter is maintained that tracks how many agents are represented by the same DNH/physical status set.

The nature of the simulation also allows for the use of the optimised update algorithms to be implemented. Within this simulation, agents that are created or move to the exposed state on the same logical day within the simulation, that have the same physical status and DNH will progress through the same set of states, changing at the same time up until they are removed from the simulation. This is a trivial update until the agent transitions to the exposed state as in the susceptible state, agents have no state information changes. Agents that become exposed on the same day will progress through the remainder of their states together. As a result of this configuration, these agents can be updated without decompres-

Figure 12. The National Model for Emerging Livestock Disease Threats running a simulation. The coloured markers represent premises that contain livestock infected with FMD. The colour represents the state of the premises.

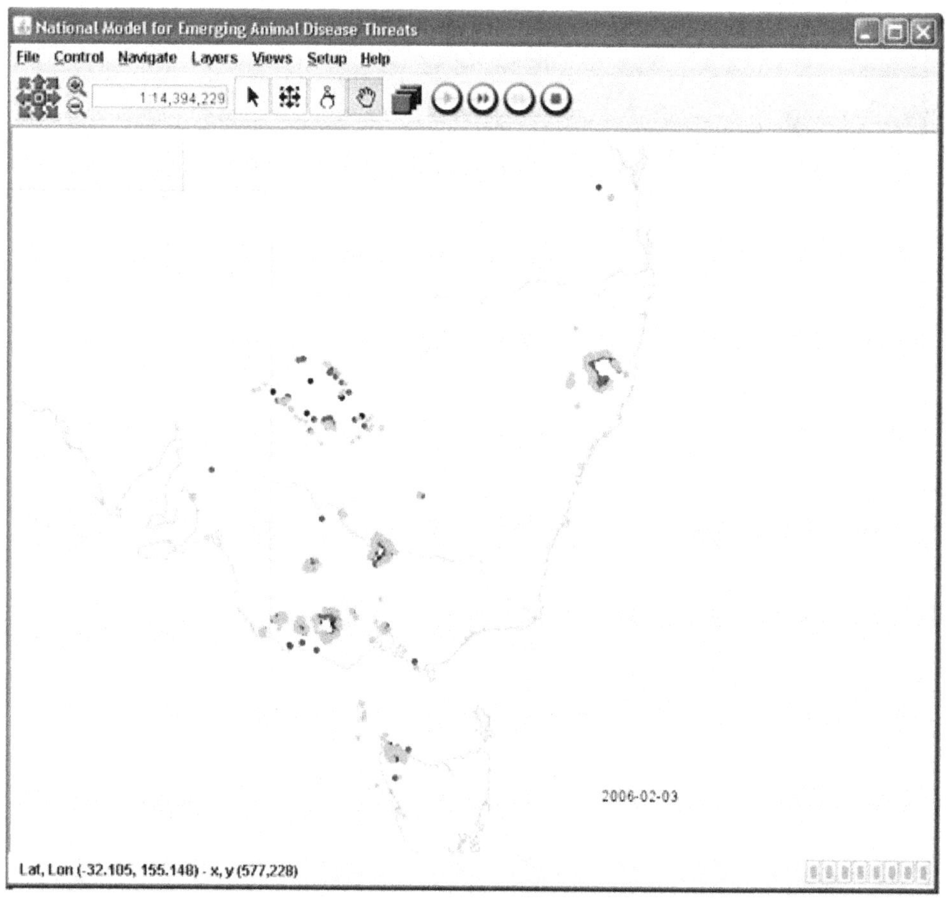

Figure 13. The agent data hierarchy scheme applied to the NMELDT

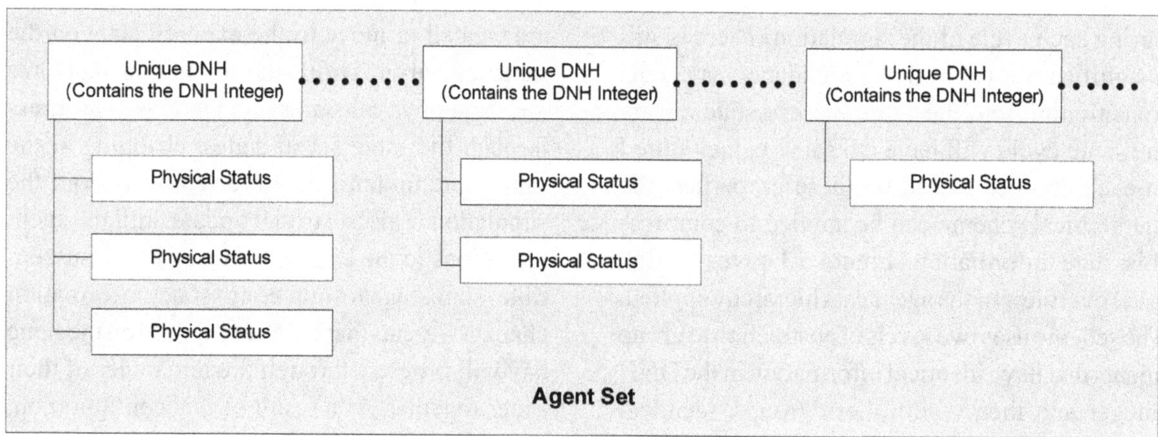

sion in the manner described in the previous section. In simple terms, the current disease state, current symptom state along with their corresponding day counters can be updated within the hierarchy directly because the update operation on the physical status/DNH combination that represents one or more logical agents will be identical across the logical agents it represents.

A complete analysis of the efficiency gains obtained from the application of DAC will be left out for brevity, but a simple experiment will be outlined here to illustrate the reduction in the amount of memory used and the improvements in the efficiency of the update process. The experiment carried out involved a simulation loop that runs for 10 cycles. At each iteration of the loop 20000 new agents were added with a 'physical Status' value unique to that iteration. This represents that agents within a simulation that become infected at different times will have different physical states. (e.g. all the agents that become infected on Day *y* will have the same physical status, but it will be different to that agents created on day *x*). 10 runs of the experiment were carried out using the dynamic agent compression with averages taken to insure validity. The results for this experiment are discussed below:

- Across the 10 simulation cycles 200,000 agents are created within the toy simulation. This means that without DAC, 200,000 × 4 bytes are used for the Disease natural history encoding, 200,000 × 4 bytes are used for the physical status encoding and 200,000 4 bytes are used for the agents pointers their parent groups. This means that at the end of the tenth cycle, the agents occupy a total of 2,400,000 bytes or 2343.75Kb of memory.
- Using the dynamic agent compression scheme, an average of 1219 DNH level data items were created, to represent the Disease lifecycles and these 1219 DNH data items contained a combined average total of 10,611 physical status data items representing the physical statuses of the all logical agents generated in the simulation. This means that at the end of the tenth cycle, using DAC, 1219 × 4 bytes were used to store that agents disease natural histories, 10,611 × 4 bytes were used to store the physical statuses of the agents, 10611 × 4 bytes were used to store the physical status data and 200,000 × 4 bytes were used to store pointers to the parent groups. This means that the 200,000 agents in the simulation occupied a total space of 889,764 bytes or ≈868.9 Kb.

Based upon the above results using DAC to update all 200,000 agents present in the simulation at the end of the 10th cycle, it will only require 10,611 update operations. This is a major improvement over the current implementation which would require 200,000 update operations (i.e. one update operation for each logical agent).

In order to compare the memory usage between a simulation using the compression scheme and a simulation without compression, simulations with increasing numbers of agents were run with different numbers of agents ranging from 25 to up to 650. Each simulation was run for a single cycle to insure that no 'new' agents were generated. At the end of each simulation run, the amount of memory used was analysed. Figure 14 shows the simulation system with compression uses significantly less memory than without the compression scheme applied. Further experimentation measured the execution time of the agent update process with increasing number of agents in the sample simulation. Figure 15 confirmed that the update execution time only rises by 10% (i.e. from 1.6ns to 1.8ns) even when the number of agents increases six-fold (i.e. from 100 to 600).

Figure 14. The memory usage as the number of agents is increased

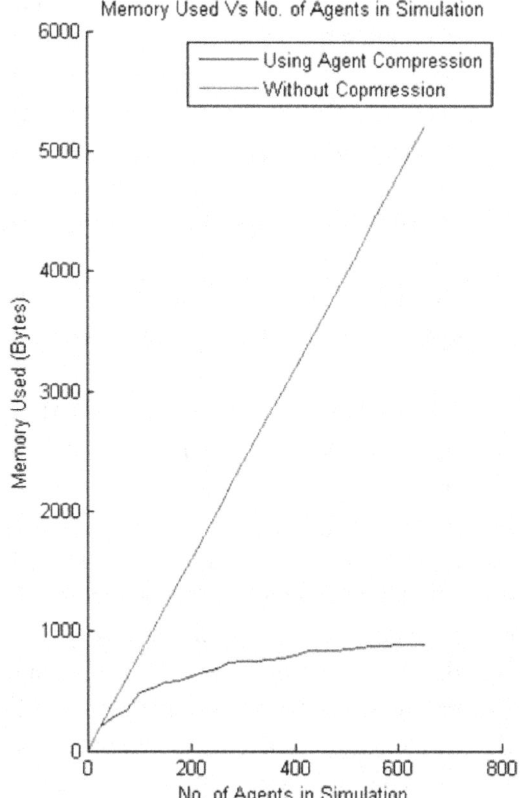

CONCLUSION

Agent based modelling is an increasingly popular approach for simulating complex phenomena and the increasing scale of ABMs have fostered the need for a scheme that effectively manages the increasing number of agents present in these systems. This chapter has outlined the techniques for improving the processing efficiency and memory usage of large scale agent based modelling systems through the use of Dynamic agent compression. The work presented here shows how a data hierarchy, that represents all of the data items contained within all the agents present in a model, can take advantage of data redundancy to reduce the storage space required and the processing overhead in an ABM. A method for accessing the hierarchy through a centralised manager that allows the individual agent's data items to be used throughout the model was outlined so that the system is usable in a wide variety of systems. The detailed case study a compression scheme's implementation to the *National Model for Emerging Livestock Disease Threats* provides a solid example of how these techniques can be applied to an existing modelling system. This implementation demonstrates the viability of the use of data compression within a real-world modelling system and how the techniques outlined for developing a compression hierarchy can be successfully applied to a complex set of agent data items. The experimental analysis shows the potential benefits that dynamic agent compression can provide in terms of memory savings and CPU clock cycles required for state update operations. The results show that a saving of approximately 2/3 on the amount of memory required to store the agent set data in the final simulation cycle and a 50% decrease in the number of CPU operation required for updating the agent's state information. Further analyses show that the system scales well as the number of agents are increased within the simulation in terms of both execution time for update operations and memory usage.

The implications of the efficiency improvements that this compression technique can deliver are twofold; the scheme allows large scale agent-based simulations to be operated on lower performing computer systems and it allows even larger scale, more highly detailed, agent-based models to be feasibly operated on high performance computing equipment. The first implication is important because the users of ABMs, such as scientists and policy makers, may not have access to high performance computing equipment. The compression scheme can allow a larger audience of users' access and make use of these large scale agent-based modelling tools. The second implication is important for model developers as it will allow them to produce models with a greater level

Figure 15. The execution time of the agent update process against increasing number of agents

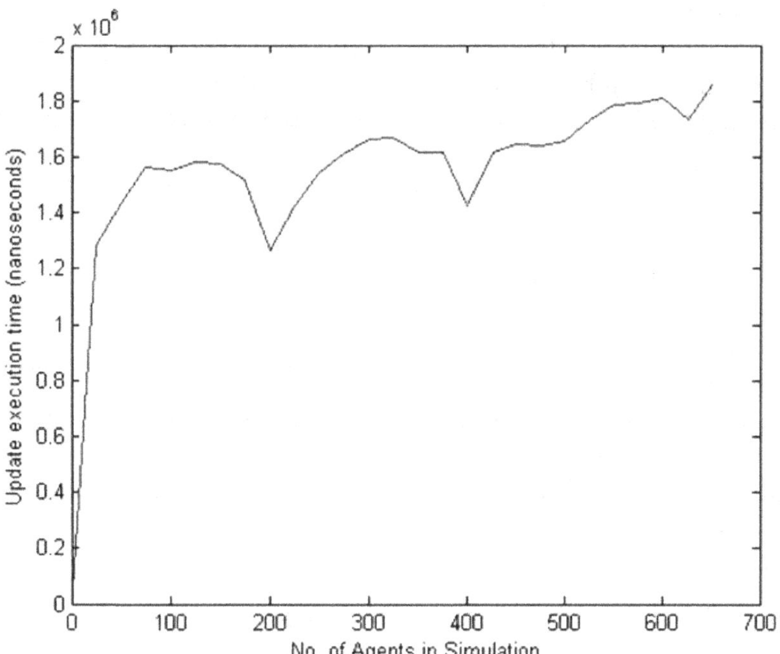

of detail without increasing the computational requirements. This will allow developers to meet policy makers and scientists increasing need for higher detail decision support tools.

FUTURE DIRECTIONS

There are three key areas for the future development of this compression scheme. The first area is the application of this system in broader agent based simulation systems and agent-based artificial intelligence systems. Applying this system to new applications will promote further development of additional features and improvements on the current design that allow the scheme to suit a range of different system types. Currently the authors of this chapter are in the early stages of developing a national-scale, geospatial simulation system for modelling the spread of insect pests within Australia. With further development, the DAC scheme outlined in this chapter will be used for the management of the large numbers of agents present in this system to improve its performance.

The second key area for further development of this DAC architecture is the application of parallel processing to the compression and update procedures that operate within the central agent manager. This was explored in NMELDT through the implementation of multiple Java threads for the agent update operation, however it was not implemented for the compression/decompression procedures. This is highly dependent upon the programming platform that is used, but most general purpose programming languages (C/C++, Java, Visual Basic etc.) offer an API to facilitate multithreading and parallel processing on the CPU. This improvement could be taken even further by making use of Graphics Processing Units found in most modern personal computers. Nvidia's CUDA or the general purpose GPU libraries (OpenGL or Direct 3D) could be used to develop a compression manager that operates partly on the CPU and main memory and partly on the GPU and graphics memory. The multi-core GPU could be used to manage the optimised update process, and the GPU memory could be used to store the data that forms the compression hierarchy. The benefits of this are twofold:

- Firstly, the large number of GPU cores can perform a large number of the compression/decompression and update processes in parallel.
- The GPU memory is much faster for to access for reading and writing than the PCs main memory. The only significant constraint on its use is its size. At the time of publication, most off-the-shelf graphics cards offer around 1 to 2 gigabytes of memory, whereas a PC has on average 4 to 8 gigabytes of RAM for use. This could limit the size of agent set within the simulation.

The final area for development is the application of this scheme to heterogeneous agent systems. In the scheme outlined, the compression hierarchy can only be used to represent the data from a set of agents that are of the same type. If this scheme was applied to a heterogeneous simulation, a separate compression hierarchy and compression manager would need to be implemented for each type of agents in the system. A method of representing multiple agent types within a single compression hierarchy will allow the scheme to make use of data redundancy across different agent types. If we take the example from the previous sections of the agents that contained the x and y coordinate data and extend this to include a second class of agents that also have x and y coordinate data, these items can be compressed across the agent types. This could improve the performance of the compression hierarchy and reduce the overhead incurred by using multiple compression managers.

REFERENCES

Animal Health Australia. (2009). *NLIS cattle*. Retrieved from http://www.animalhealthaustralia.com.au/programs/biosecurity/national-livestock-identification-system/nlis-cattle/

Berger, T. (2001). Agent-based spatial models applied to agriculture: a simulation tool for technology diffusion, resource use changes and policy analysis. *Agricultural Economics*, *25*, 245–260. doi:10.1111/j.1574-0862.2001.tb00205.x

Busing, R., & Mailly, D. (2004). Advances in spatial, Individual-based modelling of forrest dynamics. *Journal of Vegetation Science*, *15*, 831–842.

Collier, N. (2004). *RePast: An extensible framework for agent-based simulation*. Paper presented at the Swarmfest.

Commission, P. (2002). *Impact of foot and mouth disease outbreak on Australia*. Canberra.

D'Souza, R., Marino, S., & Kirschner, D. (2009, March). *Data parallel algorithms for agent-based model simulation of tuberculosis on graphics processing units*. Paper presented at the Agent-Directed Simulation Symposium.

Elliston, L., & Beare, S. (2006). Managing agricultural pest and disease incursions: An application of agent-based modelling. In Perez, P., & Batten, D. (Eds.), *Complex science for a complex world*. Canberra, Australia: ANU E-press.

Funk, P., Gerber, C., Lind, J., & Schillo, M. (1998). *SIF: An agent-based simulation toolbox using the EMS paradigm*. Paper presented at the 3rd International Congress of the Federation of EUROpean SIMulation Societies (EuroSim).

Gibbens, J. G., Sharpe, C. E., Wilesmith, J. W., Mansley, L. M., Michaelopolous, E., & Ryan, J. B. (2001). Descrriptive epidemiology of the 2001 foot-and-mouth disease epidemic in Great Britain: The first five months. *The Veterinary Record*, *149*, 729–743.

Goddeke, D. (2005). *GPGPU - Basic math tutorial*. Retrieved from http://www.mathematik.uni-dortmund.de/~goeddeke

Grecu, D., & Gonsalves, P. (2000). *Agent-based environment for UCAV mission planning and execution*. Paper presented at the AIAA Guidance, Navigation, and Control Conference and Exhibit.

Gropp, W., Lusk, E., & Skjellum, A. (1999). *Using MPI* (2nd ed.). MIT Press.

Happold, J., Garner, G., Miron, D., Sajeev, A. S. M., Kwan, P., & Welch, M. (2010). *Towards a national livestock disease model*. F. F. Australian Dept. of Agriculture.

Higgins, S. I., & Richardson, D. M. (1995). A review of models of alien plant spread. *Ecological Modelling*, *87*, 249–265. doi:10.1016/0304-3800(95)00022-4

Li, Z.-N., & Drew, M. S. (2004). *Fundamentals of multimedia*. Upper Saddle River, NJ: Prentice Hall. LLC, B. S. (2005). *OpenMap*. Retrieved from http://openmap.bbn.com/

Luke, S., Cioffi-Revilla, C., Panait, L., & Sullivan, K. (2004). *MASON: A new multi-agent simulation toolkit*. Paper presented at the Swarfest.

Lysenko, M., & D'Souza, R. M. (2008). A framework for megascale agent based meld simulations on graphics processing units. *Journal of Artificial Societies and Social Simulation*, *11*(410).

Minar, N., Burkhart, R., Langton, C., & Askenazi, M. (1996). *The swarm simulation system: A toolkit for building multi-agent simulations*. Working Papers, Santa Fe Institute. Retrieved from http://econpapers.repec.org/RePEc:wop:safiwp:96-06-042

Miron, D., Garner, G., Donald, G., & Dyall, T. (2009). *A national model for emerging livestock disease threats: User* guide.

NVIDIA. (2010). *NVIDIA CUDA: Programming guide*. Santa Clara, CA: NVIDIA Corporation.

Perumalla, K. S., & Aaby, B. G. (2008). *Data parallel execution challeneges and runtime performance of agent simulations on GPUs*. Paper presented at the Spring Simulation Multi-Conference.

Rao, A., Jain, M., & Karlapalem, K. (2007). *Towards simulating billions of agents in thousands of seconds*. Paper presented at the International Conference on Autonomous and Multiagent Systems, Honolulu.

Richmond, P., Coakley, S., & Romano, D. (2009, May, 10-15, 2009). *A high performance agent-base modelling framework on graphics card hardware with CUDA*. Paper presented at the Autonomous Agents and Multiagent Systems (AAMAS), Budapest, Hungary.

Russell, S., & Norvig, P. (2003). *Artificial intelligence: A modern approach. New Jersy*. Prentice Hall.

Schelhorn, T., O'Sullivan, D., Haklay, M., & Thurstain-Goodwin, M. (1999). *STREETS: An agent based pedestrian model*. Paper presented at the Computers in Urban Planning and Urban Management.

Sislak, D., Volf, P., Jakob, M., & Pechoucek, M. (2009). *Distributed platform for large-scale agent-based simulations* (pp. 16–32). Agents for Games and Simulations.

Sonnessa, M. (2003). JAS: Java agent-based simulation library. An open framework for algorithm-intensive simulations. *Industry and Labor Dynamics: The Agent-Based Computational Economics Approach*, (pp. 43-56).

Stage, A. R., Crookson, N. L., & Monserud, R. A. (1993). An aggregation algorithm for increasing the efficiency of population models. *Ecological Modelling, 68*(3-4), 257–271. doi:10.1016/0304-3800(93)90021-J

Strippgen, D., & Nagel, K. (2009). *Usuing common graphics hardware for multi-agent traffic simulation with CUDA*. Paper presented at the SIMUTools.

Sunderam, V. S. (1990). PVM: A framework for parallel distributed computing. *Journal of Concurrency: Practice and Experience, 2*(4), 315–339. doi:10.1002/cpe.4330020404

Tisue, S., & Wilensky, U. (2004). *NetLogo*. Paper presented at the International Conference on Complex Systems.

Wendel, S., & Dibble, C. (2007). Dynamic agent compression. *Artificial Societies and Social Simulation, 10*(2).

Yamamoto, G., Tai, H., & Mizuta, H. (2007). *A platform for massive agent-based simulation and its evaluation*. Paper presented at the 6th International Joint Conference on Autonomous Agent and Multiagent Systems (AAMAS '07).

Chapter 19
Embedded System for Heart Disease Recognition using Fuzzy Clustering and Correlation

Helton Hugo de Carvalho Júnior
Instituto Federal de Educacao, Ciencia e Tecnologia, Campus Campos do Jordão, Brazil

Robson Luiz Moreno
UNIFEI, Brazil

Tales Cleber Pimenta
UNIFEI, Brazil

ABSTRACT

This chapter presents the viability analysis and the development of heart disease identification embedded system. It offers a time reduction on electrocardiogram – ECG signal processing by reducing the amount of data samples without any significant loss. The goal of the developed system is the analysis of heart signals. The ECG signals are applied into the system that performs an initial filtering, and then uses a Gustafson-Kessel fuzzy clustering algorithm for the signal classification and correlation. The classification indicates common heart diseases such as angina, myocardial infarction and coronary artery diseases. The system uses the European electrocardiogram ST-T Database – EDB as a reference for tests and evaluation. The results prove the system can perform the heart disease detection on a data set reduced from 213 to just 20 samples, thus providing a reduction to just 9.4% of the original set, while maintaining the same effectiveness. This system is validated in a Xilinx Spartan®-3A FPGA. The FPGA implemented a Xilinx Microblaze® Soft-Core Processor running at a 50 MHz clock rate.

DOI: 10.4018/978-1-4666-1830-5.ch019

INTRODUCTION

According to the Center of Disease Control and Prevention – CDC of the United States of America, the leading cause of human death is attributed to heart illnesses, even surpassing deaths caused by cancer. More than 910 thousand U.S. citizens die every year from heart related illnesses and more than 70 million live and cope with some sort of heart condition, such as high blood pressure, strokes or angina (Carter M. (2006)). Seeking to reduce these figures, much research has been undertaken in order to make diagnoses faster, more accurate and with enough foresight to elevate the chances of patient survival through specific cardiopathy treatment.

In order to monitor patients' cardiac signals, a device known as an electrocardiograph (galvanometer) is utilized which, in turn, presents these signals in the form of an electrocardiogram – ECG. An ECG is a record of the variations in electrical potential generated by the heart's electrical activity. The diagnosis is based on the extraction of information about the peak of electrical waves and time intervals of the ECG signal. The procedure is safe, noninvasive (performed on the human body's surface without breaking the skin), reproducible, easy to obtain, low in cost and offers important indicators for analyses and diagnoses of cardiac anomalies (Brazilian Society of Cardiology (2003)). ECGs are a representation of an analog signal whose magnitude in the abscissa axis corresponds to time (normally in seconds), while the ordinate axis corresponds to electrical potential in volts (mV).

The problem herein under investigation is the possibility of application and implantation of a real system, or rather, of a device which utilizes signal processing techniques in order to obtain the most relevant characteristics of an electrocardiogram signal with greater precision and simplicity. Through such improvements, it may be possible to attain cheaper and simpler hardware with less processing, while still enabling accurate diagnoses.

In order to verify the efficacy of this research's proposal, a databank of real electrocardiogram signals was acquired, in which each signal presents the main characteristics of an electrocardiogram with some kind of cardiopathy. The databank was obtained through PhysioNet (Taddei, A. (1993)), which is a cooperative public service project for complex physiologic signals research. The project is financed by the National Center for Research Resources and the National Institutes of Health. PhysioNet offers free access via the Internet to multiple physiologic signal databases and open-source related software (Goldberger, AL. (2000)).

The general objective of this chapter is to present processing techniques for signals inserted in an embedded system, implanted in hardware, which serves to receive an electrocardiogram signal and carry out processing, while also reducing the quantity of samples, until generating a possible diagnosis. We further divide system implantation, in relation to the ECG, into acquisition, treatment, filtering, fuzzy clustering and correlation. The system is always aiming to produce accurate and fast diagnoses at a low cost with portable algorithms for the proposed implementation.

The entire process, starting from the acquisition to the probable diagnosis, is demonstrated in Figure 1 and Figure 2.

Figure 1 shows two blocks: ECG acquisition and Filters. The ECG block represents the leads. These leads are signals obtained through sensors placed on strategic points of the human body in order to capture electrical signals generated by the heart. For greater certainty in the diagnosis, normally 12 leads are analyzed in the electrocardiogram, detailed in item 2 of this chapter. However, it is known that with just two leads it is possible to generate a diagnosis (Negreiros de Andrade, PJ. (2008)). The second block separates the noise from the signal to be analyzed and removes the DC level. The DC level corresponds to the average obtained from the 213 signal

Figure 1. Acquisition and filtering blocks

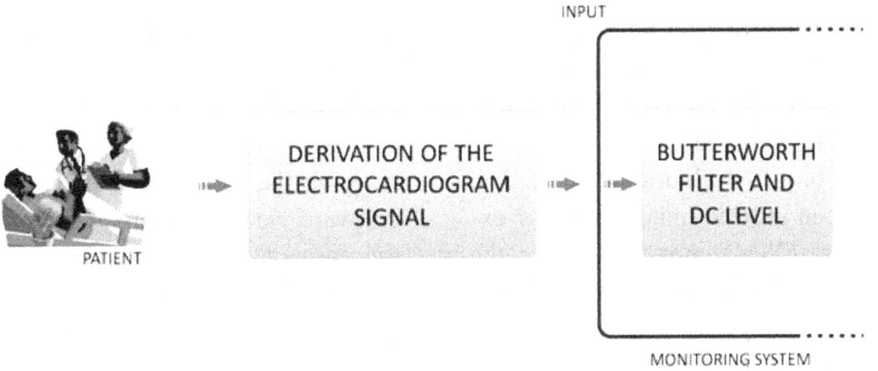

samples. The DC level is eliminated by subtracting the average from each sample. The noise is eliminated through a Butterworth filter.

Figure 2 shows the fuzzy clustering and correlation blocks along with techniques which aim to provide the diagnosis. In the first block the clusterization process is carried out, in which the points that describe the main characteristics of the electrocardiogram signal are obtained. Once the points are known, correlation is established between the signal under analysis and the databank signals in the second block to obtain the patient's diagnosis.

1. INITIAL CONSIDERATIONS

The researches on the use of computational systems in the generation of cardiac diagnoses encompass a wide range of knowledge areas. For instance, signal processing, application of filters and artificial intelligence (AI) algorithms can be used in signal identification and classification. The majority of the research in this area seeks to offer the means for automatic diagnoses, or the best preparation of the necessary stages for this purpose, as a way of supporting doctors and other healthcare professionals.

Figure 2. Fuzzy clustering and correlation blocks

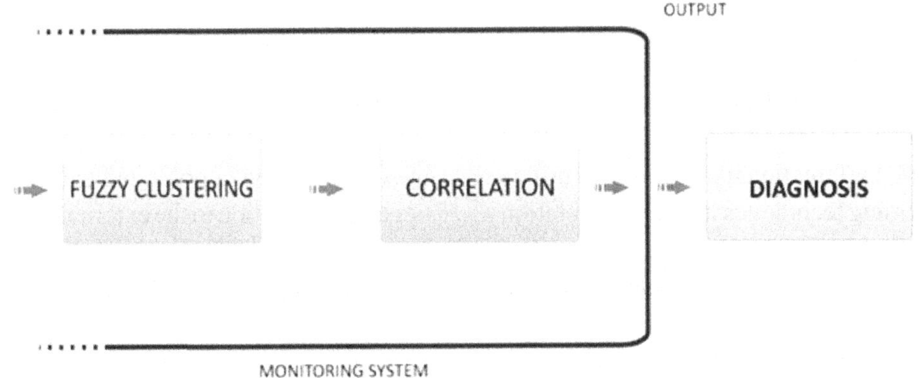

In signal processing studies, one of the topics to be dealt with is filtering. Nianqiang (2010) cites the importance of digital filter application in ECG signals, which aim to eliminate noise and reinforce the necessity for this type of processing in real time and at high speed.

The application of AI algorithms in cardiac problems has been utilized quite often. For example, Mitsakura (2004) cites that one of the main motivations and necessities for research on the medical diagnosis system is the high mortality rate caused by heart illnesses. That process is composed of two stages: ECG signal detection and classification. Yan (2010) presents a mathematical algorithm intended for the identification of the QRS complex, which shows a high level of precision that will be detailed in the next section. This identification is important as it forms the basis for cardiac illness classification. Once the ECG signal is duly filtered and identified, the next step is classification, which will be able to demonstrate (or not) the recognition of some cardiopathy. Jewajinda and Chongstitvatana (2010) demonstrate the ECG signal classification in long-term patient monitoring.

In order to obtain a probable diagnosis of the ECG signal, a correlation technique is used. In this case, a comparison is made between the ECG under analysis and the ECGs from the Physionet database which contains the cardiopathies previously defined by a medical team. In order to attain the level of efficiency shown in the algorithms in this chapter, comparisons were made with articles that possess the same statistical parameters of correct and erroneous diagnoses. These articles include Andreão (2004), (1998), Maglaveras (1998), Taddei (1995), and Vila (1997). All of them present computational systems that utilize signal processing techniques in the interpretation of electrocardiogram characteristics, which makes it possible to obtain the patient diagnoses. With the use of these techniques, it becomes possible to automatically diagnose the patient, thereby allowing, for instance, remote monitoring, in which the triggering of an alarm in real time would advise a patient, or even a medical team, that would be able to take action with reasonable notice, thus enabling the problem to be addressed before it could worsen and, in turn, increase the patient's chances of survival.

After the validation of the algorithms in the software via simulations – such as Matlab®, in the case of fuzzy clustering algorithms – the objective becomes the development of an embedded system, normally in FGPA, which carries out diagnoses or at least a part of the diagnosis process. Armato (2009) exemplifies the extraction of QRS complexes, real-time normal or pathological classification and the integration into FGPA. Therefore, due to the cost reduction seen in embedded systems over the last few years, a natural tendency of validation and application has been seen in systems that contain FGPAs due to its ease and quick implementation.

2. CONSIDERATIONS ON ELECTROCARDIOGRAPHIC LEADS

According to Thaler (2002), electrodiagrams are a record of all of the electrical activities generated by the heart. The information obtained via the electrocardiogram is greatly important for the determination of disturbances that could be occurring in the functioning or structure of the heart. The electrocardiogram is attained using a device known as a galvanometer, which measures the current between two electrodes placed on strategic points of the human body. In the human body, a polarized cell at rest is rich in potassium. The external medium which surrounds the cell is rich in sodium. Thus, a polarized cell at rest is more negative in relation to the external medium, which is more positive in relation to the cell. When the cell is activated, depolarization occurs, in which the interior of the cell becomes more positive than the external medium. Upon repolarization, the cell returns to its normal initial conditions.

Due to the electronic phenomenons generated by the heart, it is possible to measure the electrical potential differences on the surface of the human body. Depending on the location on the human body where the device's electrodes are placed, the corresponding leads are characterized for each signal. According to Stein, E. (1987), the most used leads are:

- Biopolar leads, that are obtained through the utilization of two electrodes positioned on the human body, as seen in Figure 3.
- Unipolar leads, where the electrode is placed on one of the bipolar lead points and the other electrode is connected to a central terminal, as shown in Figure 4.
- Precordial leads, which are obtained through analysis of a horizontal plane, which is a view of the human body from above, as shown in Figure 5.

With these leads it is possible to obtain signals which indicate cardiac anomalies. The system shown in this chapter utilizes two leads, indicated in the signals in the European ST-T Database (EDB).

Figure 3. Location of ECG bipolar leads I, II, III (Stein, 1987)

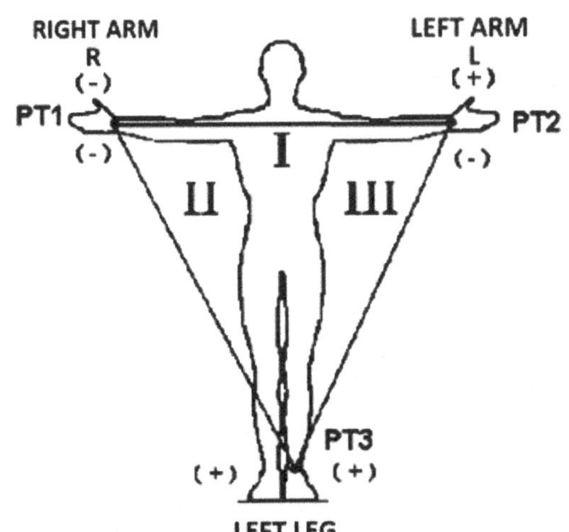

Figure 4. Location of unipolar ECG leads aVF, aVL e aVR Stein, E. (1987)

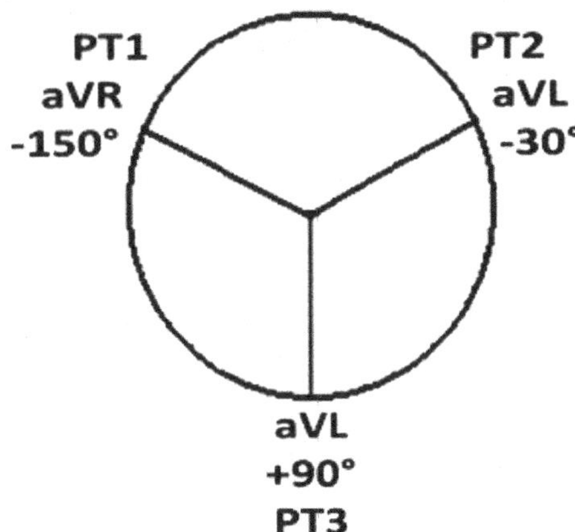

In Figure 6, a characteristic electrodiogram signal is presented, indicating its five main segments.

Each segment indicated in Figure 6 represents one stage of the cellular depolarization and repolarization processes.

The P wave represents the start of the depolarization, first in the right and then the left atrium. The segment PR describes the moment in which the electric impulse makes its way through the Bundle of His and the right and left branches. Depolarization of the ventricles is represented by the segment QRS. The segment ST represents the initial phase of ventricle repolarization and the T-wave describes the final repolarization of the ventricles. After the T-wave comes the U-wave, which is considered normal when it is positive; contrarily, when it is negative, it represents some kind of anomaly. This wave is not constant (Stein, E. (1987)).

3. PRE-PROCESSING AND FILTERING SYSTEM

In order to utilize real electrocardiogram signals, a pre-processing system needed to be used in order to remove the high-frequency noises from

Figure 5. Precordial leads V1, V2, V3, V4, V5, and V6 Stein, E. (1987)

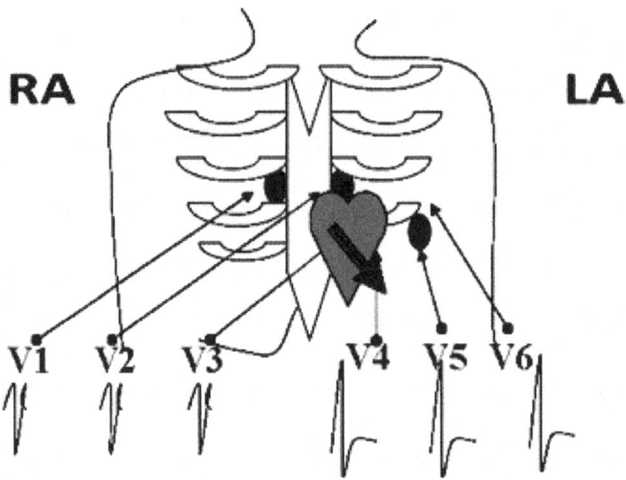

the electrocardiogram. The pre-processing system serves to prepare the signal so that it can be processed without interferences. Figure 7 shows the pre-processing system employed.

As can be seen in Figure 7, the first block of the pre-processing system represents the system entry point. The real electrocardiogram signals, obtained from the databank, had already been sampled at 0.003s intervals.

The second block represents the low pass filter, which eliminates high frequency noises. In this work, an algorithm representing the Butterworth filter was chosen after some testing in the software Matlab®.

The third block corresponds to the elimination of the DC level present in the electrocardiogram. Signal processing techniques have also been applied to eliminate DC levels.

Figure 6. Characteristics electrocardiogram signal

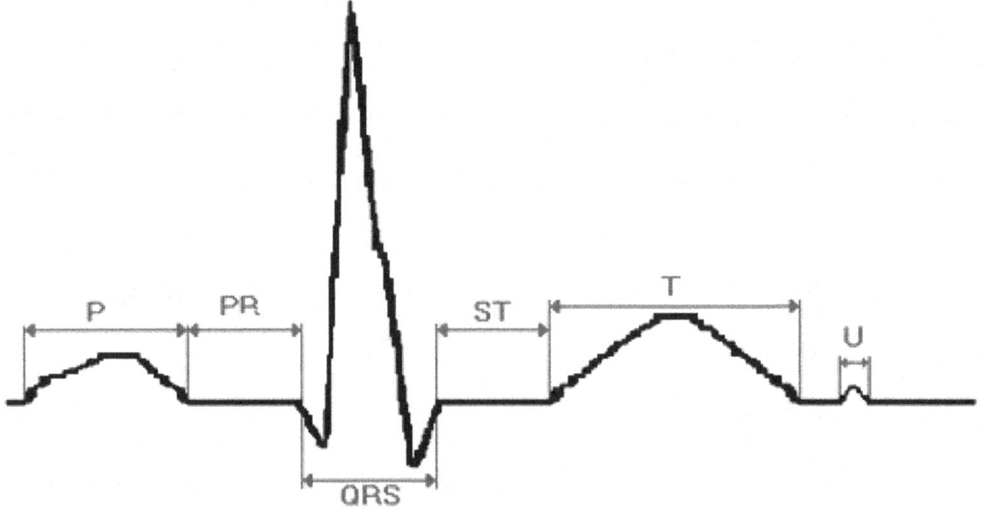

Figure 7. Pre-processing system

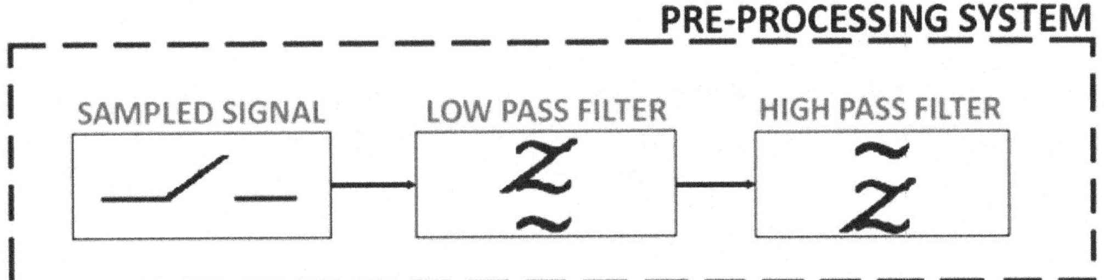

Overall, the filter aims to eliminate undesired frequency signals. There are four types of filters: high pass, low pass, passband and stopband.

In the proposed system, it was verified the need for a low pass filter to eliminate high frequency noise. The noise may cause system errors due to the alterations in the characteristics of the signal under analysis.

The software MATLAB was utilized to confirm the applicability of the Butterworth filter, which produced satisfactory results after few adjustments. It is known that the Butterworth filter presents a flat frequency response without ripples in its passband and a null response outside the passband. Another characteristic of this type of filter is that, by altering its order, only the attenuation's inclination is altered (Boylestad, R. (2005)). An order N function with a passband with a cut-off frequency w_p is given as:

$$\left|T(jw)\right| = \frac{1}{\sqrt{1 + e^2 \left(\frac{w}{w_p}\right)^{2N}}} \tag{1}$$

where N is the filter order, w is the frequency and w_p is the cutoff frequency.

Figure 8. Butterworth filter transfer function

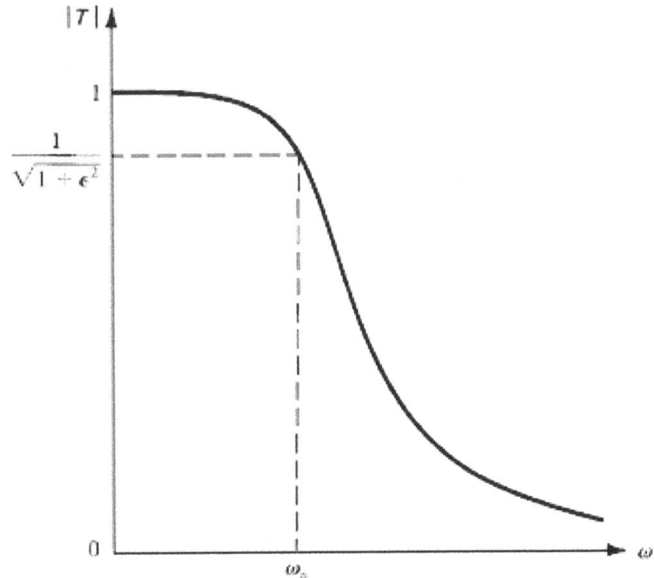

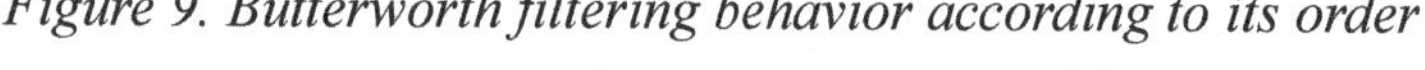

Figure 9. Butterworth filtering behavior according to its order

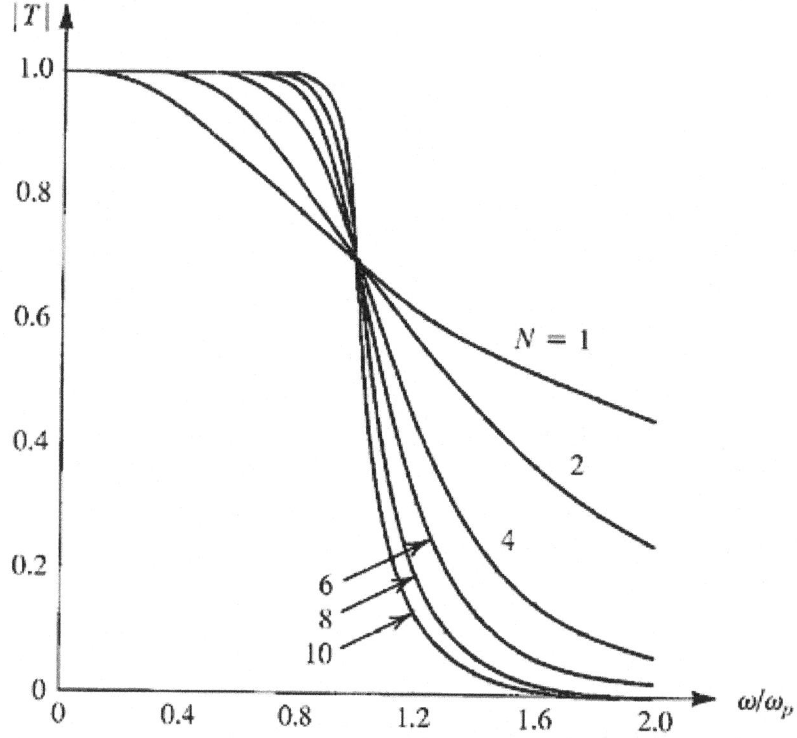

Figure 10. Butterworth frequency response

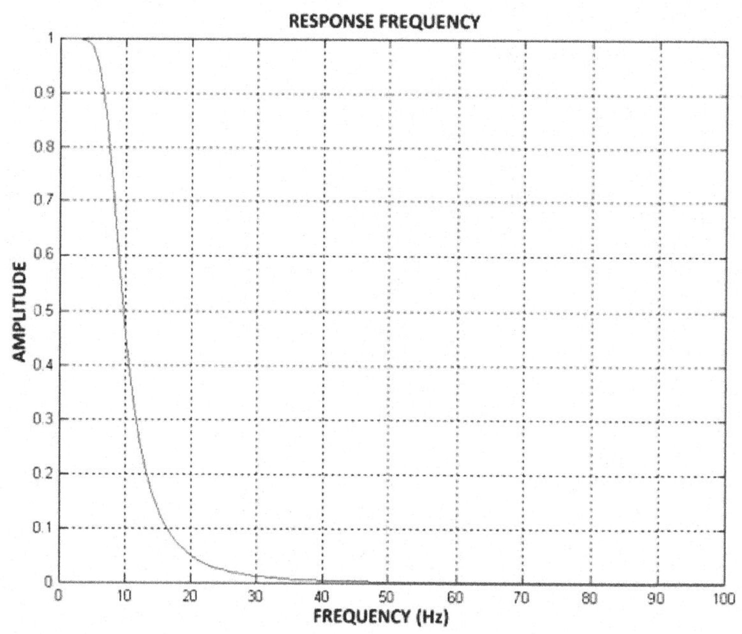

Figure 8 shows an example of the Butterworth filtering behavior.

Figure 9 presents the Butterworth filtering behavior according to its order.

Figure 10 presents the Butterworth frequency response. It is a third order filter and with a cutoff frequency of 13.8 Hz.

Figure 11 shows an original electrocardiogram signal and Figure 12 shows the signal after the filtering. The filter eliminates the higher frequency signals which alter the ECG characteristics.

The ECG signal, as seen in Figure 11, is applied to the Butterworth filter. The filtering eliminates high frequency noise in such a way that, it outputs only the heart's original signal. Through processing, the DC level present on the ECG signal is also removed. This processing is fundamental for the correlation method, since the signals will have the same reference. After the processing, the signal possesses the characteristics shown in Figure 12, and therefore the signal is ready to be analyzed.

In order to eliminate the DC level, it was initially obtained the signal average. The average was subtracted from each sample in order to cancel the DC signal present in the electrocardiogram, thus obtaining the signal in Figure 12.

4. FUZZY MEMBERSHIP FUNCTION E FUZZY CLUSTERING

The fuzzy clustering process can be divided into two steps. The membership function to be used is first chosen. Later the rule creation step is initiated, where each rule describes the tendency of the system output for each range of input signals. Those rules describe the main response of the system.

A membership function indicates the degree of pertinence of an element in relation to an event. The membership value can vary in the range [0,1]. This range represents the degree of influence

Figure 11. ECG signal with noise and DC level

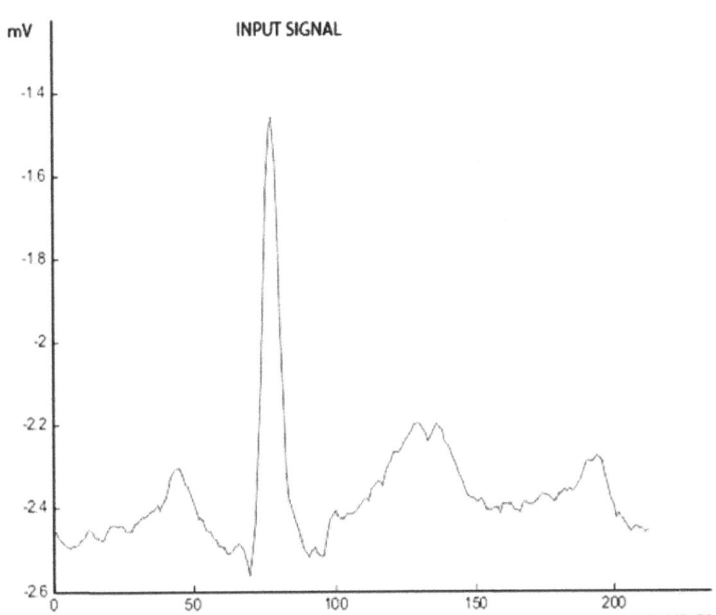

Figure 12. Filtered ECG signal

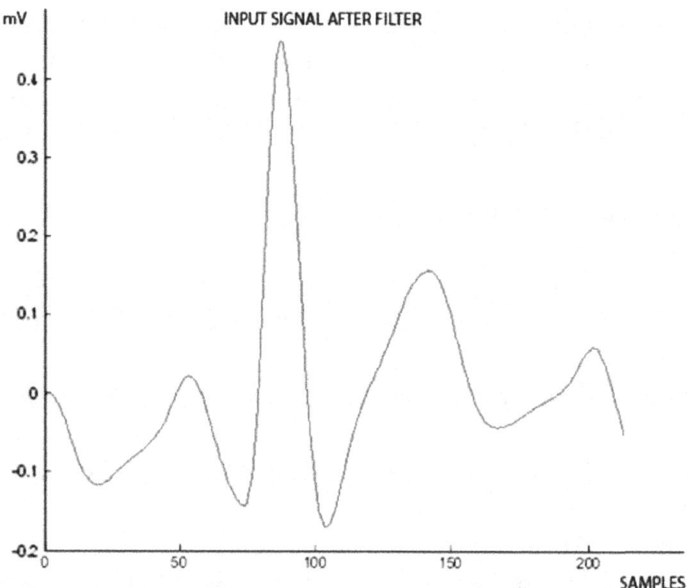

of an element due to a given event (Ian, S., and Simões, M. (1999)).

In a real system, a membership function may be based on information provided by an operator that knows the variation value range of a given event and the action to be taken for each situation. By using this information, a membership function can be obtained which provides values closed to those offered by the system operator (Ian, S., and Simões, M. (1999)).

Four types of membership function tests were carried out using MathWorks® MATLAB®. The functions are triangular, Gaussian, sigma and sine. In this chapter, only the triangular and Gaussian functions, shown in Figures 13 and 14, will be presented. It can be observed that each function has a different inclination level, which makes them more adequate for determined applications.

The membership function shown in Figure 13 is an example of triangular shape which possesses abrupt variations between a maximum value of 1 and a minimum value of 0. This function is given as:

For $x = [0, 3] \rightarrow \mu = 0;$

For $x =]3, 6[\rightarrow \mu = \frac{x - 3}{3};$

For $x = 6 \rightarrow \mu = 1;$

For $x =]6, 8[\rightarrow \mu = \frac{8 - x}{2};$

For $x \geq 8 \rightarrow \mu = 0.$

Figure 14 presents a Gaussian membership function. It shows the smoothest variation and has the best results in systems which demand smooth variations in their output, when compared with the other ones. The fuzzy Gaussian membership function is given as:σ_i

$$¼_{A^i}(x) = \exp(-\frac{(c_i - x)^2}{2\tilde{A}_i^2}) \quad (2)$$

Figure 13. Triangular membership function

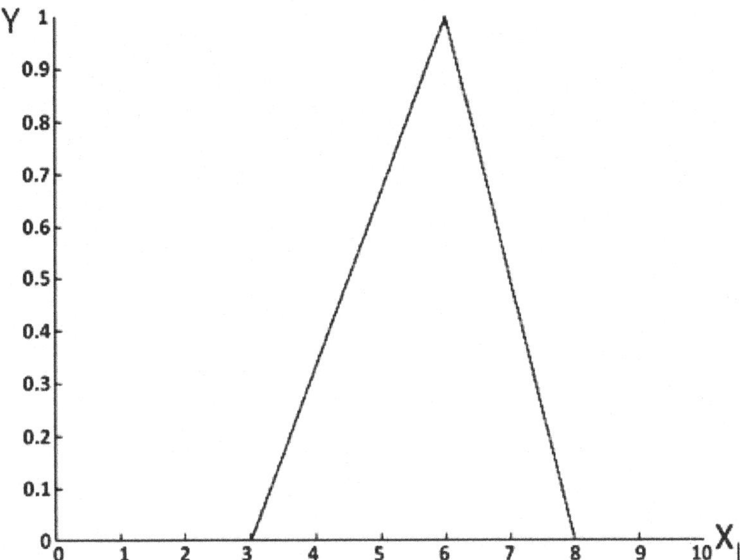

where c_i and $\tilde{A}_1$ are the center and width of the i th fuzzy set A^i, respectively.

According to Ian, S., and Simões, M. (1999), the triangular membership function is normally easier to use than others since it is ease to generate. However, in situations where smooth performance is considered very important, the membership functions may have other shapes, such as Gaussian, sigmoid or sine.

In order to verify the influence of membership function shape in a fuzzy clustering system, two different functions will be carried out for the same application. The system used for the testing utilizes membership functions in order to create the control rules. In this example, the control function should be sin(X_1.X_2), or rather, for the input values X_1 and X_2, the output should generate the result of the control function.

Initially, the system is trained, by providing the input and expected output values. After training using the supplied data, the program generates a control function that will be able to produce values in its output according to the previously conducted training. This application should utilize 14 membership functions.

The ideal membership function for the ECG signal analysis is that one with the smallest difference between the control and the membership generated functions. For example, the program must generate a function in its output that best represents the value of sin(X_1.X_2), according to the two input values X1 and X2. Figure 15 shows the output function that the program should generate, which can be used for validation.

Figure 15 shows the expected correct function at the output, where X_1 and X_2 range between [-3,3] and the result of sin(X_1.X_2) varies between [-1,1].

The Gaussian membership function obtained the best results, given that its membership function has the smoothest variation. In order to demonstrate some of the results obtained, the best and worst membership function, the Gaussian and triangular, respectively, will be presented.

Figure 16 shows the triangular membership function. It corresponds to the 14 membership functions utilized by the two input data (X_1 and X_2). Since the program generates a function that

Figure 14. Typical Gaussian membership function

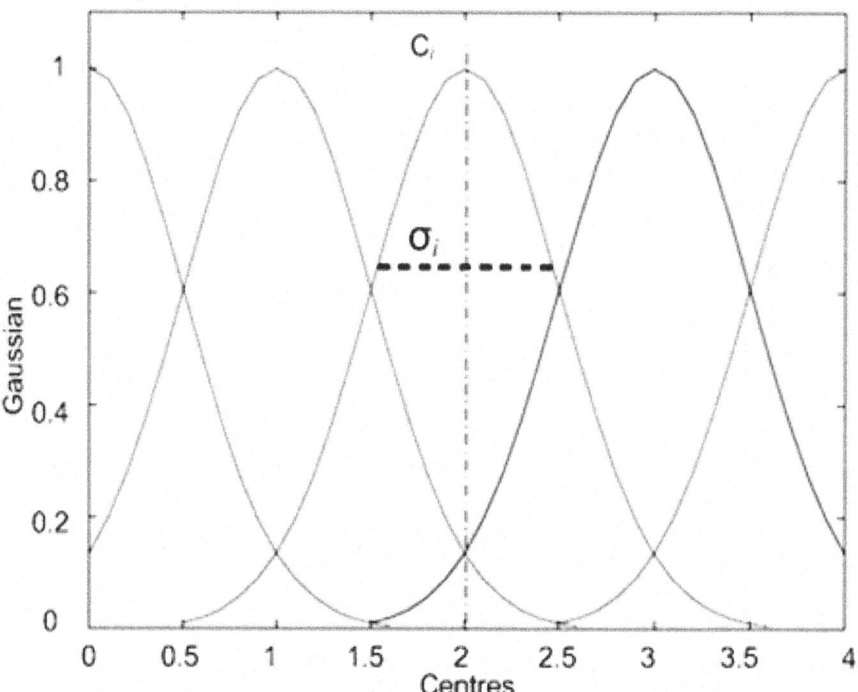

relates X_1 and X_2, given that each input works with 14 memberships, the program will relate the 14 input memberships of each input, thus resulting in a combination of 196 memberships. Figure 17 presents the graph generated by the program where, with X_1 and X_2 ranging between [-3,3], the program generated an output function which comes close to the expected function shown in Figure 15. It can be observed that the graph generated is quite deformed regarding to the original one. This deformation can be perceived by the surface waves as indicated. It occurs because the function generated by the program is a function of the smooth variation and the membership function, in triangular shape, possesses a more pronounced variation. When compared to the other two functions, the triangular function presented the greatest deformity in its output function.

The Gaussian membership function is presented in Figure 18.

It can be observed from the Gaussian membership function shown in Figure 19, that the membership function variation is smooth when compared to the triangular one. The Gaussian function yields best results, or rather, smallest errors, since it presents a smooth variation.

In the Gaussian membership function, the largest error generated between the expected and the generated functions within the interval [-3,3] was close to 0.03. In the triangular membership function, the largest error was almost 0.6, once again highlighting the fact that this function possesses much more pronounced variations.

Another characteristic that also influences the precision of the fuzzy system's response is the quantity of fuzzy sets. The quality of the system's response improves as the number of memberships increases; however, this also increases the system's computational demand. According to Ian, S., and Simões, M. (1999), a quantity between 2 and 7

Figure 15. Original plot of a $Sin(X_1.X_2)$ function

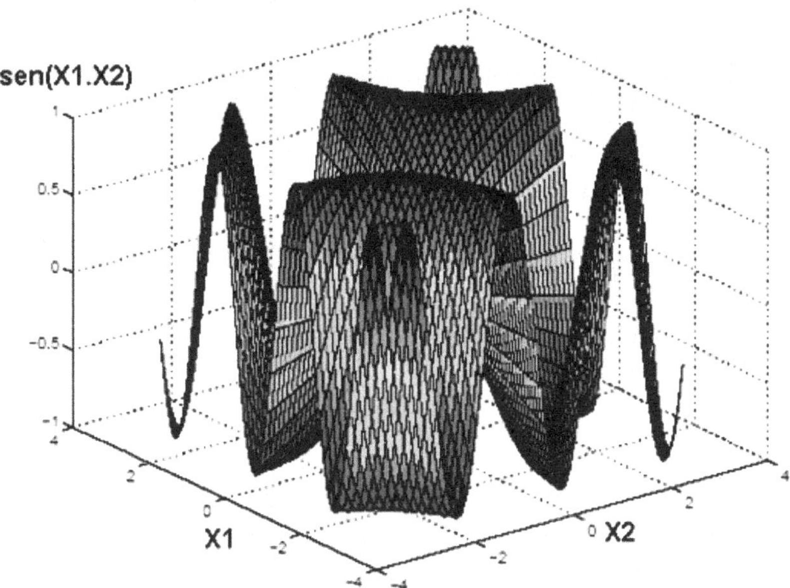

memberships is adequate; an increase from 5 to 7 triangular membership results in a 15% improvement. Significant improvements are not perceived for more than 7 memberships.

The fuzzy clustering process consists of dividing a given set of data into groups or clusters, according to the distance of their point to the prototype clusters. There are several methods that can be used to identify these clusters, and we have used the GK fuzzy clustering algorithm method (Gustafson, D., and Kessel, W. (1979)). Every cluster represents a rule within a rule set. Based on the pairs formed by inputs and their corresponding outputs, a regression matrix X and an output vector Y are formed, as shown by:

$$X^T = [x_1, x_2, \ldots\ldots\ldots, x_N],$$
$$Y^T = [y_1, y_2, \ldots\ldots\ldots, y_N] \quad (3)$$

where N indicates the number of pairs used in the identification process.

The fuzzy clustering algorithm can be summarized by the block diagram of Figure 20.

It is applied the fuzzy clustering algorithm to the filtered 213 ECG samples, shown in Figure 12, that reduces the data to just 20 samples, as indicated in Figure 21. It can be observed that the 20 samples are enough to draw a waveform that maintains the ECG information.

5. CORRELATION

It is possible to reach three outcomes from the analysis of the correlation between two phenomena, since correlation may indicate the correlation intensity and type (Bendat, J., and Piersol, A. (1993)).

A correlation factor close to -1 (negative correlation) indicates that there is a strong inverse correlation between the two phenomena. If the correlation factor is close to 0, either positive or negative, this indicates that there is no correlation between the phenomena. A correlation factor close to 1 indicates that there is a strong direct correlation between the data under analysis.

Figure 16. Triangular membership graph

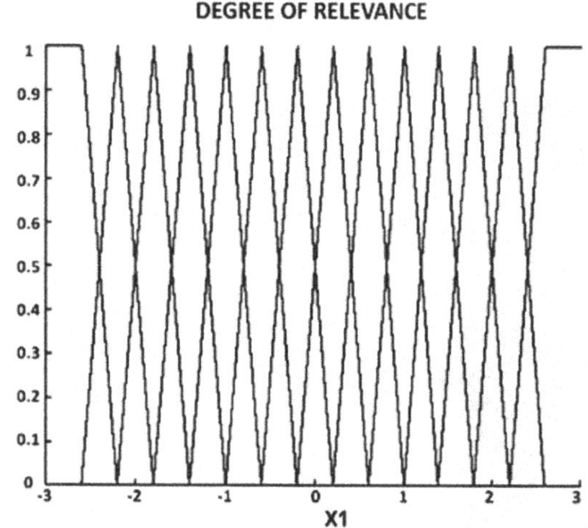

One of the main applications of correlation in signal processing is to find a similarity between an unknown signal and a known data bank.

The correlation between the data generated by the fuzzy clustering algorithm and the previously fuzzy clustered data bank is evaluated. Consider X as the signal clustered data, and Y as the clustered data from the known bank, therefore the correlation factor between them is given as (Bendat, J., and Piersol, A. (1993)).

$$\rho = \frac{\sum x \times y}{n \times \sigma x \times \sigma y} \tag{4}$$

where $x = X - MX$, $y = Y - MY$.

MX is the signal clustering average, and MY is the bank clustering average, or in other words:

$$MX = \frac{\sum X}{n} \tag{5}$$

$$MY = \frac{\sum Y}{n} \tag{6}$$

Where n is the number of clusters, σx is the standard deviation on x, and σy is the standard deviation on y, given as:

$$\sigma x = \sqrt{\frac{\sum x^2}{n}} \tag{7}$$

Figure 17. Attempt of using the triangular membership function to generate $Sin(X_1.X_2)$ function

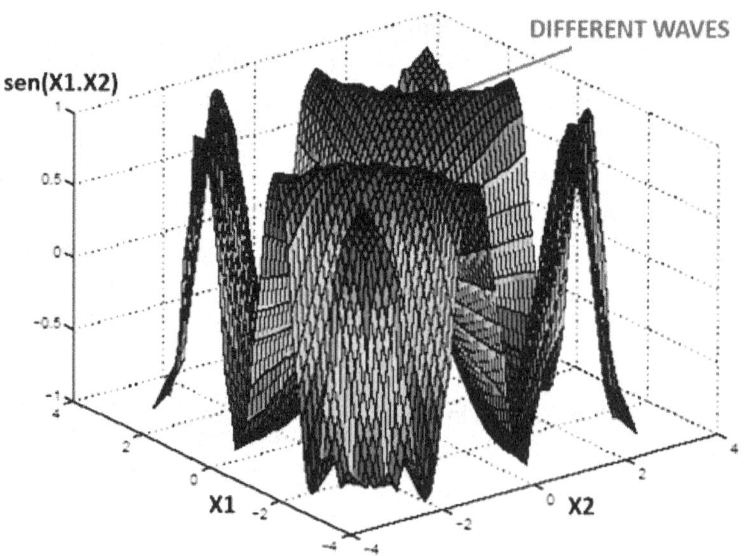

Figure 18. Gaussian membership graph

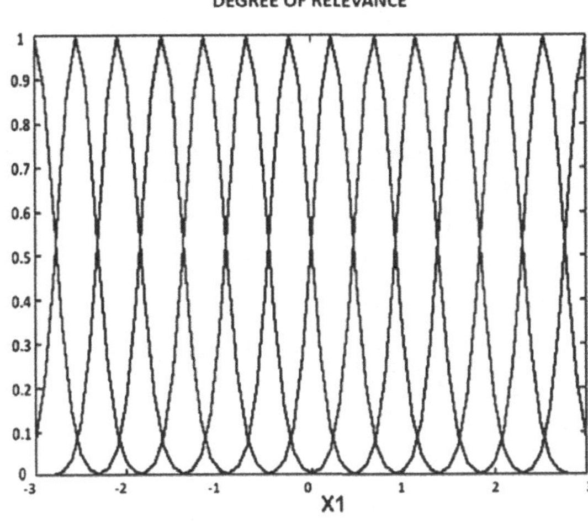

$$\sigma y = \sqrt{\frac{\sum y^2}{n}} \tag{8}$$

6. EMBEDDED SYSTEMS, FPGAS, AND MICROBLAZE

Embedded systems perform a specific and correlated set of functions and are formed by the same basic architectural components of a computer such as microprocessor, main memory, interfaces, and others, depending on the system (Oliveira, A., and Andrade, F. (2006)). There are some hardware limitations when compared with computer systems, such as the lower processing frequency and smaller memory, among others. On the other hand, the advantages of embedded systems compared to computers are cost, size, weight, energy consumption and custom application. An embedded system may be composed of one or more integrated circuits.

A Field Programmable Gate Array – FPGA is programmable integrated circuits – IC. The technology was created by XILINX Inc, and launched in 1985. They are composed of an enormous number of programmable switch matrices that may be configured to simulate the behavior of any type of digital circuit. In order to program these circuits, Hardware Description Languages – HDL are fre-

Figure 19. Attempt of using the Gaussian membership function to generate $Sin(X_1.X_2)$ function

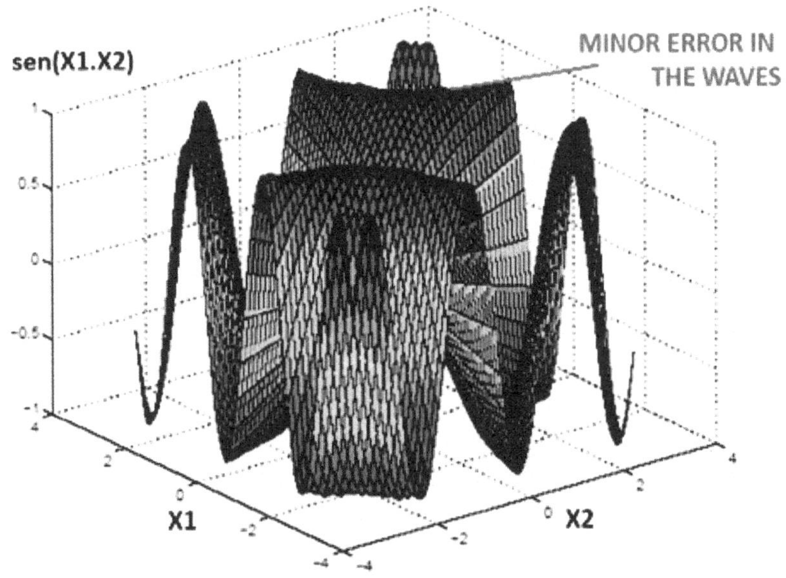

Figure 20. Simplified block diagram of the fuzzy clustering algorithm

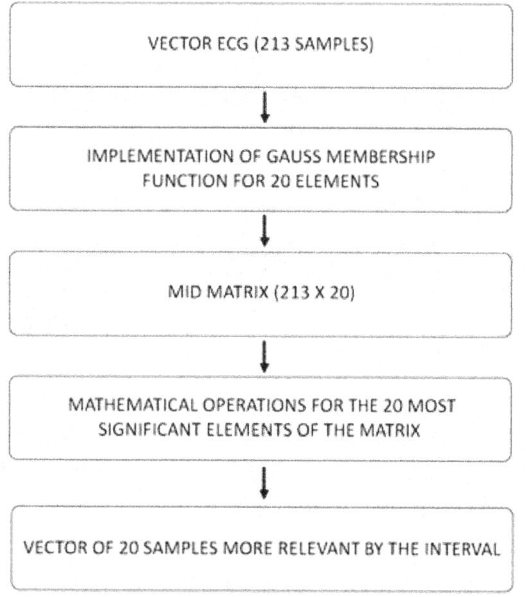

quently used. Currently, the most commonly used HDLs are VHDL, Verilog and SystemVerilog. The advantage of FPGAs over conventional ICs is their hardware performance with the software flexibility (Zeidman, B. (2002)). FPGAs are naturally more expensive than ICs; nonetheless they are a good option for low volume of productions or just few circuits. There are several FPGA manufacturers, such as XILINX and ALTERA. The system herein detailed was constructed in an XILINX FPGA from the SPARTAN Microblaze family with a soft Central Processing Unit – CPU core.

Microblaze is a 32-bit soft core Reduced Instruction Set Computer – RISC processor. RISC processors are capable of executing a handful of simple instructions. Consequently, the chips based in this architecture are much simpler and cheaper. Due to its implementation in FGPA, it is treated in some bibliographies as a virtual processor. Microblaze possesses instructions optimizing embedded applications (Xilinx Inc (2009)). It works, as a standard, with many different types of

Figure 21. Set of 20 samples after the fuzzy clustering algorithm

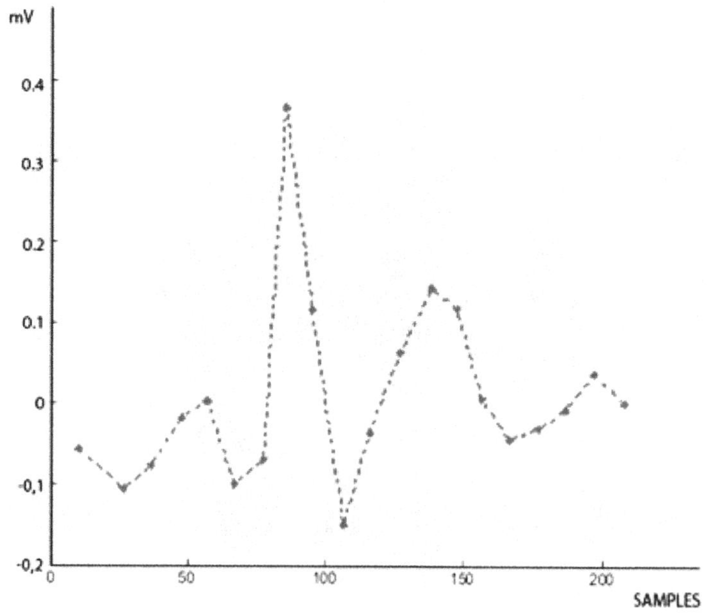

memory, such as SDR, DDR, DDR2, SRAM and Flash, and possesses a simple precision Floating Point Unit - FPU compatible with IEEE-754. FPU is essential for this implementation.

The basic Microblaze architecture consists of thirty two general purpose registers, an Arithmetic Logic Unit – ALU, a shifting unit and two interruption levels. The XILINX SPARTAN 3A Starter kit development board runs at 50 MHz.

The system development system is the XILINX Software Development Kit – SDK, which divides the development into two hardware and software design.

The software design into SDK must be carried out in C or C++ languages. Therefore the SDK compilers generate a machine code from the C or C++ listing, that are required to run the Microblaze. In this implementation we have chosen C. XILINX Platform Studio – XPS, is a suite used in the generation of all MicroBlaze intellectual property cores and their respective peripherals. XPS offers a library with few architectures already written in VHDL. The suite joins and compiles all VHDL descriptions and implants them into the FPGA.

Figure 22 shows the Spartan 3 XILINX A Starter Kit board with its components. The main features are:

- Microblaze with FPU running at 50,
- 32 MB DDR2 RAM,
- RS232 serial interface,
- Dip switches,
- LEDs,
- Buttons,
- IP clock counter.

7. SOFTWARE AND HARDWARE DEVELOPMENT

The entire system was developed in C language according to the American National Standards Institute ANSI standards. The block diagram of the main functionalities is presented in Figure 23.

The main difficulties in the embedded system software development are the hardware limitations, including its peripheries and the algorithms that must present the best performance possible. Since no operational system was inserted, nor does the hardware possess any memory management system, all the required code had to be developed.

The allocation, liberation and reuse of vectors and matrices used in the system must be efficient, since any fault of memory management may damage the data by other variables. The system is dedicated, and thus, it runs only the algorithms developed in C language and loaded in Microblaze memory, thus validating the goal of dedicated embedded system of seeking maximum efficiency. At the end of C file compilation, the SDK generate an ELF file (Xilinx standard file) that is sent to the Microblaze initialization memory, in this case, the memory DDR2 SDRAM. This ELF file contains the controller and processing codes from the C algorithm. Upon sending the ELF file, the system is operational and ready for use.

The hardware was designed and implemented according to the developed software aiming the heart illness diagnosing. All of the XPS IP cores and the Microblaze were implemented in FPGA.

The sw3, sw2, sw1 and sw0 switches are responsible for the selection of the lead input. Switch sw3 is the least significant bit and sw0 is the most, as indicated Figure 24.

The system functions with seven leads, which are available in the used databank. These leads were classified in integers, according to Table 1.

For instance, derivation V4 is selected by placing the switches into position 10, as shown in Figure 24.

It was created a communication system via HyperTerminal using the board RS-232 interface. The signals are sent to the system via Hyper Terminal. It was configured to directly receive the automatically acquired CSV (comma separated values) files in real time from the site PHYSIONET (http://www.physionet.org/cgi-bin/ATM).

Figure 22. XILINIX SPARTAN 3A Starter Kit Board, where 1 - FPGA, 2 - Switches, 3 - LEDs, 4 - Buttons, 5 - RS232 Port, 6 - USB connection and 7 - Power supply connector

The system outputs are based in LEDs. The board has the eight LEDs 1d7,1d6, 1d5, 1d4, 1d3, 1d2, 11, 1d0 as indicated in Figure 25. The LEDs indicate which lead is selected, as previously listed, and indicate a possible diagnosis for the applied signal. Table 2 lists the diagnosis provided by the LEDs.

Some of the system functionalities were implemented solely for the purpose of validation and verification, as in the case of the clock counter and the RS-232 interface.

The clock counter is used to find out the number o clock cycles required by the processor to carry out a given task. It was very important during the software implementation, as it indicates if an al-

Figure 23. Block diagram algorithm

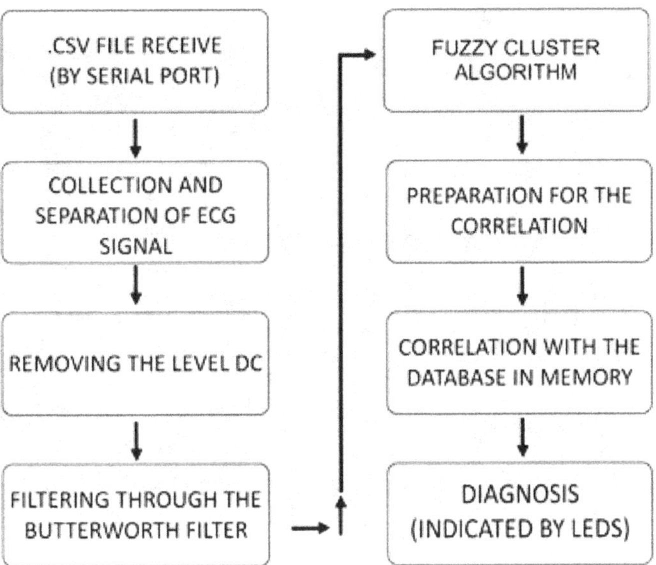

gorithm presents an adequate performance. It was also used to validate the fuzzy clustering algorithm. The RS-232 port contributed to a deeper system analysis, since several parameters may evaluated by the hyperterminal as in a debugging mode.

RESULTS

As previously described, the results were obtained by using the Physionet EBD databank. A databank of previously known ECG diagnoses was created in order to implement the proposed system. The bank consists of 50 signals of 213 samples each. The 213 samples represent a full cycle required for an ECG analysis. All data were pre-processed and only the clusters containing the main features of the signal were stored. The data are stored in the system memory at the same time the system is loaded in the Microblaze board through JTAG.

The literature presents other techniques that use the same data bank (Andreão (2004), Jager (1998) and Vila (1997)) and provides comparison parameters, or merit figures, Sensitivity – *Se* and Positive Predictive Value (or precision rate) – *PPV*, as given by (Altman, D. (1994)):

$$Se = \frac{Tp}{Tp + Fn} \tag{9}$$

where *Tp* and *Fn* are the correct and the non-detected diagnosis, respectively. The parameter *Se* indicates the percentage of correct diagnosis over the non-detected diagnosis.

$$PPV = \frac{Tp}{Tp + Fp} \tag{10}$$

where *Fp* indicates the wrong diagnosis provided. The parameter *PPV* indicates the percentage of correct diagnosis over the wrong diagnosis.

Tests were conducted to evaluate the system effectiveness based on the comparison parameters by using the described mathematic algorithms. A data bank composed of ECG sample signals with cardiopathies such as angina, infarction and high blood pressure was prepared.

Figure 24. Switch selection

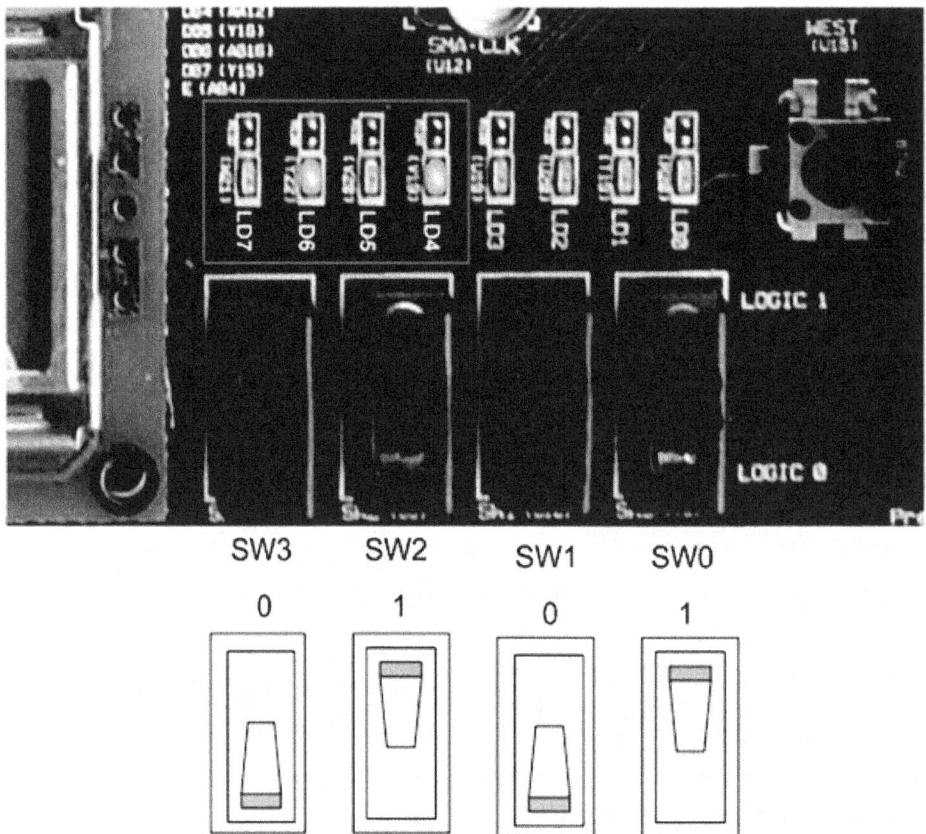

There is a set of 37 distinct diagnoses from 37 different patients. Each signal was filtered using a third order low pass Butterworth filter to eliminate noise and the DC component on the ECG signal.

The test results were compiled and compared with other work presented in the literature, as presented in Table 3. As can be observed from the table, the parameter *Se*, of 75%, is a little below the other systems, meaning that our systems do not offer a high performance on the possibility of not detecting a disease. Nevertheless, the parameter *Se* is still acceptable. On the other hand, the *PPV* parameter, of 92%, offers a better performance than other systems. The *PPV* parameter indicates that, if a cardiopathy is detected, the chance of detecting a wrong cardiopathy is smaller.

Those results were obtained using the correlation technique. The same tests were conducted for a number of samples, as indicated by the graph of Figure 26. It can be observed from the graph that the full signal with 213 samples takes ap-

Table 1. Lead classification

Lead	Classification
MLI	1
MLIII	3
V1	7
V2	8
V3	9
V4	10
V5	11

Figure 25. Diagnosis indication of angina

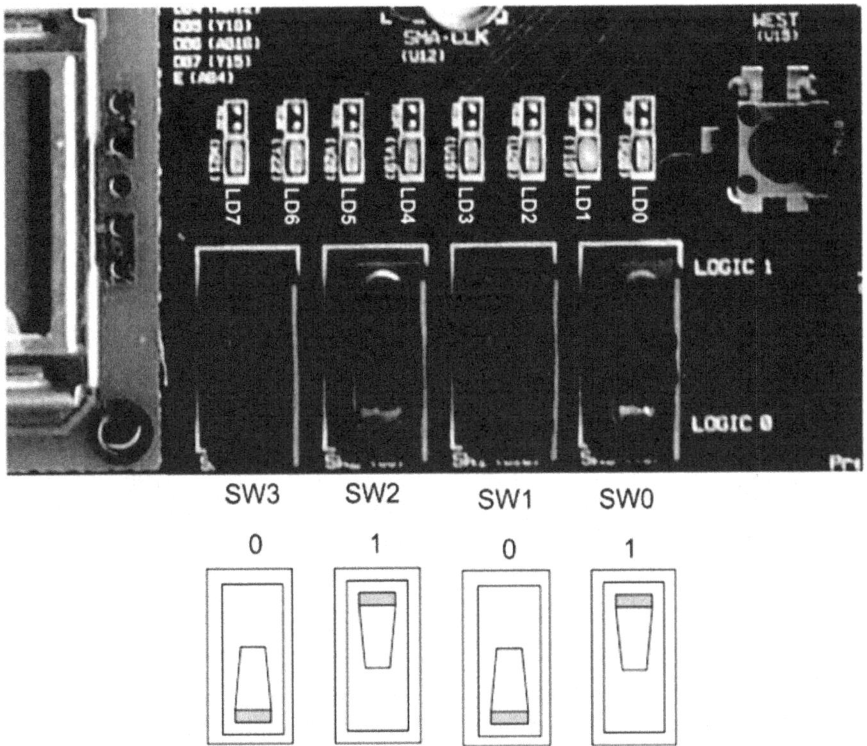

proximately 9 times clock cycles than the ECG with just 20 samples.

Since correlation is a comparison technique, the amount of clock cycles per sample was linear. Nevertheless, in other ECG detection techniques, such as neural networks (Armato (2009)), the performance improvement tends to be exponential, since the relative amount of input data is much smaller and it can reduce the processing and improve the system response.

Table 2. Final system diagnosis

Diagnosis	*LEDs*
Infarct	Ld0
Angina	Ld1
Coronary artery disease	Ld2
High arterial pressure	Ld3
None	Ld7

The system runs at a maximum frequency of 50 MHz, which is comparable to other work (Yan, L. (2010)), and very suitable for a portable embedded ECG diagnosis system.

CONCLUSION

Besides presenting a good performance compared to other work, the fuzzy clustering algorithm uses only 20 samples per signal to make a cardiopathy diagnose. It takes a smaller amount of memory to store the data bank and requires less processing, thus generating the response in a shorter period of time.

An embedded system using our solution may help physicians and other health professionals to make decisions. The proposed system does not intend at all to replace professionals, but to assist newly graduated physicians and other health

Figure 26. Clock cycles for 20 samples

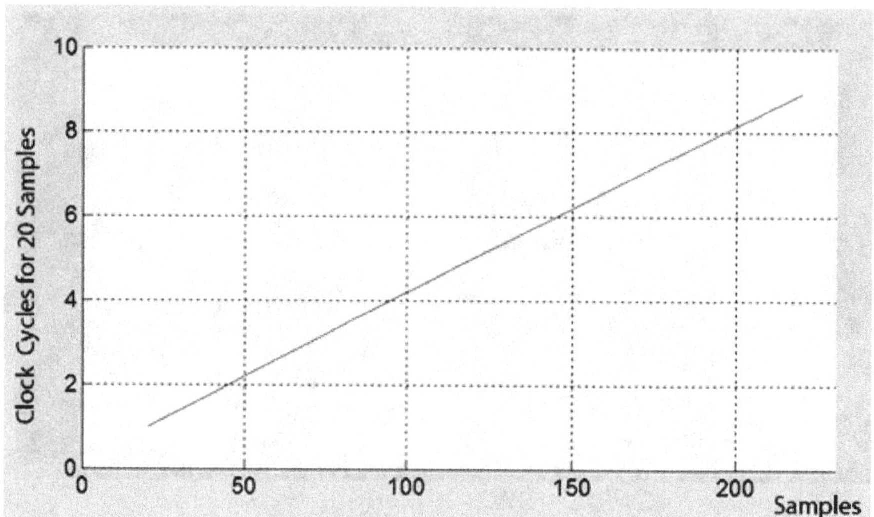

professionals. It could even be used by others in emergencies or urgencies. The system could also be used in areas far away from cardiologists or other physicians, including telehealth programs. The system could also be used for overnight "on duty" physicians, of any specialty, and could provide the first, or initial diagnose of any cardiopathy.

The methods used to implement our system offered a good rate of correct diagnosis; as can be observed form Table 2, they provide a higher confidence in the results, mainly if a cardiopathy is detected. That conclusion is due to the PPV parameter. Although the parameter Se is slightly smaller than others reported, it is still satisfactory.

Table 3. Comparison results

System	Statistic Measures	
	Sensitivity (%)	PPV (%)
Taddei	84	81
Vila	83	75
Jager	87	88
Maglaveras	89	78
Andreão	83	86
Fuzzy Clustering	75	92

Nevertheless, the parameter Se could be improved by using a larger data bank, with different characteristics.

Another important consideration of our method, compared with other techniques, is the smaller data set to be processed, which is reduced by about 10%. The presented technique can be applied to other biopotentials, or even other applications in which a reduction in the data set is essential.

REFERENCES

Altman, D., & Bland, M. (1994). Statistics notes: Diagnostic tests 1: Sensitivity and specificity. *British Medical Journal, 308*, 1552. doi:10.1136/bmj.308.6943.1552

Altman, D., & Bland, M. (1994). Statistics notes: Diagnostic tests 2: Predictive values. *British Medical Journal, 309*, 102. doi:10.1136/bmj.309.6947.102

Andreão, R. V. (2004). ST-segment analysis using hidden Markov model beat segmentation: Application to ischemia detection. *Computers in Cardiology*, 381–384. doi:10.1109/CIC.2004.1442952

Armato, A., Nardini, E., Lanatà, A., Valenza, G., Mancuso, C., Scilingo, E., & Rossi, D. (2009). An FPGA based arrhythmia recognition system for wearable applications. *Ninth International Conference on Intelligent Systems Design and Applications*, (pp. 660-664).

Bendat, J., & Piersol, A. (1993). *Engineering applications of correlation and spectral analysis*. New York, NY: John Wiley and Sons.

Boylestad, R., Nashelsky, L., & Monssen, F. (2005). *Electronic devices and circuit theory*. Upper Saddle River, NJ: Prentice Hall.

Brazilian Society of Cardiology. (2003). *Guidelines for the interpretation of the resting electrocardiogram*. Brazilian Archives of Cardiology, Retrieved January 7, 2008, from http://publicacoes.cardiol.br/consenso/2003/8002/repouso.pdf

Carter, M. (2006). *Heart disease still the most likely reason you'll die*. CNN. Retrieved January 05, 2008, from http://edition.cnn.com/2006/HEALTH/10/30/heart.overview/index.html

Goldberger, A. L., Amaral, L., Glass, L., Hausdorff, J. M., Ivanov, P. C., & Mark, R. G. ... Stanley, H. E. (2000). *PhysioBank, PhysioToolkit, and PhysioNet: Components of a new research resource for complex physiologic signals*. Retrieved March 10, 2009, from http://physionet.org/physiobank/database/edb/

Gustafson, D., & Kessel, W. (1979). Fuzzy clustering with a fuzzy covariance matrix. *Hemometrics and Intelligent Laboratory Systems - IEEE*, (pp. 761-766).

Ian, S., & Simões, M. (2007). *Controle e Modelagem Fuzzy*. São Paulo, Brazil: Editora Edgard Blucher Ltda.

Jager, F., Moody, G., & Mark, R. (1998). Detection of transient ST segment episodes during ambulatory ECG monitoring. *Computers and Biomedical Research, an International Journal, 31*, 305–322. doi:10.1006/cbmr.1998.1483

Jewajinda, Y., & Chongstitvatana, P. (2010). FPGA-based online-learning using parallel genetic algorithm and neural network for ECG signal classification. *Seventh International Conference on Electrical Engineering/Electronics, Computer, Telecommunications and Information Technology (ECTI-CON)*, (pp. 1050-1054).

Maglaveras, N., Stamkopoulos, T., Pappas, C., & Gerassimos Strintzis, M. (1998). An adaptive backpropagation neural network for real-time ischemia episodes detection: Development and performance analysis using the European ST-T database. *IEEE Transactions on Bio-Medical Engineering, 45*, 805–813. doi:10.1109/10.686788

Mitsukura, Y., Miyata, K., Mitsukura, K., Fukumi, M., & Akamatsu, N. (2004). Intelligent medical diagnosis system using the fuzzy and neural networks. *IEEE Annual Meeting of the North American Fuzzy Information Processing Society*, Vol. 2, (pp. 550-554).

National Center for Health Statistics. (2009). *Health, United States: With special feature on medical technology*. Hyattsville. Retrieved March 5, 2009, from http://www.cdc.gov/nchs/data/hus/hus09.pdf

Negreiros de Andrade, P. J. (2008). *Cardiologia para o Generalista: Uma abordagem fisiopatológica*. Fortaleza, Brazil: UFC.

Nianqiang, L., Yongbing, W., & Guoyi, Z. (2010). A preferable method on digital filter in ECG signal's processing based on FPGA. *Third International Symposium on Intelligent Information Technology and Security Informatics*, (pp. 184-187).

Oliveira, A., & Andrade, F. (2006). *Sistemas embarcados: Hardware e firmware na prática*. São Paulo, Brazil: Editora Érica.

Stein, E. (1987). *Clinical electrocardiography: A self-study course*. Philadelphia, PA: Lea and Febiger.

Taddei, A., & Constantino, G. (1995). A system for the detection of ischemic episodes in ambulatory ECG. *Computers in Cardiology*, 705–708.

Taddei, A., Distante, G., Emdin, M., Pisani, P., Moody, G. B., Zeelenberg, C., & Marchesi, C. (1992). The European ST-T database: Standard for evaluating systems for the analysis of ST-T changes in ambulatory electrocardiography. *European Heart Journal*, *13*, 1164–1172.

Thaler, M. (2002). *The only EKG book you'll ever need*. Philadelphia, PA: Lippincott Williams and Wilkins.

Vila, J., Presedo, J., Delgado, M., Barro, S., Ruiz, R., & Palacios, F. (1997). SUTIL: Intelligent ischemia monitoring system. *International Journal of Medical Informatics*, *47*, 193–214. doi:10.1016/S1386-5056(97)00095-6

Xilinx Inc. (2009). *MicroBlaze soft processor core*. Retrieved March 10, 2009, from http://www.xilinx.com/tools/microblaze.htm

Yan, L., Hang, Y., Lai, J., Lixiao, M., & Zhen, J. (2010). Adaptive lifting scheme for ECG QRS complexes detection and its FPGA implementation. *Third International Conference on Biomedical Engineering and Informatics*, (pp. 721-724).

Zeidman, B. (2002). *Designing with FPGAs and CPLDs*. London, UK: CMP Publishing.

Chapter 20
Parallel Evolutionary Computation in R

Cedric Gondro
The Centre for Genetic Analysis and Applications, University of New England, Australia

Paul Kwan
University of New England, Australia

ABSTRACT

Evolutionary Computation (EC) is a branch of Artificial Intelligence which encompasses heuristic optimization methods loosely based on biological evolutionary processes. These methods are efficient in finding optimal or near-optimal solutions in large, complex non-linear search spaces. While evolutionary algorithms (EAs) are comparatively slow in comparison to deterministic or sampling approaches, they are also inherently parallelizable. As technology shifts towards multicore and cloud computing, this overhead becomes less relevant, provided a parallel framework is used. In this chapter the authors discuss how to implement and run parallel evolutionary algorithms in the popular statistical programming language R. R has become the de facto language for statistical programming and it is widely used in biostatistics and bioinformatics due to the availability of thousands of packages to manipulate and analyze data. It is also extremely easy to parallelize routines within R, which makes it a perfect environment for evolutionary algorithms. EC is a large field of research, and many different algorithms have been proposed. While there is no single silver bullet that can handle all classes of problems, an algorithm that is extremely simple, efficient, and with good generalization properties is Differential Evolution (DE). Herein the authors discuss step-by-step how to implement DE in R and how to parallelize it. They then illustrate with a toy genome-wide association study (GWAS) how to identify candidate regions associated with a quantitative trait of interest.

INTRODUCTION

In recent years R (R Development Core Team 2011) has become *de facto* statistical programming language of choice for statisticians and it is widely used to teach statistic courses at universities. It is also arguably the most widely used environment for analysis of high throughput genomic data and in particular for microarray analyses. R's main strength lies in the literally thousands of packages freely available from repositories such as CRAN or Bioconductor (Gentleman *et al.* 2004) which build on the core platform. Chances are that there

DOI: 10.4018/978-1-4666-1830-5.ch020

already is an *off the shelf* package available for a particular task. At the end of this chapter we briefly summarize the main Evolutionary Computation packages that are available for R.

Since R is a scripted language it is very easy to essentially *assemble* various packages, add some personalized routines and chain-link it all into a full analysis pipeline all the way from raw data to final report. This of course dramatically reduces development and deployment times for complex analyses. The downside is that the development speed and ease comes along with a certain compromise in computational times because R is a scripted language and not a compiled one. But there are some tricks for writing R code which will improve performance, and we will discuss some of these later on. Alternatively, for time critical routines, R can be dynamically linked to compiled code in C or Fortran (and also other languages to various degrees), this opens the possibility of using prior code or developing code specifically tailored for solving a computationally intensive task and then sending the results back into R for further downstream analyses (Gentleman 2009).

Parallel computation has been a buzz word for a few years now, but programs and programming practices have not quite caught up with the technology and there generally is a reasonable amount of work involved in developing a program that runs in parallel. Of course this will be problem specific, but it is relatively easy to parallelize iterative routines in R; and this is especially true for evolutionary algorithms (EAs) which are inherently parallelizable.

R is also platform independent. Scripts will generally run on any operating system. When all these factors are taken together we have a perfect environment for working with complex problems. Herein we assume that the reader is reasonably familiar with R and its syntax. For those who are unfamiliar with it, two excellent texts more focused on the programming aspects of the language are Chambers (2008) and Jones *et al.* (2009). A very brief *Getting Started with R* is provided in Appendix 1 for the interested readers.

A Quick Tour of Evolutionary Algorithms

Evolution can be seen as a dynamic and opportunistic optimization process. Effectively it is a method to search through a vast solution space and find a solution that allows organisms to survive and reproduce in a certain environment. It is dynamic in the sense that solutions (organisms) can change to adapt to environmental changes and it is opportunistic in the sense that solutions are not necessarily globally optimal but rather tend to move to the next available solution that ensures viability, even if in detriment of a more globally optimal solution. Interestingly enough, the high-level rules that govern evolution and account for the great variability of organisms are quite straightforward. Organisms – which can be seen as candidate solutions – evolve through random variation due to mutation, crossover and manipulations on their genetic material; these candidates are subjected to selective pressures which evaluate their *adaptiveness* and determine their capacity of generating descendants, thus propagating better fit genotypes into the future generations. These characteristics are the inspiration of Evolutionary Computation.

Evolutionary algorithms are primarily computational methods designed for optimization of complex problems with large search spaces. These algorithms try to mimic the mechanisms of biological evolution to evolve a solution (Mitchell and Taylor 1999; Fogel 2000a; Fogel 2000b). Even though specific implementations can vary significantly and algorithms are not constrained to using only biological mechanisms, there are three common features which are shared by the different branches of EC (Bäck 2000): population, selection and search operators.

- Population: a number (n) of candidate solutions (representations of the problem) compete against each other to remain in the population and generate offspring. Since EC uses populations, it can be seen as a parallelized search of the solution space.
- Selection: candidate solutions from the population pool are selected for culling or reproduction based on their fitness. Fitness is a function that measures how good a representation is at solving the problem. The two most adopted methods for assigning fitness are as a direct mapping to the problem or as a relative measurement of performance in relation to the remainder of the population. Arguably, the choice of a fitness function that clearly states the problem is the most important step in determining the success or failure of the algorithm.
- Search Operators: EC uses stochastic methods to solve a problem; these biologically inspired operators provide the variability necessary for the EC population to explore different areas of the solution space. The two main sources of variability are mutation, which are randomly generated new sources of variability and crossover, which exploits the available variability within the population to form new combinations of candidate solutions.

Thus, a general EC algorithm combines these features and through iterations improves the overall fitness of the population, gradually converging on a solution. The following steps form the general structure of an EC algorithm:

1. Create an initial population – randomly or based on prior information
2. Assign a fitness value to all organisms (also referred to as chromosomes)
3. Select organisms for reproduction based on their fitness and a selection scheme
4. Create descendants from the selected parents
5. Modify the descendants with the search operators
6. Evaluate the fitness of the descendants
7. Cull organisms from the parental population and replace them with the descendants according to the selection scheme
8. Repeat from step 3 until a termination criterion is met, for example, a specified number of iterations or a predefined fitness value is reached

Unfortunately there is no optimal method for solving all types of optimization problems. An algorithm adequate for a certain class of problems may breakdown under a different problem. While there are no definite rules, a simple recipe for solving complex problems using EAs is illustrated in Figure 1 and would include:

- Nature of the problem: to solve a problem it is necessary to understand it. This may sound like a tautology, but EAs need to be able to evaluate how good a solution is, if not in absolute terms, at least in relation to other candidate solutions. If a problem is

Figure 1. Optimization pathway

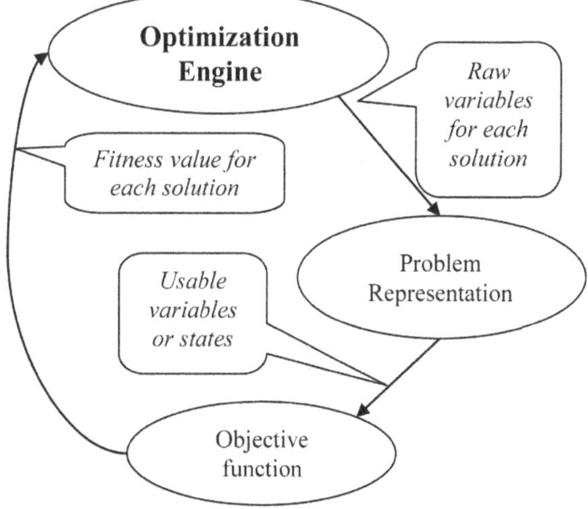

well understood, a more reliable/realistic method to evaluate solutions can be developed.

- Modeling of the problem: optimization is not carried out on the problem itself but rather on a model (representation) of the problem. This is an important distinction; a solution can be perfect for the model but, for the real problem, it is only as good as the model itself. Thus, again, it is critical to understand the nature of the problem. Knowledge of the problem allows the development of a model that captures and reflects its essential characteristics.
- Objective function: this is arguably the most important component of EAs. The objective function is a measurement of how well a solution fits the model of the problem and is used to assign a fitness value to candidate solutions, either through, for example, direct 1:1 mapping or rank based selection (based on the relative performance of solutions within the population).
- Development of an evolutionary algorithm: depending on the problem a certain EA will be better suited than others. For example, it is now generally accepted that the original binary genetic algorithm is inefficient to solve real valued numerical problems. Alternative methods such as Differential Evolution, discussed in the next section, are faster and yield better solutions. Two other important aspects are the design of efficient search operators and how to present the problem to an EA, ideally in a parameterization that *automatically* accommodates constraints.
- **Computational Implementation:** Population representation can also be an important consideration for an EA and will largely depend on the nature of the problem. A parameterization problem is usually best represented as a real-valued vector; if implementing for example an Evolutionary Strategy or an Evolutionary Programming method the vector will need to hold the solution's variables as well as variability parameters. Finite-state representations are also frequent with Evolutionary Programming. A Genetic Algorithm classically uses binary strings (albeit most modern implementations are based on real-valued GAs). Genetic Programming has to store information on the functions, the terminals and the relations between the two; lists, stacks, parse-trees and vectors are commonly used.

The choice of programming language is of secondary importance to the algorithms and they can usually be easily ported between languages. Fortran or C are natural choices due to their computational efficiency but tend to take longer to write code. EAs can also be easily written for Matlab, R and even Excel. The bottom line is that EAs can probably be coded into just about anything. The choice depends on what the objectives are.

Main Types of Evolutionary Algorithms

Below we briefly describe the main branches of EC. The purpose is neither to provide a comprehensive overview nor to suggest that these are the correct methods for a given EA; the sole intent is to give an overview of the different variants. The boundaries between these branches have blurred almost beyond recognition in modern EC. Keep in mind that the field is evolving rapidly, the binning below is simply for didactic purposes, at the end of the day one should pick the aspects of each method that seem best suited to the problem and use them. Remember: *adapt the method to the problem and not the problem to the method.*

- **Evolutionary Programming (EP):** The basic form consists of generating an initial population μ and a fitness value is assigned to each individual. The iterative loop (each loop is commonly referred to as a generation) usually consists of duplicating each parent μ_1 until a predefined number λ_1 of offspring are generated. The offspring are modified through a mutation process – commonly a Gaussian distribution with zero mean and variance of one, crossover is not used in classic EP. All offspring are evaluated as to their fitness and along with the parental population a selection operator is used to cull the population size back to μ. The main difference between EP and other EC methods is the global optimization method employed by EP. No attempt is made to break the problem down into subcomponents; the fitness evaluation is based solely on the whole solution. In this sense the genotype is of little importance and focus is on optimization of the phenotype. EP traditionally uses continuous-valued variables instead of the discrete representation common in Genetic Algorithms. Current versions of EP are self-adaptive, with the mutation parameters (variance, covariance) adapting to the current state of the population (Fogel 1999).

- **Evolution Strategies (ES):** ES were initially developed to solve technical optimization problems. There are two main general notations for the strategy: $(\mu + \lambda)$ where the ES generates λ offspring from a parental population μ and selects the best μ from all $\mu+\lambda$ individuals. Alternatively the (μ, λ) strategy generates λ offspring from μ parents and selects the μ best from the λ offspring. Weak selective pressures seem to yield a better response thus the μ/λ ratio should not be too small. Of course, a 1:1 mapping of $\mu:\lambda$ reduces the algorithm to a random walk. Typically ES use crossover between two randomly selected parents to generate the offspring; commonly adopted is the multipoint crossover. In a typical ES mutation scheme each solution, alongside the element that maps their position in the search space, can have several parameters controlling the mutation distribution which customarily follows a multivariate normal distribution with zero mean and a covariance matrix that is symmetric and positive definite. At least two mutation parameters are commonly used: angles (σ) and standard deviations (ω). These mutation parameters can be self-adaptive as in EP algorithms. The original ES strategy was $(\mu + 1)$ with a single replacement per iteration loop. Even though the steady-state approach is the preferred choice for other EC methods, modern ES adopt a generational approach similar to EP. As with Evolutionary Programming, ES does not attempt to break down the problem into smaller subcomponents. Optimization is solely based on the phenotypic values of the solution (Schwefel and Rudolph 1995).
- **Genetic Algorithms (GAs):** The most widely disseminated EC branch, GAs date back to Holland's (1975) seminal work. Traditional GA solutions are represented as linear bitstrings which are referred to as chromosomes. The value in each position of the bitstring is an allele (0 or 1) and the position itself is a gene or locus. The combination of values (alleles) in the chromosome maps to a phenotypic expression, such as a parameter to be optimized. GAs operate at two structural levels: a genotypic and a phenotypic one. Selection operators are carried out based on the overall chromosome value (phenotype) while search operators act on the genotype, modifying the chromosome which may or may not change the phenotypic expression. GAs, in the canonical form, are the class of EC which most closely mimic evolutionary processes at a genetic level. Crossover swaps chromosome parts between parents

to form the offspring and mutation changes the value of alleles at randomly selected loci. From this notion derives the concept of schema in GAs (Holland 1975); a good solution consists of a set of good small building blocks. Thus, the assumption is that the chromosomes in the population are formed by small schemas that add up to yield the final fitness. The schema theory has been widely discussed with many arguments for and against but still limited solid evidence. Crossover is often regarded as the main search operator of a GA, with mutation seen more as a mechanism of ensuring a robust gene pool to be explored by crossover (Bäck *et al.* 2000).

- **Genetic Programming (GP):** Often regarded as a specialization of Genetic Algorithms, GP has evolved to become a branch of EC in its own right. Initially GP was devised as a method to optimize data structures as executable computer programs with the fitness value assigned based on the results obtained when executing the instructions contained in each member of the population. In this context, GP evolves populations of computer programs or other algorithmic processes to solve a specific problem (Koza *et al.* 2003). Original implementations of GP used tree-structured representations implemented in LISP (rarely used nowadays). Tree-structures have the terminal nodes of the tree containing inputs (referred to as terminals) and the internal nodes holding functions. This type of construct demands significant overhead to ensure viability of the trees (to handle, for instance, division by zero or infinite loops) or correct tree structures which can break-up due to mutation and crossover. GP uses crossover and mutation in a similar fashion to GAs.

DIFFERENTIAL EVOLUTION

We have already mentioned that no optimization heuristic is superior to all others for all types of optimization problems. But, given that an algorithm is capable of finding optimal or near-optimal solutions, it should ideally also be simple to implement, fast to converge and will not overwhelm the user with a plethora of initial settings. Differential Evolution – DE (Storn and Price 1997) comes quite close to meeting these criteria. It can be implemented in approximately 20 lines of code; converges fast and uses a small number of parameter settings. DE has been successfully used in a wide range of optimization problems; frequently outperforming other heuristics (see www.icsi.berkeley.edu/~storn/code.html for a bibliography on DE).

Differential Evolution lies on the intersection between real-valued Genetic Algorithms (GAs) and Evolution Strategies (ES), using the conventional population structure of GAs and the self-adapting mutation of ES. In a sense DE can loosely be viewed as a population based Simulated Annealing (SA) with the mutation rate decreasing (analogously to the temperature in SA) as the population converges on a solution.

The principle behind DE is straightforward. An initial population of candidate solutions of user defined size is randomly generated – typically of size 10 or so. Each candidate consists of a numeric vector where each position in the vector corresponds to a numeric parameter to be optimized. The size of the vector is equivalent to the number of parameters. On initialization each candidate is assigned a fitness value according to the objective function. The population evolves by iteratively generating a challenger for each candidate using search operators (see details below). If the challenger has a higher fitness, it replaces the *title holder* in the population. If not, the challenger is discarded. Once all solutions in the population have been challenged (one generation), the process starts again with the new population formed by the surviving solutions of the original population and the challengers that had a higher fitness. *Out of the box* Differential Evolution uses discrete generations with elitism (the best solutions are always kept in the population). In each generation all solutions in the population are challenged and are only replaced if the challenger has a higher fitness than the parent solution. Since an elitist approach is adopted, at the end of each generation the average fitness of the population can only increase or remain unchanged. The process is repeated until e.g. a maximum number of generations are attained, a fitness threshold is reached or the average fitness value does not improve over a certain number of generations.

In its basic form, DE uses only four user defined parameters: number of generations, population size, crossover rate (*CR*) and mutation rate (*F*). The number of generations necessary for convergence varies from problem to problem and the user should perform some test runs to get an indication of the evolution of the process. Storn and Price (1997) suggested a population size of 5 to 20 times the number of parameters to be optimized. We have found that small populations (around 1.4 times the number of parameters to optimize) can be considerably more efficient. The other two operators are discussed below, but first let's build a challenger – it will make it easier to understand how they fit into the DE.

- **Challenger:** the key to the effectiveness and simplicity of DE resides in how the challengers are constructed. Consider that *TH* (*title holder*) is the solution to be challenged and *S1*, *S2* and *S3* are three different solutions randomly selected from the population. To create a challenger we will use these four solutions. Initially, simply copy *TH* into the challenger (*CH*) to create a template. Then, with a probability *CR,* we sequentially test each parameter in *CH* and either change (mutate) it or leave it the same as in *TH*. The parameters that change are replaced with the corresponding parameters in *S3* but mutated according to the difference (hence the differential) between *S1* and *S2* times a mutation factor *F*. So, a challenger is simply built by cycling through the parameters $I = (i_1, i_2, \ldots, i_n)$ and allocating a value CH_i with probability *CR*: $CH_i = S_3 + F * (S_1 - S_2)$ or with probability *1-CR*: $CH_i = TH_i$.
- **Crossover (CR):** Differential Evolution uses a very simple form of uniform recombination. A user defined rate defines the probability with which a parameter value is copied from the challenged candidate or a new value is generated from the other three solutions. Low crossover rates make the challenger more similar to the title holder and are more meticulous in exploring the solution space, but are also slower. Higher rates converge faster but there is the risk of getting trapped at a local optimum. An initial recombination rate of 0.5 seems to work well in most situations.
- **Mutation (F):** in DE the mutation rate is self-adapting. As shown above, the mutation operator *F* is used as a multiplier of the difference between two randomly selected solutions which is then added to a third random solution. As the optimization process converges on a solution the population variance decreases and the magnitude of the mutation reduces accordingly. This mimics the self-adapting operators used in Evolution Strategies (Beyer & Schwefel 2002) without the complexity of having to store and calculate variance and covariance information for each gene to tune the operators.

Storn and Price (1997) originally suggested a mutation operator between 0.4 and 1.0. Depending on the problem this can lead to premature convergence and entrapment in a local optimum. Lower rates tend to generate intermediates between the solutions that are used to generate the challenger and higher rates tend to extrapolate out of these bounds. To avoid entrapment at a local optimum, particularly at the latter stages of the optimization, Mayer *et al.* (2005) suggest changing the mutation rate to a higher level every few generations to provoke extrapolative mutation. For example, every ten generations the rate can be changed to 5.0 and then back again to 0.5.

In practice, if *F* is large, the algorithm is more *adventurous* – jumping around the solution space more widely to find solutions that might be good. This is useful in the early generations and helps to get a better initial coverage of the solution space. However, it will usually slow down convergence once there is a decent hill to climb (might cause too much disruption to the solutions). One strategy is to keep *F* high (say between 1 and 2) for the first several hundred generations and then bring it down.

DIFFERENTIAL EVOLUTION IN R

Implementation of DE in R is extremely simple. All we need to do is define the parameters; create a fitness function suitable for our problem; create an initial population; write a function to create the challenger; replace the title holder with the challenger if it has a better fitness and repeat until the termination criterion is met. Let's break this down:

DE Parameters

```
popsize =    10 # population size -
             number of candidate
             solutions
allelesize = 2 # number of parameters
             to optimize
numgen =     1000 # number of
             generations to iterate
CR =         0.5 # probability of
             crossover
FR =         0.8 # mutation rate
```

Notes: The # is a comment in R – everything after it is ignored. We use = instead of the usual ->notation for assignment in R, they both work in current releases of R and personally, one key stroke is better than 2 (plus *SHIFT*)!

Initial Population

```
pop=matrix(runif(popsize*allelesize),
    popsize,allelesize)
fit=apply(pop,1,fitness)
```

For most problems we can simply start with random numbers as the initial population. Sometimes it's worthwhile to *seed* the initial population with some prior knowledge (e.g. potential parameter values) but this is generally good enough.

All the first line does is create a matrix of dimensions *popsize* X *allelesize* and fills it up with random uniform numbers between 0 and 1 (that's what *runif* does). Other distributions could be tried as well. For example normal (*rnorm*) or chi-square (*rchsiq*), etc.

The second line gets this *population* matrix and computes the fitness for each candidate solution using a function called *fitness*. This function does not yet exist and we have to create it, but for the time being let's just assume that it takes as input a solution (that is, a vector of numbers) and returns a single value (which is the fitness).

Note here the first little trick to speed up R. Instead of writing a loop, we use the function *apply*. This basically does the same as a loop (calculates the fitness for each solution in the population matrix) but tends to be faster – R is extremely slow with loops. This is mainly because of the scripted nature of the language. With a loop you are each time going back and forth through the interpreter. Try to send everything as much as possible as a vector which can then be iterated through using compiled functions. Recall that most of R is written in C or Fortran, it's just a matter of presenting the data more efficiently to these functions.

Challenger

(See Box 1) This function creates a new challenger for each candidate solution in the previous generation. The parameter *x* sent to the function is simply the number of the current generation (a simple counter). Initially an *index* is created to randomly sample three solutions from the current population that will be used to construct the *challenger*. This is done for each solution in the population. In our example *index* is a matrix of 10 (popsize) x 3. Note the use of the R function *sample* to randomly select the 3 indices and the use of *[-S]* to exclude the actual solution that will be challenged from the sampling (by default *sample* returns unique values, so all 3 indices are guaranteed to be different).

Next, *crtf* creates and stores a logical matrix to define if crossover will or will not occur in each allele across the population (herein a *10 x 2* matrix). The current solutions in *pop* are then copied into *challenger* as a placeholder and an entire new *mutated* population is created and stored in *hold* using the solutions stored in *index* and the mutation *FR* factor. Note that as previously discussed, *FR* is bumped up from 0.8 to 5 every ten generations to avoid entrapment. Note also that the value of *FR* is changed within the function but this change is only valid within the scope of the function.

Finally the values in *challenger*, which is just a copy of the current population, are replaced with the values in *hold* given the probability of recombination *CR* already stored in *crtf* as a logical matrix (i.e. all *challenger[i,j]* for which *crtf[i,j]==TRUE* are replaced with *hold[i,j]*). It seems a lot of overhead to create an entire new mutated population when only some will be effectively used but it is computationally more efficient to do this in R and it also makes the code very straightforward.

These simple lines create and return an entire new population of solutions, which of course, implies a discrete generation approach to the problem. Arguably steady-state generations (each new solution is immediately tested and made available for selection) can lead to faster convergence but, again, with a trade off in speed since the process is not easily *vectorizable*.

Box 1.

```
challenge=function(x)
{
   # choose 4 candidates from current population
   # 1 title holder, 2, 3 and 4 mutators
   index=matrix(unlist(lapply(1:popsize, function (S)
   sample (c(1:popsize)[-S],3))), popsize, 3, byrow=T)
   # T/F for CR - generate random numbers for CR and then test
   crtf=matrix(CR>runif(allelesize*popsize), popsize,allelesize)
   challenger=pop # make a challenger from title holder
   if (x%%5==0) FR=5 # increase mutation every 10 generations
   hold=pop[index[,1],]+FR*(pop[index[,2],]-pop[index[,3],])
   challenger[crtf]=hold[crtf]
   challenger
}
```

Evaluate Challengers and Replace

```
rungen=function(x)
{
  challenger=challenge(x)
  fitchal=apply(challenger,1,fitness)
  index=which(fitchal>=fit)
  fit[index]<<-fitchal[index]
  pop[index,]<<-challenger[index,]
}
```

This function calls *challenge* to create a new generation of solutions as just discussed and then evaluates the fitness of each of these new candidates. Again *apply* is used to speed up the run; each solution with its alleles is sent as parameters to the *fitness* function which returns the candidate's fitness. Results are stored in the vector *fitchal* which is then compared to the fitness of the title holders from the previous generation (in the vector *fit*). Better solutions (from *challenger*) replace the current ones (in *pop*) and the new fitness values replace the old ones in *fit*. Note the use of <<- to make the changes to *pop* and *fit* permanent and not only within the scope of the function.

Running the DE

The last step we need is to iterate through the generations. A single line does the trick:

```
lapply(1:numgen,rungen) # iterate
   through generations
```

Again, just for consistency, we used the *apply* family of functions but there are no speed gains in this case since there is no real vectorization (we are simply looping in incremental units). A conventional loop takes exactly the same time to run.

```
for (i in 1:numgen) rungen[i]
```

This is the full DE. All that is missing is an objective function to represent the problem at hand and some way of evaluating the fitness of the candidate solutions. The DE itself seldom needs any further changes so it is good practice to write the objective function in a separate file and make it available to the DE using e.g. *source("fitness.r")*. Include this as the first line of the DE – recall that R is a scripted language and code is executed sequentially; a function is only available after it has been defined in the workspace.

There are two main reasons to separate the DE from the objective function. First, the DE itself can very easily be wrapped into a function with the five startup parameters (population size, number of alleles, etc.) which makes it very flexible and it can then be used as any normal R function (Appendix 2 provides full code for a parallel version of DE as an R function). The second reason is that in most real world cases the problem representation/evaluation is the most complicated aspect. While the DE itself is just around 20 lines of code, the objective function can be in the thousands. But let's start with a simple problem.

Example: Rosenbrock's Valley

Various test functions have been proposed to test optimization algorithms (for a good list of test problems see Yang (2010)). One of the most commonly used ones is Rosenbrock's function which is defined as

$$f\left(x\right)=\sum_{i=1}^{n-1}\left(x_i-1\right)^2+100\left(x_{i+1}-x_i^2\right)^2$$

This is a non-convex function also known as Rosenbrock's valley with the global minimum residing inside a long and narrow flat valley (Figure 2). There are other variants, but as presented here it has a global minimum at $x_*=\left(1,1,\ldots,1\right)$ where $f_*=0$.

Figure 2. Rosenbrock's function in two dimensions. The global minimum (0) is at the bottom of the valley with $x_* = 1$.

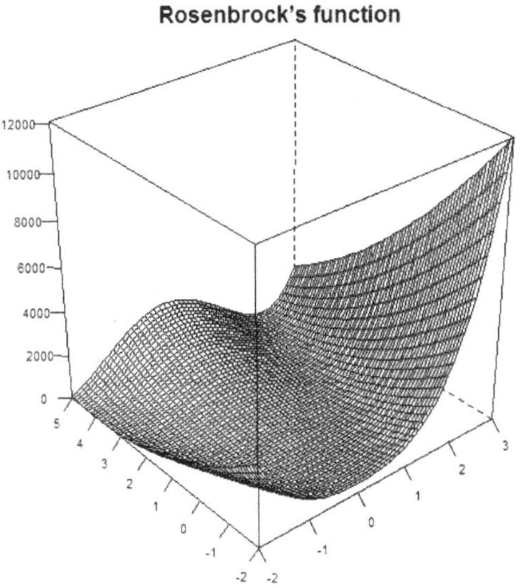

For this problem the objective function is simple and consists of finding the values of two alleles (parameters) that minimize the value of $f(x)$. So, our objective function in R could be: *(see Box 2).*

The *fitness* function receives the alleles as input parameters, calculates $f(x)$ and returns its negative (as variable *crit*) since we want to find the function's minimum. This trivial example will run in around half a second and will always converge on a perfect solution with the exact same parameters used so far. Unfortunately real world problems are much more complex and particularly the objective function can be computationally demanding to calculate. For these scenarios it makes sense to parallelize the optimization algorithm to make better use of the current trend of computer architectures and maintain runtimes within reasonable limits.

PARALLEL EVOLUTIONARY COMPUTATION

Probably the greatest limitation to the use of EC methods is the dimensionality problem. As the number of variables increases the computational effort can increase exponentially. EAs cannot compete in terms of speed with *strong arm* approaches. But by their very nature EC methods are well suited for parallelization, they are commonly referred to as *embarrassingly parallel* due to the ease with which they can be split into smaller problems. This ease meets heads on the current trend of low cost clusters and multicore processors and can potentially shift the time-cost balance since parallelization of deterministic (e.g. dynamic programming) algorithms is not such a trivial task. The main constraints to parallelization are not the EAs but getting processors/computers to communicate with each other; luckily this is quite straightforward in R.

Parallelization can be achieved at the population, individual or fitness level through different models. The two most common models are:

- **Master-slave model:** run the population on one machine (or core) and calculate the

Box 2.

```
fitness = function(allele)
{
   # rosenbrock function
   rosen=(allele[1]-1)^2 + 100*(allele[2]-allele[1]^2)^2
   crit= -1 * rosen # to minimize
}
```

fitness on other machines (or cores). Here the population manipulations (the EA per se) run on a single node but the fitness evaluation (which in more cases than not is the most demanding task) is spread out across the computational resources. This model can be particularly efficient with overlapping generations since there is no need to keep the population synchronized.

- **Island model:** each processor runs its own population and from time to time *migrants* move from one machine to the other. This model allows different areas of the search space to evolve concurrently whilst still allowing a certain level of *gene flow* which will have smaller or larger influence on the acceptor population depending on the differences between fitness. If the migrants move between neighbors the model is termed *stepping stone*.

A complete overview of parallel EAs is given in Nedjah*et al.* (2006) and a GPU specific review is given in Arenas *et al.* (2011). Here we will limit the discussion to the practical implementation of a DE *master-slave* model in R since the objective function is the most common bottleneck found in optimization problems.

Parallel DE in R

Interest in parallel computation in R has grown rapidly in the last few years. This is mainly driven by the rapid increase in the size of datasets, particularly data derived from genomic projects which are outstripping hardware performance. And also, the strong drive towards Bayesian approaches which are computationally demanding.

A variety of packages and technologies have been developed for parallel computing with R. This is a very active area of research so the landscape is changing quite rapidly; a good starting point for the current state of affairs is the *CRAN Task View: High-Performance and Parallel Computing with R* (http://cran.r-project.org/). In a nutshell, there are packages to target different platforms (multi-core machines, clusters, grid computing, GPUs) and these either provide low-level functionality (mainly communication layers) or easier to use wrappers that make the low-level packages more accessible for rapid development/deployment. Currently, the most widely used approach for parallel computing is the MPI (Message Passing Interface) which is supported in R through the *Rmpi* package. At a higher level the package *snow* (Rossini *et al.* 2007) provides easy to use functions that hide details of the communication layer and allows communication using different methods (PVM, MPI, NWS or simple sockets). An even higher level wrapper is *snowfall* which wraps the snow package. Herein we will illustrate how to parallelize Differential Evolution using snowfall and simple socket communication; a detailed overview of parallel methods/packages in R is given in Schmidberger *et al.* (2009) and a good introductory tutorial is Eugster *et al.* (2010).

Some tasks are hard to parallelize, e.g. numerical integration of systems of differential equations which depend on the previous state of all equations. On the other hand some problems are *embarrassingly parallel*. Luckily our Differential Evolution falls in this category. To parallelize the DE all that is needed is four extra lines of code and a single function change to the DE described above. Before the DE add the following code: *(see Box 3)*.

The first line loads the *snowfall* library and then the parameter *sfSetMaxCPUs* is used to change the default maximum number of CPUs that can be accessed (in this example we want to use 48 cores). If less than 32 nodes/cores will be used there's no need to change the parameter – this is simply a safeguard to avoid reckless overloading of shared resources. Next the variable *cpu* stores the number of processors to be used and finally *sfInit* initializes the *cluster*. Here we are using

Box 3.

```
library(snowfall)
# set maximum number of cpus available - default is 32
sfSetMaxCPUs(number=48)

cpu=48
sfInit(parallel=TRUE,cpus=cpu, type="SOCK",
   socketHosts=rep("localhost",cpu))
```

Box 4.

```
rungen=function(x)
{
  challenger=challenge(x)
  # fitchal=apply(challenger,1,fitness) # original sequential code
  fitchal=sfApply(challenger,1,fitness) # new parallel code
  index=which(fitchal>=fit)
  fit[index]<<-fitchal[index]
  pop[index,]<<-challenger[index,]
}
```

simple socket connections (type="SOCK") but MPI, PVM or NWS could be used for other cluster modes. Note that for these to work the packages *Rmpi*, *rpvm* or *nws* would also have to be installed (and the cluster setup in these modes). Sockets do not require any additional setup but they are slower than other modes. The argument *socketHosts* is a list of cpus/computers in the cluster, for processors on the same machine *localhost* (here repeated 48 times – once for each node) can be used but IP addresses or network computer ids can be used for distributed systems. One point of note (and common pitfall) is that socket connection is tunnelled through SSH so this has to be setup and accessible to R for between computer communication to work.

With this the cluster is up and running. When the DE run has finished, the cluster can be stopped with

```
sfStop()
```

Now all that's needed is to farm out the fitness evaluation calls to the nodes in the cluster. This can be achieved with the *sfApply* function which is a parallel version of *apply*. It's simply a matter of replacing *apply* with *sfApply*. Recall that each generation the DE calls the *rungen* function to create the challengers for the previous generation, evaluates their fitness and replaces previous solutions with better ones. So, to parallelize the fitness calls, the new *rungen* function would be *(see Box 4)*

A full parallel version of the DE is given Appendix 2. One last important function in *snowfall* is *sfExport* which exports data structures (e.g. vector of phenotypic records) from the master to the slave; a common error is that the slaves cannot *see* R structures that are only available in the master thread.

Performance of Parallel Differential Evolution in R

Before discussing a more realistic example in the next section, it is useful to briefly discuss some of the key points for parallel computing in R and the advantages and disadvantages of this parallel version of the DE.

The first point is that computation is much faster than communication between nodes. With parallel computing it is important to minimize the transfer of data between nodes. For example under the exact same conditions, consider a DE run that takes 50.6 seconds and the criterion function returns a single value. If instead, the criterion returned a vector of 10,000 numbers, the runtime increases to 91.8 seconds and with 100,000 numbers the runtime is 112.2 seconds. Considerable speed gains can be achieved by minimizing the shuffling of data between workers.

The second point is that the number of calls made to the nodes also impacts performance. In practice, the more time the workers independently spend on the computation itself, the more efficient the use of the computational resources will be. The parallel version of the DE discussed in this work implies that the objective function calculation is the slowest aspect of the computation, making it the focus point for parallelization. But this is not necessarily always the case, for example, the fitness function for the Rosenbrock saddle discussed above is computationally trivial and the workers spend hardly any time evaluating the fitness itself but do spend a lot of time communicating and transferring data. For these scenarios the parallel DE will perform worse than the sequential version of the DE.

Figure 3 illustrates this last point quite clearly. We compared the performance of the parallel DE against the sequential DE using varying numbers of workers (between 1 and 40) and with 6 different computing times (0 – 5 seconds) for the fitness function call; i.e. the number of seconds that each node spends evaluating the criterion. Results are shown as a ratio between the sequential versus the parallel DE. When the fitness function takes 0 second to compute (just calls the function and returns) the parallel DE performs extremely poorly due to the communication overhead incurred. As fitness evaluation times increase, the gains obtained through additional cores become more evident but the compromise between computation and communication is still clear.

For times 0.01 and 0.1 seconds the ideal numbers of cores are respectively 4 and 8 (1.6 and 3.7 times faster). Adding more workers after this reduces the performance. For calls of 1 and 2 seconds the performance starts to taper off after 20 workers. Take the 1 second scenario – with 20 workers the performance is 6.6 times better than the sequential DE but this only increases to 6.8 with 40 workers. Fitness evaluations of 5 seconds show the best results in terms of speed gains but while the performance has not yet plateaued there is evidence of *diminishing returns*.

It is clear that optimal performance is a balance between computational times needed to evaluate the fitness function and the number of cores used. Once performance starts to taper off there is little value in adding more workers; either performance will decline due to additional communication overhead or there will be unnecessary strain placed on computational resources, which becomes quite relevant in shared environments.

There are a few additional points worth noting. First, there is a fixed time lag to initialize the communication protocols of around 1.5 seconds. That is why the parallel DE running on a single worker performs worse than the sequential DE (Figure 3).

Second, performance gains through parallelization are not linear (e.g. 4 cores perform 4 fold better than 1 core) but rather incremental. For example, consider the 5 seconds fitness call in Figure 3 – with 40 cores the performance is 8.3 times better (instead of the wishful 40x). While this may not sound optimal, if actual runtimes are taken into consideration the picture becomes much

Figure 3. Comparison of performance of a parallel DE for varying number of nodes and various time lengths to compute the fitness function in comparison to a sequential DE. The labels on the x axis represent the actual number of cores used. The straight line through 1 (y axis) represents the sequential DE (baseline). The longer the fitness evaluation call takes the more advantageous it is to increase the number of nodes and use the parallel version of the Differential Evolution.

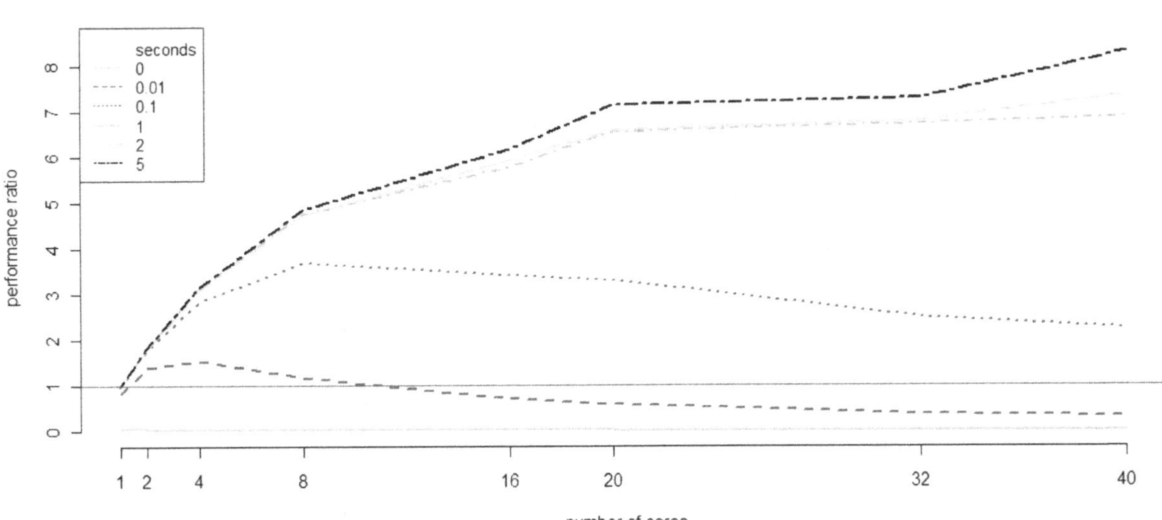

more interesting: the sequential run takes 36.7 minutes whilst the 40 core run takes 4.4 minutes.

Third, for this comparison the DE population size was set at 40. Recall that the parallel algorithm iterates through the candidate solutions and sends them off to have their fitness evaluated by the workers, results are then pooled and the next generation evaluated/built on the master. This structure places a cap on the maximum number of workers that can be used; adding more cores than the population size will have no impact on the performance – the extra cores will simply remain idle.

In summary, the key points to look out for with parallel Differential Evolution (or more broadly, most evolutionary algorithms) are:

- The longer it takes to evaluate the fitness function, the more useful it becomes to parallelize the process and the more cores can be used;
- If the fitness function is not computationally demanding an island model is more efficient than the master-slave model discussed herein, the balance then becomes between isolation (better use of computational resources – less connection between demes) and gene flow (more communication overhead – better connectivity between demes);
- Communication is more expensive than computation – minimize data transfer and calls to nodes whilst maximizing computation within workers;
- Performance gains are not linear to number of cores but actual computing times can be very significantly lower;
- The maximum number of cores effectively used will not be more than the population size. The same applies for an island model: number of nodes = number of demes (unless there's nested parallelization).

An Example: Genome-Wide Association Study using Parallel Differential Evolution in R

Evolutionary Computation is being widely employed to solve bioinformatics problems. And that is not particularly surprising; bioinformatics problems are complex, noisy and non-linear – the perfect setting for Evolutionary Computation to thrive. Some of the current efforts include sequence reconstruction from sequencing data, multiple-sequence alignment of protein or DNA sequences, tertiary protein folding inference, identification of coding regions in DNA sequences, microarray data clustering and reconstruction of metabolic and genetic pathways. Fogel and Corne (2003) and more recently Sankar (2006) provided comprehensive reviews of the main research topics in EC applied to Bioinformatics; broader computational intelligence methods applied to biological problems are discussed in Fogel *et al.* (2007) and Fogel (2008).

In this section we will illustrate the use of our parallel DE with a *toy* genome-wide association study (GWAS) to identify candidate regions associated with a quantitative trait of interest. Within the spirit of this chapter, our approach is more didactic than scientific but we have chosen this topic due to the large research efforts currently invested in association studies and the potential (or even need) they offer for applying artificial intelligence methods. Moore *et al.* (2010) argue that conventional biostatical methods applied to GWAS cannot capture the true complexity of biological systems whereas more holistic approaches could potentially help unravel the *true* genetic architecture that underlie a phenotypic expression.

Just briefly to set the background, GWAS have become pervasive across biological, medical and agricultural research over the last few years with, in humans alone, over 1,200 experiments already conducted examining more than 200 diseases and traits. These studies have identified hundreds of genetic variants associated with complex diseases in humans (e.g. diabetes, Alzheimer) and also commercially relevant traits in livestock (e.g. disease resistance, milk production). In general terms a GWAS consists of correlating genome wide genetic variability in individuals (differences in the DNA sequence) with some phenotypic variable of interest (e.g. height). And usually with the objective to identify chromosomal segments (and the DNA variation contained therein) that have a functional role in the variation observed at the phenotypic level.

Sequencing technologies are advancing at an exorbitant speed and full individual sequence data will soon become the norm for association studies but, currently, the most common platform to measure genetic polymorphism is the Single Nucleotide Polymorphism array (SNP chips). A SNP is a variation at a single nucleotide in the DNA (base substitution). SNPs are almost always bi-allelic and the most common source of genomic variation (~11 million in humans) with one found in, roughly, every 300 bases. Modern arrays measure hundreds of thousands of SNPs per assay and because of this abundance of markers tested, it is reasonably safe to assume that functional regions in the genome will have at least one SNP close enough so that it is in LD (linkage disequilibrium) with that region.

In simple terms, most human studies are based on case-control designs in which each SNP is tested for different variations associated to a discrete trait (normal versus diseased). SNPs that pass statistical significance tests are said to be associated with the trait under investigation and further studies will try to identify the actual causal genes. Note that SNPs are just *associated* (linked) to a trait, they are not necessarily *causal* (in practice they seldom are).

Interestingly, with quantitative traits the significant SNPs tend to explain only a small proportion of total variance. For example, a commonly cited case is height in humans which has a very high heritability of around 80%, yet only 5% of the genetic variance is explained by the combined effect of ~40 statistically significant SNPs (Visscher 2008). The problem is not so extreme when a large number of SNPs are used to model the trait rather than using some arbitrary threshold of statistical significance. In the same human example Yang *et al.* (2010) showed that 45% of the variance could be accounted for using 294,831 SNPs instead of only the subset of SNPs that passed significance tests. So, by simultaneously fitting all markers, a statistical model can accommodate the joint effects of *all regions* affecting a quantitative trait rather than just a single one. These models can then be used as predictors of, for example, disease outcome and susceptibility or, in the case of livestock, to estimate production potential using *genomic selection* (Goddard and Hayes 2007). This latter approach can capture the additive effects that build up to the phenotype but it cannot pick up dominance effects within a gene nor gene x gene interactions. These are exciting problems and still largely open to research; evolutionary computation and, more broadly, artificial intelligence have enormous potential to contribute to this field.

Here we will focus on a simple example, and use the DE to identify the SNPs most likely associated to a trait. The GWAS consists of simulated data with quantitative phenotypic measurements for 250 individuals and for each one there are 2,000 unlinked *SNPs* in linkage equilibrium. Out of these some are QTL – quantitative trait loci, i.e. actually have an effect on phenotype. The heritability for the trait is 0.5, meaning that 50% of the phenotype is due to the genetic constitution (additive) and 50% due to the environment. The objective is to identify which SNPs are QTL and how many there are. In a real scenario, results could provide insights into the actual genomic regions that are functionally relevant for a trait or could also be used to predict phenotypes in an independent population. So, let's just treat this as a simple additive problem and what we want to find is a model of the form $y_i = b_1x_{i1} + b_2x_{i2} + \ldots + b_nx_{in}$, where y is the phenotypic observation for individual i, n is the number of QTL (using SNPs as proxies assuming full linkage), $b_{1\ldots n}$ are the coefficients for each SNP and $x_{i1\ldots in}$ are the genotypes for each individual and each SNP. Genotypes are coded as 0, 1 or 2 with 1 being the heterozygote. The problem for the DE is then to find the number of QTL for this trait and the coefficients $b_{1\ldots n} \neq 0$ for these SNPs (non-QTL SNPs will have coefficients of zero).

The DE itself usually needs no changes, now it's a matter of designing the fitness function. Unfortunately there is no recipe for this, it depends on the objective and there are many different ways of tackling the same problem. Here is where R really comes into its own; whilst computational speed takes a hit in R it also provides access to a large range of functions which would demand a large time investment in coding from scratch and it is of course, much faster and easier to test different problem representations.

To illustrate this point let's treat this example as a model selection problem and try to find the model that best fits the data. One way forward is to evolve a ranking of the SNPs based on their association to the trait and use an additional parameter to select the number of SNPs fitted into the model (a cutoff). The fitness value will be the R^2 of the candidate model which provides an adequate indication of the goodness of fit.

For ranking the SNPs, random keys (Bean 1994) can be used. A random key is an evolvable vector of real values (alleles in the DE); here one for each SNP which are sorted in the objective function and the ranking of the key is used to rank the SNPs. In practice the QTL SNPs should evolve to high values in the key and non-explanatory SNPs to low key values. The cutoff is an additional parameter to be optimized alongside the key. Based on the cutoff parameter the ranked SNPs are fitted into a linear model and the adjusted R^2 of this model is used as the fitness value. In R this objective function is easy to write: *(see Box 5)*

The first lines are just to read in the data – a vector of phenotypes (*pheno*) and a matrix of genotypes (*geno*). More interesting is the *fitness* function. The first allele is used as the *cutoff*, i.e. number of SNPs for the model; the other alleles are the random key. Note that with just two lines of code (and the *sort* function) the key is sorted, a vector with the ranks is created and this is matched with the number of SNPs chosen in *cutoff* to create an index of the position of the SNPs of interest in the matrix *geno*. These are then written as a formula for the linear model function *lm* and the R^2 of this model is returned as the fitness value.

And finally just a little housekeeping to make the data structures available to the workers in the cluster.

```
sfExport(list=list("geno","pheno"))
```

This is a simple simulated example and not surprisingly the DE finds a perfect answer to it (correlation 0.999). We ran the DE for 100 generations with a small population size of 40 and the same parameters described above. The sequential run took 14.3 minutes and with 40 cores 7.7 minutes. In both cases the evolved model is

Box 5.

```
# read in data files
pheno = read.table("phenotypes.txt",header=T,sep="\t")$Pheno
pheno=pheno-mean(pheno)
geno = as.matrix(read.table("genotypes.txt",header=F,sep="\t"))

fitness = function(allele)
{
   # make integer number of SNPs selected for model
   cutoff=round(allele[1])
   # make sure at least one selected
   if (cutoff <1) cutoff=1

   # exclude first allele from random key
      allele=allele[-1]
   # sort key and get index for all SNPs
   rankedSNPs=sort(allele,index.return=T)$ix
   # get index of SNPs from 1 to 'cutoff'
      selected=rankedSNPs[1:cutoff]

   # build regression formula: pheno ~ geno[,1]+geno[,2]...
   pred=paste("geno[,",selected,"]", sep="",collapse="+")
   pred=paste("pheno~",pred,sep="")
   pred=as.formula(pred)
   crit=summary(lm(pred))$adj.r.squared
}
```

Figure 4. Correlation of model estimates with fitted phenotypes (~1.0) and true genetic values (~0.7)

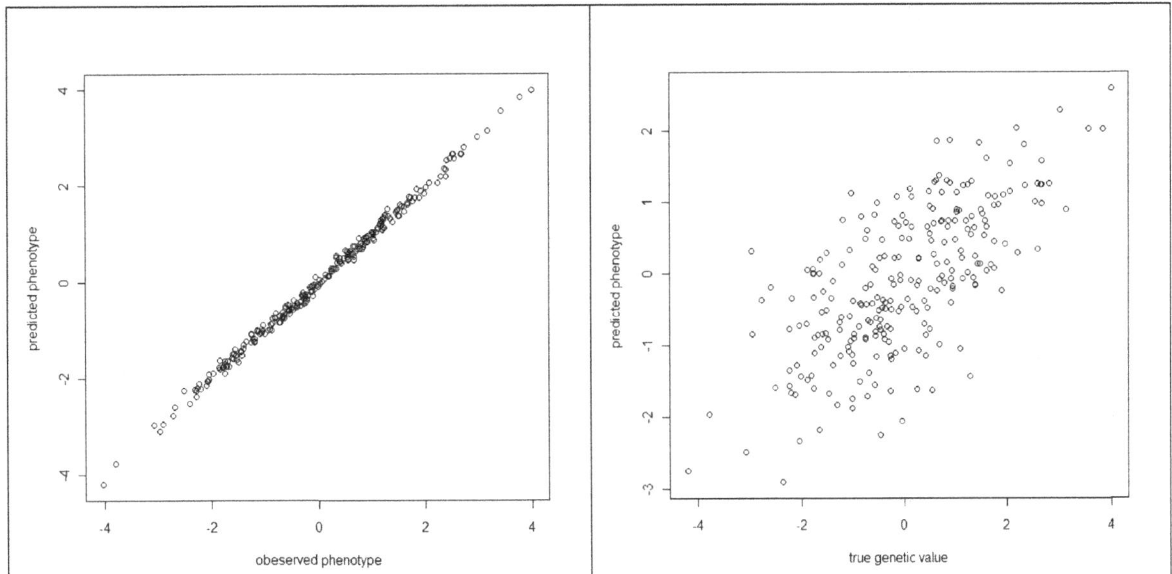

large with over 150 SNPs included. Figure 4 shows the correlation of the selected model with the phenotypes (the data used in the regression) and also the correlation with the *true* genetic value of the dataset (lower correlation of 0.7 due to over fitting). There is limited value in dwelling on these results since they are only for illustration purposes (and the model is of course over fitted to this data). But what we do want to emphasize is the ease with which robust statistical approaches can be used with very little coding. In a single line of code the fitness function runs a linear regression model and returns the adjusted R^2. Just as easily information on effects, p-values, standard errors can be extracted and used in different ways as a criterion. For example selection could be based (at least partially) on Akaike's Information Criterion (AIC) to control some of this over fitting with

```
AIC(lm(pred))
```

or some other penalty function. To illustrate, when we penalized the number of parameters in the model to approximate a prior QTL expectation the DE evolved to solutions with between 10 and 20 SNPs which reduced the correlation to the phenotypes (0.7 – 0.75) but increased the correlation with the true genetic values (0.87 – 0.83). Further, instead of fitting genotypes as fixed effects, they could be fitted as random using a mixed model instead (using e.g. *lmer*). Other covariates can be fitted concurrently; interaction terms (for epistasis) could also be included. In a nutshell, R provides an ideal platform for rapidly testing different approaches to data analysis.

PACKAGES FOR EVOLUTIONARY COMPUTATION IN R

One of the best aspects of R is the large number of add-on packages developed by the community. Optimization algorithms are also well represented among these. While we will not attempt to provide a comprehensive review of these (an excellent starting point is http://cran.r-project.org/web/views/Optimization.html), a few worth mentioning are:

Box 6.

```
begin=Sys.time()
library(DEoptim) # replace with RccpDE for C++ port of the package

fitness = function(allele)
{
   crit=(allele[1]-1)^2 + 100*(allele[2]-allele[1]^2)^2
}
outDEoptim=DEoptim(fn=fitness,lower=c(-10,-10),
upper=c(10,10),control=list(NP=40,itermax=500))

summary(outDEoptim)
plot(outDEoptim, type = 'b')
print(Sys.time()-begin) # show runtime
```

- **DEoptim:** a Differential Evolution package with the DE written in C.
- **RcppDE:** this package is a C++ port of DEoptim.
- **Rgp:** for genetic programming.
- **Rgenoud:** this package combines evolutionary algorithms with a derivative based method and supports parallel processing (Mebane and Sekhon 2011); a good choice for out of the box parallel optimization.
- **Mco:** a package for multi criteria optimization using genetic algorithms.
- **Optim:** a function in the base installation of R (the stats package) includes general optimization methods such as the gradient based BFGS for smooth functions or simulated annealing for non-smooth functions.

Out of these, *DEoptim* (Mullen *et al.* 2011) implements Differential Evolution and is easy to use. *DEoptim* is written in native C which makes it faster than the pure R implementation discussed herein. *RcppDE* is a C++ version of DEoptim and, for the examples we tested, speed and results are exactly the same for the two packages.

For the Rosenbrock example previously discussed, *DEoptim* runs in 0.22 seconds while the R code takes 0.54 seconds; roughly twice slower. Currently *DEoptim* does not run in parallel. So, if the fitness function is written in R and it is also the main computational bottleneck, there will be no speed differences between the C or R versions. For example, with fitness evaluations taking 0.1 second (as per Figure 3), both *DEoptim* and the sequential R code take almost exactly the same time to run (3.37 minutes). In contrast, using four cores the runtime is around 54 seconds, which again just highlights that the compromise between programming ease and speed is reasonably favorable towards R.

Of course, ideally, *DEoptim* would run in parallel and the fitness function would also be coded in a lower level language such as C or FORTRAN for maximum speed efficiency. The downside is an increase in programming complexity and longer development times, particularly in the parallelization steps. Just to contextualize, the Rosenbrock example fully coded in C++ as a native executable (DE and fitness function) runs in 0.05 seconds; roughly 10 times faster than the R version. Both DEoptim and RcppDE use the same syntax. The Rosenbrock example can be implemented as: *(see Box 6)*

CONCLUSION AND FUTURE DIRECTIONS

In this work we have discussed how to code and parallelize Evolutionary Algorithms in R. The ease of programming, the analytical tools built into the environment and the large number of add-on packages available makes R an ideal environment for scientific programming. This comes however at some increase in computational time since R is a scripted instead of a compiled language. As technology shifts towards multicore and cloud computing this overhead becomes less relevant, provided a parallel framework is used. Currently, applications written in R are easier to parallelize than in C or Fortran, but this should change in the near future as parallel development tools mature. On the other hand, with each new release R becomes faster as well, which brings its performance closer to these other languages.

On the EC front we can expect to see great interest in parallel implementations, particularly approaches that explore GPU architectures. Most current parallel platforms including multicore machines, clusters, grid computing, and GPUs are supported in R and are easy to setup. With proper consideration given to programming design, efficient parallel implementation of inherently parallelizable algorithms that minimizes traffic and maximizes cpu cycles can be achieved. While conventional fully compiled solutions can still beat R in terms of speed, we have demonstrated in this chapter how simple and quick it is to parallelize applications in R and that performance gains through parallelization are significant in most cases in comparison to sequential runs. Specifically for EC, the optimal performance is a balance between the computational times needed to evaluate the objective function and the number of parallel computing resources used.

ACKNOWLEDGMENT

The authors wish to acknowledge Brian Kinghorn for insights and useful comments on the chapter. Also Dorian Garrick for permission to use the simulated data used in the GWAS section of this chapter.

REFERENCES

Arenas, M. G., Mora, A. M., Romero, G., & Castillo, P. A. (2011). *GPU computation in bioinspired algorithms: a review. Advances in Computational Intelligence, LNCS 6691* (pp. 433–440). Berlin, Germany: Springer.

Bäck, T. (2000). *Introduction to evolutionary algorithms. Evolutionary Computation 1: Basic Algorithms and Operators* (pp. 59–63). Bristol, UK: Institute of Physics Publishing. doi:10.1887/0750306653

Bean, J. C. (1994). Genetic algorithms and random keys for sequencing and optimization. *ORSA Journal on Computing, 6*, 154–160. doi:10.1287/ijoc.6.2.154

Beyer, H.-G., & Schwefel, H.-P. (2002). Evolution strategies: A comprehensive introduction. *Natural Computing, 1*(1), 3–52. doi:10.1023/A:1015059928466

Chambers, J. M. (2008). *Software for data analysis – Programming with R*. New York, NY: Springer.

Eugster, M. J. A., Knaus, J., Porzelius, C., Schmidberger, M., & Vicedo, E. (2011). Hands-on tutorial for parallel computing with R. *Computational Statistics, 26*, 219–239. doi:10.1007/s00180-010-0206-4

Fogel, D. B. (1999). *Evolutionary computation: Toward a new philosophy of machine intelligence*. Piscataway, NJ: Wiley-IEEE.

Fogel, D. B. (2000a). *Introduction to evolutionary computation. Evolutionary Computation 1: Basic Algorithms and Operators* (pp. 1–3). Bristol, UK: Institute of Physics Publishing.

Fogel, D. B. (2000b). *Principles of evolutionary computation. Evolutionary Computation 1: Basic Algorithms and Operators* (pp. 23–26). Bristol, UK: Institute of Physics Publishing.

Fogel, D. B., & Corne, D. W. (Eds.). (2003). *Evolutionary computation in bioinformatics*. San Mateo, CA: Morgan Kaufmann.

Fogel, G. B. (2008). Computational intelligence approaches for pattern discovery in biological systems. *Briefings in Bioinformatics*, *9*(4), 307–316. doi:10.1093/bib/bbn021

Fogel, G. B., Corne, D. W., & Pan, Y. (Eds.). (2007). *Computational intelligence in bioinformatics*. Piscataway, NJ: Wiley-IEEE Press. doi:10.1002/9780470199091

Gentleman, R. C. (2009). *R programming for bioinformatics*. Boca Raton, FL: Chapman & Hall/CRC.

Gentleman, R. C., Carey, V. J., Bates, D. M., Bolstad, B., Dettling, M., & Dudoit, S. (2004). Bioconductor: Open software development for computational biology and bioinformatics. *Genome Biology*, *5*(10), R80. Goddard, M. E., & Hayes, B. J. (207). Genomic selection. *Journal of Animal Breeding and Genetics*, *124*(6), 323–330.

Holland, J. H. (1975). *Adaptation in natural and artificial systems*. Ann Arbor, MI: University of Michigan Press.

Jones, O., Maillardet, R., & Robinson, A. (2009). *Introduction to scientific programming and simulation using R*. Boca Raton, FL: Chapman & Hall/CRC.

Koza, J. R., Keane, M. A., Streeter, M. J., Mydlowec, W., Yu, J., & Lanza, G. (2003). *Genetic programming IV: Routine human-competitive machine intelligence*. Boston, MA: Kluwer Academic Publishers.

Mayer, D. G., Kinghorn, B. P., & Archer, A. A. (2005). Differential evolution – an easy and efficient evolutionary algorithm for model optimisation. *Agricultural Systems*, *83*, 315–328. doi:10.1016/j.agsy.2004.05.002

Mebane, W. R., & Sekhon, J. S. (2011). Genetic optimization using derivatives: The rgenoud package for R. *Journal of Statistical Software*, *42*(11), 1–26.

Mitchell, M., & Taylor, C. E. (1999). Evolutionary computation: An overview. *Annual Review of Ecology and Systematics*, *30*, 593–616. doi:10.1146/annurev.ecolsys.30.1.593

Moore, J. H., Asselbergs, F. W., & Williams, S. M. (2010). Bioinformatics challenges for genome-wide association studies. *Bioinformatics (Oxford, England)*, *26*(4), 445–455. doi:10.1093/bioinformatics/btp713

Mullen, K. M., Ardia, D., Gil, A. L., Windover, D., & Cline, J. (2011). DEoptim: An R package for global optimization by differential evolution. *Journal of Statistical Software*, *40*(6).

Nedjah, N., Alba, E., & de Macedo, L. M. (Eds.). (2006). *Parallel evolutionary computations*. Berlin, Germany: Springer. doi:10.1007/3-540-32839-4

R Development Core Team. (2011). *R: A language and environment for statistical computing*. Vienna, Austria: R Foundation for Statistical Computing.

Rossini, A. J., Tierney, L., & Li, N. M. (2007). Simple parallel statistical computing in R. *Journal of Computational and Graphical Statistics*, *16*(2), 399–420. doi:10.1198/106186007X178979

Sankar, K. P., Bandyopadhyay, S., & Ray, S. S. (2006). Evolutionary computation in bioinformatics: A review. *IEEE Transactions on Systems, Man and Cybernetics. Part C, Applications and Reviews*, *36*(5), 601–615. doi:10.1109/TSMCC.2005.855515

Schmidberger, M., Morgan, M., Eddelbuettel, D., Yu, H., Tierney, L., & Mansmann, U. (2009). State of the art in parallel computing with R. *Journal of Statistical Software*, *31*(1).

Schwefel, H. P., & Rudolph, G. (1995). *Advances in artificial life*. 3rd International Conference ALIFE. Berlin, Germany: Springer-Verlag.

Storn, R., & Price, K. (1997). Differential evolution – A simple and efficient heuristic for global optimization over continuous spaces. *Journal of Global Optimization*, *11*(4), 341–359. doi:10.1023/A:1008202821328

Visscher, P. M. (2008). Sizing up human height variation. *Nature Genetics*, *40*, 489–490. doi:10.1038/ng0508-489

Yang, J., Benyamin, B., McEvoy, B. P., Gordon, S., Henders, A. K., & Nyholt, D. R. (2010). Common SNPs explain a large proportion of the heritability for human height. *Nature Genetics*, *42*, 565–569. doi:10.1038/ng.608

Yang, X.-S. (2010). Test problems in optimization. In *Engineering optimization: An introduction with metaheuristic applications*. John Wiley & Sons. doi:10.1002/9780470640425.app1

APPENDIX 1: GETTING STARTED WITH R

R can run on most operating systems including Microsoft Windows, Mac OS and UNIX/Linux and code is reasonably platform independent (the code discussed in this chapter works across all three platforms without any changes). R derives from the S language originally created by John Chambers at Bell Labs, and was initially developed by Ross Ihaka and Robert Gentleman from the University of Auckland, New Zealand, having since become a part of the GNU project. Arguably the most popular programming language for statistical analysis, R is an interpreted language whereby a command is typed and the result returned through a command line interpreter. For example, if one types in $3 + 7$ at the command prompt (the > symbol) and presses enter, the computer returns 10 as the result.

```
> 3+7
[1] 10
```

While Linux users tend to prefer the command line, Windows and MacOS users usually interact with R through graphical interfaces. Figure 5 illustrates the Windows RGui.

R is a fully-fledged programming language and provides significant support for vector and matrix computations. It has a rich set of data structures, including scalars, vectors, matrices, data frames

Figure 5. The R program running in Microsoft Windows and an example of an R function and how to run it in the R Console

```
R Console (64-bit)
File Edit Misc Packages Windows Help
R version 2.14.0 (2011-10-31)
Copyright (C) 2011 The R Foundation for Statistical Computing
ISBN 3-900051-07-0
Platform: x86_64-pc-mingw32/x64 (64-bit)

R is free software and comes with ABSOLUTELY NO WARRANTY.
You are welcome to redistribute it under certain conditions.
Type 'license()' or 'licence()' for distribution details.

  Natural language support but running in an English locale

R is a collaborative project with many contributors.
Type 'contributors()' for more information and
'citation()' on how to cite R or R packages in publications.

Type 'demo()' for some demos, 'help()' for on-line help, or
'help.start()' for an HTML browser interface to help.
Type 'q()' to quit R.

> square <- function (x) {
+ return (x^2)
+ }
> cat ("the square of 3 is ", square(3), "\n")
the square of 3 is  9
>
```

(similar to tables in a relational database) and lists. Below, we demonstrate how each of these data structures is being created in R.

```
> a = 1.063                    # Construct a scalar 1.063
> b = c(8,6,7,3)               # Construct a vector [8 6 7 3]
> age  c(15,10,17,9)
> names = c("tom","peter","mary","susan")
> M = cbind(b,age) # Construct a matrix with columns b and age
> D = data.frame(names,b,age)        # Construct a data frame with data
> Person = list(name="susan",age=9)        # Construct a list Person
> Person$name        # Access things inside a list
[1] "susan"
> Person$age
[1] 9
```

R also supports procedural programming, in that one can write functions, use control statements like *if-else* and repetitions like *for* and *while* loops. In Figure 5, we show a simple function that outputs the square of its input, and how to call it from within the R console. The power of R also lies in the large number of packages that have been contributed by the user community. The main archive for R packages can be found at http://cran.r-project.org/web/packages/.

It is clearly impossible to cover R in this short appendix. What we have simply attempted to provide the first entry point into the language. The best way to learn more about R is through the ample online available resources and wide range of R books. These include:

- The official website of the R project (http://www.r-project.org/)
- The R wiki (http://rwiki.sciviews.org/doku.php)
- R seek, which is a custom front-end to the Google search engine for searching information related to the R language (http://rseek.org/)
- A partial annotated list of R books can be found at http://www.r-project.org/doc/bib/R-books.html

APPENDIX 2: A PARALLEL DE FUNCTION IN R

```
DE = function(crit="fitness.r", popsize=40, allelesize=2,
numgen=500, CR=0.5, FR=0.8,
cpu=4, maxcores=32, computer="localhost", farm=NA)
{
  require(snowfall)
  begin=Sys.time()
  # increase max number of cores
  sfSetMaxCPUs(number=maxcores)
  # setup number of cores in cluster
  sfInit(parallel=TRUE,cpus=cpu,socketHosts=rep(computer,cpu))
  # read fitness function
 if (is.na(crit)!=TRUE) source(crit)
  # initialize random population with random uniform numbers
  pop=matrix(runif(popsize*allelesize),popsize,allelesize)
  # calculate fitness of initial population
  fit=apply(pop,1, fitness)
  # just a plot to see how fitness evolves
  plot(max(fit),xlim=c(0,numgen),ylim=c(mean(fit),0),
    xlab="generation",ylab="fitness",cex=0.8,col="blue")
  # create a challenger for the next generation
  challenge=function(x)
  {
    # choose 4 - 1 title holder, 2 template, 3 and 4 mutators
    index=matrix(unlist(lapply(1:popsize,
      function (S) sample(c(1:popsize)[-S],3))),
    popsize,3,byrow=T)
    # T/F for CR - generate random numbers for CR and then test
    crtf=matrix(CR>runif(allelesize*popsize),popsize,allelesize)
    # make a challenger from title holder
    challenger=pop
    if (x%%5==0) FR=5
    hold=pop[index[,1],]+FR*(pop[index[,2],]-pop[index[,3],])
    challenger[crtf]=hold[crtf]
    return(challenger)
  }
  # call challenge function
  # calculate fitness of new solutions
  # evaluate against previous solutions
  rungen=function(x)
  {
    challenger=challenge(x)
```

```
    fitchal=sfApply(challenger,1,fitness)
    index=which(fitchal>=fit)
    fit[index]<<-fitchal[index]
    pop[index,]<<-challenger[index,]
    points(x,max(fit),cex=0.8,col="blue")
  }
  # list of additional data to export to slaves
  if (is.na(farm)!=TRUE) sfExport(list=farm)
  # generation loop
  lapply(1:numgen,rungen)
  # print results
  print(pop[which(fit==max(fit))[1],])
  # stop cluster
  sfStop()
  # show runtime
  print(Sys.time()- begin)
}
```

Chapter 21
Fuzzy Image Segmentation for Mass Detection in Digital Mammography:
Recent Advances and Techniques

Hajar Mohammedsaleh H. Alharbi
King Abdulaziz University, Kingdom of Saudi Arabia

Paul Kwan
University of New England, Australia

Ashoka Jayawardena
University of New England, Australia

A. S. M. Sajeev
University of New England, Australia

ABSTRACT

In the last decade, many computer-aided diagnosis (CAD) systems that utilize a broad range of diagnostic techniques have been proposed. Due to both the inherently complex structure of the breast tissues and the low intensity contrast found in most mammographic images, CAD systems that are based on conventional techniques have been shown to have missed malignant masses in mammographic images that would otherwise be treatable. On the other hand, systems based on fuzzy image processing techniques have been found to be able to detect masses in cases where conventional techniques would have failed. In the current chapter, recent advances in fuzzy image segmentation techniques as applied to mass detection in digital mammography are reviewed. Image segmentation is an important step in CAD systems since the quality of its outcome will significantly affect the processing downstream that can involve both detection and classification of benign versus malignant masses.

DOI: 10.4018/978-1-4666-1830-5.ch021

INTRODUCTION

Breast cancer is one of the most common causes of death in women worldwide, and its occurrence is still on the rise. Early detection of breast cancer has shown to be effective in improving the chance of full recovery. Mammography is a widely used breast imaging technology for the detection of masses which can develop further into breast cancer. However, a double reading of mammography images (i.e. independent readings by two radiologists) is not only costly but will also incur a significant increase of workload. In order to enhance the sensitivity of detection, thereby improving the detection rate of breast cancer, CAD systems have been utilized as a second opinion in the interpretation of mammography images.

Digital mammography is now accepted as an essential technique in early detection of breast cancer. However, due to the difficulty posed in interpreting mammography images by visual inspection even for trained radiologists, medical-imaging techniques for accurately segmenting potential cancerous masses from normal tissues have continued to be an active area of research since the turn of the century. In particular, applications of fuzzy-logic techniques have been proven very efficient in the analysis of mammography images in the past decade. Since masses appearing in mammography images often possess uncertain boundaries and low-intensity contrast, fuzzy-logic approaches for breast-cancer detection have demonstrated to be far more robust than systems that were built following a rigid approach. A major contribution of this book chapter will be an up-to-date review of current techniques for segmenting masses for cancer detection in mammographic images by applying a fuzzy logic approach. Although several review articles on topics related to the computer-aided detection and diagnosis of breast cancer have been published in the past few years, most were fairly broad in their coverage (Sampat, Markey, & Bovik, 2005; Tang, Rangayyan, Xu, El Naqa, & Yang, 2009). The current book chapter distinguishes itself from other reviews in that it has a clear focus, and that is on fuzzy image segmentation techniques for mass detection. This chapter aims to contribute a useful reference for researchers and students who would like to gain an understanding of recent advances in fuzzy logic approaches for image segmentation as applied to digital mammographic imaging.

The rest of this chapter is organized as follows. In the next section, we will review the background of cancer detection, particularly as it relates to breast cancer. We will explain what digital mammography is, followed by a general description of CAD system and its main processing stages. Next, we will introduce medical imaging in digital mammography by discussing the role of image pre-processing and mass detection and classification, before detailing how image segmentation is being performed by conventional approaches. After this, we will focus on fuzzy image segmentation for mass detection. Here, we cover fuzzy image processing, fuzzy concept for mammography images, and recent advances and techniques in this area. We will also mention performance and metrics towards the end. Finally, the last section gives the conclusions.

BACKGROUND

According to the Oxford Dictionary, *cancer* is a disease that is caused by an uncontrolled division of abnormal cells in a certain part of the body (Oxford Dictionary, n.d.). The result of this unusual growth is normally in the form of a mass or tumor. Most types of cancer are named according to the part of the body in which the cancer first arises. Breast cancer can thus be considered an uncontrolled growth of cells in the breast tissue. A human female's breast (illustrated in Figure 1) consists of lobules and ducts, which are surrounded by fatty and connective tissues. Lobules are glands that produce milk, while ducts connect lobules and carry milk to the nipple.

Figure 1. A female human breast (© 2008, Don Bliss, National Cancer Institute, Public domain)

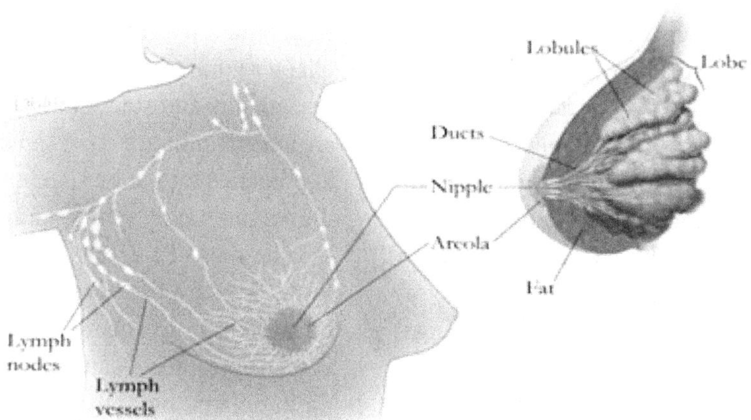

Masses detected in a female's breast can be divided into two main types: benign or malignant. The growth of a benign mass is restricted to a single cell, while a malignant mass can grow to invade the surrounding tissues. In some cases, the cancer can spread to different areas of the body. Most breast masses are found to be benign; they are not cancerous and are rarely life-threatening. Malignant masses normally begin in the lobules or ducts of the breast, but then subsequently invade the surrounding tissues through breaches in the ducts and the glandular walls.

Breast cancer is a major cause of death in women worldwide. It is the second leading cause of cancer deaths after lung cancer. In countries like the USA, one in four women is diagnosed with breast cancer, while in Australia one in nine will eventually develop breast cancer before the age of 85, according to a study conducted by the Cancer Council Australia (Cancer Australia, 2011).

Gender, age, race, family history, history of radiation therapy to the chest, breast conditions, pregnancy and breastfeeding, exposure to estrogen, etc. are well-known factors that might increase the risk of developing breast cancer. Although a man can also develop breast cancer, being a woman is unarguably one of the most fundamental risk factors for developing breast cancer. Breast cancer can occur at any age, and its incidence and death rates also increase with age. In Australia, "about 24 per cent of new breast cancer cases diagnosed in 2007 were in women younger than 50 years; 51 per cent in women aged 50-69; and 25 per cent in women aged 70 and over" (Cancer Australia, 2011). In the USA, "during 2002-2006, women aged 20-24 had the lowest incidence rate, 1.4 cases per 100,000 women; women aged 75-79 had the highest incidence rate, 441.9 cases per 100,000" (American Cancer Society, n.d.). At age 45, white women are slightly more prone to develop breast cancer than their African-American counterparts. However, African-American women have a higher incidence rate in developing breast cancer before age 45 and are more likely to die from breast cancer at any age. Women who have a first-degree relative (i.e. mother, sister, or daughter) who has had breast cancer or have many relatives diagnosed with breast or ovarian cancer before they turned age 50 are at a higher risk of developing breast cancer. Likewise, women who have had radiation therapy done to their chests, especially if they were first exposed to high doses of radiation at younger ages as part of the treatment for another cancer, are at an increased risk of developing breast cancer.

Women who have high breast density were found to have four to six times more risk of developing breast cancer than women with low breast density. In addition, unusual changes detected in breast cells removed for biopsy might point to a risk of developing breast cancer. Furthermore, women who had their first full-term pregnancy before age 30 have a decreased risk of breast cancer over the long term. Breastfeeding can also decrease a woman's risk of developing breast cancer, especially if breastfeeding is continued for a longer duration, like one-and-a-half to two years. Exposure to estrogen without any breaks over a long period of time may also increase a woman's risk of breast cancer, such as early menstruation at a younger age like before 12 years old, and late menopause at an older age, such as after 55 years old.

As long as a tumor is small, breast cancer can progress without showing any signs or symptoms. Once the tumor has grown to a size that can be felt, the most common sign of breast cancer would be a painless mass. Other signs and symptoms include changes in the shape or size of the breast, pain in the breast, change in the feel or appearance of the breast's skin or nipple, and nipple spontaneous discharge. All of these changes can be detected during self-examination of the breast. It is when a woman notices any abnormality in her breast that a medical examination will be arranged, which normally will involve X-ray mammography to determine if a breast cancer has developed.

Breast-cancer treatment aims to get rid of the cancer, and to prevent it from returning to the body. Depending on the stage of the breast cancer, the location and size of the tumor in the breast, the results of laboratory tests, the age of the patient, her preferences about treatment options, and her general health, the doctor will recommend an optimal treatment for that particular patient. Breast-cancer treatments are either local or systemic. Local treatments are useful for controlling, destroying or removing cancer cells from the breast, such as by surgery and radiation therapy. Systemic treatments, on the other hand, are useful for controlling or destroying cancer cells all over the body. Chemotherapy, hormone therapy and biological therapy are the known types of systemic treatments. Most breast-cancer patients may just need one form of treatment, usually surgery, while others may need a combination of treatments.

Early detection of breast cancer produces better results and gives the patient's health a longer-term prospect. Breast-cancer detection varies depending on a woman's age, and includes approaches like mammography, magnetic resonance imaging, and self- and clinical breast examinations. At present, mammography is considered a highly effective tool for early detection of breast cancer. It uses a special kind of X-ray to examine the breast tissue. According to American Cancer Society (n.d.), mammography may "detect about 80%-90% of the breast cancers in women without symptoms". Magnetic resonance imaging (MRI), on the other hand, uses magnetic fields to produce detailed images of the breast tissue. During an MRI exam, a contrast material is injected into a small vein in the arm to illuminate the breast tissue more clearly. MRI is recommended for women at higher risk of breast cancer along with a yearly mammogram.

Early detection of breast cancer in the opposite breast allows women to choose from different treatment options and avoid unnecessary procedures. A recent study (Lehman *et al.*, 2007) indicates that MRI has been useful for detecting cancer in the opposite breast, where breast cancer has been recently diagnosed. The likelihood of developing breast cancer is increased when women have a higher density of breast tissues. Kerlikowske *et al.* (2007) argued that the increase in breast density over time may be a future sign of breast cancer. Aligned with this argument, American Cancer Society (n.d.) suggested that "future studies will focus on identifying the best time to measure breast density and how to incorporate this information into risk prediction models". In addition, Digital Tomosynthesis (DT) – a new technology which uses an x-ray tube that moves in an arc (ranges from ±15 to ±45 degrees) around a breast, captures typically 11 to 45 images and combines them into a 3D image – is currently being developed to improve breast-cancer detection for women with dense breast tissue. DT in many ways is similar to mammography, but it uses less compression than mammograms. Not only will DT improve breast cancer detection in early stages, but it will also reduce the number of patient recalls because it is advantageous for women with dense breast tissue. The first DT device, produced by Hologic, was recently approved by the US Food and Drug Administration in early February 2011 (Freiherr, 2011).

Digital Mammography

Mammography, as mentioned earlier, is a low-dose X-ray testing method that can be used to visualise the breast's internal structure in order to detect abnormal growths or changes. A mammography test is usually performed as follows (see Figure 2): First, a woman will be asked to undress from the waist up and stand in front of an X-ray machine. Next, a radiologist will rest one breast on the film plate, place it between two radiographic breast plates, which will be pressed together gently in order to flatten the breast. The purpose of flattening and compressing the breast before radiating it with a low dose of X-ray beam, is to enable the device to take a clear image of the breast. Several X-ray images might be taken from several different angles, both horizontally and obliquely, for each breast, one at a time.

There are two main types of mammography: film mammography and digital mammography. Film mammography captures the images of the breast directly on a sheet of black and white film, while digital mammography takes an electronic image of the breast and displays it on a computer screen for viewing. Digital mammography allows radiologists to view mammogram images on the screen, highlight any suspicious areas and zoom in for a closer look. According to American Cancer Society (n.d.), digital mammography gives better results than film mammography for "pre- and peri-menopausal women younger than age 50 with dense breasts".

Figure 2. Mammography (© 2003, Alan Hoofring, National Cancer Institute, Public domain)

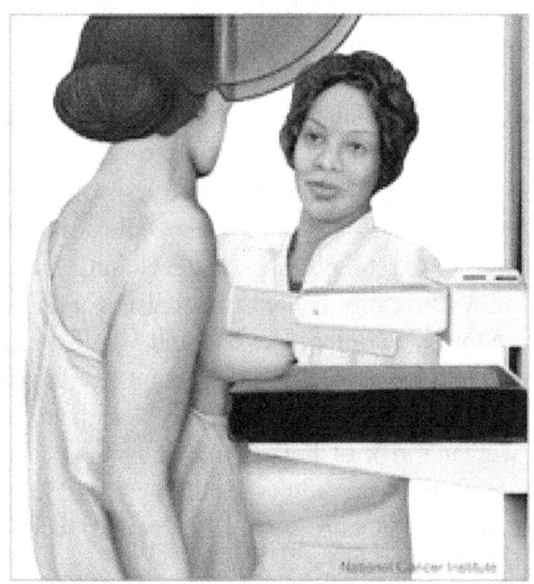

Mammography is among the most effective testing method for early detection of breast cancer because it can detect tumors before the actual symptoms occur. Despite its advantages, mammography is not perfect. Inappropriate placement of the breast on the film plate, high breast density and the failure of a radiologist to identify very tiny signs of a breast's abnormalities are among the reasons that breast cancers go undetected by mammography. In addition, mammography is not able to identify all types of breast cancers, especially in premenopausal cases. Some research has pointed out that mammography produces more accurate results in postmenopausal women than premenopausal women (Michaelson *et al.*, 2002). Moreover, in some cases mammography results are inconclusive. For example, some women may be required to have additional mammography as well as other examinations including biopsies. According to American Cancer Society (n.d.), "only one or two mammograms out of every 1,000 lead to a diagnosis of cancer" and "approximately 10% of women will require additional mammography". Among these, "only 8% to 10% of those women will need a biopsy, and 80% of those biopsies will not be cancer".

Computer-Aided Diagnosis System

Early detection of breast cancer is important for facilitating effective treatment and reducing the death rate among women, but it requires double reading of mammography images. Double reading permits two radiologists to assess the same mammography images. Not only is it costly to hire two radiologists, but it also incurs an increase in workload. CAD systems are increasingly being viewed as an alternative by providing a second opinion in interpreting the mammography images. The objectives are increasing the radiologist's sensitivity and improving the detection rate of breast cancer. In (Islam, Ahmadi, & Sid-Ahmed, 2010), the authors presented their arguments that "reports show that the estimated sensitivity of the radiologists is about 75%. To increase the rate it is especially important to use the computer-aided system."

Most CAD systems consist of the following four stages in succession: 1) *image pre-processing* of the digitised mammogram to remove noises and to improve the contrast of the image, 2) *image segmentation* for identifying the suspicious regions, 3) *feature extraction and selection* for classifying mass types and removal of false positives, and 4) *classification* of the masses as a cancerous or a normal tissue. The stages that are involved in a CAD system are illustrated in Figure 3.

The ultimate goals for a CAD system are detecting and classifying suspicious lesions (calcifications, masses and architectural distortion) with high sensitivity, while reducing the number of false positives. To evaluate the performance of any CAD system, some measures such as sensitivity, specificity, the number of false positives per image, and false positive rate are often reported. These terms are defined below. When a mass was observed in a mammography test, "positive" observation is marked; otherwise "negative" observation is marked (Dhawan, 2011). To calculate these measures, we need to know values

Figure 3. Main processing stages of a CAD system (Adapted from: Cao, Song, & Yang (2008), Breast image: © 1991, National Cancer Institute, Public domain)

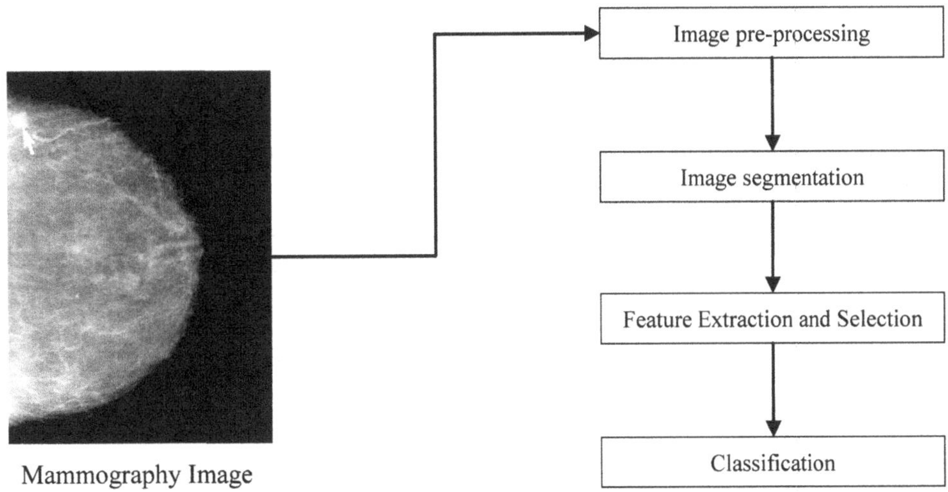

of both true conditions and observed information (illustrated in Figure 4).

Here,

- TP is the number of patients who are correctly diagnosed with breast cancer.
- FP is the number of healthy people who are incorrectly diagnosed with breast cancer.
- TN is the number of healthy people who are correctly diagnosed as healthy.
- FN is the number of patients who are incorrectly diagnosed as healthy.

Sensitivity (shown in Equation 1), is the percentage of correct cases diagnosed positively; the number of *false positives per image* (FPI) (shown in Equation 2) is used to report the performance of any CAD system. Sensitivity is also addressed as the true positive rate (TPR) of the CAD system. Other measures such as *specificity* (shown in Equation 3) and *false positive rate* (FPR) (shown in Equation 4) are also reported. Specificity is the percentage of normal cases diagnosed as normal, which is also called the true negative rate. False positive rate is the ratio of all negative cases that is incorrectly diagnosed as positive by the CAD system. A receiver operating characteristic (ROC) curve is a graph that shows the relationship between TPR and FPR (Kallergi, 2005). ROC curve is considered as the most meaningful standard to assess the accuracy of a CAD system. Any CAD system would aim to have higher ROC curves, high ratio of TPR to FPR, which implies better diagnostic accuracy of that system (Sameti, 1998).

$$\text{Sensitivity} = \frac{Number\ of\ true\ positives}{Number\ of\ true\ positives + Number\ of\ false\ negatives} \quad (1)$$

$$\text{FPI} = \frac{Number\ of\ false\ positives}{Number\ of\ images} \quad (2)$$

$$\text{Specificity} = \frac{Number\ of\ true\ negatives}{Number\ of\ true\ negatives + Number\ of\ false\ positives} \quad (3)$$

$$\text{FPR} = \frac{Number\ of\ false\ positives}{Number\ of\ false\ positives + Number\ of\ true\ negatives} \quad (4)$$

MEDICAL IMAGING IN DIGITAL MAMMOGRAPHY

Mammography uses very small doses of ionising radiation to create images of the breast. Since it was introduced, mammography has become a highly effective tool for detecting early signs of breast cancer, which can take the form of masses, calcifications and architectural distortion. Screening is conducted on two views for each of the left

Figure 4. A conditional matrix that defines four true conditions and observed information (Adapted from: Dhawan, 2011)

Observed Information	True Condition: *Object is present*	True Condition: *Object is NOT present*
Object is observed	**True Positive (TP)**	**False Positive (FP)**
Object is NOT observed	**False Negative (FN)**	**True Negative (TN)**

and right breasts. The craniocaudal (CC) view is a top-bottom view of the breast, and the mediolateral oblique (MLO) view is a side view of the breast taken at a certain angle.

Film mammography creates an image of the breast directly on film, while digital mammography captures an electronic image of the breast and displays it on a computer screen for examination by the radiologist. Digital mammography has several advantages over conventional film mammography. First, it uses less radiation and allows easier image storage and transmission to other radiologists. Digital mammography also requires a shorter examination time than film mammography.

Radiologists often look for specific signs of abnormalities such as clusters of microcalcifications, masses and architectural distortions in mammograms. According to Sampat *et al.* (2005), a mass is defined as "a space occupying lesion seen in at least two different projections". Masses can have different margins (circumscribed or well-defined, micro-lobular, obscured, ill-defined and spiculated) and shapes (round, oval, lobular, nodular and stellate). Particularly, calcifications occur as tiny calcium deposits, which appear as white spots on the mammogram. However, an architectural distortion might be difficult to ascertain as definite mass can be invisible. This can occur as spiculations radiating from a point, focal retraction or distortion of the edge of the parenchyma.

Ambiguities in the signs of abnormalities can make it hard for radiologists to provide both accurate and uniform evaluations for the enormous number of mammograms they have to deal with. Recent research has demonstrated that CAD systems can help radiologists in interpreting mammograms for mass detection and classification. Most of the CAD systems for mass detection involve four main processing steps, which were pointed out in Figure 3. However, it is important to note that for some of these systems not all four steps would have to be present.

Image Pre-Processing

Image pre-processing is an important initial step in handling low contrast digital mammograms. It aims to enhance the texture and features of masses in the images. Specifically, it enlarges the intensity difference between objects and background, thus yielding two dependable representations of breast tissue structures. Image pre-processing techniques can be categorised into global histogram modification, local processing and multi-scale processing.

The principle behind the global histogram modification approach is to reassign the intensity values of pixels in order to make the new distribution of the intensities maximally uniform. Histogram equalisation (HE) is the most commonly used technique for global histogram modification. The HE technique is effective in enhancing the entire image of low contrast. However, it works only if the image contains a single object or if there is no apparent contrast change between an object and its background. The multi-peak HE method (Cheng, Shi, Min, Hu, Cai, & Du, 2005) has been developed to improve the HE method. The main drawbacks of the global histogram modification approach include its limitation to images that have only one apparent object, and its inability to enhance texture because it cannot change the order of the gray levels in the original image. As a result, it is not suitable for mammogram enhancement.

Many local processing methods are used for image contrast enhancement by changing pixel intensities. The common one is based on non-linear mapping methods such as local histogram and bi-linear techniques (Cheng *et al.*, 2005). A feature-based method that enhances image contrast by increasing the contrast ratio using an exponent function is also widely used. Local processing methods are effective in local texture enhancement, but they cannot enhance the entire image well.

Multi-scale processing is a feature enhancement technique based on wavelet transformation (Cheng *et al.*, 2005). Although multi-scale processing is flexible in selecting local features for enhancement while suppressing noises due to its ability to detect directional features and remove unwanted perturbations, it is difficult for radiologists to select the best mother wavelet for transformation. As such, this might not result in the most effective method for enhancing every kind of mass.

Mass Detection and Classification

Usually, masses are characterised by their shapes and margins. In general, masses with regular shapes are benign, whereas irregular shapes are malignant (see Figure 5). Most mass detection algorithms consist of two successive steps: (1) detection of suspicious regions and (2) classification of each suspicious region as benign or malignant.

Generally, mass detection algorithms are either pixel-based or region-based. In the pixel-based approaches, selected features are extracted for each pixel, which is then classified as being normal or suspicious. On the other hand, in the region-based approaches, regions of interests are first segmented. Next, selected features are extracted from each region of interest that will provide input to a classifier. Finally, each region will be classified as a normal, benign or malignant mass.

Many pixel-based approaches have been proposed in the literature. Just to mention only a few recent techniques, Liu *et al.* (2001) presented a multi-resolution technique to detect speculated lesions of very different sizes. The mammography image was broken down into a multi-resolution representation, and for every pixel at each resolution, four features were extracted. Mass detection was performed using a binary tree classifier. Zhen and Chan (2001) introduced a technique that combined different artificial intelligence techniques including fractal dimension analysis and dogs-and-rabbits algorithm with the discrete wavelet transform to detect masses. The authors used the fractal dimension analysis to identify the locations of the suspicious regions, and the dogs-and-rabbits clustering algorithm (McKenzie & Alder, 1994) to start the segmentation. In the end, a tree-type classification method was applied to determine whether a given region was cancererous or not. Sampat and Bovik (2003) described a technique to detect speculated masses in digitised mammograms. Their technique first applied a filter to enhance certain features. Then, it used a radial speculation filter to detect the spatial location of these enhanced features. Campanini *et al.* (2004) proposed a technique for mass detection by making use of support vector machines. The authors codified the image with redundant information by

Figure 5. Masses have different shapes and margins. Normally, benign mass has regular shape, while malignant mass has irregular shape (© 1990, American College of Radiology, Public domain).

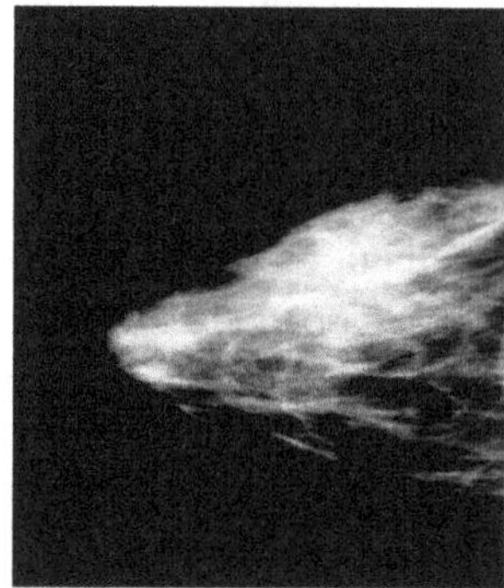

(a) Benign mass

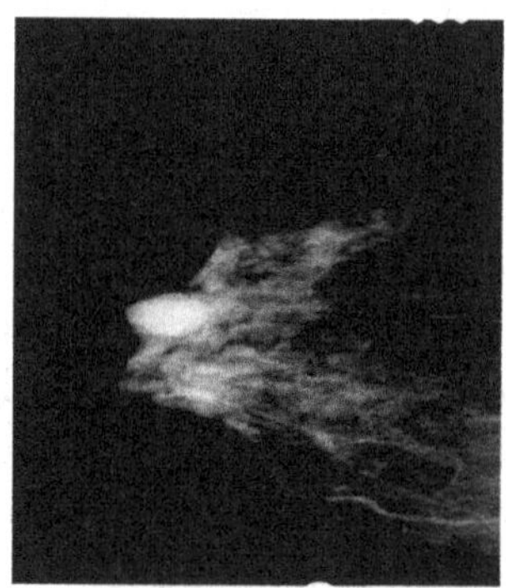

(b) Malignant mass

using a multiresolution, over-complete wavelet representation. They also used two support vector machine classifiers. The first classifier was used to find the mass candidates, while the second was applied to reduce the number of false positives. Kom *et al.* (2007) presented a technique that used a linear transformation filter to enhance the image. They developed a local adaptive thresholding technique to detect the masses in the difference image, which was formed by subtracting the original image from the enhanced image.

Eltonsy, Tourassi, & Elmaghraby (2007) introduced a mass detection algorithm that comprised three stages (see Figure 6). First, they applied segmentation and granulation techniques to pre-process the mammograms. Next, a knowledge-based reasoning method was used to detect suspicious regions. Finally, they removed the false positives by using two different criteria. Recently, De Oliveira Martins *et al.* (2009) described a mass-detection technique by using the K-means algorithm for image segmentation and a co-occurrence matrix to describe the texture of segmented regions. A support vector machine classifier was then used to classify suspicious regions into masses and non-masses, using shape and texture descriptors.

A number of researchers have proposed region-based techniques for detecting masses in mammograms. Lee *et al.* (2000) proposed a technique that detects subtle mass lesions with various contrast ranges (see Figure 7). Their technique first divides the breast image into three regions: a fat region, a fatty and glandular region, and a dense region. Next, consecutive processes of seed selection and segmentation are carried out, with different threshold values applied to each breast region. Lastly, potential masses are classified by using four features that represent shape, density and margins of the segmented regions.

Mudigonda, Rangayyan, & Desautels (2000) proposed a mass-detection technique that combines texture-based and gradient-based features to distinguish between benign masses and malignant tumors. After the features have been extracted and combined, the authors applied the Mahalanobis distance to compute a posterior probability that is used to classify breast masses as benign or malignant.

Baeg and Kehtarnavaz (2002) proposed a technique to assist radiologists to reduce the number of benign breast cancer biopsies. First, a radiologist is asked to detect mass abnormality and mark the suspicious regions. Next, for each suspicious region, the technique extracts two texture features, namely denseness and architectural distortion. Depending on the texture features within each region of interests, a neural network classifier decides whether the region is benign or malignant. This technique, however, assumes that the radiologist will be able to spot all areas of suspicion. Wei *et al.* (2005) developed a CAD system for mass detection. First, they used multi-scale methods to enhance raw full-field digital mammography images. Second, they detected suspicious masses on the full-field digital mammography images using a two-stage segmentation method, which combined gradient field information and gray-level information. Third, for each suspicious mass they extracted morphological and spatial gray-level dependence texture features. Last, they applied the stepwise linear discriminant analysis with simplex optimisation to select the most useful features. The classifier and the most useful feature set were used to distinguish masses from the normal tissues.

Another automated CAD system for mass detection was developed by Bellotti *et al.* (2006). First, the system used an edge-based segmentation algorithm to select the suspicious regions. Next, for each region of interest, eight gray-level texture features were derived from the Gray-Level Co-Occurrence Matrix at four different angles. Finally, they used a supervised two-layered feed forward neural network to classify masses from the normal tissues.

Timp, Varela, Karssemeijer, & Dacolian (2007) proposed an automated technique to detect tem-

Figure 6. Block diagram of the pixel-based mammographic mass detection technique (Adapted from: Eltonsy, Tourassi, & Elmaghraby, 2007)

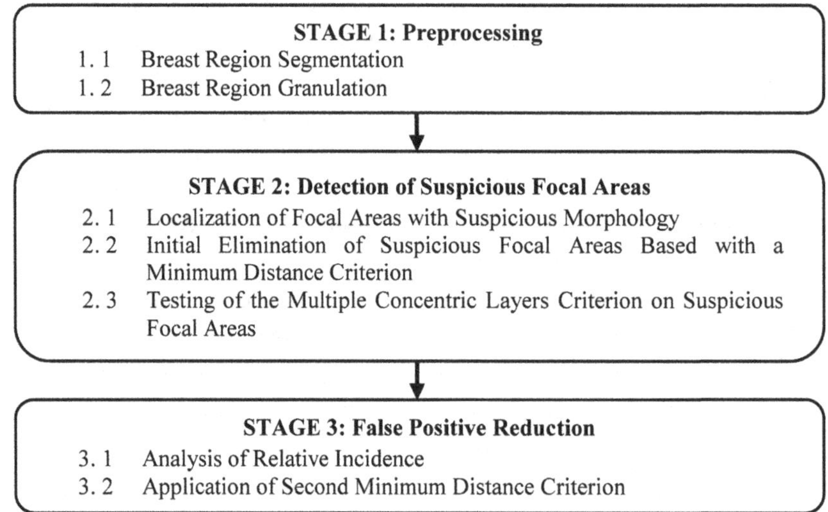

Figure 7. Block diagram of the region-based mammographic mass detection method (Adapted from: Lee, Park, & Park, 2000)

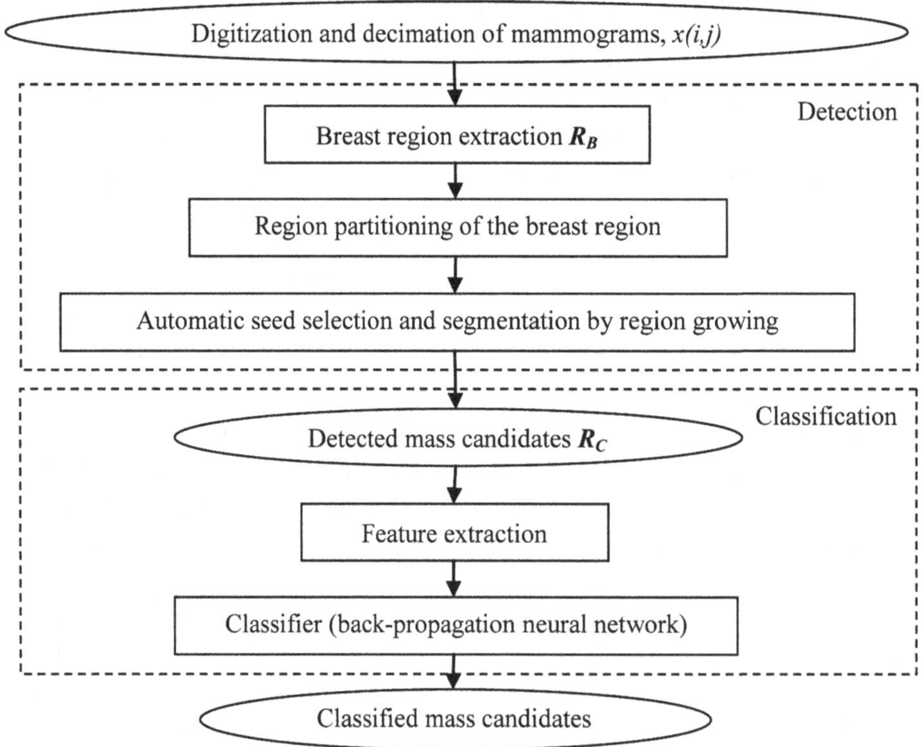

poral changes in mammographic masses between two sequential screening rounds. The authors designed two kinds of temporal features: difference features and similarity features. Difference features were useful for detecting lesions that are visible on both views, while similarity features were useful for identifying lesions that are visible on the prior view as well as for newly developing lesions. The authors employed a support vector machine classifier to detect the temporal changes in the mammographic masses.

Hupse and Karssemeijer (2009) developed a technique that used a set of multiple context features and a neural network classifer to detect suspicious regions. For each suspicious region, three normal reference areas were defined in the primary image. In the contralateral image, corresponding areas were similarly defined in different projections. The 10-fold cross validation and case-based bootstrapping were used to evaluate the context features.

Muralidhar *et al.* (2010) presented a novel, model-based active contour algorithm called "snakules". For each suspicious spiculated mass region, the authors deployed snakules that could deform, grow and adapt to the true spicules in the image. Recently, Samulski and Karssemeijer (2011) proposed a new learning technique for multiview CAD systems. The method builds on a single-view lesion detection system and a correspondence classifier. The classifier's output is used to bias the selection of training patterns for the multiview CAD system. Table 1 gives a summary of all the previous mass-detection approaches.

Image Segmentation (The Conventional Approach)

Image segmentation, in the context of breast cancer diagnosis, is the process of separating suspicious regions that may contain masses from the background parenchyma. The result of image segmentation is assumed to include all the regions that might contain masses, even with some false positives (FPs) that can be removed at a later stage. Although image segmentation is a critical step that determines the sensitivity of the entire CAD system, the result of a good segmentation depends mainly on using a suitable algorithm for finding the desired features. If the algorithm is fixed, the result can be improved by enhancement techniques. Segmentation techniques are classified into four types: classical, bilateral image subtraction, multi-scale and fuzzy.

The classical algorithms are further divided into six sub-categories: global thresholding, local thresholding, iterative pixel classification, edge detection, template matching and stochastic relaxation (Cheng *et al.*, 2005).

Global thresholding techniques have been widely used for image segmentation. They are based on global information, such as the histograms of the mammograms. Global thresholding is easy to implement, but it is not good for identifying regions of interests (ROIs) because mammograms are 2D projections of 3D breasts. Moreover, the false negatives (FNs) and false positives (FPs) could be too high. Due to the drawbacks of global thresholding, the output of these techniques is mainly used as an input to the next step in most diagnosis systems.

Local thresholding (LT) can refine the results of global thresholding. It also performs better than global thresholding for mass detection because a thresholding value is determined locally for each pixel, based on the intensity values of the surrounding pixels (Kom, Tiedeu, & Kom, 2007). Because LT cannot accurately separate the pixels into suitable sets, it is often used as an initialisation step for other segmentation algorithms.

There are three kinds of segmentation algorithms based on pixel classification: Markov random field (MRF) or Gibbs random field (GRF), region growing, and region clustering. (1) MRF/GRF uses the local neighbourhood relationship to represent the global relationship. MRFs/GRFs are statistical methods and powerful modelling tools, and they have been the bases for the development

Table 1. Summary of selective mass detection approaches

Mass Type	Author(s)	Year	Detection Method	Number of Images	Sensitivity	FPI
-	Lee *et al.*	2000	Region	204	92.3%	3.2
Circumscribed & spiculated	Mudigonda *et al.*	2000	Region	54	-	-
Spiculated	Liu *et al.*	2001	Pixel	19	84.2%	< 1
Circumscribe, spiculated & ill-defined	Zhen and Chan	2001	Pixel	322	97.3%	3.92
-	Baeg and Kehtarnavaz	2002	Region	404	-	-
Spiculated	Sampat and Bovik	2003	Pixel	-	-	-
-	Campanini *et al.*	2004	Pixel	512	80%	**FPR** 1.1
All	Wei *et al.*	2005	Region	**Mass dataset (MD)** 110 (220) **No-mass dataset (ND)** 90 (180)	70% 80% 90%	**MD** / **ND** 0.72 / 0.82 1.08 / 1.31 1.82 / 2.14
All	Bellotti *et al.*	2006	Region	3369	80%	4.23
-	Timp *et al.*	2007	Region	465	-	-
-	Kom *et al.*	2007	Pixel	61	95.91%	0.033
All	Eltonsy *et al.*	2007	Pixel	540	92% 88% 81%	5.4 2.4 0.6
-	De Oliveira Martins *et al.*	2009	Pixel	433	86%	1.2
-	Hupse and Karssemeijer	2009	Region	-	-	-
Spiculated	Muralidhar *et al.*	2010	Region	52	-	-
-	Samulski and Karssemeijer	2011	Region	454	-	-

of a number of methods. For example, a model-based technique based on a modified Markov random field (MRF) is used to segment mammogram images by using the statistical properties of the pixel and its neighbours. Another method to find the abnormalities in a mammogram image, based on the Gibbs model, assumes that the abnormalities are statistical restorations of noisy images. The MRF/GRF algorithms lead to good segmentation results. However, they are computationally expensive and time-consuming. (2) Region growing is one of the most popular algorithms for segmenting masses in digitised mammograms. The basic idea of this algorithm is to find a set of seed pixels in the image first, and then to grow iteratively and aggregate with pixels that have similar properties (Lee, Park, & Park, 2000). The key challenge of region growing is finding suitable seeds. (3) Region clustering searches for regions directly without any prior information (De Oliveira Martins, Braz Junior, Correa Silva, Cardoso de Paiva, & Gattass, 2009). Region clustering and region growing are very similar. Examples include the K-means and other adaptive clustering algorithms that have been used for mass segmentation.

Edge detection is a conventional method for image segmentation. It has been used to detect discontinuity in mammograms. There are five edge detector techniques in related literature: density-weighted contrast enhancement (DWCE), logic filter, Iris filter, Gaussian filter, and deformable models.

Template matching is the most commonly used technique for medical image segmentation. It uses the prior information of possible masses of mammograms and segments from the background by referencing the prototypes. Template matching may result in a high number of FPs.

Stochastic relaxation is an unsupervised segmentation method with an evidential constrained optimisation that aims to detect all different lesions. It is often used in a statistical model by building an optimal label map to separate normal tissues from suspicious areas. It is computational intensive, time consuming and requires complex parameter estimation.

Bilateral image subtraction has been used in detecting suspicious regions. It is also called the asymmetry approach as it is based on the normal symmetry between the left and right breasts. Bilateral image subtraction is easy to implement. However, it cannot remove the FPs. Neither can it classify true positive regions into benign and malignant masses because it is difficult to differentiate the left and right breasts correctly.

The multi-scale technique applies discrete wavelet transform filters to transform the mammogram images from the spatial domain to the frequency domain before image segmentation (Zhen & Chan, 2001). It can improve the detection rate when suspicious regions are detected correctly. The main drawbacks of this technique are selecting suitable mother wavelets and weighting the modifying functions.

Fuzzy logic techniques have been used for segmenting suspicious masses when the conventional segmentation methods might not work well; it is especially effective when the contrast in mammograms is very low and the boundaries between normal tissue and tumors are unclear. There are two kinds of fuzzy techniques: fuzzy thresholding and fuzzy region clustering or growing. (1) Fuzzy thresholding techniques try to segment ROIs, but it can only handle unclear boundaries effectively (Sameti, 1998), (2) Fuzzy region growing techniques try to define ROIs, but it is not easy to find a criterion because most malignant tumors with fuzzy boundaries extend from a dense core region to the surrounding tissues (Guliato, Rangayyan, Carnielli, Zuffo, & Desautels, 2003; Sun, Qian, & Song, 2004; Hassinen, 2007; Oliver *et al.*, 2008). Although fuzzy logic techniques are effective, it is difficult to determine the suitable fuzzy membership functions and rules. A summary of these fuzzy image segmentation techniques will be provided in Table 2, towards the end of the chapter.

FUZZY IMAGE SEGMENTATION FOR MASS DETECTION

Fuzzy set theory was introduced by Lotfi A. Zadeh (Zadeh, 1965). It is an extension of conventional or *crisp* set theory, which is a collection of elements that have a number of common properties. Any element x in a *crisp* set A is assigned a value of 0 or 1 as follows:

$$f(x) = \begin{cases} 1\, if\, x \in A \\ 0\, if\, x \notin A \end{cases} \tag{5}$$

A *fuzzy* set, on the other hand, is unlike a crisp set. Each element x in the *fuzzy* set A in X has a grade of membership $f_A(x)$, which is a real number in the interval [0.0, 1.0]. In fuzzy set theory, the closer the value of $f_A(x)$ is to unity, the larger the grade of membership of x in A.

Fuzzy set theory has been proven very efficient in solving real-life problems in a variety of fields such as artificial intelligence and robotics, image processing and pattern recognition, biological and medical sciences, applied operations research, economics and geography. The most popular fuzzy set models as applied in different fields are the fuzzy membership function, fuzzy clustering, fuzzy-rule based systems, fuzzy entropy (measure of fuzziness), fuzzy measure and the fuzzy integral.

Table 2. A summary of fuzzy techniques developed for masses detection and classification

Author(s)	Method description	Application	Evaluation results	
Guliato *et al.*, 2003	Two segmentation methods incorporating fuzzy concepts were proposed to determine the boundary of a mass by region growing. The first method used classical region-growing with fuzzy sets pre-processed image, while the second segmentation method based on fuzzy region-growing.	Mass segmentation	Sensitivity 80% Specificity 90%	
Cheng and Cui, 2004	Self-adjusting fuzzy neural network consisting of four layers. The output layer has a maximum of two fuzzy neurons and one competitive fuzzy neuron.	Mass detection	Sensitivity	FPI
			92%	1.33
			100%	2.15
Sun *et al.*, 2004	An ipsilateral multi-view method used to detect masses by using an adaptive fuzzy c-means algorithm for image segmentation.	Mass detection	-	
Mousa *et al.*, 2005	The proposed technique based on wavelet analysis and fuzzy-neural approaches. A wavelet transform function is used for image enhancement and feature extraction; a combination of adaptive neuro-fuzzy inference system algorithms is used for the classification process.	Mass detection and classification	-	
Hassanien, 2007	A hybrid scheme combining fuzzy sets for image enhancement and rough sets for generating a minimal number of attributes and rules is then used as a classifier for the different regions of interest.	Mass detection and classification	Classification accuracy rate 98%	
Moayedi *et al.*, 2007	The algorithm combined support vector machines and fuzzy logic, as well as the learning ability of neural networks to deal with mass detection and classification.	Mass detection and classification	-	
Oliver *et al.*, 2008	A fuzzy c-means algorithm used to segment fatty tissues from dense tissues.	Mass detection and classification	Classification accuracy rate 77% using 831 images from DDSM database.	
Cao *et al.*, 2008	A robust information clustering technique using the fuzzy margin of a mass and noisy data.	Mass detection	Sensitivity	FPI
			90.7%	2.57

Fuzzy set operations include:

1. **Empty set:** A fuzzy set A is said to be empty if and only if its membership function is zero, $f_A(x) = 0,\ \forall x \in X$.
2. **Equality:** Two fuzzy sets A and B are said to be equal, written as $A = B$, if and only if $f_A(x) = f_B(x),\ \forall x \in X$.
3. **Complement:** The complement of a fuzzy set A is written as $\bar{A}$ and is defined as $\bar{A}(x) = 1 - f_A(x), \forall x \in X$.
4. **Union:** The union of two fuzzy sets A and B with their respective membership functions $f_A(x)$ and $f_B(x)$ is a fuzzy set C, written as $C = A \cup B$, with membership function $f_C(x) = \max[f_A(x), f_B(x)],\ \forall x \in X$.
5. **Intersection:** The intersection of two fuzzy sets A and B with their respective membership functions $f_A(x)$ and $f_B(x)$ is a fuzzy set C, written as $C = A \cap B$, with membership function $f_C(x) = \min[f_A(x), f_B(x)],\ \forall x \in X$.

In addition, the union and intersection operations of fuzzy set satisfy the following properties as in the conventional set theory:

1. **Commutativity:**
   $A \cup B = B \cup A; A \cap B = B \cap A$
2. **Associativity:**
   $(A \cup B) \cup C = A \cup (B \cup C); (A \cap B) \cap C = A \cap (B \cap C)$
3. **Idempotency:**
   $A \cup A = A; A \cap A = A$
4. **Distributivity:**
   $A \cup (B \cap C) = (A \cup B) \cap (A \cup C); A \cap (B \cup C) = (A \cap B) \cup (A \cap C)$
5. **Absorption:**
   $A \cup (A \cap B) = A; A \cap (A \cup B) = A$
6. **De Morgan's laws:**
   $\overline{(A \cup B)} = \bar{A} \cap \bar{B}; \overline{(A \cup B)} = \bar{A} \cup \bar{B}$
7. **Equivalence formula:**
   $(A \cup B) \cap (A \cup C) = (A \cap B) \cup (A \cap C)$
8. **Symmetrical difference formula:**
   $(A \cap B) \cup (A \cap C) = (A \cup B) \cap (A \cup C)$

Fuzzy Image Processing

Fuzzy image processing includes techniques that are used to process and represent an image's features and regions as fuzzy sets. Depending on both the problem to be solved and the chosen fuzzy technique, image processing and representation methods are determined (Tizhoosh, 2004). Fuzzy image processing is important for two main reasons. First, fuzzy set theory and fuzzy logic are powerful tools to represent and process human knowledge as a series of fuzzy if-then rules. Second, in image processing, difficulties arise due to the randomness, ambiguity and vagueness of data and fuzzy techniques can manage them efficiently. Moreover, images by nature possess a degree of fuzziness due to their borders being not always well defined. Imperfection problems in image processing such as grayness ambiguity and geometrical fuzziness are *fuzzy* as well. Examples include questions of whether a certain pixel should become brighter or darker than its current value, and where a particular object is located in a scene analysis problem.

When using fuzzy techniques on images, three main steps should be followed (see Figure 8). The first step is *fuzzification*, which is transferring image data – from gray-level to the membership plane – into a specific format suitable for fuzzy techniques. Modification of membership values is the second step. In this step, suitable fuzzy techniques are selected. The third step is *defuzzification*, which is decoding the image and evaluating the result. Although both the first and the last steps are essential in fuzzy image processing, modification of membership value is the most critical step (see Figure 9).

A fuzzy set of a gray-scale image I is a mapping of every pixel p in I into their corresponding real values ranging between 0.0 and 1.0. For any pixel $p \in I, f_I(p)$ is called the grade of membership of p.

$$f_I(p) \rightarrow [0.0, 1.0] \tag{6}$$

Fuzzy Concept for Mammography Images

Many CAD systems have been used to demonstrate a variety of performances in the detection and diagnosis of abnormalities. Since mammography images feature ill-defined shapes, imprecise borders, and different densities and textures, they are inherently "fuzzy". Therefore, image processing techniques which apply fuzzy set theory to deal with uncertain edges, boundaries and contrast are considered to be perfect tools for enhancing, isolating and classifying lesions in mammography images.

A mammography image f in a fuzzy set based system is considered as an array of fuzzy singletons, each having a value in the interval [0,1] that represents its degree of membership for a certain

Figure 8. Fuzzy image processing steps (Adapted from: http://pami.uwaterloo.ca)

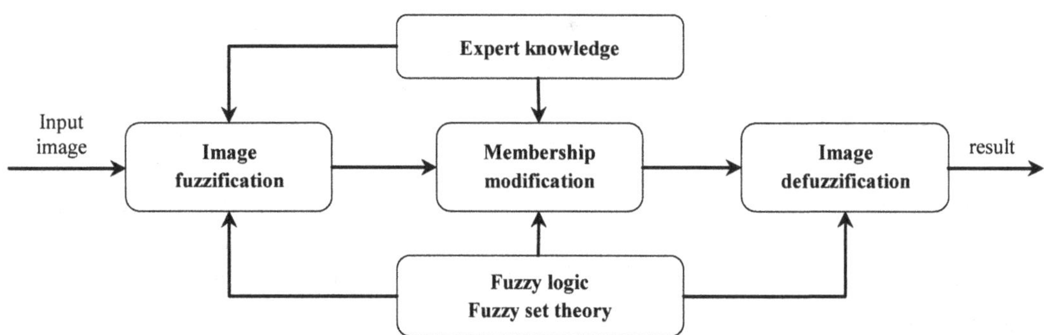

image property such as brightness, on an edge, etc. (Sahba, Venetsanopoulos, & Schaefer, 2010). A fuzzy notation is as follows:

$$f = \cup_i \cup_j \frac{\mu_{ij}}{p_{ij}} \qquad i, j \in f \tag{7}$$

where p_{ij} is the property of the ij^{th} pixel, and μ_{ij} is a membership function. Different membership functions have been used to transform a mammography image from the spatial domain to the fuzzy property space.

Performance Efficiency

In the previous sections, we commented on the computational intensity of a number of algorithms. Researchers for some time have investigated parallel computing as a strategy to achieve performance efficiency in image segmentation (Pal and Pal, 1993). As examples, Chen *et al.* (2001) describe parallel edge detection techniques for colour image segmentation. Similarly, Rahimi *et al.* (2004) has proposed a parallel fuzzy algorithm for image segmentation, and Han and Shi (2007) studied, for fuzzy clustering, the use of ant colony algorithm which is inherently parallel. While these works are not specifically in the

Figure 9. Example of fuzzy image processing. (Adapted from: http://pami.uwaterloo.ca)

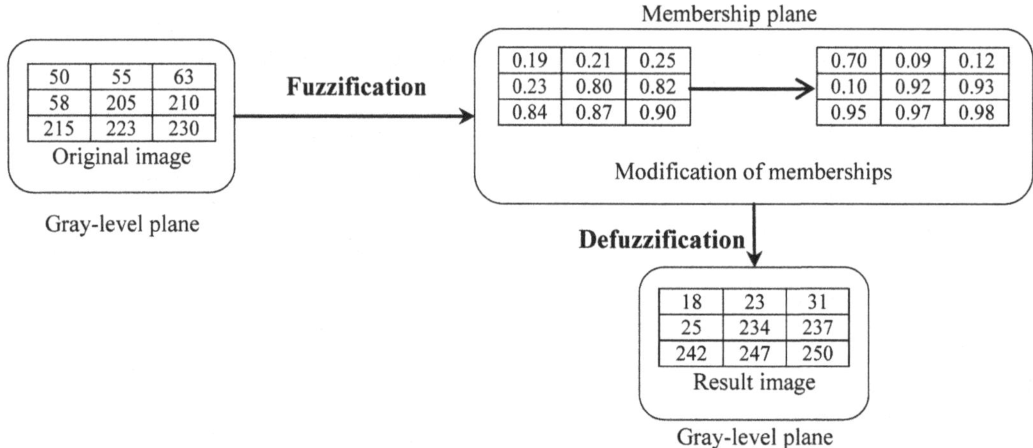

context of breast cancer detection, the principles are general enough to solve performance issues arising from computational complexity in image segmentation. Until recently, parallel processing has been a very expensive technique requiring special purpose servers and sometimes dedicated networks, however, with the advent of multi-core CPUs and general purpose graphical programming units (Harvey, 2008), parallel computing is becoming mainstream and increasingly will be used to address performance issues.

Recent Advances and Techniques

Masses are an important indicator for abnormalities in mammography images. Radiologists classify breast masses into three categories, according to their shapes and margins: benign, which represents tumor with a regular shape but without cancerous cells; malignant, which represents a tumor with an irregular shape that is highly likely to have cancerous cells; and normal tissues.

Guliato *et al.* (2003) proposed two segmentation methods that incorporate fuzzy concepts. The first method determines the regional boundary of a tumor or a growing mass after employing a preprocessing step based on fuzzy sets to enhance the ROI. The second segmentation method is a fuzzy region-growing method that takes the uncertainty present around the boundaries of tumors into account.

A work presented by Cheng and Cui (2004) introduces a fuzzy neural network based approach to detect malignant masses in mammography images. The fuzzy neural network is modelled as a self-adjusting system consisting of four layers. The first and second layers have ordinary neurons, but the third layer consists of a maximum of N fuzzy neurons, where N is determined during the training process and is adjusted with the network parameters and data distribution. The output layer has a maximum of two fuzzy neurons and one competitive fuzzy neuron. Regions of interest are extracted and randomly divided into two sets of training and testing data. It can incorporate expert knowledge in the detection of malignant mass lesions. The co-occurrence matrix of each region is computed and its entropy, uniformity, contrast and maximum matrix element features are extracted. Feature differences are computed for each feature to discriminate between malignant masses and normal tissues. The authors stated that expert knowledge can be incorporated in the system as fuzzy neurons based on IF-THEN rules.

An ipsilateral multi-view CAD system was presented by Sun *et al.* (2004). This method is designed to detect masses in digital mammograms by using correlative information of suspicious lesions between mammograms of the same breast (see Figure 10). The method uses tree-structured filtering for image noise suppression, directional wavelet transform and tree-structured wavelet transform for image enhancement, and an adaptive K algorithm for segmentations, which is applied to each mammogram taken of the same breast. Using inter-projective feature matching analysis, a concurrent analysis is developed for evaluating the ipsilateral multi-view mammograms. An artificial back-propagation neural network, combined with Kalman filtering, is used as a classifier to train the algorithm. Performance comparison demonstrates the advantages of this mutli-view CAD method over a single-view CAD system on false positives reduction.

Mousa, Munib, & Moussa (2005) proposed a technique based on wavelet analysis and fuzzy-neural approaches that distinguishes normal lesions from abnormal ones, masses from microcalcifications, and categorised abnormal severity as either benign or malignant. A wavelet transform function is used for image enhancement and feature extraction; a combination of adaptive neuro-fuzzy inference system algorithms is used for the classification process. The classifier is built in three phases and used to classify images into normal or abnormal—containing mass or microcalcification—categories. Abnormal images are passed on to the next stage to verify if

Figure 10. Flowchart of ipsilateral multi-view CAD system (Adapted from: Sun, Qian, & Song, 2004)

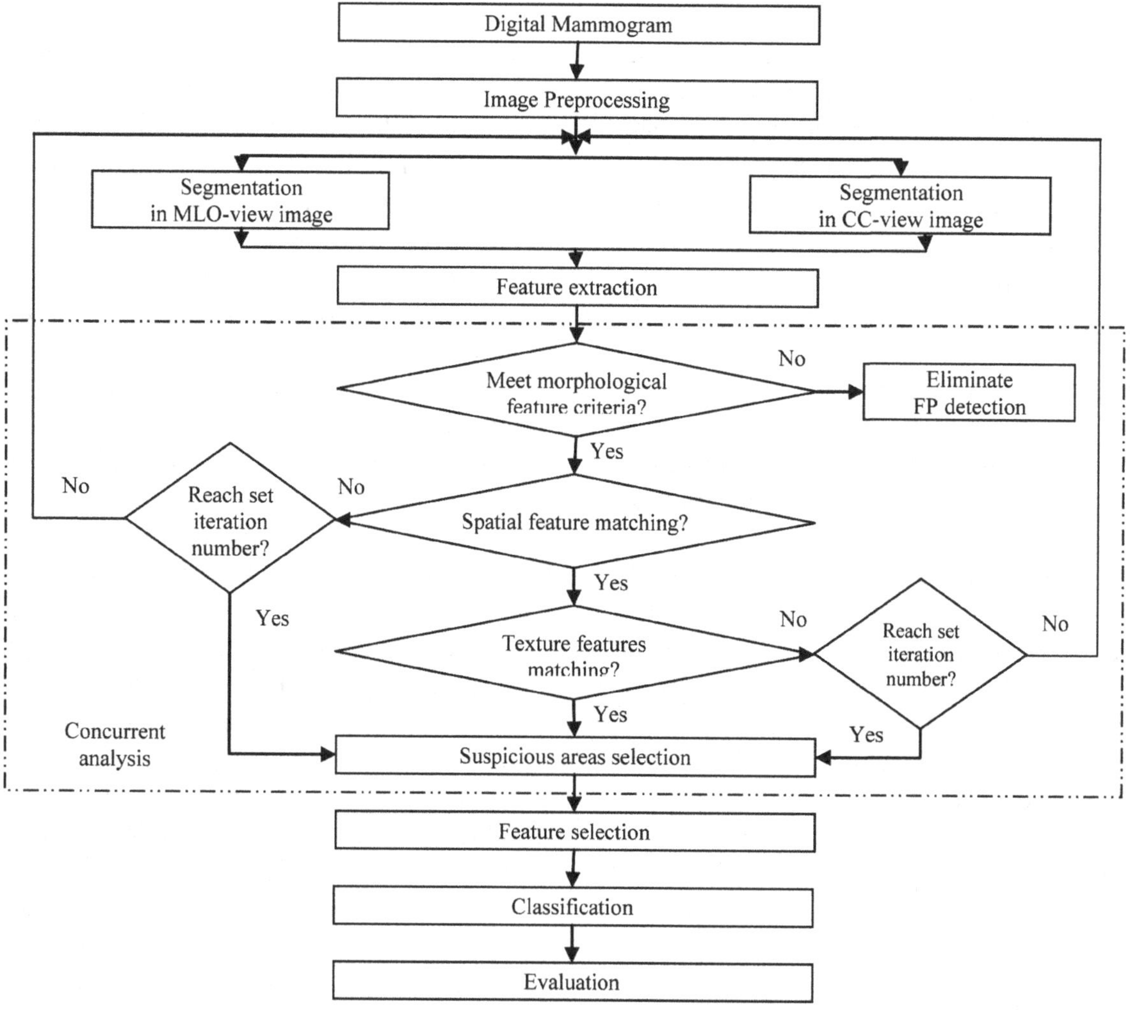

they contain a mass or microcalcification tumors. In the last stage, the abnormal mammograms are classified into malignant or benign. The authors stated that the result of each classifier is computed by evaluating the tested features and then computing the minimum error between features and the output results of each classifier.

Hassanien (2007) introduced a hybrid scheme, combining fuzzy and rough sets and statistical feature extraction techniques (shown in Figure 11). This approach has been applied to breast cancer images to classify them into two groups: cancer or non-cancer images. The authors used a fuzzy technique for pre-processing the image to enhance the contrast, identify the region of interest (ROI), and enhance the edges surrounding the ROI. A gray-level co-occurrence matrix is used to extract features from the segmented regions of interest. A rough set approach for generating a minimal number of attributes and rules is then used as a classifier for the discrimination of different regions of interest. This can indicate whether a region is benign or malignant.

Figure 11. Block diagram of fuzzy rough hybrid system (Adapted from: Hassanien (2007). Breast image: © 1993, National Cancer Institute, Public domain)

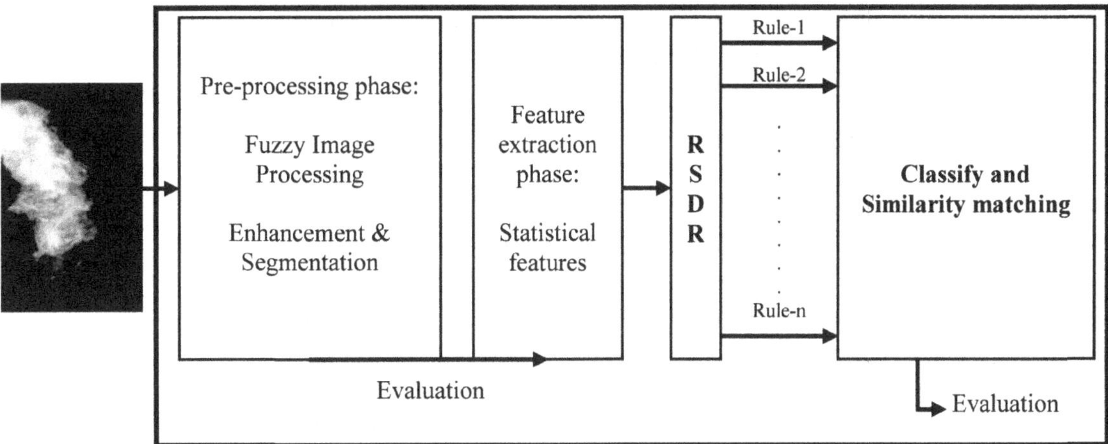

An approach based on contour-let texture features and support-vector-based fuzzy neural-network classifiers for mass classification was proposed by Moayedi *et al.* (2007). This algorithm combines support vector machines and the human-like reasoning of fuzzy logic in handling uncertainty, as well as the learning ability of neural networks to deal with this problem. Mammograms are first segmented into regions of interest, and then features are extracted by contour-let coefficients in the frequency domain.

In the work presented by Oliver *et al.* (2008), an automatic breast tissue classification method based on the following three steps is described: (1) segmentation of the breast area based on gray-level information, followed by the use of a fuzzy c-means algorithm to segment fatty and dense tissues; (2) extraction of morphological and texture features from the segmented breast areas, for each tissue region; and lastly (3) classification of the mammograms into four categories by applying a Bayesian approach and a combination of a number of classifiers. The evaluation, based on a number of cases from two different mammographic datasets shows a correlation between automatic and expert-based density assessment.

Cao *et al.* (2008) introduced a robust information clustering technique for breast mass detection. The detection system applies a two-step adaptive thresholding on the raw region of interest extracted from a mammogram. The information clustering technique identified pixels on the fuzzy margin of a mass and noisy data through a two-phase minimax optimisation process that incorporates spatial information that takes the influence of a neighbourhood window into account. In this algorithm, the pixels corresponding to a valley in an image intensity histogram are clustered adaptively around the image content. This algorithm is shown to locate suspicious regions of mass in mammograms.

Performance and Metrics

The performance of any CAD system is reported using different measures such as sensitivity, FPI, specificity and FPR. In Table 2, we provide a summary of the fuzzy techniques for mass detection and classification that are described above. The missing results in the evaluation fields are due to the absence of values for these well-known measures.

FUTURE RESEARCH DIRECTIONS

An important future direction would be digital tomosynthesis (DT), which is a new 3D breast imaging technology capable of capturing multiple images of the breast from at least 11 different angles and combines them into a single 3D image. DT has the potential to reduce the recall rates for women who did not have breast cancer detected previously. Whereas the limitation of spatial superposition of a breast tissue in digital mammography can be attributed to the use of two dimensional (2D) images to represent a 3D structure of the breast, DT removes the obscuring effects of superimposed normal tissue. In addition, DT eliminates false positives that could occur in conventional screening mammography which is caused by the superimposed normal structures projected on a 2D image. Moreover, in DT the multiple projected views obtained from different acquisition angles that are used to reconstruct the 3D slices might reduce the number of false negatives caused by the superimposition of normal breast tissue on the cancerous region. Furthermore, DT utilizes effectively the volume, shape, and spatial relation features derived from the 3D structures of candidate cancerous regions in the analysis. Because DT is a 3D breast imaging method that has the potential to overcome the limitations of conventional screening mammography, we will explore the use of fuzzy image segmentation to detect masses in images generated by this new technique in our future work.

CONCLUSION

Digital mammography as applied in CAD systems goes a long way in facilitating radiologists in the detection of potential cancerous masses in breast images. A critical step in the overall detection process is image segmentation which determines the sensitivity of the entire CAD system. Many image segmentation techniques have been proposed to date, and it is still an active area of research in cancer detection and classification. Since mammographic images often possess uncertain boundaries and low intensity contrast, fuzzy set theory have been demonstrated to be very efficient in the analysis of these images. Over the past decade, a number of advances in fuzzy image segmentation techniques have been made. However, much still needs to be done. This chapter attempts to document these recent advances and techniques for ease of comparison and reference.

REFERENCES

American Cancer Society. (n.d.). *Breast cancer facts & figures 2009-2010*. Atlanta, GA: American Cancer Society, Inc. Retrieved August 21, 2011, from http://www.cancer.org/Research/CancerFactsFigures/BreastCancerFactsFigures/breast-cancer-facts--figures-2009-2010

Baeg, S., & Kehtarnavaz, N. (2002). Classification of breast mass abnormalities using denseness and architectural distortion. *Electronic Letters on Computer Vision and Image Analysis*, *1*(1), 1–20.

Bandyopadhyay, S. K. (2011). Diagnosis of breast abnormalities in mammographic image. *International Journal of Computer Science and Technology*, *2*(1), 69–71.

Bellotti, R., Carlo, F. D., Tangaro, S., Gargano, G., Maggipinto, G., & Castellano, M. (2006). A completely automated CAD system for mass detection in a large mammographic database. *Medical Physics*, *33*(8), 3066–3075. doi:10.1118/1.2214177

Benign mass with regular shape. (n.d.). Retrieved December 21, 2011 from http://visualsonline.cancer.gov/

Breastcancer.org. (2011). Retrieved August 21, 2011 from http://www.breastcancer.org/

Campanini, R., Dongiovanni, D., Iampieri, E., Lanconelli, N., Masotti, M., & Palermo, G. (2004). A novel featureless approach to mass detection in digital mammograms based on support vector machines. *Physics in Medicine and Biology*, *49*(6), 961–975. doi:10.1088/0031-9155/49/6/007

Cancer Australia. (2011). Retrieved August 22, 2011 from http://canceraustralia.nbocc.org.au/breast-cancer/home/home

Cao, A., Song, Q., & Yang, X. (2008). Robust information clustering incorporating spatial information for breast mass detection in digitized mammograms. *Computer Vision and Image Understanding*, *109*(1), 86–96. doi:10.1016/j.cviu.2007.07.004

Cheng, H. D., & Cui, M. (2004). Mass lesion detection with a fuzzy neural network. *Pattern Recognition*, *37*(6), 1189–1200. doi:10.1016/j.patcog.2003.11.002

Cheng, H. D., Jiang, X. H., Sun, Y., & Wang, J. (2001). Color image segmentation: Advances and prospects. *Pattern Recognition*, *34*(12), 2259–2281. doi:10.1016/S0031-3203(00)00149-7

Cheng, H. D., Shi, X. J., Min, R., Hu, L. M., Cai, X. P., & Du, H. N. (2005). Approaches for automated detection and classification of masses in mammograms. *Pattern Recognition*, *39*(4), 646–668. doi:10.1016/j.patcog.2005.07.006

De Oliveira Martins, L., Braz Junior, G., Correa Silva, A., Cardoso de Paiva, A., & Gattass, M. (2009). Detection of masses in digital mammograms using k-means and support vector machine. *Electronic Letters on Computer Vision and Image Analysis*, *8*(2), 39–50.

Dhawan, A. (2011). *Medical image analysis* (2nd ed.). Wiley-IEEE Press. doi:10.1002/9780470918548

Eltonsy, N. H., Tourassi, G. D., & Elmaghraby, A. S. (2007). A concentric morphology model for the detection of masses in mammography. *IEEE Transactions on Medical Imaging*, *26*(6), 880–889. doi:10.1109/TMI.2007.895460

Example of fuzzy image processing (n.d.). Retrieved September 4, 2011 from http://pami.uwaterloo.ca/tizhoosh/images/steps.gif

Frank, Y. S. (2010). *Image processing and pattern recognition: fundamentals and techniques*. Wiley-IEEE Press. Retrieved from http://www.ius.edu.ba/rkoker/cs415/0470404612.pdf

Freiherr, G. (2011, March 22). Tomosynthesis: A new era in breast imaging. *Medscape*. Retrieved October 12, 2011 from http://www.medscape.com

Fuzzy image processing steps (n.d.). Retrieved September 4, 2011 from http://pami.uwaterloo.ca/tizhoosh/images/fuzzbv.gif

Gonzalez, R. C., & Woods, R. E. (2007). *Digital image processing* (3rd ed.). Prentice-Hall.

Guliato, D., Rangayyan, R. M., Carnielli, W. A., Zuffo, J. A., & Desautels, J. E. (2003). Segmentation of breast tumors in mammograms using fuzzy sets. *Journal of Electronic Imaging*, *12*(3), 369–378. doi:10.1117/1.1579017

Han, Y., & Shi, P. (2007). An improved ant colony algorithm for fuzzy clustering in image segmentation. *Neurocomputing*, *70*(4-6), 665–671. doi:10.1016/j.neucom.2006.10.022

Harvey, N., Luke, R., Keller, J. M., & Anderson, D. (2008). Speedup of fuzzy logic through stream processing on graphics processing units. *Evolutionary Computation: IEEE World Congress on Computational Intelligence*, (pp. 3809-3815).

Hassanien, A. E. (2007). Fuzzy rough sets hybrid scheme for breast cancer detection. *Image and Vision Computing*, *25*(2), 172–183. doi:10.1016/j.imavis.2006.01.026

http://pastel.archives-ouvertes.fr/docs/00/50/06/02/PDF/PhD_GP.pdf

Human female breast (n.d.). Retrieved December 21, 2011 from http://visualsonline.cancer.gov/

Hupse, R., & Karssemeijer, N. (2009). Use of normal tissue context in computer-aided detection of masses in mammograms. *IEEE Transactions on Medical Imaging*, *28*(12), 2033–2041. doi:10.1109/TMI.2009.2028611

Islam, M., Ahmadi, M., & Sid-Ahmed, M. (2010). Computer-aided detection and classification of masses in digitized mammograms using artificial neural network. In Tan, Y., Shi, Y., & Tan, K. (Eds.), *Advances in swarm intelligence* (pp. 327–334). doi:10.1007/978-3-642-13498-2_43

Kallergi, M. (2005). Evaluation strategies for medical-image analysis and processing methodologies. In Costaridou, L. (Ed.), *Medical image analysis methods*. doi:10.1201/9780203500453.ch12

Kerlikowske, K., Ichikawa, L., Miglioretti, D., Buist, D., Vacek, P., & Smith-Bindman, R. (2007). Longitudinal measurement of clinical mammographic breast density to improve estimation of breast cancer risk. *Journal of the National Cancer Institute*, *99*(5), 386–395. doi:10.1093/jnci/djk066

Kom, G., Tiedeu, A., & Kom, M. (2007). Automated detection of masses in mammograms by local adaptive thresholding. *Computers in Biology and Medicine*, *37*(1), 37–48. doi:10.1016/j.compbiomed.2005.12.004

Lee, Y. J., Park, J. M., & Park, H. W. (2000). Mammographic mass detection by adaptive thresholding and region growing. *International Journal of Imaging Systems and Technology*, *11*(5), 340–346. doi:10.1002/ima.1018

Lehman, C. D., Gatsonis, C., Kuhl, C. K., Hendrick, R. E., Pisano, E. D., & Hanna, L. (2007). MRI evaluation of the contralateral breast in women with recently diagnosed breast cancer. *The New England Journal of Medicine*, *356*(13), 1295–1303. doi:10.1056/NEJMoa065447

Liu, S., Babbs, C. F., & Delp, E. J. (2001). Multiresolution detection of spiculated lesions in digital mammograms. *IEEE Transactions on Image Processing*, *10*(6), 874–884. doi:10.1109/83.923284

Malignant mass with irregular shape. (n.d.). Retrieved August 18, 2011 from http://marathon.csee.usf.edu/Mammography/Database.html

Mammography test (n.d.). Retrieved December 21, 2011 from http://visualsonline.cancer.gov/

McKenzie, P., & Alder, M. (1993). *The EM algorithm used for Gaussian mixture modeling and its initialization*. University of Western Australia.

Mediolateral oblique view of left breast (n.d.). Retrieved August 18, 2011 from http://www.radiologyteacher.com/id/3381/1005-0-0-1.jpg

Michaelson, J., Satija, S., Moore, R., Weber, G., Halpern, E., & Garland, A. (2002). The pattern of breast cancer screening utilization and its consequences. *Cancer*, *94*(1), 37–43. doi:10.1002/cncr.10154

Moayedi, F., Boostani, R., Azimifar, Z., & Katebi, S. (2007). A support vector based fuzzy neural network approach for mass classification in mammography. Paper presented at 15th International conference on digital signal processing. Cardiff, UK: IEEE

Mousa, R., Munib, Q., & Moussa, A. (2005). Breast cancer diagnosis system based on wavelet analysis and fuzzy-neural. *Expert Systems with Applications*, *28*(4), 713–723. doi:10.1016/j.eswa.2004.12.028

Mudigonda, N. R., Rangayyan, R. M., & Desautels, J. E. L. (2000). Gradient and texture analysis for the classification of mammographic masses. *IEEE Transactions on Medical Imaging*, *19*(10), 1032–1043. doi:10.1109/42.887618

Muralidhar, G. S., Bovik, A. C., Giese, J. D., Sampat, M. P., Whitman, G. J., & Haygood, T. M. (2010). Snakules: A model-based active contour algorithm for the annotation of spicules on mammography. *IEEE Transactions on Medical Imaging*, *29*(10), 1768–1780. doi:10.1109/TMI.2010.2052064

Oliver, A., Freixenet, J., Martí, R., Pont, J., Pérez, E., & Denton, E. R. (2008). A novel breast tissue density classification methodology. *IEEE Transactions on Information Technology in Biomedicine*, *12*(1), 55–65. doi:10.1109/TITB.2007.903514

Oxford Dictionaries. (n.d.). *Definition of cancer*. Retrieved September 20, 2011 from http://oxforddictionaries.com/definition/cancer

Pain Free Mammogram. (2007). Retrieved August 28, 2011 from http://www.sciencedaily.com/videos/2007/0907-pain_free_mammogram.htm

Pal, N. R., & Pal, S. K. (1993). A review of image segmentation techniques. *Pattern Recognition*, *26*(9), 1277–1294. doi:10.1016/0031-3203(93)90135-J

Peters, G. (2007). *Computer-aided detection for digital breast tomosynthesis*. Doctoral dissertation, Paris Institute of Technology, 2007. Retrieved October 13, 2011, from

Rahimi, S., Zarham, M., Thakre, A., & Chillar, D. (2004). *A parallel fuzzy C-mean algorithm for image segmentation. Fuzzy Information* (pp. 234–237). IEEE.

Rangayyan, R. M. (2005). *Biomedical image analysis*. CRC Press LLC.

Sahba, F., Venetsanopoulos, A., & Schaefer, G. (2010). *A review of recent fuzzy-based methods for computer-aided detection and classification of breast cancer using mammography*. Paper presented at the 2010 International Conference on Image Processing, Computer Vision, and Pattern Recognition, Las Vegas, Nevada, USA.

Sameti, M. (1998). *Detection of soft tissue abnormalities in mammographic images for early diagnosis of breast cancer*. Doctor of philosophy, The University of British Columbia, 1998. Retrieved March 21, 2011, from https://circle.ubc.ca/bitstream/handle/2429/9987/ubc_1999-389723.pdf?sequence=1

Sampat, M. P., & Bovik, A. C. (2003). Detection of spiculated lesions in mammograms. Paper presented at *Proceedings of the 25th Annual International Conference of the IEEE Engineering in Medicine and Biology Society*.

Sampat, M. P., Markey, M. K., & Bovik, A. C. (2005). Computer-aided detection and diagnosis in mammography. In Bovik, A. (Ed.), *Handbook of image and video processing* (pp. 1195–1217). doi:10.1016/B978-012119792-6/50130-3

Samulski, M., & Karssemeijer, N. (2011). Optimizing case-based detection performance in a multiview cad system for mammography. *IEEE Transactions on Medical Imaging*, *30*(4), 1001–1009. doi:10.1109/TMI.2011.2105886

Sun, X., Qian, W., & Song, D. (2004). Ipsilateral-mammogram computer-aided detection of breast cancer. *Computerized Medical Imaging and Graphics*, *28*, 151–158. doi:10.1016/j.compmedimag.2003.11.004

Tang, J., Rangayyan, R., Xu, J., El Naqa, E., & Yang, Y. (2009). Computer-aided detection and diagnosis of breast cancer with mammography: Recent advances. *IEEE Transactions on Information Technology in Biomedicine, 13*(2), 236–251. doi:10.1109/TITB.2008.2009441

Timp, S., Varela, C., Karssemeijer, N., & Dacolian, B. (2007). Temporal change analysis for characterization of mass lesions in mammography. *IEEE Transactions on Medical Imaging, 26*(7), 945–953. doi:10.1109/TMI.2007.897392

Tizhoosh, H. R. (2004). *Homepage of fuzzy image processing*. Retrieved September 3, 2011, from http://pami.uwaterloo.ca/tizhoosh/fip.htm

Wei, J., Sahiner, B., Hadjiiski, L., Chan, H., Petrick, N., & Helvie, M. A. (2005). Computer aided detection of breast masses on full field digital mammograms. *Medical Physics, 32*(9), 2827–2837. doi:10.1118/1.1997327

Zadeh, L. A. (1965). Fuzzy sets. *Information and Control, 8*(3), 338–353. doi:10.1016/S0019-9958(65)90241-X

Zhen, L., & Chan, A. K. (2001). An artificial intelligent algorithm for tumor detection in screening mammogram. *IEEE Transactions on Medical Imaging, 20*(7), 559–567. doi:10.1109/42.932741

Compilation of References

Abd. Malik, N. N. N., Esa, M., Yusof, S. K., & Hamzah, S. A. (2010). Evaluation on optimum geometrical of linear node array for self-organization in a wireless sensor network. *Proceedings of IEEE Asia-Pacific Conf. on Applied Electromagnetics (APACE 2010),* IEEE Computer Soc., 2010, (pp. 1 – 4).

Abraham, A., Das, S., & Roy, S. (2007). Swarm intelligence algorithms for data clustering. In Maimon, O. Z., & Rokach, L. (Eds.), *Soft computing for knowledge discovery and data mining* (pp. 279–313). New York, NY: Springer-Verlag.

Adams, J., Rothman, E. D., Kerr, W. E., & Paulino, Z. L. (1972). Estimation of the number of sex alleles and queen matings from diploid male frequencies in a population of apis mellifera. *Genetics, 86*, 583–596.

Adjare, S. O. (1990). Beekeeping in Africa. *FAO Agricultural Services Bulletin, 68*(6). FAO of the United Nations.

Adriana, D. S. J., & José Maria, P. (2008). An ontology-based architecture for intelligent tutoring system. *Interdisciplinary Studies in Computer Science,* (pp. 25-35). Retrieved from http://www.unisinos.br/publicacoes_cientificas/images/stories/Publicacoes / scientiavol19n1/25a35_art03_jacinto% 5Brev_ok%5D.pdf

Agent Markup Language, D. A. R. P. A. (DAML). (n.d.). *Homepage*. Retrieved from http://www.daml.org

Agha, B., Yehya, M., Jerman, M., Hattab, T., & Sidawi, K. (2004). *2005). Arabic optical character recognition system* (pp. 5–19). Beirut Arab University.

Ahn, C. W., & Ramakrishna, R. S. (2004, January). QoS provisioning dynamic connection- admission control for multimedia wireless networks using a Hopfield neural network. *IEEE Transactions on Vehicular Technology, 53*(1), 106–117. doi:10.1109/TVT.2003.822000

Ahn, D. H., Conrad, J., & Dittmar, R. F. (2009). Basis assets. *Review of Financial Studies, 22*(12), 5133–5174. doi:10.1093/rfs/hhp065

Ahrendt, P., Meng, A., & Larsen, J. (2004). Decision time horizon for music genre classification using short time features. *European Signal Processing Conference (EUSIPCO),* (pp. 1293–1296).

Akyildiz, I. F., Su, W., Sankarasubramaniam, Y., & Cayirci, E. (2002). Wireless sensor networks: A survey. *IEEE Communications Magazine*, 102–114. doi:10.1109/MCOM.2002.1024422

Alam, S., Dobbie, G., & Riddle, P. (2008). An evolutionary particle swarm optimization algorithm for data clustering. In *Swarm Intelligence Symposium*, (pp. 1-6).

Almustafa, K., Zantout, R., & Obeid, H. (2010, November, December). *Pixel density: Recognizing characters in a Saudi license plate*. The 2010 International Conference on Intelligent Systems Design and Applications Cairo, Egypt.

Alrifai, M., & Risse, T. (2009). Combining global optimization with local selection for efficient QoS-aware service composition. *Proceedings of the 18th International Conference on World Wide Web*, (pp. 881-890).

Al-Sbou, Y. A. (2010, December). Fuzzy logic estimation system of quality of service for multimedia transmission. *International Journal of QoS Issues in Networking, 1*(1).

Al-Sultan, K. S., & Khan, M. M. (1996). Computational experience on four algorithms for the hard clustering problem. *Pattern Recognition Letters*, *17*(3), 295–308. doi:10.1016/0167-8655(95)00122-0

Altman, D., & Bland, M. (1994). Statistics notes: Diagnostic tests 1: Sensitivity and specificity. *British Medical Journal*, *308*, 1552. doi:10.1136/bmj.308.6943.1552

Altman, D., & Bland, M. (1994). Statistics notes: Diagnostic tests 2: Predictive values. *British Medical Journal*, *309*, 102. doi:10.1136/bmj.309.6947.102

Altschul, K. (1997). Gapped BLAST and PSI-BLAST: A new generation of protein database search programs. *Nucleic Acids Research*, *25*, 3389–3402. doi:10.1093/nar/25.17.3389

Amazon EC2. (n.d.). Retrieved on January 12, 2012, from http://aws.amazon.com/ec2/

Amazon. (2011). *Amazon elastic compute cloud*. Retrieved September 24, 2011, from http://aws.amazon.com/ec2/

American Cancer Society. (n.d.). *Breast cancer facts & figures 2009-2010*. Atlanta, GA: American Cancer Society, Inc. Retrieved August 21, 2011, from http://www.cancer.org/Research/CancerFactsFigures/BreastCancerFactsFigures/breast-cancer-facts--figures-2009-2010

Anderson, R. J., & Spong, M. W. (1989). Bilateral control of teleoperation with time delay. *IEEE Transactions on Automatic Control*, *34*, 494–501. doi:10.1109/9.24201

Andreão, R. V. (2004). ST-segment analysis using hidden Markov model beat segmentation: Application to ischemia detection. *Computers in Cardiology*, 381–384. doi:10.1109/CIC.2004.1442952

Andrews, D. F., & Pregibon, D. (1978). Finding the outliers that matter. *Journal of the Royal Statistical Society. Series-B*, *40*, 85–93.

Angiulli, F., Basta, S., & Pizzuti, C. (2006). Distance-based detection and prediction of outliers. *IEEE Transactions on Knowledge and Data Engineering*, *18*(2), 145–160. doi:10.1109/TKDE.2006.29

Animal Health Australia. (2009). *NLIS cattle*. Retrieved from http://www.animalhealthaustralia.com.au/programs/biosecurity/national-livestock-identification-system/nlis-cattle/

Annesi, P., Basili, R., Gitto, R., Moschitti, A., & Petitti, R. (2007). Audio feature engineering for automatic music genre classification. In *Large Scale Semantic Access to Content (Text, Image, Video, and Sound) (RIAO '07)*, (pp. 702-711).

Antoniou, G., & van Harmelen, F. (2004). *A Semantic Web primer*. MIT Press.

API. (2011). *Apis mellifera*. Retrieved September 25, 2011, from http://en.wikipedia.org/wiki/Apis_mellifera/

Arabshahi, P., Gray, A., et al. (2001). Adaptive routing in wireless communication networks using swarm intelligence. In *9th AIAA Int. Communications Satellite Systems Conference*, (pp. 17-20).

Araujo, J., Rodrigues, J., Fraiha, S., Gomes, H., Cavalcante, G., & Frances, C. R. (2010). Strategy for WLAN planning and performance evaluation through Bayesian networks as computational intelligence approach. In Rebai, A. (Ed.), *Bayesian network*. doi:10.5772/10066

Arenas, M. G., Mora, A. M., Romero, G., & Castillo, P. A. (2011). *GPU computation in bioinspired algorithms: a review. Advances in Computational Intelligence, LNCS 6691* (pp. 433–440). Berlin, Germany: Springer.

Armato, A., Nardini, E., Lanatà, A., Valenza, G., Mancuso, C., Scilingo, E., & Rossi, D. (2009). An FPGA based arrhythmia recognition system for wearable applications. *Ninth International Conference on Intelligent Systems Design and Applications*, (pp. 660-664).

Arulampalam, M., Maskell, S., Gordon, N., & Clapp, T. (2002). A tutorial on particle filters for online nonlinear/non-Gaussian Bayesian tracking. *IEEE Transactions on Signal Processing*, *2*(50), 174–188. doi:10.1109/78.978374

Asimakopoulou, E., Bessis, N., Varaganti, R., & Norrington, P. (2009). A personalized forest fire evacuation data grid push service – The FFED-GPS approach. In Asimakopoulou, E., & Bessis, N. (Eds.), *Advanced ICTs for disaster management and threat detection: Collaborative and distributed frameworks* (pp. 279–295). Hershey, PA: IGI Global.

Atkinson, A. C. (1986). Masking unmasked. *Biometrika*, *73*, 533–541. doi:10.1093/biomet/73.3.533

Bäck, T. (2000). *Introduction to evolutionary algorithms. Evolutionary Computation 1: Basic Algorithms and Operators* (pp. 59–63). Bristol, UK: Institute of Physics Publishing. doi:10.1887/0750306653

Baeg, S., & Kehtarnavaz, N. (2002). Classification of breast mass abnormalities using denseness and architectural distortion. *Electronic Letters on Computer Vision and Image Analysis*, *1*(1), 1–20.

Ball, G., & Hall, D. (1967). A clustering technique for summarizing multivariate data. *Behavioral Science*, *12*, 153–155. doi:10.1002/bs.3830120210

Bandyopadhyay, S. (2003). *Simulated annealing for fuzzy clustering: Variable representation, evolution of the number of clusters and remote sensing applications.* unpublished, private communication.

Bandyopadhyay, S. K. (2011). Diagnosis of breast abnormalities in mammographic image. *International Journal of Computer Science and Technology*, *2*(1), 69–71.

Bandyopadhyay, S., & Maulik, U. (2002). Genetic clustering for automatic evolution of clusters and application to image classification. *Pattern Recognition*, *35*, 1197–1208. doi:10.1016/S0031-3203(01)00108-X

Banz, R. W. (1981). The relationship between return and market value of common stocks. *Journal of Financial Economics*, *9*(1), 3–18. doi:10.1016/0304-405X(81)90018-0

Banz, R. W., & Breen, W. J. (1986). Sample-dependent results using accounting and market data: Some evidence. *The Journal of Finance*, *41*(4), 779–793. doi:10.2307/2328228

Barbancho, J., Leon, C., Molina, F. J., & Barbancho, A. (2007). Using artificial intelligence in routing scheme for wireless networks. *Computer Communications*, *30*, 2802–2811. doi:10.1016/j.comcom.2007.05.023

Barbedo, J. G. A., & Lopes, A. (2007). Automatic genre classification of musical signal. *EURASIP Journal on Applied Signal Processing*, *1*, 157–169.

Barnett, V., & Lewis, T. B. (1995). *Outliers in statistical data*. New York, NY: Wiley.

Barros, H. (2011). Steps, techniques, and technologies for the development of intelligent applications based on Semantic Web Services: A case study in e-learning systems. *Engineering Applications of Artificial Intelligence*, *24*(8). doi:10.1016/j.engappai.2011.05.007

Baskar, S., Alphones, A., Suganthan, P. M., & Liang, J. J. (2005). Design of Yagi-Uda antennas using comprehensive learning particle swarm optimisation. *IEE Proceedings. Microwaves, Antennas and Propagation*, *152*, 340–346. doi:10.1049/ip-map:20045087

Basu, S. (1983). The relationship between earnings yield, market value and return for NYSE common stocks: Further evidence. *Journal of Financial Economics*, *12*(1), 129–156. doi:10.1016/0304-405X(83)90031-4

Bateman, A., Birney, E., Durbin, R., Eddy, S. R., Howe, K. L., & Sonnhammer, E. L. (2000). The Pfam protein families database. *Nucleic Acids Research*, *28*, 263–266. doi:10.1093/nar/28.1.263

Baum, L. E., & Eagon, J. A. (1967). An inequality with applications to statistical estimation for probabilistic functions of Markov processes and to a model for ecology. *Bulletin of the American Mathematical Society*, *73*(3), 360–363. doi:10.1090/S0002-9904-1967-11751-8

Bean, J. C. (1994). Genetic algorithms and random keys for sequencing and optimization. *ORSA Journal on Computing*, *6*, 154–160. doi:10.1287/ijoc.6.2.154

Beckett, D. (2004). *RDF/XML syntax specification (revised).* W3C Recommendation 10th February 2004. Retrieved from http://www.w3.org/TR/rdf-syntax-grammar/

Bellotti, R., Carlo, F. D., Tangaro, S., Gargano, G., Maggipinto, G., & Castellano, M. (2006). A completely automated CAD system for mass detection in a large mammographic database. *Medical Physics*, *33*(8), 3066–3075. doi:10.1118/1.2214177

Belsley, D. A., Kuh, E., & Welsch, R. E. (1980). *Regression diagnostics: Identifying influential data and sources of collinearity*. New York, NY: Wiley.

Bemani, M., & Nikmehr, S. (2009). A novel wide-band microstrip Yagi-Uda array antenna for WLAN applications. *Progress in Electromagnetics Research B*, *16*, 389–406. doi:10.2528/PIERB09053101

Bendat, J., & Piersol, A. (1993). *Engineering applications of correlation and spectral analysis*. New York, NY: John Wiley and Sons.

Benign mass with regular shape. (n.d.). Retrieved December 21, 2011 from http://visualsonline.cancer.gov/

Bennett, C., Bernstein, E., Brassard, G., & Vazirani, U. (1997). Strengths and weaknesses of quantum computing. *SIAM Journal on Computing, 26*, 1510–1523. doi:10.1137/S0097539796300933

Benson, D. A., Karsch-Mizrachi, I., Lipman, D. J., Ostell, J., & Wheeler, D. L. (2006). GenBank. *Nucleic Acids Research, 34*, D16–D20. doi:10.1093/nar/gkj157

Berger, T. (2001). Agent-based spatial models applied to agriculture: a simulation tool for technology diffusion, resource use changes and policy analysis. *Agricultural Economics, 25*, 245–260. doi:10.1111/j.1574-0862.2001.tb00205.x

Bergstra, J., Casagrande, N., & Eck, D. (2005). *Two algorithms for timbre- and rhythm-based multi-resolution audio. Tech. Report, Music Information Retrieval Exchange*. MIREX.

Berk, J. B. (2000). Sorting out sorts. *The Journal of Finance, 55*(1), 407–427. doi:10.1111/0022-1082.00210

Berners-Lee, T., Hendler, J., & Lassila, O. (2001, May 17). The Semantic Web. *Scientific American*.

Bessis, N., Asimakopoulou, E., & Xhafa, F. (2011). A next generation emerging technologies roadmap for enabling collective computational intelligence in disaster management. *International Journal of Space-Based and Situational Computing, 1*(1), 76–85. doi:10.1504/IJSSC.2011.039109

Beyer, H.-G., & Schwefel, H.-P. (2002). Evolution strategies: A comprehensive introduction. *Natural Computing, 1*(1), 3–52. doi:10.1023/A:1015059928466

Bezdek, J. C., Keller, J., Krishnampuram, R., & Pal, N. R. (1999). *Fuzzy models and algorithms for pattern recognition and image processing*. Dordercht, The Netherlands: Kluwer Academic Publishers.

Billor, N., Hadi, A. S., & Velleman, F. (2000). BACON: Blocked adaptive computationally efficient outlier nominator. *Computational Statistics & Data Analysis, 34*, 279–298. doi:10.1016/S0167-9473(99)00101-2

Bitam, S., Batouche, M., & Talbi, E.-G. (2010). A survey on bee colony algorithms. *24th IEEE International Parallel and Distributed Processing Symposium, NIDISC Workshop,* Atlanta, Georgia, USA, (pp. 1-8).

Bittencourt, E. C., Silva, M., & Soares, E. (2009). A computational model for developing semantic web-based educational systems. *Knowledge-Based Systems, 22*, 302–315. doi:10.1016/j.knosys.2009.02.012

Blaisdell, B. (1989). Average values of a dissimilarity measure not requiring sequence alignment are twice the averages of conventional mismatch counts requiring sequence alignment for a computer-generated model system. *Journal of Molecular Evolution, 29*, 538–547. doi:10.1007/BF02602925

Blaisdell, B. E. (1986). A measure of the similarity of sets of sequences not requiring sequence alignment. *Proceedings of the National Acdemy of Sciences USA, 83*, 5155–5159. doi:10.1073/pnas.83.14.5155

Bleicher, A. (2010). Forgotten Soviet moon rover beams light back to Earth. *IEEE Spectrum,* August.

Boeringer, D. W., & Werner, D. H. (2006). Bezier representations for the multiobjective optimization of conformal array amplitude weights. *IEEE Transactions on Antennas and Propagation, 54*(7), 1964–1970. doi:10.1109/TAP.2006.877173

Bong, C. W. (2006). *Multiple objectives hybrid metaheuristic for spatial-based redistricting: The framework and algorithms*. Ph.D. Thesis, University Malaysia Sarawak.

Bong, C. W., & Mandava, R. (2010). Multiobjective optimization approaches in image segmentation – The directions and challenges. *International Journal of Advances in Soft Computnig Applications, 2*(1), 40–64.

Bouzeghoub, A., Defude, B., Ammour, S., Duitama, J. F., & Lecocq, C. (2004). A RDF description model for manipulating learning objects. *Proceedings International Conference on Advanced Learning Technologies, IV,* Joensuu, ICALT, (pp. 81-85).

Boylestad, R., Nashelsky, L., & Monssen, F. (2005). *Electronic devices and circuit theory*. Upper Saddle River, NJ: Prentice Hall.

Bozkurt, B., Ozturk, O., & Dutoit, T. (2003). Text design for TTS speech corpus building using a modified greedy selection. In *Proceedings of Eurospeech, 2003*, 277–280.

Brad, R. (2001). *License plate recognition system*. Computer Science Department, Lucian Blaga University, Sibiu, Romania. Retrieved from http://remus.ulbsibiu.ro/publications/papers/icics2001.pdf

Bradski, G. R. (1998). Computer vision face tracking for use in a perceptual user interface. *Intel Technology Journal, Q2*, 15.

Brazilian Society of Cardiology. (2003). *Guidelines for the interpretation of the resting electrocardiogram*. Brazilian Archives of Cardiology, Retrieved January 7, 2008, from http://publicacoes.cardiol.br/consenso/2003/8002/repouso.pdf

Breastcancer.org. (2011). Retrieved August 21, 2011 from http://www.breastcancer.org/

Breiman, L., Meisel, W., & Purcell, E. (1977). Variable kernel estimates of multivariate densities. *Technometrics*, *19*(2), 135–144.

Breunig, M., Kriegel, H. P., Ng, R., & Sander, J. L. O. F. (2000). Identifying density-based local outliers. In *Proceedings of the 2000 ACM SIGMOD International Conference on Management of Data* (pp. 93–104). New York, NY: ACM Press.

Brickley, D., & Guha, R. V. (2004). *RDF vocabulary description language 1.0: RDF schema*. W3C Recommendation 10th February 2004. Retrieved from http://www.w3.org/TR/rdf-schema/

Broumandnia, A., & Fathy, M. (2005, January). Application of pattern recognition for Farsi license plate recognition. *International Journal on Graphics, Vision and Image Processing*, *5*(2), 25–31.

Brown, S. J., & Goetzmann, W. N. (1997). Mutual fund styles. *Journal of Financial Economics*, *43*(3), 373–399. doi:10.1016/S0304-405X(96)00898-7

Brown, S. J., & Goetzmann, W. N. (2003). Hedge funds with style. *Journal of Portfolio Management*, *29*(2), 101–112. doi:10.3905/jpm.2003.319877

Brown, S. J., Lajbcygier, P., & Li, B. (2008). Going negative: What to do with negative book equity stocks? *Journal of Portfolio Management*, *35*(1), 98–102. doi:10.3905/JPM.2008.35.1.95

Brusilovsky, P. (1999). Adaptive and intelligent technologies for web-based education. In C. Rollinger & C. Peylo (Eds.) *Künstliche Intelligenz Special Issue on Intelligent Systems and Teleteaching, 4*, 19-25.

Brusilovsky, P., & Miller, P. (2001). Course delivery systems for the virtual university. In Tschang, F. T., & Della Senta, T. (Eds.), *Access to knowledge: New information technologies and the emergence of the virtual university* (pp. 167–206). Amsterdam, The Netherlands: Elsevier Science and International Association of Universities.

Bui, T., & Lee, J. (1999). An agent-based framework for building decision support systems. *Decision Support Systems, International Journal (Toronto, Ont.)*, *25*(3).

Burred, J. J. (2005). *A hierarchical music genre classifier based on user-defined taxonomies. Proceedings of Music Information Retrieval Evaluation Exchange*. MIREX.

Busing, R., & Mailly, D. (2004). Advances in spatial, Individual-based modelling of forrest dynamics. *Journal of Vegetation Science*, *15*, 831–842.

Buzolic, J., Mladineo, N., & Knezic, S. (2009). Decision support system for disaster communications in Dalmatia. *International Journal of Emergency Management*, *1*(2), 191–201. doi:10.1504/IJEM.2002.000520

Campanini, R., Dongiovanni, D., Iampieri, E., Lanconelli, N., Masotti, M., & Palermo, G. (2004). A novel featureless approach to mass detection in digital mammograms based on support vector machines. *Physics in Medicine and Biology*, *49*(6), 961–975. doi:10.1088/0031-9155/49/6/007

Campbell, J. Y., Hilscher, J. D., & Szilagyi, J. (2008). In search of distress risk. *The Journal of Finance*, *63*(6), 1467–1484. doi:10.1111/j.1540-6261.2008.01416.x

Cancer Australia. (2011). Retrieved August 22, 2011 from http://canceraustralia.nbocc.org.au/breast-cancer/home/home

Cao, A., Song, Q., & Yang, X. (2008). Robust information clustering incorporating spatial information for breast mass detection in digitized mammograms. *Computer Vision and Image Understanding, 109*(1), 86–96. doi:10.1016/j.cviu.2007.07.004

Cao, L., & Zheng, H. (2005). Distributed spectrum allocation via local bargaining. In *IEEE SECON 2005 Proceedings* (*Vol. 5*, pp. 119–127). China: IEEE Communications.

Carle, B., Vermeersch, F., & Palma, C. R. (2004). *Systems improving communication in case of a nuclear emergency.* International Community on Information Systems for Crisis Response Management (ISCRAM2004) Conference, 3–4 May 2004, Brussels, Belgium.

Carter, M. (2006). *Heart disease still the most likely reason you'll die.* CNN. Retrieved January 05, 2008, from http://edition.cnn.com/2006/HEALTH/10/30/heart.overview/index.html

Chamaani, S., Mirtaheri, S. A., & Abrishamian, M. S. (2011). Improvement of time and frequency domain performance of antipodal Vivaldi antenna using multi-objective particle swarm optimization. *IEEE Transactions on Antennas and Propagation, 59*(5), 1738–1742. doi:10.1109/TAP.2011.2122290

Chamaani, S., Mirtaheri, S. A., Teshnehlab, M., Shoorehdeli, M. A., & Seydi, V. (2008). Modified multi-objective particle swarm optimization for electromagnetic absorber design. *Progress in Electromagnetics Research-Pier, 79*, 353–366. doi:10.2528/PIER07101702

Chambers, J. M. (2008). *Software for data analysis – Programming with R.* New York, NY: Springer.

Chandel, A., Madathingal, M., Parate, A., Pant, H., Rajput, N., Ikbal, S., ... Verma, A. (2007). Sensei: Spoken language assessment for call center agents. *ASRU 2007.*

Chang, Y., & Yan, H. (2003). An effective multilevel thresholding approach using conditional probability entropy and genetic algorithm. In Jin, J. S., Eaqdes, P., Feng, D. D., & Yan, H. (Eds.), *Conferences in Research and Practice in Information Technology* (*Vol. 22*, p. 21).

Chan, K. C., & Chen, N. (1991). Structural and return characteristics of small and large firms. *The Journal of Finance, 46*(4), 1467–1484. doi:10.2307/2328867

Chatterjee, S., & Hadi, A. S. (1986). Influential observations, high leverage points, and outliers in regression. *Statistical Science, 1*, 379–416. doi:10.1214/ss/1177013622

Chatterjee, S., & Hadi, A. S. (1988). *Sensitivity analysis in linear regression.* New York, NY: Wiley.

Chatterjee, S., & Hadi, A. S. (2006). *Regression analysis by examples.* New York, NY: Wiley.

Chava, S., & Jarrow, R. A. (2004). Bankruptcy prediction with industry effects. *Review of Finance, 8*(4), 537–569. doi:10.1093/rof/8.4.537

Chen, J. C., Yao, K., & Hudson, R. E. (2002). Source localization and beamforming. *IEEE Signal Processing Magazine.*

Chen, L. J., Sun, T., Chen, B., Rajendran, V., & Gerla, M. (2004). A smart decision model for vertical handoff. *Proceedings of the 4th International Workshop on Wireless Internet and Re-configurability*, Athens, Greece.

Chen, C. A., & Cheng, D. K. (1975). Optimum element lengths for Yagi-Uda arrays. *IEEE Transactions on Antennas and Propagation, AP-23*(1), 8–15. doi:10.1109/TAP.1975.1141001

Cheng, D. K. (1991). Gain optimization for Yagi-Uda arrays. *IEEE Antennas and Propagation Magazine, 33*(3), 42–45. doi:10.1109/74.88220

Cheng, D. K., & Chen, C. A. (1973). Optimum element spacings for Yagi-Uda arrays. *IEEE Transactions on Antennas and Propagation, AP-21*(5), 615–623. doi:10.1109/TAP.1973.1140551

Cheng, H. D., & Cui, M. (2004). Mass lesion detection with a fuzzy neural network. *Pattern Recognition, 37*(6), 1189–1200. doi:10.1016/j.patcog.2003.11.002

Cheng, H. D., Jiang, X. H., Sun, Y., & Wang, J. (2001). Color image segmentation: Advances and prospects. *Pattern Recognition, 34*(12), 2259–2281. doi:10.1016/S0031-3203(00)00149-7

Cheng, H. D., Shi, X. J., Min, R., Hu, L. M., Cai, X. P., & Du, H. N. (2005). Approaches for automated detection and classification of masses in mammograms. *Pattern Recognition, 39*(4), 646–668. doi:10.1016/j.patcog.2005.07.006

Cheng, H., & Yang, S. (2011). Joint multicast routing and channel assignment in multi radio multichannel wireless mesh networks using intelligent computational methods. *International Journal of Applied Soft Computing*, *34*(2).

Chen, N.-S., Kinshuk, Wei, C.-W., & Yang, S.J.H. (2008). Designing a self-contained group area network for ubiquitous learning. *Journal of Educational Technology & Society*, *11*(2), 16–26.

Choo, H., Rogers, R. L., & Ling, H. (2005). Design of electrically small wire antennas using a Pareto genetic algorithm. *IEEE Transactions on Antennas and Propagation*, *53*(3), 1038–1046. doi:10.1109/TAP.2004.842404

Chopra, N., Spong, M. W., Ortega, R., & Barabanov, N. E. (2004). *Position and force tracking in bilateral teleoperation* (pp. 269–280). Advances in Communication Control Networks.

Chou, H. T., Hung, K. L., & Chen, C. Y. (2009). Utilization of a yagi antenna director array to synthesize a shaped radiation pattern for optimum coverage in wireless communications. *Journal of Electromagnetic Waves and Applications*, *23*(7), 851–861. doi:10.1163/156939309788355298

Chu-Yu, C., & Cheng-Ying, H. (2006). A simple and effective method for microstrip dual-band filters design. *IEEE Microwave and Wireless Components Letters*, *16*(5), 246–248. doi:10.1109/LMWC.2006.873584

Clarridge, J. E. (2004). Impact of 16S rRNA gene sequence analysis for identification of bacteria on clinical microbiology and infectious diseases. *Clinical Microbiology Reviews*, *17*, 840–862. doi:10.1128/CMR.17.4.840-862.2004

Clerc, M. (1999). The swarm and the queen: Towards a deterministic and adaptive particle swarm optimization. In *Proceedings of the 1999 IEEE Congress on Evolutionary Computation*, Washington DC, (pp. 1951–1957).

Cocea, M. (2006). *Assessment of motivation in online learning environments. Adaptive Hypermedia and Adaptive Web-based Systems, LNCS 4018*. Berlin, Germany: Springer-Verlag.

Coello Coello, C. A. (2006). Evolutionary multi-objective optimization: A historical view of the field. *IEEE Computational Intelligence Magazine*, February, 28-36.

Coello Coello, C. A. (1999). A comprehensive survey of evolutionary-based multiobjective optimization techniques. *Knowledge and Information Systems*, *1*(3), 129–156.

Coello Coello, C. A., Pulido, G. T., & Lechuga, M. S. (2004). Handling multiple objectives with particle swarm optimization. *IEEE Transactions on Evolutionary Computation*, *8*(3), 256–279. doi:10.1109/TEVC.2004.826067

Collier, N. (2004). *RePast: An extensible framework for agent-based simulation*. Paper presented at the Swarmfest.

Collins, R., Liu, Y., & Leordeanu, M. (2005). Online selection of discriminative tracking features. *IEEE Transactions on Pattern Analysis and Machine Intelligence*, *1*(27), 1631–1643. doi:10.1109/TPAMI.2005.205

Comaniciu, D., & Meer, P. (2002). Mean shift: A robust approach toward feature space analysis. *IEEE Transactions on Pattern Analysis and Machine Intelligence*, *5*(24), 603–619. doi:10.1109/34.1000236

Comaniciu, D., Ramesh, V., & Meer, P. (2003). Kernel-based object tracking. *IEEE Transactions on Pattern Analysis and Machine Intelligence*, *5*(25), 564–575. doi:10.1109/TPAMI.2003.1195991

Commission, P. (2002). *Impact of foot and mouth disease outbreak on Australia*. Canberra.

Coniam, D. (1999). Voice recognition software accuracy with second language speakers of English. *System*, *27*, 49–64. doi:10.1016/S0346-251X(98)00049-9

Conrad, J., Cooper, M., & Kaul, G. (2003). Value versus glamour. *The Journal of Finance*, *58*(5), 1969–1996. doi:10.1111/1540-6261.00594

Cook, R. D. (1977). Detection of influential observations in linear regression. *Technometrics*, *19*, 15–18. doi:10.2307/1268249

Cook, R. D. (1979). Influential observations in regression. *Journal of the American Statistical Association*, *74*, 169–174.

Cook, R. D., & Weisberg, S. (1982). *Residuals and influence in regression*. London, UK: Chapman and Hall.

Cristianini, N., & Taylor, J. S. (2000). *An introduction to support vector machines and other kernel-based learning methods*. New York, NY: Cambridge University Press.

Cristian, T. I. (2003). The particle swarm optimization algorithm: Convergence analysis and parameter selection. *Information Processing Letters*, *85*(6), 317–325. doi:10.1016/S0020-0190(02)00447-7

Culler, D., Estrin, D., & Srivastava, M. (2004). Overview of sensor networks. *Computer*, *37*(8). doi:10.1109/MC.2004.93

Daniel, K., & Titman, D. (2005). *Testing factor-model explanations of market anomalies*. Working Paper, Kellogg School of Management, Northwestern University.

Daniel, K., & Titman, D. (2006). Market reactions to tangible and intangible information. *The Journal of Finance*, *61*(4), 1605–1643. doi:10.1111/j.1540-6261.2006.00884.x

Das, S., Chowdhury, A., & Abraham, A. (2009). A bacterial evolutionary algorithm for automatic data clustering. *IEEE Congress on Evolutionary Computation, CEC 09*, (pp. 2403-2410).

Das, S., Abraham, A., & Konar, A. (2008). Automatic kernel clustering with multi-elitist particle swarm optimization algorithm. *Pattern Recognition Letters*, *29*, 688–699. doi:10.1016/j.patrec.2007.12.002

Das, S., Abraham, A., & Konar, A. (2008). Particle swarm optimization and differential evolution algorithms: Technical analysis, applications and hybridization perspectives. In Liu, Y. L., Sun, A. S., Lim, E. P. L., Loh, H. T. L., & Lu, W. F. L. (Eds.), *Studies in computational intelligence* (*Vol. 116*, pp. 1–38). doi:10.1007/978-3-540-78297-1_1

Das, S., & Konar, A. (2009). Automatic image pixel clustering with an improved differential evolution. *Applied Soft Computing*, *1*, 226–236. doi:10.1016/j.asoc.2007.12.008

David, W. C., & Joshua, D. K. (2003). *No free lunch and free leftovers theorems for multiobjective optimisation problems*. Paper presented at the 2nd International Conference on Evolutionary Multi-Criterion Optimization, EMO 03, Faro, Portugal.

Davies, P., Imon, A. H. M. R., & Ali, M. M. (2004). A conditional expectation method for improved residual estimation and outlier identification in linear regression. *International Journal of Statistical Sciences, Special issue*, 191 – 208.

Dayhoff, M. O., Schwartz, R. M., & Orcutt, B. C. (1978). A model of evolutionary change in proteins. *Atlas of protein sequence and structure,* Vol. 5, (pp. 345-351).

De Jong Van Coevorden, C. M., Garcia, S. G., Pantoja, M. F., Bretones, A. R., & Martin, R. G. (2005). Microstrip-patch array design using a multiobjective GA. *IEEE Antennas and Wireless Propagation Letters*, *4*(1), 100–103. doi:10.1109/LAWP.2005.845907

De Oliveira Martins, L., Braz Junior, G., Correa Silva, A., Cardoso de Paiva, A., & Gattass, M. (2009). Detection of masses in digital mammograms using k-means and support vector machine. *Electronic Letters on Computer Vision and Image Analysis*, *8*(2), 39–50.

Dean, M., Schreiber, G., van Harmelen, F., Hendler, J., Horrocks, I., & McGuinness, D. L. ... Stein, D. L. (2004). *OWL Web ontology language reference*. W3C Recommendation 10th February 2004. Retrieved from http://www.w3.org/TR/owl-ref/

Deb, K., Thiele, L., Laumanns, M., & Zitzler, E. (2005). Scalable test problems for evolutionary multiobjective optimization. In *Evolutionary Multiobjective Optimization* (pp. 105-145).

Deb, K. (2001). *Multi-objective optimization using evolutionary algorithms*. England: John Wiley and Sons, Ltd.

Deb, K. (2002). A fast elitist non-dominated sorting genetic algorithm for multiobjective optimization: NSGA II. *IEEE Transactions on Evolutionary Computation*, *5*(3), 115–148.

Deb, K., Pratap, A., Agarwal, S., & Meyarivan, T. (2002). A fast and elitist multiobjective genetic algorithm: NSGA-II. *IEEE Transactions on Evolutionary Computation*, *6*(2), 182–197. doi:10.1109/4235.996017

DeCarlo, D., & Metaxas, D. (2000). Optical flow constraints on deformable models with applications to face tracking. *International Journal of Computer Vision*, *2*(38), 99–127. doi:10.1023/A:1008122917811

Dede, M. I. C., & Tosunoglu, S. (2007). *Parallel position/force controller for teleoperation systems*. 5th IFAC Workshop on Technology Transfer in Developing Countries: Automation in Infrastructure Creation, DECOM-TT, Izmir, Turkey.

Deng, Y., Yang, Q., Lin, X., & Tang, X. (2007). Stereo correspondence with occlusion handling in a symmetric patch-based graph-cuts model. *IEEE Transactions on Pattern Analysis and Machine Intelligence*, *6*(29), 1086–1079.

Derwing, T. M., Munro, M. J., & Carbonaro, M. (2000). Does popular speech recognition software work with ESL speech? *TESOL Quarterly*, *34*(3), 592–603. doi:10.2307/3587748

Deutsch, D. (1985). Quantum theory, the Church-Turing principle and the universal quantum computer. *Proceedings of the Royal Society of London. Series A: Mathematical and Physical Sciences*, *400*, 97–117. doi:10.1098/rspa.1985.0070

Devedzic, V. (2006). *IASTED International Conference on Artificial Intelligence and Applications, part of the 24th Multi-Conference on Applied Informatics*, Innsbruck, Austria, February 13-16, 2006 IASTED/ACTA Press 2006.

Devedzic, V. (2004). Education and the Semantic Web. *International Journal of Artificial Intelligence in Education*, *14*(2), 39–65.

Dhawan, A. (2011). *Medical image analysis* (2nd ed.). Wiley-IEEE Press. doi:10.1002/9780470918548

Din, N. M., & Fisal, N. (2008). Fuzzy logic bandwidth prediction and policing in a DiffServ aware network. *Journal of Computers*, *3*, 18–23. doi:10.4304/jcp.3.5.18-23

Dirac, P. (1939). A new notation for quantum mechanics. *Proceedings of the Cambridge Philosophical Society*, *35*, (p. 416).

Djerou, L., Dehimi, H., Khelil, N., & Batouche, M. (2009). Automatic multilevel thresholding using binary particle swarm optimization for image segmentation. In the *Proceeding of the International Conference of Soft Computing and Pattern Recognition*, (pp. 67-71).

Djerou, L., Khelil, N., & Batouche, M. (2011). Numerical integration method based on particle swarm optimization. In Tan, Y. (Eds.), *Part I, LNCS 6728* (pp. 221–226). Berlin, Germany: Springer-Verlag. doi:10.1007/978-3-642-21515-5_26

Dong, S. L., Bullard, M. J., Meurer, D. P., Colman, I., Blitz, S., Holroyd, B. R., & Rowe, B. H. (2008). Emergency triage: Comparing a novel computer triage program with standard triage. *Academic Emergency Medicine*, *12*, 28. Retrieved from http://onlinelibrary.wiley.com/doi/10.1197/j.aem.2005.01.005/pdf

Dote, Y. (1998). Soft computing (immune networks) in artificial intelligence. *Proceedings of IEEE International Symposium on Industrial Electronics*, ISIE'98, Vol. 1, (pp. 1 –7).

Draper, N. R., & John, J. A. (1981). Influential observations and outliers in regression. *Technometrics*, *32*, 21–26.

D'Souza, R., Marino, S., & Kirschner, D. (2009, March). *Data parallel algorithms for agent-based model simulation of tuberculosis on graphics processing units.* Paper presented at the Agent-Directed Simulation Symposium.

Duch, W. (2007). What is computational intelligence and where is it going? In W. Duch, & J. Mandziuk (Eds.), *Challenges for Computational Intelligence, volume 63 of Studies in Computational Intelligence,* 2007, (pp. 1–13). Berlin, Germany: Springer.

Duda, R. O., & Hart, P. E. (1973). *Pattern classification and scene analysis*. Chichester, UK: John Wiley and Sons.

Dunham, M. H., Meng, Y., & Huang, J. (2004). *Extensible Markov model* (pp. 371–374).

Durbin, R. (1998). *Biological sequence analysis: Probabilistic models of proteins and nucleic acids*. Cambridge University Press. doi:10.1017/CBO9780511790492

Eberhart, R. C., & Kennedy, J. (1995). A new optimizer using particles swarm theory. In *Sixth International Symposium on Micro Machine and Human Science*, Nagoya, Japan, (pp. 39–43).

Eberhart, R. C., & Shi, Y. (1998). *Parameter selection in particle swarm optimization.*

Eberhart, R. C. (1996). *Computational intelligence PC tools*. Boston, MA: Academic Press Professional.

Eddy, S. R. (1998). Profile hidden Markov models. *Bioinformatics (Oxford, England)*, *14*, 755–763. doi:10.1093/bioinformatics/14.9.755

Educational Modelling Language (EML). (n.d.). *Homepage*. Retrieved from http://eml.ou.nl/eml-ou-nl.htm

Edutella Project. (n.d.). *Homepage*. Retrieved from http://edutella.jxta.org/

Ellison, P., Ash, G., & McDonald, C. (1998). An expert system for the management of Botrytis cinerea in Australian vineyards. *Agricultural Systems*, *56*, 185–207. doi:10.1016/S0308-521X(97)00035-8

Elliston, L., & Beare, S. (2006). Managing agricultural pest and disease incursions: An application of agent-based modelling. In Perez, P., & Batten, D. (Eds.), *Complex science for a complex world*. Canberra, Australia: ANU E-press.

Elmusrati, M., & Hasu, V. (2007). Random switched beamforming for uplink wireless sensor Networks. *IEEE 65th Vehicular Technology Conference VTC2007-Spring*, 22-25 April 2007 (pp. 3150 – 3154).

Eltonsy, N. H., Tourassi, G. D., & Elmaghraby, A. S. (2007). A concentric morphology model for the detection of masses in mammography. *IEEE Transactions on Medical Imaging*, *26*(6), 880–889. doi:10.1109/TMI.2007.895460

English Across Taiwan (EAT). (n.d.). Retrieved from http://www.aclclp.org.tw/use_mat.php#eat

Erdem, C. E., Tekalp, A. M., & Sankur, B. (2003). Video object tracking with feedback of performance measures. *IEEE Transactions on Circuits and Systems for Video Technology*, *4*(13), 310–324. doi:10.1109/TCSVT.2003.811361

Eskenazi, M. (1996). Detection of foreign speakers' pronunciation errors for second language training - preliminary results. In *Proceedings International Conference on Spoken Language Processing*, (pp. 1465-1468). Philadelphia, USA

Eugster, M. J. A., Knaus, J., Porzelius, C., Schmidberger, M., & Vicedo, E. (2011). Hands-on tutorial for parallel computing with R. *Computational Statistics*, *26*, 219–239. doi:10.1007/s00180-010-0206-4

European Union. (2010). *Reinforcing the European Union's disaster response capacity*. Retrieved on 12, January, 2012, from http://ec.europa.eu/governance/impact/planned_ia/docs/28_echo_eu_disaster_response_capacity_en.pdf

Example of fuzzy image processing (n.d.). Retrieved September 4, 2011 from http://pami.uwaterloo.ca/tizhoosh/images/steps.gif

Faceli, K., De-Carvalho, A. C. P. L. F., & De-Souto, M. C. P. (2007). Multi-objective clustering ensemble with prior knowledge. *Lecture Notes in Computer Science*, ▪▪▪, 4643.

Fama, E. F., & French, K. R. (1988). Dividend yields and expected stock returns. *Journal of Financial Economics*, *33*(1), 3–56. doi:10.1016/0304-405X(93)90023-5

Fama, E. F., & French, K. R. (1993). Common risk factors in the returns on stocks and bonds. *Journal of Financial Economics*, *33*(1), 3–56. doi:10.1016/0304-405X(93)90023-5

Fama, E. F., & French, K. R. (1995). Size and book-to-market sectors in earnings and returns. *The Journal of Finance*, *50*(1), 131–155. doi:10.2307/2329241

Fama, E. F., & French, K. R. (1996). Multifactor explanation of asset pricing anomalies. *The Journal of Finance*, *51*(1), 55–84. doi:10.2307/2329302

Fama, E. F., & French, K. R. (2001). Disappearing dividends: Changing firm characteristics or lower propensity to pay? *Journal of Applied Corporate Finance*, *14*(1), 67–79. doi:10.1111/j.1745-6622.2001.tb00321.x

Fang, L., Song-Yu, Z., & Lin-Jing, H. (2009, December). *Image extraction and segment arithmetic of license plate recognition.* 2nd International Conference on Power Electronics and Intelligent Transportation System, Shenzhen, China.

Fayed, G. (2006). E-learning model based on Semantic Web technology. *International Journal of Computing & Information Sciences*, *4*(2), 63–71.

FEKO. (2003). *User's manunal, FEKO suite 5.2.* Retrieved from www.feko.info

Feng, H., Shu, Y., Wang, S., & Ma, M. (2006). SVM-based models for predicting WLAN traffic. *IEEE International Conference on Communications* (pp. 597-602).

Finn, R. D., Tate, J., Mistry, J., Coggill, P. C., Sammut, S. J., & Hotz, H.-R. (2008). The Pfam protein families database. *Nucleic Acids Research*, *36*, D281–D288. doi:10.1093/nar/gkm960

Fitzgerald, J., & Dennis, A. (2010). *Fundamentals of business data communications* (10th ed.). John Wiley & Sons, Inc.

Fogel, D. B. (1999). *Evolutionary computation: Toward a new philosophy of machine intelligence*. Piscataway, NJ: Wiley-IEEE.

Fogel, D. B. (2000a). *Introduction to evolutionary computation. Evolutionary Computation 1: Basic Algorithms and Operators* (pp. 1–3). Bristol, UK: Institute of Physics Publishing.

Fogel, D. B. (2000b). *Principles of evolutionary computation. Evolutionary Computation 1: Basic Algorithms and Operators* (pp. 23–26). Bristol, UK: Institute of Physics Publishing.

Fogel, D. B., & Corne, D. W. (Eds.). (2003). *Evolutionary computation in bioinformatics*. San Mateo, CA: Morgan Kaufmann.

Fogel, G. B. (2008). Computational intelligence approaches for pattern discovery in biological systems. *Briefings in Bioinformatics*, *9*(4), 307–316. doi:10.1093/bib/bbn021

Fogel, G. B., Corne, D. W., & Pan, Y. (Eds.). (2007). *Computational intelligence in bioinformatics*. Piscataway, NJ: Wiley-IEEE Press. doi:10.1002/9780470199091

Forgy, E. W. (1965). Cluster analysis of multivariate data: Efficiency versus interpretability of classification. *Biometrics*, *21*, 768–769.

Fourie, P. C., & Groenwold, A. A. (2000). Particle swarms in size and shape optimization. In *Proceedings of the International Workshop on Multi-disciplinary Design Optimization*, Pretoria, South Africa, August 7-10, (pp. 97–106).

Fourie, P. C., & Groenwold, A. A. (2001). Particle swarms in topology optimization. In *Extended Abstracts of the Fourth World Congress of Structural and Multidisciplinary Optimization*, Dalian, China, June 4-8, (pp. 52–53).

Fox, J. (1993). Regression diagnostics. In Beck, M. S. L. (Ed.), *Regression analysis* (pp. 245–334). London, UK: Sage Publications.

Franco, H., Abrash, V., Precoda, K., Bratt, H., Rao, R., & Butzberger, J. (2000). The SRI EduSpeak system: Recognition and pronunciation scoring for language learning. In *Proceedings InSTILL 2000*, (pp. 123-128). Dundee, Scotland.

Frank, Y. S. (2010). *Image processing and pattern recognition: fundamentals and techniques*. Wiley-IEEE Press. Retrieved from http://www.ius.edu.ba/rkoker/cs415/0470404612.pdf

Freiherr, G. (2011, March 22). Tomosynthesis: A new era in breast imaging. *Medscape*. Retrieved October 12, 2011 from http://www.medscape.com

Frigo, L. B., Cardoso, J., & Bittencourt, G. (2005). *Adaptive interaction in intelligent tutoring systems. Proceedings Methods/ Techniques in Web Based Education Systems, XXVI* (pp. 33–38). Salzburg: CIAH.

Funk, P., Gerber, C., Lind, J., & Schillo, M. (1998). *SIF: An agent-based simulation toolbox using the EMS paradigm*. Paper presented at the 3rd International Congress of the Federation of EUROpean SIMulation Societies (EuroSim).

Furht, B., & Escalante, A. (2010). Cloud computing fundamentals. In *Handbook of cloud computing*. Springer. doi:10.1007/978-1-4419-6524-0_1

Fuzzy image processing steps (n.d.). Retrieved September 4, 2011 from http://pami.uwaterloo.ca/tizhoosh/images/fuzzbv.gif

Gadomski, A. M., Bologna, S., & Costanzo, G. D. (2001). Towards intelligent decision support systems for emergency managers: The IDA approach. *International journal of Risk Assessment and Management, 2*, 224-242.

Gentleman, R. C. (2009). *R programming for bioinformatics*. Boca Raton, FL: Chapman & Hall/CRC.

Gentleman, R. C., Carey, V. J., Bates, D. M., Bolstad, B., Dettling, M., & Dudoit, S. (2004). Bioconductor: Open software development for computational biology and bioinformatics. *Genome Biology, 5*(10), R80. Goddard, M. E., & Hayes, B. J. (207). Genomic selection. *Journal of Animal Breeding and Genetics*, *124*(6), 323–330.

Gibbens, J. G., Sharpe, C. E., Wilesmith, J. W., Mansley, L. M., Michaelopolous, E., & Ryan, J. B. (2001). Descrriptive epidemiology of the 2001 foot-and-mouth disease epidemic in Great Britain: The first five months. *The Veterinary Record*, *149*, 729–743.

Godara, L. C. (1997). Application of antenna arrays to mobile communications, Part II: Beam-forming and directional-of–arrival considerations. *Proceedings of the IEEE*, *85*(8), 1195–1245. doi:10.1109/5.622504

Goddeke, D. (2005). *GPGPU - Basic math tutorial*. Retrieved from http://www.mathematik.uni-dortmund.de/~goeddeke

Goldberger, A. L., Amaral, L., Glass, L., Hausdorff, J. M., Ivanov, P. C., & Mark, R. G. … Stanley, H. E. (2000). *PhysioBank, PhysioToolkit, and PhysioNet: Components of a new research resource for complex physiologic signals*. Retrieved March 10, 2009, from http://physionet.org/physiobank/database/edb/

Gonzalez, R. C., & Woods, R. E. (2007). *Digital image processing* (3rd ed.). Prentice-Hall.

Google App Engine. (n.d.). Retrieved on January 12, 2012, from http://code.google.com/appengine/

Google. (2011). *Google app engine*. Retrieved September 24, 2011, from http://code.google.com/appengine/

Goscinski, A., & Brock, M. (2010). Toward dynamic and attribute based publication, discovery and selection for cloud computing. *Future Generation Computer Systems*, *26*, 947–970. doi:10.1016/j.future.2010.03.009

Goudos, S. K., Zaharis, Z. D., Baltzis, K. B., Hilas, C. S., & Sahalos, J. N. (2009, June). *A comparative study of particle swarm optimization and differential evolution on radar absorbing materials design for EMC applications*. Paper presented at the International Symposium on Electromagnetic Compatibility - EMC Europe, 2009

Goudos, S. K., & Sahalos, J. N. (2006). Microwave absorber optimal design using multi-objective particle swarm optimization. *Microwave and Optical Technology Letters*, *48*(8), 1553–1558. doi:10.1002/mop.21727

Goudos, S. K., & Sahalos, J. N. (2010). Pareto optimal microwave filter design using multiobjective differential evolution. *IEEE Transactions on Antennas and Propagation*, *58*(1), 132–144. doi:10.1109/TAP.2009.2032100

Goudos, S. K., Siakavara, K., Vafiadis, E. E., & Sahalos, J. N. (2010). Pareto optimal Yagi-Uda antenna design using multi-objective differential evolution. *Progress in Electromagnetics Research*, *105*, 231–251. doi:10.2528/PIER10052302

Goudos, S. K., Zaharis, Z. D., Kampitaki, D. G., Rekanos, I. T., & Hilas, C. S. (2009). Pareto optimal design of dual-band base station antenna arrays using multi-objective particle swarm optimization with fitness sharing. *IEEE Transactions on Magnetics*, *45*(3), 1522–1525. doi:10.1109/TMAG.2009.2012695

Goudos, S. K., Zaharis, Z. D., Salazar-Lechuga, M., Lazaridis, P. I., & Gallion, P. B. (2007). Dielectric filter optimal design suitable for microwave communications by using multiobjective evolutionary algorithms. *Microwave and Optical Technology Letters*, *49*(10), 2324–2329. doi:10.1002/mop.22755

Graf, S., & List, B. (2005). An evaluation of open source e-learning platforms stressing adaptation issues. In P. Goodyear, D. G. Sampson, D. J.-T. Yang, Kinshuk, T. Okamoto, R. Hartley & N.-S. Chen (Eds.), *Proceedings of the 5th International Conference on Advanced Learning Technologies* (pp. 163-165). Los Alamitos, NM: IEEE Computer Science.

Graf, S., Yang, G., & Liu, T. C., & Kinshuk. (2009). Automatic, global and dynamic student modeling in a ubiquitous learning environment. *International Journal on Knowledge Management and E-Learning*, *1*(1), 18–35.

Grant, J., & Beckett, D. (2004). *RDF test cases*. W3C Recommendation 10th February 2004. Retrieved from http://www.w3.org/TR/rdf-testcases/

Graves, R. J. (2004). *Key technologies for emergency response*. International Community on Information Systems for Crisis Response (ICSCRAM2004) Conference, 3–4 May 2004, Brussels, Belgium.

Grecu, D., & Gonsalves, P. (2000). *Agent-based environment for UCAV mission planning and execution*. Paper presented at the AIAA Guidance, Navigation, and Control Conference and Exhibit.

Gropp, W., Lusk, E., & Skjellum, A. (1999). *Using MPI* (2nd ed.). MIT Press.

Grover, L. K. (1996). A fast quantum mechanical algorithm for database search. *Proceedings of the ACM Symposium on the Theory of Computing*, (pp. 212-219).

Guaus, E., & Herrera, P. (2007). *A basic system for music genre classification*. International Conference on Music Information Retrieval.

Guliato, D., Rangayyan, R. M., Carnielli, W. A., Zuffo, J. A., & Desautels, J. E. (2003). Segmentation of breast tumors in mammograms using fuzzy sets. *Journal of Electronic Imaging*, *12*(3), 369–378. doi:10.1117/1.1579017

Gustafson, D., & Kessel, W. (1979). Fuzzy clustering with a fuzzy covariance matrix. *Hemometrics and Intelligent Laboratory Systems - IEEE*, (pp. 761-766).

Gutierrez-Estrada, J. C., De Pedro Sanz, E., Lopez-Luque, R., & Pulido-Calvo, I. (2005). SEDPA, an expert system for disease diagnosis in eel rearing systems. *Aquacultural Engineering*, *33*, 110–125. doi:10.1016/j.aquaeng.2004.12.003

Guturu, P. (2007). *Computational intelligence in multimedia networking and communications-Trends and future directions. Computational Intelligence in Multimedia Processing: Recent Advances in the series 'Studies in Computational Intelligence*. Heidelberg, Germany: Springer Verlag.

Hadi, A. S. (1992). A new measure of overall potential influence in linear regression. *Computational Statistics & Data Analysis*, *14*, 1–27. doi:10.1016/0167-9473(92)90078-T

Hadi, A. S., & Simonoff, J. S. (1993). Procedures for the identification of outliers. *Journal of the American Statistical Association*, *88*, 1264–1272.

Halkidi, M., Batistakis, Y., & Vazirgiannis, M. (2001). On clustering validation techniques. *Journal of Intelligent Information Systems*, *17*(2-3), 107–145. doi:10.1023/A:1012801612483

Hall, M., Frank, E., Holmes, G., Pfahringer, B., & Reutemann, I. (2009). The WEKA data mining software: An update. *SIGKDD Explorations*, *11*(1). doi:10.1145/1656274.1656278

Hamada, H., Miki, S., & Nakatsu, R. (1993). Automatic evaluation of English pronunciation based on speech recognition techniques. *Transactions of the IEICE of Japan. E (Norwalk, Conn.)*, *76-D*(3), 352–359.

Hamer, H., Schindler, K., Koller-Meier, E., & Van Gool, L. (2009). Tracking a hand manipulating an object. *12th International Conference Computer Vision*, (pp. 1475-1482).

Hamerly, G. (2003). *Learning structure and concepts in data using data clustering*. Unpublished doctoral dissertation, University of California, San Diego.

Hammouche, K., Diaf, M., & Siarry, P. (2008). A multilevel automatic thresholding method based on a genetic algorithm for a fast image segmentation. *Journal of Computer Vision and Image Understanding*, *109*(2), 163–175. doi:10.1016/j.cviu.2007.09.001

Hammouche, K., Diaf, M., & Siarry, P. (2010). A comparative study of various meta-heuristic techniques applied to the multilevel thresholding problem. *Journal of Engineering Applications of Artificial Intelligence*, *23*(5), 676–688. doi:10.1016/j.engappai.2009.09.011

Hampel, F. R., Ronchetti, E. M., Rousseeuw, P. J., & Stahel, W. A. (1986). *Robust statistics: The approach based on influence function*. New York, NY: Wiley.

Hamza, A., & Elghoneimy, M. (2010). On the effectiveness of using genetic algorithm for spectrum allocation in cognitive radio networks. In *High-Capacity Optical Networks and Enabling Technologies (HONET), 2010* (pp. 183–189). Cairo, Egypt: IEEE. doi:10.1109/HONET.2010.5715770

Han, B., & Davis, L. (2004) Object tracking by adaptive feature extraction. *Proceedings International Conference on Image Processing (ICIP)*, (Vol. 3, pp. 638–644).

Han, X., Wang, L., Shi, X., & Liang, Y. (2008). *SOM2W and RBF neural network-based hybrid models and their applications to new share pricing*. Paper presented at the meeting of the IEEE International Conference on Natural Computation, Washington, DC.

Handl, J., & Knowles, J. (2007). An evolutionary approach to multiobjective clustering. *IEEE Transactions on Evolutionary Computation*, *11*, 56–76. doi:10.1109/TEVC.2006.877146

Han, Y., & Shi, P. (2007). An improved ant colony algorithm for fuzzy clustering in image segmentation. *Neurocomputing*, *70*(4-6), 665–671. doi:10.1016/j.neucom.2006.10.022

Happold, J., Garner, G., Miron, D., Sajeev, A. S. M., Kwan, P., & Welch, M. (2010). *Towards a national livestock disease model*. F. F. Australian Dept. of Agriculture.

Hartigan, J. A. (1975). *Clustering algorithms*. New York, NY: John Wiley and Sons.

Harvey, N., Luke, R., Keller, J. M., & Anderson, D. (2008). Speedup of fuzzy logic through stream processing on graphics processing units. *Evolutionary Computation*: *IEEE World Congress on Computational Intelligence*, (pp. 3809-3815).

Hassanien, A. E. (2007). Fuzzy rough sets hybrid scheme for breast cancer detection. *Image and Vision Computing*, *25*(2), 172–183. doi:10.1016/j.imavis.2006.01.026

Hayes, P. (2004). *RDF semantics*. W3C Recommendation 10th February 2004. Retrieved from http://www.w3.org/TR/rdf-mt/

Heflin, J. (2004). *Web ontology language (OWL) use cases and requirements*. W3C Recommendation 10th February 2004. Retrieved from http://www.w3.org/TR/webont-req/

Henikoff, S., & Henikoff, J. G. (1992). Amino acid substitution matrices from protein blocks. *Proceedings of the National Academy of Sciences of the United States of America*, *89*, 10915–10919. doi:10.1073/pnas.89.22.10915

Hernandez, J. Z., & Serrano, J. M. (2001). Knowledge-based models for emergency management systems. *Expert Systems with Applications*, *20*, 173–186. doi:10.1016/S0957-4174(00)00057-9

Heyes, B. (2008). Cloud computing as software migrates from local PCs to distant Internet servers, users and developers alike go along for the ride. *Communications of the ACM*, *51*(7), 9–11.

Higgins, S. I., & Richardson, D. M. (1995). A review of models of alien plant spread. *Ecological Modelling*, *87*, 249–265. doi:10.1016/0304-3800(95)00022-4

Hiller, S., Rooney, E., Laver, J., & Jack, M. (1993). SPELL: An automated system for computer-aided pronunciation teaching. *Speech Communication*, *13*, 463–473. doi:10.1016/0167-6393(93)90045-M

Hirche, S. (2005). *Haptic telepresence in packet switched communication networks*. PhD thesis, TU-Munich, Germany.

Hoaglin, D. C., & Welsch, R. E. (1978). The hat matrix in regression and ANOVA. *The American Statistician*, *32*, 17–22.

Hocking, R. R., & Pendleton, O. J. (1983). The regression dilemma. *Communications in Statistics Theory and Methods*, *12*, 497–527. doi:10.1080/03610928308828477

Holland, J. H. (1975). *Adaptation in natural and artificial systems*. Ann Arbor, MI: University of Michigan Press.

Hoorfar, A., Zhu, J., & Nelatury, S. (2003). Electromagnetic optimization using a mixed-parameter self-adaptive evolutionary algorithm. *Microwave and Optical Technology Letters*, *39*(4), 267–271. doi:10.1002/mop.11187

Horng, M. H. (2009). A multilevel image thresholding using the honey bee mating optimization. *Journal of Applied Mathematics and Computation*, *215*(9), 3302–3310. doi:10.1016/j.amc.2009.10.018

Hosmer, D. W., & Lemeshow, S. (2000). *Applied logistic regression*. New York, NY: Wiley. doi:10.1002/0471722146

Hosung, C., Hao, L., & Liang, C. S. (2008). On a class of planar absorbers with periodic square resistive patches. *IEEE Transactions on Antennas and Propagation*, *56*(7), 2127–2130. doi:10.1109/TAP.2008.924766

Howard, R., Kiviniemi, A., & Samuelson, O. (2002). *The latest developments in communications and e-commerce IT barometer in 3 Nordic countries*. CIB w87 Conference, 12–14 June 2002, Aarhus School of Architecture. International Council for Research and Innovation in Building and Construction.

Hruschka, E. R., Campello, R. J. G. B., Freitas, A. A., & de Carvalho, A. C. P. L. F. (2009). A survey of evolutionary algorithms for clustering. *IEEE Transactions on Systems, Man, and Cybernetics, Part C: Applications and Reviews*, *39*(2), 133-155. ISSN 1094-6977

Hsu, Y., & Chen, A. (2008). *Clustering time series data by SOM for the optimal hedge ratio estimation.* Paper presented at the meeting of the IEEE International Conference on Convergence and Hybrid Information Technology, Busan, Korea.

http://pastel.archives-ouvertes.fr/docs/00/50/06/02/PDF/PhD_GP.pdf

Huang, T., & Sanagavarapu Mohan, A. (March 2007). A microparticle swarm optimizer for the reconstruction of microwave images. *IEEE Transactions on Antennas and Propagation, 55*(3 I), 568-576.

Huang, J., Berry, R., & Honig, M. (2006). Auction-based spectrum sharing. *Mobile Networks and Applications, 11*(3), 405–418. doi:10.1007/s11036-006-5192-y

Huang, K. (2002). A synergistic automatic clustering technique (Syneract) for multispectral image analysis. *Photogrammetric Engineering and Remote Sensing, 1*(1), 33–40.

Huber, P. J. (1981). *Robust statistics.* New York, NY: Wiley.

Human female breast (n.d.). Retrieved December 21, 2011 from http://visualsonline.cancer.gov/

Hupse, R., & Karssemeijer, N. (2009). Use of normal tissue context in computer-aided detection of masses in mammograms. *IEEE Transactions on Medical Imaging, 28*(12), 2033–2041. doi:10.1109/TMI.2009.2028611

Ian, S., & Simões, M. (2007). *Controle e Modelagem Fuzzy.* São Paulo, Brazil: Editora Edgard Blucher Ltda.

Ibrahim, Z., Dimitrova, V., & Boyle, R. (2005). A schema-based pedagogical agent to support children's conceptual understanding. *Proceedings International Conference on Artificial Intelligence in Education,* V, Amsterdam, AIED, (pp. 51-58).

Imon, A. H. M. R. (2005). Identifying multiple influential observations in linear regression. *Journal of Applied Statistics, 32,* 73–90.

Imon, A. H. M. R. (2006). Identification of high leverage points in logistic regression. *Pakistan Journal of Statistics, 22,* 147–156.

Imon, A. H. M. R., & Hadi, A. S. (2008). Identification of multiple outliers in logistic regression. *Communications in Statistics Theory and Methods, 37,* 1967–1709. doi:10.1080/03610920701826161

IMS Global Learning Consortium. (n.d.). *Homepage.* Retrieved from http://www.imsglobal.org/

Islam, M., Ahmadi, M., & Sid-Ahmed, M. (2010). Computer-aided detection and classification of masses in digitized mammograms using artificial neural network. In Tan, Y., Shi, Y., & Tan, K. (Eds.), *Advances in swarm intelligence* (pp. 327–334). doi:10.1007/978-3-642-13498-2_43

ISO. (2011). *ISO 8402:1994: Quality management and quality assurance.* Retrieved September 24, 2011, from http://www.iso.org/iso/ iso_catalogue/catalogue_tc/catalogue_detail.htm?csnumber=20115/

Isogai, M., Mizuno, H., & Mano, K. (2005). Recording script design for corpus-based TTS system based on coverage of various phonetic elements. In *Proceedings of ICASSP 2005.*

Jaffe, J., Keim, D. B., & Westerfield, R. (1989). Earnings yields, market values, and stock returns. *The Journal of Finance, 44*(1), 135–148. doi:10.2307/2328279

Jager, F., Moody, G., & Mark, R. (1998). Detection of transient ST segment episodes during ambulatory ECG monitoring. *Computers and Biomedical Research, an International Journal, 31,* 305–322. doi:10.1006/cbmr.1998.1483

Jain, A. K., Murty, M. N., & Flynn, P. J. (1999). Data clustering: A review. *ACM Computing Surveys, 31*(3), 264–323. doi:10.1145/331499.331504

Jaques, P. A., & Viccari, R. M. (2006). Considering student's emotions in computer-mediated learning environments. In Ma, Z. (Ed.), *Web-based intelligent-learning systems: Technologies and applications* (pp. 122–138). Hershey, PA: Information Science Publishing.

Jevtic, N. (2001). *Interactive tutorial on neural networks.* Retrieved from http://sydney.edu.au/engineering/it/~irena/ai01/nn/som.html

Jewajinda, Y., & Chongstitvatana, P. (2010). FPGA-based online-learning using parallel genetic algorithm and neural network for ECG signal classification. *Seventh International Conference on Electrical Engineering/Electronics, Computer, Telecommunications and Information Technology (ECTI-CON),* (pp. 1050-1054).

Jeyakar, J., Babu, R. V., & Ramakrishnan, K. R. (2008). Robust object tracking with background-weighted local kernels. *Journal of Computer Vision and Image Understanding, 3*(112), 296–309. doi:10.1016/j.cviu.2008.05.005

Ji, H., & Grishman, R. (2006). Data selection in semi-supervised learning for name tagging. In *Proceedings of ACL 06 Workshop on Information Extraction Beyond Document*, Sydney, Australia.

Jia, W., He, X., & Piccardi, M. (2004). Automatic license plate recognition: A review. *Proceedings of International Conference on Imaging Science, Systems and Technology* (pp. 43-49). Las Vegas, Nevada.

Jiang, L., Cui, J., Shi, L., & Li, X. (2009). Pareto optimal design of multilayer microwave absorbers for wide-angle incidence using genetic algorithms. *IET Microwaves Antennas & Propagation, 3*(4), 572–579. doi:10.1049/iet-map.2008.0059

Jiang, S., Fang, L., & Huang, X. (2009). An idea of special cloud computing in forest pests' control. *Lecture Notes in Computer Science, 5931*, 615–620. doi:10.1007/978-3-642-10665-1_61

Jones, E. A., & Joines, W. T. (1997). Design of yagi-uda antennas using genetic algorithms. *IEEE Transactions on Antennas and Propagation, 45*(9), 1386–1392. doi:10.1109/8.623128

Jones, O., Maillardet, R., & Robinson, A. (2009). *Introduction to scientific programming and simulation using R.* Boca Raton, FL: Chapman & Hall/CRC.

Kalikow, D. N., & Swets, J. A. (1972). Experiments with computer-controlled displays in second-language learning. *IEEE Transactions on Audio and Electroacoustics, 20*, 23–28. doi:10.1109/TAU.1972.1162353

Kallergi, M. (2005). Evaluation strategies for medical-image analysis and processing methodologies. In Costaridou, L. (Ed.), *Medical image analysis methods*. doi:10.1201/9780203500453.ch12

Kapur, J. N., Sahoo, P. K., & Wong, A. K. C. (1985). A new method for gray-level picture thresholding using the entropy of the histogram. *Journal of Computer Vision Graphics Image Processing, 29*, 273–285. doi:10.1016/0734-189X(85)90125-2

Karampiperis, P., & Sampson, D. (2004). Adaptive instructional planning using ontologies. In *Proceedings International Conference on Advanced Learning Technologies, IV*, Joensuu, ICALT, (pp. 126-130).

Karlin, S., & Altschul, S. F. (1990). Methods for assessing the statistical significance of molecular sequence features by using general scoring schemes. *Proceedings of the National Academy of Sciences of the United States of America, 87*, 2264–2268. doi:10.1073/pnas.87.6.2264

Kasiolas, A., & Makrakis, D. (1999). A fuzzy-based traffic controller for high-speed ATM networks using realistic traffic models. *IEEE Transactions on Multimedia Computing and Systems, 2*, 389–394.

Katari, V., Satapathy, S. C., Murthy, J., & Reddy, P. P. (2007). Hybridized improved genetic algorithm with variable length chromosome for image clustering. In *International Journal of Computer Science and Network Security, 7*(11), 21–131.

Kayalvizhi, R., & Sathya, P. D. (2011). Optimal segmentation of brain MRI based on adaptive bacterial foraging algorithm. *Journal of Neurocomputing, 74*, 2299–2313. doi:10.1016/j.neucom.2011.03.010

Kennedy, J. (1998). The behaviour of particles. *Proceedings of the 7th Annual Conference on Evolutionary Programming,* (pp.581–587).

Kennedy, J., & Eberhart, R. (1995). Particle swarm optimization. *Proceedings of IEEE International Conference on Neural Networks*, Perth, Australia, Vol. 4, (pp. 1942-1948).

Kennedy, J., & Eberhart, R. (1997). A discrete binary version of the particle swarm algorithm. *Proceedings of the Conference on Systems, Man, and Cybernetics*, (pp. 4104-4109).

Kennedy, J., & Eberhart, R. C. (1997). *Discrete binary version of the particle swarm algorithm.* Paper presented at the IEEE International Conference on Systems, Man and Cybernetics.

Kennedy, J., & Eberhart, R. C. (Eds.). (2001). *Swarm intelligence*. San Francisco, CA: Morgan Kaufmann Publishers.

Kerlikowske, K., Ichikawa, L., Miglioretti, D., Buist, D., Vacek, P., & Smith-Bindman, R. (2007). Longitudinal measurement of clinical mammographic breast density to improve estimation of breast cancer risk. *Journal of the National Cancer Institute*, *99*(5), 386–395. doi:10.1093/jnci/djk066

Khan, Z. H. Genon-Catalot, D., & Thiriet, J. M. (2011). Drive-by-wireless teleoperation with network QoS adaptation. *International Journal of Advanced Engineering Sciences and Technology*, *2*(2). ISSN: 2230-7818

Khan, Z. H., Genon-Catalot, D., & Thiriet, J. M. (2010). A co-design approach for bilateral teleoperation over hybrid networks. *18th Mediterranean Conference on Control and Automation (MED)*, Marakesh, Morroco

Khelil N., & al. (2009). Improvement of Gregory's formula using particle swarm optimization. In *The Proceeding of International Conference on Computer and Applied Mathematics,* Vol. 58, (pp. 940–942).

Kim, J. M., Wang, C., Peabody, M., & Seneff, S. (2004). An interactive English pronunciation dictionary for Korean learners. In *Proceedings of the 8th International Conference on Spoken Language Processing*, Jeju Island, Korea.

Kim, B. G., Shim, J. I., & Park, D. J. (2003). Fast image segmentation based on multi-resolution analysis and wavelets. *Pattern Recognition Letters*, *24*, 2995–3006. doi:10.1016/S0167-8655(03)00160-0

Kittler, J., & Illingworth, J. (1986). Minimum error thresholding. *Pattern Recognition*, *19*(1), 41–47. doi:10.1016/0031-3203(86)90030-0

Kjelds, J. T., & Müller, H. G. (2008). *Integrated flood plain & disaster management using the MIKE 11 decision support system.* Retrieved on May 21, 2011, from http://www.icimod.org/?opg=949&document=1248

Kloeck, C., Jaekel, H., & Jondral, F. (2005). Dynamic and local combined pricing, allocation and billing system with cognitive radios. In *2005 First IEEE International Symposium on New Frontiers in Dynamic Spectrum Access Networks, DySPAN 2005* (pp. 73-81). Baltimore, MD: IEEE.

Klyne, G., & Carroll, J. (2004). *Resource description framework (RDF): Concepts and abstract syntax.* W3C Recommendation 10th February 2004. Retrieved from http://www.w3.org/TR/rdf-concepts/

Knorr, M. E., Ng, T. R., & Tucakov, V. (2000). Distance-based outlier: Algorithms and applications. *The VLDB Journal*, *8*(3-4), 237–253. doi:10.1007/s007780050006

Kohonen, T. (2001). *Self-organizing maps*. Espoo, Finland: Springer-Verlag.

Koivunen, M.-R., & Miller, E. (2001). W3C Semantic Web activity. *Proceedings of the Semantic Web Kick-off Seminar in Finland.* Retrieved from http://www.w3.org/2001/12/semweb-fin/w3csw

Kolodner, J. L. (1992). An introduction to case-based reasoning. *Artificial Intelligence Review*, *6*, 3–34. doi:10.1007/BF00155578

Kom, G., Tiedeu, A., & Kom, M. (2007). Automated detection of masses in mammograms by local adaptive thresholding. *Computers in Biology and Medicine*, *37*(1), 37–48. doi:10.1016/j.compbiomed.2005.12.004

Kotamarti, R. M., & Dunham, M. H. (2010). *Alignment-free sequence analysis using extensible Markov models.* Presented paper at 9th International Workshop on Data Mining in Bioinformatics (BIOKDD).

Kotamarti, R. M., Raiford, D. W., Hahsler, M., Wang, Y., McGee, M., & Dunham, M. H. (Nov 2009). *Targeted genomic signature profiling with quasi-alignment statistics.* COBRA Preprint Series, Article 63.

Kotamarti, R., Hahsler, M., Raiford, D., & Dunham, M. (2010). Sequence transformation to a complex signature form for consistent phylogenetic tree using extensible Markov model. *Computational Intelligence in Bioinformatics and Computational Biology (CIBCB)* (pp. 1 - 8). Montreal: ieeexplore.ieee.org.

Kotamarti, R. M., Hahsler, M., Raiford, D., McGee, M., & Dunham, M. H. (2010). Analyzing taxonomic classification using extensible Markov models. *Bioinformatics (Oxford, England)*, *26*(18), 2235–2241. doi:10.1093/bioinformatics/btq349

Koulouridis, S., Psychoudakis, D., & Volakis, J. L. (2007). Multiobjective optimal antenna design based on volumetric material optimization. *IEEE Transactions on Antennas and Propagation*, *55*(3), 594–603. doi:10.1109/TAP.2007.891551

Koza, J. R., Keane, M. A., Streeter, M. J., Mydlowec, W., Yu, J., & Lanza, G. (2003). *Genetic programming IV: Routine human-competitive machine intelligence*. Boston, MA: Kluwer Academic Publishers.

Koziel, S., & Bandler, J. W. (2008). Space mapping with multiple coarse models for optimization of microwave components. *IEEE Microwave and Wireless Components Letters*, *18*(1), 1–3. doi:10.1109/LMWC.2007.911969

Kukkonen, S., & Lampinen, J. (2005). *GDE3: The third evolution step of generalized differential evolution.* Paper presented at 2005 IEEE Congress on Evolutionary Computation, (CEC 2005).

Kukkonen, S., & Lampinen, J. (2006). *An empirical study of control parameters for the third version of generalized differential evolution (GDE3).* Paper presented at the IEEE Congress on Evolutionary Computation, CEC 2006.

Kukkonen, S., & Lampinen, J. (2007). *Performance assessment of generalized differential evolution 3 (GDE3) with a given set of problems.* Paper presented at the IEEE Congress on Evolutionary Computation, 2007. CEC 2007.

Kukkonen, S., Jangam, S. R., & Chakraborti, N. (2007). *Solving the molecular sequence alignment problem with generalized differential evolution 3 (GDE3).* Paper presented at the IEEE Symposium on Computational Intelligence in Multicriteria Decision Making.

Kukkonen, S., & Deb, K. (2006). A fast and effective method for pruning of non-dominated solutions in many-objective problems. *Lecture Notes in Computer Science*, *4193*, 553–562. doi:10.1007/11844297_56

Kuncheva, L., & Bezdek, J. (1998). Nearest prototype classification: Clustering, genetic algorithms, or random search? *IEEE Transactions on Systems, Man and Cybernetics. Part C, Applications and Reviews*, *28*(1), 160–164. doi:10.1109/5326.661099

Kuwahara, Y. (2005). Multiobjective optimization design of Yagi-Uda antenna. *IEEE Transactions on Antennas and Propagation*, *53*(6), 1984–1992. doi:10.1109/TAP.2005.848501

Kwasnicka, H., & Wawrzyniak, B. (2002, November). *License plate localization and recognition in camera pictures.* Artificial Intelligence Methods Conference, Gliwice, Poland.

Lai, C. C. (2005). A novel clustering approach using hierarchical genetic algorithms. *Intelligent Automation and Soft Computing*, *11*(3), 143–153.

Laidlaw, H. H., & Page, R. E. (1986). Mating designs. In Rinderer, T. E. (Ed.), *Bee genetics and breeding* (pp. 323–341). Academic Press, Inc.

Larose, D. T. (2005). *Discovering knowledge in data: An introduction to data mining*. John Wiley & Sons, Inc.

Lassila, O., & Swick, R. (1999). *Resource description framework (RDF) model and syntax specification.* W3C Recommendation, 22nd February 1999. Retrieved from http://www.w3.org/TR/1999/REC-rdf-syntax-19990222

Learning Object Metadata (LOM). (n.d.). *Homepage*. Retrieved from http://ltsc.ieee.org/wg12/

Lee, J., Bharosa, N., Yang, J., Janssen, M., & Rao, H. R. (2011). Group value and intention to use — A study of multi-agency disaster management information systems for public safety. *Decision Support Systems*, *50*, 404–414. doi:10.1016/j.dss.2010.10.002

Lee, Y. H., Cahill, B. J., Porter, S. J., & Marvin, A. C. (2004). A novel evolutionary learning technique for multi-objective array antenna optimization. *Progress in Electromagnetics Research-Pier*, *48*, 125–144. doi:10.2528/PIER04012202

Lee, Y. J., Park, J. M., & Park, H. W. (2000). Mammographic mass detection by adaptive thresholding and region growing. *International Journal of Imaging Systems and Technology*, *11*(5), 340–346. doi:10.1002/ima.1018

Lehman, C. D., Gatsonis, C., Kuhl, C. K., Hendrick, R. E., Pisano, E. D., & Hanna, L. (2007). MRI evaluation of the contralateral breast in women with recently diagnosed breast cancer. *The New England Journal of Medicine*, *356*(13), 1295–1303. doi:10.1056/NEJMoa065447

Li, S. Z., & Guo, G. (2000). *Content-based audio classification and retrieval using SVM learning*. IEEE Pacific-Rim Conf. on Multimedia.

Li, S., Shen, P., & Yang, S. (2011). A grouping particle swarm optimization algorithm for Web service selection based on user preference. *IEEE International Conference on Computer Science and Automation Engineering (CSAE)* Shanghai, China, (pp. 315-327).

Li, Z.-N., & Drew, M. S. (2004). *Fundamentals of multimedia*. Upper Saddle River, NJ: Prentice Hall. LLC, B. S. (2005). *OpenMap*. Retrieved from http://openmap.bbn.com/

Liang, Y. C., Chen, A. L., & Chyu, C. C. (2006). Application of a hybrid ant colony optimization for the multilevel thresholding in image processing. *Lecture Notes in Computer Science, 4233*. ISSN 0302-9743

Liao, P. S., Chen, T. S., & Chung, P. C. (2001). A fast algorithm for multilevel thresholding. *Journal of Information Science Engineering*, *17*, 713–727.

Li, H., & Zhang, Q. (2009). Multiobjective optimization problems with complicated pareto sets, MOEA/ D and NSGA-II. *IEEE Transactions on Evolutionary Computation*, *13*(2), 284–302. doi:10.1109/TEVC.2008.925798

Li, J. Y., & Guo, J. L. (2009). Optimization technique using differential evolution for Yagi-Uda antennas. *Journal of Electromagnetic Waves and Applications*, *23*(4), 449–461. doi:10.1163/156939309787612356

Lin, K. C. (2001). Fast thresholding computation by searching for zero derivates of images between-class variance. In *27th Annual Conference on IEEE Industrial Electronics Society* (pp. 393–397).

Lin, H. J., Yang, F. W., & Kao, Y. T. (2005). An efficient GA-based clustering technique. *Tamkang Journal of Science and Engineering*, *8*(2), 113–122.

Litva, J., & Kwok-Yeung Lo, T. (1996). *Digital beamforming in wireless communications*. Boston, MA: Artech House, Inc.

Liu, W., Chih, C. H., Kuo, B. C., & Coleman, T. (2008). An adaptive clustering algorithms based on the possibility clustering and ISODATA for multispectral image classification. *Proceedings of the International Society for Photogrammetry and Remote Sensing (ISPRS – XXI Congress)*, Beijing, China, July 3 – 11.

Liu, S., Babbs, C. F., & Delp, E. J. (2001). Multiresolution detection of spiculated lesions in digital mammograms. *IEEE Transactions on Image Processing*, *10*(6), 874–884. doi:10.1109/83.923284

Li, Z., Wang, W., & Jiang, Y. (2009). Managing quality-of-control and requirement-of-bandwidth in networked control systems via fuzzy bandwidth scheduling. *International Journal of Control Automation and Systems*, *7*(2), 289–296. doi:10.1007/s12555-009-0215-7

Lu, C. H., Wu, S. H., Tu, L. Y., & Hsu, W. L. (2004). The design of an intelligent tutoring system based on the ontology of procedural knowledge. In *Proceedings International Conference on Advanced Learning Technologies, IV*, Joensuu, ICALT, (pp. 525-530).

Lukashin, A. V., & Fuchs, R. (2001). Analysis of temporal gene expression profiles: Clustering by simulated annealing and determining the optimal number of clusters. *Bioinformatics (Oxford, England)*, *17*(5), 405–414. doi:10.1093/bioinformatics/17.5.405

Luke, S., Cioffi-Revilla, C., Panait, L., & Sullivan, K. (2004). *MASON: A new multi-agent simulation toolkit*. Paper presented at the Swarfest.

Lu, Y., & Yang, D. (2011). Information exchange in virtual communities under extreme disaster conditions. *Decision Support Systems*, *50*, 529–538. doi:10.1016/j.dss.2010.11.011

Lysenko, M., & D'Souza, R. M. (2008). A framework for megascale agent based meld simulations on graphics processing units. *Journal of Artificial Societies and Social Simulation*, *11*(410).

MacQueen, J. (1967). Some methods for classification and analysis of multivariate observations. In *Proceedings of the Fifth Berkely Symposium on Mathematical Statistics and Probability*, (pp. 281–297).

Maglaveras, N., Stamkopoulos, T., Pappas, C., & Gerassimos Strintzis, M. (1998). An adaptive backpropagation neural network for real-time ischemia episodes detection: Development and performance analysis using the European ST-T database. *IEEE Transactions on Bio-Medical Engineering*, *45*, 805–813. doi:10.1109/10.686788

Maio, C. D., Fenza, G., Gaeta, M., Loia, V., & Orciuoli, F. (2011). A knowledge-based framework for emergency DSS. *Knowledge-Based Systems*, *24*(8).

Mak, B., Siu, M., Ng, M., Tam, Y. C., Chan, Y. C., & Chan, K. W. (2003). PLASER: Pronunciation learning via automatic speech recognition. In *Proceedings of HLT-NAACL*, *2003*, 23–29.

Malignant mass with irregular shape (n.d.). Retrieved August 18, 2011 from http://marathon.csee.usf.edu/Mammography/Database.html

Mammography test (n.d.). Retrieved December 21, 2011 from http://visualsonline.cancer.gov/

Manola, F., & Miller, E. (2004). *RDF primer*. W3C Recommendation 10th February 2004. Retrieved from http://www.w3.org/TR/rdf-primer/

Marinescu, D. C., & Marinescu, G. M. (2005). *Approaching quantum computing*. France: Pearson Prentice-Hall.

Markus, M., & Grani, M. (2009). Automatic cluster number selection using a split and merge k-means approach. *20th International Workshop on Database and Expert Systems Application*, (pp. 363-367).

Marler, R. T., & Arora, J. S. (2004). Survey of multi-objective optimization methods for engineering. *Structural and Multidisciplinary Optimization*, *26*(6), 369–395. doi:10.1007/s00158-003-0368-6

Marston, S., Li, Z., Bandyopadhyay, S., Zhang, J., & Ghalsasi, A. (2011). Cloud computing — The business perspective. *Decision Support Systems*, *51*, 176–189. doi:10.1016/j.dss.2010.12.006

Matake, N., Hiroyasu, T., Miki, M., & Senda, T. (2007). Multiobjective clustering with automatic k-determination for large-scale data. *Genetic and Evolutionary Computation Conference*, London, England, (pp. 861-868).

Matthews, B. (2005). *Semantic Web technologies*. CCLRC Rutherford Appleton Laboratory, JISC Technology and Standards Watch. Retrieved from http://www.jisc.ac.uk/uploaded_documents/jisctsw_05_02bpdf.pdf

Mayer, D. G., Kinghorn, B. P., & Archer, A. A. (2005). Differential evolution – an easy and efficient evolutionary algorithm for model optimisation. *Agricultural Systems*, *83*, 315–328. doi:10.1016/j.agsy.2004.05.002

McEnnis, D., McKay, C., & Fujinaga, I. (2005). jAudio: Additions and improvements. *Proceedings of the International Conference on Music Information Retrieval*, (pp. 385–386).

McKay, C., & Fujinaga, I. (2005). *Automatic music classification and similarity analysis*. International Conference on Music Information Retrieval.

McKay, C., & Fujinaga, I. (2006). jSymbolic: A feature extractor for MIDI files. *Proceedings of the International Computer Music Conference*, (pp. 302–305).

McKay, C., & Fujinaga, I. (2009). jMIR: Tools for automatic music classification. *Proceedings of the International Computer Music Conference*.

McKenzie, P., & Alder, M. (1993). *The EM algorithm used for Gaussian mixture modeling and its initialization*. University of Western Australia.

Mebane, W. R., & Sekhon, J. S. (2011). Genetic optimization using derivatives: The rgenoud package for R. *Journal of Statistical Software*, *42*(11), 1–26.

Mechraoui, A., Khan, Z. H., Thiriet, J.-M., & Gentil, S. (2009). *Co-design for wireless networked control of an intelligent mobile robot*. In International Conference on Informatics in Control, Automation and Robotics (ICINCO), Milan, Italy.

Mechraoui, A., Thiriet, J.-M., & Gentil, S. (2010). *Online distributed Bayesian decision and diagnosis of wireless networked mobile robots*. In 18th Mediterranean Conference on Control and Automation, Marrakech, Morocco.

Mediolateral oblique view of left breast (n.d.). Retrieved August 18, 2011 from http://www.radiologyteacher.com/id/3381/1005-0-0-1.jpg

Menasce, D. A. (2004). Composing Web services: A QoS view. *IEEE Internet Computing*, *8*(6), 88–90. doi:10.1109/MIC.2004.57

Menzel, W., Herron, D., Bonaventura, P., & Morton, R. (2000). Automatic detection and correction of non-native English pronunciations. In *Proceedings of InSTILL 2000*, Dundee, Scotland.

Mezura-Montes, E., Velazquez-Reyes, J., & Coello Coello, C. A. (2006). *A comparative study of differential evolution variants for global optimization*. Paper presented at the GECCO 2006 - Genetic and Evolutionary Computation Conference, Seattle, WA.

Michaelson, J., Satija, S., Moore, R., Weber, G., Halpern, E., & Garland, A. (2002). The pattern of breast cancer screening utilization and its consequences. *Cancer*, *94*(1), 37–43. doi:10.1002/cncr.10154

Michalowski, W., Rubin, S., Slowinski, R., & Wilk, S. (2003). Mobile clinical support system for pediatric emergencies. *Decision Support Systems*, *36*(2), 161–176. doi:10.1016/S0167-9236(02)00140-9

Michielssen, E., Sajer, J.-M., Ranjithant, S., & Mittra, R. (1993). Design of lightweight, broad-band microwave absorbers using genetic algorithms. *IEEE Transactions on Microwave Theory and Techniques*, *41*(6-7), 1024–1030. doi:10.1109/22.238519

Microsoft Azure Services. (n.d.). Retrieved on January 12, 2012, from http://www.microsoft.com/azure/default.mspx

Minar, N., Burkhart, R., Langton, C., & Askenazi, M. (1996). *The swarm simulation system: A toolkit for building multi-agent simulations*. Working Papers, Santa Fe Institute. Retrieved from http://econpapers.repec.org/RePEc:wop:safiwp:96-06-042

Mirfenderesk, H. (2009). Flood emergency management decision support system on the Gold Coast, Australia. *Australian Journal of Emergency Management*, *24*, 2.

Miron, D., Garner, G., Donald, G., & Dyall, T. (2009). *A national model for emerging livestock disease threats: User* guide.

Misra, I. S., Chakrabarty, R. S., & Mangaraj, B. B. (2006). Design, analysis and optimization of V-dipole and its three-element Yagi-Uda array. *Progress in Electromagnetics Research*, *66*, 137–156. doi:10.2528/PIER06102604

Mitchell, M., & Taylor, C. E. (1999). Evolutionary computation: An overview. *Annual Review of Ecology and Systematics*, *30*, 593–616. doi:10.1146/annurev.ecolsys.30.1.593

Mitsukura, Y., Miyata, K., Mitsukura, K., Fukumi, M., & Akamatsu, N. (2004). Intelligent medical diagnosis system using the fuzzy and neural networks. *IEEE Annual Meeting of the North American Fuzzy Information Processing Society*, Vol. 2, (pp. 550-554).

Mittra, R., & Varadarajan, V. (2007). A technique for solving 2D method-of-moments problems involving large scatterers. *Microwave and Optical Technology Letters*, *8*(3), 127–132. doi:10.1002/mop.4650080304

Moayedi, F., Boostani, R., Azimifar, Z., & Katebi, S. (2007). A support vector based fuzzy neural network approach for mass classification in mammography. Paper presented at 15th International conference on digital signal processing. Cardiff, UK: IEEE

Monga, O., & Wrobel, B. (1987). Segmentation d'images: Vers une méthodologie. *Traitement du Signal*, *4*(3), 169–193.

Moore, J. H., Asselbergs, F. W., & Williams, S. M. (2010). Bioinformatics challenges for genome-wide association studies. *Bioinformatics (Oxford, England)*, *26*(4), 445–455. doi:10.1093/bioinformatics/btp713

Mousa, R., Munib, Q., & Moussa, A. (2005). Breast cancer diagnosis system based on wavelet analysis and fuzzy-neural. *Expert Systems with Applications*, *28*(4), 713–723. doi:10.1016/j.eswa.2004.12.028

Mudigonda, N. R., Rangayyan, R. M., & Desautels, J. E. L. (2000). Gradient and texture analysis for the classification of mammographic masses. *IEEE Transactions on Medical Imaging*, *19*(10), 1032–1043. doi:10.1109/42.887618

Mullen, K. M., Ardia, D., Gil, A. L., Windover, D., & Cline, J. (2011). DEoptim: An R package for global optimization by differential evolution. *Journal of Statistical Software*, *40*(6).

Muller, A., Weber, P., & Salem, A. B. (2004). *Process model based dynamic Bayesian networks for prognostic.* Fourth International Conference on Intelligent Systems Design and Applications, ISDA 2004, Budapest, Hungary.

Munir, S. A., Bin, Y., Biao, R., & Jian, M. (2007). Fuzzy logic based congestion estimation for QoS in wireless sensor network. *IEEE International Symposium on Wireless Communications and Networking* (pp. 4336–4341).

Muralidhar, G. S., Bovik, A. C., Giese, J. D., Sampat, M. P., Whitman, G. J., & Haygood, T. M. (2010). Snakules: A model-based active contour algorithm for the annotation of spicules on mammography. *IEEE Transactions on Medical Imaging*, *29*(10), 1768–1780. doi:10.1109/TMI.2010.2052064

Nakagawa, S., Mori, K., & Nakamura, N. (2003). A statistical method of evaluation pronunciation proficiency for English words spoken by Japanese. In *Proceedings Eurospeech 2003*, Geneva, Switzerland, (pp. 3193-3196).

Nakib, A., Oulhadj, H., & Siarry, P. (2007). Image histogram thresholding based on multiobjective optimization. *Signal Processing*, *87*, 2516–2534. doi:10.1016/j.sigpro.2007.04.001

Nakib, A., Oulhadj, H., & Siarry, P. (2008). Non-supervised image segmentation based on multiobjective optimization. *Pattern Recognition Letters*, *29*, 161–172. doi:10.1016/j.patrec.2007.09.008

Nakib, A., Oulhadj, H., & Siarry, P. (2009). Fractional differentiation and non-Pareto multiobjective optimization for image thresholding. *Engineering Applications of Artificial Intelligence*, *22*, 236–249. doi:10.1016/j.engappai.2008.07.005

Nakib, A., Oulhadj, H., & Siarry, P. (2010). Image thresholding based on Pareto multiobjective optimization. *Engineering Applications of Artificial Intelligence*, *23*, 313–320. doi:10.1016/j.engappai.2009.09.002

National Center for Health Statistics. (2009). *Health, United States: With special feature on medical technology*. Hyattsville. Retrieved March 5, 2009, from http://www.cdc.gov/nchs/data/hus/hus09.pdf

Nedjah, N., Alba, E., & de Macedo, L. M. (Eds.). (2006). *Parallel evolutionary computations*. Berlin, Germany: Springer. doi:10.1007/3-540-32839-4

Negreiros de Andrade, P. J. (2008). *Cardiologia para o Generalista: Uma abordagem fisiopatológica*. Fortaleza, Brazil: UFC.

Neri, A., Cucchiarini, C., & Strik, H. (2004). Segmental errors in Dutch as a second language: How to establish priorities for CAPT. In *Proceedings InSTIL/ICALL Symposium*, (pp. 13-16).

Neri, A., Cucchiarini, C., & Strik, H. (2006a). ASR corrective feedback on pronunciation: Does it really work? In *Proceedings Interspeech*, (pp. 1982–1985).

Neri, A., Cucchiarini, C., & Strik, H. (2006b). Selecting segmental errors in L2 Dutch for optimal pronunciation training. *International Review of Application in Linguistics Language Teaching*, *44*, 357–404. doi:10.1515/IRAL.2006.016

Neumeyer, L., Franco, H., Weintraub, M., & Price, P. (1996). Pronunciation scoring of foreign language student speech. In *Proceedings International Conference on Spoken Language Processing*, (pp. 1457-1460). Philadelphia, USA.

Nianqiang, L., Yongbing, W., & Guoyi, Z. (2010). A preferable method on digital filter in ECG signal's processing based on FPGA. *Third International Symposium on Intelligent Information Technology and Security Informatics*, (pp. 184-187).

Nielsen, M. A., & Chuang, I. L. (2000). *Quantum computation and quantum information*. Cambridge University Press.

Nie, N., & Comaniciu, C. (2006). Adaptive channel allocation spectrum etiquette for cognitive radio networks. *Mobile Networks and Applications*, *11*(6), 779–797. doi:10.1007/s11036-006-0049-y

Noy, N. F., & Mcguinness, D. L. (2001). *Ontology development 101: A guide to creating your first ontology.* Retrieved from http://protege.stanford.edu/publications/ontology_development/ ontology101.pdf

Nurmi, D., Wolski, R., Grzegorczyk, C., Obertelli, G., Soman, S., Youseff, L., & Zagorodnow, D. (2010). *The eucalyptus open-source cloud-computing system*. The 9th IEEE/ACM International Symposium on Cluster Computing and the Grid. Retrieved April 22, 2011, from http://www.cca08.org/papers/Paper32-Daniel-Nurmi.pdf

Nurunnabi, A. A. M., Imon, A. H. M. R., & Nasser, M. (2010). Identification of multiple influential observations in logistic regression. *Journal of Applied Statistics*, *37*(10), 1605–1624. doi:10.1080/02664760903104307

Nurunnabi, A. A. M., Imon, A. H. M. R., & Nasser, M. (2011). A diagnostic measure for influential observations in linear regression. *Communications in Statistics Theory and Methods*, *40*(7), 1169–1183. doi:10.1080/03610920903564727

Nurunnabi, A. A. M., Imon, A. H. M. R., Shawkat, A. B. M., & Nasser, M. (2011). Outlier detection in linear regression. In Igelnik, B. (Ed.), *Computational modelling and simulation of intellect: Current state and future perspectives* (pp. 510–550). Hershey, PA: IGI Global. doi:10.4018/978-1-60960-551-3.ch020

NVIDIA. (2010). *NVIDIA CUDA: Programming guide*. Santa Clara, CA: NVIDIA Corporation.

Obeid, H., & Zantout, R. (2007, May). *Line processing: An approach to ALPR character recognition.* ACS/IEEE International Conference on Computer Systems and Applications. Amman, Jordan

Obeid, H., Zantout, R., & Sibai, F. (2007, November). *License plate localization in ALPR systems*. 4th International Conference on Innovations in Information Technology Dubai, United Arab Emirates.

Oliveira, A., & Andrade, F. (2006). *Sistemas embarcados: Hardware e firmware na prática*. São Paulo, Brazil: Editora Érica.

Oliveira, D., & Ramos, R. (2007). Quantum bit string comparator: Circuits and applications. *Quantum Computers and Computing*, *7*(1), 17–26.

Oliver, A., Freixenet, J., Martí, R., Pont, J., Pérez, E., & Denton, E. R. (2008). A novel breast tissue density classification methodology. *IEEE Transactions on Information Technology in Biomedicine*, *12*(1), 55–65. doi:10.1109/TITB.2007.903514

Oliver, T., Yeow, L. Y., & Schmidt, B. (2008). Integrating FPGA acceleration into HMMer. *Parallel Computing*, *34*, 681–691. doi:10.1016/j.parco.2008.08.003

Omran, M., Salman, A., & Engelbrecht, A. (2006). Dynamic clustering using particle swarm optimization with application in image segmentation. *Pattern Analysis and Applications Journal, 8*(4).

Othman, R. M., Deris, S., Illias, R. M., Zakaria, Z., & Mohamad, S. M. (2006). Automatic clustering of gene ontology by genetic algorithm. *International Journal of Information Technology*, *3*(1), 37–46.

Otsu, N. (1979). A threshold selection method from gray-level histograms. *IEEE Transactions on Systems, Man, and Cybernetics*, *9*(1), 62–66. doi:10.1109/TSMC.1979.4310076

Otten, J., Heijningen, B., & Lafortune, J. F. (2004). *The virtual crisis management centre. An ICT implementation to canalise information.* International Community on Information Systems for Crisis Response (ISCRAM2004) Conference, 3–4 May 2004, Brussels, Belgium.

Oxford Dictionaries. (n.d.). *Definition of cancer*. Retrieved September 20, 2011 from http://oxforddictionaries.com/definition/cancer

Ozbay, S., & Ercelebi, E. (2005, November). Automatic vehicle identification by plate recognition. *Transactions on Engineering, Computing and Technology, 9.*

Pachet, F., & Roy, P. (2009). Analytical features: A knowledge-based approach to audio feature generation. *EURASIP Journal on Audio, Speech, and Music Processing.*

Padmanabhan, N., Burstein, F., Churilov, L., Wassertheil, J., Hornblower, B., & Parker, N. (2006). A mobile emergency triage decision support system evaluation. *Proceedings of the 39th Hawaii International Conference on System Sciences* – 2006. Retrieved January 12, 2012, from http://www.computer.org/portal/web/csdl/doi/10.1109/HICSS.2006.17

Pain Free Mammogram. (2007). Retrieved August 28, 2011 from http://www.sciencedaily.com/videos/2007/0907-pain_free_mammogram.htm

Pal, N. R., & Pal, S. K. (1993). A review on image segmentation techniques. *Pattern Recognition*, *9*(26), 1277–1294. doi:10.1016/0031-3203(93)90135-J

Pal, S., Das, S., & Basak, A. (2011). Design of time-modulated linear arrays with a multi-objective optimization approach. *Progress in Electromagnetics Research B, 23*, 83–107. doi:10.2528/PIERB10052401

Pal, S., Das, S., Basak, A., & Suganthan, P. N. (2011). Synthesis of difference patterns for Monopulse antennas with optimal combination of array-size and number of subarrays - A multi-objective optimization approach. *Progress in Electromagnetics Research B, 21*, 257–280.

Pal, S., Qu, B., Das, S., & Suganthan, P. N. (2010). Linear antenna array synthesis with constrained multi-objective differential evolution. *Progress in Electromagnetics Research B, 21*, 87–111.

Panduro, M. A., Brizuela, C. A., Balderas, L. I., & Acosta, D. A. (2009). A comparison of genetic algorithms, particle swarm optimization and the differential evolution method for the design of scannable circular antenna arrays. *Progress in Electromagnetics Research B, 13*, 171–186. doi:10.2528/PIERB09011308

Papalexidis, N., Walker, T. O., Gkionis, C., Tummala, M., & McEachen, J. (2007). *A distributed approach to beamforming in a wireless sensor network*. Forty-First Asilomar Conference on Signals, Systems and Computers, IEEE, 4-7 Nov. 2007.

Park, K. I. (2005). QoS in packet networks. *Springer*, 2005.

Parker, J. R., & Federl, P. (1996). *An approach to license plate recognition.* University of Calgary. Retrieved from http://pages.cpsc.ucalgary.ca/~federl/Publications/LicencePlate1996/licence-plate-1996.pdf

Parrilla, E., Ginestar, D., Hueso, J. L., Riera, J., & Torregrosa, J. R. (2008). Handling occlusion in optical flow algorithms for object tracking. *Computers & Mathematics with Applications (Oxford, England), 3*(56), 733–742. doi:10.1016/j.camwa.2008.02.008

Parrilla, E., Riera, J., Torregrosa, J. R., & Hueso, J. L. (2008). Handling occlusion in object tracking in stereoscopic video sequences. *Journal of Mathematical and Computer Modelling, 5-6*(50), 823–830.

Parsopoulos, K. E., et al. (2001a). Stretching technique for obtaining global minimizers through particle swarm optimization. In *Proceedings of the PSO Workshop*, Indianapolis, USA, (pp. 22–29).

Parsopoulos, K. E., et al. (2001b). Objective function stretching to alleviate convergence to local minima. *Non linear Analysis TMA, 47*, 3419–3424.

Parsopoulos, K. E., & Vrahatis, M. N. (2001). Modification of the particle swarm optimizer for locating all the global minima. In Kurkova, V. (Eds.), *Artificial Neural Networks and Genetic Algorithms* (pp. 324–327). New York, NY: Springer.

Passin, T. B. (2004). *Explorer's guide to the Semantic Web*. USA: Manning Publications Co.

Patel, V. C., McClendon, R. W., & Goodrum, J. W. (1998). Development and evaluation of an expert system for egg sorting. *Computers and Electronics in Agriculture, 20*, 97–116. doi:10.1016/S0168-1699(98)00009-X

Pearl, J. (1988). *Probabilistic reasoning in intelligent systems: Networks of plausible inference*. Morgan Kaufman Publishers.

Pelleg, D., & Moore, A. (2000). X-means extending K-means with efficient estimation of the number of clusters. In *Proceedings of the 17th International Conference on Machine Learning*, 2000, (pp. 727–734).

Peng, C., Zheng, H., & Zhao, B. (2006). Utilization and fairness in spectrum assignment for opportunistic spectrum access. *Mobile Networks and Applications, 11*(4), 555–576. doi:10.1007/s11036-006-7322-y

Peng, Y., Zhang, Y., Tang, Y., & Li, S. (2011). An incident information management framework based on data integration, data mining, and multi-criteria decision making. *Decision Support Systems, 51*, 316–327. doi:10.1016/j.dss.2010.11.025

Perumalla, K. S., & Aaby, B. G. (2008). *Data parallel execution challeneges and runtime performance of agent simulations on GPUs*. Paper presented at the Spring Simulation Multi-Conference.

Peters, G. (2007). *Computer-aided detection for digital breast tomosynthesis*. Doctoral dissertation, Paris Institute of Technology, 2007. Retrieved October 13, 2011, from

Petersen, M. A. (2009). Estimating standard errors in finance panel data sets: Comparing approaches. *Review of Financial Studies, 22*(1), 435–480. doi:10.1093/rfs/hhn053

Petko, J. S., & Werner, D. H. (2008). The pareto optimization of ultrawideband polyfractal arrays. *IEEE Transactions on Antennas and Propagation*, *56*(1), 97–107. doi:10.1109/TAP.2007.913147

Petko, J. S., & Werner, D. H. (2011). Pareto optimization of thinned planar arrays with elliptical mainbeams and low sidelobe levels. *IEEE Transactions on Antennas and Propagation*, *59*(5), 1748–1751. doi:10.1109/TAP.2011.2122212

Pirmez, L., Delicato, F. C., Pires, P., Mostardinha, A., & de Rezende, N. (2007). Applying fuzzy logic for decision-making on wireless sensor networks. *IEEE International Symposium on Fuzzy Systems* (pp. 1-6).

Ponce, P., Wang, S. S., & Wang, D. L. (2001). *License plate recognition*. Report, Department of Electrical and Computer Engineering, Carnegie Mellon University. Retrieved from http://www.ece.cmu.edu/~ee551/Final_Reports/Gr18.551.S00.pdf

Pregibon, D. (1981). Logistic regression diagnostics. *Annals of Statistics*, *9*, 977–986. doi:10.1214/aos/1176345513

Protégé. (2006). *The Protégé ontology editor and knowledge acquisition system*. Retrieved from http://Protege.Stanford.Edu

Pye, D. (2000). Content-based methods for the management of digital music. *IEEE International Conference on Acoustics, Speech, and Signal Processing (ICASSP)*, *4*, (pp. 2437–2440).

Quanquan, L., Dongfeng, Y., Yong, W., & Ruihua, Z. (2006). A new sensor antenna-array selecting method in wireless sensor networks. *Proceedings 2006 International Conference on Communications, Circuits and Systems*, Vol. 3, 25-28 June (pp. 1523 – 1529).

Qu, B. Y., & Suganthan, P. N. (2010). Multi-objective evolutionary algorithms based on the summation of normalized objectives and diversified selection. *Information Sciences*, *180*(17), 3170–3181. doi:10.1016/j.ins.2010.05.013

R Development Core Team. (2011). *R: A language and environment for statistical computing*. Vienna, Austria: R Foundation for Statistical Computing.

Rae, S. (2004). *Using telerobotics for remote kinematics experiments*. Honors Thesis, School of Mechanical Engineering, University of Western Australia.

Rafea, A., Hassen, H., & Hazman, M. (2003). Automatic knowledge acquisition tools for irrigation and fertilization expert systems. *Expert Systems with Applications*, *24*, 49–57. doi:10.1016/S0957-4174(02)00082-9

Rahimi, S., Zarham, M., Thakre, A., & Chillar, D. (2004). *A parallel fuzzy C-mean algorithm for image segmentation. Fuzzy Information* (pp. 234–237). IEEE.

Ramos, R. M., Saldanha, R. R., Takahashi, R. H. C., & Moreira, F. J. S. (2003). The real-biased multiobjective genetic algorithm and its application to the design of wire antennas. *IEEE Transactions on Magnetics*, *39*(3 I), 1329-1332.

Rangayyan, R. M. (2005). *Biomedical image analysis*. CRC Press LLC.

Rao, A., Jain, M., & Karlapalem, K. (2007). *Towards simulating billions of agents in thousands of seconds*. Paper presented at the International Conference on Autonomous and Multiagent Systems, Honolulu.

Rattan, M., Patterh, M. S., & Sohi, B. S. (2008). Optimization of Yagi-Uda antenna using simulated annealing. *Journal of Electromagnetic Waves and Applications*, *22*(2-3), 291–299. doi:10.1163/156939308784160749

RDF Core Working Group. (n.d.). *Homepage*. Retrieved from http://www.w3.org/2001/sw/RDFCore/

Reimann, P., Yacef, K., & Kay, J. (2011). Analyzing collaborative interactions with data mining methods for the benefit of learning. In Puntambekar, S., Hmelo-Silver, C., & Erkens, G. (Eds.), *Analyzing interactions in CSCL: Methodology, approaches and issues* (pp. 161–185). Springer. doi:10.1007/978-1-4419-7710-6_8

Reinganum, M. R. (1981). Misspecification of capital asset pricing: Empirical anomalies based on earnings' yields and market values. *Journal of Financial Economics*, *9*(1), 19–46. doi:10.1016/0304-405X(81)90019-2

Rekanos, I. T. (2007, March 19-23). *Conducting Scatterer reconstruction using differential evolution and particle swarm optimization*. Paper presented at the 23rd Annual Review of Progress in Applied Computational Electromagnetics (ACES), Verona, Italy.

Rekanos, I. T. (2008). Shape reconstruction of a perfectly conducting scatterer using differential evolution and particle swarm optimization. *IEEE Transactions on Geoscience and Remote Sensing*, *46*(7), 1967–1974. doi:10.1109/TGRS.2008.916635

Reyes-Sierra, M., & Coello, C. A. C. (2006). Multiobjective particle swarm optimizers: A survey of the state-of-the-art. *International Journal of Computer Intelligence Research*, *2*(3), 287–308.

Richmond, P., Coakley, S., & Romano, D. (2009, May, 10-15, 2009). *A high performance agent-base modelling framework on graphics card hardware with CUDA*. Paper presented at the Autonomous Agents and Multiagent Systems (AAMAS), Budapest, Hungary.

Rinderer, T. E., & Collins, A. M. (1986). Behavioral genetics. In Rinderer, T. E. (Ed.), *Bee genetics and breeding* (pp. 155–176). Academic Press, Inc.

Rivest, R. L., Shamir, A., & Adleman, L. (1978). A method for obtaining digital signatures and public-key cryptosystems. *Communications of the ACM*, *21*, 120–126. doi:10.1145/359340.359342

Romeo, F., & Sangiovanni-Vincentelli, A. (1991). A theoretical framework for simulated annealing. *Algorithm*, *6*, 302–345. doi:10.1007/BF01759049

Ronen, O., Neumeyer, L., & Franco, H. (1997). Automatic detection of mispronunciation for language instruction. In *Proceedings Eurospeech '97*, Vol. 2, Rhodes, Greece, (pp. 649-652).

Rosenberger, C., & Chehdi, K. (2000). Unsupervised clustering method with optimal estimation of the number of clusters: Application to image segmentation. In *Proceedings IEEE International Conference on Pattern Recognition (ICPR)*, Vol. 1, Barcelona, (pp. 1656–1659).

Rossini, A. J., Tierney, L., & Li, N. M. (2007). Simple parallel statistical computing in R. *Journal of Computational and Graphical Statistics*, *16*(2), 399–420. doi:10.1198/106186007X178979

Rousseeuw, P. J., & Leroy, A. M. (1987). *Robust regression and outlier detection*. New York, NY: Wiley.

Roussel, O., Cavelier, A., & van der Werf, H. M. G. (2000). Adaptation and use of a fuzzy expert system to assess the environmental effect of pesticides applied to field crops. *Agriculture Ecosystems & Environment*, *80*, 143–158. doi:10.1016/S0167-8809(00)00142-0

Ruiz, P. M., Botía, J. A., & Gómez-Skarmeta, A. (2004). Providing QoS through machine-learning-driven adaptive multimedia applications. *IEEE Transactions on Systems, Man, and Cybernetics B*, *33*(4), 1398–1411. doi:10.1109/TSMCB.2004.825912

Russell, S., & Norvig, P. (2003). *Artificial intelligence: A modern approach. New Jersy*. Prentice Hall.

Ryan, T. P. (1997). *Modern regression methods*. New York, NY: Wiley.

Saha, S., & Bandyopadhyay, S. (2008). *Unsupervised pixel classification in satellite imagery using a new multiobjective symmetry based clustering approach*. IEEE Region 10 Annual International Conference.

Saha, S., & Bandyopadhyay, S. (2010). A new symmetry based multiobjective clustering technique for automatic evolution of clusters. *Pattern Recognition*, *43*(3). doi:10.1016/j.patcog.2009.07.004

Sahba, F., Venetsanopoulos, A., & Schaefer, G. (2010). *A review of recent fuzzy-based methods for computer-aided detection and classification of breast cancer using mammography*. Paper presented at the 2010 International Conference on Image Processing, Computer Vision, and Pattern Recognition, Las Vegas, Nevada, USA.

Sahoo, P. K., Soltani, S., & Wong, A. K. C. (1988). A survey of thresholding techniques. *Computer Vision Graphics and Image Processing*, *41*, 233–260. doi:10.1016/0734-189X(88)90022-9

Salazar-Lechuga, M., & Rowe, J. E. (2005). *Particle swarm optimization and fitness sharing to solve multi-objective optimization problems*. Paper presented at the Congress on Evolutionary Computation.

Sameti, M. (1998). *Detection of soft tissue abnormalities in mammographic images for early diagnosis of breast cancer*. Doctor of philosophy, The University of British Columbia, 1998. Retrieved March 21, 2011, from https://circle.ubc.ca/bitstream/handle/2429/9987/ubc_1999-389723.pdf?sequence=1

Sampat, M. P., & Bovik, A. C. (2003). Detection of spiculated lesions in mammograms. Paper presented at *Proceedings of the 25th Annual International Conference of the IEEE Engineering in Medicine and Biology Society*.

Sampat, M. P., Markey, M. K., & Bovik, A. C. (2005). Computer-aided detection and diagnosis in mammography. In Bovik, A. (Ed.), *Handbook of image and video processing* (pp. 1195–1217). doi:10.1016/B978-012119792-6/50130-3

Samulski, M., & Karssemeijer, N. (2011). Optimizing case-based detection performance in a multiview cad system for mammography. *IEEE Transactions on Medical Imaging, 30*(4), 1001–1009. doi:10.1109/TMI.2011.2105886

San Pedro, J., Burstein, F., Wassertheil, J., Arora, N., Churilov, L., & Zaslavsky, A. (2005). On the development and evaluation of prototype mobile decision support for hospital triage. *Proceedings of the 38th Hawaii International Conference on System Sciences*, 2005.

Sankar, K. P., Bandyopadhyay, S., & Ray, S. S. (2006). Evolutionary computation in bioinformatics: A review. *IEEE Transactions on Systems, Man and Cybernetics. Part C, Applications and Reviews*, *36*(5), 601–615. doi:10.1109/TSMCC.2005.855515

Santos, N., Gummadi, K. P., & Rodrigues, R. (2009). Towards trusted cloud computing. Retrieved April 22, 2011, from http://www.mpi-sws.org/~gummadi/papers/trusted_cloud.pdf

Santos, O. C., Gaudioso, E., Barrera, C., & Boticario, J. G. (2003). An adaptive elearning platform. In *Proceedings of mICTE Multimedia, Information and Communication Technologies*. Badajoz, Spain: ALFANET.

Saraireh, M., Saatchi, R., Al-Khayatt, S., & Strachan, R. (2007). Assessment and improvement of quality of service in wireless networks using fuzzy and hybrid genetic fuzzy approaches. *Journal of Artificial Intelligence Research*, *27*(2-3), 95–111. doi:10.1007/s10462-008-9090-5

Sarfraz, M., Ahmed, M. J., & Ghazi, S. A. (2003, July). *Saudi Arabian license plate recognition system*. International Conference on Geometric Modeling and Graphics. International Conference on Geometric Modeling and Graphics, London, England.

Schaffer, J. D. (1985). Multiple objective optimization with vector evaluated genetic algorithm. In the *Proceedings of the First International Conference on Genetic Algorithms*, (pp. 93-100). July, Pittsburgh (USA).

Schapire, R. E. (1990). The strength of weak learnability. *Machine Learning*, *5*(2), 197–227. doi:10.1007/BF00116037

Scheffer, T., Decomain, C., & Wrobel, S. (2001). Active hidden Markov models for information extraction. In *Proceedings of the Fourth International Symposium on Intelligent Data Analysis*, (pp. 301-109). Lisbon.

Schelhorn, T., O'Sullivan, D., Haklay, M., & Thurstain-Goodwin, M. (1999). *STREETS: An agent based pedestrian model*. Paper presented at the Computers in Urban Planning and Urban Management.

Schmidberger, M., Morgan, M., Eddelbuettel, D., Yu, H., Tierney, L., & Mansmann, U. (2009). State of the art in parallel computing with R. *Journal of Statistical Software*, *31*(1).

Schwefel, H. P., & Rudolph, G. (1995). *Advances in artificial life*. 3rd International Conference ALIFE. Berlin, Germany: Springer-Verlag.

Seeley, T. D. (1995). *The wisdom of the hive*. Cambridge, MA: Harvard University Press.

Selim, S. Z., & Ismail, M. A. (1984). K-means type algorithms: a generalized convergence theorem and characterization of local optimality. *IEEE Transactions on Pattern Analysis and Machine Intelligence*, 81–87. doi:10.1109/TPAMI.1984.4767478

Semnani, A., Kamyab, M., & Rekanos, I. T. (2009, Oct.). Reconstruction of one-dimensional dielectric scatterers using differential evolution and particle swarm optimization. *IEEE Geoscience and Remote Sensing Letters*, *6*(4), 671–675. doi:10.1109/LGRS.2009.2023246

Settles, M. (2005). *An introduction to particle swarm optimization* (pp. 1–8). Moscow, Idaho: University of Idaho.

Sezgin, M., & Sankur, B. (2004). Survey over image thresholding techniques and quantitative performance evaluation. *Journal of Electronic Imaging*, *13*(1), 146–165. doi:10.1117/1.1631315

Sezgin, M., & Tasaltin, R. (2000). A new dichotomization technique to multilevel thresholding devoted to inspection applications. *Pattern Recognition Letters, 21*, 151–161. doi:10.1016/S0167-8655(99)00142-7

Shi, Y. H., & Eberhart, R. C. (1998a). A modified particle swarm optimizer. In *Proceedings of the 1998 IEEE International Conference on Evolutionary Computation*, Anchorage, Alaska, May 4-9.

Shi, Y. H., & Eberhart, R. C. (2001). Fuzzy adaptive particle swarm optimization. In *IEEE International Conference on Evolutionary Computation*, (pp. 101–106).

Shin, J., Kim, S., Kang, S., Lee, S., Paik, J., Abidi, B., & Abidi, M. (2005). Optical flow-based real-time object tracking using non-prior training active feature model. *Real-Time Imaging, 3*(11), 204–218. doi:10.1016/j.rti.2005.03.006

Shi, Y. H., & Eberhart, R. C. (1998b). Parameter selection in particle swarm optimization. In Porto, V. W., & Waagen, D. (Eds.), *EP 1998, LNCS* (*Vol. 1447*, pp. 591–600). Heidelberg, Germany: Springer.

Silla, C. N., Koerich, A. L., & Kaestner, C. A. A. (2008). A machine learning approach to automatic music genre classification. *Journal of the Brazilian Computer Society, 14*(3), 7–18. doi:10.1007/BF03192561

Simon, B., Dolog, P., Miklos, Z., Olmeda, D., & Sintek, M. (2004). Conceptualizing smart spaces for learning. *Journal of Interactive Media in Education, Special Issue on the Educational Semantic Web.* Retrieved from http://www-jime.open.ac.uk/jime/article/viewArticle/78

Sislak, D., Volf, P., Jakob, M., & Pechoucek, M. (2009). *Distributed platform for large-scale agent-based simulations* (pp. 16–32). Agents for Games and Simulations.

Smith, D. M. (2010). *Hype cycle for cloud computing*. Gartner Rep. no.: G00201557.

Smith, M. K., McGuinness, D., Volz, R., & Welty, C. (2004). *OWL Web ontology language guide*. W3C Recommendation 10th February 2004. Retrieved from http://www.w3.org/TR/owl-guide/

Smith, K. A. (1999). *Introduction to neural networks and data mining for business applications*. Australia: Eruditions Publishing.

SoKNOS. (2011). *Service-oriented architectures supporting networks of public security sector*. Retrieved May 20, 2011, from http://www.soknos.de/index.php?id=197&L=0

Sonnessa, M. (2003). JAS: Java agent-based simulation library. An open framework for algorithm-intensive simulations. *Industry and Labor Dynamics: The Agent-Based Computational Economics Approach*, (pp. 43-56).

Srinivas, M., & Patnaik, L. M. (1994). Adaptive probabilities of crossover and mutation in genetic algorithms. *IEEE Transactions on Systems, Man, and Cybernetics, 24*(4). doi:10.1109/21.286385

Srinivas, N., & Deb, K. (1995). Multiobjective optimization using non-dominated sorting in genetic algorithms. *Evolutionary Computation, 2*(8), 221–248.

Stage, A. R., Crookson, N. L., & Monserud, R. A. (1993). An aggregation algorithm for increasing the efficiency of population models. *Ecological Modelling, 68*(3-4), 257–271. doi:10.1016/0304-3800(93)90021-J

Stahel, W., & Weisberg, S. (1991). *Direction in robust statistics and diagnostics, (Preface)*. New York, NY: Springer-Verlag.

Stair, R., & Reynolds, G. (2005). *Fundamentals of information systems* (3rd ed.). Thomson Course Technology.

Stein, M. R., & Madden, C. P. (2005). *The Puma Paint Project: Long term usage trends and the move to three dimensions.* IEEE International Conference on Robotics and Automation, ICRA.

Stein, E. (1987). *Clinical electrocardiography: A self-study course*. Philadelphia, PA: Lea and Febiger.

Stein, J. (1996). Rational capital budgeting in an irrational world. *The Journal of Business, 69*(4), 429–455. doi:10.1086/209699

Storn, R., & Price, K. (1995). *Differential evolution—A simple and efficient adaptive scheme for global optimization over continuous spaces*. Tech. Rep. TR-95-012, from http://citeseer.ist.psu.edu/article/storn95differential.html

Storn, R. (2008). Differential evolution research - Trends and open questions. *Studies in Computational Intelligence, 143*, 1–31. doi:10.1007/978-3-540-68830-3_1

Storn, R., & Price, K. (1997). Differential evolution - A simple and efficient heuristic for global optimization over continuous spaces. *Journal of Global Optimization*, *11*(4), 341–359. doi:10.1023/A:1008202821328

Strippgen, D., & Nagel, K. (2009). *Using common graphics hardware for multi-agent traffic simulation with CUDA*. Paper presented at the SIMUTools.

Stutt, A., & Motta, E. (2004). Semantic Webs for learning: A vision and its realization. *Proceedings of EKAW 2004, LNCS 3257*, (pp.132-143). Springer-Verlag.

Su, H. Y., Wu, C. H., & Tsai, P. J. (2008). *Automatic assessment of articulation disorders using confident unit-based model adaptation* (pp. 4513–4516). ICASSP.

Sun, B. H., Zhou, S. G., Wei, Y. F., & Liu, Q. Z. (2010). Modified two-element Yagi-uda antenna with tunable beams. *Progress in Electromagnetics Research*, *100*, 175–187. doi:10.2528/PIER09111501

Sunderam, V. S. (1990). PVM: A framework for parallel distributed computing. *Journal of Concurrency: Practice and Experience*, *2*(4), 315–339. doi:10.1002/cpe.4330020404

Sun, X., Qian, W., & Song, D. (2004). Ipsilateral-mammogram computer-aided detection of breast cancer. *Computerized Medical Imaging and Graphics*, *28*, 151–158. doi:10.1016/j.compmedimag.2003.11.004

Taddei, A., & Constantino, G. (1995). A system for the detection of ischemic episodes in ambulatory ECG. *Computers in Cardiology*, 705–708.

Taddei, A., Distante, G., Emdin, M., Pisani, P., Moody, G. B., Zeelenberg, C., & Marchesi, C. (1992). The European ST-T database: Standard for evaluating systems for the analysis of ST-T changes in ambulatory electrocardiography. *European Heart Journal*, *13*, 1164–1172.

Tan, K. C. (2008). CEC 2007 Conference report. *IEEE Computational Intelligence Magazine*, *3*(2), 72-73.

Tang, J., Rangayyan, R., Xu, J., El Naqa, E., & Yang, Y. (2009). Computer-aided detection and diagnosis of breast cancer with mammography: Recent advances. *IEEE Transactions on Information Technology in Biomedicine*, *13*(2), 236–251. doi:10.1109/TITB.2008.2009441

Tao, W. B., Tian, J. W., & Liu, J. (2003). Image segmentation by three level thresholding based on maximum fuzzy entropy and genetic algorithm. *Pattern Recognition Letters*, *24*, 3069–3078. doi:10.1016/S0167-8655(03)00166-1

Teisbaek, H. B., & Jakobsen, K. B. (2009). Koch-fractal Yagi-Uda antenna. *Journal of Electromagnetic Waves and Applications*, *23*(2-3), 149–160. doi:10.1163/156939309787604337

Tepperman, J., & Narayanan, S. (2005). *Automatic syllable stress detection using prosodic features for pronunciation evaluation of language learners*. In ICASSP 2005, Philadelphia, PA, March.

Terrell, G. R., & Scott, D. W. (1992). Variable kernel density estimation. *Annals of Statistics*, *20*(3), 1236–1265. doi:10.1214/aos/1176348768

Thaler, M. (2002). *The only EKG book you'll ever need*. Philadelphia, PA: Lippincott Williams and Wilkins.

Theodoridis, S., & Koutroumbas, K. (2003). *Pattern recognition* (2nd ed.). Amsterdam, the Netherlands: Elsevier Academic Press.

Thompson, J. D., Higgins, D. G., & Gibson, T. J. (1994). CLUSTAL W: Improving the sensitivity of progressive multiple sequence alignment through sequence weighting, position-specific gap penalties and weight matrix choice. *Nucleic Acids Research*, *22*, 4673–4680. doi:10.1093/nar/22.22.4673

TIMIT Corpus. (n.d.). Retrieved from http://www.ldc.upenn.edu/Catalog/CatalogEntry.jsp?catalogId=LDC93S1

Timp, S., Varela, C., Karssemeijer, N., & Dacolian, B. (2007). Temporal change analysis for characterization of mass lesions in mammography. *IEEE Transactions on Medical Imaging*, *26*(7), 945–953. doi:10.1109/TMI.2007.897392

Tisue, S., & Wilensky, U. (2004). *NetLogo*. Paper presented at the International Conference on Complex Systems.

Tizhoosh, H. R. (2004). *Homepage of fuzzy image processing*. Retrieved September 3, 2011, from http://pami.uwaterloo.ca/tizhoosh/fip.htm

Trucco, E. L., & Plakas, K. (2006). Video tracking: A concise survey. *IEEE Journal of Oceanic Engineering*, *2*(31), 520–529. doi:10.1109/JOE.2004.839933

Tseng, L. Y., & Yang, S. B. (2001). A genetic approach to the automatic clustering algorithm. *Pattern Recognition*, *34*(2), 415–424. doi:10.1016/S0031-3203(00)00005-4

Tsubota, Y., Kawahara, T., & Dantsuji, M. (2002). CALL system for Japanese students of English using pronunciation error prediction and formant structure estimation. In *Proceedings InSTILL 2002.*

Tummala, M., Wai, C. C., & Vincent, P. (2005). Distributed beamforming in wireless sensor networks. *Conference Record of the Thirty-Ninth Asilomar Conference on Signals, Systems and Computers,* October 28 - November 1, 2005 (pp. 793 – 797).

Turchenko, V. Kochan, V., Koval, V., Sachenko, A., & Markowsky, G. (2003, May). Smart vehicle screening system using artificial intelligence methods. *Proceedings of 2003 Spring IEEE Conference on Technologies for Homeland Security*, Cambridge, Massachusetts (pp. 182-185).

Turi, R. (2001). *Clustering-based colour image segmentation.* Unpublished Doctoral dissertation, Monash University, Australia.

Turi, R. H. (2001). *Clustering-based color image segmentation.* Ph.D Thesis, Monash University, Australia.

Tzanetakis, G. (2005). *Tempo extraction using beat histograms. Music Information Retrieval Evaluation eXchange*. MIREX.

UDDI. (2011). Universal discovery, description, integration. Retrieved September 24, 2011, from http://uddi.org/pubs/uddi-v3.0.2-20041019. htm/

Umarani, R., & Selvi, V. (2010). Particle swarm optimization-evolution, overview and applications. *International Journal of Engineering Science*, *2*(7), 2802–2806.

United Nations. (2005). *Hyogo framework for action 2005-2015: Building the resilience of nations and communities to disasters.* World Conference on Disaster Reduction, January, Kobe, Hyogo, Japan.

Van den Bergh, F. (2002). *An analysis of particle swarm optimizers*. PhD Thesis, Department of Computer Science, University of Pretoria.

Van Heerden, R. P., & Botha, E. C. (2010, November). *Optimization of vehicle license plate segmentation and symbol recognition.* The 21st Annual International Symposium of the Pattern Recognition Association of South Africa, Stellenbosch, South Africa.

Van Veen, B. D., & Buckley, K. M. (1988). Beamforming: A versatile approach to spatial filtering. *IEEE ASSP Magazine*.

Velleman, P. F., & Welsch, R. E. (1981). Efficient computing in regression diagnostics. *The American Statistician*, *35*, 234–242.

Venkatarayalu, N. V., & Ray, T. (2003). Single and multi-objective design of Yagi-Uda antennas using computational intelligence. *Congress on Evolutionary Computing, 2*, 1237-1242.

Venkatarayalu, N. V., & Ray, T. (2004). Optimum design of Yagi-Uda antennas using computational intelligence. *IEEE Transactions on Antennas and Propagation*, *52*(7), 1811–1818. doi:10.1109/TAP.2004.831338

Venkatarayalu, N. V., Ray, T., & Gan, Y. B. (2005). Multilayer dielectric filter design using a multiobjective evolutionary algorithm. *IEEE Transactions on Antennas and Propagation*, *53*(11), 3625–3632. doi:10.1109/TAP.2005.858565

Vesterstrom, J., & Thomsen, R. (2004). *A comparative study of differential evolution, particle swarm optimization, and evolutionary algorithms on numerical benchmark problems.* Paper presented at the Congress on Evolutionary Computation, CEC2004 Portland, USA.

Vila, J., Presedo, J., Delgado, M., Barro, S., Ruiz, R., & Palacios, F. (1997). SUTIL: Intelligent ischemia monitoring system. *International Journal of Medical Informatics*, *47*, 193–214. doi:10.1016/S1386-5056(97)00095-6

Vincent, P., Tummala, M., & McEachen, J. (2008). A new method for distributing power usage across a sensor network. *Ad Hoc Networks*, *6*(8), 1258–1280. Retrieved from http://www.sciencedirect.com/science/journal/15708705doi:10.1016/j.adhoc.2007.11.014

Vinga, S., & Almeida, J. (2003). Alignment-free sequence comparison-a review. *Bioinformatics (Oxford, England)*, *19*, 513–523. doi:10.1093/bioinformatics/btg005

Visscher, P. M. (2008). Sizing up human height variation. *Nature Genetics*, *40*, 489–490. doi:10.1038/ng0508-489

Vouk, M. A. (2008). Cloud computing – Issues, research and implementations. *Journal of Computing and Information Technology – CIT*, *16*(4), 235–246.

Vouk, M. A., Bitzer, D., & Klevans, R. (1999). Workflow and end-user quality of service issues in web-based education. *IEEE Transactions on Knowledge and Data Engineering*, *11*(4). doi:10.1109/69.790839

W3C. (2000). *Semantic Web advanced development*. Retrieved from http://www.w3.org/2000/01/sw/

W3C. (2001). *Semantic Web activity*. Retrieved from http://www.w3.org/2001/sw/

W3C. (2001). *Semantic Web advanced development in Europe*. Retrieved from http://www.w3.org/2001/sw/Europe/

W3C. (2001). *Web Ontology Working Group*. Retrieved from http://www.w3.org/2001/sw/WebOnt/

Wang, S., Zheng, Z., Sun, Q., Zou, H., & Yang, F. (2011). Cloud model for service selection. *Proceedings of INFOCOM2011 Workshop on Cloud Computing*, Shanghai, China, (pp. 677-682).

Wang, X., Han, T. X., & Yan, S. (2009). An HOG-LBP human detector with partial occlusion handling. In *IEEE 12th International Conference on Computer Vision*, (pp. 32–39).

Wang, Y., Zhang, H., Fang, X., & Guo, J. (2009, February). *Low-resolution Chinese character recognition of vehicle license plate based on ALBP and Gabor filters*. Seventh International Conference on Advances in Pattern Recognition, Kolkata, India.

Wang, W., Sun, Q., Zhao, X., & Yang, F. (2010). An improved particle swarm optimization algorithm for QoS-aware web service selection in service oriented communication. *International Journal of Computational Intelligence Systems*, *3*(1), 18–30. doi:10.2991/ijcis.2010.3.s1.2

Wang, X.-H. (2004). Numerical integration study based on triangle basis neural network algorithm. *Journal of Electronics and Information Technology*, *26*(3), 394–399.

Wang, X., Qu, H., Liu, P., & Cheng, Y. (2004). A self-learning expert system for diagnosis in traditional Chinese medicine. *Expert Systems with Applications*, *26*, 557–566. doi:10.1016/j.eswa.2003.10.004

Weber, P., Theilliol, D., & Aubrun, C. (2008). Component reliability in fault diagnosis decision-making based on dynamic Bayesian networks. *Proceedings of the Institution of Mechanical Engineers Part O, Journal of Risk and Reliability*, (pp. 161-172).

Wei, J., Sahiner, B., Hadjiiski, L., Chan, H., Petrick, N., & Helvie, M. A. (2005). Computer aided detection of breast masses on full field digital mammograms. *Medical Physics*, *32*(9), 2827–2837. doi:10.1118/1.1997327

Weile, D. S., Michielssen, E., & Goldberg, D. E. (1996). Genetic algorithm design of Pareto optimal broadband microwave absorbers. *IEEE Transactions on Electromagnetic Compatibility*, *38*(3), 518–525. doi:10.1109/15.536085

Weisburg, W. G., Barns, S. M., Pelletier, D. A., & Lane, D. J. (1991). 16S ribosomal DNA amplification for phylogenetic study. *Journal of Bacteriology*, *173*(2), 697–703.

Welsch, R. E. (1982). Influence functions and regression diagnostics. In Launar, R. L., & Siegel, A. F. (Eds.), *Modern data analysis*. New York, NY: Academic Press.

Wendel, S., & Dibble, C. (2007). Dynamic agent compression. *Artificial Societies and Social Simulation*, *10*(2).

Wikipedia. (n.d.). *Beat (acoustics)*. Retrieved January 5, 2012, from http://en.wikipedia.org/wiki/Beat_(acoustics)

Wikipedia. (n.d.). *Music of Bangladesh*. Retrieved January 5, 2012, from http://en.wikipedia.org/wiki/Music_of_Bangladesh

Witt, S. M., & Young, S. J. (2000). Phone-level pronunciation scoring and assessment for interactive language learning. *Speech Communication*, *30*, 95–108. doi:10.1016/S0167-6393(99)00044-8

Wolpert, D. H., & Macready, W. G. (1997). No free lunch theorems for optimization. *IEEE Transactions on Evolutionary Computation*, *1*(1), 67–82. doi:10.1109/4235.585893

Wu, B. F., Chen, Y. L., & Chiu, C. C. (2004). Recursive algorithms for image segmentation based on a discriminant criterion. *International Journal of Signal Processing*, *1*, 55–60.

Wu, C. H., Hsia, C. C., Chen, J. F., & Wang, J. F. (2007). Variable-length unit selection in TTS using structural syntactic cost. *IEEE Trans. Audio, Speech, and Language Processing*, *15*(4), 1227–1235. doi:10.1109/TASL.2006.889752

Wu, C. H., Su, H. Y., & Shen, H. P. (2011). Articulation-disordered speech recognition using speaker-adaptive acoustic models and personalized articulation patterns. *ACM Transactions on Asian Language Information Processing*, *10*(2). doi:10.1145/1967293.1967294

Xia, F., Zhao, W. H., Sun, Y. X., & Tian, Y. C. (2007). Fuzzy logic control based QoS management in wireless sensor/actuator networks. *Sensors (Basel, Switzerland)*, *7*(12), 3179–3191. doi:10.3390/s7123179

Xie, J. (2009). Optimal control of chaotic system based on LS-SVM with mixed kernel. *Third International Symposium on Intelligent Information Technology Application*, Vol. 1, (pp. 622-625).

Xilinx Inc. (2009). *MicroBlaze soft processor core*. Retrieved March 10, 2009, from http://www.xilinx.com/tools/microblaze.htm

Xu, L. (1994). Theories for unsupervised learning: PCA and its nonlinear extensions. *Proceedings of IEEE International Conference on Neural Networks*, ICNN'94, Orlando, Florida, Vol. 2, (pp. 1252a, 1253 –1257).

Xu, R., & Wunsch, D. (2005). Survey of clustering algorithms. *IEEE Transactions on Neural Networks*, *16*, 645–678. doi:10.1109/TNN.2005.845141

Yamamoto, G., Tai, H., & Mizuta, H. (2007). *A platform for massive agent-based simulation and its evaluation.* Paper presented at the 6th International Joint Conference on Autonomous Agent and Multiagent Systems (AAMAS '07).

Yan, L., Hang, Y., Lai, J., Lixiao, M., & Zhen, J. (2010). Adaptive lifting scheme for ECG QRS complexes detection and its FPGA implementation. *Third International Conference on Biomedical Engineering and Informatics*, (pp. 721-724).

Yang, B., Lim, D., & Tan, A. C. C. (2005). VIBEX: An expert system for vibration fault diagnosis of rotating machinery using decision tree and decision table. *Expert Systems with Applications*, *28*, 735–742. doi:10.1016/j.eswa.2004.12.030

Yang, J., Benyamin, B., McEvoy, B. P., Gordon, S., Henders, A. K., & Nyholt, D. R. (2010). Common SNPs explain a large proportion of the heritability for human height. *Nature Genetics*, *42*, 565–569. doi:10.1038/ng.608

Yang, Q., Wang, L., Yang, R., & Stewenius, H., & Nister. (2009). Stereo matching with colour-weighted correlation, hierarchical belief propagation, and occlusion handling. *IEEE Transactions on Pattern Analysis and Machine Intelligence*, *3*(31), 492–504. doi:10.1109/TPAMI.2008.99

Yang, X.-S. (2010). Test problems in optimization. In *Engineering optimization: An introduction with metaheuristic applications*. John Wiley & Sons. doi:10.1002/9780470640425.app1

Yanofsky, N. S., & Mannucci, M. A. (2008). *Quantum computing for computer scientists*. Cambridge University Press.

Yao, K., Hudson, R. E., Reed, C. W., Chen, D., & Lorenzelli, F. (1998). Blind beamforming on a randomly distributed sensor array system. *IEEE Journal on Selected Areas in Communications*, *16*(8), 1555–1567. doi:10.1109/49.730461

Yasuhiro, T., & Mitsuo, G. E. (1998). Entropy-based genetic algorithm for solving TSP. *The Second International Conference on Knowledge-based Intelligent Electronic Systems*, (pp. 285–290).

Yen, C., Chang, F. J., & Chang, S. (1995). A new criterion for automatic multilevel thresholding. *IEEE Transactions on Image Processing*, *4*, 370–378. doi:10.1109/83.366472

Yeung, S. H., Man, K. F., Luk, K. M., & Chan, C. H. (2008). A trapeizform u-slot folded patch feed antenna design optimized with jumping genes evolutionary algorithm. *IEEE Transactions on Antennas and Propagation*, *56*(2), 571–577. doi:10.1109/TAP.2007.915473

Yick, J., Mukherjee, B., & Ghodal, D. (2008). Wireless sensor network survey. *Computer Networks*, *52*(12). doi:10.1016/j.comnet.2008.04.002

Yilmaz, A., Javed, O., & Shah, M. (2006). Object tracking: A survey. *ACM Computing Surveys (CSUR)*, *4*(38). DOI=10.1145/1177352.1177355

Yin, P. Y., & Chen, L. H. (1997). A fast iterative scheme for multilevel thresholding methods. *Journal Signal Process*, *60*, 305–313. doi:10.1016/S0165-1684(97)00080-7

Young, S. (2000). *The HTK book*. Microsoft Corporation.

Yourui, H., & Shuang, W. (2008). Multilevel thresholding methods for image segmentation with Otsu based on QPSO. *Congress on Image and Signal Processing*, (pp. 701-705).

Yu, T., Zhang, Y., & Lin, K.-J. (2007). Efficient algorithms for Web services selection with end-to-end QoS constraints. *ACM Transactions on the Web (TWEB)*, *1*(1).

Yuan, X., Nie, H., Su, A., Wang, L., & Yuan, Y. (2009). An improved binary particle swarm optimization for unit commitment problem. *Expert Systems with Applications*, *36*(4), 8049–8055. doi:10.1016/j.eswa.2008.10.047

Zadeh, L. A. (1965). Fuzzy sets. *Information and Control*, *8*(3), 338–353. doi:10.1016/S0019-9958(65)90241-X

Zahara, E., Fan, S. K. S., & Tsai, D. M. (2005). Optimal multi-thresholding using a hybrid optimization approach. *Pattern Recognition Letters*, *26*(8), 1082–1095. doi:10.1016/j.patrec.2004.10.003

Zantout, R., & Almustafa, K. (2011, November). *Automatic recognition of Saudi license plates*. Technical Report, Prince Sultan University, Kingdom of Saudi Arabia.

Zeidman, B. (2002). *Designing with FPGAs and CPLDs*. London, UK: CMP Publishing.

Zerarka, A., & Khelil, N. (2006). A generalized integral quadratic method: improvement of the solution for one dimensional Volterra integral equation using particle swarm optimization. *International Journal of Simulation and Process Modelling*, *2*(1-2), 152–163.

Zerarka, A., Soukeur, A., & Khelil, N. (2009). The particle swarm optimization against the Runge's phenomenon: Application to the generalized integral quadrature method. *International Journal of Mathematical and Statistical Sciences*, *1*(3), 171–176.

Zhang, X., Hu, W., Li, W., Qu, W., & Maybank, S. (2009). Multi-object tracking via species based particle swarm optimization. *Computer Vision Workshops (ICCV Workshops) IEEE 12th International Conference*, *20*(11), 1105-1112.

Zhang, C., Su, S., & Chen, J. (2007). DiGA: Population diversity handling genetic algorithm for QoS-aware web services selection. *Computer Communications*, *30*, 1082–1090. doi:10.1016/j.comcom.2006.11.002

Zhao, S. Z., & Suganthan, P. N. (2010). Two-lbests based multi-objective particle swarm optimizer. *Engineering Optimization*, *43*(1).

Zhao, Z., Peng, Z., Zheng, S., & Shang, J. (2009). Cognitive radio spectrum allocation using evolutionary algorithms. *IEEE Transactions on Wireless Communications*, *8*(9), 4421–4425. doi:10.1109/TWC.2009.080939

Zheng, H., & Peng, C. (2005). Collaboration and fairness in opportunistic spectrum access. In *2005 IEEE International Conference on Communications, ICC 2005* (Vol. 5, pp. 3132-3136). Beijing, China: IEEE.

Zhen, L., & Chan, A. K. (2001). An artificial intelligent algorithm for tumor detection in screening mammogram. *IEEE Transactions on Medical Imaging*, *20*(7), 559–567. doi:10.1109/42.932741

Zhou, H., Yuan, Y., & Shi, C. (2008). Object tracking using SIFT features and mean shift. *Journal of Computer Vision and Image Understanding*, *3*(113), 345–352.

Zhu, X. (2005). *Semi-supervised learning literature survey*. University of Wisconsin – Madison.

Zmijewski, M. E. (1984). Methodological issues related to the estimation of financial distress prediction models. *Journal of Accounting Research*, *22*, 59–82. doi:10.2307/2490859

About the Contributors

Shawkat Ali is currently with School of Information and Communication Technology, CQUniversity, Australia. He received his PhD in Information Technology from Clayton School of Information Technology, Monash University. His research interests include computational intelligence, data mining, smart grid, cloud computing, and biomedical engineering. In particular, he is currently leading in a research group on computational intelligence. He has published more than 85 research papers in international journals and conferences, most of them are IEEE/ELSEVIER journals/conferences, such as *IEEE Transactions on Intelligent Transportation Systems*, *Future Generation Computer Systems,* ELSEVIER, *WSEAS Transactions on Information Science and Applications, Journal of Medical Systems*, Springer, and *Renewable Energy*, ELSEVIER. He has also published several book chapters and books. His Data Mining book is being used as text in more than two dozen universities around the globe. Dr. Ali has chaired many conferences including DMAI, NSS, ICDKE, and ISDA. He has been a program committee member for about 40 international conferences such as IEEE TrustCom, IEEE ICCIT, IEEE/ACIS, IEEE ICARCV, and IEEE AINA. Currently he is the Editor-in-Chief for *International Journal of Emerging Technologies in Sciences and Engineering* (IJETSE), Canada. He is an IEEE Senior Member. Dr. Ali has received a couple of awards including the Post Graduation Publication Award, Monash University, 2004, the Excellence in Supervision Award, CQUniversity, 2007 and the Top 10 Course Designers, CQUniversity, 2010.

Noureddine Abbadeni is currently Associate Professor of Computer Science and vice-chair of the Software Engineering department at the College of Computer and Information Sciences at King Saud University. He received the B.Eng. degree in Computer Science (Software Engineering) from USTHB-Algiers-Algeria, the M.Sc. degree in Computer Science and the M.Sc degree in Computational Linguistics, both from University of Grenoble-France, the DESS degree in Management from HEC Montreal-Canada, and the PhD degree in Computer Science from University of Sherbrooke-Canada. Dr. Abbadeni has an experience of more than 14 years in both academia and IT industry in Canada, USA, UAE, and KSA. Dr. Abbadeni conducted research projects for several years and has several papers published in international refereed conferences and journals such as *IEEE Trans. on IP*, Elsevier's *JVCIR, IEEE ICME, IEEE ICIP*, etc. His research fields include multimedia computing, information retrieval, data mining, and pattern recognition & image processing.

Mohamed Batouche is currently full Professor of Computer Science at University of Constantine, Algeria. He was full Professor in the College of Computer and Information Sciences at King Saud University, Saudi Arabia between 2007 and 2011. He holds a Ph.D. in Computer Science from University of Nancy - INPL, France. He published over 150 refereed journal and conference papers in the areas of complex systems, nature inspired computing, bioinformatics, image processing, machine learning, and telecommunication.

* * *

Hisham Abdelsalam holds a Master of Science and a Ph.D. in Mechanical Engineering (Old Dominion University, Norfolk, Virginia, USA). He obtained his Bachelor degree with honors in Mechanical Engineering from Cairo University (Cairo, Egypt). Dr. Abdelsalam is an Associate Professor in the Operations Research and Decision Support Department, Faculty of Computers and Information, Cairo University. In 2009, Dr. Abdelsalam was appointed as the director of the Decision Support and Future Studies Center in Cairo University. During the past four years, Dr. Abdelsalam has led several consultancy and research projects and published eight scholarly articles on e-government.

Hajar Mohammedsaleh H Alharbi received her Bachelor of Science degree in Computer Science with first class honours from King Abdulaziz University (KAU), Jeddah, Kingdom of Saudi Arabia, in 2001. She completed her Master's degree in Computer Science at the University of New England (UNE), Armidale, Australia, in 2011. Currently, she is a Ph.D. student in the School of Science and Technology at UNE. Since 2007, she has been a teacher's assistant at the Department of Computer Science, Faculty of Computing and Information, KAU. Her current research interests include image processing, fuzzy logic, neural network, pattern recognition and their applications to medical image analysis.

Khaled Almustafa received his B.E.Sc. in Electrical Engineering, M.E.Sc and Ph.D. in Wireless Communication from the University of Western Ontario, London, Ontario, Canada in 2003, 2004, and 2007, respectively. He is currently the Chairman of the Department of Communication and Networks Engineering, College of Engineering at Prince Sultan University (PSU), Riyadh, K.S.A. Also he is the General Supervisor for the Information Technology and Computer Services Center (ITCS) at PSU. His research interests include error performance evaluation of MIMO communication systems in partially known channels, adaptive modulation, and channel security, as well as text recognition models.

Abdoul Rahman M. AlShaar received the B.S. degree in Operations Research and Decision Support, Cairo, Egypt, in 2010. He is currently studying towards the M.Sc. degree in the same major in the Cairo University. Eng. AlShaar is a research assistant in the Decision Support and Future Studies Center, Faculty of Computers and Information, Cairo University.

Salahuddin A. Azad received the B.Sc. Eng. (hons.) degree in Computer Science & Engineering from Bangladesh University of Engineering & Technology (BUET), Bangladesh, in 1999 and the Ph.D. degree in Information Technology from Monash University Australia, in 2007. Dr. Azad has research experiences in multiple disciplines. He has published nine refereed conference papers and two IEEE journals. Currently, he is working as a postdoctoral research fellow with Power Engineering Group in Central Queensland University of Technology. His major research interests are in the fields of renewable energy, smart grid, image processing, machine learning, data mining, control systems, and robotics. Besides, he has extensive teaching experiences in Australia and overseas. His courses of interest for teaching are Web application development, mobile application development, computer communications & networks, computer systems & microprocessors, Internet commerce, and computer graphics.

Salim BITAM received the State Engineer degree in computer science from Mentouri University, Constantine, Algeria, in 1999 and the Magister and Doctorate in Science degrees in Computer Science from Mohamed Khider University, Biskra, Algeria, in 2002 and 2011, respectively. In December 2002, he has been an Assistant Professor and since January 2011 he is an Associate Professor in Computer Science department in University of Biskra. His main research interests are cloud computing, mobile ad hoc networks, vehicular ad hoc networks, wireless sensor networks, and bio-inspired methods for optimization. Dr. Salim Bitam has served as a reviewer of several journals such as Elsevier and Springer and on the program committees of several international conferences.

Yee Ling Boo is currently an Associate Lecturer at School of Information Systems, Faculty of Business and Law, Deakin University. Her research interests include data mining, artificial neural networks, brain inspired cognitive systems, business intelligence, and health informatics. She worked as a Software Engineer for Intel (Malaysia) after graduating with a Bachelor of Information Technology (Honours) from Multimedia University, Malaysia. She received her Ph.D in Information Technology from Clayton School of Information Technology, Faculty of Information Technology, Monash University.

Farjana Z. Eishita was born in Rajshahi, Bangladesh in 1984. She completed her Bachelors in Computer Science and Engineering from American International University Bangladesh (AIUB) in 2007. Immediately after completing her Bachelor's, she started her Master's program in Computer Science at the same university. Her area of Master's research program was Intelligent Systems. In parallel to her Master's program, she served as a Lecturer at AIUB as well. After completing her Master's, she started her PhD program in January 2010 at the University of Saskatchewan, Canada. Currently she is continuing her PhD program in the area of Augmented Reality Games.

M. Esa received the BEE (Hons.), MSc in RF Engineering, and PhD in Electrical and Electronics Engineering from Universiti Teknologi Malaysia, Univ. of Bradford (UK), and Univ. of Birmingham (UK), in 1984, 1987, and 1996, respectively. She is attached with the Faculty of Electrical Engineering, UTM, since 1984. She has served several key administrative posts, and is currently a full professor. Her research interests are RF/microwave and antenna engineering, THz/PHz technology, wireless power transmission, CAD/CAE, qualitative research, and quality engineering education. She is a co-founder of IEEE Malaysia AP/MTT/EMC Chapter and IEEE Malaysia Section, and has served various posts of Executive Committee in the Chapter. She was the Chapter Chair from 2007 to Jan 2011. She is currently the Counselor of IEEE UTM Student Branch. She is an active Senior Member of IEEE. She has also served various key portfolios in international conferences organized by the Chapter including General Chair, Technical Program Chair, and Tutorial Chair. She also serves as Int. Steering Committee member of Int. Sym. on Antennas and Propagation (ISAP) and Asia-Pacific Microwave Conference (APMC), representing Malaysia. She will lead APMC 2017 in Malaysia.

Graeme Garner is a Senior Principal Research Scientist and manages the Epidemiology Program in the Animal Health Policy Branch of the Australian Department of Agriculture, Fisheries and Forestry. The Epidemiology Program provides technical support to national disease surveillance and reporting programs, undertakes studies on endemic and foreign animal diseases, and provides technical advice to address regional, national and international animal health issues. During his career, Dr Garner has worked on a range of animal health projects both in Australia and overseas. His research interests include simulation modelling of infectious diseases (with particular focus on emergency animal diseases), analysis of disease information, and use of computer mapping and geographical information systems in epidemiological studies.

Cedric Gondro is a Senior Lecturer in Animal Genetics at the University of New England in Australia. His current research interests lie in the development and application of statistical and artificial intelligence methods, particularly evolutionary computation, applied to analysis of high-throughput genomic data.

Sotirios K. Goudos was born in Thessaloniki, Greece in 1968. He received the B.Sc. degree in Physics in 1991 and the M.Sc. degree in Electronics in 1994 both from the Aristotle University of Thessaloniki. In 2001 he received the Ph.D. degree in Physics from the Aristotle University of Thessaloniki and in 2005 the Master in Information Systems degree from the University of Macedonia, Greece. In 2011 he obtained the Diploma degree in Electrical and Computer Engineering from the Aristotle University of Thessaloniki. Since 1996 he has been working in the Telecommunications Center of the Aristotle University of Thessaloniki, Greece. He has authored or co-authored more than 70 papers in peer reviewed journals and international conferences. His research interests include antenna and microwave structures design, electromagnetic compatibility of communication systems, evolutionary computation algorithms, mobile communications and semantic web technologies. Dr. Goudos is a member of the IEEE, the Greek Physics Society, the Technical Chamber of Greece, and the Greek Computer Society.

Lama Hamandi received her B.E. degree in Electrical Engineering from the American University of Beirut in 1988 and her M.S. and Ph.D. degrees from the Ohio State University in 1995 with a major in Computer Engineering and minor in Computer Science. She taught for five years in the Computer Applications Department in King Saud University and was an academic consultant of Al-Alamiya and New Horizon Colleges in Saudi Arabia. She returned to Lebanon in 2000 where she taught in the Computer Science department in Beirut Arab University, and then she was the Chairperson of the Computer Science and Computer Communication departments in the Business and Computer University College for two years. After that she joined the Electrical and Computer Engineering department in the American University of Beirut. Her research interests include parallel architecture, parallel processing, digital image processing, and natural language processing involving the Arabic language.

Abdelbaset S. Hamza received the B.S. (Hons.) degree in Electronics and Communication Engineering from the Institute of Aviation Engineering and Technology, Cairo, Egypt, in 2008. In 2011, he received the M.Sc. degree in Electronics and Communications Engineering from Cairo University, Cairo, Egypt. He is currently studying towards the Ph.D. degree in Computer Science and Computer Engineering at the University of Nebraska-Lincoln. In addition, he works as a Graduate Teaching at the University of Nebraska-Lincoln.

Haitham S. Hamza received the B.S. (Hons.) and the M.S. degree in electronics and communication engineering from Cairo University, Cairo, Egypt, in 1998 and 2002,respectively. He received the M.S. and Ph.D. degree in computer science from the University of Nebraska-Lincoln in 2002 and 2006, respectively. Dr. Hamza is a Fling Fellow of the University of Nebraska-Lincoln. He is currently is an Assistant Professor of Information Technology at Cairo University. Dr. Hamza has more than 50 papers published in international journals and conferences such as *IEEE/ACM Transaction on Networking, IEEE/OSA Journal of Lightwave Technology, Journal of Photonic Network Communications, IEEE Globecom, IEEE ICC*, and *Broadnets*. He is the recipient of the Best Paper Award for the Optical Networking Track in Broadnets 2005. Dr. Hamza is the author of a new book entitled "Wavelength Exchanging Switching Networks" published in 2010. His research interests include wireless and cognitive radio networks, design and analyses of photonic switches, optical interconnect architectures, and WDM networks protection algorithms.

S. A. Hamzah received the Bachelor of Electrical Engineering from Universiti Teknologi Malaysia (UTM), Malaysia in September 1998 and Master of Engineering in Communication and Computer System from National University of Malaysia (UKM), Selangor, Malaysia, in 2000. He is currently working towards a Ph.D. degree at the Department of Radio Communication Engineering, Faculty of Electrical Engineering, Universiti Teknologi Malaysia. From 1998 to 2004, he worked as a Lecturer at Kolej UNITI Sdn. Bhd, Malaysia. Since April 2004, he has been working as a Lecturer at the Faculty of Electrical and Electronic Engineering, Universiti Tun Hussein Onn Malaysia (UTHM). He is a student member of IEEE.

Helton Hugo de Carvalho Júnior received his B.S. in Computer Engineering from the Universidade Federal de Itajuba – Brazil in 2005 and his MsC and PhD from the Universidade Federal de Itajuba – Brazil, in 2007 and 2011, respectively. Since 2009, he has been a Professor at IFSP.

Chung-Hsien Wu received the Ph.D. degree in Electrical Engineering from National Cheng Kung University (NCKU), Tainan, Taiwan, in 1991. Since 1991, he has been with the Department of Computer Science and Information Engineering, NCKU. He became Professor and Distinguished Professor in 1997 and 2004, respectively. Currently, he is the Deputy Dean of the College of Electrical Engineering and Computer Science, NCKU. He also worked at Computer Science and Artificial Intelligence Laboratory in Massachusetts Institute of Technology, Cambridge, MA USA, in summer 2003 as a visiting scientist. He received the Outstanding Research Award of National Science Council in 2010 and the Distinguished Electrical Engineering Professor of the Chinese Institute of Electrical Engineering in 2011, Taiwan. He is currently Associate Editor Of *IEEE Trans. Audio, Speech and Language Processing*, *IEEE Trans. Affective Computing*, and *ACM Trans. Asian Language Information Processing*. His research interests include speech recognition, text-to-speech, and spoken language processing.

A.H.M. Rahmatullah Imon was born in Rajshahi, Bangladesh in 1967. He graduated with Honors in Statistics in 1987 and obtained his M.Sc. in Statistics in 1988 from the University of Rajshahi. He got his PhD in Mathematics and Statistics from the University of Birmingham, U.K. in 1996. Dr. Imon began his academic career as a Lecturer at the University of Rajshahi in 1992 and was promoted to a Full Professor position in 2004. He joined the Department of Mathematical Science, Ball State University in fall, 2008 and has been serving this department since then. Dr. Imon's areas of specialization are regression diagnostics, robust regression, and outlier detection. Dr. Imon has published 70 research articles in refereed journals and proceedings of international conferences. He got several awards for his outstanding academic records and research. He has been an elected member of the International Statistical Institute since 2005.

M. K. H. Ismail received the B. Eng. (Electrical-Telecommunication) and the M. Eng. (Electrical). degrees from Universiti Teknologi Malaysia, Malaysia in 2001 and 2004, respectively. He is currently pursuing PhD at Universiti Teknologi Malaysia, majoring in radio communication engineering. From January 2005, he joined Department of Space Systems and Operations, as a research officer of Malaysia

Space Agency (ANGKASA). As a research officer, he has been involved in satellite design projects such as RF system and electrical power system. He also conducted research and design on Electrical Power System for CubeSat project. In 2006, he joined a research project called MAGDAS (Magnetic Data Acquisitions System) to expand Global Monitoring of the Earth's Magnetic Field along Magnetic Equator with Space Environment Research Centre, Kyushu University, Japan. He is a student member of IEEE.

Suraiya Jabin is an Assistant Professor in Computer Science at the Jamia Millia Islamia (Central University), India. Her research interests are machine learning, intelligent tutoring systems, and data mining. She received her PhD in Machine Learning from the Hamdard University of India. She has published 2 papers in international journals and presented more than 5 research papers at International Conferences in India and abroad. She is a member of several professional bodies including ACM SIGCSE and life member of Indian Society for Technical Education (ISTE) apart from conference and journal review committees.

Ashoka Jayawardena holds a PhD in Computer Science specializing in wavelet signal/image processing. He is currently a Lecturer in Computer Science at University of New England. His past research work includes design of double-density wavelets, M-band wavelets, digital watermarking, and trust in peer to peer systems. His current research interests include computer vision, pattern recognition, image processing, and game programming.

Arsalan H. Khan received his first degree in Industrial Electronics from NED University of Engineering and Technology, Karachi in 2004 and M.Sc Computer Engineering from the University of Engineering and Technology, Taxila, Pakistan in 2008. Currently, he is pursuing his PhD degree in Control and automation on Chinese government scholarship in Northwestern Polytechnical University (NPU), Xi'an, China. His research interest includes fault tolerant control, intelligent optimization in flight controller design and computational intelligence in automation systems. He has more than 7 year industrial experience. He is a member of IEEE and professional member of Pakistan Engineering Council.

Salman H. Khan is a final year student of Electrical Engineering (B.E) at College of Electrical and Mechanical Engineering, National University of Science & Technology (NUST), Rawalpindi, Pakistan. He was selected for participation in the Global Undergraduate Exchange Program for Pakistan in 2011, organized by the Bureau of Educational and Cultural Affairs of the US state department and administered by IREX (International Research & Exchanges Board). He has been working as a research assistant at the Research laboratory for Communication, Networks & Multimedia (Connekt), School of Electrical Engineering & Computer Science (SEECS), NUST for two years. He is a student member of IEEE.

Zeashan H. Khan earned his MS (by research) in 2007 and PhD in 2010 from University of Grenoble, France. His major interest includes system identification, nonlinear control, artificial intelligence, teleoperation, and networked control system. He has actively contributed in the co-design conception for networked teleoperation by implementing a dynamic adaptation scheme for drive-by-wireless applications. He has published his work in more than 15 international conferences and 3 journals up till now. He has 10 years of industrial experience in control system design, implementation and validation. He is an active member of IEEE, ASME, SIAM, and ACM.

Rao M Kotamarti received the B.S in Computer Science from Concordia University, Montreal, Quebec and M.B.A. in General Management from Duke Fuqua School of Business, Durham, NC, and the Ph.D. degree in Computer Science from Southern Methodist University. From January 2011 to the present, he has been on adjunct faculty in the department of Computer Science and Engineering at Southern Methodist University in Dallas. Dr. Kotamarti's current research interests are in the areas of bioinformatics and data visualization. He had been in Telecom industry for twenty five years working in the research and development of several wireless network infrastructure products based on fault tolerant embedded systems.

Paul Kwan is currently a Senior Lecturer in Computer Science in the School of Science and Technology at University of New England, Australia. He received a BSc and an MSc degree in Computer Science from Cornell University and University of Arizona (USA) in 1986 and 1988, respectively. He was awarded PhD degree in Advanced Engineering Systems in 2003 from University of Tsukuba, Japan. His current research interests include Multimedia Information Processing and Analysis, Hand-based Biometrics, Pattern Recognition and Machine Learning, Bioinformatics and Biomedical Data Mining. He is a Senior member of IEEE and a Senior member of ACM.

Bob Li has academic experience well balanced with commercial expertise. He started his career as a research engineer in the commodity industry and later became a futures analyst. He also worked as an investment analyst in banking and utility industries. The last industry position he held before turning into academics was senior research analyst. He has deep understandings of financial markets, instruments, and equity/portfolio analysis/management. Bob has a hybrid education background. He holds a PhD in Finance, Master's in Economics, and Bachelor's in Engineering (Honours). He works at Deakin as a Lecturer in Finance.

Chao-Hong Liu received the B.S. degree in Earth Science (with minor in Civil Engineering) from National Cheng Kung University, Tainan, Taiwan, in 1998, and the M.S. degree in Computer Science and Information Engineering from National Dong Hwa University, Hualien, Taiwan, in 2005. He served as a Geologist and Civil Engineer in Central Geological Survey, National Cheng Kung University, and National Taiwan University during 1998 to 2003. Since 2005 he joined the department of Computer Science and Information Engineering, National Cheng Kung Universty, and he is currently a Ph.D. candidate in Computer Science. His research interests include speech and natural language processing, machine translation, and machine learning.

N. N. N. Abd. Malik graduated with B. Eng (Electrical-Telecommunication) and M. Eng. (Radio Frequency and Microwave Communications) from Universiti Teknologi Malaysia (UTM), Malaysia and University of Queensland (UQ), Australia, in 2003 and 2005, respectively. In 2003, she served as a research and development (R&D) Electrical Engineer for Motorola Technology Malaysia. At the end of 2003, she joined UTM as a Tutor and has been a Lecturer with the Faculty of Electrical Engineering, UTM since 2005. She is currently pursuing her PhD study in Universiti Teknologi Malaysia (UTM), Malaysia. She is a student member of IEEE.

Shah Jahan Miah is working as a Lecturer in Information Systems at Victoria University, Melbourne, Australia. Prior to this position, Shah has worked as an academic at Griffith University, James Cook University and University of the Sunshine Coast. He has received his PhD in Information Systems from Griffith University, in the area of decision support systems (DSS) development. Shah has lead authored more than 45 papers in different IS areas. He has published in many academic journals including *Australasian Journal of Information Systems, Electronic Journal of Information Systems Evaluations, Journal of Org. and End User Computing, Expert Systems with Applications,* and *Knowledge Based Systems*, and presented his research in many prominent academic conferences including *Americas Conference on Information Systems (AMCIS)* and *Australasian Conference on Information Systems (ACIS)*. His current research interests include cloud-based app design, industry oriented DSS design, and design science research in IS.

Robson L. Moreno received his B.S. in Electrical Engineering from the Universidade Federal de Itajuba – Brazil in 1988 and his MsC from the UNICAMP – Brazil in 1996. He received his PhD from the USP – Brazil in 2002. Since 2002, he has been a Professor at Universidade Federal de Itajuba.

K. Mustafa, an alumnus of IIT Delhi, is presently heading the Department of Computer Science at Jamia Millia Islamia (Central University), India. His research interests are software quality assurance and intelligent tutoring systems. He has large number of publications and two books to his credit, apart from international exposure to teaching of more than 15 years. In addition, he is member of several professional bodies including ACM & ISTE, apart from conference, review, and editorial committees.

Mohammed Nasser (1960-) is now Professor and Chairman at Department of Statistics, University of Rajshahi, Rajshahi – 6205, Bangladesh. He got Honours and M.Sc degree in Statistics from Jahangirnagar University, Bangladesh and did his Ph.D degree on *"Continuity and Differentiability of Statistical Functionals; Its Relation to Robustness in Boostrapping"* at Research Centre for Mathematical and Physical Sciences, Chittagong University, Bangladesh. He is the founder chairman of Statistical Learning Group (SLG) that has members working in several national-international universities and research organizations. He has already published more than forty articles in national and international journals in statistics, mathematics and sociology. His current research interest is in mathematics of kernel methods, bioinformatics, machine learning, data mining, robust estimation, and globalization. He is a life member of both Bangladesh Statistical Society and Bangladesh Mathematical Society, and editorial board members of three national journals and a member of Board of Global Advisors of The International Federation of Non-Linear Analysis (IFNA).

A. A. M. Nurunnabi received BSc (Hons), MSc and MPhil degrees in Statistics from the Department of Statistics, University of Rajshahi, Bangladesh. In his MPhil degree he carried out research into robust and diagnostic statistical techniques for outlier investigation in regression analysis. He started his profession as a Lecturer and later served as Principal at IMIT, Dhaka. He served (2003-2009) as an Assistant Professor at School of Business, Uttara University, Dhaka. He is a member of the Statistical Learning Group (SLG), Rajshahi University, Bangladesh. He has authored more than thirty five research articles in referred journals and conference proceedings, and three book chapters. He has edited a journal and reviewed many journal and conference papers. He is the member of several national and international statistical, computer sciences and engineers' association. His research interests are in regression diagnostics, robust statistical techniques, outlier detection, feature extraction, data mining, pattern recognition, photogrammetry, and remote sensing.

Hasan Obeid received his B.S. and M.S. in Computer Science from the Hariri Canadian University in 2004 and 2006, respectively. He acquired a number of publications related to image processing and in automatic license plate recognition in particular. Hasan joined Zawya in 2007 and currently holding a Technical Lead position in web development. Although Hasan has a web development career, but he is an automation enthusiast with a passion for image processing.

Tales C Pimenta received his B.S. and M.S. degrees in Electrical Engineering from the Universidade Federal de Itajuba – Brazil, in 1985 and 1988, respectively. He received his PhD from the Ohio University – USA in 1992. Since 1985, he has been a Professor at the Universidade Federal de Itajuba. He was a visiting scholar at The Ohio State University and Virginia Polytechnic and State University in 1997 and 2005, respectively.

Akhlaqur Rahman is currently an undergraduate student at the department of Electronic Engineering of American International University Bangladesh. Akhlaqur has participated in a number of programming language contests and won prizes. He is a student member of IEEE Bangladesh Section. He secured a grade of A+ in Higher and Secondary School Certificate examinations. He is in the final year of his studies. His research interest includes signal processing and renewable engineering. He is currently undertaking a thesis on renewable energy.

Ashfaqur Rahman is currently working as a Research Fellow at the Centre for Intelligent and Networked Systems (CINS) at Central Queensland University (CQUni), Australia. He received his Ph.D. degree in Information Technology from Monash University, Australia in 2008. His major research interests are in the fields of data mining, multimedia signal processing, and communication and artificial intelligence. He has published around 30 peer-reviewed journal articles, book chapters, and conference papers. Dr. Rahman is the recipient of numerous academic awards including CQU Seed Grant, the International Postgraduate Research Scholarship (IPRS), Monash Graduate Scholarship (MGS) and FIT Dean Scholarship by Monash University, Australia.

A. S. M. Sajeev is the Chair in IT/Computer Science at the University of New England, Armidale, Australia. He holds a Bachelor of Engineering degree with Honours in Electrical Engineering from Cochin University, India, a Master of Technology with Honours in Computer Science from the Indian Statistical Institute, Calcutta, and a PhD in Computer Science from Monash University. He is also a Fellow of the Institution of Engineers, Australia. Professor Sajeev's research interests include software engineering, security, and computational modelling. Before joining the University of New England he has held positions at Monash University and the University of Newcastle.

Hung-Yu Su received the B.S., M.S. and Ph.D. degrees from the Department of Computer Science and Information Engineering, National Cheng Kung University, Tainan, Taiwan, in 2001, 2003, and 2009, respectively. In 2009 and 2010, he conducted one-year post-doctoral research on speech recognition applications about computer assistant pronunciation training and pronunciation training assistant for the articulation disordered, at Multimedia Human-Machine Communication (MHMC) Laboratory in National Cheng Kung University. Since 2010, he works for Openfind Information Technology, Inc. in Taipei. His research interests include natural language processing, machine translation, and sign language processing for the hearing impaired.

El-Ghazali Talbi received the Ph.D degrees in Computer Science from the Institut National Polytechnique de Grenoble in France. Since 2001, he is a full Professor at the University of Lille. He is the founder and head of the INRIA Dolphin project. He has many collaborative national, European and international projects. His current research interests are in the field of multi-objective optimization, parallel algorithms, metaheuristics, combinatorial optimization, and cloud computing, hybrid and cooperative optimization, and application to logistics/transportation and networks. Professor Talbi has to his credit more than 150 publications in journals, books and conferences. He was a guest editor of more than 15 special issues in different journals (*Journal of Heuristics, Journal of Parallel and Distributed Computing, European Journal of Operational Research, Theoretical Computer Science, Computers and Operations Research, Journal of Global Optimization*). He is the co-founder and the coordinator of the research group dedicated to Metaheuristics: Theory and Applications (META). He served in different capacities on the programs of more than 100 national and international conferences. His work on metaheuristics (e.g. his book entitled "Metaheuristics: From Design to Implementation") has a large impact and visibility in the field of optimization.

Mitchell A. Thornton is a Professor of Computer Science and Engineering at Southern Methodist University in Dallas, Texas, USA. Prior to his appointment at SMU, he has served on the faculties of Mississippi State University and the University of Arkansas. Before entering academia, Mitch was employed by ESystems, Inc (now L-3 Communications) for 5 years and the Cyrix Corporation for 1 year. His research interests include quantum logic and computing, all aspects of digital systems design and analysis, and formal and spectral methods in system design. Mitch is a Professional Engineer in Texas, Mississippi, and Arkansas and is a Senior Member of the IEEE and the ACM.

S. K. Yusof received BSc (cum laude) in Electrical Engineering from George Washington University USA in 1988 and obtained her MEE and PhD in 1994 and 2006, respectively, from Universiti Tecknologi Malaysia. She is currently Associate Professor with the department of Radio Communication, Faculty of Electrical Engineering Universiti Teknologi Malaysia. Her research interest includes OFDMA based system, software define radio, and cognitive radio.

Rached Zantout received his B.E. from The American University of Beirut, Lebanon in 1988, his MSc from the University of Florida in 1990, and Ph.D. from the Ohio State University in 1994, all degrees in Electrical Engineering. Directly after finishing his PhD he joined Scriptel Corporation and worked on several R&D projects to develop a new generation of graphic input devices. Dr. Zantout taught at King Saud University (Saudi Arabia) and at the University of Balamand, Hariri Canadian University, American University of Beirut, Lebanese American University and Beirut Arab University (Lebanon). Dr. Zantout is currently an Associate Professor at Prince Sultan University, Riyadh, Saudi Arabia. Dr. Zantout's research interests are in Robotics and Artificial Intelligence He currently works on developing components for Arabic machine translation and natural language processing. He also has active research in the area of autonomous robot navigation, computer vision, and embedded systems design.

Index